# IN CONCERT

## Reading and Writing

D0025499

### KATHLEEN T. McWHORTER

Niagara County Community College

**PEARSON**

Boston   Columbus   Indianapolis   New York   San Francisco   Upper Saddle River
Amsterdam   Cape Town   Dubai   London   Madrid   Milan   Munich   Paris   Montreal   Toronto
Delhi   Mexico City   São Paulo   Sydney   Hong Kong   Seoul   Singapore   Taipei   Tokyo

**Senior Acquisitions Editor:** Nancy Blaine
**Editorial Assistant:** Jamie Fortner
**Senior Development Editor:** Gillian Cook
**Executive Market Development Manager:** Donna Kenly
**Marketing Manager:** Kurt Massey
**Senior Supplements Editor:** Donna Campion
**Executive Digital Producer:** Stefanie A. Snajder
**Digital Project Manager:** Janell Lantana
**Digital Editor:** Robert St. Laurent
**Production Manager:** Ellen MacElree
**Project Coordination, Text Design, and Electronic Page Makeup:**
  PreMediaGlobal
**Cover Design Manager:** John Callahan
**Cover Designer:** Laura Shaw
**Cover Images:** Marcus Amon/Getty Images
**Senior Manufacturing Buyer:** Dennis J. Para
**Printer/Binder:** Courier/Kendallville
**Cover Printer:** Lehigh-Phoenix Color/Hagerstown

This title is restricted to sales and distribution in North America only.

Credits and acknowledgments borrowed from other sources, and reproduced, with permission, in this textbook, appear on pages 613–619.

**Library of Congress Cataloging-in-Publication Data**
McWhorter, Kathleen T.
 In concert : reading and writing / Kathleen T. McWhorter.
   p. cm.
 Includes bibliographical references and index.
 ISBN-13: 978-0-321-83862-9
 ISBN-10: 0-321-83862-9
1.  English language—Rhetoric—Study and teaching.   2.  Report writing—Study and teaching.   3.  Critical thinking—Study and teaching.   I. Title.
 PE1404.M396 2012
 808'.04207 dc23                                                    2012013634

10  9  8  7  6  5  4—V011—15   14  13

www.pearsonhighered.com

|  | Student Edition | Annotated Instructor's Edition |
| --- | --- | --- |
| ISBN-13: | 978-0-321-83862-9 | 978-0-321-84441-5 |
| ISBN-10: | 0-321-83862-9 | 0-321-84441-6 |

# Brief Contents

# Detailed Contents

# Preface to the Instructor

Having taught both reading and writing to beginning college students for over 30 years, it is clear to me that these essential skills work together and can be effectively taught together. Readers must develop skills to comprehend and analyze the message put forth by the writer. The writer must express ideas clearly, concisely, and correctly while using various writing conventions to guide the reader and to ensure that the message is understood.

The thought that reading and writing might be best taught together was suggested by a student one day in my classroom. I was teaching a reading class on main ideas and topic sentences when a student remarked, "This is the same stuff I just learned in my writing class."

Several decades ago, along with a co-author, I wrote and published a combined reading and writing text, *Write to Read: Read to Write*. The peer reviews were positive, but the book had few adoptions. It was a book ahead of its time, since many reading and writing programs were still in the development stages then. Now, the time has come. I am pleased to apply many more years of teaching experience and textbook writing expertise to create a book that integrates these skills—a book that demonstrates that reading and writing do work together—in concert.

## Purpose

*In Concert* features a comprehensive, integrated approach to reading and writing that is developed through structured, sequential instruction and guided practice. The text emphasizes paragraph- and essay-level reading and writing skills and makes them relevant to students through everyday, academic, and workplace examples. The text emphasizes the complementary nature of the reading and writing processes, demonstrating to students that reading and writing are best learned together. The text also features critical thinking and explores and reinforces its relationship to the reading and writing processes. Visual literacy is emphasized with students learning how to read and respond to images and photographs.

## Emphases

The book has three primary emphases:

- **The Reading-Writing Connection** The book provides an overview of the reading and writing processes and presents skills and strategies for reading and writing paragraphs and essays. Many chapters offer complementary instruction, first examining how readers approach a skill and then moving to how writers use the same skill. For example, in Chapter 5 students learn how to identify topics and main ideas in paragraphs and then move immediately to learning how to choose manageable topics and write effective topic sentences for paragraphs. Models of student and professional writing are included in most chapters. Students read the models, examine their features and characteristics, demonstrate their comprehension of the content through completing related exercises, and then write in response to what they have read.

- **Critical Thinking** The text emphasizes the role and benefits of critical thinking in reading and writing. Students learn skills and strategies for thinking critically while reading. They also learn to write critical responses to what they read. The apparatus for each full-length reading contains a section titled "Thinking and Writing Critically."

- **Visual Literacy** Print and electronic sources, including textbooks, are becoming increasingly more visual. This book features comprehensive instructional material on thinking critically about visuals. Students read and write about visuals and analyze how they contribute meaning to text. Visuals with related writing prompts also accompany each professional reading.

# Approach to the Integration of Reading and Writing

The following features distinguish this text from other developmental books and make its approach unique:

- **Reading and Writing Process Instruction** This book teaches both reading and writing skills by demonstrating how they work together and complement one another. **Part One** provides an introduction to both reading and writing skills. Chapter 1 focuses on active reading skills, showing students how to preview, form guide questions, handle difficult reading material, and build vocabulary. It also provides an introduction to critical thinking and reading. Chapter 2 walks students through the writing process, demonstrating how to generate and organize ideas, write a draft, revise, and proofread. Because college success hinges upon students' abilities to read college textbooks and write about what they read through summarizing, paraphrasing, and essay exam writing, students need to learn how to read college textbooks effectively and develop these necessary writing strategies. Chapter 3 focuses on these skills. Chapter 4 teaches students to read and think critically about visuals.

  **Part Two** guides students in reading, writing, organizing and revising paragraphs. **Part Three** focuses on reading and writing essays, discussing how to read, plan, draft, and organize essays. A full chapter on multimodal essay writing is included. **Part Four** discusses essential critical thinking and writing skills, and **Part Five** concentrates on reading and writing papers using sources. Chapters in these Parts open with a "Focusing on Reading and Writing" section in which students learn what the skill involves for both readers and writers, then develop specific, but complementary reading and writing skills.

- **Extensive Coverage of Critical Thinking** To handle college level work and to be well prepared for freshman composition classes, students need to be able to think critically about what they read as well as respond in writing to what they have read. **Part Four**, Chapters 13–15, addresses specific critical thinking skills for both reading and writing and focuses on reading and writing arguments. The apparatus for each professional reading contains a section titled "Thinking and Writing Critically." Many chapters contain a section "Thinking Critically About . . . " that links chapter skills with related critical thinking skills.

- **Metacognitive Approach to Reading and Writing** Both reading and writing are approached as thinking processes—processes in which students read, write, and assess their performance of the task. They are encouraged to be aware of, control, assess, and adjust how they are reading and writing.

- **Emphasis on Textbook Reading and Writing** Chapter 3 presents skills for reading textbook chapters and describes the SQ3R system. Students learn recall strategies and use writing to highlight, annotate, map, outline, paraphrase, and summarize ideas they read.

- **Visual Literacy** Chapter 4 teaches students essential visual literacy skills. Students learn to read and interpret various types of visuals, integrate text and visuals, and think critically about visuals. Additionally, each chapter opens with a visual that demonstrates the purpose of the chapter; within chapters, the feature "Visualize It!" identifies useful maps and diagrams; and the apparatus of each professional reading contains a thinking visually question.

- **Emphasis on Student Success** The book begins with an introduction, "Reading and Writing Success Starts Here!," that focuses on the skills students need to be successful not only in their reading and writing classes but also in all their college courses. Topics include time management, the management of technology, concentration, journal writing, and collaboration with other students.

- **Vocabulary Coverage** Because a strong vocabulary is important to both readers and writers, vocabulary building skills are emphasized throughout the book. Chapter 1 presents an introduction to vocabulary; it discusses dictionary usage and offers general strategies for figuring out unfamiliar words. Four Vocabulary Workshops immediately follow Chapter 1, providing instruction and practice on expanding vocabulary, using context clues, learning specialized vocabulary, and using word parts. The apparatus following each professional reading includes a "Strengthening Your Vocabulary" section that focuses on learning words used in the reading.

- **Coverage of Organizational Patterns** Two chapters in Part Two cover eight patterns of organization, showing students how to identify each pattern to guide their reading and demonstrating how to write using these patterns to explain their ideas.

- **Multimodal Essay Chapter** This chapter recognizes that writers often rely on several methods of development in a single essay and offers strategies for combining and integrating two or more rhetorical modes.

- **Introductory Material on Reading and Writing Using Sources** As preparation for college courses that require the use of sources in writing academic papers, Chapter 16 offers an overview of research, synthesis, and documentation of sources.

# Chapter Features

- **Visual and Engaging Chapter Openers** Each chapter opens with a photograph or other image that is intended to capture students' attention, generate interest, and connect the topic of the chapter to their experience. This feature gets students writing immediately about chapter-related content.

- **Learning Objectives Tied to Interactive Summaries** Learning objectives at the beginning of each chapter identify what students can expect to learn and correspond directly to the interactive summaries that students can use to check their recall of chapter content at the end of each chapter.

- **Reading and Writing Connections** Examples of everyday, academic, and workplace situations are presented to demonstrate the relevance and importance of chapter skills.

- **Linked Writing Exercises** Writing in Progress exercises guide students step-by-step through the writing process.

- **Visualize It!** Many chapters contain idea maps that show how paragraphs and essays are organized from both a reading and a writing perspective. The professional readings in earlier chapters also contain partially completed maps for students to finish.

- **Need to Know boxes** These boxes summarize key concepts and strategies in an easy reference format.

- **Read and Respond: A Student Essay** Most chapters contain an annotated student essay. These student samples provide realistic models of the writing process and set realistic, attainable expectations for students. Students also read and respond to each model.

- **Read and Respond: A Professional Essay** This feature presents a brief professional essay. The exercises following each reading guide students in assessing their comprehension, building their vocabulary, examining the structure of the essay, thinking critically about the essay, and writing about the essay.

**Complete** this Exercise

- **Writing About the Reading at MySkillsLab** The paragraph and essay writing options that follow each of the professional readings can now be completed online. Students are directed to MSL in the print text and can click on a direct link to the site in the eBook using the icon shown here in the margin.

- **Self-Test Summary** Included at the end of each chapter is a Self-Test Summary that corresponds to the learning goals stated at the beginning of the chapter. This summary allows students to test their recall of chapter content and mastery of each learning goal. The summary also provides a means by which students can review immediately upon completion of their first reading of the chapter.

- **MySkillsLab** For each chapter, students are directed to the corresponding section in MySkillsLab for further practice and review.

- **Grammar Handbook** For students who need review of basic principles and rules of grammar, a handbook, "Reviewing the Basics," is provided at the end of the book. Topics include a review of the parts of speech as well as sentence parts and instruction on avoiding sentence errors, writing effective sentences, using punctuation correctly, and managing mechanics and spelling. Error correction exercises are also included.

- **Reading Levels in Annotated Instructor's Edition** A Lexile® measure—the most widely used reading metric in U.S. schools—provides valuable information about a student's reading ability and the complexity of text. It helps match students with reading resources and activities that are targeted to their ability level. Lexile measures indicate the reading levels of content in MySkillsLab and the longer selections in the Annotated Instructor's Editions of all Pearson's reading books. See the Annotated Instructor's Edition of *In Concert* and the *Instructor's Manual* for more details.

# Book-Specific Ancillary Materials

**Annotated Instructor's Edition** (ISBN 9780321844415/0321844416). Identical to the student text, but with answers printed directly on the pages where questions and exercises appear.

**Instructor's Manual and Test Bank** (ISBN 9780321844408/0321844408). The instructor's manual features lecture hints, in-class activities, handouts, and quizzes to accompany each chapter, as well as sample course outlines and a primer on teaching an integrated reading and writing course. Available both in print and for download from the Instructor Resource Center. Instructor's manual by Mary Dubbé of Thomas Nelson Community College, Virginia; test bank by Jeanne Jones.

**MyTest Test Bank** (ISBN 9780321844392/0321844394). Pearson MyTest is a powerful assessment generation program that helps instructors easily create and print quizzes, study guides, and exams. Select questions from the test bank to accompany *In Concert* or from other developmental reading test banks; supplement them with your own questions. Save the finished test as a Word document or PDF or export it to WebCT or Blackboard. Available at www.pearsonmytest.com.

**PowerPoint Presentation** (ISBN 9780321844439/0321844432). PowerPoint presentations to accompany each chapter consist of classroom-ready lecture outline slides, lecture tips and classroom activities, and review questions. Available for download from the Instructor Resource Center. Created by Sarah Jane Gilliam of Mountain Empire Community College, Virginia.

**Answer Key** (ISBN 9780321858801/0321858808). The Answer Key contains the solutions to the exercises in the student edition of the text. Available for download from the Instructor Resource Center.

**MySkillsLab®**

## Where better practice makes better readers and writers!

## What makes the practice in MySkillsLab better?

- **Diagnostic Testing** MySkillsLab's diagnostic Path Builder test comprehensively assesses proficiency in reading skills as well as basic grammar, sentence grammar, punctuation and mechanics, and usage and style. Students are provided an individualized learning path based on the diagnostic's results, identifying the areas where they most need help.

- **Progressive Learning** MySkillsLab's learning path offers Open sequence or Preset sequence. The Open sequence allows students to freely access all resources and assessment at any point. The Preset sequence prompts students to build knowledge by first reading, viewing, and listening to instructional material before they can move forward to a series of activities and then a post test. This progressive path from preparation (Overview, Animation) to literal comprehension (Recall) to critical understanding (Apply) to written knowledge (Write) to mastery (Posttest) is not available in any other online resource. MySkillsLab enables students to truly master the skills and concepts they need to become successful readers and writers.

- **eText** The *In Concert* eText is accessed through MySkillsLab. Students now have the eText at their fingertips while completing the various exercises and activities within MySkillsLab, including those specific to this text.

# Acknowledgements

I wish to express my gratitude to the many instructors who reviewed *In Concert* for their excellent ideas, suggestions, and advice on preparing this text:

Regina (Gina) Barnett, Tidewater Community College–Virginia Beach
Craig Barto, Southern University
Robyn Browder, Tidewater Community College–Virginia Beach
Sandi Buschmann, Cincinnati State
Maureen Cahill, Tidewater Community College–Virginia Beach
Sharon M. Cellemme, South Piedmont Community College
Helen Chester, Milwaukee Area Technical College

Karen Cowden, Valencia College
Amber Cristan, Kinonen Bay College
Christopher Deal, Piedmont Community College
Margaret DeSalvo, Kingsborough Community College
Genevieve Dibua, Baltimore City Community College
Joanne Diddlemeyer, Tidewater Community College–Norfolk
Barbara Doyle, Arkansas State University–Jonesboro

Mary Dubbe, Thomas Nelson Community College

Kim Edwards, Tidewater Community College–Chesapeake

Jennifer Ferguson, Cazenovia College

Lisa Ferrell, Arkansas State University

Mindy Flowers, Midland College

Tarasa Gardner, Moberly Area Community College

Susan Givens, Northern Virginia–Manassas

Sharon Green, Niagara University

Beth Gulley, Johnson County Community College

Barbara Hampton, Rend Lake College

Tom Hargrove, Tidewater Community College–Chesapeake

Curtis Harrell, North West Arkansas Community College

Carlotta Hill, Oklahoma City Community College

Wayne Johnson, Odessa College

Frank Lammer, Northeast Iowa Community College

Erlinda Legaspi, City College of San Francisco

Glenda Lowery, Rappahannock Community College

Maureen Maas-Feary, Finger Lakes Community College

Agnes Malicka, Northern Virginia–Alexandria Campus

Jennifer McCann, Bay College

Margaret McClain, Arkansas State University

Chante McCormick, City College of San Francisco

Brenda Meisel, Northern Virginia Community College–Woodbridge

Debbie Nacquin, Northern Virginia Community College

Carl Olds, University of Central Arkansas

Debbie Ousey, Penn State University–Brandywine

Michelle Palmer, Pulaski Technical College

Catherine Parra, Northern Virginia–Loudoun

Pat Pierce, Pulaski Technical College

Betty Raper, Pulaski Technical College

Joan Reeves, Northeast Alabama Community College

Linda Robinett. Oklahoma City Community College

Tony Rogers, Benjamin Franklin Institute of Technology

Dianna Rottinghaus, Johnson County Community College

Charis Sawyer, Johnson County Community College

Syble Davis Simon, Houston Community College

Benjamin Sloan, Piedmont Virginia Community College

Catherine Swift, University of Central Arkansas

Colleen Weeks, Arapahoe Community College

Michelle Zollars, Patrick Henry Community College

I wish to thank Hilda Barrow, Department Chair of Development Studies at Pitt Community College, who has worked with me as a consultant on the project. She has been teaching combined reading and writing courses for several years and provided valuable guidance, advice, and insights for development of this book. Nancy Blaine, Senior Acquisitions Editor, deserves special thanks for her enthusiastic support of the project and for providing advice and resources for the book's development. I also wish to thank Jeanne Jones for her assistance in drafting and preparing the manuscript and Gillian Cook, Senior Development Editor, for helping me carry out the vision of this book through essential day-to-day collaboration.

I would also like to thank the following students who provided samples of their writing for the student essays and shared personal tips on how to be a successful student:

Kate Atkinson

Jordan Bobbitt

Yesenia De Jesus

Nora Edge

Santiago Quintana Garcia

Aurora Gilbert

DeJohn Harris

Ben Howard

Elizabeth Lawson

Doug Mello

Jessica Nantka

Nina Paus-Weiler

Ted Sawchuck

Quinne Sember

Adam Simmons

James Sturm

Sharlinda Thompson

I also value the professional and creative efforts of Melissa Sacco and her team at PreMediaGlobal.

# Reading and Writing Success Starts Here!

Regardless of your curriculum or major, reading and writing are an important part of your everyday life, your college career, and your workplace. Knowing how to read effectively and being comfortable expressing yourself in writing in each of these areas can add a whole new dimension to your life and increase your potential for success. In this section you will learn numerous success strategies for becoming a better reader and writer.

Success in any college course involves accepting responsibility for your own learning. Your reading and writing instructor is your guide, but you are in charge. It is not enough to attend class and do what you are asked. You have to decide what to learn and how to learn it.

## Use the Help Features in This Book

Although your instructor and your classmates are your most important sources for learning, this book also contains numerous features to help you become a successful reader and writer.

### Learning Goals

These lists of topics tell you what you should expect to learn in each chapter and correspond to the major headings in each chapter.

### Think About It!

Each chapter opens with a photograph or other visual image that is intended to capture your attention, generate interest, and connect the topic of the chapter to your own experience. This "Think About It!" feature encourages you to start writing immediately about chapter-related content using a relevant topic. It also makes clear the close connection between reading and writing.

**THINK About It!**

This photograph shows fans attending a sporting event. Can you sense their excitement and team spirit? The fans demonstrate *active* involvement with the team and the game. The fans in the photograph are reacting to a play on the field. Fans often direct plays, criticize calls, encourage the players, and reprimand the coaches. They become part of the game, and the team is *their* team.

## Reading and Writing Connections

**EVERYDAY CONNECTIONS**

- **Reading** You read your monthly credit card statement.
- **Writing** You write a letter to your credit card company about a questionable charge you find on it.

**ACADEMIC CONNECTIONS**

- **Reading** You read an assigned article in *Newsweek* on taser guns for a class discussion.
- **Writing** You write a summary of the assigned article in an essay on the unnecessary use of force by police officers.

**WORKPLACE CONNECTIONS**

- **Writing** You write a cover letter to accompany your résumé and application for a new job.
- **Reading** You read the worker safety regulations before starting the new job.

## Reading and Writing Connections

Each chapter begins with three brief examples that show how reading and writing work together. These situations demonstrate how everyday, academic, and workplace situations require you to use the reading and writing skills taught in the chapter. These connections help answer a question that is often asked: "Why do I need to learn this?"

## Idea Maps

Idea maps, labeled "Visualize It!" are digrams that show the content and organization of a piece of writing. You can use these maps in several ways:

**VISUALIZE IT!**

- ■ **As an aid to understanding a professional reading that you have been assigned.** By filling in an idea map or creating your own, you can assure yourself that you have understood the reading; the process of completing or drawing an idea map will also help you to remember what you read.

- ■ **To organize and guide your own writing.** Think of them as models you can follow.

- ■ **To help you analyze a paragraph or essay you have written.** Drawing a map of your writing will help you identify problems in organization or spot ideas that do not belong in a paragraph or essay.

**Model for Idea Map**

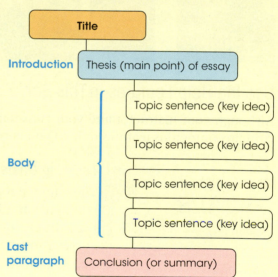

## Student Writing Samples

Sentences, paragraphs, and essays written by students appear throughout this book. These pieces of student writing are included to illustrate particular writing techniques. Chapter 6, for example, includes sample paragraphs that illustrate how to organize details effectively. Study each of these samples to see how each writing technique works.

## Organize Details Effectively

Nan had an assignment to write a paragraph about travel. She drafted the paragraph and then revised it. As you read each version, pay particular attention to the order in which she arranged the details.

**FIRST DRAFT**

   This summer I had the opportunity to travel extensively. Over Labor Day weekend I backpacked with a group of friends in the Allegheny Mountains. When spring semester was over, I visited my seven cousins in Florida. My friends and I went to New York City over the Fourth of July to see fireworks and explore the city. During June I worked as a wildlife-preservation volunteer in a Colorado state park. On July 15 I celebrated my twenty-fifth birthday by visiting my parents in Syracuse.

**REVISION**

   This summer I had the opportunity to travel extensively in the United States. When the spring semester ended, I went to my cousins' home in Florida to relax.

## Read and Respond: A Student Essay

Most chapters include a sample student essay. These essays were written by real college students who were writing in response to classroom writing assignments. The essays are realistic models of good writing, but they are not perfect. They show you how the writer applied the techniques taught in the chapter to produce a good essay. Before each essay, the writer and his or her writing task are described. The essays are annotated to call your attention to particular writing features or techniques. Questions follow the essay to help you further examine the writer's techniques, and writing assignments are suggested.

Here are some suggestions for reading and learning from student writing:

- **Read the piece of writing more than once.** Read it once to understand the writer's message. Read it again to examine the writing techniques it illustrates.

- **Read the piece to answer this question:** What does this writer do that I can use in my own writing?

- **Highlight as you read.** Mark words, sentences, or paragraphs that you want to study further or that you feel work particularly well.

## Read and Respond: A Professional Essay

The professional essays in this book were written by expert writers and have been published in books, textbooks, news magazines, and journals. A professional essay appears at the end of most chapters. By studying the writing of professional writers, you can improve your own writing. As with the student writing, plan on reading each essay several times. Be sure to look for techniques that the writer uses that you can use in your own writing. Both before and after each reading, you will find questions and activities intended to guide you in reading, examining, and writing about the reading. You should complete these, even if they are not assigned by your instructor, because doing so will help you be better prepared to discuss and write about the reading.

---

### INTEGRATING READING AND WRITING

#### READ AND RESPOND: A Student Essay

*Kate Atkinson is a sophomore at Beloit College in Wisconsin where she is studying Health and Education and Russian.*

*Atkinson wrote this essay for her writing class in response to the article "School of Hard Knocks." Atkinson studied Russia during high school and used her study abroad experience in responding to the article.*

---

### READ AND RESPOND: A Professional Essay

#### Thinking Before Reading

The author of this article has written several books on the link between diet and health. In the following reading, he examines a new partnership between a famous fried chicken restaurant chain and a breast cancer advocacy group. Before you read:

1. Preview the reading, using the steps discussed in Chapter 1, page. 15.
2. Connect the reading to your own experience by answering the following questions:
   a. How often do you eat fast food? Are you concerned about the effects of fast food on your health?
   b. What do you already know about Susan G. Komen for the Cure?
3. Mark and annotate as you read.

### Greed, Cancer, and Pink KFC Buckets

#### John Robbins

1   We live in a world of profound contradictions. Some things are just unbelievably strange. At times I feel like I've found a way to adapt to the weirdness of the world, and then along comes something that just boggles my mind. It is ironic that the largest **grassroots** breast cancer advocacy group in the world, a group called "Susan G. Komen for the Cure," has now partnered with the fast food chain KFC, known for its high-fat foods and questionable treatment of its chickens, in a national "Buckets for the Cure" campaign. The program began last month and runs through the end of May.

2   KFC is taking every chance it can manufacture to trumpet the fact that it will donate 50 cents to Komen for every pink bucket of chicken sold. For its part, Komen is announcing on its website that "KFC and Susan G. Komen for the Cure are teaming up . . . to . . . spread educational messaging via a major national campaign which will reach thousands of communities served by nearly 5,000 KFC restaurants."

**grassroots**
involving ordinary people at a local or community level

## Need to Know Boxes

In many chapters you will find boxes titled "Need to Know." Pay particular attention to these boxes because they present or summarize important information. They are a quick way to review information, so refer to them often. You may want to mark boxes that you find particularly valuable.

### ! NEED TO KNOW

#### How to Integrate Text and Visuals

When reading text and visuals together, be sure to do the following:

1. **Notice the type and number of visuals included in the material as you preview the chapter** (see Chapter 1).
2. **Refer to the visual when the author directs you to.** Writers tell you when they want you to look at a visual by saying "See Figure 17-2" or by introducing the visual with a phrase like "Table 12-7 displays . . . ."
3. **Read the visual, using steps listed on page 118.**
4. **Move back and forth between the text and visual.** As you study the visual, refer back to the text as needed, following the explanation of the visual provided by the author. This technique is particularly effective with illustrations and diagrams, which often show the meaning or function of particular terms or parts.
5. **Determine why the author included the visual.** Ask these questions:
   - What am I supposed to learn from this visual?
   - Why was it included?
   - What new information does the visual contain?
   - On what topic(s) does the visual provide more detail or further explanation?

## Self-Test Summary

Appearing at the end of every chapter, the self-test summaries provide **you with an opportunity to test your recall of chapter content and mastery of each learning goal.** Use them as a review, both immediately upon finishing the chapter, and later.

### SELF-TEST SUMMARY

To test yourself, cover the Answer column with a sheet of paper and answer each question in the left column. Evaluate each of your answers as you work by sliding the paper down and comparing your answer with what is printed in the Answer column.

| QUESTION | ANSWER |
|---|---|
| ■ GOAL 1 Structure a paragraph<br><br>What is a paragraph and what are its three key elements? | A paragraph is a group of related sentences that develop one thought or idea. The three key elements are the *topic, topic sentence,* and *supporting details.* |
| ■ GOAL 2 Identify the topic of a paragraph<br>How do I identify the topic of a paragraph? | Look for the one thing the author is discussing throughout the paragraph. |
| ■ GOAL 3 Locate main ideas<br>How do I locate the main idea of a paragraph? | Find the topic and then locate the sentence in the paragraph that is the most general. Check to be sure this one sentence brings all the other details together under one common concept. |
| ■ GOAL 4 Think critically about main ideas<br>How can I think critically about main ideas? | Ask if there are other views that can be held about the topic. |

## MySkillsLab

Next to the Write About the Reading section after every professional reading, a marginal Exercise icon directs you to MySkillsLab where you can complete specific exercises online. At the end of each chapter, the MSL box directs you to MySkillsLab, where you can find additional instruction and practice the skills taught in the chapter.

**An Overview of Active Reading**
For more help in meeting the goals of this chapter, go to your learning path in MySkillsLab at www.myskillslab.com.

MySkillsLab®

Complete this Exercise

### Writing About the Reading

#### Paragraph Options

1. Think of a situation in which you tried to help someone who was unwilling or unable to be helped. Write a paragraph describing that experience.
2. Try to put yourself in the author's shoes and imagine what you would have done. Do you think you would have been able to let your brother (or sister, or other loved one) go? Write a paragraph explaining your answer.
3. Do you agree with the author that the news media would have been more interested in her disappearance than that of her mentally ill brother? Write a paragraph explaining your answer.

# Reading and Writing Success | Tips

## Manage Your Time and Identify a Place to Study

Many students say they do not have enough time to pay adequate attention to classes, studying, jobs, family, and friends. They also find it difficult to find a good place to study. You can avoid or overcome these problems by managing your time effectively and organizing a place to read and write.

### How to Manage Your Time

- **Develop a weekly study plan.** Set aside time for reading assignments, writing and revising papers, reviewing what you have learned, and studying for exams. Identify specific times each week for working on each of your courses.

- **As a rule of thumb, reserve two study hours for each hour you spend in class.**

- **Work on difficult assignments first.** It is tempting to get the easy tasks out of the way first, but then you are left with the more challenging ones when you are tired. Work on difficult tasks, like brainstorming ideas for an essay, when your mind is fresh. When you are tired, do more routine tasks such as organizing lecture notes.

- **Schedule study for a particular course close to class time.** By studying close to class time, you will find it easier to relate what goes on in class to what you have been reading and writing about.

- **Include short breaks in your study time.** Studying for long, uninterrupted periods of time leads to fatigue. Taking periodic, short breaks refreshes you and helps you to focus when you resume working.

**Nora Edge**
*St. John's College, Annapolis, MD*
Nora just graduated from St. John's College where she took a double major in literature and philosophy. She is planning to join the Peace Corps this summer: she wants to apply what she has learned, gain work experience, and decide on her future plans.

**Advice on scheduling:** I found writing a schedule was the most useful way to deal with time management. I wrote it out on paper, carried it with me all the time, and checked it constantly. When I had time between classes I knew what I was doing. For example, I would read ahead of time if there was no break between classes, and read for the next class when I did have a break. I found the best way to be successful was give myself time to breathe. I made sure I was exercising three times a week and got 6–8 hours of sleep a night.

## Planning a Weekly Schedule

Plan a weekly schedule using the tips provided. Try it for one week, evaluate what worked and what did not, and then revise it.

## How to Organize a Place to Read and Write

You will find that it is easier to read and write if you do so in the same place, as well as at the same time, each day.

- **Try to find a quiet area that you can reserve for reading and writing.** If possible, avoid areas used for other purposes, such as the dining room or kitchen table, because you'll have to move or clean up your materials frequently. If you live in a dorm, your desk is an ideal place to write, unless the dorm is too noisy. If it is, find a quiet place elsewhere on campus.

- **Use a table or desk.** Do not try to write on the arm of a comfortable chair. Choose a space where you can spread out your papers.

- **Eliminate distractions from your writing area.** Get rid of photos or stacks of bills to pay that may take your mind off your writing.

- **Be sure that the lighting is adequate and your chair is straight and not too comfortable.**

- **Collect and organize supplies.** You will need plenty of paper, pens, pencils, erasers, a ruler, a stapler, and so forth. If you write on a computer, keep a flash or thumb drive on hand.

- **Organize completed and returned papers, quizzes, class handouts, and other course materials in separate folders.**

**Nina Paus-Weiler**
*Occidental College*
*Eagle Rock, CA*
Nina is a sophomore at Occidental College, where she is working toward a bachelor's degree in urban and environmental policy.

**Advice on organizing a place to study:** I go to the library because it makes me work, no distractions. I find a spot that's secluded, usually near a window so I don't feel trapped. My dorm is far away from the library, so I bring everything I need to work, including drinks and snacks. I also write in my room a lot at my desk. If my roommate and I are both working, we'll be quiet, use headphones.

## Getting Organized

Choose one place at home (or in your dorm) and organize it. Write a list of supplies you need. Try using this location for one week. Do you notice a difference in your ability to get down to work and get things done?

# Manage Your Electronic Life

Computers offer convenient ways of writing and revising, while the Internet offers a world of information at your fingertips. Cell phones and other high-tech items like the iPhone and Android smartphones serve not only as communication devices (through voice and text messaging) but also as powerful, portable computers. The challenge, of course, is making these tools work for you. Many students report losing hours of their time to instant messaging and Facebook when they should have been working on their writing assignments. So how do you get rid of the *distractions* of technology and turn them to your advantage? Here are some suggestions:

## Avoid Distractions and Make Technology Work for You

1. **Cell Phones.** To write effectively, you need to concentrate, so turn off the ringer, vibrator, and IM "ding." Avoid the temptation to check for messages constantly.

2. **E-mail.** Set up two e-mail addresses: one for friends, another for "serious" matters. Communicate with classmates or teachers on the serious e-mail. Leave that e-mail account on during the day and check it occasionally, because e-mails to this account can be valuable in terms of sharing ideas or important information. Use your serious e-mail *only* for school- or work-related matters, and check your "fun" e-mail only at night or during meal breaks. Use the fun e-mail address for *all* social matters.

3. **Instant Messages (IMs) and Text Messages.** Typing on a cell phone or a tiny keypad can be very time-consuming—which can make it difficult to convey information efficiently. For most college students, text messages are almost purely social. Don't read, write, or respond to text messages when you should be working on your writing assignments. Keep in mind, too, that the abbreviations used in text messages are not acceptable in college writing. In a text message, "how r u" may be the norm, but such abbreviations are never acceptable in college writing.

4. **Apps.** Many high-tech devices and phones offer applications, or "apps," that may prove useful in your studies. You can download free (or inexpensive) dictionaries, encyclopedias, grammar guides, and a host of other apps that can help with your writing. Put these apps on your initial screen, and put your social apps (such as Facebook) on a later screen.

5. **Technology for Peer Review Groups.** In some classes, you will be expected to get together as a group to discuss your writing (see Success Tip #5, p. 12). Programs like Skype make it easy for a group to "meet" when everyone is online at the same time. Such group chats are often preferable to walking a mile in the rain to participate in person!

## Examining Your Electronic Distractions

**Try It Out!**

Answer the following questions to get a sense of the type and number of electronic distractions in your life and how they affect your ability to focus and write:

1. How many **text messages** do you send and receive per day? _____ How many of these are "important"? _____ Do you stop what you are doing to check your cell phone every time a text message arrives? _____ Have you ever texted while driving? _____

2. How many **e-mails** do you send and receive per day? _____ How many of these convey important information? _____ How many are purely for entertainment or socializing? _____ How much time do you spend each day on e-mail unrelated to your studies or job? _____

3. How many **calls** do you receive on your cell phone each day? _____ Do you leave your cell phone on all the time? _____ Do you answer it every time it rings, even when you're in class or studying? _____ Do you ever use your cell phone as a way to procrastinate? _____

4. How many hours a day do you spend surfing the **Internet** or posting on social networking sites like **Facebook**? _____ Does this socializing affect your studying, concentration, and grades? _____

**Ben Howard**
*Brown University,*
*Providence, RI*
Ben graduated from Brown, where he majored in mechanical engineering. He would like to apply his skills in mechanical engineering to video technology.

**Advice on using technology:** Google Documents is really useful. You go to the site, sign up for your own account, and then either import an existing document or set up a new document, spreadsheet, or slide show for a presentation. It's really cool, because then you can e-mail everyone in the same study project as you, they can sign up as collaborators, and you can all work on the document simultaneously. If you're working in a cell on a spreadsheet you will see it highlighted in one color and as other people work on cells you'll see their work highlighted in a different color. When you're done, you can save the project as a Word file on your computer.

Success
**TIP 3**

# Build Your Concentration

No matter how intelligent you are, how serious you are, or what skills and talents you possess, reading and writing will be difficult and frustrating if you cannot keep your mind on the task at hand. Improving your concentration involves two tasks: eliminating distractions and building your attention span.

## Eliminate Distractions

There are several steps you can take to eliminate distractions.

- **Choose a place to study with minimal distractions.** Try it out and identify any distractions that occur. If you cannot eliminate them, find a different place to work.

- **Control noise levels.** Determine how much background noise you need or can tolerate, and choose a place best suited to those requirements.

- **Write down bothersome thoughts.** When you think of an errand you need to do or a call you need to make, write it down on a separate notepad to follow up on later. Once you have written it down, you will be able to stop thinking about it.

■ **Ask for cooperation.** Your family, friends, and roommates need to understand that you need to be by yourself in order to get your work done.

■ **Shut off your cell phone.**

### Focus Your Attention

To focus your attention on your work, try the following:

■ **Establish goals and time limits for each assignment.** Deadlines will keep you motivated, and you will be less likely to daydream.

■ **Use writing to keep mentally and physically active.** Highlighting, outlining, and note taking will force you to keep your mind on what you are doing.

■ **Reward yourself.** Use rewards such as texting with a friend or ordering a pizza when you complete an evening of study or a particularly challenging assignment.

**Jordan Bobbitt**
*Beloit College*
*Beloit, Wisconsin*
Jordan is a freshman at Beloit College. She is currently studying for her bachelor's degree.

"If I need to concentrate in order to get work done, I feel like staying in my room gets in the way; all my stuff is in my room so there are lots of opportunities to do other things, like clean. So I look for someplace that doesn't feel like I'm in solitary confinement—I find absolute silence distracting—but isn't too busy, like the library. If I'm working on a particularly intense project, I turn off my phone. I usually like some background music, but it has to be mellow, so it doesn't pull me away from what I'm doing. I find it helps to tell friends when I have a big project; they remind me not to fall behind. Once I get everything done, then I can do what I want, like play video games."

**Try It Out!**

### Building Your Concentration

Place a check mark in front of three suggestions in the two preceding lists that may work for you. Choose three days this week and try to build one of these suggestions into your routine each day.

**Success**
**TIP**

**4**

# Keep a Writing Journal

A journal can be a fun and meaningful way to explore ideas and improve your writing. Writing in your journal daily will change how you think about events in your life. Writing regularly will also make you a more confident writer.

### Setting Up Your Journal

Use the following suggestions for setting up your journal.

1. **Create a computer file or buy a spiral-bound notebook and use it exclusively for journal writing.** If you are using the college computer lab, save your file on a flash or thumb drive.

2.  **Take 10 or 15 minutes a day to write in your journal.** You can do this during "downtime"—waiting for a bus or for class to begin, for example. Some students prefer to do their journal writing at the end of the day, to reflect on the day's events.

3.  **Record your feelings, ideas, and impressions of the day.** Don't just record events; analyze what they mean to you.

4.  **Don't worry about perfect spelling.** A journal is a "safe space" that is not evaluated or graded for punctuation or grammar. It is a place for you to reflect on your life and experiences.

## Getting Started

Some writers have difficulty facing a blank page or computer screen. If you don't know what to write about, try answering some of these thought-provoking questions:

- **What new ideas did I encounter today?** Perhaps you started thinking about poverty or world peace. Describe your thoughts.

- **What interesting conversations did I have?** Jot down some of the dialogue.

- **What am I worrying about?** Describe the problem and brainstorm possible solutions.

- **What was the best/worst/most unusual thing that happened to me today?** Describe how you feel about it.

- **What was a particularly pleasurable or upsetting experience?** Describe your reactions.

## A Sample Journal Entry

Today in my biology class we talked about animal-organ transplants. I was surprised that research is going on about this. My instructor told us that scientists have experimented with putting pigs' hearts into baboons. It didn't work because the baboons' immune systems rejected the hearts. The reason for doing this is the shortage of human organs. I wonder why more people don't donate? And would I ever let a pig's heart be put into me? Maybe, if it was my only choice!

## Why It Works

Keeping a journal doesn't come naturally to all students, but it has many benefits.

1.  **Keeping a journal gives you practice in writing.** The more you write, the better your writing becomes.

2.  **Journal writing allows you to write for yourself.** Class assignments are written for someone else to read. Your journal is for you. Think of it as a conversation with yourself, a place to ponder, vent, and think.

3. **Journal writing helps you think, react to problems, and discover solutions.** Through your journal, you'll learn to use writing to discover and evaluate ideas.

4. **Your journal will become a valuable source of writing topics.** When your instructor asks you to write a paragraph or essay on a topic of your choice, you can turn to your journal for ideas.

5. **Many students find they enjoy journal writing and continue it long after they complete their writing courses.** Reading a journal you wrote several years ago is like looking at old photographs—it brings back memories and helps you preserve the past.

**Try It Out!**

### Keeping a Journal

Write in your journal for five minutes on one of the following topics:

1. The place you would most like to visit and why
2. Your dream job or dream career (don't be afraid to dream)
3. The stresses of modern life

**Sharlinda Thompson**
*Valencia College*
*Orlando, Florida*
Sharlinda is a freshman at Valencia College, where she is studying for an associate's degree in dental hygiene. She has taken a writing class both semesters and uses a journal to improve her writing skills.

"Last semester our teacher had us write in our journals in class and at home every day. This semester we use journals in class to improve our writing. The teacher puts things on the board for us to write about. For example, she put up a picture of army guys peeing on four dead people, and we wrote about how it made us feel. Writing in the journal helps me express my feelings, but it helps me more with grammar and punctuation. It sometimes involves critical thinking, such as looking things up I don't know about on the Internet. We get graded on the journals and my grades have got a lot better from using a journal."

**Success TIP 5**

# Collaborate for Success

While *you* are responsible for your college success, you'll need the help of others along the way. Instructors will offer feedback on your work, and you'll sometimes need to work closely with classmates as well.

### Learn from Peer Review

In writing classes, you'll often participate in **peer review**, in which you comment on your classmates' writing and they comment on yours. How can you make peer reviewing as valuable as possible?

## *When You Are the Writer*

1. Prepare your draft in readable form. Double-space your work and print it on standard 8.5" × 11" paper. Use only one side of the paper.

2. When you receive your peers' comments, weigh them carefully. Keep an open mind, but do not feel that you must accept every suggestion that is made.

3. If you have questions or are uncertain about your peers' advice, talk with your instructor.

## *When You Are the Reviewer*

1. Read the draft through at least once before making any suggestions.

2. As you read, keep the writer's intended audience in mind (see Chapters 7, 9, and 11). The draft should be appropriate for that audience.

3. Offer positive comments first. Say what the writer did well.

4. Use the Revision Checklists in Chapter 9 to guide your reading and comments. Be specific in your review and offer suggestions for improvement.

**Santiago Quintana Garcia**
*Beloit College*
*Beloit, Wisconsin*

Santiago is in his first year at Beloit College, where he will be completing a joint major in biochemistry and literature. After graduation, he plans to attend graduate school for an advanced degree in biochemistry. He uses both peer review and teacher feedback to improve his written work.

"Whenever I write a paper or article I ask other people to read it and critique it. It helps bring out things I would otherwise overlook. I ask my roommate, who is a senior in a different field from me, sociology, to look at my papers and he looks at them from a very different point of view and finds things I haven't addressed. I've taken a paper I've written for biochemistry to my English teacher and asked her what she thinks. If she can understand what I'm saying, I know I am writing clearly. I have also paired up with people having trouble with a problem from a class, even if I'm blurry on it, and find that I can find better ways to explain it so they understand it and that helps me get clearer in my thinking. If I can't understand what a teacher has said, I'll find someone who does and sit down for an hour with coffee and music and talk through what I need to know."

**Try It Out!**

Exchange writing samples with a classmate.

1. List two things the writer did well.

   a. _____

   b. _____

2. List two areas for improvement.

   a. _____

   b. _____

# An Overview of Active Reading

**1**

## LEARNING GOALS

Learn how to . . .

- **GOAL 1**
  Read actively

- **GOAL 2**
  Preview before reading

- **GOAL 3**
  Form guide questions

- **GOAL 4**
  Develop strategies for understanding what you read

- **GOAL 5**
  Build your vocabulary

- **GOAL 6**
  Think critically

## THINK About It!

This photograph shows fans attending a sporting event. Can you sense their excitement and team spirit? The fans demonstrate *active* involvement with the team and the game. The fans in the photograph are reacting to a play on the field. Fans often direct plays, criticize calls, encourage the players, and reprimand the coaches. They become part of the game, and the team is *their* team.

In a similar way, *active* readers get involved with the material they read. They think, question, challenge, and criticize the author's ideas. They try to make the material *their* material. This chapter will give you some strategies for becoming an active, successful reader. The skills you learn to become an active reader will also help you as you write in response to what you read.

13

# Reading and Writing Connections

### EVERYDAY CONNECTIONS

- **Reading** You read your monthly credit card statement.
- **Writing** You write a letter to your credit card company about a questionable charge you find on it.

### ACADEMIC CONNECTIONS

- **Reading** You read an assigned article in *Newsweek* on taser guns for a class discussion.
- **Writing** You write a summary of the assigned article in an essay on the unnecessary use of force by police officers.

### WORKPLACE CONNECTIONS

- **Writing** You write a cover letter to accompany your résumé and application for a new job.
- **Reading** You read the worker safety regulations before starting the new job.

## FOCUSING ON READING AND WRITING

# What Is Active Reading?

■ **GOAL 1**
Read actively

Active readers are involved with what they are reading. They interact with the author and his or her ideas. Table 1-1 contrasts the active strategies of successful readers with the passive ones of less successful readers. Throughout the remainder of this chapter and this book, you will discover specific strategies for becoming a more active reader and learner. Not all strategies work for everyone. Experiment to discover those that work for you.

### TABLE 1-1   ACTIVE VERSUS PASSIVE READING

| Active Readers . . . | Passive Readers . . . |
|---|---|
| Tailor their reading strategies to suit each assignment. | Read all assignments the same way. |
| Analyze the purpose of a reading assignment. | Read an assignment *because* it was assigned. |
| Adjust their reading speed to suit their purposes. | Read everything at the same speed. |
| Question ideas in the assignment. | Accept whatever is in print as true. |
| Skim the headings or introduction and conclusion to find out what an assignment is about before beginning to read. | Check the length of an assignment and then begin reading. |
| Make sure they understand what they are reading as they go along. | Read until the assignment is completed. |
| Read with pencil in hand, highlighting, jotting notes, and marking key vocabulary. | Simply read. |
| Develop personalized strategies that are particularly effective. | Follow routine, standard methods. |

## EXERCISE 1-1

*WORKING TOGETHER*

# Reading Actively

**Directions:** Rate each of the following items as either helpful (H) or not helpful (NH) in reading actively. Then discuss with a classmate how each of the items marked NH could be changed to be more helpful.

_____  1. Beginning to write an essay without reviewing the chapter in which is it assigned

_____  2. Giving yourself a maximum of one hour to write an essay

_____  3. Using different techniques to read different types of essays

_____  4. Highlighting important new words in an essay

_____  5. Rereading an essay the same way as many times as necessary to understand it

# Preview Before Reading

■ GOAL 2
Preview before reading

You probably would not jump into a pool without checking its depth. You would not buy clothes without trying them on. You would not purchase a CD if you knew nothing about the artist.

Similarly, you should not begin reading a textbook chapter without knowing what it is about and how it is organized. **Previewing** is a way of quickly familiarizing yourself with the organization and content of a chapter or article *before* beginning to read it. Once you try previewing, you will discover that it makes a dramatic difference in how effectively you read and how much you can remember.

## How to Preview

Think of previewing as getting a sneak peek at what a reading will be about.

### Previewing Textbook Chapters

1. **Read the title and subtitle of the selection.** The title provides the overall topic of the chapter. The subtitle suggests the specific focus, aspect, or approach toward the overall topic.
2. **Check the author's name.** If it is familiar, what do you know about the author?
3. **Read the introduction or the first paragraph.** The introduction or first paragraph introduces the subject, establishing the overall subject and suggesting how it will be developed.
4. **Read each boldfaced (dark print) heading.** Headings label the contents of each section, announcing the major topic of the section.
5. **Read the first sentence under each heading.** The first sentence often states the central thought of the section.

6. **If the reading lacks headings, read the first sentence of each of a few paragraphs on each page.** You will discover many of the main ideas in the selection.

7. **Note any graphic aids.** Graphs, charts, photographs, and tables often suggest what is important in the selection. Be sure to read the captions for photographs and the legends on graphs, charts, or tables.

8. **Read the last paragraph or summary.** This may provide a condensed view of the selection, often reviewing key points or it may draw the reading to a close. If the last paragraph is lengthy, read only the last few sentences.

## Demonstration of Previewing

The following selection is a section from a business textbook. The parts of the text that should be read during previewing are highlighted.

### Alternative Scheduling Arrangements

An increasing number of employees are finding that managing the demands of work and personal life results in doing neither well. The added stresses that face employees today from child care, elder care, commuting, and other work/life conflicts have led to a decrease in productivity and an increase in employee absenteeism and tardiness. As a result, more and more employers are offering alternatives to the traditional 9 AM to 5 PM, Monday to Friday workweek. In fact, according to the U.S. Bureau of Labor and Statistics, over one-quarter of U.S. employees take advantage of some form of flexible work arrangement. The most popular flexible work arrangements include the following:

### Alternative Scheduling Plans (Flextime)

In *alternative scheduling plans* or **flextime,** management defines a total number of required hours as a core workday and is flexible with starting and ending times. Managers must rise to the challenge of ensuring that required hours are met and monitoring employee performance. However, overall, flexible arrangements allow for increased productivity due to reductions in absenteeism and tardiness.

### Permanent Part-Time

**Permanent part-time employees** are hired on a permanent basis to work a part-time week. Unlike temporary part-time workers who are employed to fill short-term needs, permanent part-time employees enjoy the same benefits that full-time employees receive.

### Job Sharing

**Job sharing** is an arrangement in which two employees work part-time sharing one full-time job. Those who share a job have been found to be very motivated to make this flexible situation work, so productivity and employee satisfaction increase. On the other hand, conflicts may arise if the job sharers don't have a clear understanding of who is in charge of what or if there is confusion from other employees about whom to contact and when. Therefore, job sharers must carefully coordinate and communicate both with one another and their employer to ensure that all responsibilities are met.

### Compressed Workweek

A **compressed workweek** allows employees to work four 10-hour days instead of five 8-hour days or nine days (not ten) in a two-week schedule for 80 hours. Such arrangements can reduce worker overtime, make more efficient use of facilities, and provide employees with longer blocks of personal time and less commuting time. The disadvantages are a potential increase in employee fatigue and conflicts with state labor laws that cite overtime requirements for hours worked in excess of eight a day.

### Telecommuting

**Telecommuting** allows employees to work in the office part-time and work from home part-time, or to work completely from home, making only occasional visits to the office. Telecommuting reduces commuting costs and allows employees to take care of home needs while also fulfilling work responsibilities. Telecommuting arrangements are also necessary for those employees dealing with clients, colleagues, or suppliers who are on the other side of the globe. Taking calls at 2 AM is much easier at home than at the office. The disadvantages of telecommuting include monitoring employees' performance at a distance, servicing equipment for off-site employees, and communication issues. Additionally, employees who telecommute may become isolated from other employees.

Despite the costs associated with designing and implementing flexible working arrangements, employers can expect positive bottom-line results due to increases in employee satisfaction, decreases in absenteeism, and increases in worker productivity. Similarly, reductions in employee turnover lead to a decrease in time and costs associated with employee recruiting and replacement training.

—Solomon et al., *Better Business*, pp. 279–280

| EXERCISE 1-2 | Evaluating Your Previewing |

**Directions:** Indicate whether each of the following statements is true (T) or false (F) based on what you learned by previewing the selection above.

_____  1. A decrease in worker productivity is tied to work/life conflicts.

_____  2. Most U.S. employees take advantage of some sort of flexible work arrangement.

_____  3. Flextime means that workers can choose how many hours they want to work.

_____  4. Compressed workweeks allow employees to fit a full workweek into fewer days.

_____  5. Alternative scheduling has not been shown to improve employee absenteeism.

This exercise tested your recall of some of the important ideas in the article. Check your answers by referring back to the article. Did you get most or all of the items correct? This exercise demonstrates, then, that previewing helps you learn the key ideas in a selection before actually reading it.

## Making Predictions

While previewing a reading assignment, you can make predictions about its content and organization. Specifically, you can anticipate what topics will be covered and how they will be presented. Ask the following questions to sharpen your previewing skills and strengthen your recall of what you read:

- How difficult is the material?
- How is it organized?
- What is the overall subject and how is it approached?
- What type of material is it (for example, practical, theoretical, historical background, or a case study)?
- Where are the logical breaking points where you might divide the assignment into portions, perhaps reserving a portion for a later study session?
- At what points should you stop and review?
- Why was this material assigned?

EXERCISE 1-3

# Practicing Previewing

**Directions:** Preview Chapter 5 in this book. After you have previewed it, complete the items below.

1. What are the subjects of Chapter 5?

   _____

2. List the five major topics Chapter 5 covers.

   a. _____

   b. _____

   c. _____

   d. _____

   e. _____

EXERCISE 1-4

# Practicing Previewing

**Directions:** Preview a chapter from one of your other textbooks. After you have previewed it, without referring to the chapter write a list of topics it covers.

**EXERCISE 1-5**    ## Previewing a Reading

**Directions:** Preview the professional essay "A Brother Lost," on page 28, using the steps listed in the "How to Preview" section, and answer the following questions:

1. What is the topic of the reading?
2. What main point does the reading make about the topic?
3. What did you already know about the topic?

# Form Guide Questions

■ **GOAL 3**
Form guide questions

Did you ever read an entire page or more and not remember anything you read? Have you found yourself going from paragraph to paragraph without really thinking about what the writer is saying? Guide questions can help you overcome these problems. **Guide questions** are questions you expect to be able to answer while or after you read. Most students form them mentally, but you can jot them in the margin if you prefer.

The following tips can help you form questions to guide your reading. It is best to develop guide questions *after* you preview but *before* you read.

■ **Turn each major heading into a series of questions.** The questions should ask something that you feel is important to know.

■ **As you read a section, look for the answers to your questions.** Highlight the answers as you find them.

■ **When you finish reading a section, stop and check to see whether you can recall the answers.** Place check marks by those you cannot recall. Then reread.

■ **Avoid asking questions that have one-word answers, like** yes **or** no. Questions that begin with *what*, *why*, or *how* are more useful.

Here are a few textbook headings and some examples of questions you might ask:

| HEADING | QUESTIONS |
|---|---|
| **Reducing Prejudice** | How can prejudice be reduced? |
| | What type of prejudice is discussed? |
| **The Deepening Recession** | What is a recession? Why is it deepening? |
| **Newton's First Law of Motion** | Who was Newton? What is his First Law of Motion? |

## EXERCISE 1-6

# Writing Guide Questions

**Directions:** Write at least one guide question for each of the following headings.

| HEADING | QUESTIONS |
| --- | --- |
| 1. World War II and Black Protest | 1. _____ <br> _____ |
| 2. Foreign Policy Under Obama | 2. _____ |
| 3. The Increase of Single-Parent Families | 3. _____ <br> _____ |
| 4. Changes in Optical Telescopes | 4. _____ <br> _____ |
| 5. Causes of Violent Behavior | 5. _____ |

## EXERCISE 1-7

# Writing Guide Questions

**Directions:** Preview Chapter 5 of this book. Then write a question for each major heading.

1. _____

2. _____

3. _____

4. _____

5. _____

## EXERCISE 1-8

# Writing Guide Questions

**Directions:** For the chapter you choose for Exercise 1-4, write a list of guide questions.

_____

_____

_____

_____

# Keys to Understanding What You Read

■ GOAL 4
Develop strategies for
understanding what
you read

Each semester you will spend many hours reading a variety of material, from textbooks to student essays to professional readings. In order to get the most from the material, you will need to develop strategies for understanding what you read.

## Using Idea Maps

An **idea map** is a visual picture of the organization and content of an essay. It is a drawing that enables you to see what is included in an essay in a brief outline form. Idea maps are used throughout this book for both reading and writing. For reading, you can use them to help you understand a selection—discover how it is organized and study how ideas relate to one another. For writing, an idea map can help you organize your own ideas and check to be sure that all the ideas you have included belong in the essay.

By filling in an idea map for a reading, you are reviewing the reading and analyzing its structure. Both of these activities will help you remember what you read. Though it takes time to draw, an idea map will save you time in the long run. You can avoid rereading, and the content of the essay will stick in your mind, preparing you for class discussions and writing about the reading. Use the model that follows to draw idea maps. You may need to add extra boxes or you may not need all the boxes included, depending on the number of ideas and details in the essay. The following model shows only the essay's main point (thesis) and the key ideas. You can draw idea maps that include details as well, if it suits your purpose.

**VISUALIZE IT!**

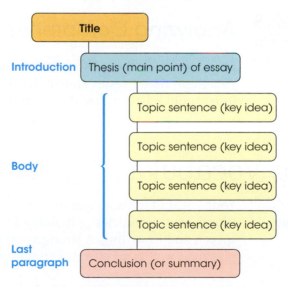

**Model for Idea Map**

Title

Introduction — Thesis (main point) of essay

Body
- Topic sentence (key idea)
- Topic sentence (key idea)
- Topic sentence (key idea)
- Topic sentence (key idea)

Last paragraph — Conclusion (or summary)

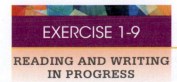

**EXERCISE 1-9**

READING AND WRITING
IN PROGRESS

## Drawing an Idea Map

**Directions:** Read the professional essay on page 28. Draw an idea map of the essay. Use the model shown above as a guide.

## Tips for Understanding Difficult Assignments

The professional readings that end each chapter are intended to be challenging as well as models of good writing. Depending on your background knowledge and experience, you may encounter one or more readings that are difficult. Use the following suggestions to help you find new strategies for approaching a difficult reading:

1. **Analyze the time and place in which you are reading.** If you've been working for several hours, mental fatigue may be the source of the problem. If you are reading in a place with distractions or interruptions, you might not be able to understand what you are reading.

2. **Rephrase each paragraph in your own words.** You might need to approach complicated material sentence by sentence, expressing each in your own words.

3. **Read aloud sentences or sections that are particularly difficult.** Reading out loud sometimes makes complicated material easier to understand.

4. **Reread difficult or complicated sections.** In fact, sometimes several readings are appropriate and necessary.

5. **Slow down your reading rate.** On occasion, simply reading more slowly and carefully will provide you with the needed boost in comprehension.

6. **Write a brief outline of major points.** This will help you see the overall organization and progression of ideas.

7. **Highlight key ideas.** After you have read a section, go back and think about and highlight what is important. Highlighting forces you to sort out what is important, and this sorting process builds comprehension and recall.

**EXERCISE 1-10**

**READING AND WRITING IN PROGRESS**

## Analyzing Comprehension Strategies

**Directions:** Consider the professional essay you read for Exercise 1-9. Write a paragraph that assesses and analyzes how using any of the techniques just outlined could have improved your understanding of the reading.

# Build Your Vocabulary Through Reading

■ **GOAL 5**
Build your vocabulary

Your vocabulary is an important asset, both in college and in the workplace. Words are the vehicles or building blocks with which you express ideas both in speech and in writing. A strong vocabulary identifies you as a learned, educated person as well as an effective communicator.

## Using a Dictionary

Every writer needs to use a dictionary, whether it is an online or a print version, because it is a basic tool for expanding vocabulary. In addition to being used for looking up unfamiliar words and for checking spelling, a dictionary is also useful for pronouncing words, learning about word origins, and finding variant (alternative) spellings and synonyms.

For quick reference when in class, access an online dictionary using your smartphone, or carry a pocket dictionary. When working at your desk, use either a print collegiate dictionary or an online version. Two popular dictionaries that are available both in print and online are those by Merriam-Webster (http://www.m-w.com) and American Heritage (http://www.ahdictionary.com). Both online versions feature an audio component that allows you to hear how a word is pronounced.

## Figuring Out Unfamiliar Words

One of the best ways to improve your vocabulary is to read! Reading essays, by both professional and student authors, is an excellent way to build your vocabulary. As you read them, you will encounter words that you can use to expand your vocabulary. Use the "Strengthening Your Vocabulary" exercise that follows each reading to learn new words in the reading. You may also encounter other words in the reading that are unfamiliar to you or you may come upon uncommon uses for words you already know. As you find words that you want to make part of your writing vocabulary, circle or highlight them as you read, and use the tips on page 24 to learn their meanings. Notice that the first step is not what you expect, which would be to look words up in a dictionary.

In addition to adding words to your vocabulary, you can also learn about creative and interesting ways to use language. As you read, look for the following:

1. **Euphemisms** These are words that hide or disguise the importance, reality, or seriousness of something. ("Ladies' room" is a euphemism for toilet; "victim of friendly fire" is a euphemism for a soldier shot by his or her own comrades.)

2. **Connotative meanings** Words have shades of meaning called connotations. These are the emotional associations that accompany words for some readers. The word *mother* has many connotative meanings. For some it means a warm, loving caregiver. For others it may suggest a strict disciplinarian.

3. **Jargon** Jargon is specialized terminology used in a particular field of study. Football has its own jargon: *linebackers, kickoff, touchdown,* and so on. Academic disciplines also have their own language (psychology: *drive, motivation, stressor*).

4. **Foreign words and phrases** Many Latin, French, and Spanish words have entered our language and are used as if they are part of our language. Here are a few examples:

| | |
|---|---|
| **aficionado** | (Spanish)—someone enthusiastic and knowledgeable about something |
| **et cetera** | (Latin)—and so forth |
| **faux pas** | (French)—embarrassing social blunder |
| **guerrilla** | (Spanish)—freedom fighter |
| **status quo** | (Latin)—the way things are, an existing state of affairs |
| **tête-à-tête** | (French)—a private conversation between two people |

5. **Figurative language** Figurative language consists of words and phrases that make sense creatively or imaginatively but not literally. The expression "The exam was a piece of cake" means, creatively, that the exam was easy, as eating cake is easy. But the exam did not literally resemble a cake.

6. **Neologisms** Neologisms are new words that have recently entered our language. As technology and society change, new words are created. Here are a few examples: *blogs* (Web logs or diaries), *spamming* (sending unwanted e-mail to someone), and *egosurfing* (searching online for information about yourself).

## How to Figure Out Unfamiliar Words

Use the following steps to figure out the meaning of a word you do not know:

1. **Pronounce the word.** Often, by "hearing" the word, you will recall its meaning.

2. **Try to figure out the word from its context—the words and sentences around the unfamiliar word.** Often there is a clue in the context that will help you figure out a meaning.

   **Example:** During her lecture, the **ornithologist** described her research on western spotted owls as well as other species of birds.

   The context reveals that an ornithologist is a person who studies birds.

   Be sure to look for clues to meaning after the word, as well as before it.

   **Example:** The elderly man walked with the help of a **prosthesis.** He was proud that his artificial limb enabled him to walk without assistance.

   The context reveals that a prosthesis is an artificial limb. Refer to Vocabulary Workshop #2 (p. 39) for more practice using context clues.

3. **Look for parts of the word that are familiar.** You may spot a familiar root (for example, in the word *improbability* you may see a variant spelling of the word *probable*), or you may recognize a familiar beginning (for example, in the word *unconventional*, knowing that *un-* means "not" lets you figure out that the word means not conventional). Refer to Vocabulary Workshop #4 (p. 47) for more practice using word parts.

4. **If you still cannot figure out the word, mark it and keep reading, unless the sentence does not make sense without knowing what the word means.** If it does not, then stop and look up the word in a print or online dictionary.

5. **When you finish reading, look up all the words you have marked.**

6. **After reading be sure to record, in a vocabulary log notebook or computer file, the words you figured out or looked up so you can review and use them frequently.**

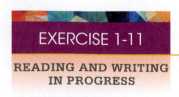

## EXERCISE 1-11

**READING AND WRITING IN PROGRESS**

## Analyzing Words

**Directions:** For the professional essay you read in Exercise 1-9, list any words for which you did not know the meaning. For each word listed, write the meaning and indicate what method you used to figure it out (context, words parts, or dictionary).

| Word | Meaning | Method |
|------|---------|--------|
| 1. _____ | _____ | _____ |
| 2. _____ | _____ | _____ |
| 3. _____ | _____ | _____ |

# Think Critically

■ GOAL 6
Think critically

The biggest difference between high school and college is the difference in your instructors' expectations of how you should *think*. High school classes focus on developing a basic foundation of knowledge, often built through memorization. In college, however, you are expected not only to learn and memorize new information, but also to *analyze* what you are learning: In other words, your college instructors expect you to be a **critical thinker.**

*Critical* does not mean "negative." Critical thinking means evaluating and reacting to what you read, rather than accepting everything as "the truth." Thinking critically sometimes requires you to consult multiple sources of information to develop perspective on a topic. For example, when writing an essay on how post-traumatic stress disorder affects returning veterans, you might read several accounts written by vets and consult several research studies, gleaning ideas from each.

## The Benefits of Critical Thinking

The ability to think critically offers many benefits. In your college courses, critical thinking allows you to

- Do well on essay exams, particularly those that ask for analysis.
- Write effective essays and term papers.
- Distinguish good information from incomplete, inaccurate, or misleading information.

In everyday life and in the workplace, a good set of critical thinking skills will help you

- Make informed, reasonable decisions.
- Spend money wisely and make good financial choices.
- Understand issues in the news, including business and political issues.
- Expand your interests beyond "passive entertainment" (such as watching TV or movies) to active entertainment that engages your mind and creativity.

## Critical Thinking Is Active Thinking

Critical thinking is essential to effective reading. For example,

- When reading a college textbook, you might ask yourself if the author is trying to influence your opinions.
- When reading a newspaper, you might ask yourself if the article is telling the full story or if the journalist is leaving something out.
- When reading an advertisement, you might ask yourself what message the ad is sending to get you to buy the product.

To help you strengthen your critical reading skills, Chapters 14 and 15 are devoted entirely to critical thinking.

## EXERCISE 1-12    Understanding Critical Thinking

**Directions:** Indicate whether each of the following statements is true (T) or false (F) based on your understanding of critical thinking.

_____  1. Thinking critically about a reading selection means finding ways to criticize it and show all the ways it is wrong.

_____  2. Critical reading is not necessary unless the instructor specifically assigns some sort of "critical thinking" exercise to go along with the reading.

_____  3. While textbooks offer good opportunities for critical reading, so do other reading materials, such as magazines and Web sites.

_____  4. Critical thinking skills are important in college but do not have much relevance in the "real world."

_____  5. Engaging in critical thinking sometimes requires you to consult additional sources of information beyond what you are currently reading.

## EXERCISE 1-13    Thinking Critically

**Directions:** Read the paragraph and answer the questions that follow.

> In survey after survey, 60 to 80 percent of food shoppers say they read food labels before selecting products; they consume more vegetables, fruits, and lower-fat foods; and they are cutting down on portion sizes and total calories. Diet-book sales are at an all-time high as millions of people make the leap toward what they think is healthy eating. But we still have a long way to go. In fact, although reports indicate that increasing numbers of us read labels and are trying to eat more healthfully, nearly 78% of all adults indicate that they are not eating the recommended servings of fruits and vegetables and that they are still eating too many refined carbohydrates and high-fat foods.
>
> —Donatelle, *Health: The Basics*, p. 255

(Hint: Think analytically and critically to answer the following questions.)

1. The passage talks about *surveys*, which is another word for *questionnaires*. Why might the survey results not truly reflect reality?

_____

_____

_____

2. Does the fact that diet-book sales are at an all-time high mean that more people are going on diets and/or eating more healthfully? Why or why not?

_____

_____

_____

3. Based on this passage, what do you think the author sees as the most important parts of a healthy diet?

_____

_____

4. What phrase does the author use to imply that people may have good intentions but don't necessarily understand how to eat more healthfully?

_____

_____

# INTEGRATING READING AND WRITING

## READ AND RESPOND: A Professional Essay

### Thinking Before Reading

The following reading first appeared in *Salon* magazine in July 2010. In the reading, the author describes how her perception of homelessness changed after her own brother became homeless. This essay is a good example of the kind of professional essay you will be asked to read in this book.

1. Preview the reading.
2. Connect the reading to your own experience by answering the following questions:
    a. What experience have you had with homeless people?
    b. How would you describe the homeless people you have seen in your city?
    c. Have you ever tried to help someone who did not want your help?

# A Brother Lost

## Ashley Womble

1    Like any New Yorker, I was no stranger to homeless people. I passed by them on my way to the shiny glass tower where I worked for a glossy women's magazine: the older lady perched atop a milk crate in the subway station, the man curled up in a dirty sleeping bag and clutching a stuffed animal. They were unfortunate ornaments of the city, unlucky in ways I never really considered.

2    Until one hot summer day in 2009 when my little brother Jay left his key on the coffee table and walked out of his house in West Texas to live on the streets. In the days that followed I spent hours on the phone with detectives, social workers, and even the FBI, frantically trying to track him down. A friend designed a "Missing" poster using the most recent picture I had of him; he was wearing a hoodie and a Modest Mouse T-shirt, a can of beer in his hand and a deer-in-headlights expression on his face. I created a Facebook group and contacted old acquaintances still living in our hometown of Lubbock, begging everyone I even remotely knew to help me find him. No luck. If it had been me, a pretty young white woman, chances are my face would have been all over the news—but the sudden disappearance of a 20-year-old guy with paranoid schizophrenia didn't exactly warrant an **Amber Alert**.

**Amber Alert**

a public alert system that spreads information about a missing person through broadcast media and electronic billboards on highways

3    In the year and a half that mental illness had ravaged my brother's mind, I'd learned to lower my expectations of what his life would be like. The smart kid who followed politics in elementary school probably wouldn't become a lawyer after all. Instead of going to college after high school, Jay became obsessed with 9/11 conspiracy theories. What began as merely eccentric curdled into something manic and disturbing: He believed the planners of 9/11 were a group of people called "the Cahoots" who had created a 24-hour television network to monitor his actions and control his thoughts. Eventually, his story expanded until the Cahoots became one branch of the New World Order, a government whose purpose was to overturn Christianity, and he had been appointed by God to stop it.

4    This made it hard for him to act normal, even in public. He'd lost his job busing tables after yelling "Stop the filming and hand over the tapes" to everyone dining in the restaurant. Having friends or even a coherent conversation wouldn't be possible unless he took the antipsychotic medication he'd been prescribed while he was in the mental hospital. A legal adult, he was allowed to refuse treatment, and he did. Otherwise the Cahoots would win.

5    I counted each day he'd been missing until they became weeks, until the number was so high I wondered if he was even still alive. That number was about the only thing I continued to keep track of. Dirty clothes and dishes piled up at home, I missed deadlines at work, and I got out of bed only if it was absolutely necessary. I cried often, but especially during thunderstorms, a reminder that wherever my

brother was, he was unprotected. Eventually it became clear that I was losing it, too. So I did what my brother wouldn't allow himself to do: I started taking a pill that helped usher away my anxiety and depression.

6      Weeks after Jay disappeared, police in Maryland found him talking to a spider and had him hospitalized. He stayed for 72 hours. Then he went missing again.

7      September 11, 2009, was one of those drizzling mornings when I thought of my brother. There was the usual undertone of reverent sadness in the city, but for me, the date was a reminder of all that had gone wrong inside Jay's mind. And on that day my phone finally rang.

8      "Hello." Jay's Southern drawl was unmistakable. I sat straight up in my desk chair at work wondering what I should do. Record the call? Take notes?

9      "Where are you?" I asked, as images of him sitting in a jail cell or stranded alone in an alley flashed in my head.

10      "Manhattan," he said.

11      My heart filled with hope. Then he asked me if I'd gone to the witchcraft celebration at the World Trade Center, where the Sorcerers had ordered the wind and the rain to destroy the ceremony. Once again, I just felt like a helpless stranger.

12      I asked nervously if I could buy him dinner. To my surprise, he agreed. Twenty minutes later I met him near Penn Station; he was hunched under an awning next to a big blue tarp that covered his backpack and the paisley duffel he'd once borrowed. His pale skin had tanned and hair covered his face. He was staring at people as they walked by, but he didn't see me until I said his name. Standing face-to-face with him, I could see that he had lost a lot of weight. His cheekbones jutted out from his once-full face. If I had seen his picture I would have gasped. Instead, I just held out my arms.

**Zagat**
a guide to restaurants in a particular city

13      **Zagat** has no recommendations for where to take your homeless brother to dinner. We settled on the Mexican chain Chevys and sat in a booth near the back. He told me about hitchhiking to New York and sleeping in Central Park until the cops kicked him out. He grinned as he talked about sleeping on the steps of a downtown school, his smile still as charming as it had been when he was 7.

14      "Do you consider yourself homeless?" I asked.

15      "Oh, yes!" he answered proudly.

16      I wondered if the constant motion of wandering from town to town helped quiet the voices he heard. If it was his own kind of medication and, if so, could I really tell him that was the wrong way to live?

17      Earlier in the year I'd bribed him with a trip to visit me on the condition that he took his meds. Now he was sitting in front of me, and as much as I wanted to let him stay in my apartment, I knew I couldn't let him (my therapist discouraged it and my roommate rightly put her foot down). I approached the topic cautiously, my voice shaking as I asked, "Do you know why you can't stay with me?" His voice small and shamed, he answered, "Because I won't take my medication." He had always denied that he had schizophrenia, but his admission gave me hope that maybe some day that would change.

18      I tried to quiet my own inner voice, which told me Jay needed to be in the hospital where a team of psychiatrists could experiment with medications that would fix his mind. I could do some things for my brother: I could give him a little

money for cigarettes. I could buy him a new backpack, a sleeping bag, good walking shoes. But the more I pushed him to get help, the more my own sanity escaped me.

19      So I let him go. He went to New Jersey. Florida. Louisiana. To a place where he told me from a pay phone he wouldn't call anymore because he didn't want me to know his whereabouts. I can only imagine what he looks like after a year on the streets: His hair must be long, skin tan and hardened, and his rail-thin body caked in dirt. He probably doesn't look much different from the homeless people I pass by on the streets of New York City. Seeing them makes my heart ache, makes me think about those they may have left behind, people who long to dust them off and put them on the right path but who know, in the end, it's not their choice.

## Getting Ready to Write

### Checking Your Comprehension

1. Explain who Jay is. How old was he when he disappeared and what mental illness does he have?
2. What does Jay believe about 9/11? Explain the term "the Cahoots."
3. What caused Jay to lose his job?
4. How did the author eventually handle her anxiety and depression?
5. When does Jay finally contact the author? Why can't he stay with her?
6. What does the author do for Jay? What is she unable to do?

### Strengthening Your Vocabulary

Using the word's context, word parts, or a dictionary, write a brief definition of each of the following words as it is used in the reading:

1. warrant (paragraph 2) _____
2. ravaged (paragraph 3) _____
3. eccentric (paragraph 3) _____
4. coherent (paragraph 4) _____
5. reverent (paragraph 7) _____

### Examining the Reading: Drawing Idea Maps

As described on page 21, an idea map can help you grasp the content and organization of an essay. Drawing an idea map is also an excellent way to check your understanding and review the reading in preparation for discussing or writing about it.

Complete the following idea map of "A Brother Lost" by filling in the missing information. Because this essay relates events in story form, this map takes the form of a time line. Time lines are used to show the sequence of events.

**VISUALIZE IT!**

**Time Line for "A Brother Lost"**

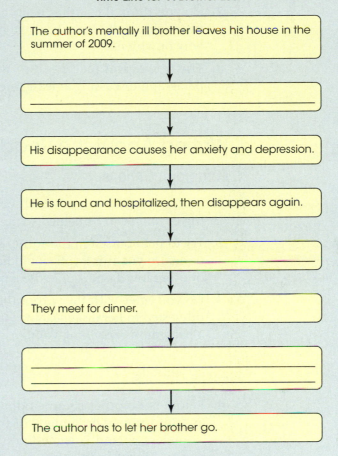

The author's mentally ill brother leaves his house in the summer of 2009.

⬇

_____

⬇

His disappearance causes her anxiety and depression.

⬇

He is found and hospitalized, then disappears again.

⬇

_____

⬇

They meet for dinner.

⬇

_____
_____

⬇

The author has to let her brother go.

## Reacting to Ideas: Discussion and Journal Writing

1. How do you typically react when you see a homeless person? Will the author's story change how you react next time? Write a journal entry explaining your answers and describing how this essay makes you feel about homelessness and homeless people.

2. Discuss the opening paragraph of "A Brother Lost." Did you find yourself agreeing with the author's view of homeless people?

3. Consider the author's choice of descriptive words such as *ravaged* and *curdled*. How do these words help make her story more effective?

4. Discuss the author's purpose in writing this essay. Do you think she achieves her purpose? Why or why not?

5. How does the author conclude this essay? How would you describe her feelings in the last paragraph?

**THINKING VISUALLY**

6. What is the purpose of the illustration that accompanies the reading? What details do you notice about it that reflect the author's story?

### Thinking and Writing Critically

1. The author describes the homeless as the "unfortunate ornaments of the city" (paragraph 1). Write a sentence or two explaining what she means by this figurative expression.

2. Do you think the author believes that mentally ill people should be institutionalized and forced to take medication? Write a paragraph explaining why or why not.

3. The title of this piece, "A Brother Lost," has multiple meanings. Write a paragraph discussing at least three of these meanings.

MySkillsLab®

**Complete** this Exercise

# Writing About the Reading

## Paragraph Options

1. Think of a situation in which you tried to help someone who was unwilling or unable to be helped. Write a paragraph describing that experience.

2. Try to put yourself in the author's shoes and imagine what you would have done. Do you think you would have been able to let your brother (or sister, or other loved one) go? Write a paragraph explaining your answer.

3. Do you agree with the author that the news media would have been more interested in her disappearance than that of her mentally ill brother? Write a paragraph explaining your answer.

## Essay Options

4. Before her brother became homeless, the author viewed homeless people as "unfortunate ornaments of the city." Her experience shows that each homeless person is someone's brother, sister, daughter, son—in other words, a real person. Write an essay explaining how you viewed homeless people before reading this article, and how you view them now, after reading this article.

5. We sometimes make assumptions or generalizations about a certain group until we meet a member of that group who changes our opinion. Think of an individual who changed your viewpoint toward a group, perhaps an elderly person or someone with a disability, a person from another culture or political party, or even a homeless or mentally ill person. Write an essay about your experience.

6. In this article, the author must come to terms with letting her brother make his own choice about what is the "right path" for him. Write an essay about freedom of choice. You may focus on a difficult choice you made for yourself, or one that you believed represented the right path for another person. How did the choice work out in the end?

# SELF-TEST SUMMARY

To test yourself, cover the Answer column with a sheet of paper and answer each question listed in the left column. Evaluate each of your answers as you work by sliding the paper down and comparing your answer with what is printed in the Answer column.

| QUESTION | ANSWER |
|---|---|
| **GOAL 1 Read actively**<br>What is active reading? | Active reading is a method of thinking about a text as you read it, and becoming engaged with the text. |
| **GOAL 2 Preview before reading**<br>Why is previewing important? | Previewing helps you become familiar with a reading or chapter's content and organization and enables you to make predictions. |
| **GOAL 3 Form guide questions**<br>What are guide questions? | Based on headings, guide questions are questions you expect to be able to answer while or after reading. |
| **GOAL 4 Develop strategies for understanding what you read**<br>What strategies can I use for understanding what I read? | Use idea maps, which are diagrams that show the content and organization of an essay. Also, refer to the numbered list under "Tips for Understanding Difficult Assignments" on page 22. |
| **GOAL 5 Build your vocabulary**<br>How can I improve my vocabulary? | Use context, word parts, and a dictionary to figure out words you do not know. Keep track of new words in a vocabulary log or computer file. Use the Vocabulary Workshops on pages 34–54. |
| **GOAL 6 Think critically**<br>What is critical thinking? | Critical thinking means evaluating and reacting to what you read, rather than accepting everything as the truth. |

 **MySkillsLab**® For more help with **Active Reading**, go to your learning path in MySkillsLab at www.myskillslab.com.

# VOCABULARY WORKSHOPS

Vocabulary is important for both readers and writers:

- Readers need a strong vocabulary to grasp what an author means.
- Writers need a strong vocabulary to express their ideas clearly and effectively.

The following set of workshops focuses on vocabulary building strategies. Each workshop offers a technique for increasing your speaking, reading, writing, and listening vocabularies:

- **Vocabulary Workshop 1:** Expanding Your Vocabulary
- **Vocabulary Workshop 2:** Using Context Clues
- **Vocabulary Workshop 3:** Learning Specialized and Technical Vocabulary
- **Vocabulary Workshop 4:** Using Word Parts

Each workshop explains a technique and gives you practice using it. Be sure to apply these techniques to everything you read for college, on the job, or for leisure or everyday reading. The more often you use these techniques, the faster your vocabulary will improve.

## VOCABULARY WORKSHOP: EXPANDING YOUR VOCABULARY

### How to Expand Your Vocabulary

Expanding your vocabulary requires motivation, a positive attitude, and skills. Of these, motivation is the most important. To improve your vocabulary, you must be willing to work at it, spending both time and effort to notice and learn new words and meanings.

Expanding your vocabulary is important because

- A strong vocabulary will contribute to both academic and career success.
- Broadening your vocabulary will improve the clarity of your thinking.
- Your reading and writing skills will improve as your vocabulary improves.
- Your vocabulary is a reflection of you, and a strong vocabulary creates a positive image.

This workshop focuses on the skills you need to build your vocabulary.

## Reading Widely

One of the best ways to improve your vocabulary is by reading widely and diversely, sampling many different subjects and styles of writing. Through reading, you encounter new words and new uses for familiar words. You also see words used in contexts that you have not previously considered.

## Using Words You Already Know

Most people think they have just one level of vocabulary and that this can be characterized as large or small, strong or weak. Actually, everyone has at least four levels of vocabulary, and each varies in strength.

1. Words you use in everyday speech or writing
   Examples: *laptop, leg, lag, lead, leave, lost*

2. Words you know but seldom or never use in your own speech or writing
   Examples: *lethal, legitimate, leverage, locomotion, luscious*

3. Words you've heard or seen before but cannot fully define
   Examples: *logistics, lament, lackadaisical, latent, latitude*

4. Words you've never heard or seen before
   Examples: *lanugo, lagniappe, laconic, lactone, lacustrine*

---

**EXERCISE 1**

# Levels of Vocabulary

**Directions:** In the spaces provided below, list five words that fall under each of the four categories listed above. It will be easy to think of words for category 1. Words for categories 2 through 4 may be taken from the following list.

| | | | |
|---|---|---|---|
| activate | credible | garbanzo | logic |
| alien | deletion | gastronome | manual |
| attentive | delicate | havoc | meditate |
| congruent | delve | heroic | osmosis |
| connive | demean | impartial | resistance |
| continuous | focus | impertinent | voluntary |
| contort | fraught | liberate | |

| *Category 1* | *Category 2* | *Category 3* | *Category 4* |
|---|---|---|---|
| _____ | _____ | _____ | _____ |
| _____ | _____ | _____ | _____ |
| _____ | _____ | _____ | _____ |
| _____ | _____ | _____ | _____ |
| _____ | _____ | _____ | _____ |

To build your vocabulary, try to shift as many words as possible from a less familiar to a more familiar category. This task is not easy. You start by noticing words. Then you question, check, and remember their meanings. Finally, and most important, you use these new words often in your speech and writing.

## Looking for Five-Dollar Words to Replace One-Dollar Words

Some words in your vocabulary are general and vague. Although they convey meaning, they are not precise, exact, or expressive. Try to replace these one-dollar words with five-dollar words that convey your meaning more directly. The word *good* is an example of a much-overused word that has a general, unclear meaning in the following sentence:

> The movie was so good, it was worth the high admission price.

Try substituting the following words for *good* in the preceding sentence: *exciting, moving, thrilling, scary, inspiring.* Each of these gives more information than the word *good.* These are the types of words you should strive to use in your speech and writing.

## Actively Practicing Vocabulary

The *bad news* about vocabulary is that if you don't use it, you will lose it. If you don't play a sport for several years, you forget some of the plays and moves and have to relearn them. If you don't perform a certain function on your computer for several months, you forget the commands to use. If you don't use a new word you just learned, you are likely to forget it. The *good news* is that you can prevent this from happening.

Here are some suggestions for learning and retaining words. Depending on your learning style, some of the suggestions will work better than others.

- **Learn a word each day.** No matter how busy you are, find a new word to learn on the TV news or in the newspaper or book you are reading. The Dictionary.com and Merriam-Webster sites also offer a new word every day.

- **Write the word immediately.** If you find the word in a textbook, you will have a better chance of remembering it if you write it rather than just highlight it. In fact, write it several times, once in the margin of the text, then again on an index card or in your vocabulary log. Write it again as you test yourself.

- **Write a sentence using the word.** Make the sentence personal, about you or your family or friends. The more meaningful the sentence is, the more likely you are to remember the word.

- **Try to visualize a situation involving the word.** For instance, for the word *restore* (to bring back to its original condition), visualize an antique car restored to its original condition.

- **Draw a picture or diagram that involves the word.** For example, for the word *squander* (to waste), draw a picture of yourself squandering money by throwing dollar bills out of an open car window.

- **Talk about the word.** With a classmate, try to hold a conversation in which each of you uses at least ten new words you have learned. Your conversation may become comical, but you will get practice using new words.

- **Play word games.** Various Web sites offer word games that heighten your word awareness and introduce you to new words. The Merriam-Webster site (http://www.m-w.com) offers a word game that changes daily, and at Freerice.com, every vocabulary quiz item you answer correctly means a donation of 20 grains of rice to the United Nations World Food Program.

- **Try to use the word in your own academic speech or writing as soon as you have learned it.**

- Give yourself vocabulary tests or, working with a friend, make up tests for each other.
- Use the "Strengthening Your Vocabulary" exercises that accompany each professional reading in this book.

**EXERCISE 2**

## Using Newly Learned Words

**Directions:** Choose five new words you have recently encountered in your textbooks or class lectures. Use several of the preceding suggestions to learn each of the words.

## Develop a System for Learning Unfamiliar Words

You have to make a deliberate effort to remember and use new words, or they will fade from your memory.

### The Vocabulary Card System

One of the most practical and easy-to-use systems for expanding your vocabulary is the index card system. It works like this:

1. Whenever you hear or read a new word that you intend to learn, jot it down in the margin of your notes or mark it in some way in the material you are reading.

2. Later, write each new word on the front of an index card, then look up the meaning (or meanings) of the word and write it on the back. You might also record the word's pronunciation or a sample sentence in which the word is used. Your cards should look like the ones shown in Figure 1.

3. Whenever you have a few spare minutes, go through your pack of index cards. For each card, look at the word on the front and try to recall its meaning. Then check the back of the card to see if you were correct. If you were unable to recall the meaning or if you confused it with another word, retest yourself. Shuffle the cards after each use.

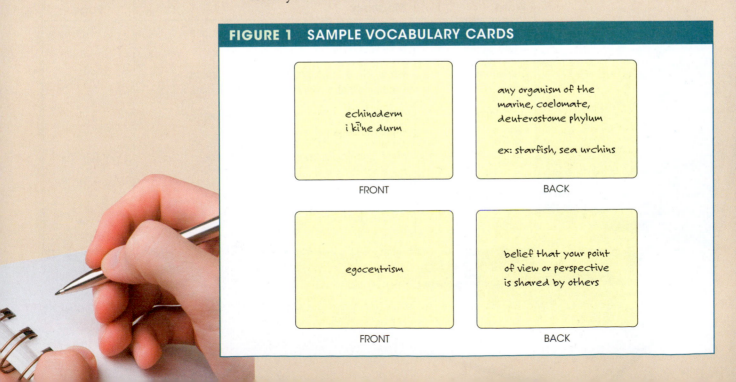

**FIGURE 1    SAMPLE VOCABULARY CARDS**

echinoderm
i kī'ne durm

FRONT

any organism of the marine, coelomate, deuterostome phylum

ex: starfish, sea urchins

BACK

egocentrism

FRONT

belief that your point of view or perspective is shared by others

BACK

4. **After you have gone through your pack of cards several times, sort the cards into two piles;** separate the words you know from those that you have not learned. Then, putting the "known words" aside, concentrate on the words still to be learned. Shuffle the cards to change their order.

5. **Once you have mastered the entire pack of cards, periodically review them to refresh your memory and to keep the words current in your mind.**

This word card system of learning vocabulary is effective for these reasons:

■ It can be used in the spare moments that are often wasted waiting for a return phone call, waiting for a class to begin, or riding a bus.

■ The system enables you to spend time learning what you do *not* know rather than wasting time studying what you already know.

■ It prevents you from learning the material in a fixed order.

## The Computerized Vocabulary Log

Using a word processing program, create a computer log for each of your courses. Daily or weekly, review both textbook chapters and lecture notes and enter specialized and technical terms that you need to learn. Use a three-column format, entering the word in one column, its meaning in the second, and a page reference in the third. You might subdivide or code your file by textbook chapter so that you can review easily when exams or quizzes on particular chapters are announced. A sample is shown below.

Your files can be used in several different ways. If you alphabetize the words, you have created a glossary that will serve as a handy reference. Keep a print copy handy as you read new chapters and review lecture notes. When studying the words in your file, try scrambling the words to avoid learning them in a fixed order.

### FIGURE 2    SAMPLE VOCABULARY LOG FOR A PSYCHOLOGY COURSE

| Word | Meaning | Page |
|------|---------|------|
| intraspecific aggression | attack by one animal upon another member of its species | 310 |
| orbitofrontal cortex | region of the brain that aids in recognition of situations that produce emotional responses | 312 |
| modulation | an attempt to minimize or exaggerate the expression of emotion | 317 |
| simulation | an attempt to display an emotion that one does not really feel | 319 |

## EXERCISE 3 — Using Vocabulary Cards

**Directions:** Select two or three sets of notes on a particular topic from any course you are taking. Prepare a set of vocabulary cards for the new terms introduced. Review and study the cards.

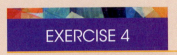

## EXERCISE 4 — Using Vocabulary Cards for Academic Terms

**Directions:** Select one chapter from any of the textbooks you are currently using. Prepare a vocabulary card for each new term introduced in the chapter. Review and study the cards.

## VOCABULARY WORKSHOP: USING CONTEXT CLUES

**2**

One of the best and fastest ways to figure out meanings of words you don't know is to use the context around the unfamiliar word. **Context** refers to other words and phrases around a given word, either in the same sentence, or in surrounding sentences. Often you can use context to figure out a word you do not know. Try it in the following sentence:

> **Phobias**, such as a fear of heights, water, or confined spaces, are difficult to overcome.

From the clues in the rest of the sentence, you can figure out that *phobias* are fears of specific objects or situations. Such clues are called **context clues**. There are five types of context clues that can help you figure out a word you do not know: *definition, synonym, example, contrast,* and *inference.* These are summarized in the following box:

### Five Useful Types of Context Clues

| Type of Context Clue | How It Works | Examples |
|---|---|---|
| **Definition** | Writers often define a word after using it. Words and phrases such as *means, refers to,* and *can be defined as* provide an obvious clue that the word's meaning is to follow. | *Corona* refers to <u>the outermost part of the sun's atmosphere</u>.<br><br><u>Broad flat noodles</u> that are served covered with sauce or butter are called fettuccine. |
| | Sometimes writers use dashes, parentheses, or commas to separate a definition from the rest of the sentence. | The judge's candor—<u>his sharp, open frankness</u>—shocked the jury.<br><br>Audition, <u>the process of hearing</u>, begins when a sound wave reaches the ear. |
| **Synonym** | Rather than formally define a word, some writers include a word or brief phrase that is close in meaning to a word you may not know. | The main character in the movie was an amalgam, <u>or combination</u>, of several real people the author met during the war. |

*(continued)*

*(continued)*

| Type of Context Clue | How It Works | Examples |
|---|---|---|
| **Example** | Writers often include examples to help explain a word. From the examples, you can often figure out what the unknown word means. | Toxic materials, such as <u>arsenic, asbestos, pesticides, and lead</u>, can cause bodily damage. (You can figure out that *toxic* means "poisonous.") |
| | | Many pharmaceuticals, including <u>morphine and penicillin</u>, are not readily available in some countries. (You can figure out that *pharmaceuticals* are drugs.) |
| **Contrast** | Sometimes a writer gives a word that is opposite in meaning to a word you don't know. From the opposite meaning, you can figure out the unknown word's meaning. (Hint: watch for words such as *but, however, though, whereas*.) | Uncle Sal was quite portly, <u>but his wife was very thin</u>. (The opposite of *thin* is *fat*, so you know that *portly* means "fat.") |
| | | The professor advocates the testing of cosmetics on animals, <u>but many of her students oppose it</u>. (The opposite of *oppose* is *favor*, so you know that *advocates* means "favors.") |
| **Inference** | Often your own logic or reasoning skills can lead you to the meaning of an unknown word. | Bob is quite versatile: <u>he is a good student, a top athlete, an excellent auto mechanic, and a gourmet cook</u>. (Because Bob excels at many activities, you can reason that *versatile* means "capable of doing many things.") |
| | | <u>On hot, humid afternoons</u>, I often feel languid. (From your experience you may know that you feel drowsy or sluggish on hot afternoons, so you can figure out that *languid* means "lacking energy.") |

Context clues do not always appear in the same sentence as the unknown word. They may appear anywhere in the passage, or in an earlier or later sentence. So if you cannot find a clue immediately, look before and after the word. Here is an example:

> Betsy took a *break* from teaching in order to serve in the Peace Corps. Despite the **hiatus**, Betsy's school was delighted to rehire her when she returned.

Notice that the clue for the word *hiatus*, *break*, appears in the sentence before the one containing the word you want to define.

**EXERCISE 5**

## Using Definition and Synonym Clues

**Directions:** Write a brief definition of each boldfaced word using the definition or synonym clues in each sentence.

1. After taking a course in **genealogy**, Diego was able to create a record of his family's history dating back to the eighteenth century. _____

2. Louie's **dossier** is a record of his credentials, including college transcripts and letters of recommendation. _____

3. There was a **consensus**—or unified opinion—among the students that the exam was difficult. _____

4. After each course heading there was a **synopsis**, or summary, of the content and requirements for the course. _____

5. When preparing job application letters, Serena develops one standard letter or **prototype**. Then she changes that letter to fit the specific jobs for which she is applying. _____

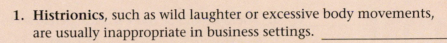
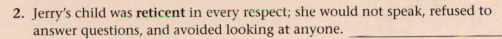

**EXERCISE 6**

# Using Example Clues

**Directions:** Write a brief definition of each boldfaced word using the example clues in each sentence.

1. **Histrionics**, such as wild laughter or excessive body movements, are usually inappropriate in business settings. _____

_____

2. Jerry's child was **reticent** in every respect; she would not speak, refused to answer questions, and avoided looking at anyone. _____

3. Most **condiments**, such as pepper, mustard, and catsup, are used to improve the flavor of foods. _____

4. Dogs, cats, parakeets, and other **sociable** pets can provide senior citizens with companionship. _____

5. Paul's grandmother is a **sagacious** businesswoman; once she turned a small ice cream shop into a popular restaurant and sold it for a huge profit. _____

**EXERCISE 7**

# Using Contrast Clues

**Directions:** Write a brief definition of each boldfaced word using the contrast clues in each sentence.

1. Freshmen are often **naive** about college at first, but by their second semester they are usually quite sophisticated in the ways of their new school. _____

2. Although most members of the class agreed with the instructor's evaluation of the film, several strongly **objected**. _____

3. L'Tanya hid shyly behind her mother when she met new people, yet her brother Matthew was very **gregarious**. _____

4. The child remained **demure** while the teacher scolded, but became loud and assertive afterward. _____

5. Some city dwellers are **affluent**; others live in or near poverty. _____

EXERCISE 8

# Using Logic and Reasoning to Determine Meaning

**Directions:** Choose the correct definition of each boldfaced word in the following sentences using logic and your own reasoning skills.

_____ 1. To **compel** Lin to hand over her wallet, the mugger said he had a gun.

   **a.** discourage          **c.** force
   **b.** entice             **d.** imagine

_____ 2. Student journalists are taught how to be **concise** when writing in a limited space.

   **a.** peaceful           **c.** proper
   **b.** clear and brief     **d.** wordy

_____ 3. There should be more **drastic** penalties to stop people from littering.

   **a.** extreme            **c.** dirty
   **b.** suitable           **d.** dangerous

_____ 4. To **fortify** his diet while weightlifting, Jose took 12 vitamins a day.

   **a.** suggest            **c.** avoid
   **b.** strengthen         **d.** approve of

_____ 5. On our wedding anniversary, my husband and I **reminisced** about how we first met.

   **a.** sang               **c.** argued
   **b.** forgot             **d.** remembered

EXERCISE 9

# Using Context Clues in a Passage

**Directions:** Read the following passage and then choose the answer that best defines each boldfaced word.

> _Worms_ and _viruses_ are rather unpleasant terms that have entered the **jargon** of the computer industry to describe some of the ways that computer systems can be invaded.
>
> A worm can be defined as a program that transfers itself from computer to computer over a network and plants itself as a separate file on the target computer's disks. One worm was **injected** into an electronic mail network where it multiplied uncontrollably and clogged the memories of thousands of computers until they could no longer function.
>
> A virus is a set of illicit instructions that passes itself on to other programs or documents with which it comes in contact. It can change or delete files, display words or obscene messages, or produce bizarre screen effects. In its most **vindictive** form, a virus can slowly **sabotage** a computer system and remain undetected for months, contaminating data or wiping out an entire hard drive. A virus can be dealt with using a vaccine, or antivirus, which is a computer program that stops the virus from spreading and often **eradicates** it.
>
> —adapted from Capron, _Computers_

_____ 1. jargon

    **a.** security    **b.** system    **c.** confusion    **d.** language

_____ 2. injected

    **a.** avoided    **b.** introduced    **c.** removed    **d.** discussed

_____ 3. vindictive

    **a.** creative    **b.** simple    **c.** spiteful    **d.** typical

_____ 4. sabotage

    **a.** prevent    **b.** disable    **c.** transfer    **d.** produce

_____ 5. eradicates

    **a.** eliminates    **b.** allows    **c.** repeats    **d.** produces

---

**EXERCISE 10**

*WORKING TOGETHER*

# Using Context Clues in Passages

**Directions:** Working with a classmate, use context clues to determine the meaning of each boldfaced word in the following passages. Write a synonym or brief definition for each. Use a dictionary, if necessary.

1.    If you have ever tried to perform heavy manual labor on a hot summer day, you may have become weak and dizzy as a result. If your **exertions** were severe, you may have even collapsed and lost **consciousness** momentarily. If this has happened to you, then you have experienced *heat exhaustion.* Heat exhaustion is a **consequence** of the body's effort to regulate its temperature—in particular, its efforts to get rid of **excess** heat. When the body must get rid of a large quantity of heat, **massive** quantities of sweat can be produced, leading to a significant **reduction** in blood volume. In addition, blood flow to the skin increases markedly, which **diverts** blood from other areas of the body. Together, these changes produce a reduction in blood pressure, which reduces blood flow to the brain and **precipitates** the symptoms just described.

    A far more serious condition is *heat stroke,* in which the body's temperature rises out of control due to failure of the **thermoregulatory** system. The skin of individuals experiencing heat stroke has a flushed appearance but will also be dry, in contrast to the **profuse** sweating of heat exhaustion. If someone is experiencing heat stroke, immediate medical attention is of the utmost importance.

    —adapted from Germann and Stanfield, *Principles of Human Physiology,* p. 9

1. exertions _____    6. reduction _____

2. consciousness _____    7. diverts _____

    _____    8. precipitates _____

3. consequence _____    9. thermoregulatory _____

4. excess _____    _____

5. massive _____    10. profuse _____

2.    The homeless are among the extremely poor. They are by definition people who sleep in streets, parks, shelters, and places not intended as **dwellings,** such as bus stations, lobbies, or **abandoned** buildings. Homelessness is not new. There have always been homeless people in the United States. But the

homeless today differ in some ways from their **counterparts** of the 1950s and 1960s. More than 30 years ago, most of the homeless were old men, only a **handful** were women, and **virtually** no families were homeless. Today the homeless are younger, and include more women and families with young children. Today's homeless also are more **visible** to the general public because they are much more likely to sleep on the streets or in other public places in great numbers. They also suffer greater **deprivation.** Although in the past homeless men on Skid Row were **undoubtedly** poor, their average income from casual and **intermittent** work was three to four times more than what the current homeless receive. In addition, many of the older homeless had small but **stable** pensions, which today's homeless do not have.

—Thio, *Sociology*, p. 235

1. dwellings _____

2. abandoned _____

3. counterparts _____

4. handful _____

5. virtually _____

6. visible _____

7. deprivation _____

8. undoubtedly _____

9. intermittent _____

10. stable _____

**3.**    Some **visionaries** say that we can **transform** nursing homes into warm, inviting places. They started with a clean piece of paper and asked how we could redesign nursing homes so they **enhance** or maintain people's quality of life. The model they came up with doesn't look or even feel like a nursing home. In Green Houses, as they are called, elderly people live in a homelike setting. Instead of a **sterile** hallway lined with rooms, 10 to 12 residents live in a carpeted ranch-style house. They receive medical care suited to their personal needs, share meals at a **communal** dining table, and, if they want to, they can cook together in an open kitchen. They can even play **virtual** sports on plasma televisions. This homelike setting **fosters** a sense of community among residents and staff.

—adapted from Henslin, *Sociology: A Down-To-Earth Approach*, p. 386

1. visionaries _____
   _____

2. transform _____

3. enhance _____

4. sterile _____

5. communal _____

6. virtual _____

7. fosters _____

**4.**    Marketers and consumers **coexist** in a complicated, two-way relationship. It's often hard to tell where marketing efforts leave off and "the real world" begins. One result of these **blurred** boundaries is that we are no longer sure (and perhaps we don't care) where the line separating this **fabricated** world from reality begins and ends. Sometimes, we **gleefully** join in the illusion. A story line in a Wonder Woman comic book featured the usual out-of-this-world **exploits** of a **vivacious** superhero. But it also included the real-world proposal of the owner of a chain of comic book stores, who persuaded DC Comics to let him **woo** his beloved in the issue.

—Solomon, *Consumer Behavior*, p. 19

1. coexist _____

2. blurred _____

3. fabricated _____

4. gleefully _____

5. exploits _____

6. vivacious _____

7. woo _____

5.     Rising tuition; roommates who bug you; social life drama; too much noise; no privacy; long lines at the bookstore; pressure to get good grades; never enough money; worries about the economy, terrorism, and natural disaster all add up to: STRESS! You can't run from it, you can't hide from it, and it can affect you in **insidious** ways that you aren't even aware of. When we try to sleep, it **encroaches** on our **psyche** through outside noise or internal worries over all the things that need to be done. While we work at the computer, stress may interfere in the form of noise from next door, strain on our eyes, and **tension** in our back. Even when we are out socializing with friends, we feel guilty, because there is just not enough time to do what needs to be accomplished. The **precise** toll that stress exacts from us over a lifetime is unknown, but increasingly, stress is recognized as a major threat to our health.

—Donatelle, *Health: The Basics*, p. 57

1.  insidious _____    3.  psyche _____

_____    4.  tension _____

2.  encroaches _____    5.  precision _____

---

## EXERCISE 11

**Working with Context Clues**

**Directions:** Bring to class a brief textbook excerpt, editorial, or magazine article that contains difficult vocabulary. Working with another student, each of you locate and underline at least three words in the passage that your partner can define by using context clues. Then work together to reason out each word, checking a dictionary to verify meanings.

## EXERCISE 12

**Using Context Clues**

**Directions:** Bring to class three sentences, each containing a word whose meaning is suggested by the context of the sentence. The sentences can come from textbooks or other sources, or you can write them yourself. Underline the words, and write each one on a separate index card.

Form groups of three to five students. Each student should create a definition sheet to record meanings.

Pass the index cards around the group. For each card, each student should list the word and write its meaning on the definition sheet. When everyone has read each card, compare meanings.

## EXERCISE 13

**A Nonsense Words Activity**

**Directions:** Each student should write five sentences, each containing a nonsense word whose meaning is suggested by the context of the sentence. Here is an example:

Before I went out to pick up a pizza, I put on my purplut. I buttoned up my purplut and went outside, glad that it was filled with down.

(Can you figure out the meaning of a purplut?)

Form groups of three to five students. Students should take turns reading aloud their sentences as group members guess the meanings of the nonsense words.

## VOCABULARY WORKSHOP: LEARNING SPECIALIZED AND TECHNICAL VOCABULARY

Have you noticed that each sport and hobby has its own language—a specialized set of words and phrases with very specific meanings? Baseball players and fans talk about slides, home runs, errors, and runs batted in, for example. Each academic discipline also has its own language. For each course you take, you will encounter an extensive set of words and terms that have a particular, specialized meaning in that subject area. In this reading and writing course, you will learn terms such as *topic sentence*, *supporting details*, *idea map*, and *transitions*.

One of the first tasks you will face in a new college course is to learn its specialized language. This is particularly true of introductory courses in which a new discipline or field of study is explained.

### How to Learn Specialized and Technical Vocabulary

The first few chapters in a textbook are introductory, too. They are written to familiarize students with the subject of study and acquaint them with its specialized language. In one economics textbook, 34 new terms were introduced in the first two chapters (40 pages). In the first two chapters (28 pages) of a chemistry book, 56 specialized words were introduced. A sample of the words introduced in each of these texts is given below. Some of the terms are common, everyday words that take on a specialized meaning; others are technical terms used only in that subject area.

| New Terms: Economics Text | New Terms: Chemistry Text |
| --- | --- |
| capital | matter |
| ownership | element |
| opportunity cost | halogen |
| distribution | isotope |
| productive contribution | allotropic form |
| durable goods | nonmetal |
| economic system | group (family) |
| barter | burning |
| commodity money | toxicity |

Recognition of specialized terminology is only the first step in learning the language of a course. More important is the development of a systematic way of identifying, marking, recording, and learning the specialized terms. Use the suggestions listed in Vocabulary Workshop 1 on page 37.

**EXERCISE 14**

### Finding Specialized Vocabulary

**Directions:** Select any two textbooks you are currently using. In each, turn to the first chapter and check to see how many specialized terms are introduced. List the total number of such terms. Then list several examples.

## Specialized Terminology in Class Lectures

As a part of your note-taking system, develop a consistent way of separating new terms and definitions from other facts and ideas. You might circle or draw a box around each new term; or, as you edit your notes (make revisions, changes, or additions to your notes after taking them), underline each new term in red; or mark "def." in the margin each time a definition is included. The mark or symbol you use is a matter of preference. Be sure to use a system to organize the terms for efficient study. One such system will be suggested later in this chapter.

## Specialized Terminology in Textbooks

Textbook authors use various means to emphasize new terminology; these include italics, boldfaced type, colored print, marginal definitions, and a new-terms list or vocabulary list at the beginning or end of each chapter.

While you are reading and highlighting important facts and ideas, you should also mark new terminology. Be sure to mark definitions and to separate them from other chapter content. (The mark or symbol you use is your choice.)

If you encounter a new term that is not defined or for which the definition is unclear, check the glossary at the back of the book for its meaning. Make a note of the meaning in the margin of the page.

At the end of the course, use the glossary to test yourself; read an entry, cover up the meaning, and try to remember it; then check to see whether you were correct.

## VOCABULARY WORKSHOP: USING WORD PARTS

**4**

Suppose you want to learn 50 new words. For each word you learn, your vocabulary increases by one word; if you learn all 50, then you've increased your vocabulary by 50 words. The vocabulary of the average young adult is 30,000 words. Adding 50 words is equal to a 0.17 percent increase—negligible at best. You may be thinking, "There must be a better way," and fortunately, there is. If you learn word parts—prefixes, roots, and suffixes (beginnings, middles, and endings of words)—instead of single words, your vocabulary will multiply geometrically rather than increase by one word at a time.

Learning word parts, then, produces a multiplier effect. A single prefix can unlock the meaning of 50 or more words. Think of the prefix *inter-*. Once you learn that it means "between," you can define many new words. Here are a few examples:

| | | |
|---|---|---|
| intercede | interrupt | interstellar |
| interconnect | interscholastic | intertribal |
| interracial | intersperse | intervene |
| interrelate | | |

Similarly, knowledge of a single root unlocks numerous word meanings. For instance, knowing that the root *spec* means "to look or see" enables you to understand words such as:

| | | |
|---|---|---|
| inspect | perspective | spectator |
| inspector | retrospect | speculate |
| introspection | retrospection | speculation |
| introspective | | |

Learning word parts is a much more efficient means of building vocabulary than learning single words. The following sections list common prefixes, roots, and suffixes and provide practice in learning them. Before you begin to learn specific word parts, study the following guidelines:

1. **In most cases, a word is built on at least one root.**

2. **Words can have more than one prefix, root, or suffix.**
   a. Words can be made up of two or more roots (*geo-logy*).
   b. Some words have two prefixes (*in-sub-ordination*).
   c. Some words have two suffixes (*beauti-ful-ly*).

3. **Words do not always have both a prefix and a suffix.**
   a. Some words have neither a prefix nor a suffix (*read*).
   b. Others have a suffix but no prefix (*read-ing*).
   c. Others have a prefix but no suffix (*pre-read*).

4. **Roots may change in spelling as they are combined with suffixes (*arid*, *arable*).**

5. **Sometimes, you may identify a group of letters as a prefix or root but find that it does not carry the meaning of the prefix or root.** For example, the letters *m-i-s* in the word *missile* are part of the root and are not the prefix *mis-*, which means "wrong or bad."

## Prefixes

Prefixes appear at the beginning of many English words and alter the meaning of the root to which they are connected. Table 1 (p. 49) groups 36 common prefixes according to meaning.

Learning word parts is particularly useful for science courses. Many scientific words are built from a common core of prefixes, roots, and suffixes.

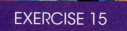

**EXERCISE 15**    ## Using Prefixes

**Directions:** Using the list of common prefixes in Table 1, write the meaning of each of the following boldfaced words. If you are unfamiliar with the root, check its meaning in a dictionary.

1. a **multinational** corporation_____

2. **antisocial** behavior_____

3. **inefficient** study habits_____

4. **postglacial** period_____

5. **unspecialized** training_____

6. housing **subdivision**_____

7. **redefine** one's goals_____

8. a **semifinalist**_____

9. **retroactive** policies_____

10. a sudden **transformation**_____

## TABLE 1    COMMON PREFIXES

| Prefix | Meaning | Example |
|---|---|---|
| **Amount or Number** | | |
| bi- | two | bimonthly |
| centi- | hundred | centigrade |
| deci- | ten | decimal |
| equi- | equal | equidistant |
| micro- | small | microscope |
| milli- | thousand | milligram |
| mono- | one | monocle |
| multi- | many | multipurpose |
| poly- | many | polygon |
| semi- | half | semicircle |
| tri- | three | triangle |
| uni- | one | unicycle |
| **Negative** | | |
| a- | not | asymmetrical |
| anti- | against | antiwar |
| contra- | against, opposite | contradict |
| dis- | apart, away, not | disagree |
| in-/il-/ir-/im- | not | illogical |
| mis- | wrongly | misunderstood |
| non- | not | nonfiction |
| pseudo- | false | pseudoscientific |
| un- | not | unpopular |
| **Direction, Location, or Placement** | | |
| circum- | around | circumference |
| com-/col-/con- | with, together | compile |
| de- | away, from | depart |
| ex-/extra- | from, out of, former | ex-wife |
| hyper- | over, excessive | hyperactive |
| inter- | between | interpersonal |
| intro-/intra- | within, into, in | introduction |
| post- | after | posttest |
| pre- | before | premarital |
| re- | back, again | review |
| retro- | backward | retrospect |
| sub- | under, below | submarine |
| super- | above, extra | supercharge |
| tele- | far | telescope |
| trans- | across, over | transcontinental |

## EXERCISE 16

**WORKING TOGETHER**

# Listing Words with Prefixes

**Directions:** Select two classmates and, working as a team, record as many words as you can that begin with one of the following prefixes. Compare your findings with those of other classroom teams.

1. pre-                2. de-                3. mis-

## Roots

Roots carry the basic or core meaning of a word. Hundreds of root words are used to build words in the English language. Table 2 lists 30 of the most common and most useful roots.

### TABLE 2    COMMON ROOTS

| Root | Meaning | Example |
|------|---------|---------|
| aster/astro | star | astronaut |
| aud/audit | hear | audible |
| bio | life | biology |
| cap | take, seize | captive |
| chron(o) | time | chronology |
| corp | body | corpse |
| cred | believe | incredible |
| dict/dic | tell, say | predict |
| duc/duct | lead | introduce |
| fact/fac | make, do | factory |
| geo | earth | geophysics |
| graph | write | telegraph |
| log/logo/logy | study, thought | psychology |
| mit/miss | send | dismiss |
| mort/mor | die, death | immortal |
| path | feeling | sympathy |
| phono | sound, voice | telephone |
| photo | light | photosensitive |
| port | carry | transport |
| sen/sent | feel | insensitive |
| scop | see | microscope |
| scrib/script | write | inscription |
| spec/spic/spect | look, see | retrospect |
| tend/tent/tens | stretch or strain | tension |
| terr/terre | land, earth | territory |
| theo | god | theology |
| ven/vent | come | convention |
| vert/vers | turn | invert |
| vis/vid | see | invisible |
| voc | call | vocation |

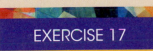

## EXERCISE 17    Using Roots

**Directions:** Use the list of common roots in Table 2 to determine the meanings of the following boldfaced words. Write a brief definition or synonym for each, checking a dictionary if necessary.

1. **bioethical** issues _____

    _____

2. **terrestrial** life _____

3. to **desensitize** _____

4. to study **astronomy** _____

5. **synchronize** your watches _____

6. **visualize** the problem _____

7. a religious **missionary** _____

8. **biographical** data _____

9. a **geology** course _____

10. **pathological** behavior _____

## Suffixes

**Suffixes** are word endings that often change the part of speech of a word. For example, adding the suffix *-y* to the noun *cloud* produces the adjective *cloudy*, meaning overcast. Accompanying the change in part of speech is a shift in meaning. Often, several different words can be formed from a single root word with the addition of different suffixes, for example,

> **Root:** *class (number of persons or things that share characteristics)*
>
> root + suffix = *class-ify, class-ification, class-ic*
>
> The students were asked to **classify** the rock specimens based on how they were formed. (verb)
>
> In biology, **classification** means systematically grouping organisms into categories. (noun)
>
> The Beatles album *Sergeant Pepper's Lonely Heart's Club Band* is a considered a rock **classic.** (adjective)

If you know the meanings of root words and the ways in which different suffixes affect those meanings, you will be able to work out the meanings of unfamiliar words. (A list of common suffixes and their meanings appears in Table 3.) When you find a word you do not know, look for the root. Then, using the sentence the word appears in, its context, work out how the word's meaning changes with the suffix added.

## TABLE 3  COMMON SUFFIXES

| Suffix | Root | Example | Meaning |
|---|---|---|---|
| **State, Condition, or Quality** | | | |
| -able | touch (v) | touchable (v) | can be touched |
| -ance | assist (v) | assistance (n) | act of helping |
| -ation | confront (v) | confrontation (n) | hostile interaction |
| -ence | refer (v) | reference (n) | mention something |
| -ible | collect (v) | collectible (adj) | able to be collected |
| -ion | discuss (v) | discussion (n) | informal debate |
| -ity | superior (adj) | superiority (n) | condition of being superior |
| -ive | permit (v) | permissive (adj) | allows behavior others would not |
| -ment | amaze (v) | amazement (n) | total astonishment |
| -ness | kind (adj) | kindness (n) | being kind |
| -ous | prestige (n) | prestigious (adj) | esteemed or honored |
| -ty | loyal (adj) | loyalty (n) | being faithful to commitments |
| -y | cream (n) | creamy (adj) | smooth and soft |
| **"One Who"** | | | |
| -ee | pay (v) | payee (n) | one to whom money is payable |
| -eer | engine (n) | engineer (n) | person skilled in working with machines |
| -er | teach (n) | teacher (n) | person who instructs |
| -ist | active (adj) | activist (n) | strong advocate for a cause |
| -or | advise (v) | advisor (n) | person who gives advice |
| **Pertaining to or Referring to** | | | |
| -al | autumn (n) | autumnal (adj) | autumn-like |
| -hood | brother (n) | brotherhood (n) | being like a brother(s) |
| -ship | friend (n) | friendship (n) | state of being a friend |
| -ward | home (n) | homeward (adv) | toward home |
| -ic | horror (n) | horrify (v) | cause someone to feel horror |

| EXERCISE 18 | **Using Suffixes** |
|---|---|

**Directions:** For each of the words listed, add a suffix so that the word will complete the sentence. Write the new word in the space provided.

1. **behavior**

   _____ therapy attempts to change habits and illnesses by altering people's responses to stimuli.

2. **atom**

   Uranium, when bombarded with neutrons, explodes and produces a heat reaction known as _____ energy.

3. **advertise**

   One important purpose of an _____ is to inform potential customers about the service or product and familiarize the public with the brand name.

4. **uniform**

The _____ of a law requires that it must be applied to all relevant groups without bias.

5. **evolution**

Darwin's theory of natural selection tied the survival of a species to its _____ fitness—its ability to survive and reproduce.

6. **compete**

When food sources are not large enough to support all the organisms in a habitat, environmental _____ occurs.

7. **religion**

During the Age of Reason in American history, _____ revivals swept the nation.

8. **perform**

Perhaps an administrator's most important duty is establishing conditions conducive to high employee motivation, which results in better job _____ .

9. **effective**

A critical factor in evaluating a piece of literature or art is its _____ —how strongly and clearly the artist's message has been conveyed to the audience.

10. **theory**

_____ have spent decades studying the theory of relativity.

---

**EXERCISE 19**     ## Using Word Parts

**Directions:** Read each of the following paragraphs and determine the meaning of each boldfaced word. Write a brief definition for each.

1.      The values and norms of most **subcultures** blend in with mainstream society. In some cases, however, some of the group's values and norms place it at odds with the dominant culture. **Sociologists** use the term **counterculture** to refer to such groups. To better see this distinction, consider motorcycle enthusiasts and motorcycle gangs. Motorcycle **enthusiasts**—who emphasize personal freedom and speed and **affirm** cultural values of success through work or education—are members of a subculture. In contrast, the Hell's Angels, Pagans, and Bandidos not only stress freedom and speed but also value dirtiness and contempt toward women, work, and education. This makes them a counterculture. Countercultures do not have to be negative, however. Back in the 1800s, the Mormons were a counterculture that challenged the dominant culture's core value of **monogamy**.

—Henslin, *Sociology: A Down-to-Earth Approach*, p. 52

1. subcultures _____

2. sociologists _____

3. counterculture _____

4. enthusiasts _____

5. affirm _____

6. monogamy _____

**2.**    Our **perception** of the richness or quality of the material in clothing, bedding, or upholstery is linked to its "feel," whether rough or smooth, flexible or **inflexible**. We **equate** a smooth fabric, such as silk, with luxury, whereas we consider denim to be practical and **durable**. Fabrics composed of **scarce** materials or that require a high degree of processing to achieve their smoothness or fineness tend to be more expensive and thus we assume they are of a higher class.
—adapted from Solomon, *Consumer Behavior*, pp. 62–63

1. perception _____

2. inflexible _____

3. equate _____

4. durable _____

5. scarce _____

**3.**    The college years mark a critical **transition** period for young adults as they move away from families and establish themselves as **independent** adults. The transition to independence will be easier for those who have successfully accomplished earlier developmental tasks, such as learning how to solve problems, make and evaluate decisions, define and **adhere** to personal values, and establish both casual and **intimate** relationships. People who have not fulfilled these earlier tasks may find their lives interrupted by **recurrent** "crises" left over from earlier stages. For example, if they did not learn to trust others in childhood, they may have difficulty establishing intimate relationships as adults.
—Donatelle, *Health: The Basics*, p. 34

1. transition _____

2. independent _____

3. adhere _____

4. intimate _____

5. recurrent _____

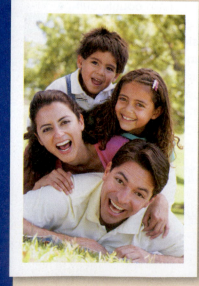

**4.**    In the U.S. legal system, the family has traditionally been defined as a unit consisting of a **heterosexual** married couple and their child or children. Many **scholars** have a more flexible definition of "family" taking into account the **extended** family of grandparents, aunts and uncles, and cousins, and sometimes even people who are not related by blood at all. Class, race, and **ethnicity** are important factors to consider as we define what makes a family.
—adapted from Kunz, *THINK Marriages and Families*, pp. 278–279

1. heterosexual _____

2. scholars _____

3. extended _____

4. ethnicity _____

# An Overview of the Writing Process

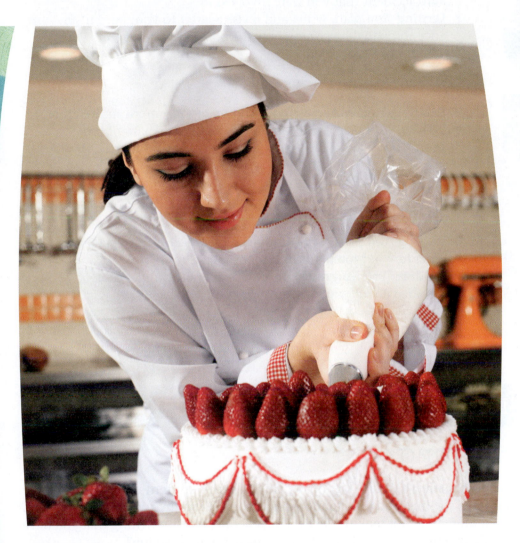

LEARNING
## GOALS

Learn how to . . .

- **GOAL 1**
  Use the writing
  process

- **GOAL 2**
  Generate ideas

- **GOAL 3**
  Organize ideas

- **GOAL 4**
  Write a first draft

- **GOAL 5**
  Revise and rewrite

- **GOAL 6**
  Proofread for
  correctness

- **GOAL 7**
  Consider your
  audience and
  purpose

## THINK About It!

Study the photograph above showing a chef decorating a cake. The chef follows a process—a series of steps taken in a particular order. First, the chef reads the customer's order for a cake. To prepare the cake, the chef reads the recipe and mixes the batter, which she then places into baking pans. Next, she prepares the frosting and other decorations. Then final assembly occurs. In much the same ways as a cake is made and assembled, writers must also follow a series of steps—which usually include reading—when writing a paragraph or an essay.

This chapter will explain what good writing is, show you five steps for writing well, and discuss two important factors you should consider when writing anything: your audience and your purpose. Approaching writing as a process is important in everyday life, in the classroom, and in the workplace.

# Reading and Writing Connections

### EVERYDAY CONNECTIONS

- **Reading** You read the summary on a police report describing an auto accident that you were involved in.
- **Writing** You plan, write, and revise a letter to your auto insurance company explaining how the police report supports your account of the accident.

### ACADEMIC CONNECTIONS

- **Reading** You read an assigned short story in American literature.
- **Writing** You plan, write, and revise a plot summary of the short story.

### WORKPLACE CONNECTIONS

- **Writing** You plan, write, and revise your yearly self-evaluation letter for your job performance review.
- **Reading** You read the performance appraisal your manager prepared about you for your review.

# FOCUSING ON READING AND WRITING

# What Is Good Writing?

To the question "What is good writing?" many students answer, "Correct grammar, spelling, and punctuation—no errors." Actually, good writing involves much more than not making errors. Think about pieces of writing that you have enjoyed reading or found helpful. What made them satisfying?

■ **Good writing requires thinking.** Good writing is a thinking process. As you read this book, you'll see that writers do a great deal of work before they actually begin writing. They think about their audience and topic, develop ideas and supporting material, and plan how best to say what they want to say. Once they have written a draft, they reevaluate their ideas to see if there is a better way to express them.

■ **Good writing involves revision.** Finding the best way to express your ideas involves experimentation and change. This process is called *revision*. When you revise, you rethink ideas and improve what you have said and how you have said it. All good writers revise, sometimes many times.

■ **Good writing expresses ideas clearly.** Good writers communicate with their readers in a direct and understandable way, making their main points clearly and supporting these points with details, facts, reasons, and examples. Good writers also arrange their main points logically. This book contains a variety of techniques to help you arrange ideas logically.

■ **Good writing is directed toward an audience.** Suppose you were going to an interview for a job. Would you wear the same clothes you wear to stop by a friend's apartment? Of course not; you modify your appearance in keeping with the situation and the people you will be seeing. Similarly, when you write, you must consider your audience. Ask yourself: Who will be reading what I write? How should I express myself so that my readers will understand what I write? Considering your audience is essential to good writing. You will learn more about this process in the "Considering Your Audience" section later in the chapter.

■ **Good writing achieves a purpose.** In written communication, you write for a specific reason or purpose. Sometimes, in college, you write for yourself: to record an assignment, to take notes in class, or to help yourself learn or remember information for an exam. Many other times, you write to communicate information, ideas, or feelings to a specific audience. You will learn more about "Writing for a Purpose" later in the chapter.

■ **Good writing requires practice.** To improve your writing, you need to practice using the three basic building blocks of written language: the sentence, the paragraph, and the essay. A **sentence** expresses one or more complete thoughts. A **paragraph** expresses one main idea and is usually made up of several sentences that explain or support that idea. An **essay** consists of multiple paragraphs that explain related ideas, all of which support a larger, broader idea. This text focuses on writing paragraphs and essays. However, Part Six, "Reviewing the Basics," will help you write more effective sentences by answering your questions about grammar, mechanics, and punctuation. The chart that follows shows how the parts of paragraphs are very much like the parts of an essay.

**VISUALIZE IT!**

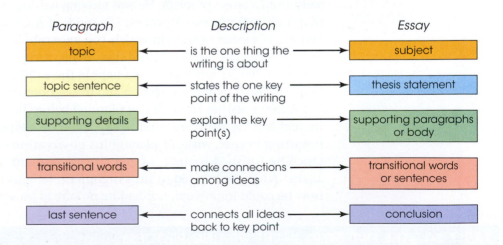

| Paragraph | Description | Essay |
|---|---|---|
| topic | is the one thing the writing is about | subject |
| topic sentence | states the one key point of the writing | thesis statement |
| supporting details | explain the key point(s) | supporting paragraphs or body |
| transitional words | make connections among ideas | transitional words or sentences |
| last sentence | connects all ideas back to key point | conclusion |

Good writing helps readers. By expressing your ideas clearly, logically, and concisely, you are helping readers understand what you are writing about.

# The Five Steps in the Writing Process

■ GOAL 1
Use the writing process

Alfredo was given his first writing assignment by his sociology instructor. This was the assignment:

> Visit the local zoo and spend at least one hour in the primate house. Write a description of what you see, and explain how it relates to our introductory unit on group behavior.

This assignment did not make much sense to Alfredo, but on Sunday afternoon he and a friend went to the primate house and he found that he actually had fun watching the monkeys' antics. Because the assignment was due Tuesday, he decided that he would begin writing later that day. He sat down at the computer and said to himself, "Well, I might as well get started," and began his assignment with the following sentence:

> I visited the primate house over the weekend and saw many interesting things.

At that point Alfredo was in trouble; he didn't know what to say next. He stared at the blank paper for a while. Realizing that he *had* to write something, he tried to describe some of what three individual monkeys did while he was there. When he finished writing a page or so of description, Alfredo printed out what he'd done, put it in his notebook, and handed it in on Tuesday. The next week, when the professor returned the papers, Alfredo was angry and disappointed when he saw his grade. The instructor's note said, "I know you tried. Next time, though, plan out your essay, write a draft, and then revise it." Alfredo thought, "I really tried. This is really disappointing. I need to learn a different way to go about writing!"

Where did Alfredo go wrong? Actually, he made several mistakes, but they all stem from a larger problem. He was viewing writing as a single-step activity instead of a multistep process. A **process** is a series of steps you follow in a specific order. Writing is a series of steps in which you **generate ideas** on what to say, **plan** how you will organize your ideas, and then **write, revise,** and **proofread** what you have written. Table 2-1 summarizes the steps in the writing process. You will get plenty of help with each step in this section and throughout the entire book.

Alfredo neither thought nor planned before he began writing; consequently, he had trouble knowing what to say. Then, in desperation, he ended up simply reporting events, without placing his observations into a unifying framework. Once he finished writing, he put the assignment away and did not look at it again. When he handed in his assignment, he hadn't reread it even once to see how he could improve it, nor had he proofread for errors. In this chapter, you will

| TABLE 2-1   THE FIVE STEPS IN THE WRITING PROCESS | |
|---|---|
| **Step** | **What It Involves** |
| 1. Generate ideas | Coming up with ideas that explain and support your topic |
| 2. Plan and organize your ideas | Deciding what ideas to include and in what order to place them |
| 3. Write a first draft | Putting your ideas in sentence, paragraph, and essay form |
| 4. Revise | Rewriting, rearranging your ideas; deleting some ideas, adding others |
| 5. Proofread | Looking for errors in typing, spelling, grammar, and punctuation |

learn to approach writing as a process and avoid making Alfredo's mistakes. Don't be concerned if this process is not entirely clear by the end of this chapter; the rest of the book will go into more detail on each step. You'll understand more and more as you work through each chapter and apply each step to your own writing.

When writing, people frequently find that some of these steps overlap or that some circling back to earlier steps is necessary. For example, you may continue to organize your ideas while writing your first draft, or you may need to generate more ideas while revising. This circling back is fine; the writing process does not always go in a straight line.

If you use each of these steps, you will find that writing will be easier and more successful for you than it was for Alfredo. You will not find yourself frustrated, staring at a blank sheet of paper, or writing something that doesn't seem to hang together or say much. Instead, you will feel as if you are developing and focusing your ideas, shaping them into words, and making a point that will hold and interest your reader. You will be well on your way to producing a good paper.

# Generate Ideas

■ GOAL 2
Generate ideas

Before you begin to write a paper, the first step is to generate ideas about your topic. Although Alfredo spent time in the primate house, he did not spend time thinking about what he saw or how it related to what he had learned in his course. He did not develop any ideas to write about.

Four good techniques you can use to generate ideas are

- freewriting
- brainstorming
- branching
- questioning

These techniques can help you overcome the feeling that you have nothing to say. They can unlock ideas you already have and help you discover new ones.

Since each of these four techniques provides a different way to generate ideas, feel free to choose from among them. At times, you may use several at different points in your writing process, or you may need to use only one of them for a particular writing assignment. Experiment to see what works best for you.

## Freewriting

**Freewriting** is writing nonstop for a limited period, usually around five or ten minutes. Write whatever comes into your mind, whether it is about the topic or not. If nothing comes to mind, you can just write, "I'm not thinking of anything."

As you write, don't be concerned with grammar, punctuation, or spelling, or with writing in complete sentences. Words and phrases are fine. Focus on recording your thoughts as they come to you. The most important thing is to keep writing without stopping. Work fast; don't think about whether what you are writing is worthwhile or makes sense. Darken your computer screen if seeing errors is distracting. After you finish, reread what you have written. Start to think about what your main point could be, a point that would unify various details and observations and fit them into an interesting framework. Highlight everything that you might be able to use in your paper.

Alfredo discussed his sociology assignment with his writing instructor, who explained how to use freewriting to generate ideas. He suggested that Alfredo redo the assignment to see how freewriting works.

*Alfredo's Freewriting*

The monkeys are behind bars like prisoners. They leap and jump and play but seem to know they can't get out. They eat with their hands—they look like impolite humans. There's an old monkey who has been there forever and he's crabby and nasty to the others. People like to go there during feeding time. Monkeys eat bananas. I can't think of anything. I can't think. It smells in the monkey house. The monkeys seemed to enjoy being watched by us. They seemed to be showing off for us. The monkey house is located next to the reptile house. I hate going there. Some monkeys threw things at us and at other monkeys and they looked angry. One monkey stole another's food but the monkey whose food was stolen didn't fight back. Most people go to the zoo during the summer. Sometimes I wonder if the zoo is really humane. Monkeys were grooming each other by picking through each other's hair. Monkeys in the zoo don't act like they would in the wild though either. I felt sorry for some of them they looked so confused. Sometimes they seemed to compete with each other to see who could do the most antics.

Alfredo reviewed what he had written and highlighted all the points having to do with his topic, *group behavior*—how the monkeys interacted with each other and with zoo visitors. The other topics in his freewriting—zoos as depressing places, how zoos differ from the wild, the eating habits of monkeys—did not relate to group behavior.

Freewriting is a creative way to begin translating ideas and feelings into words without being concerned about their value or worrying about correctness. You will often be pleasantly surprised, as Alfredo was, by the number of usable ideas this technique uncovers. Some ideas may be too broad or too personal or may stray from the topic. Still, once you have some ideas down on paper, you can begin to shape your material and select what you need. You can also do additional freewriting—or use another technique for generating ideas—once your topic or direction has become clear.

**EXERCISE 2-1**

# Using Freewriting

**Directions:** Choose three of the following topics and then, using a clock or timer, freewrite for at least five minutes on each. Be sure to write without stopping. After you finish each freewriting, reread carefully. Underline ideas that have a common thread, as you look for a group of usable ideas that would be a good focus for a paper.

1. Today's heroes
2. Rap music—its influence on attitudes and behavior, if any
3. Changes you would make where you work
4. A friend's annoying or bad habit that you wish you could break
5. The physical environment of your campus—what it is like, how it makes you feel

## Brainstorming

Brainstorming is a way of developing ideas by making a list of everything you can think of about a topic. You might list feelings, ideas, facts, examples, or problems. There is no need to write in sentences; instead, list words and phrases. Don't try to organize your ideas; just list them as you think of them. Give yourself a time limit. You'll find ideas come faster that way.

You can brainstorm alone or with friends. With your friends, you will discover a lot more ideas, because their ideas will trigger more of your own. When you've finished, read your list and mark usable ideas. One group of students came up with the following list on the topic of sports fans:

| | |
|---|---|
| sit in bleachers | baseball card collections |
| stadiums and ballparks | beer |
| have tailgate parties | betting |
| do the "wave" | cost of tickets |
| excitement and shouting | parking |
| disappointment | traffic jams in and out |
| restrooms, long lines | dress in team colors |
| food costs | chanting |
| fanatical | cold and snow |
| radio sports talk show | hotseats |

The topic of sports fans is too broad for a paragraph or short essay, but there are several groups of usable ideas here: the behavior and attitude of fans at games, the high cost of being a fan, tailgate parties, and radio sports talk shows. A student could develop a good paper on any one of these ideas, doing more brainstorming as necessary.

**EXERCISE 2-2**

# Using Brainstorming

**Directions:** For two of the following topics, brainstorm for about five minutes each. When you finish, review your list and mark ideas that seem closely connected enough to use in writing a paragraph.

1. What makes a good commercial?
2. Why is talking to strangers sometimes fun (or not fun)?
3. Why are cell phones so popular?
4. Why are some people always late—and what consequences does this have?
5. What is road rage?

## Branching

**Branching** is a visual way of generating ideas. To begin, write your topic in the middle of a whole sheet of paper and draw a circle around it. Next, think of related ideas and write them near the circle. Connect each to the circle with a line. These ideas are called the primary branches. Your topic is like a tree trunk, and your ideas are like limbs that branch out from it. You can connect other related ideas to the primary branches with smaller, or secondary, branches. The following is an example of a branching diagram that one student did for the topic "shopping at convenience stores." After the student looked at his first branching diagram, labeled Branching: Step 1, he decided to focus on the limited selection at convenience stores.

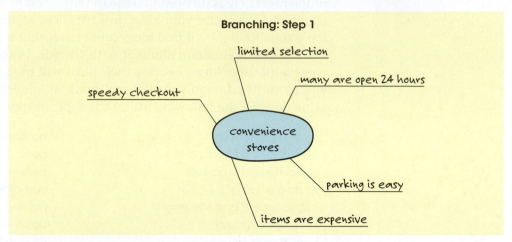

Then, the student used "limited selection" as the trunk and created three primary branches: poor-quality fresh fruit, limited veggies, and limited brand selection, as shown in the diagram Branching: Step 2.

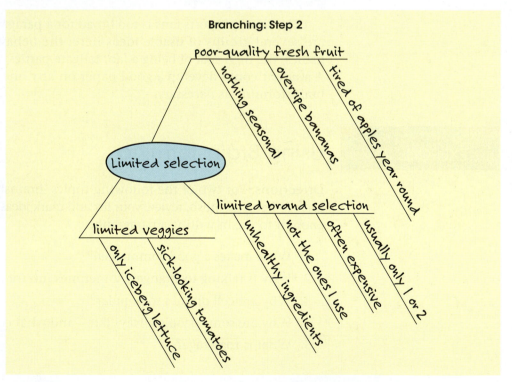

He drew secondary branches onto each of these primary ones and could have kept going.

If you use this technique, you can branch from your branches almost indefinitely. If you run out of room, you can attach extra sheets of paper. On the other hand, you don't have to develop branches for every main branch. It is often fine to choose one branch and ignore all the others.

When you have finished branching, use a highlighter or colored pencil to mark those branches that seem like good possibilities to write about.

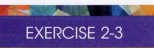

## EXERCISE 2-3 — Using Branching

**Directions:** Draw branching diagrams for two of the following topics. Then highlight those branches that could be the basis of a paragraph or essay.

1. The lives of professional athletes (choose one sport to focus on)
2. Homeless people's rights
3. Tourists who litter or display a lack of respect for the site they are visiting
4. Destination weddings
5. Waiting in hospital emergency rooms (or a location of your choice)

## Questioning

Another way to generate ideas about a given topic is to write down questions about it. As with freewriting and brainstorming, write any question that comes to mind. Don't worry if it seems silly, and don't stop to evaluate whether it is related to the topic. If you can think of answers, include them as well, but don't limit yourself to questions to which you know the answers.

The key words *Who? What? When? Where? Why?* and *How?* can help you get started in your questioning of a topic. When you have finished, read your questions carefully. Underline those questions or answers that bring out interesting angles on a topic and that you might be able to use for writing a paragraph or an essay. Here are the questions one student wrote on the topic of dreams:

| | |
|---|---|
| Why do we dream? | Do I remember all of my dreams? |
| Do dreams have meaning in our everyday life? | Are dreams predictions? |
| How do you interpret a dream? | Are dreams warnings? |
| Why are they so frightening when they hardly make sense? | What are the most common dreams? |
| | How are dreams studied? |

## EXERCISE 2-4 — Using Questioning

**Directions:** Use questioning to generate ideas on two of the following topics. Afterward, underline the questions or answers that could form the basis of an interesting paragraph or essay.

1. Giving gifts for Valentine's Day
2. The best job you ever had
3. An incident of racial profiling you have experienced, observed, or heard about
4. Drinking on campus
5. The importance of music in your life

## When to Use Which Technique

Now that you have tried freewriting, brainstorming, branching, and questioning, you are probably wondering when to use each technique. In general, there are no rules to follow. The best advice is to give them all a good chance and use the technique, or techniques, with which you are most comfortable.

You may also find that for certain topics, one technique works better than the others. For example, suppose you decide to write a paragraph about your mother's sense of humor. While it might be difficult to think of questions, freewriting might help you remember humorous events from your life with her. Suppose, however, that you are studying types of discrimination in your sociology class. Your instructor has assigned a paper that requires you to explain the effects of one type of discrimination. Asking questions about the specific topic is likely to produce useful ideas to include in your paper.

The four techniques are summarized in Table 2-2.

## Sorting Usable Ideas

Freewriting, brainstorming, branching, and questioning each produces a wide range of usable ideas. You will need to sort through them to decide which ones you can put together and expand upon to produce a paper that is unified and interesting to your reader. You will read more about this process in the upcoming section "Organizing Your Ideas."

## Choosing Your Own Topic

When your instructor assigns a topic or provides a choice of topics, part of your paper, in a sense, has been done for you. You may not like the topic(s), or you may need to narrow the topic down to make it more manageable, but at least you have a point from which to start. If your instructor directs you to choose a topic, you have greater freedom, but sometimes your first reaction may be "I don't know what to write about!"

Don't be tempted to grab just any topic in order to get on with writing. Remember that the most important element in clear writing is clear *thinking*. Invest your time in thinking about what you want to write. Use one—or several—of the four techniques you just learned for generating topics—freewriting,

| TABLE 2-2 TECHNIQUES FOR GENERATING IDEAS | |
|---|---|
| **Technique** | **How to Do It** |
| *Freewriting* | 1. Write nonstop about your topic. <br> 2. Write whatever comes to mind without concern for correctness. <br> 3. Give yourself a time limit; then stop, review, and repeat as necessary. |
| *Brainstorming* | 1. List all ideas about your topic that come to mind. <br> 2. List words and phrases, observations, and thoughts without attention to correctness. <br> 3. Give yourself a time limit; then stop, review, and repeat as necessary. |
| *Branching* | 1. Write and circle your topic in the middle of your page. <br> 2. As you think of related ideas, write them down around the circle. Connect with lines. <br> 3. Draw additional branches as you think of additional ideas. |
| *Questioning* | 1. Ask *Who? What? When? Where? Why?* and *How?* questions about your topic. <br> 2. Ask any other questions that come to mind. <br> 3. Include answers, if you know them. |

brainstorming, branching, or questioning. You can also generate ideas by reacting to the world around you. Here are some suggestions to get you involved in your world:

1. **Think of an interesting topic that was discussed in one of your classes or a topic that relates to your major.** Nursing students might, for example, think of genetic counseling for prospective parents, and accounting students of new computer software.

2. **Think of activities you have participated in over the past week.** Going to work or to church, playing softball, taking your child to the playground, shopping at a mall, or seeing a horror film could produce the following topics: communication patterns among co-workers; why attendance at church is rising (or falling); the problem with pitchers; how toddlers develop language skills; the mall as an adult playground; the redeeming value of horror films.

3. **Look around you or out the window.** What do you see? Perhaps it is the television, a dog lying at your feet, traffic, or children playing tag. Possible topics are the influence of television on what we buy, pets as companions, cars as noise polluters (or entertainment), and play as a form of learning.

4. **Think of the time of year.** Think about what you do on holidays or vacation, what is happening around you in the environment, or what this season's sports or upcoming events might mean to you.

5. **Use a writing journal.** A writing journal is a notebook or computer file in which you record your thoughts and ideas on a regular basis. Many students try to write daily and find that a journal is a useful way to spur their thinking and become a more effective writer.

6. **Think of a controversial topic you have read about, heard about on the radio or on television, or argued about with a friend.** A political candidate up for reelection, a terminally ill patient's right to euthanasia, and reforms in public education are examples.

7. **As you read, listen to the news, or go about your daily life, be alert for possible topics and write them down.** Keep the list and refer to it when your next paper is assigned.

If you choose a topic that interests you, one that you know something about or are willing to read about, you will feel more like writing. You will also find that you have more to say and that what you write will be more engaging and memorable for your reader.

**EXERCISE 2-5**

# Evaluating Techniques for Generating Ideas

**Directions:** Select one of the topics listed below. Try all four techniques—freewriting, brainstorming, branching, and questioning—on the same topic.

### TOPICS

1. Is violence a necessary part of sports?

2. What do you think of people who bring babies to adult-oriented concerts, and why?

3. How can we eat well without spending a lot of money?

4. What should a person do (or not do) when he or she loses a job or is laid off?

5. Why is it so difficult to save money?

When you have tried all four techniques, read the list of ideas produced by using each one. Mark the usable ideas. Then write short answers to the following questions:

**QUESTIONS**

1. Which technique produced the most usable ideas?

2. Which technique were you most comfortable using?

3. Which technique were you least comfortable using? Why?

# Organize Your Ideas

■ GOAL 3
Organize ideas

Once you have generated ideas about your topic, the next step is to decide how to organize them. Ideas in a paragraph or essay should progress logically from one to another. Group or arrange your ideas in a way that makes them clear and understandable to your reader. Imagine someone picking up what you have written and reading it for the first time: will that person be able to follow your train of thought easily? That should be your goal.

Assume you have been asked to write an essay about your experience in the workplace and how it has affected your life. Here is the brainstorming list that one student, Doug Mello, wrote. He worked at three places so he did some brainstorming about each.

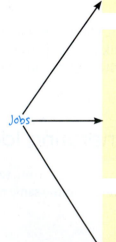

**BURGER KING:**

inconvenient hours—holidays, weekends

rude customers—I felt unappreciated

pressured and rushed work environment

other workers not serious—I hated it there

**WALMART:**

large and confusing, responsibilities not clear

supervisor was too bossy—thought she was better than us

co-workers tried to cheat the company

went home with a headache most days

customers were always in a hurry, so I felt I should be, too

never wanted to make a career of this—looked for another job

**TRUCK DRIVER:**

liked working by myself making deliveries

working with equipment and machinery was fun

job responsibilities were clear

worked on scheduling and job routing, which I enjoyed

eventually I learned that there was no future driving a truck

I decided to leave and go back to school

Jobs

As Mello reviewed his brainstorming ideas, he realized that his most positive experience had been as a truck driver and that it was the job that had the most impact on his life. He decided to write about how his experience as a truck driver changed the direction of his life. Mello reread his list of ideas and did more brainstorming to collect additional details. As he reread his additional brainstorming, he decided the best way to organize his ideas was in the order in which they happened.

## Using an Idea Map to Organize Your Ideas

One effective way to organize your ideas is to draw an idea map. Recall from Chapter 1 that an idea map is a visual picture of the organization and content of an essay. Just as a campus map shows the relationship of various buildings on campus to one another, an idea map shows the relationship of ideas to one another. When you are beginning to write, an idea map can help you organize your ideas into paragraphs and see how paragraphs fit together to form essays. Here is an idea map that Mello drew for his essay on the workplace. He developed his ideas further as he drew the map.

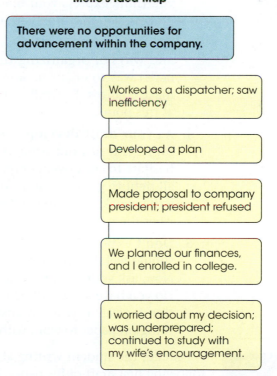

**Mello's Idea Map**

There were no opportunities for advancement within the company.

Worked as a dispatcher; saw inefficiency

Developed a plan

Made proposal to company president; president refused

We planned our finances, and I enrolled in college.

I worried about my decision; was underprepared; continued to study with my wife's encouragement.

**EXERCISE 2-6**

**WRITING IN PROGRESS**

## Arranging Ideas Logically

**Directions:** Use a topic that you developed in any of the previous exercises. Determine which ideas are usable and interrelated, and arrange them in a logical order.

# Write a First Draft

■ GOAL 4
  Write a first draft

Suppose you are taking a weekend trip and are about to pack your suitcase. You have in mind what you'll be doing and whom you'll see. You look through your entire closet, then narrow your choices to several outfits. You mix and match the outfits, figure out how much will fit in the suitcase, and finally decide what to take.

Writing a draft of a paragraph or an essay is similar to packing for a trip. You have to try out different ideas, see how they work together, express them in different ways, and, after several versions, settle upon what your paper will include. Drafting is a way of trying out ideas to see if and how they work.

A first draft expresses your ideas in sentence form. Work from your list of ideas, and don't be concerned with grammar, spelling, or punctuation at this point. Instead, focus on expressing and developing each idea fully. The following suggestions will help you write effective first drafts:

1. **After you have thought carefully about the ideas on your list, write one sentence that expresses the main point of your paragraph (working topic sentence) or essay (thesis statement).**

2. **Concentrate on explaining your topic sentence or thesis statement, using ideas from your list.** Focus first on those ideas you like best or that you think express your main point particularly well. Later in the writing process, you may find you need to add other ideas from your list.

3. **Think of a first draft as a chance to experiment with different ideas and ways of organizing them.** While you are working, if you think of a better way to organize or express your ideas, or if you think of new ideas, make changes. Be flexible. Do not worry about getting your exact wording at this point.

4. **As your draft develops, feel free to change your focus or even your topic, if it has not been assigned.** If your draft is not working out, don't hesitate to start over completely. Go back to generating ideas. It is always all right to go back and forth among the steps in the writing process. Most writers make a number of "false starts" before they produce a draft that satisfies them.

5. **Don't expect immediate success.** When you finish your first draft, you should feel that you have the *beginnings* of a paper you will be happy with. Now, ask yourself if you have a sense of the direction your paper will take. Do you have a main idea? Do you have supporting details? Is the organization logical? If you can answer "yes" to these questions, you have something on paper to work with and revise.

Mello, the student writing about his experience as a truck driver, wrote the following first draft of his paper. The highlighting indicates the main point that he developed as he wrote.

*First Draft*

   I came from a working-class family, so I had no choice but to go to work right after high school. One of the jobs was as a truck driver. At the age of twenty-nine, a company hired me that I thought offered a promising career future. After several years I knew that there were no opportunities for advancement within the company.
   After five years with the company I was frequently asked for advice on routing schedules and was assigned the job of dispatching when the plant manager was

on vacation. Being involved in the operations of the company allowed me to see the constant waste of time and money that resulted from day-to-day planning. I finally came up with a plan I thought would allow me to advance within the company and get out of my truck and off the road. I went to the president of the company with my proposal, which could have saved the company twice my wages each year in transportation costs. He said no, and that made me realize that I needed an education to have a future.

My wife and I devised a plan to organize our finances so I could return to school. I gave a six-month notice to my employer and told him why I had decided to return to school. I applied to Modesto Junior College and started in January.

I didn't know how to study and was not prepared for college courses. My major was civil engineering. Almost immediately I wondered if I had made the right decision to return to school; it was much more work than driving a truck. One of the biggest problems I am faced with is what, or how, I am contributing to my family. My wife continually encourages me in my studies and assures me that I am contributing to our family's future.

**EXERCISE 2-7**

**WRITING IN PROGRESS**

## Writing a Draft

**Directions:** Write the first draft of a paragraph (or two) using the topic you chose in Exercise 2-6 and the ideas you put in logical order in that exercise.

# Revise and Rewrite Drafts

■ **GOAL 5**
Revise and rewrite

Let's think again about the process of packing a suitcase. At first you may think you have included everything you need and are ready to go. Then, a while later, you think of other things that would be good to take. But because your suitcase is full, you have to reorganize everything. When you repack, you take everything out and rethink your selections and their relationships to each other. You might eliminate some items, add others, and switch around still others.

A similar thing often happens as you revise your first draft. When you finish a first draft, you are more or less satisfied with it. Then you reread it later and see you have more work to do. When you revise, you have to rethink your entire paper, reexamining every part and idea. Revising is more than changing a word or rearranging a few sentences, and it is not concerned with correcting punctuation, spelling errors, or grammar. Make these editing changes later when you are satisfied that you have presented your ideas in the optimal way. Revision is your chance to make significant improvements to your draft. It might mean changing, adding, deleting, or rearranging whole sections.

Mello's final draft appears on page 75, along with annotations showing the changes he made.

## How to Know What to Revise: Peer Review

**Peer review** means asking one or more of your classmates to read and comment on your writing. It is an excellent way to find out what is good in your draft and what needs to be improved in your draft. For more information on how to find a reviewer, what to ask your reviewer, and how to be a good reviewer, see "Success Tip #5" on page 11.

## EXERCISE 2-8

**WORKING TOGETHER**

## Using Peer Review

**Directions:** Pair up with a classmate for this exercise. Read and evaluate each other's paragraphs written for Exercise 2-7, page 69.

### Tips for Revising

Use these suggestions to revise effectively:

1. **Reread the sentence that expresses your main point.** It must be clear, direct, and complete. Experiment with ways to improve it.

2. **Reread each of your other sentences.** Does each relate directly to your main point? If not, cross it out or rewrite it to clarify its connection to the main point. If all your sentences suggest a main point that is different from the one you've written, rewrite the topic sentence or thesis statement.

3. **Make sure your writing has a beginning and an end.** A paragraph should have a clear topic sentence and concluding statement. An essay should have introductory and concluding portions, their length depending on the length of your essay.

4. **Replace words that are vague or unclear with more specific or descriptive words.**

5. **Seek advice.** If you are unsure about how to revise, visit your writing instructor during office hours and ask for advice, or try peer review. Ask a classmate or friend to read your paper and mark ideas that are unclear or need further explanation.

6. **When you have finished revising, you should feel satisfied with what you have said and with the way you have said it.** You will learn additional strategies for revising in Chapter 9.

## EXERCISE 2-9

**WRITING IN PROGRESS**

## Revising a Draft

**Directions:** Revise the first draft you wrote for Exercise 2-7, following steps 1 through 6 in the Tips for Revising box.

# Proofread Your Final Draft

■ GOAL 6
Proofread for correctness

**Proofreading** is a final reading of your paper to check for errors. In this final polishing of your work, the focus is on correctness, so don't proofread until you have done all your rethinking of ideas and revision. When you are ready to proofread your writing, you should check for errors in

■ sentences (run-ons or fragments)
■ grammar

- spelling
- punctuation
- capitalization

The following tips will ensure that you don't miss any errors:

1. **Review your paper once for each type of error.** First, read it for run-on sentences and fragments. Take a short break, and then read it four more times, each time paying attention to one of the following: *spelling, punctuation, grammar,* and *capitalization.*

2. **To find spelling errors, read your paper from last sentence to first sentence and from last word to first word.** Reading in this way, you will not get distracted by the flow of ideas, so you can focus on finding errors. Also use the spell-checker on your computer, but be sure to proofread for the kinds of errors it cannot catch: missing words, errors that are themselves words (such as *of* for *or*), and homonyms (for example, using *it's* for *its*).

3. **Read each sentence aloud, slowly and deliberately.** This technique will help you catch endings that you have left off verbs or missing plurals.

4. **Check for errors one final time after you print out your paper.** Don't do this when you are tired; you might introduce new mistakes. Ask a classmate or friend to read your paper to catch any mistakes you missed.

Here is a paragraph that shows the errors that a student corrected during proofreading. Notice that errors in grammar, punctuation, and spelling were corrected.

> The Robert Burns said that the dog is mans best friend. To a large extent, this statement may be ~~more true~~ *truer* than we thinks. What makes dogs so special to human is ~~they're~~ *their* unending loyalty and their unconditional love. Dogs have been known to cross the entire United states to return home. *They* Never make fun of you or criticize you, *or* throw fits, and they are always happy to see you. Dogs never ~~lye~~ *lie* to you, never betray your confidences, and never stays angry with you for more than five minutes. *The* World would be a better place if only people could be more like dogs.

Chapter 9, page 291, includes a proofreading checklist.

**EXERCISE 2-10**

**WRITING IN PROGRESS**

## Proofreading

**Directions:** Prepare and proofread the final version of the paragraph you have developed throughout this chapter.

# Consider Your Audience and Purpose

- **GOAL 7**
  Consider your audience and purpose

In an earlier section of the chapter, you saw that among the characteristics of good writing are "Good writing is directed toward an audience" and "Good writing achieves a purpose."

## Considering Your Audience

When you write, ask yourself, Who will be reading what I write? How should I express myself so that my readers will understand what I write? Considering your audience is essential to good writing.

What is appropriate for one audience may be inappropriate for another. For example, if you were writing about a car accident that you were involved in, you would write one way to a close friend and another way to your professor. Because your friend knows you well, she would be interested in all of the details. Conversely, because you and your professor don't know each other well, she would want to know less about your feelings about the accident and more about how it would affect your course work. Study the following excerpts. What differences do you notice?

### E-mail to a Friend

Jeff was driving the car. As we got to Cedar Road, the light turned red. Jeff was changing the radio station because Sue hates country music, and I guess he didn't notice. I yelled, "Stop!" but he went through the intersection and a van hit the back of the car. I was terrified and I felt sick. Fortunately, we were all OK. Jeff felt really terrible, especially because by the time we got to school, I had missed my biology exam.

### Note to a Professor

I missed the exam today because I was involved in a car accident. Although I was not injured, I didn't arrive on campus in time for class. Please allow me to make up the exam. I will stop by your office tomorrow during your office hours to talk.

While the e-mail to the friend is casual and personal, the note to the professor is businesslike and direct. The writer included details and described his feelings when telling his friend about the car accident, but focused on missing the exam in his note to his professor.

Writers make many decisions based on the audience they have in mind. As you write, consider:

- How many and what kinds of details are appropriate
- What format is appropriate (for example, paragraph, essay, letter, or memo)
- How many and what types of examples should be used
- How formal the writing should be
- What kinds of words should be used (straightforward, technical, or emotional)
- What tone the writing should have; that is, how it should sound to readers (for example, friendly, distant, knowledgeable, or angry)

Audience is as important in the workplace as it is in personal and academic writing. You would write differently to a manager within your company than you would to a customer outside it, as the following two e-mail messages show.

### E-mail Message 1: Salesperson to Customer

| | |
|---|---|
| From: | Jim Watts [Jwatts@pcs.net] |
| Sent: | Wednesday, April 04, 2012 9:46AM |
| To: | Tim Rodney |
| Subject: | Replacement Shipment of Norfolk Pine Trees |

Hi, Tim,

I am sorry that you were displeased with our recent shipment of Norfolk pines. I cannot imagine how they could have become infested with aphids, since they were insect free at point of shipment. Because we value your continued business, we are happy to ship a replacement order. The new shipment should arrive in the next 3–5 business days. If I can be of further help, please be sure to call or e-mail.

Jim Watts

Farm Manager

Highland Tree Farms

(123) 555-7596

### E-mail Message 2: Salesperson to District Manager

| | |
|---|---|
| From: | Jim Watts [jwatts@pcs.net] |
| Sent: | Wednesday, April 04, 2012 10:13AM |
| To: | Brown, Thomas |
| Subject: | Replacement Shipment to Rodney's Nursery |

Tim at Rodney's Nursery claims to have received an aphid-infested shipment of Norfolk pines, but of course we know they were infested after delivery. (The conditions are so bad there that I am amazed any plant survives more than a few weeks.) Because Tim is one of our best customers, I decided to ship a replacement order, even though he's trying to con us on this one. Hope this decision is OK with you.

Jim Watts

Farm Manager

Highland Tree Farms

(123) 555-7596

Both messages are casually written, since e-mail is a less formal method of communication than letters. Notice, however, that the information in each differs, as does the tone.

Here are four key questions that will help you address your audience appropriately in the workplace as well as in academic situations:

- Who is your audience and what is your relationship with that audience?
- How is the audience likely to react to your message?
- What does the audience already know about the situation?
- What does the audience need to know about the situation?

In later chapters, you will learn more about adapting your writing to your audience and see how writers address specific audiences.

## Writing for a Purpose

When you call a friend on the phone, you have a reason for calling, even if it is just to stay in touch. When you ask a question in class, you have a purpose for asking. When you describe to a friend an incident you were involved in, you are relating the story to make a point or share an experience. These examples demonstrate that you use spoken communication to achieve specific purposes.

Good writing must also achieve your *intended purpose*. If you write a paragraph on how to change a flat tire, your reader should be able to change a flat tire after reading the paragraph. Likewise, if your purpose is to describe the sun rising over a misty mountaintop, your reader should be able to visualize the scene. If your purpose is to argue that the legal age for drinking alcohol should be twenty five, your reader should be able to follow your reasoning, even if he or she is not won over to your view.

Purpose is important in both workplace writing and academic writing. The two e-mail messages just shown reveal two very different purposes. The first message, to the nursery, is intended to keep good relations with a customer who claims that he received infested trees. The second e-mail, to the district manager, is intended to explain why a replacement shipment was sent, even though the claim was not legitimate.

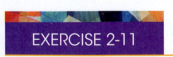

EXERCISE 2-11

## Writing a Paragraph

**Directions:** Think of a public event you have attended recently, such as a concert or film showing. Complete two of the following activities:

1. Write a paragraph describing the event to a friend.
2. Write a paragraph describing the event to your English instructor.
3. Write a paragraph describing the event as the movie or music critic for your local newspaper.

# INTEGRATING READING AND WRITING

## READ AND RESPOND: A Student Essay

*This student essay is a later draft of the essay shown on page 68. In this draft, you can see that Doug Mello expands his ideas (underlined), adds details (underlined), and writes a title and a conclusion. You can see that he added a sentence (highlighted) that states the main point of his essay, his thesis statement. After you have read the essay once, study the annotations. They will help you see the changes Doug made.*

*Doug Mello graduated from Modesto Junior College and went straight to work for a civil engineer. This job ended with the recession, but Doug was able to return to the trucking industry and is now a dispatcher for a "great company" and really enjoys his job.*

**Title: suggests thesis**

**Background information on his life**

**Background on job as truck driver**

**Thesis**

**Quotation added**

**More detail added**

# Education: The Open Road

1    Because I came from a working-class family, the option of pursuing an education was not a choice. Going to work after high school was my only choice and also what my parents expected of me. One of the first jobs I had provided me with the opportunity to acquire a commercial driver's license, which allowed me to become a truck driver. Due to a good driving record and work history, my employment and wages always seemed to get better as I searched for the perfect truck-driving job. At the age of twenty-nine, a company hired me that I thought offered a promising career future. However, I failed to see where this particular road would take me. After several years I found that there were no opportunities for advancement within the company. I realized, at this point in my life, that an education could offer challenges, opportunities, and a career that would last a lifetime.

2    There was one particular event that led to my decision to get an education. After five years with the company I was frequently asked for advice on routing schedules and was assigned the job of dispatching when the plant manager was on vacation. Being involved in the operations of the company allowed me to see the constant waste of time and money that resulted from day-to-day planning. I finally came up with a plan I thought would allow me to advance within the company and get out of my truck and off the road. I went to the president of the company with my proposal, which could have saved the company twice my wages each year in transportation costs. His response was, "our company is not large enough to have a transportation manager and you have no education." Obviously he believed that without an education driving trucks was the only job I was qualified to do. However, for me, driving trucks for thirty-five more years was not a career; it was only a job that was never finished. I realized that with an education, the open road could have a completely different meaning; education is a through road not a dead end.

Details about financial plan added

3    After making the decision to return to school, my wife and I devised a plan to organize our finances. Returning to school is not something you "just do" when you have financial obligations and a family. Our plan consisted of using my income for the next two years to pay off our vehicles, and saving enough money to cover college tuition for four years by investing with a financial advisor. The two years before starting college really prepared us for what it would be like to live on one income.

Giving employer notice developed into full paragraph

4    I gave a six-month notice to my employer and told him why I had decided to return to school. I explained that his comment on education and advancing within the company influenced my decision. He was quite shocked and said, "you're smarter than most of the people working here." I lost a lot of respect for him that day because he had great employees who were very smart and did an outstanding job for the company. I applied to Modesto Junior College and started in January.

5    Because I had been out of school for seven years, I had no study skills and was in no way prepared for college courses. My major was civil engineering. Almost immediately I wondered if I had made the right decision to return to school; it was much more work than driving a truck. The list of classes that I needed in order to transfer to a four-year college was long due to my low scores on the college placement test. After completing an educational plan, I decided to complete four years at Modesto before transferring as a second semester junior to a university.

Details added about beginning college

Now a full paragraph is devoted to the challenges of starting college

6    There are real challenges in returning to school after working for over twenty years. One of the biggest I am faced with is what, or how, I am contributing to my family. My wife continually encourages me in my studies and assures me that I am contributing to our family's future. Furthermore, her education has allowed her to have a job as a schoolteacher that provides wages and benefits that support our family as I attend school. My parents have become very supportive as they realize the importance of an education. Also, the hard work is much more rewarding than truck driving ever was. At the end of each semester the challenge is rewarded with a completed class and a good grade.

New details

Conclusion added: he reflects on his experience

7    In conclusion, though it is clear to me that work was easier than school, I believe the reward at the end of the academic road will be greater. To complete a semester and maintain a 3.9 GPA is more rewarding to me than a paycheck at the end of the week. As I travel to and from school each day I pass by the company I used to work for; occasionally I stop and visit. I miss the work, however, I don't miss the idea that there was nothing else in life. I now realize that work actually prepared me for college. I feel that older students have an advantage over young students. Professors know I am here for "me" not "my parents," and I have something to contribute to their classes. Work experience is the best foundation for many courses offered in college, and the biggest advantage to being an older student is applying that experience to my education.

## Examining Writing

1. Evaluate Doug's decision to organize his ideas in the order in which they happened. Do his ideas progress logically from one to another?

2. Evaluate Doug's thesis statement. How could it be revised to be more effective?

3. Evaluate the revisions Doug made to his draft. Which paragraphs could be improved and how?

## Writing Assignments

1. Think about your own experiences in the workplace. Choose one and write a paragraph describing how the experience affected your life.

2. Use brainstorming or freewriting to generate ideas for the topic "The Perfect Job." Then write a paragraph describing your perfect job.

3. Doug Mello's essay explains why he made the decision to return to school. Write a paragraph describing what made you decide to pursue an education after high school.

## READ AND RESPOND: A Professional Essay

### Thinking Before Reading

In the following reading, the College Board offers some valuable tips on using credit cards and protecting your finances. Before you read:

1. Preview the reading using the steps discussed in Chapter 1, page 15.

2. Connect the reading to your own experience by answering the following questions:

   a. Do you currently use a debit card and/or credit card to pay for your purchases?

   b. How much do you generally pay in finance or interest charges per month?

   c. Do you use credit cards to buy things you really cannot afford?

# Credit Card Smarts: Take Charge of Your Cards

1    Imagine being 30 years old and still paying off a slice of pizza you bought when you were in college. It may sound crazy, but problems with credit card debt can lead to this scenario. Learning how to use credit cards responsibly now can save you from having to dig yourself out of debt after you graduate. It also helps prevent you from having a bad credit history in the future that will affect other things you want to do. You know that the loans you take out for college need to be paid back once you graduate. If you add a large monthly credit card bill (avoid the temptation to charge your tuition!) to that amount, you may find yourself in a very difficult situation financially.

**Credit Cards and College Students**

2    Credit cards are an indisputable fact of life and there are many good reasons to have one. They give you protection for your purchases, allow you to shop online,

and provide a cushion in case of emergencies. The secret is to use the credit card as a tool to help you when you need it, but not to excess. Discuss with your family what kind of expenses it is reasonable to charge.

3    Credit card abuse has become such a problem that, in February 2010, the federal government recognized the importance of protecting college students from the consequences of misusing credit cards. They enacted legislation changing how credit card companies can do business with students. Although the law provides some protection, it's still up to you to manage credit wisely.

4    The law bans credit card companies from issuing cards to people under the age of 18. If you're under 21 years old, you need an adult cosigner to get a card, unless you can prove that you have the financial means to pay your bill. Other provisions in the law limit some of the fees credit card companies can charge—and, in response, the companies are raising interest rates to avoid losing income. Anyone without an established credit history may face the highest interest rates—and that group typically includes students.

### Credit Card Offers on Campus

5    If you don't already have a card, you'll have plenty of opportunities to apply for one once you hit campus. It shouldn't surprise you that the companies are allowed on campus; many colleges earn money by permitting this practice and from creating affinity cards—credit cards that include the name of your college. The law requires that educational institutions and credit card companies let you know about these agreements, but the messages may be subtle. Learn about fees and interest rates to protect yourself.

### Carrying a Balance Can Be Very Expensive

6    Credit cards are actually high-interest loans in disguise. Companies may lend you money, but they get it all back and a lot more by charging you fees. Finance charges on the unpaid portion of your bill can be as much as 25 percent each month, and cash-advance fees have even higher interest rates. Annual fees just to carry the card in your wallet range from $20 to $100; there are also late-payment fees, typically $25–$50.

7    Not paying off the entire amount in your account each month can lead to big finance charges. Take the story of Joe: Joe's average unpaid credit card bill during

a year is $500, and his finance charge is 20 percent—so he has to pay $100 in interest for the year. He pays a $20 annual fee per year, plus a $25 late fee one month (he was up late studying and forgot to mail in his check). After a year, Joe ends up owing $145 in interest and fees to his credit card company, and he still hasn't paid for any of his actual purchases!

### Your Credit Report Matters

8    Your college years are an important time to build the good credit history you need after you graduate. You need to provide a credit report to

apply for an apartment or finance a large purchase, such as a car. Employers often review a credit report when they hire and evaluate employees. Problems with credit cards, such as late or missed payments, stay in your credit report for seven years.

**Be Credit Smart**

9       When you sign up for a credit card, you are responsible for paying the bills. Follow these rules of credit management to lead a financially healthy life:

- Consider using a debit card instead of a credit card. Money is deducted directly from your checking account, so you can't spend more than you actually have.

- Read all application materials carefully—especially the fine print. What happens after the "**teaser rate**" expires? What happens to your interest rate if you're late with a payment or fail to make a payment? What's the interest rate for a cash advance?

- Pay bills promptly to keep finance and other charges to a minimum; pay the balance off if you can.

- Use credit only if you're certain you are able to repay the debt.

- Avoid impulse shopping on your credit card.

- Save your credit card for a money emergency.

**teaser rate**
a low interest rate that increases drastically when the introductory period expires

**Additional Credit Card Advice**

10      The Federal Trade Commission provides free information to consumers on dozens of topics related to credit and credit cards.

# Getting Ready to Write

## Checking Your Comprehension

Answer each of the following questions using complete sentences.

1. What is the key difference between a debit card and a credit card?

2. What are three good reasons to own and use a credit card?

3. How are credit card companies responding to new legislation, and how do these changes affect students?

4. Why is it important to have a good credit history?

5. What is an affinity card?

## Strengthening Your Vocabulary

Using the word's context, word parts, or a dictionary, write a brief definition of each of the following words as it is used in the reading.

1. indisputable (paragraph 2) _____

2. consequences (paragraph 3) _____

3. means (paragraph 4) _____

4. affinity (paragraph 5) _____

## Examining the Reading: Using an Idea Map

Review the reading by completing the missing parts of the idea map shown below.

**VISUALIZE IT!**

**Title**    Credit Card Smarts: Take Charge of Your Cards

**Thesis**    Learning how to use credit cards responsibly now can save you from having to dig yourself out of debt after you graduate.

Credit Cards and College Students

There are three benefits to using credit cards: _____ _____ _____

New laws provide some protection for students, but it's still up to you to manage your credit wisely.

To maintain profits, credit card companies are _____ _____

Credit Card Offers on Campus

Credit card companies work with colleges to offer credit cards to students.

Proceed with caution.

_____

Credit cards are high-interest loans in disguise.

_____ _____

Your Credit Report Matters

You need good credit to make large purchases and sometimes to get a job.

Be Credit Smart

Use a _____ instead of a credit card.

Read application materials carefully.

_____

Use credit only when you can repay the debt.

_____

Save your card for emergencies.

**Conclusion**    The _____ provides good advice on using credit cards.

## Reacting to Ideas: Discussion and Journal Writing

Get ready to write about the reading by discussing the following.

1. How did the author capture your attention in the opening paragraph?

2. What is the author's purpose in providing the example of Joe's experience with credit-card debt?

3. How would you describe the author's attitude toward or opinion of credit-card companies?

4. What is the relationship between using a credit card and being able to finance large purchases later in life?

5. The photo shows credit cards spilling out of a wallet. Do you think the author of this reading would approve of carrying this many credit cards? What argument might she make in favor of carrying so many credit cards? What argument might she make against carrying multiple credit cards?

**THINKING VISUALLY**

## Thinking and Writing Critically

1. Write a sentence that summarizes the author's opinion of owning and using credit cards.

2. What words would you use to describe the author's tone? Does this tone add or detract from the reading?

3. What other information about credit cards would you like to have that was not discussed in the reading?

**MySkillsLab®**

**Complete** this Exercise

# Writing About the Reading

## Paragraph Options

1. Write a paragraph summarizing the pros and cons of carrying and using a credit card.

2. Describe your own experiences with credit cards. Have they been positive, negative, or both? How?

3. Suppose you are offered an affinity card for one of the following organizations: Greenpeace (an environmental, activist group), PETA (People for the Ethical Treatment of Animals), or the NRA (National Rifle Association). Which would you be most likely to choose, and why? (If none of these groups appeals to you, write about an organization whose affinity card you would be willing to carry.)

## Essay Options

4. Do you think your college should allow credit card companies to advertise on campus? Why or why not? What are the benefits and drawbacks to this practice for both you and the college?

5. The reading is about using credit cards to live a financially secure and successful life. Write an essay in which you offer additional advice on how to live within your means and achieve financial security.

6. Add up your expenses for a typical day. How much do you spend on food, snacks, entertainment, gas, and the like? Now write an essay exploring the ways in which you can save half that money by making different choices. (For example, instead of buying a bottle of water, you can bring an empty bottle to campus and fill it from the water fountain.)

# SELF-TEST SUMMARY

To test yourself, cover the Answer column with a sheet of paper and answer each question in the left column. Evaluate each of your answers as you work by sliding the paper down and comparing your answer with what is printed in the Answer column.

| QUESTION | ANSWER |
|---|---|
| ■ GOAL 1  Use the writing process<br><br>What are the steps in the writing process? | The five steps are<br>■ generating ideas<br>■ organizing ideas<br>■ writing a first draft<br>■ revising<br>■ proofreading |
| ■ GOAL 2  Generate ideas<br><br>What techniques can help you generate ideas? | The techniques are freewriting, brainstorming, branching, and questioning. |
| ■ GOAL 3  Organize ideas<br><br>How can you organize your ideas? | Look for relationships among ideas, and present ideas logically, building upon one another. Use idea maps to create a visual diagram of the relationships among your ideas. |
| ■ GOAL 4  Write a first draft<br><br>When writing a first draft, what is your goal? | A first draft should express your ideas in sentence and paragraph form. Focus on ideas, not on grammar, spelling, and punctuation. |
| ■ GOAL 5  Revise and rewrite<br><br>What does revision involve? | Revision involves rethinking your ideas and evaluating how effectively you have expressed them. Revise your draft by adding, deleting, changing, and reorganizing your ideas. |
| ■ GOAL 6  Proofread for correctness<br><br>What is proofreading? | Proofreading is checking your paper for errors in sentence structure, grammar, spelling, punctuation, and capitalization. |
| ■ GOAL 7  Consider your audience and purpose<br><br>What two factors should you consider regardless of what you write? | You should consider the audience for whom you are writing; what is appropriate for one audience may not be appropriate for another. You should also consider your purpose for writing: your reasons for writing will affect the type of information you include and how you present it. |

 MySkillsLab®    For more help with the **Writing Process**, go to your learning path in MySkillsLab at www.myskillslab.com.

# Reading and Learning from Textbooks

# 3

## THINK About It!

Why is the student in the photograph so obviously overwhelmed? What reading, writing, and study strategies would help him cope with the heavy reading and study workload of college? This chapter focuses on strategies that can help all college students. You will learn several strategies for identifying what to learn and numerous techniques for remembering what you read. These include highlighting and annotating textbooks, mapping and outlining to organize ideas, and writing paraphrases and summaries of what you read. All of these skills will also help you to prepare for writing essays and taking exams.

## Reading and Writing Connections

### EVERYDAY CONNECTIONS

- **Reading** You read an article in the newspaper about a proposed high-rise development in a historically significant part of town.
- **Writing** You write a letter to the editor arguing against the proposed development and proposing the area be listed in the National Register of Historic Places.

### ACADEMIC CONNECTIONS

- **Reading** You read a section of a world history text titled "China's Golden Age: The Tang and Song Dynasties."
- **Writing** In an essay exam question for the same class, you are asked to describe events that led to the end of the Tang Dynasty and the rise of the Song Dynasty.

### WORKPLACE CONNECTIONS

- **Reading** You read in the company newsletter that a new management training program is being offered for existing employees.
- **Writing** You write a summary of your qualifications and your history with the company so that you can be considered for the management training program.

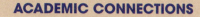

# FOCUSING ON READING AND WRITING

# Why Write As You Read and Study?

■ **GOAL 1**
Use writing as a learning tool

As a college student, you are expected to learn large amounts of textbook material. Rereading to learn is *not* an effective strategy. Writing *is* an effective strategy. In fact, writing is an excellent means of improving both your comprehension and your retention.

Writing during and after reading has numerous advantages:

1. **Writing focuses your attention.** If you are writing as well as reading, you are forced to keep your mind on the topic.
2. **Writing forces you to think.** Highlighting or writing forces you to decide what is important and understand relationships and connections.

3. **Writing tests your understanding.** One of the truest measures of understanding is your ability to explain an idea in your own words. When you have understood an idea, you will be able to write about it, but when an idea is unclear or confusing, you will be at a loss for words.

4. **Writing facilitates recall.** Research studies indicate that information is recalled more easily if it is elaborated on. Elaboration involves expanding and thinking about the material by drawing connections and associations, seeing relationships, and applying what you have learned. Writing is a form of elaboration.

This chapter describes six learning strategies that use writing as a learning tool: *highlighting, annotating, mapping, outlining, paraphrasing,* and *summarizing*.

## READING

# Strategies for Reading Textbooks

■ GOAL 2
Use strategies for
reading textbooks

While textbooks may seem to be long and impersonal, they are actually carefully crafted teaching and learning systems. They are designed to work with your instructor's lecture to provide you with reliable and accurate information and to help you practice your skills.

## Why Buy and Study Textbooks?

Did you know the following facts about textbooks?

- **Nearly all textbook authors are college teachers.** They work with students daily and understand students' needs.

- **Along with your instructor, your textbook is the single best source of information for the subject you are studying.**

- **The average textbook costs only about $7 a week.** For the price of a movie ticket, you are getting a complete learning system that includes not only a textbook but also a companion Web site and other study materials.

- **Your textbook can be a valuable reference tool in your profession.** For example, many nursing majors keep their textbooks and refer to them often when they begin their career.

Textbooks are an investment in your education and in your future. A textbook is your ally—your partner in learning.

## Textbook Learning Aids and How to Use Them

Most textbooks are written by college professors who are experienced teachers. They know their subject matter and they also know their students. They know what topics you may have difficulty with and know the best way to explain them. Because textbooks are written by teachers, they contain numerous features to help you learn. Table 3-1 on page 86 summarizes these features and explains how to use each.

| TABLE 3-1   TEXTBOOK AIDS TO LEARNING | |
|---|---|
| **Feature** | **How to Use It** |
| Preface or "To the Student" | ■ Read it to find out how the book is organized, what topics it covers, and what learning features it contains. |
| Chapter Opener (may include chapter objectives, photographs, and chapter outlines) | ■ Read it to find out what the chapter is about.<br>■ Use it to test yourself later to see if you can recall the main points. |
| Marginal Vocabulary Definitions | ■ Learn the definition of each term.<br>■ Create a vocabulary log (in a notebook or computer file) and enter words you need to learn. |
| Photographs and Graphics | ■ Determine their purpose: what important information do they illustrate?<br>■ For diagrams, charts, and tables, note the process or trend they illustrate. Make marginal notes.<br>■ Practice redrawing diagrams without referring to the originals. |
| Test Yourself Questions (after sections within the chapter) | ■ Always check to see if you can answer them before going on to the next section.<br>■ Use them to check your recall of chapter content when studying for an exam. |
| Special Interest Inserts (can include profiles of people, coverage of related issues, critical thinking topics, etc.) | ■ Discover how the inserts are related to the chapter content: what key concepts do they illustrate? |
| Review Questions/Problems/ Discussion Questions | ■ Read them once *before* you read the chapter to discover what you are expected to learn.<br>■ Use them after you have read the chapter to test your recall. |
| Chapter Summary | ■ Test yourself by converting summary statements into questions using the words *Who? Why? When? How?* and *So What?* |
| Chapter Review Quiz | ■ Use this to prepare for an exam. Pay extra attention to items you get wrong. |

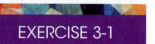

**EXERCISE 3-1**     ## Evaluating Textbook Learning Aids

**Directions:** Using this textbook or a textbook from one of your other courses, use Table 3-1 to analyze the features the author includes to guide your learning. Identify particularly useful features and decide how you will use each when you study.

# Use the SQ3R System for Learning from Textbooks

■ GOAL 3
Use the SQ3R system

SQ3R is an established method of actively learning while you read. Instead of reading now and studying later when an exam is scheduled, the SQ3R method enables you to integrate reading and learning by using the five steps listed on page 87. By using SQ3R, you will strengthen your comprehension, remember more of what you read, and need less time to prepare for an exam. Don't get discouraged if you don't see dramatic results the first time you use it. It may take a few practice sessions to get used to the system.

Feel free to adapt the SQ3R method to suit how you learn and the type of material you are studying. For example, if writing helps you recall information, you might add an *Outline* step and make the *Review* step a *Review of Outline* step. Or if you are studying a course in which terminology is especially important, such as biology, then add a *Vocabulary Check* step.

## Steps in the SQ3R System

**S**urvey Become familiar with the overall content and organization of the material using the steps for previewing from Chapter 1 on page 15.

**Q**uestion Ask questions about the material that you expect to be able to answer as you read. As you read each successive heading, turn it into a question.

**R**ead As you read each section, actively search for the answers to your guide questions. When you find the answers, underline or mark the portions of the text that concisely state the information.

**R**ecite Probably the most important part of the system, "recite" means that after each section or after each major heading you should stop, look away from the page, and try to remember the answer to your question. If you are unable to remember, look back at the page and reread the material. Then test yourself again by looking away from the page and "reciting" the answer to your question.

**R**eview Immediately after you have finished reading, go back through the material again, reading headings and summaries. As you read each heading, recall your question and test yourself to see whether you can still remember the answer. If you cannot, reread that section. Once you are satisfied that you have understood and recalled key information, move toward the higher-level thinking skills. Ask application, analysis, evaluation, and creation questions. Some students like to add a fourth "R" step—for "React."

**EXERCISE 3-2**

## Using SQ3R

**Directions:** Apply the SQ3R system to a section of a chapter in one of your textbooks. List your questions in the margin or on a separate sheet of paper, and highlight the answers in your textbook. After you have finished the section, evaluate how well SQ3R worked for you, and note how you might adapt it.

# Use Learning and Recall Strategies

■ **GOAL 4**
Use learning and recall strategies

Some students think that as long as they spend time studying they will get good grades. However, spending time is not enough. You have to plan when to study and use the right techniques to get the most out of the time you spend. Use the following strategies.

## Immediate Review

Forgetting occurs most rapidly right after learning. **Immediate review** means reviewing new information as soon as possible after you hear or read it.

Think of immediate review as a way of fixing in your mind what you have just learned. Here are some ways to use immediate review:

- **Review your lecture notes as soon as possible after taking them.** This review will help the ideas stick in your mind.
- **Review a textbook chapter as soon as you finish reading it.** Do this by rereading each chapter heading and then rereading the summary.
- **Review all new course materials again at the end of each day of classes.** This review will help you pull together information and make it more meaningful.

## Periodic Review

To keep from forgetting material you have learned, you will need to review it several times throughout the semester. **Periodic review**, then, means returning to and quickly reviewing previously learned material on a regular basis. Suppose you learned the material in the first three chapters of your criminology text during the first two weeks of the course. Unless you review that material regularly, you are likely to forget it and have to relearn it by the time your final exam is given. Therefore, you should establish a periodic review schedule in which you quickly review these chapters every three weeks or so.

## Final Review

**Final review** means making a last check of material before a test or exam. This should not be a lengthy session; instead, it should be a quick once-over of everything you have learned. A final review is helpful because it fixes in your mind what you have learned. Be sure to schedule your final review as close as possible to the exam in which you will need to recall the material.

## Building an Intent to Remember

Very few people remember things that they do not intend to remember. Before you begin to read an assignment, define as clearly as possible what you need to remember. Your decision will depend on the type of material, why you are reading it, and how familiar you are with the topic. For instance, if you are reading an essay assigned in preparation for a class discussion, plan to remember not only key ideas but also points of controversy, applications, and opinions with which you disagree. Your intent might be quite different in reviewing a chapter for an essay exam. Here you would be looking for important ideas, trends, and significance of events.

As you read a text assignment, sort important information from that which is less important. Continually ask and answer questions such as:

1. How important is this information?
2. Will I need to know this for the exam?
3. Is this a key idea or is it an explanation of a key idea?
4. Why did the writer include this?

## Organizing and Categorizing

Information that is organized, or that has a pattern or structure, is easier to remember than material that is randomly arranged. One effective way to organize information is to *categorize* it, to arrange it in groups according to similar characteristics. Suppose, for example, that you had to remember the following list of items to buy for a picnic: *cooler, candy, 7-Up, Pepsi, napkins, potato chips, lemonade, peanuts, paper plates.* The easiest way to remember this list would be to divide it into groups. You might arrange it as follows:

| DRINKS | SNACKS | PICNIC SUPPLIES |
|---|---|---|
| 7-Up | peanuts | cooler |
| Pepsi | candy | paper plates |
| lemonade | potato chips | napkins |

By grouping the items into categories, you are putting similar items together. Then, rather than learning one long list of unorganized items, you are learning three shorter, organized lists.

Now imagine you are reading an essay on discipline in public high schools. Instead of learning one long list of reasons for disruptive student behavior, you might divide the reasons into groups such as peer conflicts, teacher-student conflicts, and so forth.

## Associating Ideas

Association involves connecting new information with previously acquired knowledge. For instance, if you are reading about divorce in a sociology class and are trying to remember a list of common causes, you might try to associate each cause with a person you know who exhibits that problem. Suppose one cause of divorce is lack of communication between the partners. You might remember this by thinking of a couple you know whose lack of communication has caused relationship difficulties.

## Using a Variety of Sensory Modes

Your senses of sight, hearing, and touch can all help you remember what you read. Most of the time, most of us use just one sense—sight—as we read. However, if you are able to use more than one sense, you will find that recall is easier. Activities such as highlighting, note taking, and outlining involve your sense of touch and reinforce your learning. Or, if you are having particular difficulty remembering something, try to use your auditory sense as well. You might try repeating the information out loud or listening to someone else repeat it.

## Visualizing

Visualizing, or creating a mental picture of what you have read, often aids recall. In reading about events, people, processes, or procedures, visualization is relatively simple. However, visualization of abstract ideas, theories, philosophies, and concepts may not be possible. Instead, you may be able to create a visual picture of the relationship of ideas in your mind or on paper. For example, suppose you are reading about the invasion of privacy and learn that there are arguments for and against the storage of personal data about each citizen by online companies like Google. You might create a visual image of two lists of information—advantages and disadvantages.

## Using *Mnemonic* Devices

Memory tricks and devices, often called **mnemonics**, are useful in helping you recall lists of factual information. You might use a rhyme, such as the one used for remembering the number of days in each month: "Thirty days hath September, April, June, and November. . . ." Another device involves making up a word or phrase in which each letter represents an item you are trying to remember. If you remember the name *Roy G. Biv,* for example, you will be able to recall the colors in the light spectrum: **r**ed, **o**range, **y**ellow, **g**reen, **b**lue, **i**ndigo, **v**iolet.

EXERCISE 3-3

# Using Recall Strategies

**Directions:** Five study-learning situations follow. Indicate which of the strategies described in this section—organization/categorization, association, sensory modes, visualization, and mnemonic devices—might be most useful in each situation.

1. In a sociology course, you are assigned to read about and remember the causes of child abuse. How might you remember them easily?

   _____

2. You are studying astronomy and you have to remember the names of the eight planets: Mercury, Venus, Earth, Mars, Jupiter, Saturn, Uranus, and Neptune. What retention aid(s) could help you remember them?

   _____

3. You are taking a course in anatomy and physiology and must learn the name and location of each bone in the human skull. How could you learn them easily?

   _____

4. You have an entire chapter to review for a history course, and your instructor has told you that your exam will include 30 true/false questions on Civil War battles. What could you do as you review to help yourself remember the details of various battles?

   _____

5. You are taking a course in twentieth-century history and are studying the causes of the Vietnam War in preparation for an essay exam. You find that there are many causes, some immediate, others long-term. Some have to do with international politics; others, with internal problems in North and South Vietnam. How could you organize your study for this exam?

   _____

## WRITING

# Select and Organize What to Learn

■ GOAL 5
Select and organize
what to learn

As you read textbooks and other college assignments, you will be able to read them more effectively, remember more of what you read, and review more efficiently if you use the following strategies for selecting and organizing what to learn.

## Highlight and Annotate

Highlighting and annotating important facts and ideas as you read are effective ways to keep track of information. They are also big time-savers for college students. Suppose it took you four hours to read an assigned chapter in sociology. One month later you might need to review that chapter to prepare for an exam. If you did not highlight or annotate the chapter the first time, then you would have to spend another four hours rereading it. However, if you had highlighted and annotated as you read, you could review the chapter fairly quickly.

### *Highlighting to Identify What to Learn*

Here are a few basic suggestions for highlighting effectively:

1. **Read a paragraph or section first.** Then go back and highlight what is important.
2. **Highlight important portions of any topic sentence.** Also highlight any supporting details you want to remember (see Chapter 6).
3. **Be accurate.** Make sure your highlighting reflects the content of the passage.
4. **Highlight the right amount.** If you highlight too little, you may miss valuable information. On the other hand, if you highlight too much, you are not zeroing in on the most important ideas, and you will wind up rereading too much material when you study. As a general rule of thumb, highlight no more than 20 to 30 percent of the material.

Read the following paragraph. Notice that you can understand its meaning from the highlighted parts alone.

The results of resistance training in men and women are quite different. Women don't normally develop muscle to the same extent that men do. The main reason for the difference between the sexes is that men and women have different levels of the hormone testosterone in their blood. Before puberty, testosterone levels in blood are similar for both boys and girls. During adolescence, testosterone levels in boys increase dramatically, about ten-fold, but testosterone levels in girls are unchanged. Women's muscles will become larger as a result of resistance training exercise but typically not to the same degree as in adult males.

—Donatelle, *Health: The Basics*, p. 286

## EXERCISE 3-4    Using Highlighting

**Directions:** Read the following paragraph, which has been highlighted two different ways. Look at each highlighted version and then answer the questions that follow.

### Example 1

Chemistry begins defining **matter** by dividing it into two broad types, *pure substances* and *mixtures*. In **pure substances**, only a single type of matter is present. **Mixtures** occur when two or more pure substances are intermingled with each other. For example, table salt is a pure substance. So is water. And so is table sugar. If you put salt and sugar in a jar together and shake, however, you have a mixture. Dissolve sugar in water and you have another mixture. Some things that you might not think of as mixtures actually do fit the definition—a rock, for example. In most rocks, you'll see a mixture of different minerals, each a different pure substance.

—Russo and Silver, *Introductory Chemistry Essentials*, pp. 3–4

### Example 2

Chemistry begins defining **matter** by dividing it into two broad types, *pure substances* and *mixtures*. In **pure substances**, only a single type of matter is present. **Mixtures** occur when two or more pure substances are intermingled with each other. For example, table salt is a pure substance. So is water. And so is table sugar. If you put salt and sugar in a jar together and shake, however, you have a mixture. Dissolve sugar in water and you have another mixture. Some things that you might not think of as mixtures actually do fit the definition—a rock, for example. In most rocks, you'll see a mixture of different minerals, each a different pure substance.

1.  The topic sentence begins with the word _____.

2.  Is Example 1 or Example 2 the better example of effective highlighting?

    _____

3.  Why isn't the highlighting in the other example effective?

    _____

4.  According to the writer, what two broad types of matter are there in chemistry?

    a. _____

    b. _____

### Annotating to Record Your Thinking

**Annotating** is a way to keep track of your impressions, ideas, reactions, and questions as you read. You have already learned how to highlight, which is a way of identifying key information. In contrast to highlighting, annotating is a way of recording *your* thinking about these key ideas. It allows you to interact with the reading as a critical reader, almost as if you are having a conversation with the writer—questioning, challenging, agreeing with, disagreeing with, or commenting on what he or she is saying.

There is only one rule of annotating:

> Read with a pen or pencil in your hand, and take notes in the margin as you read.

Let's consider an example of a student writer and how she used annotations to record her ideas and impressions as she read. In her mass-media course, Lin was given an assignment:

> Write an essay on how the media, such as TV, radio, and magazines, shape people's thinking.

In a textbook, she found a section on how the media portray men and women differently, and she thought it might contain excellent information to use in her essay.

As Lin read the discussion carefully, highlighter in hand, all kinds of questions and thoughts came to mind. By annotating as she read, she was able to record her questions and reactions—all of which would help her when it came time to write her essay. Here is the excerpt Lin read, along with her marginal annotations.

### Excerpt from Reading

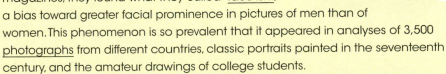

*All media?*

<u>Media</u> images of men and women also differ in other subtle ways. In any visual representation of a person—such as a photograph, drawing, or painting—you can measure the relative prominence of the face by calculating the percentage of the vertical dimension occupied by the model's head. When Dane Archer and his colleagues (1983) inspected 1,750 photographs from *Time, Newsweek*, and other magazines, they found what they called "<u>face-ism</u>," a bias toward greater facial prominence in pictures of men than of women. This phenomenon is so prevalent that it appeared in analyses of 3,500 <u>photographs</u> from different countries, classic portraits painted in the seventeenth century, and the amateur drawings of college students.

*Who selected them? Were they selected randomly?*

*Aren't men's faces larger?*

*Stereotyping*

*Stereotyping*

*Why?*

<u>Why is the face more prominent in pictures of men than of women?</u> One possible interpretation is that face-ism reflects historical conceptions of the sexes. The face and head symbolize the mind and *intellect*—which are traditionally associated with men. With respect to women, more importance is attached to the heart, emotions, or perhaps just the body. Indeed, when people evaluate models from photographs, <u>those pictured with high facial prominence are seen as smarter and more assertive, active, and ambitious—regardless of their gender</u> (Schwarz & Kurz, 1989). Another interpretation is that facial prominence signals power and *dominance*.

—Brehm and Kassin, *Social Psychology*

Many readers develop their own style of annotating, using underlining, asterisks, exclamation points, and other marks to express their ideas, as shown in the box on page 94.

## Ways to Annotate Text

- <u>Underline</u> or ==highlight== key ideas
- Mark key terms or definitions with a star *
- Number key supporting points (1, 2, 3 . . .)
- Circle and define unfamiliar words
- Indicate useful examples with brackets [ ]
- Mark useful summary statements with an asterisk (*)
- Draw arrows ←→ connecting ideas
- ==Highlight== statements that reveal the author's feelings, attitudes, or biases
- Indicate confusing statements with a question mark (?)
- Argue with the author by placing an exclamation point (!) next to assertions or statements with which you disagree

In recording your responses in the margin, you might include

| | |
|---|---|
| Questions | Why would . . . ? |
| Challenges to the author's ideas | If this is true, wouldn't . . . ? |
| Inconsistencies | But the author earlier said . . . |
| Examples | For instance . . . |
| Exceptions | This wouldn't be true if . . . |
| Disagreements | How could . . . ? |
| Associations with other sources | This is similar to . . . |
| Judgments | Good point . . . |

## EXERCISE 3-5   Practicing Annotating

**Directions:** Choose any essay-length reading from this book and annotate it. Did you find yourself creating your own system of symbols and marginal annotations?

## Map

In Chapter 1 you learned a little bit about **mapping** (p. 21), which is a visual method of organizing information. It involves drawing diagrams to show how ideas in a paragraph or chapter are related. Some students prefer mapping to outlining because they feel it is freer and less tightly structured.

Maps can take many forms. You can draw them in any way that shows the relationships between ideas. Read the following paragraph about homeschooling and then study the two sample maps of the paragraph in Figures 3-1 (p. 95) and 3-2 (p. 96).

With the increase in comprehensive online learning providers, a growing number of parents are choosing to educate their children at home. The number of homeschooled students rose from an estimated 300,000 in 1990 to more than a million just a decade later. Common reasons for homeschooling include avoiding the negative influences of public schools, concern with the quality of public school education, and a desire to include religious teachings in the curriculum. Although most studies agree that there is little difference in student achievement between homeschooled and public-schooled students, three factors appear to influence academic achievement: Students who are homeschooled by more educated parents do better than those who are taught by less educated parents; students who are homeschooled by more conservative parents do better on standardized tests than those taught by more liberal parents; and children of parents who homeschool due to family needs have lower levels of achievement than those who are homeschooled for other reasons. However, the primary factor directly linked to student achievement can best be attributed to the approach and teaching style of the parent. For example, in the case of students who are taught by more conservative parents and do better on standardized tests than those taught by more liberal parents, this is most likely attributed to the conservative teaching style of teaching specific knowledge, whereas the more liberal parent might teach in an experimental or less formal approach, which would not be rewarded or recognized by standardized testing.

—Kunz, *Think Marriages & Families*, p. 207

## FIGURE 3-1    SAMPLE HAND-DRAWN MAP

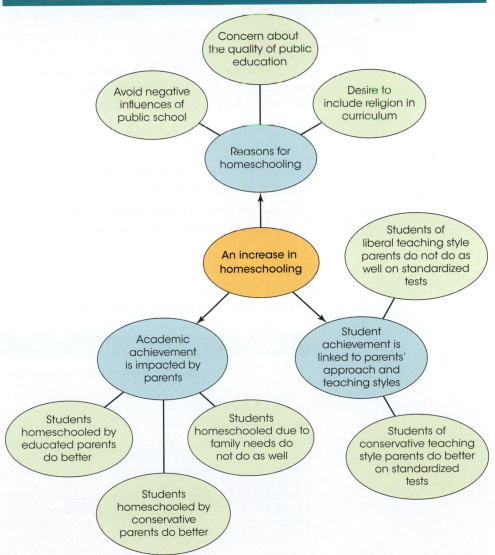

**FIGURE 3-2 SAMPLE COMPUTER-DRAWN MAP**

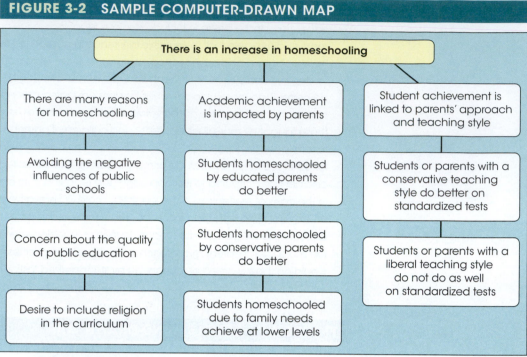

Notice how important information is included using each method—it's just presented differently.

As you draw a map, think of it as a picture or diagram that shows how ideas are connected. You can hand draw maps or use a word processer. Use the following steps, which can be seen in Figures 3-1 and 3-2:

1. **Identify the overall topic or subject.** Write it in the center or at the top of the page.

2. **Identify major ideas that relate to the topic.** Using a line, connect each major idea to the central topic.

3. **As you discover supporting details that further explain an idea already mapped, connect those details with new lines.**

Once you are skilled at drawing maps, you can become more creative, drawing different types of maps to fit what you are reading. For example, you can draw a *time line* (see Figure 3-3) to show historical events in the order in which they occurred. A time line starts with the earliest event and ends with the most recent.

**FIGURE 3-3 SAMPLE TIME LINE**

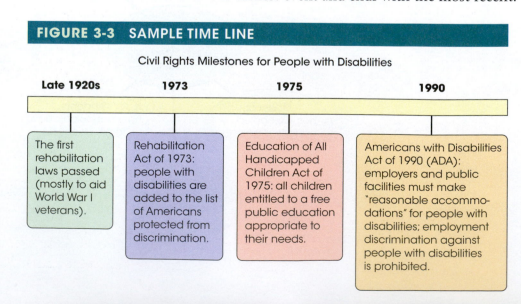

**FIGURE 3-4    SAMPLE PROCESS MAP**

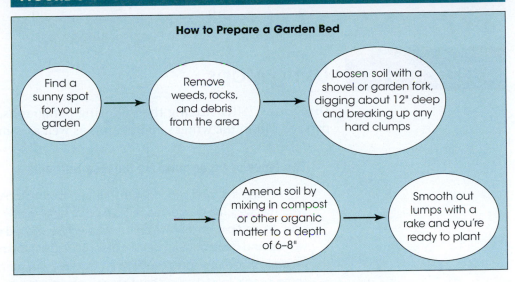

Another type of map is one that shows a process—the steps involved in doing something (see Figure 3-4). When you study chronological order and process in Chapter 7, p. 211), you will discover more uses for these kinds of maps.

| EXERCISE 3-6 | # Understanding Maps |

**Directions:** Read the paragraph and complete the map that follows, filling in the writer's main points in the spaces provided. Then answer the question that follows the map.

Because complaints are often preludes to conflict in the workplace, they need to be listened to and responded to appropriately. Here are some suggestions for dealing with complaints. First, let the person know that you're open to complaints; you view them as helpful sources of information, and you're listening. (Be careful not to fall into the trap of seeing someone who voices a complaint as someone to avoid.) Second, try to understand both the thoughts and the feelings that go with the complaint. Express not only your concern about the problem but also your understanding of the frustration this person is feeling. Third, respect confidentiality. Let the person know that the complaint will be treated in strict confidence or that it will be revealed only to those he or she wishes. Fourth, ask the person what he or she would like you to do. Sometimes all a person wants is for someone to hear the complaint and appreciate its legitimacy. Other times, the complaint is presented in hopes that you will do something specific. Finally, thank the person for voicing the complaint, and assure him or her of your intention to follow up.

—adapted from DeVito, *Messages,* p. 317

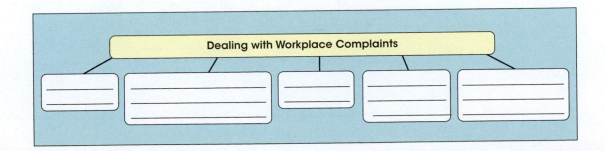

What five transition words does the writer use to introduce the main points?

a. _____ b. _____ c. _____ d. _____ e. _____

## Using Maps

**Directions:** After reading the following paragraphs, complete the map of the passage. Fill in the writer's main points as well as some supporting details.

### Two Types of Organisms That Release Nutrients

Among the most important strands in a food web are the detritus feeders and decomposers. The detritus feeders are an army of mostly small and often unnoticed animals and protists that live on the refuse of life: molted exoskeletons, fallen leaves, wastes, and dead bodies. (Detritus means "debris.") The network of detritus feeders is complex; in terrestrial ecosystems it includes earthworms, mites, centipedes, some insects, land-dwelling crustaceans, nematode worms, and even a few large vertebrates such as vultures. These organisms consume dead organic matter, extract some of the energy stored in it, and excrete it in a further decomposed state. Their excretory products serve as food for other detritus feeders and for decomposers.

The decomposers are primarily fungi and bacteria (the black coating or gray fuzz you may notice on decaying tomatoes and bread crusts are fungal decomposers). Decomposers digest food outside their bodies by secreting digestive enzymes into the environment. They absorb the nutrients they need, and the remaining nutrients are released to the environment.

—Audesirk, Audesirk, and Byers, *Life on Earth*, pp. 584–585

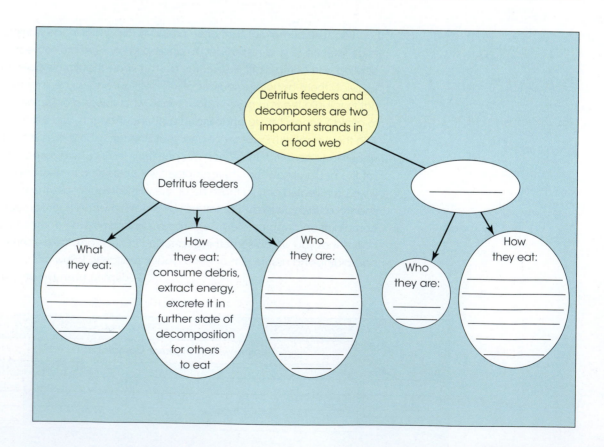

## Outline

Making an outline is another good way to keep track of what you have read. **Outlining** involves listing major and minor ideas and showing how they are related. When you make an outline, follow the writer's organization. An outline usually follows a format like the one below:

I. Major topic
  A. First major idea
    1. First key supporting detail
    2. Second key supporting detail
  B. Second major idea
    1. First key supporting detail
      a. Minor detail or example
      b. Minor detail or example
    2. Second key supporting detail
II. Second major topic
  A. First major idea

Suppose you had just read a brief essay about your friend's vacation in San Francisco. An outline of the essay might begin like this:

I. Favorite places
  A. Chinatown
    1. Restaurants and markets
      a. Fortune cookie factory
      b. Dim sum restaurants
    2. Museums
      a. Chinese Culture Center
      b. Pacific Heritage Museum
  B. Fisherman's Wharf
    1. Pier 39
      a. Street performers
      b. Sea lions sunning themselves on the docks
    2. Ghiradelli Square

Notice that the most important ideas are closer to the left margin. The rule of thumb to follow is this: The less important the idea, the more it should be indented.

Here are a few suggestions for using the outline format:

1. **Don't worry about following the outline format exactly.** As long as your outline shows an organization of ideas, it will work for you.

2. **Use words and phrases or complete sentences,** whichever is easier for you.

3. **Use your own words, and don't write too much.**

4. **Pay attention to headings.** Be sure that all the information you place underneath a heading explains or supports that heading. In the outline above, for instance, the entries "Chinatown" and "Fisherman's Wharf" are correctly placed under the major topic "Favorite Places." Likewise, "Pier 39" and "Ghiradelli Square" are under "Fisherman's Wharf," since they are located in the Wharf area.

Reread the paragraph about homeschooling on page 94, and then study its outline. In this outline, the major topic of the paragraph is listed first. The writer's main ideas are listed as A, B, and C. Supporting details are then listed under the ideas. When you look at this outline, you can easily see the writer's most important points.

I. There is an increase in the number of parents who choose to homeschool their children.

A. Reasons for homeschooling
1. Avoiding the negative influences of public schools
2. Concern about the quality of public school educations
3. Desire to include religious teachings in the curriculum

B. There is little difference between home and public schooling, but students' academic achievement is impacted by the parents
1. Students homeschooled by educated parents do better than those taught by less educated parents
2. Students homeschooled by conservative parents do better on standardized tests than those taught by liberal parents
3. Students homeschooled because of family needs achieve at lower levels than students homeschooled for other reasons

C. Student achievement is linked to the parents' approach and teaching styles
1. Conservative parent-teachers have students who achieve better on standardized tests due to the conservative teaching style of specific knowledge
2. Liberal parent-teachers have students who do not do as well on standardized tests because of a less formal or experiential approach

## EXERCISE 3-8   Using Outlines

**Directions:** After reading the passage and the incomplete outline that follows, fill in the missing information in the outline.

### Clearance and Conviction Rates

The efficiency of our criminal justice system is determined by varying standards. To a great extent, police effectiveness is still judged by rates of arrest, of either an entire agency or an individual investigator. Although it may not always be fair or even logical to judge police effectiveness by this standard alone, it continues to be the criterion used by much of the public.

As a national average, police are successful in clearing by arrest approximately 20 percent of all serious felonies reported to their agencies. Police departments judge solution rate by counting clearances; that is, the number of cases in which a known criminal offense has resulted in the arrest, citation, or judicial summoning of an individual in connection with the offense. The success of a particular investigation is not, however, a uniform factor among all crimes. Some investigations have a naturally higher probability of success than others. For example, criminal homicide investigations generally involve perpetrators who know their victims and who make little or no real effort to avoid apprehension. In addition, the extreme seriousness of the crime dictates maximum investigative effort, with an exhaustive search for forensic evidence. On the other hand, there is traditionally a much lower rate of arrest in cases of burglary. Many factors contribute to this unfortunate fact, including heavy caseloads and the large amount of stolen property that is unidentifiable when recovered. The main reason for the low rate of clearance is, however, the lack of a suspect identification, as this type of criminal purposely avoids contact with victims or witnesses.

Of those cases successfully concluded by an arrest, an unfortunately large number are not carried onward into the judicial process (see Figure A). National studies indicate that approximately 40 percent of all felony arrests brought by police for prosecution are rejected in some manner. Some investigations are either dropped outright by a prosecutor prior to court examination or dismissed by a judge in one of the various judicial screenings. Prosecutors tend to reject cases because of problems of insufficient evidence, whereas judges tend to dismiss cases because of legal violations relating to due process. However, those cases that are carried forward to the trial stage are typically strong, as evidenced by only 2 percent not resulting in conviction.

## FIGURE A   TYPICAL OUTCOME OF 100 FELONY CRIME INVESTIGATIONS RESULTING IN ARREST AND BROUGHT FOR PROSECUTION

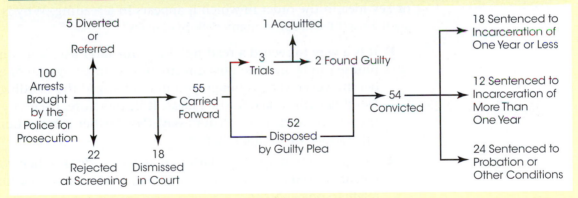

(*Source:* U.S. Department of Justice, Bureau of Justice Statistics.)

Such data can be very helpful to the investigator, demonstrating that, in many cases, evidence linking a suspect to an offense is not located, collected, or processed effectively. Although it is true that certain types of investigations are inherently difficult in this regard, there is considerable room for improvement. On the positive side, research indicates that the screening process is quite effective in predicting which cases will result in conviction.

—Gilbert, *Criminal Investigation*, pp. 64–65

    I. Police effectiveness is judged by rates of arrests

   II. 20% of felonies are cleared by arrest

      A. Criminal homicide has a higher rate of clearance

         1. Perpetrators know their victims

         2. _____

      B. Burglary cases have a lower rate of arrests.

         1. There are heavy caseloads

         2. _____

         3. _____

            _____

  III. 40% of arrests are not moved forward into the judicial process

      A. _____

      B. Judges can dismiss cases due to legal violations of due process

      C. _____

## Paraphrase

A **paraphrase** is a restatement, in your own words, of a paragraph, passage, or reading selection. It is a condensed (shortened) rewording of each sentence or key idea in the order in which it appears in a reading. Why is paraphrasing such a useful skill for so many college courses?

- **It is a way to record a reading's ideas for later use.** Sometimes your paraphrase can be incorporated directly into your paragraph or essay. Remember, however, that although you have changed the wording, you are still working with someone else's ideas. It is, therefore, necessary to document the source at the end of your essay. (For further information about documentation, see Chapter 16.)

- **Paraphrasing helps you clarify an author's ideas.** When you paraphrase, you are forced to work with each idea individually and see how these ideas relate to one another.

- **Paraphrasing is a useful study and learning strategy.** When you paraphrase a reading, you think through and learn the information it contains.

- **Because a paraphrase requires you to use different words from those in the reading, writing paraphrases helps you develop your vocabulary.** The "Strengthening Your Vocabulary" exercises in this book will prove very helpful when you write paraphrases.

- **By paraphrasing, you are practicing your own writing skills.**

    Writing a paraphrase involves two skills: (1) substituting synonyms and (2) rewording and rearranging sentence parts, as detailed in the box on the next page.

## Writing A Paraphrase

1. **Substitute synonyms.** A **synonym** is a word that has the same general meaning as another word. For example, *thin* and *lanky* are synonyms. When selecting synonyms, use the following guidelines:

   - **Make sure the synonym you choose fits the context (overall meaning) of the sentence.** Suppose the sentence you are paraphrasing is "The physician attempted to *neutralize* the effects of the drug overdose." All of the following words are synonyms for *neutralize*: *negate, nullify, counteract*. However, *counteract* fits the context, but *negate* and *nullify* do not. *Negate* and *nullify* suggest the ability to cancel, and a drug overdose, once taken, cannot be canceled. It can, however, be counteracted.

   - **Refer to a dictionary.** Use a print or online dictionary to check the exact meanings of words; refer to a thesaurus (a dictionary of synonyms) to get ideas for alternative or equivalent words.

   - **Do not try to replace every word in a sentence with a synonym.** Sometimes a substitute does not exist. In the sentence "Archaeologists study fossils of extinct species," the term *fossils* clearly and accurately describes what archaeologists study. Therefore, it does not need to be replaced.

   - **Consider connotation.** A word's *connotation* is the feelings it invokes. Some words have positive connotations, while others have negative connotations. When writing a paraphrase, select words with connotations that mirror the original. For instance, if the original reading uses the word *adorable*, which has a positive connotation, do not paraphrase with the word *sticky-sweet*, which has a negative connotation.

   - **Be sure to paraphrase—that is, do not change only a few words.**

2. **Reword and rearrange sentence parts.** When rearranging sentence parts, use the following guidelines:

   - Split lengthy, complicated sentences into two or more shorter sentences.

   - Be sure you understand the author's key ideas as well as related ideas, and include both in your paraphrase.

| ORIGINAL | Many judges believe that television cameras should not be permitted in a court of law because the defendant's right to a fair trial may be jeopardized. |
|---|---|
| CORRECT PARAPHRASE | Because cameras may prevent a defendant from being treated fairly, many judges feel television cameras should not be allowed in the courtroom. |
| INCORRECT PARAPHRASE | Many judges feel television cameras should not be allowed in the courtroom. |

The incorrect paraphrase does not include the reason many judges feel cameras should not be allowed in the courtroom.

### A Sample Paraphrase

Marcie was writing an essay on animal communication for her biology class. In a reading, she found one passage that contained exactly the information she needed. To help herself remember both the author's main point and the details, she decided to paraphrase. Here is an excerpt from the reading, followed by Marcie's paraphrase:

| Communication in the Animal Kingdom | Marcie's Paraphrase of "Communication in the Animal Kingdom" |
|---|---|
| Animal species have complex forms of communication. Ants send chemical signals secreted from glands to share information about food and enemies with other members of the colony. When honeybees discover a source of nectar, they return to the hive and communicate its location to the other worker bees through an intricate dance that signals both direction and distance. Male songbirds of various species sing in the spring to attract a female mate and also to warn other males to stay away from their territory to avoid a fight. Dolphins talk to each other at great depths of the ocean by making a combination of clicking, whistling, and barking sounds.<br>—Kassin, *Psychology,* p. 252 | According to Kassin (252), animals have complicated ways of communicating. Ants can tell one another about food and enemies by secreting chemicals from their glands. Honeybees tell others in their hive that they have found a source of nectar by a detailed dance that indicates both where the nectar is located and how far away it is. In the spring, male songbirds sing to draw females and to warn other males to stay away so as to avoid a dispute. Using clicks, whistles, and barking sounds, dolphins communicate with one another. |

Look closely at Marcie's paraphrase and the original reading, noticing how she substituted synonyms. For example, in the first sentence, she substituted *complicated* for *complex*, *ways* for *forms*, and so forth. She also included all of the author's important main ideas and supporting details.

**EXERCISE 3-9**

WORKING TOGETHER

## Writing a Paraphrase

**Directions:** Working with a classmate, choose several paragraphs from one of the end-of-chapter readings in this text. Working sentence by sentence, write a paraphrase. Then compare your work and combine both of your paraphrases to produce a revised paraphrase.

## Summarize

A **summary** is a brief statement of the major points of a reading, and it is always shorter than the original. Unlike a paraphrase, a summary does not attempt to cover all of the reading's key points and details. Rather, it is a brief statement of major points and main ideas. Usually a summary is about one-fifth the length of the original or less.

Writing summaries has four main benefits:

1. **Writing a summary improves your grasp of a writer's ideas.** Writing a summary clarifies your thinking because you must identify key ideas and explain how they relate to one another.

2. **Writing a summary saves you time when you are reviewing or studying for an exam.** Summaries make it easier to keep track of and focus on important ideas while eliminating less important information.

3. **College instructors across the disciplines—not just writing instructors—assign summaries.** For example, you may be asked to write a plot summary of a short story, a summary of a news article for an economics course, or a summary of your findings for a science laboratory experiment.

4. **Summarizing is an important workplace skill.** Today's workplace values precise, concise information. You might be asked to summarize a meeting, condense a lengthy report, or briefly describe the outcomes of a sales conference you attended.

To write an effective summary, follow these guidelines:

## Writing a Summary

1. **Complete the reading before writing your summary.** Feel free to highlight and/or annotate as you read.

2. **Review the reading.** Review your highlighting and/or annotations, or use your review to highlight and annotate for the first time.

3. **Write an opening sentence that states the author's thesis or main point.** For a review of thesis statements, see Chapter 11, page 337.

4. **Explain the author's most important supporting ideas.** Refer to text you have underlined or highlighted. Be sure to express the author's main ideas in your own words; don't copy phrases or sentences. If you can't express an idea in your own words, you probably don't fully understand it. In that case, look up words, reread, talk to someone about the passage, or seek other information about the passage to clarify its meaning.

5. **Include restated definitions of key terms, important concepts, procedures, or principles.** Do not include examples, descriptive details, quotations, or anything not essential to the main point. Do not include your opinion.

6. **Present the ideas in the order in which they appear in the original source.**

7. **Reread your summary to determine if it contains sufficient information.**

8. **Ask yourself this question:** If someone had not read the article, would your summary be a good substitute that covers all the author's main points? If not, revise your summary to include additional information.

9. **Indicate the source of the material you summarized.** See Chapter 16, p. 493 for more information on how to cite sources.

## EXERCISE 3-10    Using Summaries

**Directions:** After reading the following paragraphs, select the choice that best summarizes each one.

_____ 1.      The tourist potential of any spot depends upon its "three A's": accessibility, accommodations, and attractions. The rich bird life on the islands of Lake Nicaragua, the lions of Kenya, and the tropical vegetation in many countries are important tourist destinations. Overall, the countries best endowed for tourism have both natural and cultural attractions, pleasant climates, good beaches, and reasonably well-educated populations. Political stability is a necessity. Despite Africa's wealth of ecological and cultural attractions, political instability and lack of accommodations have restricted its income to only 2.2 percent of global tourist dollars.

—adapted from Bergman and Renwick, *Introduction to Geography*, pp. 495–496

     **a.** The tourist potential of a place depends upon its accessibility, accommodations, and attractions. Important tourist destinations include Lake Nicaragua, Kenya, and tropical countries. However, despite Africa's many attractions, its income is only 2.2 percent of global tourist dollars due to political instability and lack of accommodations.

     **b.** Tourists typically want to visit places that offer the three A's. They also want pleasant weather, nice beaches, and an educated population.

     **c.** A country's ability to attract tourism is determined by how accessible it is and by the accommodations and attractions it provides. Countries that are tourist destinations offer a variety of activities, mild weather, attractive beaches, and a population that is educated and politically stable.

     **d.** Tourists are interested in places that offer political stability, excellent beaches, nice weather, and well-educated people. A tourist spot has to have natural and cultural attractions and a variety of accommodations.

_____ 2.      The common cold is responsible for more days lost from work and more uncomfortable days spent at work than any other ailment. Caused by any number of viruses (some experts claim there may be over 200 different viruses responsible for the common cold), colds are always present to some degree among people throughout the world. In the course of a year, Americans suffer over 1 billion colds. Cold viruses are carried in the nose and throat most of the time. These viruses are held in check until the host's resistance is lowered. It is possible to "catch" a cold—from the airborne droplets of another person's sneeze or from skin-to-skin or mucous membrane contact—though recent studies indicate that the hands may be the greatest avenue of colds and transmission of other viruses. Although many people believe that a cold results from exposure to cold weather or from getting chilled or overheated, experts believe that such things have little or no effect on cold development. Stress, allergy disorders that affect the nasal passages, and menstrual cycles do, however, appear to increase susceptibility.

—adapted from Donatelle, *Health: The Basics*, p. 350

a. More workers are affected by the common cold than by any other illness. Colds are caused by viruses and result from exposure to another person's virus through the air or by physical contact. Stress, nasal allergies, and certain stages of the menstrual cycle may make people more susceptible to colds.

b. People who suffer from the common cold often miss work or are uncomfortable at work. Experts say that over 200 different viruses may be responsible for the common cold, which is always present in people all over the world. In America, people suffer over 1 billion colds every year.

c. The common cold is caused by different viruses that are carried in the nose and throat most of the time. These viruses wait until a person's resistance is low; then the person may catch a cold from someone else, through either a sneeze or some other contact.

d. Cold viruses exist all over the world, and Americans suffer more than 1 billion colds each year. More than 200 different viruses may be responsible for causing the common cold.

---

**EXERCISE 3-11**

*WORKING TOGETHER*

# Writing a Summary

**Directions:** Using the steps listed in the Writing a Summary box on page 105, write a summary of one of the end-of-chapter readings in this text. Compare and discuss your summary with that of a classmate.

---

**EXERCISE 3-12**

*WORKING TOGETHER*

# Evaluating Summaries

**Directions:** The instructor of a speech communication class assigned a reading selection from the book *You Just Don't Understand: Women and Men in Conversation* by Deborah Tannen. He also asked students to write a summary of a particular passage.

The original passage is printed below, along with the summaries written by two students, Carlos and James. Working with a classmate, compare the two student summaries and decide which is better. Explain your choice.

### Original Selection

Differences in physical alignment, or body language among friends talking to each other, leap out at anyone who looks at segments of videotapes one after another. At every age, the girls and women sit closer to each other and look at each other directly. At every age, the boys and men sit at angles to each other—in one case, almost parallel—and never look directly into each other's faces. I developed the term *anchoring gaze* to describe this visual home base.

*(continued)*

The girls and women anchor their gaze on each other's faces, occasionally glancing away, while the boys and men anchor their gaze elsewhere in the room, occasionally glancing at each other.

The boys' and men's avoidance of looking directly at each other is especially important because researchers, and conventional wisdom, have emphasized that girls and women tend to be more indirect than boys and men in their speech. Actually, women and men tend to be indirect about different things. In physical alignment, and in verbally expressing personal problems, the men tend to be more indirect.

—Tannen, *You Just Don't Understand: Women and Men in Conversation*

### Carlos's Summary

Although researchers and others have traditionally believed men to be more direct than women, videotapes of friends interacting show that this is an overgeneralization. The truth is that men and women tend to be indirect about different things. Specifically, men tend to be indirect in body language and in talking about personal problems. In each of these tapes, women sit closer to each other than men and look more directly at each other than men do.

### James's Summary

There are many differences in physical alignment as seen on videotapes of men and women. Women and girls sit closer than men and boys. Men and boys sit not facing or looking at each other's faces. Girls and women anchor their gaze on each other's faces, but boys and men often anchor their gaze everywhere else in the room.

The fact that boys and men avoid looking into each other's faces is interesting because the idea that girls and women are usually more indirect than boys and men has always been universally accepted. Also researchers have advocated the idea that girls and women have a tendency to be less direct in their speech than boys and men. In reality, men and women are both indirect about different things. In the verbal expression of problems and in physical alignment, men tend to be less direct.

# Think Critically About Information in Textbooks

■ GOAL 6
Think critically about information in textbooks

We live in a society bombarded with information. Everywhere you look, you will see written materials, from newspapers and magazines to billboards and Web sites. Some experts estimate that the amount of information available to society is increasing by 66 percent every year.

That's a lot of information for a person to take in. So how do you cut through the clutter to find and learn the information you need? Here are some suggestions.

■ **Practice selective reading.** You do not have to read everything you see. (College assignments are the exception, of course.) Learn to quickly skim material to see if it interests you and then read the material that does.

■ **Understand the goal of what you are reading.** Is it to educate you or to convince you of something? In advertising, lovely words and images are used to make products seem desirable. In the news, politicians rant and rave about the issues. Evaluate the purpose of what you are reading by asking yourself what the writer's goal is.

■ **Adjust your reading speed to match the task.** If you are reading an article in *People* magazine, you probably can skim through it quickly. However, if you are filling out paperwork for financial aid or medical claims, you will want to read the forms slowly and carefully to make sure you are doing everything right.

■ **Read the "fine print."** When dealing with important paperwork, look to see if important information is buried in large amounts of text or in small print so that you'll be less likely to read it. Never sign anything without reading it completely first.

## Thinking Critically About Information

**Directions:** Read the passage and then answer the question that follows.

> **Hidden Information**
>
> Banks and credit card companies make a huge amount of money each year by charging interest to their customers. When you use a credit card, you are actually borrowing money from the credit card company. Unless you pay the borrowed amount back within one month, you start paying interest charges. By law, credit card companies are required to tell you on your credit card statement how much interest they are charging you.
>
> Have you ever looked at your credit card statement? It is filled with information and can have pages of "fine print" (that is, very small print) with the information required by law. How many people take the time to read this information? Not many. The credit card companies have effectively buried important information that they don't want you to know.

The back side of your credit card statement is filled with tiny print. Somewhere in the middle it says, "You are not responsible for paying for any purchases made if your credit card is stolen." You receive a phone call from the credit card company offering you "protection against unauthorized use of your card." If you pay them $99 a year, they will cover any purchases that are made if your card is stolen. Should you pay the $99 for the protection plan? Why or why not?

_____

_____

_____

## INTEGRATING READING AND WRITING

### READ AND RESPOND: A Textbook Excerpt

#### Thinking Before Reading

The following reading, "How to Remember What You Study," originally appeared in an introductory psychology textbook.

This is an example of how textbook chapters are organized and of the features they contain. As you read, notice how the authors use typographical aids (in this case, **boldface**) to make the steps in the process clear. The authors distinguish between two types of memory: *short-term memory* (information that is held in the mind for a short period of time) and *long-term memory* (information that your brain can recall months or years later). The entire excerpt is about improving your long-term memory.

1. Preview the reading, using the steps discussed in Chapter 1, page 15.
2. Connect the reading to your own experience:
   a. How good do you think your memory is? Have you ever tried any techniques to improve it?
   b. Which study techniques work best for you?
3. Mark and annotate as you read.

# How to Remember What You Study

## Carole Wade and Carol Tavris

1    Someday, a "memory pill" may be available to perk up our memories. For the time being, however, those of us who hope to improve our memories must rely on mental strategies. Some simple **mnemonics** can be useful, but complicated ones are often more bother than they're worth. A better approach to improving your memory is to practice the principles outlined below.

2    **Pay attention.** It seems obvious, but often we fail to remember because we never encoded the Information in the first place. For example, which of these is the real Lincoln penny?

(a)  (b)  (c)
(d)  (e)  (f)
(g)  (h)  (i)

3    Most Americans have trouble recognizing the real penny because they have never attended to the details of a penny's design (Nickerson & Adams, 1979). We are not advising you to do so, unless you happen to be a coin collector or a counterfeiting expert. Just keep in mind that when you do have something to remember, you will do better if you **encode** it well. (The real penny, by the way, is the left one in the bottom row.)

4    **Add meaning.** The more meaningful the material, the more likely it is to link up with

**mnemonics**
systems for improving memory or recall

**encode**
to convert incoming information for storage

information already in long-term memory. Meaningfulness also reduces the number of chunks of information you have to learn. Common ways of adding meaning include making up a story about the material, thinking of examples, and forming visual images. (Some people find that the odder the image, the better.) If your license plate happens to be 236MPL, you might think of 236 maples. If you are trying to remember the concept of **procedural memory**, you might make the concept meaningful by thinking of an example from your own life, such as your ability to ride a mountain bike, and then imagine a *p* superimposed on an image of yourself on your bike.

**procedural memory**
memory of how to do things

5   **Take your time.** Leisurely learning, spread out over several sessions, usually produces better results than harried cramming (although reviewing material just before a test can be helpful). In terms of hours spent, "distributed" (spaced) learning sessions are more efficient than "massed" ones; in other words, three separate one-hour study sessions may result in more retention than one session of three hours.

6   **Take time out.** If possible, minimize interference by using study breaks for rest or recreation. A good night's sleep or an afternoon nap reduces such interference and improves the chances that a new memory will be consolidated.

7   **Overlearn.** You can't remember something you never learned well in the first place. Overlearning—studying information even after you think you know it—is one of the best ways to ensure that you'll remember it.

**rehearse**
talk through the material in your head

8   **Read, recite, review.** Test yourself frequently, **rehearse** thoroughly, and review periodically to see how you are doing. Don't just evaluate your learning immediately after reading the material, though, because the information is still in short-term memory and you are likely to feel a false sense of confidence about your ability to recall it later. If you delay making judgment for at least a few minutes, your evaluation will probably be more accurate (Nelson & Dunlosky, 1991).

9   Most of all, you will find that active learning produces more comprehension and better retention than does passive reading or listening. Even then, you should not expect to remember everything you read or hear. Nor should you want to. Piling up facts without distinguishing the important from the trivial is just confusing. Popular books and tapes that promise to give you a perfect or photographic memory, or instant recall of everything you learn, fly in the face of what psychologists know about how the mind operates. Our advice: Forget them.

## Getting Ready to Write

### Checking Your Comprehension

1.  Why do most people have trouble identifying the real Lincoln penny in the photograph on page 110?

2.  List three common methods of adding meaning to information.

3.  Why do the authors advise against evaluating your learning immediately after you've read an assignment?

4.  Is it possible to achieve perfect recall? Why or why not?

### Strengthening Your Vocabulary

The excerpt makes use of many psychological terms that are defined either indirectly or not at all. Using context, word parts, or a psychology dictionary, write a brief definition of each of the following psychological terms as it is used in the reading:

1. distributed learning sessions (paragraph 5) _____

   _____

2. massed learning sessions (paragraph 5) _____

   _____

3. interference (paragraph 6) _____

4. consolidated information (paragraph 6) _____

   _____

5. overlearning (paragraph7) _____

6. photographic memory (paragraph 9) _____

   _____

## Examining the Reading: Using Sequence Maps

Complete the sequence map for "How to Remember What You Study" by filling in the blanks.

**VISUALIZE IT!**

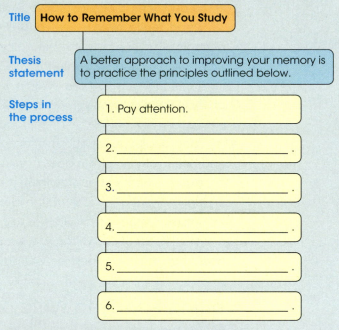

**Title** | How to Remember What You Study

**Thesis statement** | A better approach to improving your memory is to practice the principles outlined below.

**Steps in the process**

1. Pay attention.

2. _____ .

3. _____ .

4. _____ .

5. _____ .

6. _____ .

## Reacting to Ideas: Discussion and Journal Writing

1. Do you have any experience with cramming before an exam? In general, how effective have your cram sessions been in terms of your exam grades and your final course grades?

2. Create a list of three simple mnemonics you currently use or could start using. For example, many students remember the names of the U.S. Great Lakes by using the mnemonic HOMES: Huron, Ontario, Michigan, Erie, and Superior.

3. In your daily life, to what types of information do you tend to pay the most attention? The least attention? For example, do you read every billboard or advertisement, or do you ignore most of them? Which characteristics in an advertisement will make you pay more attention to it?

**THINKING VISUALLY**

4. What illustrations, other than the pennies, could be used to illustrate the same principle of memory?

### Thinking and Writing Critically

1. In paragraph 3, the authors explicitly state that they are not advising you to pay attention to the details of a penny's design. Why do they offer this advice?

2. Though the tone of the reading is basically serious, the authors try to lighten the material by using humor. Where is humor used? Is it effective?

3. Which one of the memory techniques seems most useful? Which seems least useful? Explain your reasons.

**MySkillsLab®**

**Complete** this Exercise

## Writing About the Reading

### Paragraph Options

1. Write a paragraph describing the differences between passive learning and active learning.

2. Two psychological terms not used in the reading are *internal locus of control* and *external locus of control*. A person with an *internal* locus of control believes that she has some control over the events that affect her life. A person with an *external* locus of control believes that other forces (such as the environment, her genetics, or other people) control her life.

    Write a paragraph explaining how you would add meaning to these terms to make them relevant to your life and move them into your long-term memory.

3. The authors advise you to take "time out" from your studies to maximize your learning. In what other areas of life can a time out be useful? Write a paragraph exploring how a time out can improve your performance or effectiveness in one or two specific activities.

### Essay Options

4. The authors refer to the hope that someday a "memory pill" will help all of us improve our memory. Suppose you could create the magic pill of your choice. What type of pill would you create? (For example, it might be a pill that makes you a more patient person, or a pill that makes you more friendly.) Write an essay explaining your choice and exploring the pros and cons of taking that pill.

5. Learning often occurs when we are paying attention to something we particularly enjoy. For example, many sports fans learn players' "stats" (statistics) just by watching their favorite team play. Write an essay explaining how the memory-improvement tips in this essay could help sports fans learn more about the sport and the players. (You can choose any sport you like.)

## SELF-TEST SUMMARY

To test yourself, cover the Answer column with a sheet of paper and answer each question in the left column. Evaluate each of your answers as you work by sliding the paper down and comparing your answer with what is printed in the Answer column.

*(continued)*

*(continued)*

| QUESTION | ANSWER |
|---|---|
| ■ **GOAL 1** Use writing as a learning tool<br><br>Why write as you read and study? | Writing focuses your attention, forces you to think, tests your understanding, and facilitates recall. |
| ■ **GOAL 2** Use strategies for reading textbooks<br><br>How can you use textbooks effectively? | Textbooks are designed and selected to work with your instructor's lecture. Refer to Table 3-1 on page 86 for a list of textbook features and how to use them. |
| ■ **GOAL 3** Use the SQ3R system<br><br>What are the five steps in the SQ3R system? | The steps are Survey, Question, Read, Recite, and Review. |
| ■ **GOAL 4** Use learning and recall strategies<br><br>What strategies can you use for learning and recalling what you read? | Learning and recall strategies include immediate review, periodic review, final review, building an intent to remember, organizing and categorizing, association, using a variety of sensory modes, visualization, and mnemonic devices. |
| ■ **GOAL 5** Select and organize what to learn<br><br>What are five strategies for selecting and organizing information? | 1. Highlight important parts of topic sentences as well as key supporting details, be accurate, and highlight the right amount.<br>2. Use mapping to show how ideas in a paragraph or chapter are related.<br>3. Use outlining to list major and minor ideas and to show how they are related.<br>4. Use paraphrasing, a restatement, in your own words, of a paragraph, passage, or reading selection. Use it to condense ideas.<br>5. A summary is a brief statement of the major points of a reading. To write an effective summary, refer to the guidelines in the "Writing a Summary" box on page 105. |
| ■ **GOAL 6** Think critically about information in textbooks<br><br>How do you think critically about information in textbooks? | To find and learn the information you need in textbooks, practice selective reading, understand the goal of what you are reading, adjust your reading speed to match the task, and read the "fine print." |

**MySkillsLab** ®

For more help with **Reading and Learning from College Textbooks**, go to your learning path in MySkillsLab at www.myskillslab.com.

# Reading and Evaluating Visuals

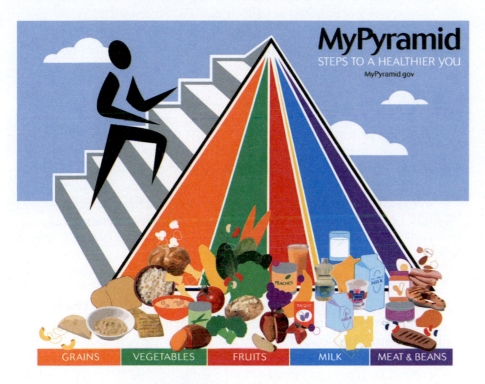

## LEARNING GOALS

Learn how to . . .

- **GOAL 1**
  Understand the function of visuals

- **GOAL 2**
  Read and interpret visuals

- **GOAL 3**
  Integrate text and visuals

- **GOAL 4**
  Read and interpret different types of visuals

- **GOAL 5**
  Think critically about visuals

## THINK About It!

The diagram shown above appeared in a college textbook on health in a chapter focusing on nutrition. Write a sentence explaining why you think the textbook authors chose to include it.

Today's textbooks, Web sites, articles, essays, and research sources contain plenty of diagrams, as well as other types of visuals—maps, graphs, charts, photographs, and infographics. To read these materials effectively you need to read, interpret, and analyze the visuals they contain. Writers also find visuals useful. You might include and label a diagram when writing an essay exam, or you might choose to include photographs or other visuals in a research paper you are writing. You can use visuals to help you organize your own writing (see "Using Idea Maps," p. 21). Drawing your own visuals is also a good way to check your recall of chapter content. The purpose of this chapter is to equip you with the skills to read, analyze, interpret, and think critically about graphics.

# Reading and Writing Connections

### EVERYDAY CONNECTIONS

- **Reading** You are trying to decide between three used cars to purchase. You do some online research on gas mileage and find tables comparing the mileages of various models, organized by year.
- **Writing** When sharing your findings with your partner by e-mail, you interpret and summarize the findings of the tables you have located.

### ACADEMIC CONNECTIONS

- **Reading** You are reading a chapter in your human anatomy textbook on the digestive system and find numerous diagrams of the digestive process that you must read and understand.
- **Writing** In preparation for an exam in this course, you decide to draw a diagram of the digestive process and label various functions, without referring to the text, as a means of checking your recall and understanding.

### WORKPLACE CONNECTIONS

- **Writing** You are a sales representative for a Web design company and are making a presentation to the chef and owner of a local restaurant. You decide to create and display a graph showing how sales at other local restaurants increased when their owners have created Web sites and posted their menus online.
- **Reading** As chef and owner of the restaurant, you need to examine the graphic and determine whether it does indeed offer reliable, accurate, and convincing evidence that Web sites increase profitability.

## FOCUSING ON READING AND WRITING

# Why Use Visuals?

■ **GOAL 1**
Understand the function of visuals

**Visuals** are any type of photograph, drawing, or graphic that presents information in a visual format. Writers include visuals in many forms of writing, including textbooks, articles and essays, research reports, manuals, and magazines and newspapers. Visuals help writers present complex information in a simple, readable format that readers can easily understand. Visuals, especially graphics, enable readers to grasp and interpret lengthy or complicated sets of information more easily than if presented in sentence and paragraph format. Visuals serve a number of important functions for both readers and writers:

■ **Visuals consolidate information and display it in an easy-to-read format.** Figure 4-1, for example, compares poverty in the United States by age and racial/ethnic status. Can you imagine how lengthy and cumbersome it would be to present all this information in paragraph form?

■ **Visuals explain and illustrate.** Diagrams in biology textbooks, for example, make it easy to explain how complex processes such as photosynthesis or transpiration work.

■ **Visuals dramatize information.** Writers can use photographs and other graphics to emphasize content and create an emotional response in readers. What could more clearly and dramatically emphasize the differences in levels of poverty faced by Latinos and African Americans as compared to other groups than the graph shown in Figure 4-1?

■ **Visuals display trends, patterns, and variations.** Graphics make it easy to see differences and changes. Readers can easily recognize trends and patterns. In Figure 4-1 you can clearly see that Latino and African American children experience higher levels of poverty than other groups.

## FIGURE 4-1   A VISUAL CONSOLIDATING INFORMATION

### POVERTY IN THE UNITED STATES, BY AGE AND RACE-ETHNICITY

> To ensure that the reader sees the exact percentage for each group, the creator of this graphic has included that number at the top of each bar.

> Note that the graph is reporting on *percentages* of the population, not the *number* of U.S. residents (in millions) who live in poverty.

Legend: All racial/ethnic groups, White Americans, Asian Americans, Latinos, African Americans

Overall: 13, 11, 10, 22, 25
The elderly age 65 and over: 10, 8, 14, 19, 24
Children under age 18: 18, 15, 10, 29, 34

Henslin, *Sociology: A Down-to-Earth Approach, Core Concepts*, p. 222. Data source: U.S. Census Bureau, *Statistical Abstract of the United States 2007*, Table 694.

**EXERCISE 4-1**    # Reading Visuals

**Directions:** Locate one visual in one of your textbooks or in a newspaper (*USA Today* frequently includes numerous visuals). Identify which function(s) the visual fulfills.

# Use Strategies for Reading and Interpreting Visuals

■ GOAL 2
Read and interpret visuals

Because graphics clarify, summarize, or emphasize important facts, concepts, and trends, you need to study them closely.

## How to Read Visuals

Following are some general suggestions that will help you get the most out of graphic elements in the material you read.

1. **Read the title or caption and legend.** The title tells you what situation or relationship is being described. The legend is the explanatory caption that may accompany the visual. The legend may also function as a key, indicating what particular colors, lines, or pictures mean. For example, in Figure 4-1, the legend shows the color bar associated with each ethnic group (red for Latinos, purple for African Americans, and so on).

2. **Determine how the visual is organized.** If you are working with a table, note the column headings. For a graph, notice the labels on the vertical axis (the top-to-bottom line on the left side of the graph) and the horizontal axis (the left-to-right line at the bottom of the graph). In Figure 4-1, for example, the vertical axis shows percentages from 0 percent to 40 percent.

3. **Determine what variables (quantities or categories) the visual is illustrating.** Identify the pieces of information that are being compared or the relationship that is being shown. Note any symbols and abbreviations used.

4. **Determine the scale or unit of measurement.** Note how the variables are measured. For example, does a graph show expenditures in dollars, thousands of dollars, or millions of dollars?

5. **Identify any trends, patterns, or relationships the visual is intended to show.** The following sections discuss this step in greater detail.

6. **Read any footnotes and identify the source.** Footnotes, printed at the bottom of a graph or chart, indicate how the data were collected, explain what certain numbers or headings mean, and describe the statistical procedures used. Identifying the source is helpful in assessing the reliability of the data.

7. **Make a brief summary note.** In the margin, jot a brief note about the key trend or pattern emphasized by the visual. Writing will crystallize the idea in your mind, and your note will be useful when you review.

# Integrate Text and Visuals

■ GOAL 3
Integrate text and visuals

In both textbooks and reference sources, most visuals do not stand alone; they have corresponding printed text that may introduce, explain, summarize, or analyze the visual. Be sure to consider the text and the visual together to get their complete meaning as outlined in the following Need to Know box.

## NEED TO KNOW

### How to Integrate Text and Visuals

When reading text and visuals together, be sure to do the following:

1. **Notice the type and number of visuals included in the material as you preview the chapter** (see Chapter 1).

2. **Refer to the visual when the author directs you to.** Writers tell you when they want you to look at a visual by saying "See Figure 17-2" or by introducing the visual with a phrase like "Table 12-7 displays . . . ."

3. **Read the visual, using steps listed on page 118.**

4. **Move back and forth between the text and visual.** As you study the visual, refer back to the text as needed, following the explanation of the visual provided by the author. This technique is particularly effective with illustrations and diagrams, which often show the meaning or function of particular terms or parts.

5. **Determine why the author included the visual.** Ask these questions:
   - What am I supposed to learn from this visual?
   - Why was it included?
   - What new information does the visual contain?
   - On what topic(s) does the visual provide more detail or further explanation?

# Types of Visuals

■ **GOAL 4**
Read and interpret different types of visuals

Many types of visuals are used in textbooks. In addition to describing some type of relationship or illustrating a particular point, each type is intended to achieve a particular purpose. When you *read* the visual, you view the information it contains. When you *interpret* the visual, you look more closely at the information and identify trends, patterns, or key ideas.

## Photographs

Photographs are included in texts for a variety of reasons:

- **To introduce a new idea.**
- **To add interest or to help you visualize an event, concept, or feeling.**
- **To provide an example of a concept.** For example, photographs in a biology textbook may be used to illustrate variation among species.
- **To create emotional responses or provide perspective.** For example, a photograph of a malnourished child may help readers visualize the conditions and sympathize with the victims of poverty.

When studying a photograph, read the caption. It may provide clues to the importance or meaning of the photograph. The purpose of the photograph in Figure 4-2 (p. 120), taken from a psychology textbook, could be unclear without the caption. This caption helps you understand how and why peer groups form and how the members of these groups act.

### FIGURE 4-2   A SAMPLE PHOTOGRAPH

Being a social outcast as an adolescent is often seen as a fate worse than death, resulting in groups of teen clones all anxious to fit in by talking, dressing, and acting like their peers. For many parents, the possibility of negative peer pressure luring their child into a world of alcohol, drugs, and casual sex is a constant source of worry. Research suggests that these fears are well-founded—teenagers of the same friendship group usually indulge in similarly risky behaviors, and teens who start smoking usually do so because one of their friends offered them a cigarette or made it look cool. But peer pressure can also have positive effects. Conforming to a peer group can help adolescents form a sense of identity. And peer groups of ambitious students can meet to do homework together and encourage one another to do well academically.

### EXERCISE 4-2    Interpreting a Photograph

**Directions:** Study the photograph in Figure 4-3, taken from a sociology textbook, and answer the following questions.

1. What is this photograph intended to illustrate?

   _____

2. What does it show that a verbal description could not?

   _____

   _____

### FIGURE 4-3    A PHOTOGRAPH

An *in-group* is a group with which people identify and have a sense of belonging. In contrast, an *out-group* is a group that people do not identify with and consider less worthy and desirable than their own. Sports fans provide excellent examples of in-group and out-group behavior. Do you have a favorite sports team to which you feel allegiance and, hence, a sense of belonging?

## Maps

There are two types of maps: *locational* and *thematic*. **Locational maps** show the exact positions of physical objects: countries, cities, states, rivers, mountains, and so forth. You will find these maps in history, astronomy, geography, archaeology, and anthropology textbooks. To read these types of maps, concentrate on each item's position in relation to other objects. For instance, when referring to a map of our solar system in an astronomy text, concentrate on the locations of planets relative to one another, of the planets to the sun and to their moons, and so forth.

**Thematic maps** provide statistical or factual information about a particular area or region. For example, a color-coded map of the United States may be used to show average income levels within each state. A map of Africa may be coded to represent each country's form of government.

When reading thematic maps, look for trends or patterns. For example, when studying a map of the United States showing average income levels, you should look for regional clusters or patterns. Are incomes higher in the North or South? Are they higher in highly populated states such as New York and California or in lower-population states such as Montana or Idaho? When reading a map of Africa showing types of government, you should look for the most and least common forms and try to discover regional similarities. Do the northern or eastern African countries, for example, have similar forms of government?

### FIGURE 4-4   A SAMPLE MAP

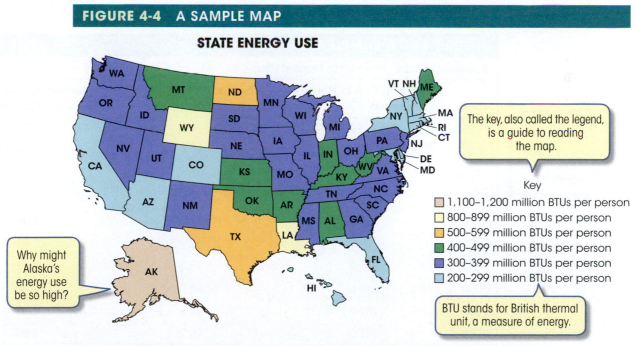

STATE ENERGY USE

The key, also called the legend, is a guide to reading the map.

Why might Alaska's energy use be so high?

**Key**
- 1,100–1,200 million BTUs per person
- 800–899 million BTUs per person
- 500–599 million BTUs per person
- 400–499 million BTUs per person
- 300–399 million BTUs per person
- 200–299 million BTUs per person

BTU stands for British thermal unit, a measure of energy.

Bennett, Briggs, and Triola, *Statistical Reasoning for Everyday Life,* p. 118.

# Interpreting a Map

**Directions:** Study the map in Figure 4-4 and answer the following questions.

1. What is the purpose of this map?

   _____

2. What type of map is this? _____

3. Which state uses the largest amount of energy per person? Which use the least?

   _____

   _____

---

## Tables

A **table** displays facts, figures, statistics, and other data in a condensed orderly sequence for convenience of reference and clarity. The information in tables is classified or organized in rows and columns so that the data can easily be compared. Figure 4-5, a table taken from a sociology text, displays data about the number of television sets in American households. By scanning the table, you can easily see how ownership of televisions has grown in America over the period 1950–2008. Use the steps in the Need to Know box to read tables.

### FIGURE 4-5   A SAMPLE TABLE

Television Sets in American Households

| Year | Television Sets in Homes (in Millions) | Percentage of Households with Television Sets | Number of Television Sets per Household |
|---|---|---|---|
| 1950 | 3.9 | 9.0 | 1.01 |
| 1960 | 45.8 | 87.1 | 1.13 |
| 1970 | 81.0 | 94.9 | 1.39 |
| 1980 | 128.0 | 97.9 | 1.68 |
| 1990 | 193.0 | 98.2 | 2.00 |
| 2000 | 245.0 | 98.2 | 2.40 |
| 2003 | 260.0 | 98.2 | 2.40 |
| 2004 | 268.0 | 98.2 | 2.50 |
| 2005 | 287.0 | 98.2 | 2.60 |
| 2008 | 301.0 | 98.2 | 2.80 |

> In the early days of TV, which households were most likely to own televisions?

> List three possible reasons why 100% of U.S. households do not own at least one TV set.

> How is it possible for a household to own 2.8 television sets?

Thompson and Hickey, *Society in Focus: 2010 Census Update*, p. 9. Data source: Table 1090, U.S. Census Bureau, *Statistical Abstract of the United States 2011*: Table 1131. Utilization and Number of Selected Media, 2000 to 2008.

# NEED TO KNOW

### How to Read a Table

1. **Determine how the data are classified or divided.** Look closely at column headings.
2. **Make comparisons and look for trends.**
3. **Draw conclusions.**

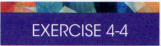

EXERCISE 4-4

## Interpreting a Table

**Directions:** Answer the following questions based on the table shown in Figure 4-5.

1. For what period has the percentage of American households with TV sets remained unchanged? _____

2. In which year did the number of TV sets in American households exceed 300 million for the first time? _____

3. The largest increase in the number of TV sets in American households took place between which two years? _____

4. The number of television sets in an American household hit 2.0 for the first time in which year? _____

## Graphs

A **graph** clarifies the relationship between two or more sets of information. A graph often reveals a trend or pattern that is easily recognizable in visual form but is not as obvious when the data appear in list or paragraph form. Graphs are often divided into four categories: *bar graphs, stacked bar graphs, line graphs*, and *circle graphs*.

### Bar Graphs

A **bar graph** compares quantities or amounts using bars of different lengths. Bar graphs are especially useful in showing changes that occur over time, and they are often included in textbooks to emphasize differences. The graph in Figure 4-6 (p. 124) displays the breakdown of the elderly population in the United States by race and ethnicity. Note that two bars are included for each racial/ethnic group: the actual percentages for 1990 and the estimated percentages for 2050. Use the following steps when reading a bar graph:

# NEED TO KNOW

### How to Read a Bar Graph

1. **Pay particular attention to differences in the lengths of the bars** (which show data for the variables)
2. **Notice which variables have the largest and smallest values**, and try to think of reasons that account for the differences

### FIGURE 4-6 A SAMPLE BAR GRAPH

**PERCENTAGE OF ELDERLY, BY RACE AND HISPANIC ORIGIN: 1990 AND 2050**

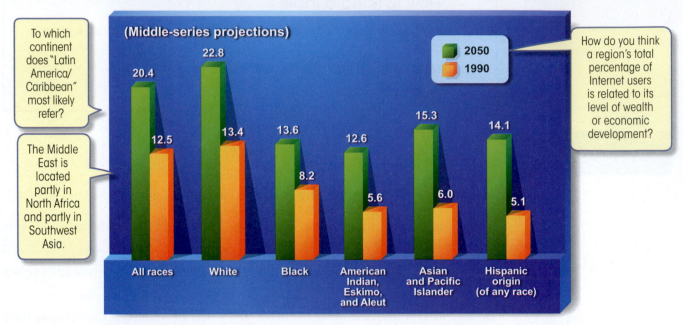

Kunz, *Think Marriages & Families*, p. 173. Data source: U.S. Census Bureau.

---

**EXERCISE 4-5**

## Interpreting a Bar Graph

**Directions:** Study the bar graph shown in Figure 4-6 and answer the following questions.

1. What is the purpose of the graph?

   _____

2. Which group is expected to see the largest increase in longevity?

   _____

3. Which groups were above the average longevity (all races) and which were below average in 1990? Did the position change in the projections for 2050?

   _____

   _____

4. Why might this graph be included in a textbook titled "Marriage and Family"?

   _____

   _____

---

### Stacked Bar Graphs

In a **stacked bar graph**, as shown in Figure 4-7, bars are placed on top of one another instead of being side by side.

A **stacked bar graph** is often used to emphasize whole/part relationships. That is, it shows the component parts that make up a total. Because stacked bar

## FIGURE 4-7 A SAMPLE STACKED BAR GRAPH

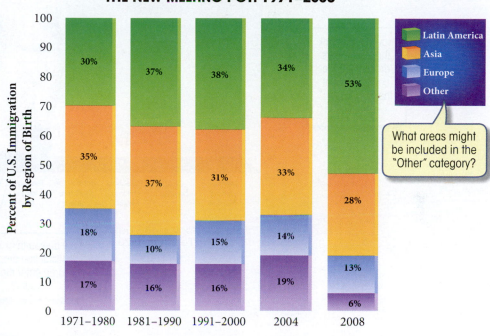

Which two world areas showed only a 5–7% decrease in immigration to the United States between 1971–1980 and 2008?

What areas might be included in the "Other" category?

What exactly does this footnote mean? Does it apply to any of the periods shown in the graph?

Because of rounding, percentages may not add up to 100.

Thompson and Hickey, *Society in Focus: An Introduction to Sociology*, p. 282. Data source: Office of Immigration Statistics, U.S. Department of Homeland Security, *2008 Yearbook of Immigration Statistics.*

graphs are intended to make numerous comparisons, study the graph carefully to be sure you "see" all possible relationships. For example, in Figure 4-7 you can see differences in how immigration patterns into the United States have changed between the period 1971–1980 and 2008. From 1971–1980, 30 percent of immigrants to the United States came from Latin America, but by 2008 that number had increased to 53 percent. Every other group represented in the stacked bar graph had reduced immigration to the United States between the two periods.

### Line Graphs

In **line graphs**, information is plotted along a vertical and a horizontal axis, with one or more variables plotted on each axis. A line graph connects points along these axes. A line graph usually includes more data points than a bar graph. Consequently, it is often used to present detailed and/or large quantities of information. If a line graph compares only two variables, then it consists of a single line. Often, however, line graphs compare two or more variables, in which case multiple lines are used. The line graph in Figure 4-8 shows how marital satisfaction (that is, how happy married people are) varies over the course of a long-term marriage.

Line graphs are often used to display data that occur in a sequence. You can see this in Figure 4-8 (p. 126), which displays a sequence starting with the early days of marriage without children and progressing through "empty nest" and the death of the first spouse.

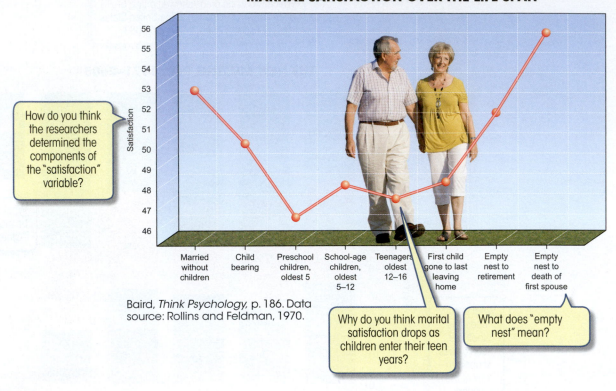

FIGURE 4-8  A SAMPLE LINE GRAPH

MARITAL SATISFACTION OVER THE LIFE SPAN

Baird, *Think Psychology*, p. 186. Data source: Rollins and Feldman, 1970.

How do you think the researchers determined the components of the "satisfaction" variable?

Why do you think marital satisfaction drops as children enter their teen years?

What does "empty nest" mean?

---

**EXERCISE 4-6**

## Interpreting a Line Graph

**Directions:** Study the line graph shown in Figure 4-8 and answer the following questions.

1. How many stages of married life are used to draw the line graph? _____

2. At which stage of life are married people the most satisfied and happy with their marriage?

   _____

3. At which stage of life do married people report the least satisfaction with their marriage?

   _____

4. What trends are illustrated by this graph?

   _____

   _____

   _____

   _____

### Circle Graphs

A **circle graph**, also called a **pie chart**, is used to show whole/part relationships or to show how parts of a unit have been divided or classified. Circle graphs often emphasize proportions or emphasize the relative size or importance of various parts (see Figure 4-9, which shows how people spend their time each day). Use the steps in the following box to read circle graphs.

---

 **NEED TO KNOW**

#### How to Read a Circle Graph

1. **Determine the subject of the circle graph.** What is being divided into parts or slices?

2. **Notice how the subject is divided and how the slices are arranged.** Are they arranged from largest to smallest pieces? What labels or headings are used?

3. **Notice trends and patterns.** What does the circle graph reveal about the subject?

---

**FIGURE 4-9    A SAMPLE CIRCLE GRAPH**

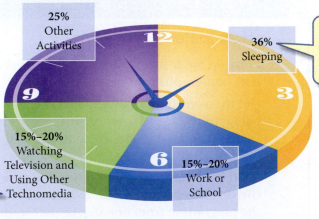

What year does this pie graph summarize?

**AVERAGE TIME SPENT AT VARIOUS ACTIVITIES**

25% Other Activities

36% Sleeping

There are 24 hours in a day. Therefore, 36% equals approximately 8.6 hours of sleep per day. (24 × 0.36 = 8.64)

15%–20% Watching Television and Using Other Technomedia

15%–20% Work or School

What does "technomedia" mean?

Adapted from Thompson and Hickey, *Society in Focus: An Introduction to Sociology*, p. 10. Data source: U.S. Census Bureau, *Statistical Abstract of the United States 2009*, Table 1089.

**EXERCISE 4-7**

# Interpreting a Circle Graph

**Directions:** Use the circle graph in Figure 4-9 to answer the following questions.

1. Which activity do people spend the largest portion of their day doing?

   _____

2. On which two sets of activities do humans spend roughly equal time each day?

   _____

3. What activities might fall into the "Other Activities" category?

   _____

## Diagrams

A **diagram** is a drawing that explains an object, idea, or process by outlining parts or steps or by showing the object's organization. Use the steps listed in the box below to read diagrams effectively.

The diagram from a biology textbook in Figure 4-10 illustrates the structure of two common viruses. This diagram clearly explains their structures while showing their differences.

To read a diagram, focus on its purpose. What is it intended to illustrate? Why did the author include it? To study a diagram, cover the diagram and try to draw it and label its parts without referring to the text. This activity will provide a good test of whether or not you truly understand the process or concept illustrated.

## NEED TO KNOW

### How to Read a Diagram

1. **Plan on switching back and forth between the diagram and the text paragraphs that describe it.**

2. **Get an overview.** Study the diagram and read the corresponding text paragraphs once to discover what process the diagram is illustrating. Pay particular attention to the heading of the textbook section and the diagram's title.

3. **Read both the diagram and the text several more times, focusing on the details of the process.** Examine each step or part and understand the progression from one step or part to the next.

4. **Try to redraw the diagram without referring to the original, including as much detail as possible.**

5. **Test your understanding and recall by explaining the diagram, step by step, using your own words.**

**FIGURE 4-10    A SAMPLE DIAGRAM**

Viruses are extremely small particles that infect cells and cause many human diseases. Their basic structure includes an outer envelope, composed of lipid and protein, a protein capsid, and genetic material that is enclosed within the capsid.

From the caption, how do you know that both RNA and DNA are types of genetic material?

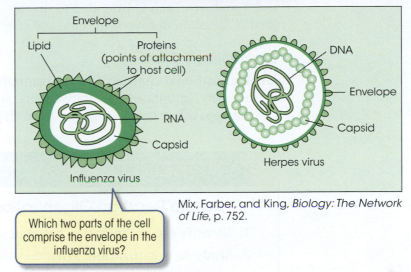

THE STRUCTURE OF VIRUSES

Mix, Farber, and King, *Biology: The Network of Life*, p. 752.

Which two parts of the cell comprise the envelope in the influenza virus?

EXERCISE 4-8

# Interpreting Diagrams

**Directions:** Study the diagram shown in Figure 4-10 and answer the following questions.

1. What are the two viruses shown in the diagram? _____

2. Identify two similarities between the virus structures.

   _____

3. What is the difference between the genetic material contained within each virus?

   _____

4. Cover the diagrams and try to draw each virus structure without referring to the text. Compare your drawing with the diagram.

EXERCISE 4-9

# Drawing a Diagram

**Directions:** Draw a diagram that illustrates one of the following, and then compare your diagram with those of several classmates.

1. The registration process at your college

2. A process explained in one of your textbooks

3. The floor plan of one of your college's buildings

4. An object described in one of your textbooks

## Charts

Two types of charts are commonly used in college textbooks: *organizational charts* and *flowcharts*. Each is intended to display a relationship, either quantitative (that is, based on numbers) or cause and effect.

### Organizational Charts

An **organizational chart** divides an organization, such as a corporation, hospital, or university, into its administrative parts, staff positions, or lines of authority. Use the steps below to read organizational charts effectively.

 **NEED TO KNOW**

### How to Read an Organizational Chart

1. **Identify the organization being described.**
2. **Study its organization.** What do various boxes and arrows represent?
3. **Identify lines of authority and responsibility.** Determine who is in charge of what.

Figure 4-11 shows the organization of Atlantic College. It depicts how authority flows in this college.

**FIGURE 4-11   A SAMPLE ORGANIZATION CHART**

**ADMINISTRATION AND FACULTY OF ATLANTIC COLLEGE**

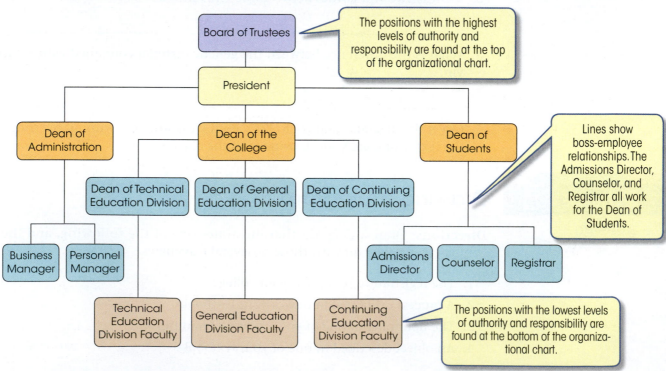

Bovée and Thill, *Business Communication Today,* p. 379.

### Flowcharts

A **flowchart** shows how a process or procedure works. Use the steps in the box below to read flowcharts effectively. Lines or arrows are used to indicate the direction (route or routes) through the procedure. Various shapes (boxes, circles, rectangles) enclose what is done at each stage or step. You could draw a flowchart, for example, to describe how to apply for a student loan or how to locate a malfunction in your car's electrical system. The flowchart shown in Figure 4-12 shows a processing procedure used in an accounting department.

## NEED TO KNOW

### How to Read a Flowchart

1. **Figure out what process the flowchart shows.**

2. **Next, follow the chart, using the arrows and reading each step.** Start at the top or far left of the chart.

3. **When you've finished, describe the process in your own words.** Try to draw the chart from memory without referring to the text. Compare your drawing with the chart and take note of anything you forgot or misplaced.

### FIGURE 4-12   A SAMPLE FLOWCHART

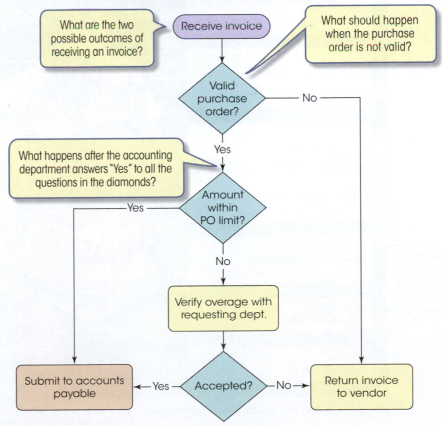

Bovée and Thill, *Business Communication Today*, p. 379.

## Infographics

Graphic designers are always looking for new, visually interesting ways to present information. In recent years, a new type of visual aid called an *infographic* has become popular. While the definition is not precise, **infographics** usually combine several types of visual aids into one, often merging photos with text, diagrams, or tables.

Unlike other graphics, infographics are sometimes designed to stand on their own; they do not necessarily repeat or summarize what is in the text. Consider the following excerpt from a health textbook:

> Cigarette smoking adversely affects the health of every person who smokes, as well as the health of everyone nearby. Each day, cigarettes contribute to more than 1,000 deaths from cancer, cardiovascular disease, and respiratory disorders. In addition, tobacco use can negatively impact the health of almost every system in your body. Figure 4-13 summarizes some of the physiological and health effects of smoking.
> —Donatelle, *Health: The Basics, Green Edition*, p. 129

### FIGURE 4-13 A SAMPLE INFOGRAPHIC

#### EFFECTS OF SMOKING ON BODY AND HEALTH

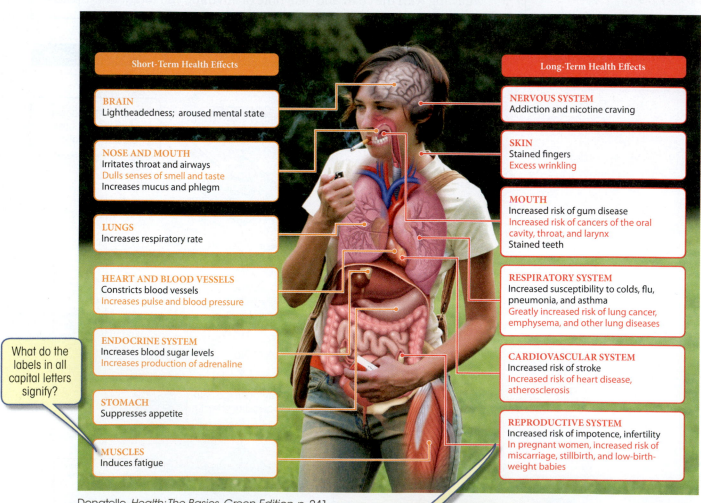

Donatelle, *Health: The Basics, Green Edition*, p. 241.

What do the labels in all capital letters signify?

Why are some of the effects of smoking in black type and other effects in colored type? Do you see a pattern here?

Figure 4-13 lists many effects of smoking that are *not* listed in the text. To understand this material, you must carefully read and learn from the infographic, because the information cannot be found in the text. Use the suggestions in the following box to read infographics effectively.

## NEED TO KNOW

### How to Read an Infographic

1. **Identify the subject.** What is the purpose of the infographic?

2. **Identify how you should follow the "flow" of the infographic.** Should you read it from top to bottom, left to right, clockwise or counterclockwise? Look for visual clues, such as arrows or headings, to determine where you should start.

3. **Examine how the artist has chosen to present the information.** That is, how is the infographic organized? Does it fit into any particular pattern?

4. **How do the words and pictures work together?** How close is the correspondence between the words and the visual elements?

5. **When you've finished, describe the infographic and its information in your own words.** Try to draw it from memory. Compare your drawing with the chart and take note of anything you forgot or misplaced.

**EXERCISE 4-10**

## Interpreting an Infographic

**Directions:** Study Figure 4-13 and answer the following questions.

1. What two major categories is the infographic exploring? How can you tell?

   _____

   _____

   _____

2. Why do you think the artist has shown the body's interior anatomy superimposed on the photo of the woman?

   _____

3. What are the effects of smoking on pregnant women?

   _____

4. Are people who smoke more likely to gain weight or lose weight? How can you tell from the infographic?

   _____

   _____

**5.** Is smoking more likely to keep you looking young or to make you look older than you are? How can you tell from the infographic?

_____

_____

## Cartoons

Cartoons are included in textbooks and other materials to make a point quickly or simply to lighten the text by adding a touch of humor about the topic at hand. Cartoons usually appear without a title or legend and there is usually no reference within the text to the cartoon.

Cartoons can make abstract ideas and concepts concrete and real. Pay close attention to cartoons, especially if you are a visual learner. They may help you remember ideas easily by serving as a recall clue that triggers your memory of related material.

The cartoon shown in Figure 4-14 appears in a U.S. history textbook chapter titled "A Global Nation for the New Millennium." It appears in a text section that discusses the growth of the Internet. The cartoon effectively makes the point that you cannot always be sure whom you are communicating with on the Internet.

### FIGURE 4-14 . A SAMPLE CARTOON

*"On the Internet, nobody knows you're a dog."*

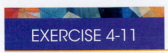

**EXERCISE 4-11**    ## Selecting an Appropriate Visual

**Directions:** Indicate what type of visual(s) would be most useful in presenting each of the following sets of information.

1. The effects of flooding on a Midwestern town

_____

2. The top five soft drink brands by percent of market share

_____

3. Changes in yearly income per person from 2005 to 2010 in Germany, France, Japan, and the United States

_____

4. The suicide rates for various age groups

_____

5. The top 20 places to live in the United States and their average income, cost of housing, quality of schools, level of taxes, amount of crime, and availability of cultural and recreational activities

_____

6. Government spending in 2010 and 2011 for payments to individuals, defense, interest on debt, grants to state and local governments, and all other spending

_____

7. The basic parts of a solar-powered automobile

_____

8. A description of how acid rain affects the environment

_____

9. The main areas of earthquakes and volcanic activity throughout the world

_____

10. Book sales in each of ten categories for the years 2008 through 2010

_____

# Think Critically About Visuals

■ **GOAL 5**
Think critically about visuals

Because writers choose the visual aids to accompany their text, they can select photos that reflect their opinions or beliefs. Consider the following excerpt and the photo that accompanies it.

Everyone knows that drinking and driving don't mix. Here's what's left of a Ferrari in Newport Beach, California. The driver of the other car was arrested for drunk driving and vehicular manslaughter.

Alcohol is the standard recreational drug of Americans. The average adult American drinks 25 gallons of alcoholic beverages per year—about 21 gallons of beer, 2 gallons of wine, and almost 2 gallons of whiskey, vodka, and other distilled spirits. Beer is so popular that Americans drink more of it than they do tea and fruit juices combined.

Is alcohol bad for health? This beverage cuts both ways. One to two drinks a day for men and one drink for women reduces the risk of heart attacks, strokes, gallstones, and diabetes. Beyond these amounts, however, alcohol scars the liver, damages the heart, and increases the risk of breast cancer. It also increases the likelihood of birth defects. One-third of the 43,000 Americans who die each year in vehicle accidents are drunk. Each year, 700,000 Americans seek treatment for alcohol problems.

—adapted from Henslin, *Sociology: A Down-to-Earth Approach*, pp. 580–581

Note that the passage is very matter-of-fact. It talks about alcohol consumption in the United States, then summarizes the benefits and drawbacks of alcohol. But also note how intense the photo is. Just looking it at, you know that a horrible accident has occurred and someone has died. Thus the photo has the effect of making the author's message about the drawbacks of alcohol much stronger than his message about the benefits of alcohol. If the author had wanted to emphasize the benefits of alcohol, he would have perhaps included a photo showing friends enjoying a drink together with a caption emphasizing its positive effects when people drink it in moderation.

**EXERCISE 4-12**

# Thinking Critically About Visuals

**Directions:** Refer to the visuals in this chapter to answer the following questions.

1. Figure 4-3 (p. 120) portrays an in-group. Suppose the authors wanted to show a photo of an out-group instead. What type of photo might they choose to use?

_____

_____

2. How might a politician take advantage of the information found in Figure 4-7 (p. 125)?

_____

_____

3. How could Figure 4-8 (p. 126) be used to argue that married people should not have children?

_____

_____

4. The source note for Figure 4-9 (p. 127) reports that the graph represents "a sample of the U.S. population." What further information would be useful about the sample population in order to better understand and interpret the graph?

_____

_____

# INTEGRATING READING AND WRITING

## READ AND RESPOND: A Professional Essay

### Thinking Before Reading

The following essay appeared in 2010 in *Working Mother* magazine. Writer Leah McLaughlin addresses the question, "Are You Hooked?" by discussing a variety of common habits that may be addictions.

1. Preview the reading using the steps discussed in Chapter 1, p. 15.
2. Connect the reading to your own experience by answering the following questions:
   a. What is the difference between a habit and an addiction?
   b. Would you say that you are "hooked" on anything?
3. Mark and annotate as you read.

## Are You Hooked?

### Leah McLaughlin

1   Padding across her kitchen floor in the predawn darkness, Mary Curley hits the start button on her coffee machine and begins her day with a steaming mug. By the time she gets to her post as a nurse at an assisted living facility, she's had two more doses of caffeine. Budget cutbacks have resulted in understaffing at the Woodcliff Lake, NJ, center where she works, and Mary knows she'll spend the morning dashing from one patient's room to another. Then she hides, she says, to have another cup of coffee. "I can hear people looking for me," she admits. "But I really need to sit with that warm cup. These days I'm doing that more and more." By the time this mom of six heads home, she's had, "well, let's just say too much coffee."

2   Tired, stressed, anxious. It's not surprising this working mom savors those caffeine fixes. It's a bad habit, for sure. But could it be something more? Increasingly, experts say that certain seemingly harmless habits—taken to excess—are actually soft addictions. What starts out as a soothing activity can wind up numbing your feelings and draining your energy. Though these soft addictions feel like a solution to a problem, they can get in the way of leading a more fulfilling life.

3   "Soft addictions are an escape from uncomfortable feelings," says Judith Wright, who wrote a book on the subject, *The Soft Addiction Solution.* A hot cup of coffee becomes a Band-Aid for work stress. More stress means more coffee. "If it leads to an unsustainable emotional high, or a feeling of numbness," says Wright, "that's a soft addiction." Unlike "hard" addictions, like drugs or alcohol, which can pose grave health risks, soft addictions aren't life-threatening. However, they can act as roadblocks that people aren't aware of. According to a Harris poll of more than 1,000 people, up to 90 percent of respondents suffered from soft addictions. Some of the most common: watching a lot of television, stress snacking, drinking too much

"On days when things are really bad, I'll reach for another handful of M&M's and realize the bowl is empty."

caffeine, shopping, emailing and social networking. "Whenever you place something—be it caffeine or an email—above the important people in your life, you're causing harm," says Jennifer Ginsberg, MSW, an addiction specialist with more than 15 years of experience. "You're telling your child or husband or friend that a latte or an email is more important. That's a tiny hurt that you inflict every day, and in the case of a true addict, several times a day." Ultimately, these actions can strain relationships, productivity and your own well-being.

4    Often associated with stress, soft addictions may become even more prevalent in shaky economic times like these. "I keep a bowl of M&M's on my desk at work," says Maryann Reiper, a properties manager in Lincoln Park, NJ, and mom of two. "On days when things are really bad—too many vacant apartments, unpaid rents, eviction notices—I'll reach for another handful and realize the bowl is empty. Only I have no memory of having eaten them all," she confesses. "I call it a chocolate blackout."

5    When you understand what soft addictions enable you to avoid—and when you learn to control these cravings—you're more likely to get what you really want out of life. Are you watching TV late at night to avoid your spouse? Does negative feedback from your boss send you on a shopping spree? We spoke with experts about why activities that seem harmless can obstruct happiness, and how to turn the tide.

## From Coping to Copping Out

6    Julie Donahue, a 40-year-old mother of three and self-described online addict, started out frequenting message boards, "I could limit what people knew about me and focus only on my good qualities, like leadership, competence and confidence," she explains. "Over time, it fed my ego. When I was feeling overwhelmed at home, I could log on and feel like I was in control of my world again,"

7    Web surfing became a haven for Julie. When she started a product review blog that stole hours away from her family, her husband pulled the plug on her online activities. "At first I was angry," she says. "He was taking away my comfort zone!" But gradually she became aware of how much time she was wasting in front of the computer. "I started to realize that my 'friends' on the boards didn't even realize I was no longer there, and that's what finally made me see that I was better off fulfilling myself in other, more productive ways."

## Hijacked Brain Waves

8    Soft addictions seize control of the reward system in your brain, explains Cassandra Vieten, PhD, associate scientist at the Mind-Body Medicine Research Group at the California Pacific Medical Center Research Institute, "It's basically the reward system gone haywire," she says. Here's how it works. You initially gravitate

toward an activity, like shopping, because it makes you feel good. You buy a great dress (on sale!), and you feel a terrific high that lasts long enough to help you forget about your crumbling 401(k) plan. That high occurs in your middle brain, which is focused on survival. "The middle brain is always on the lookout for good species-perpetuating things like food, love, sex," says Dr. Vieten. But it only identifies these things by the chemical signals they produce. If shopping feels as good as sex, the brain tags it as an easy go-to activity in times of stress. And every time you go shopping, you reinforce that middle-brain connection between shopping and survival. Simply swap shopping with Web surfing, TV watching or texting and the effect is the same, Dr. Vieten says. Stress only exacerbates a budding soft addiction. It literally silences your higher brain, the reason-driven part that reminds you that you can't afford another dress or that compulsively checking your PDA at the dinner table is obnoxious.

## Addiction Aftermath

9    A clear downside of soft addictions is that they block intimacy, much like hard addictions, such as alcoholism. "Instead of facing your difficult emotions—the fear of losing control or your sense of self, worry over money matters—you're burying yourself in Facebook," says Wright. "It's a lost opportunity to connect with the people who mean the most to you." Soft addictions can also have long-term consequences. Stress snacking can cause you to pack on pounds and put you at an unhealthy weight. A shopping addiction can destroy your finances. Excessive caffeine drinking can cause insomnia, anxiety, headaches and irritability.

10    Interestingly, most people have no trouble owning up to a soft addiction, says Wright: "They'll readily admit they have a problem. The real question is whether the problem is bad enough to stop."

## Road to Recovery

11    Before you can kick the addiction, you have to figure out what made you vulnerable to it in the first place, says Elizabeth Lombardo, PhD, a Pennsylvania-based psychologist. For instance, Mary turns to coffee to ease overwork anxiety. Maryann eats chocolate to cope with stress. Julie surfs the Web looking for control over chaos. Start by noting how you feel before, during and after you engage in an addictive behavior, Wright suggests. Once you identify the emotion, you can break the addiction by confronting what you're feeling.

12    What were you really looking for when you signed on to Facebook, turned on your TV or stayed glued to your email? Did you want to feel connected? Once you get in touch with your true wants and needs, you can look for a healthy substitute activity. Want to feel more in touch? Call a friend or make lunch plans with a family member. "When you add more family time, more reading instead of watching TV, more time with your friends instead of texting, you naturally veer away from energy-draining soft addictions as you create new reward connections in your brain," says Wright.

13    Kicking an addiction—even a soft one—can be tricky, so the key is moderation. "Herbal tea just isn't the same as a cup of coffee," admits Mary. "And going cold turkey was too difficult." Reduce the behavior but don't cut it out completely, experts advise. Wean yourself, so it loses its grip on your middle brain. For instance, if you check your BlackBerry every two minutes, limit the number of times you check it in a single day and stick to your plan. "It can feel extremely uncomfortable and stressful," says Dr. Lombardo, "But every day you do this, it will get easier. It's just one day at a time."

| Soft Addiction | You might have a problem if . . . | How to kick it |
|---|---|---|
| Watching TV | The TV goes on at night like clockwork; you often fall asleep on the sofa in front of it; you can't fall asleep without it. | Set a timer to limit it to just one hour a night. Unplug the TV one night a week and have a family game night instead. |
| Checking email | You reach for the BlackBerry whether you're breast-feeding or talking to friends; you pull over to check email when driving. | Restrict checks to certain times and turn off the PDA after 8:00 p.m. Check it only twice on weekends; never bring it on vacation. |
| Stress snacking | You often reach for food when you're feeling anxious or stressed; you feel numb while eating, you eat a lot of food without realizing it. | Before you eat, write down what you're hungry for; then call a friend and share how you're feeling. Swap in healthy snacks. |
| Caffeine | You need coffee first thing in the a.m.; you're angry if the office coffeepot is empty. | Wean yourself off caffeine slowly by gradually switching to decaf. |
| Shopping | Your credit cards are maxed out; you hide purchases from your spouse, friends or family. | Set a weekly cash budget. Record every purchase. Cancel your credit cards (yes, really). |
| Web surfing | You feel closer to strangers online than to friends and family. | Restrict screen time; get a mobile phone that's not Net ready. |

## Getting Ready to Write

### Checking Your Comprehension

Answer each of the following questions using complete sentences.

1. How does Judith Wright define soft addictions?
2. Name one difference and one similarity between hard and soft addictions.
3. According to a Harris poll, what percentage of respondents suffer from soft addictions?
4. List four of the most common soft addictions.
5. Which part of the brain is focused on survival? Which part is reason-driven?
6. According to the author, what is the key to kicking an addiction?

### Strengthening Your Vocabulary

Using the word's context, word parts, or a dictionary, write a brief definition of each of the following words as it is used in the reading.

1. savors (paragraph 2) _____
2. prevalent (paragraph 4) _____
3. haven (paragraph 7) _____
4. exacerbates (paragraph 8) _____
5. vulnerable (paragraph 11) _____
6. veer (paragraph 12) _____

## Examining the Reading: Creating Idea Maps

To analyze this essay, create an idea map. You might organize it by listing the causes and effects of soft addictions, as well as techniques to overcome soft addictions.

## Reacting to Ideas: Discussion and Journal Writing

Get ready to write about the reading by discussing the following:

1. What other soft addictions can you think of? Write a journal entry listing soft addictions you may have observed in others or have experienced yourself.
2. Discuss the warning signs and the effects of soft addictions.
3. How would you describe the author's tone in this selection? How well does her tone suit the topic?
4. What connotative language can you identify in this selection?
5. Discuss the tips given in paragraphs 11–13 for kicking an addiction. Can you add any tips or suggestions?
6. What is the purpose of the chart that accompanies the reading? Evaluate its effectiveness.
7. What concept is illustrated by the photo of candy spilling out of a wine glass?

**THINKING VISUALLY**

## Thinking and Writing Critically

1. According to the article, what is the number-one reason people turn to their soft addictions for comfort? Write a thesis sentence answering this question.
2. The author provides a table summarizing some common soft addictions. Write a paragraph in which you examine at least one or two soft addictions not included in the table.

**MySkillsLab®**

**Complete** this Exercise

# Writing About the Reading

## Paragraph Options

1. Do you or does someone you know have a soft addiction? Write a paragraph describing it. If it is your addiction, how do you plan to kick it?
2. What do you consider a haven in your life? Write a paragraph describing a place or activity that is a haven for you.
3. Write a paragraph that summarizes the steps for kicking an addiction, given under the heading "Road to Recovery."

## Essay Options

4. According to the reading, soft addictions are often associated with stress. Write an essay describing different types of stress in your life and your methods for coping with stress.
5. Write an essay about your approach to kicking a habit. Do you favor moderation or do you go cold turkey? Why?
6. The author refers to soft addictions as roadblocks. What other types of roadblocks can you think of? How do you typically overcome such obstacles in your life? Write an essay explaining your answers.

# SELF-TEST SUMMARY

To test yourself, cover the Answer column with a sheet of paper and answer each question in the left column. Evaluate each of your answers as you work by sliding the paper down and comparing your answer with what is printed in the Answer column.

| QUESTION | ANSWER |
|---|---|
| **■ GOAL 1 Understand the function of visuals**<br><br>Why are visuals included in textbooks, classroom lectures, and other course materials? | Visuals serve a number of different functions in your courses. They are used to<br>■ consolidate information<br>■ explain and illustrate ideas<br>■ dramatize information<br>■ display trends, patterns, and variations |
| **■ GOAL 2 Read and interpret visuals**<br><br>What steps should you take to read visuals effectively? | To get the most from all types of visuals, you should begin by reading the title or caption and determining how a visual is organized; what symbols, abbreviations, and variables are presented; and what scale, values, or units of measurement are being used. You should then study the data to identify trends, patterns, and relationships within the visual. Note any explanatory footnotes and the source of the data. Finally, make marginal summary notes to aid your further reading or review. |
| **■ GOAL 3 Integrate text and visuals**<br><br>How can you integrate visuals with their corresponding printed text? | To integrate text and visuals:<br>■ Be alert to the visuals as you preview chapters.<br>■ Refer to each visual when you are directed to.<br>■ Read the visual carefully.<br>■ Move back and forth between the text and graphic frequently.<br>■ Figure out why the visual was included. |
| **■ GOAL 4 Read and interpret different types of visuals**<br><br>What types of visuals are commonly used in textbooks and academic sources? | Many types of visuals are used in conjunction with print materials. They include photographs, maps, tables, graphs, diagrams, charts, infographics, and cartoons. |
| **■ GOAL 5 Think critically about visuals**<br><br>How can you think critically about visuals? | Be aware of the images and other visuals that the author chooses to include with a piece of writing. They may provide clues regarding the author's attitude or opinion toward the topic. |

**MySkillsLab®** For more help with **Reading and Evaluating Visuals**, go to your learning path in MySkillsLab at www.myskillslab.com.

# Topics, Main Ideas, and Topic Sentences

**5**

## LEARNING GOALS

Learn how to . . .

■ **GOAL 1**
Structure a paragraph

■ **GOAL 2**
Identify the topic of a paragraph

■ **GOAL 3**
Locate main ideas

■ **GOAL 4**
Think critically about main ideas

■ **GOAL 5**
Write effective topic sentences

## THINK About It!

Look at the photograph on this page. What do think is happening? Create a story or scenario in your mind. Then write a sentence describing what you think is happening.

The sentence you have written states the main idea—or main point—the photograph conveys. It expresses your view of what is happening. When others read the sentence you wrote, they understand your interpretation of the situation. They may agree or disagree with your view, but they will understand it. Both readers and writers, then, communicate and exchange ideas through the effective use of sentences that state a main point, which are called topic sentences.

## Reading and Writing Connections

### EVERYDAY CONNECTIONS

- **Writing** You are sending an e-mail to the technical support personnel of a computer manufacturer asking for help with a problem. Your **topic sentence** should directly state the problem.
- **Reading** As a support technician, you need to read an e-mail complaint or question and identify the customer's problem before you can provide assistance.

### ACADEMIC CONNECTIONS

- **Reading** You are reading a section of a sociology text titled "Communities: Goals and Structures." You try to find a paragraph that defines what a community is.
- **Writing** When answering an essay exam question for the same class, you are asked to briefly define and provide examples of a community. Your **topic sentence** should give a brief definition of *community*.

### WORKPLACE CONNECTIONS

- **Writing** You are the manager of a chain restaurant and must write an incident report for corporate headquarters about a theft that occurred on the premises. Your **topic sentence** should state the time, location, date, and item stolen.
- **Reading** As a director at corporate headquarters, you begin reading the report by looking for a sentence in the first paragraph that concisely states what happened.

## FOCUSING ON READING AND WRITING

# What Is a Paragraph?

■ **GOAL 1**
Structure a paragraph

A **paragraph** is a group of related sentences that develop a main thought, or idea, about a single topic. The structure of a paragraph is not complex. There are usually three basic elements: (1) a topic, (2) a main idea, or topic sentence, and (3) supporting details. The **topic sentence** states the main point or controlling idea. The sentences that explain this main point are called **supporting details**. These details may be facts, reasons, or examples that provide further information about the topic sentence.

As a writer, these paragraph elements provide you with an easy-to-follow structure for expressing your ideas clearly and effectively. As a reader, these same elements help you know what to look for and ensure that you will understand and remember what you read. This chapter will show you how to identify main ideas as you read and how to write clear and concise topic sentences. Chapters 6–8 will show you how to recognize key details as you read and how to provide and organize details as you write.

Read the following paragraph, noticing how all the details relate to one point, and explain the topic sentence, which is highlighted and labeled:

Topic sentence

> ==There is some evidence that colors affect you physiologically.== For example, when subjects are exposed to red light, respiratory movements increase; exposure to blue decreases respiratory movements. Similarly, eye blinks increase in frequency when eyes are exposed to red light and decrease when exposed to blue. This seems consistent with the intuitive feelings about blue being more soothing and red being more arousing. After changing a school's walls from orange and white to blue, the blood pressure of the students decreased while their academic performance improved.
>
> —DeVito, *Human Communication: The Basic Course*, p. 182

In this paragraph, look at the highlighted topic sentence. It identifies the topic as color and states that colors affect people physiologically. The remaining sentences provide further information about the effects of color.

You can think about and visualize a paragraph this way:

VISUALIZE IT!

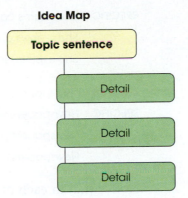

**Idea Map**

Topic sentence

Detail

Detail

Detail

Here's how you might visualize the paragraph on color:

**Idea Map**

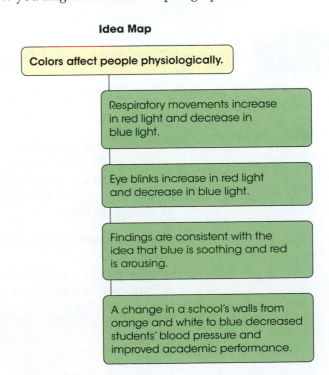

Colors affect people physiologically.

Respiratory movements increase in red light and decrease in blue light.

Eye blinks increase in red light and decrease in blue light.

Findings are consistent with the idea that blue is soothing and red is arousing.

A change in a school's walls from orange and white to blue decreased students' blood pressure and improved academic performance.

Notice how well the topic sentence and details in the above paragraph work together to develop a main idea. The more general topic sentence is explained by the more specific details. You might ask, "How can I tell what is 'general' and what is 'specific' when I am reading?" Here are a few examples. The first three use one-word topics and details; the last two use topic sentences and detail sentences.

| | |
|---|---|
| GENERAL | emotions |
| SPECIFIC | love, fear, anger |
| | |
| GENERAL | pollution |
| SPECIFIC | air pollution, water pollution, solid waste |
| | |
| GENERAL | house building materials |
| SPECIFIC | lumber, bricks, wall board |
| | |
| GENERAL | Our insurance agent is very professional. |
| SPECIFIC | She returns calls promptly. |
| | She reviews our needs every year. |
| | She explains insurance policies in plain language. |
| | |
| GENERAL | Newspapers include a wide variety of different types of information. |
| SPECIFIC | Newspapers report world and local news events. |
| | Newspapers publish human interest stories. |
| | Newspapers advertise products and services. |

Notice that in each of these examples, the specific points explain the general by giving examples, reasons, or further information. In the same way, supporting details in a paragraph explain or support a topic sentence.

## EXERCISE 5-1    Using General and Specific Terms

**Directions:** For each list of items, select the choice that best describes that grouping.

_____ 1. for money, for experience, to meet people
  **a.** reasons to attend a party
  **b.** reasons to get a part-time job
  **c.** reasons to apply for loans
  **d.** reasons to date

_____ 2. U.S. Constitution, Bill of Rights, Federalist Papers, Twenty-fifth Amendment
  **a.** policies          **c.** historical documents
  **b.** historical events    **d.** party politics

_____ 3. Mars, Saturn, Jupiter, Mercury
  **a.** asteroids        **c.** galaxies
  **b.** solar systems    **d.** planets

**EXERCISE 5-2** | # Adding Specific Details

**Directions:** Complete the following sets by supplying the missing information.

1. GENERAL   Advertisements are often misleading.

   SPECIFIC   **a.** Products often appear larger than they really are.

   **b.** _____

   **c.** _____

2. GENERAL   Television provides several types of entertainment.

   SPECIFIC   **a.** _____

   **b.** _____

   **c.** _____

3. GENERAL   _____

   SPECIFIC   **a.** Flexible work hours permit employees to work at their peak times of efficiency.

   **b.** Flexible work hours help reduce line-ups at equipment (fax machine and copier, for example).

   **c.** Flexible work hours help reduce rush hour traffic near the office.

4. GENERAL   Many careers require specialized training.

   SPECIFIC   **a.** Nurses must learn anatomy and physiology.

   **b.** _____

   **c.** _____

5. GENERAL   _____

   SPECIFIC   **a.** Some television commercials use humor to sell their product.

   **b.** Other commercials use famous people to persuade their audience to buy their product.

   **c.** Some commercials use the message "Everyone's buying it, so why don't you?"

---

## ! NEED TO KNOW

### Important Terms

**Paragraph:** a group of sentences that focus on a single idea

**Topic:** the one thing a paragraph is about

**Main idea:** the point the paragraph makes about a topic

**Topic sentence:** the sentence that states the paragraph's main idea

**Supporting details:** those sentences that explain the topic sentence

## READING

# Locate the Topic

■ **GOAL 2**
Identify the topic of a paragraph

You already know that the topic is the general subject of an entire paragraph. Every sentence in a paragraph in some way discusses or explains this topic. To find the topic of a paragraph, ask yourself: What is the one idea the author is discussing throughout the paragraph? Read the following paragraph with that question in mind:

> The major motive for excuse making seems to be to maintain our self-esteem, to project a positive image to ourselves and to others. Excuses are also offered to reduce stress that may be created by a bad performance. We feel that if we can offer an excuse—especially a good one that is accepted by those around us—it will lessen the negative reaction and the subsequent stress that accompanies poor performance.
>
> —DeVito, *Human Communication: The Basic Course*, p. 178

In this example, the author is discussing one topic—making excuses—throughout the paragraph. Notice that the word *excuse* is used several times. As you can see, the repeated use of a word often serves as a clue to the topic.

---

**EXERCISE 5-3**

## Locating Topics

**Directions:** After reading each of the following paragraphs, select the choice that best represents the topic of the paragraph.

_____ 1.    You've probably heard that older men die before older women virtually everywhere in the world. In the United States, women are expected to live an average of 80.4 years, while men live only 75.2 years. Sociologists attribute many factors to this trend. For example, men have higher testosterone levels than women, which may make men more likely to abuse alcohol and tobacco, drive aggressively, and engage in other life-threatening behaviors. Men also choose riskier types of work and become involved in wartime aggression, which are connected to men's decreased life expectancy. Studies also show that women are less likely to experience life-threatening illnesses and health problems than men are.
—Carl, *Think Sociology*, p. 211

**a.** women's health
**b.** men and risky behaviors
**c.** testosterone and age
**d.** men's life expectancy

_____ 2.    Many people look back to the 1950s as the golden age of the traditional family, but was it really? Teenage pregnancy rates were higher in the 1950s than they are today, although a higher proportion of teenage mothers were married (primarily due to "shotgun weddings," a colloquialism that developed from the idea that many fathers of pregnant girls had to force, possibly with a weapon, a man to marry his daughter once she became pregnant). Many families were unable to survive the traumas of war and its aftermath, and the divorce rate rose from one in six in 1940 to one in four marriages in 1946. Although many families prospered in the years following World War II, many others suffered from economic hardship. In 1948, *Newsweek* reported that most of the 27 million schoolchildren in the United States were badly in need of medical or dental care, while more than 900 thousand children were malnourished.

—Kunz, *Think Marriages & Families*, p. 8

**a.** teenage pregnancy rates
**b.** the effect of war on divorce
**c.** family problems in the 1950s
**d.** golden age

_____ **3.**     In the past few years, social networking sites such as MySpace, Facebook, and Twitter have become hugely popular across all ages. Despite the opinions of some that young people are in danger of turning into crouching androids glued to their computers, research shows that the majority of friendships are still maintained offline. Offline friendships are characterized by more interdependence, depth, understanding, and commitment, but online friendships can gain some of these qualities with time. Most online friends tend to be rather cautious about disclosing personal information. However, this does not apply to people with a negative view of themselves and others; they instead seem to share more information, possibly in an attempt to become more self-confident in their interactions. Interestingly, even in online friendships people seem to gain more satisfaction when befriending people of a similar age and place of residence.

—Kunz, *Think Marriages & Families*, p. 82

**a.** offline vs. online friendships
**b.** technology and self-image
**c.** personal information sharing online
**d.** satisfaction in online friendships

_____ **4.**     A century ago politicians used to say, "Vote early and often." Cases such as West Virginia's 159,000 votes being cast by 147,000 eligible voters in 1888 were not that unusual. Largely to prevent corruption associated with stuffing ballot boxes, states adopted voter registration laws around the turn of the century, which require individuals to first place their name on an electoral roll in order to be allowed to vote. Although these laws have made it more difficult to vote more than once, they have also discouraged some people from voting at all. Voter registration requirements in the United States are, in part, to blame for why Americans are significantly less likely to go to the polls than citizens of other democratic nations.

—Edwards, *Government in America*, p. 313

**a.** voter turnout
**b.** voter registration
**c.** voter eligibility
**d.** voter fraud

_____ 5. Compared with the technical resources of a theater of today, those of a London public theater in the time of Queen Elizabeth I seem hopelessly limited. Plays had to be performed by daylight, and scenery had to be kept simple: a table, a chair, a throne, perhaps an artificial tree or two to suggest a forest. But these limitations were, in a sense, advantages. What the theater of today can spell out for us realistically, with massive scenery and electric lighting, Elizabethan playgoers had to imagine and the playwright had to make vivid for them by means of language. Not having a lighting technician to work a panel, Shakespeare had to indicate the dawn by having Horatio, in _Hamlet_, say in a speech rich in metaphor and descriptive detail:

> But look, the morn in russet mantle clad
> Walks o'er the dew of yon high eastward hill.

—Kennedy, _Literature_, p. 1243

**a.** impact of technological limitations on Elizabethan theater
**b.** benefits of modern technology in theater performances
**c.** effects of Shakespeare's writing style
**d.** the use of language to make ideas vivid

# Locate the Main Idea

■ GOAL 3
Locate main ideas

You learned earlier that the _main idea_ of a paragraph is its most important point. The main idea is also the most _general_ statement the writer makes about the topic. Pick out the most general statement among the following sentences.

1. Animals differ according to when they sleep.
2. Some animals sleep during daylight while others sleep during darkness.
3. Animals' sleeping habits differ in a number of ways.
4. Hibernation is another kind of sleep for some animals.

Did you choose sentence 3 as the most general statement? Now we will change this list into a paragraph by rearranging the sentences and adding a few facts.

> [1]Animals' sleeping habits differ in a number of ways. [2]They differ according to what time of day they sleep. [3]Some animals sleep during daylight hours while others sleep during darkness. [4]They also differ in the length of time they sleep. [5]Other animals sleep for weeks or months at a time when they hibernate.

In this brief paragraph, the main idea is expressed in the first sentence. This sentence, known as the **topic sentence**, is the most general statement in the paragraph. All the other sentences are specific details that explain this main idea.

## Tips for Finding the Main Idea

Here are some tips that will help you find the main idea.

1. **Identify the topic.** As you did earlier, figure out the general subject of the entire paragraph. In the preceding sample paragraph, "animals' sleeping habits" is the topic.

2. **Locate the most general sentence (the topic sentence).** This sentence must be broad enough to include all of the other ideas in the paragraph. The topic sentence in the sample paragraph ("Animals' sleeping habits differ in a number of ways.") covers all of the other details in that paragraph. The tips in the next section will help you locate topic sentences.

3. **Study the rest of the paragraph.** The main idea must make the rest of the paragraph meaningful. It is the one idea that ties all of the other details together. In the sample paragraph, sentences 2, 3, 4, and 5 all give specific details about how animals' sleeping habits differ.

## Tips for Locating the Topic Sentence

Although a topic sentence can be located anywhere in a paragraph, it is usually *first* or *last*.

### Topic Sentence First

In most paragraphs, the topic sentence comes first. The author states his or her main point and then explains it.

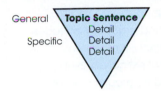

A **focus group** is a small group, usually consisting of about seven to ten people who are brought together to discuss a subject of interest to the researcher. Focus groups are commonly used today in business and politics; that flashy slogan you heard for a political campaign or a new toothpaste was almost certainly tested in a focus group to gauge people's reactions. Social researchers may use a focus group to help design questions or instruments for quantitative research or to study the interactions among group members on a particular subject. In most cases, researchers ask predetermined questions, but the discussion is unstructured. Focus groups are a relatively cheap method of research and can be completed quickly. They also allow for the flexible discussions and answers that are desirable in qualitative research. However, they definitely require a skilled leader to avoid leading participants in a predetermined direction, to establish an atmosphere in which all participants feel comfortable speaking, and to allow discussion of uncomfortable or challenging topics. It is also possible for two different researchers to analyze the discussion in different ways.

—Kunz, *THINK Marriages & Families*, p. 36

Here, the writer first defines a focus group. The rest of the paragraph provides more details about focus groups.

### Topic Sentence Last

The second most likely place for a topic sentence to appear is last in a paragraph. When using this arrangement, a writer leads up to the main point and then states it at the end.

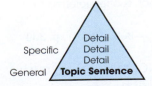

In the developing world 1.1 billion people still lack access to safe drinking water, 2.6 billion do not have access to adequate sanitation services, and more than 1.6 million deaths each year are traced to waterborne diseases (mostly in children under five). All too often in developing countries, water is costly or inaccessible to the poorest in society, while the wealthy have it piped into their homes. In addition, because of the infrastructure that is used to control water, whole seas are being lost, rivers are running dry, millions of people have been displaced to make room for reservoirs, groundwater aquifers are being pumped down, and disputes over water have raised tensions from local to international levels. Fresh water is a limiting resource in many parts of the world and is certain to become even more so as the 21st century unfolds.

—Wright, *Environmental Science*, p. 247

In this paragraph, the author discusses water as a limiting resource and concludes that water will become more limited throughout the 21st century.

### Topic Sentence in the Middle

If a topic sentence is placed neither first nor last, then it may appear somewhere in the middle of a paragraph. In this arrangement, the sentences before the topic sentence lead up to or introduce the main idea. Those that follow the main idea explain or describe it.

In colonial days, huge flocks of snowy egrets inhabited the coastal wetlands and marshes of the southeastern United States. In the 1800s, when fashion dictated fancy hats adorned with feathers, egrets and other birds were hunted for their plumage. By the late 1800s, egrets were almost extinct. In 1886, the newly formed National Audubon Society began a press campaign to shame "feather wearers" and end the practice. The campaign caught on, and gradually, attitudes changed; new laws followed. Government policies that protect animals from overharvesting are essential to keep species from the brink of extinction. Even when cultural standards change due to the efforts of individual groups (such as the National Audubon Society), laws and policy measures must follow to ensure that endangered populations remain protected. Since the 1800s, several important laws have been passed to protect a wide variety of species.

—Wright and Boorse, *Environmental Science: Toward a Sustainable Future*, p. 150

In this paragraph, the author discusses how one species nearly became extinct and concludes that government regulations are necessary to prevent this from happening again.

### Topic Sentence First and Last

Occasionally writers put the main idea at the beginning of a paragraph and again at the end. Writers may do this to emphasize the main point or to clarify it.

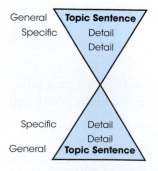

The National Cancer Institute (NCI) has taken a brute-force approach to screening species for cancer-suppressing chemicals. NCI scientists receive frozen samples of organisms from around the world, chop them up, and separate them into a number of extracts, each probably containing hundreds of components. These extracts are tested against up to 60 different types of cancer cells for their efficacy in stopping or slowing growth of the cancer. Promising extracts are then further analyzed to determine their chemical nature, and chemicals in the extract are tested singly to find the effective compound. This approach is often referred to as the "grind 'em and find 'em" strategy.

—Belk, *Biology*, p. 334

The first and last sentences together explain that the NCI takes an aggressive strategy to finding and testing samples for cancer-suppression.

## EXERCISE 5-4    Locating Topic Sentences

**Directions:** Underline the topic sentence in each of the following paragraphs.

1.    Crime is a major concern in the United States. The possibility of becoming a victim of crime, particularly of a violent assault, is the number one fear of millions of Americans. This concern is well founded, as 5.3 million people over the age of 12 annually will be victimized by violent crimes. That nearly 14 million serious crimes are reported yearly to the police indicates only part of the situation. An annual study by the Bureau of Justice Statistics surveys American households to determine the extent of serious crime not being reported to law-enforment authorities. Initiated in 1973, the National Crime Survey measures the number of crimes unreported to the police as opposed to reported crime, which is documented annually by the FBI's *Uniform Crime Reports Bulletin.* The results of the National Crime Survey are disturbing to the entire criminal justice system, indicating that people and households in the United States face 49 million crime attempts a year when unreported and reported crime occurences are combined.

—Gilbert et al., *Criminal Investigation,* p. 33

2.    A living will is a legal document prepared by a patient. This document gives instructions about the health care to be provided if the patient becomes terminally ill or falls into a permanent coma or persistent vegetative state. A living will is a way for the patient to make health-care decisions before experiencing a health-care emergency. A living will specifies whether the patient wants to be kept on life-support machines. It specifies whether the patient wants tube feedings or artificial (IV) hydration when the patient is in a coma or persistent vegetative state. It may also contain other instructions related to health care. For example, the living will may contain a Do Not Resuscitate (DNR) order. This order instructs any health-care worker not to use cardiopulmonary resuscitation if the comatose or terminally ill patient experiences a life threatening event, such as heart attack or stroke.

—adapted from Badasch, *Health Science Fundamentals,* p. 88

3.    The United States has a severe fire problem that if not addressed, will continue to worsen drastically. Fire statistics show that our nation, one of the richest and most technologically sophisticated countries in the world, lags behind its peer nations in fire security. Nationally, there are millions of fires, thousands of deaths, tens of thousands of injuries, and billions of dollars lost each year—figures which far exceed comparable statistics for other industrialized countries. In 2001, for example, the direct value of property destroyed in fires was $11 billion ($44 billion if the World Trade Center loss is included). More recently in 2004, direct property losses from fires were estimated at over $9.8 billion.

—Loyd and Richardson, *Fundamentals of Fire and Emergency Services,* p. 12

4.    Vitamin B12 (cyanocobalamin) is found in mollusks, clams, beef liver, rainbow trout, and fortified cereals. Vitamin B12 is needed for healthy nerve cells, to make DNA, and for the formation of red blood cells. Vitamin B12 is bound to the protein in food, and hydrochloric acid in the stomach releases B12 from the protein during digestion. Once released, B12 combines with a substance called intrinsic

factor (IF) before it is absorbed into the bloodstream. Deficiency is a very serious problem, ultimately leading to irreversible nerve damage signified by numbness and tingling in the hands and feet. Signs and symptoms include fatigue, weakness, nausea, constipation, flatulence, loss of appetite, weight loss, difficulty in maintaining balance, depression, confusion, poor memory, and soreness of the mouth or tongue. The RDI is 2.4 mg/day for both males and females.

—Johnson, *Pharmacy Technician*, p. 455

5.   The star system has been the backbone of the American film industry since the mid 1910s. Stars are the creation of the public, its reigning favorites. Their influence in the fields of fashion, values, and public behavior has been enormous. "The social history of a nation can be written in terms of its film stars," Raymond Durgnat has observed. Stars confer instant consequence to any film they appear in. Their fees have staggered the public. In the 1920s, Mary Pickford and Charles Chaplin were the two highest paid employees in the world. Contemporary stars such as Julia Roberts and Tom Cruise command salaries of many millions per film, so popular are these box-office giants. Some stars had careers that spanned five decades: Bette Davis and John Wayne, to name just two.

—Giannetti, *Understanding Movies*, p. 251

6.   For decades, we have looked at our steadily increasing life expectancy rates and proudly proclaimed that Americans health has never been better. Recently, however, health organizations and international groups have attempted to quantify the number of years a person lives with a disability or illness, compared with the number of healthy years. The World Health Organization summarizes this concept as **healthy life expectancy**. Simply stated, *healthy life expectancy* refers to the number of years a newborn can expect to live in full health, based on current rates of illness and mortality and also on the quality of their lives. For example, if we could delay the onset of diabetes so that a person didn't develop the disease until he or she was 60 years old, rather than developing it at 30, there would be a dramatic increase in this individual's healthy life expectancy.

— Donatelle, *Health: The Basics*, p. 6

7.   The functions of desktop publishing software are similar to those of word processing programs, except that some capabilities are more sophisticated. A user can enter text using the desktop publishing program in the same way that he or she can enter text with a word processing program. In addition, the user can retrieve text from a file created by another program. For example, the user may enter, edit, and save text using a word processing program and then retrieve the saved text using the desktop publishing program.

—Nickerson, *Business and Information Systems*, p. 249

8.   Are you "twittered out"? Is all that texting causing your thumbs to seize up in protest? If so, you're not alone. Like millions of others, you may find that all of the pressure for contact is more than enough stress for you! Known as *technostress*, the bombardment is defined as stress created by a dependence on technology and the constant state of being plugged in or wirelessly connected, which can include a perceived obligation to respond, chat, or tweet.

—Donatelle, *Health: The Basics*, p. 66

9.    In the past, exposure to liability made many doctors, nurses, and other medical professionals reluctant to stop and render aid to victims in emergency situations, such as highway accidents. Almost all states have enacted a **Good Samaritan law** that relieves medical professionals from liability for injury caused by their ordinary negligence in such circumstances. Good Samaritan laws protect medical professionals only from liability for their *ordinary negligence*, not for injuries caused by their gross negligence or reckless or intentional conduct. Most Good Samaritan laws protect licensed doctors and nurses and laypersons who have been certified in CPR. Good Samaritan statutes generally do not protect laypersons who are not trained in CPR—that is, they are liable for injuries caused by their ordinary negligence in rendering aid.

—Goldman, *Paralegal Professional*, p. 459

10.    At some time or another, many close relationships go through a conflict phase. "We're always fighting," complains a newlywed. But if she were to analyze these fights, she would discover important differences among them. According to communication researchers Miller and Steinberg, most conflicts fit into three different categories. There is (1) pseudoconflict—triggered by a lack of understanding. There is (2) simple conflict—stemming from different ideas, definitions, perceptions, or goals. Finally there is (3) ego conflict—which occurs when conflict gets personal.

—adapted from Beebe, Beebe, and Redmond, *Interpersonal Communication*, pp. 243, 248

# Think Critically About Main Ideas

■ **GOAL 4**
Think critically about main ideas

A main idea is the most general statement a writer makes about a topic. Often, main ideas are simple statements of fact that cannot be disputed. However, not all main ideas and topic sentences are completely factual. Sometimes a main idea presents an opinion about a topic, and that statement may not offer all sides of the story. (To learn more about distinguishing fact and opinion, refer to Chapter 13.) Look at the following passage:

No doubt about it, lobbying is a growth industry. Every state has hundreds of public relations practitioners whose specialty is representing their clients to legislative bodies and government agencies. In North Dakota, hardly a populous state, more than 300 people are registered as lobbyists in the capital city of Bismarck. The number of registered lobbyists in Washington, D.C., exceeds 10,000 today. In addition, there are an estimated 20,000 other people who have slipped through registration requirements but who nonetheless ply the halls of government to plead their clients' interests.

In one sense, lobbyists are expediters. They know local traditions and customs, and they know who is in a position to affect policy. Lobbyists advise their clients, which include trade associations, corporations, public interest groups and regulated utilities and industries, on how to achieve their goals by working with legislators and government regulators. Many lobbyists call themselves "government relations specialists."

—Vivian, *The Media of Mass Communication*, pp. 278–279

The main idea of the first paragraph is a statement of fact; the author can prove without a doubt that "lobbying is a growth industry." The main idea of the second paragraph is: "Lobbyists are expediters." That is, lobbyists help their clients influence the government in their favor. But this main idea presents *only "one sense"* of the topic. What is the other sense or view? Lobbying is actually a controversial activity, and many people believe that lobbyists spend large amounts of money influencing government employees in unethical or illegal ways. However, that belief is not reflected in the main idea of this passage.

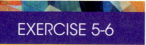

## EXERCISE 5-5

# Identifying Topics

**Directions:** For each of the following sets of topic sentences, specify the topic that is being discussed. Note that each topic sentence presents a different facet of (or opinion about) the topic.

1. ■ "The continued flow of immigrants into the United States has created a rich, diverse society that has been beneficial to the country."

   ■ "The presence of guest workers from South America in states like Arizona and California has a positive effect on the U.S. economy."

   ■ "Because the country is suffering from high unemployment, we must reduce the number of people who come here looking for jobs."

   Topic: _____

2. ■ "Most scientists agree that temperatures now are warmer than they were 20 years ago."

   ■ "It is hard to draw any definite conclusions from the hundreds of studies that have considered whether climate change is occurring or not."

   ■ "People who claim that the Earth is now hotter miss the point that the Earth has been getting warmer over the last several thousand years, not just the last 50 years."

   Topic: _____

## EXERCISE 5-6

# Expressing Viewpoints About a Topic

**Directions:** For each of the following topic sentences, write another topic sentence that expresses a different opinion or point of view about the topic.

1. It is better to live in a city than in the country because the city offers many more activities and opportunities to its residents.

   _____

   _____

2. Because tobacco products harm people's health, all tobacco products should be banned.

   _____

   _____

3. Social networking sites like Facebook and MySpace create communities of close-knit friends.

_____

_____

4. *Dancing with the Stars* entertains us by allowing celebrities to exhibit their unknown dance talents.

_____

_____

## WRITING

# Write Effective Topic Sentences

■ **GOAL 5**
Write effective topic sentences

As a writer, it is important to develop clear and concise topic sentences that help your readers understand your main ideas and guide them through your paragraphs.

### The Function of Topic Sentences

A good topic sentence does two things:

- ■ It makes clear what the paragraph is about—the topic.
- ■ It expresses a view or makes a point about the topic.

In the following examples, the topic is circled and the point about the topic is underlined.

1. The first week of college is a frustrating experience.
2. State-operated lotteries are growing in popularity.
3. Time management is a vital skill in college and on the job.

**EXERCISE 5-7**

*WORKING TOGETHER*

## Expressing Viewpoints About a Topic

**Directions:** Working with a classmate, create two topic sentences that offer differing or opposing points of view about each of the following topics.

1. Shopping malls _____

_____

2. Most fast-food restaurants _____

_____

3. Monday morning _____

   _____

4. Violence on television _____

   _____

   _____

5. College professors _____

   _____

## Choosing a Manageable Topic

To write a good paragraph, you need a manageable topic, one that is the right size. Your topic must be general enough to allow you to add interesting details that will engage your reader. It must also be specific or narrow enough that you can cover it adequately in a few sentences. If your topic is too general, you'll end up with a few unrelated details that do not add up to a specific point. If your topic is too narrow, you will not have enough to say.

Suppose you have decided to write a paragraph about sports. You write the following topic sentence:

> Sports are a favorite activity for many people.

This topic is much too broad to cover in one paragraph. Think of all the different aspects you could write about. Which sports would you consider? Would you write about both playing sports and watching them? Would you write about both professional and amateur sports? Would you write about the reasons people enjoy sports? The topic sentence must be more specific:

> My whole family likes to watch professional football on Sunday afternoons.

Here you have limited your topic to a specific sport (football), a specific time (Sunday afternoon), and some specific fans (your family).

Here are other examples of sentences that are too general. Each has been revised to be more specific.

| | |
|---|---|
| TOO GENERAL | My parents have greatly influenced my life. |
| REVISED | My parents helped me make the decision to attend college. |

| | |
|---|---|
| TOO GENERAL | Sex education is worthwhile. |
| REVISED | Sex-education courses in high school allow students to discuss sex openly. |

If your topic is *too* specific (narrow), you will not have enough details to use in the paragraph, or you may end up including details that do not relate directly to the topic. Suppose you decide to write a paragraph about the Internet and come up with this topic sentence:

> The Internet allows me to stay in touch with friends in other parts of the country.

What else would your paragraph say? You might name some specific friends and where they are, but this list wouldn't be very interesting. This topic sentence is too specific. It might work as a detail, but not as a main idea. To correct the problem, ask, "What else does the Internet allow me to do?" You might say that it allows you to stay in touch with friends by e-mail, that it makes doing research for college papers easier, and that the World Wide Web has information on careers and even specific job openings. Here is a possible revised topic sentence:

> The Internet is an important part of my personal, college, and work life.

Here are a few other examples of topic sentences that are too narrow, along with revisions for each one:

| | |
|---|---|
| TOO NARROW | Only 36 percent of Americans voted in the last election. |
| REVISED | Many Americans do not exercise their right to vote. |
| TOO NARROW | Markel Carpet Company offers child-care leave to both men and women. |
| REVISED | The child-care leave policy at Markel Carpet Company is very flexible. |
| TOO NARROW | A yearly subscription to *Appalachian Voice* costs $25. |
| REVISED | *Appalachian Voice*, a magazine devoted to environmental issues, is a bargain, considering the information it provides. |

How can you tell if your topic sentence is too general or too specific? Try brainstorming or branching to generate ideas. If you find you can develop the topic in many different directions, or if you have trouble choosing details from a wide range of choices, your topic is probably too general. If you cannot think of anything to explain or support it, your topic sentence is too specific.

## EXERCISE 5-8    Evaluating Topic Sentences

**Directions:** Evaluate the following topic sentences. Label each "G" for too general or "S" for too specific. Then rewrite each to create an effective topic sentence.

_____ 1. Learning a new sport is challenging.

_____ 2. Dinner for two at my favorite Italian restaurant costs $25.

_____ 3. The new day-care center opens earlier than most.

_____ 4. Many rules of etiquette have changed over the past 25 years.

_____ 5. Passive cigarette smoke makes me feel sick.

## Tips for Writing Effective Topic Sentences

Use the following suggestions to write clear topic sentences:

1. **Your topic sentence should state the main point of your paragraph.** It should identify your topic and express a view toward it.

2. **Be sure to choose a manageable topic**—one that is neither too general nor too specific.

3. **Make sure your topic sentence is a complete thought.** Be sure your topic sentence is not a fragment or run-on sentence (see pp. 547 and 552).

4. **Place your topic sentence first in the paragraph.** Topic sentences often appear in other places in paragraphs, as described earlier, or their controlling idea is implied, not stated. For now, it will be easier for you to put yours at the beginning. That way, as you write, you can make sure you stick to your point, and your readers will immediately be alerted to that point.

5. **Avoid announcing your topic.** Sentences that sound like announcements are usually unnecessary. Avoid such sentences as "This paragraph will discuss how to change a flat tire," or "I will explain why I object to legalized abortion." Instead, directly state your main point: "Changing a flat tire involves many steps," or "I object to abortion on religious grounds."

Not all expert or professional writers follow all of these suggestions. Sometimes, a writer may use one-sentence paragraphs or include topic sentences that are fragments to achieve a special effect. You will find these paragraphs in news and magazine articles and other sources. Although professional writers can use these variations effectively, you probably should not experiment with them too early. It is best while you are polishing your skills to use a more standard style of writing.

---

**EXERCISE 5-9**

# Evaluating Topic Sentences

**Directions:** Evaluate each of the following topic sentences and mark them as follows:

E = effective        G = too general
A = announcement    N = not complete thought
S = too specific

_____ 1. This paper will discuss the life and politics of Simón Bolívar.

_____ 2. Japanese culture is fascinating to study because its family traditions are so different from American traditions.

_____ 3. The admission test for the police academy includes vocabulary questions.

_____ 4. The discovery of penicillin was a great step in the advancement of modern medicine.

_____ 5. I will talk about the reasons for the popularity of reality television shows.

_____ 6. A habit leading to weight gain.

_____ 7. Each year Americans are the victims of more than 1 million auto thefts.

_____ 8. The White House has many famous rooms and an exciting history.

_____ 9. There are three factors to consider when buying a flat screen TV.

_____ 10. Iraq has a long and interesting history.

---

**EXERCISE 5-10**

# Revising Topic Sentences

**Directions:** Analyze the following topic sentences. If a sentence is too general or too specific, or if it makes a direct announcement or is not a complete thought, revise it to make it more effective.

1. World hunger is a crime.

   REVISED _____

   _____

2. E-mail is used by a great many people.

   REVISED _____

   _____

3. I will point out the many ways energy can be saved in the home.

   REVISED _____

4. Because Congress is very important in the United States.

   REVISED _____

   _____

5. In 2010, over 10,000 people died in alcohol-impaired driving crashes.

   REVISED _____

   _____

---

**EXERCISE 5-11**

# Writing a Paragraph

**Directions:** Write a topic sentence for four of the following topics, using the tips given on page 160. Then select one of your topic sentences and use it to develop a paragraph.

1. Should suicide be legal under certain circumstances?
2. Who deserves college scholarships?
3. Why do children need parental supervision when using the Internet?
4. Why are baseball games fun to watch?
5. Is space exploration valuable or a waste of money?
6. Does the news coverage of presidential campaigns unfairly influence voters?

## EXERCISE 5-12    Writing a Paragraph

**Directions:** Suppose you are taking a sociology course this semester. In preparation for class discussions that will focus on issues, your instructor has assigned the following topics. Choose *one* of the following topics and write a one-paragraph response to it.

1. **Educational reform:** If you could make one significant change in the public education system, what would it be?

2. **Gender differences:** Describe one way in which the behavior of men is different from that of women.

3. **The family:** What do you think is the most important function of a family? That is, why do we live in family groups? What is one key advantage? Support your answer with examples from your own experience.

4. **Discrimination:** Describe one instance of discrimination (sexual, racial, religious, class, or age) that you have witnessed or experienced.

# INTEGRATING READING AND WRITING

## READ AND RESPOND: A Student Essay

*Kate Atkinson is a sophomore at Beloit College in Wisconsin where she is studying Health and Education and Russian.*

*Atkinson wrote this essay for her writing class in response to the article "School of Hard Knocks." Atkinson studied Russia during high school and used her study abroad experience in responding to the article.*

*Title straightforwardly announces the subjects of the essay*

# The Russian and U.S. School Systems

### Kate Atkinson

*Introduction draws the reader in through discussing the ways Russia and the United States view each other*

1    Russia and the U.S. share a complex history riddled with conflict and mutual mistrust. In the years since the Cold War and collapse of the Soviet Union, the two countries have worked to set aside their differences but tension still simmers beneath the surface. Russia is still viewed by many Americans as remote, mysterious, and even dangerous. Similarly, Russians harbor both admiration and contempt for America's economic prowess and superpower status. One thing both countries have in common, however, is an excellent system of education and

impressive literacy rates (both above ninety-nine percent). Writes Mark H. Teeter for *The Moscow News*, "Russians and Americans share a long tradition of dimly perceiving each other's societies, and recent developments on both countries' school fronts neatly illustrate this through-a-glass-darkly effect." Though both systems are highly-acclaimed, they are each as different as the countries they belong to.

Thesis statement

First subject is introduced: Russia

Topic sentence: attendance in Russia

2    In Russia, primary and secondary school education is compulsory from around age seven to age fifteen. At fifteen, students either go on to vocational school, join the work force, or remain in secondary school for two more years in order to graduate and go on to higher education. This decision is usually not made by the student, but by a combination of factors including family standards and expectations, class, and location. Students who come from a family of industrial workers, for example, will usually go on to become one themselves. Russian students specialize early on in school, and as a result they know from a young age what type of career they are headed for. In recent years, specialized schools called "gymnasia" have become increasingly common in which students can focus on subjects such as music and foreign languages.

Topic sentence: curriculum in Russia

3    The Russian Ministry of Education determines the curriculum and as a result, all schools meet a certain national standard of education (Teeter). Along with the usual requirements, the Russian curriculum emphasizes oral communication, memorization, and recitation. Russian school children are well-versed in the poetry of the beloved poet Pushkin, and can recite famous lines without hesitation.

Topic sentence: classroom conduct in Russia

4    In the classroom, the code of conduct between students and teachers is formal and respectful. When a teacher enters the room at the beginning of class, all students hastily rise and wait for the teacher's greeting. Personal relationships are discouraged and the teacher's sole responsibility is to relay information to be memorized by the students.

Author switches to second topic: U.S.

Topic sentence: attendance in U.S.

5    In the U.S., students must attend school between the ages of six and seventeen. After passing all required courses, students graduate and either go on to higher education or join the military or work force. The number of students who go on to higher education has increased dramatically in the past decade as job opportunities have become more competitive and college degrees more accessible to people of all ages and backgrounds. U.S. students have a vast network of private and public universities, liberal arts colleges, and community colleges at their fingertips and therefore, a great deal of choice in the course of their education.

Topic sentence: U.S. curriculum

6    Unlike Russia, the United States does not have a country-level curriculum. Instead, independent city, state, and community boards determine curriculums and each state has its own Department of Education (Teeter). The boards work closely with the schools they monitor and can work to tackle problems such as bullying more effectively than a national ministry. However, the flexibility in curriculum from state to state has led to some schools not meeting the national literacy standard, and issues such as what is an appropriate approach to sex education and whether to teach creation science versus evolution are widely debated (Teeter).

Topic sentence: classroom conduct in U.S.

7    In general, American students have more freedom in the classroom and the student teacher relationship is less rigid. Teachers are generally more tolerant of laid back behavior in class but often do not get the respect they deserve.

Conclusion: a final discussion
about the two different
systems

8   The similarities and differences in these two systems of education closely mirror the history and values of the countries themselves. Russia still clings to rigid national control and standards while the U.S. allows for more freedom in the learning exchange. Both countries could learn from the other and work to smooth out the wrinkles in their acclaimed systems. In order for this to happen however, the two super powers would have to put the past aside and work to perceive each another through less biased lenses.

## Works Cited

Teeter, Mark H. "School of Hard Knocks." themoscownews. *The Moscow News,* 29 Mar. 2010. Web. 26 Feb. 2011.

## Examining Writing

1. How does Atkinson indicate to her readers that she will be addressing two topics in her essay?

2. Evaluate the effectiveness of her topic sentences.

3. In each paragraph, does Atkinson provide enough details to explain and support the topic sentence?

4. What overall attitude toward education in the two countries does Atkinson reveal throughout the essay?

## Writing Assignments

1. In her essay Atkinson compares and contrasts two different but highly successful systems of education. Create a summary of the main points she addresses in the essay.

2. Write a paragraph about an aspect of American education (or that of another country, if you have experienced it) that you think makes the system valuable and important.

## READ AND RESPOND: A Professional Essay

### Thinking Before Reading

The author of this article has written several books on the link between diet and health. In the following reading, he examines a new partnership between a famous fried chicken restaurant chain and a breast cancer advocacy group. Before you read:

1. Preview the reading, using the steps discussed in Chapter 1, page. 15.

2. Connect the reading to your own experience by answering the following questions:

   a. How often do you eat fast food? Are you concerned about the effects of fast food on your health?

   b. What do you already know about Susan G. Komen for the Cure?

3. Mark and annotate as you read.

# Greed, Cancer, and Pink KFC Buckets

## John Robbins

**grassroots**
involving ordinary people at a local or community level

1    We live in a world of profound contradictions. Some things are just unbelievably strange. At times I feel like I've found a way to adapt to the weirdness of the world, and then along comes something that just boggles my mind. It is ironic that the largest **grassroots** breast cancer advocacy group in the world, a group called "Susan G. Komen for the Cure," has now partnered with the fast food chain KFC, known for its high-fat foods and questionable treatment of its chickens, in a national "Buckets for the Cure" campaign. The program began last month and runs through the end of May.

2    KFC is taking every chance it can manufacture to trumpet the fact that it will donate 50 cents to Komen for every pink bucket of chicken sold. For its part, Komen is announcing on its website that "KFC and Susan G. Komen for the Cure are teaming up . . . to . . . spread educational messaging via a major national campaign which will reach thousands of communities served by nearly 5,000 KFC restaurants."

3    Educational messaging, indeed. How often do you think this "messaging" provides information about the critical importance a healthy diet plays in maintaining a healthy weight and preventing cancer? How often do you think it refers in any way to the many studies that, according to the National Cancer Institute's website, "have shown that an increased risk of developing colorectal, pancreatic, and breast cancer is associated with high intakes of well-done, fried or barbecued meats?" If you guessed zero, you're right.

4    Meanwhile, the American Institute for Cancer Research reports that 60 to 70 percent of all cancers can be prevented with lifestyle changes. Their number one dietary recommendation is to: "Choose predominantly plant-based diets rich

**egregious**
outrageously bad

**pinkwashing**
using support for breast cancer research to sell products, especially products that can be linked with cancer

in a variety of vegetables and fruits, legumes and minimally processed starchy staple foods." Does that sound like pink buckets of fried chicken?

5    Pardon me for being cynical, but I have to ask, if Komen is going to partner with KFC, why not take it a step further and partner with a cigarette company? They could sell pink packages of cigarettes, donating a few cents from each pack while claiming "each pack you smoke brings us closer to the day cancer is vanquished forever."

6    Whose brilliant idea was it that buying fried chicken by the bucket is an effective way to fight breast cancer? One breast cancer advocacy group, Breast Cancer Action, thinks the Komen/KFC campaign is so **egregious** that they call it "**pinkwashing**," another sad example of commercialism draped in pink ribbons. "Make no mistake," they say, "every pink bucket purchase will do more to benefit KFC's bottom line than it will to cure breast cancer."

7    One thing is hard to dispute. In partnering with KFC, Susan G. Komen for the Cure has shown itself to be numbingly oblivious to the role of diet in cancer prevention. Of course it's not hard to understand KFC's motives. They want to look good. But recent publicity the company has been getting hasn't been helping. For one thing, the company keeps taking hits for the unhealthiness of its food. Just last month, when KFC came out with its new Double Down sandwiches, the products were derided by just about every public health organization for their staggering levels of salt, calories and artery-clogging fat.

8    Then there's the squeamish matter of the treatment of the birds who end up in KFC's buckets, pink or otherwise. People for the Ethical Treatment of Animals (PETA) has an entire website devoted to what it calls Kentucky Fried Cruelty, but you don't have to be an animal activist to be horrified by how the company treats chickens, if you lift the veil of the company's PR and see what actually takes place.

9    When PETA sent investigators with hidden cameras into a KFC "Supplier of the Year" slaughterhouse in Moorefield, West Virginia, what they found was enough to make KFC choke on its own pink publicity stunts. Workers were caught on video stomping on chickens, kicking them and violently slamming them against floors and walls. Workers were also filmed ripping the animals' beaks off, twisting their heads off, spitting tobacco into their eyes and mouths, spray-painting their faces, and squeezing their bodies so hard that the birds expelled feces—all while the chickens were still alive.

10    KFC, naturally, did everything they could to keep the footage from being aired, but their efforts failed. In fact, the video from the investigation ended up being broadcast by TV stations around the world, as well as on all three national evening news shows, *Good Morning America*, and every one of the major cable news networks. Plus, more than a million people subsequently watched the footage on PETA's website.

11    It wasn't just animal activists who condemned the fast food chain for the level of animal cruelty displayed at KFC's "Supplier of the Year" slaughterhouse.

**ethology**
the branch of zoology that studies the behavior of animals in their natural habitats

Dr. Temple Grandin, perhaps the meat industry's leading farmed-animal welfare expert, said, "The behavior of the plant employees was atrocious." Dr. Ian Duncan, a University of Guelph professor of applied **ethology** and an original member of KFC's own animal-welfare advisory council, wrote, "This tape depicts scenes of the worst cruelty I have ever witnessed against chickens . . . and it is extremely hard to accept that this is occurring in the United States of America."

12    KFC claims, on its website, that its animal-welfare advisory council "has been a key factor in formulating our animal welfare program." But Dr. Duncan, along with five other former members of this advisory council, say otherwise. They all resigned in disgust over the company's refusal to take animal welfare seriously. Adele Douglass, one of those who resigned, said in an SEC filing reported on by the *Chicago Tribune* that KFC "never had any meetings. They never asked any advice, and then they touted to the press that they had this animal-welfare advisory committee. I felt like I was being used."

13    You can see why KFC would be eager to jump on any chance to improve its public image, and why the company would want to capitalize on any opportunity to associate itself in the public mind with the fight against breast cancer. What's far more mystifying is why an organization with as much public trust as Susan G. Komen for the Cure would jeopardize public confidence in its authenticity. As someone once said, it takes a lifetime to build a reputation, but only 15 minutes to lose it.

# Getting Ready to Write

## Checking Your Comprehension

Answer each of the following questions using complete sentences.

1. Describe the "Buckets for the Cure" campaign.

2. According to the American Institute for Cancer Research, what percentage of all cancers can be prevented with lifestyle changes?

3. What is the number one dietary recommendation of the American Institute for Cancer Research?

4. What is "pinkwashing" and what does it have to do with the Komen/KFC campaign?

5. Give a brief summary of what PETA investigators found at the KFC "Supplier of the Year" slaughterhouse in West Virginia. How did KFC's animal-welfare advisory council react?

## Strengthening Your Vocabulary

Using the word's context, word parts, or a dictionary, write a brief definition of each of the following words as it is used in the reading.

1. profound (paragraph 1) _____

2. contradictions (paragraph 1) _____

3. advocacy (paragraph 1) _____

4.  predominantly (paragraph 4) _____

5.  cynical (paragraph 5) _____

6.  vanquished (paragraph 5) _____

7.  derided (paragraph 7) _____

8.  atrocious (paragraph 11) _____

9.  jeopardize (paragraph 13) _____

10.  authenticity (paragraph 13) _____

### Examining the Reading: Drawing Idea Maps

Create an idea map of the reading that starts with the title and thesis and then lists the author's main points. Use the guidelines on page 21.

### Reacting to Ideas: Discussion and Journal Writing

Get ready to write about the reading by discussing the following:

1.  Discuss why Komen chose to partner with KFC. Do you think the "Buckets for the Cure" campaign will be considered successful?

2.  Write a journal entry that summarizes the author's opinion regarding the partnership between Komen and KFC. Do you agree or disagree with his opinion?

3.  Evaluate the introduction of the essay. What does it add to the piece of writing? How successful is it in capturing your interest?

4.  How does the photo accompanying this essay add to or detract from the material? Do you think a different photo would be more effective? What would it show?

**THINKING VISUALLY**

### Thinking and Writing Critically

1.  Did the description of animal abuse at KFC's supplier affect your opinion of fast food in general and KFC in particular? Why or why not?

2.  The author included both facts and opinions to support his thesis in this essay. Find examples of both and evaluate their effectiveness.

3.  What is the author's purpose for writing this essay? Who is his intended audience?

**MySkillsLab®**

**Complete** this Exercise

## Writing About the Reading

### Paragraph Options

1.  How would this essay be different if it were written as a strictly factual report? Write a paragraph in which you summarize the facts of the essay in objective language.

2.  Write a paragraph explaining whether you agree or disagree that Susan G. Komen for the Cure has "jeopardize[d] public confidence in its authenticity" by partnering with KFC.

3. The author points to the importance of a healthy diet in preventing cancer. Do you think most people (including yourself) make that connection? Write a paragraph explaining your answer.

### Essay Options

4. Is it appropriate for advocacy organizations such as Komen to promote their causes using commercial means? Write an essay explaining why or why not. Try to think of other advocacy groups that have formed such partnerships, on either a national or a local level.

5. What responsibility do restaurants and other commercial enterprises have toward consumer health? Write an essay exploring this question. In your own experience, what effect does "educational messaging" from advertising campaigns have on your lifestyle choices?

6. Imagine that you are a member of an animal-welfare advisory council for a large company. What guidelines would you promote for the company to follow regarding animal welfare? Write an essay describing your ideas for animal welfare in a commercial setting.

## SELF-TEST SUMMARY

To test yourself, cover the Answer column with a sheet of paper and answer each question in the left column. Evaluate each of your answers as you work by sliding the paper down and comparing your answer with what is printed in the Answer column.

| QUESTION | ANSWER |
| --- | --- |
| ■ GOAL 1 **Structure a paragraph**<br><br>What is a paragraph and what are its three key elements? | A paragraph is a group of related sentences that develop one thought or idea. The three key elements are the *topic, topic sentence,* and *supporting details.* |
| ■ GOAL 2 **Identify the topic of a paragraph**<br><br>How do I identify the topic of a paragraph? | Look for the one thing the author is discussing throughout the paragraph. |
| ■ GOAL 3 **Locate main ideas**<br><br>How do I locate the main idea of a paragraph? | Find the topic and then locate the sentence in the paragraph that is the most general. Check to be sure this one sentence brings all the other details together under one common concept. |
| ■ GOAL 4 **Think critically about main ideas**<br><br>How can I think critically about main ideas? | Ask if there are other views that can be held about the topic. |

*(continued)*

*(continued)*

| QUESTION | ANSWER |
|---|---|
| ■ GOAL 5 Write effective topic sentences<br><br>How can I write effective topic sentences? | Write a sentence that identifies your topic and expresses a view or makes a point about the topic. Choose a manageable topic and be sure the sentence expresses a complete thought. |

For more help with **Topics, Main Ideas, and Topic Sentences**, go to your learning path in MySkillsLab at www.myskillslab.com.

# Details, Transitions, and Implied Main Ideas

**6**

## LEARNING GOALS

Learn how to . . .

- **GOAL 1**
  Understand details, transitions, and implied main ideas

- **GOAL 2**
  Identify supporting details

- **GOAL 3**
  Think critically about details

- **GOAL 4**
  Use transitions to guide your reading

- **GOAL 5**
  Find implied main ideas

- **GOAL 6**
  Select and organize details to support your topic sentence

- **GOAL 7**
  Use transitional words and phrases to connect details

## THINK About It!

The photograph on this page shows the menu from a coffee shop. Providing information about breakfast options is the main point of the menu. All the listed items are breakfast choices, the details related to that main point. The coffee shop owner had to plan what details to include on the menu, as well as how to organize these details, so that his customers could read it and make decisions about what to order.

To avoid customer confusion or dissatisfaction, the menu was written so as to clearly indicate what is offered as what is not. Notice, for example, that the kinds of juices that are available are listed. The menu writer, in order to convey the impression that the coffee shop was careful and conscientious, presented the menu accurately and correctly and included prices. We might assume that informal abbreviations, such as "CZ" for cheese, "Scrmbld" for scrambled, and "E" for English were necessary to due to space limitations on the menu board. As you will see in this chapter, details are important to both readers and writers.

# Reading and Writing Connections

## EVERYDAY CONNECTIONS

- **Reading** You read your auto insurance policy for coverage information and instructions on how to file a claim for an auto accident in which you were involved.
- **Writing** You write the accident claim report, including clear and accurate details that are essential to proving you were not at fault.

## ACADEMIC CONNECTIONS

- **Reading** You read a section of a psychology text titled, "What Happens When We Sleep?"
- **Writing** For an exam in psychology, you answer an essay question that asks you to explain the stages of sleep. By giving clear, accurate details about each stage, you will earn full credit.

## WORKPLACE CONNECTIONS

- **Reading** As a sales rep for a mechanical supply company, you read e-mails from several customers saying that a valve you sell has been malfunctioning.
- **Writing** You write a report about the faulty valve for the manufacturing department of your company, including full details describing the problem.

# FOCUSING ON READING AND WRITING

# What Are Details, Transitions, and Implied Main Ideas?

■ **GOAL 1**
Understand details, transitions, and implied main ideas

**Supporting details** are those facts and ideas that prove or explain the main idea of a paragraph as expressed in the topic sentence. **Transitions** are linking words and phrases that connect the details and pull the paragraph together. **Implied main ideas** are thoughts suggested, but not directly stated in a topic sentence.

As a reader, your task is to examine how details support and explain a topic sentence. You can use transitions to guide you through a paragraph and help you recognize when a writer is moving from one important detail to the next. When you find a paragraph without a topic sentence, use the details to reason out the implied main idea.

As a writer, your task is to select appropriate details to fully explain and support your topic sentence. Use transitions to guide your readers and help them identify your important details. Unless you have a specific reason for writing a paragraph with an implied main idea, it is usually better to write paragraphs that do have clear topic sentences.

## READING

# Identify Supporting Details

■ GOAL 2
Identify supporting
details

**Supporting details** are those facts and ideas that prove or explain the main idea of a paragraph. While all the details in a paragraph support the main idea, not all details are equally important. As you read, try to identify and pay attention to the most important details. Pay less attention to details of lesser importance. The **major details** directly explain the main idea. Other **minor details** may provide additional information, offer an example, or further explain one of the major details.

The diagram in Figure 6-1 shows how details relate to the main idea and how details vary in degree of importance. In the diagram, less important details appear below the important details they explain.

VISUALIZE IT!

**FIGURE 6-1**

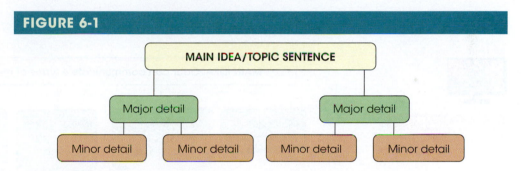

Read the following paragraph and study the diagram that follows.

The skin of the human body has several functions. First, it serves as a protective covering. In doing so, it accounts for 17 percent of the body weight. Skin also protects the organs within the body from damage or harm. The skin serves as a regulator of body functions. It controls body temperature and water loss. Finally, the skin serves as a receiver. It is sensitive to touch and temperature.

VISUALIZE IT!

**FIGURE 6-2**

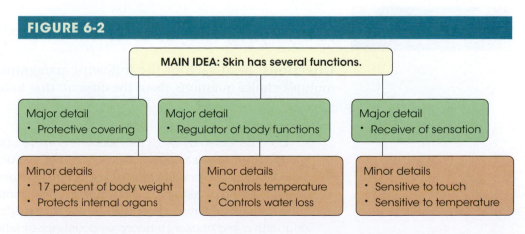

From the diagram in Figure 6-2 you can see that the details that state the three functions of skin are the major details. Other details, such as "protects internal organs," provide further information and are at a lower level of importance.

Read the following paragraph and try to pick out the more important details.

> Communication occurs with words and gestures but did you know it also occurs through the sense of smell? Odor can communicate at least four types of messages. First, odor can signal attraction. Animals give off scents to attract members of the opposite sex. Humans use fragrances to make themselves more appealing or attractive. Smell also communicates information about tastes. The smell of popcorn popping stimulates the appetite. If you smell a chicken roasting you can anticipate its taste. A third type of smell communication is through memory. A smell can help you recall an event that occurred months or even years ago, especially if the event was an emotional one. Finally, smell can communicate by creating an identity or image for a person or product. For example, a woman may wear only one brand of perfume. Or a brand of shaving cream may have a distinct fragrance, which allows users to recognize it.
>
> —DeVito, *Messages*, p. 159

This paragraph could be diagrammed as follows:

**VISUALIZE IT!**

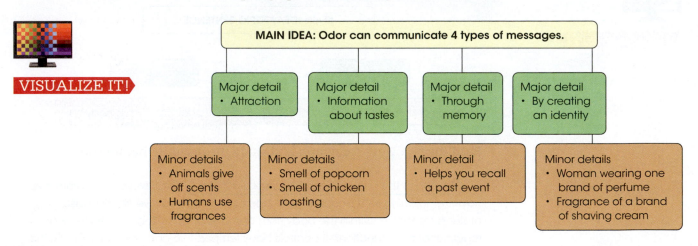

**MAIN IDEA: Odor can communicate 4 types of messages.**

| Major detail • Attraction | Major detail • Information about tastes | Major detail • Through memory | Major detail • By creating an identity |

| Minor details • Animals give off scents • Humans use fragrances | Minor details • Smell of popcorn • Smell of chicken roasting | Minor detail • Helps you recall a past event | Minor details • Woman wearing one brand of perfume • Fragrance of a brand of shaving cream |

## EXERCISE 6-1    Identifying Major and Minor Details

**Directions:** Read each of the following paragraphs, and then answer the multiple-choice questions about the diagram that follows.

**Paragraph 1**

Don't be fooled by words that sound impressive but mean little. Doublespeak is language that fails to communicate; it comes in four basic forms. **Euphemisms** make the negative and unpleasant appear positive and appealing, for example, calling the firing of 200 workers "downsizing" or "reallocation of resources." **Jargon** is the specialized language of a professional class (for example, the computer language of the hacker); it becomes doublespeak when used to communicate with people who aren't members of the group and who don't know this specialized language. **Gobbledygook** is overly complex language that overwhelms the listener

instead of communicating meaning. **Inflated language** makes the mundane seem extraordinary, the common exotic ("take the vacation of a lifetime; explore unsurpassed vistas"). All four forms can be useful in some situations, but, when spoken or listened to mindlessly, they may obscure meaning and distort perceptions.
—DeVito, *Messages: Building Interpersonal Communication Skills*, p. 130

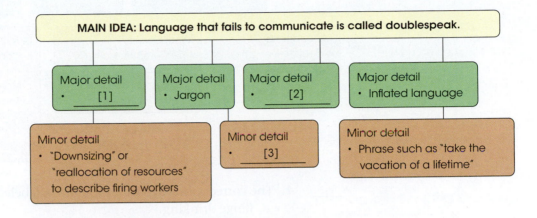

_____ 1. The correct word to fill in the blank labeled [1] is
    **a.** Doublespeak.
    **b.** Euphemisms.
    **c.** Negative.
    **d.** Positive.

_____ 2. The correct word or phrase to fill in the blank labeled [2] is
    **a.** Complex language.
    **b.** Specialized language.
    **c.** Gobbledygook.
    **d.** Mundane.

_____ 3. The correct phrase to fill in the blank labeled [3] is
    **a.** Obscure meanings.
    **b.** Distort perceptions.
    **c.** A professional class.
    **d.** The computer language of the hacker.

**Paragraph 2**

The risks associated with the consumption of alcohol are determined in part by how much an individual drinks. An **occasional drinker** is a person who drinks an alcoholic beverage once in a while. The occasional drinker seldom becomes intoxicated, and such drinking presents little or no threat to the health of the individual. A **social drinker** is someone who drinks regularly in social settings but seldom consumes enough alcohol to become intoxicated. Social drinking, like occasional drinking, does not necessarily increase health risks. **Binge drinking** is defined as having five drinks in a row for men or four in a row for women. Binge drinking can cause significant health and social problems. In comparison to nonbinge drinkers, binge drinkers are much more likely to have unprotected sex, to drive after drinking, and to fall behind in school.
—Pruitt and Stein, *Health Styles*, pp. 108, 110

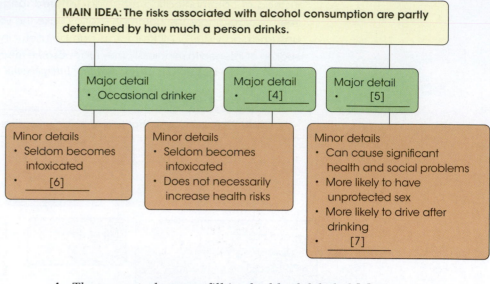

_____ 4. The correct phrase to fill in the blank labeled [4] is
   **a.** Binge drinking.
   **b.** Alcohol consumption.
   **c.** Health risks.
   **d.** Social drinker.

_____ 5. The correct phrase to fill in the blank labeled [5] is
   **a.** Social drinker.
   **b.** Binge drinking.
   **c.** Health problems.
   **d.** Social problems.

_____ 6. The correct phrase to fill in the blank labeled [6] is
   **a.** Occasional drinker.
   **b.** Social drinker.
   **c.** Little or no health threat.
   **d.** Drinks regularly in social settings.

_____ 7. The correct phrase to fill in the blank labeled [7] is
   **a.** More likely to fall behind in school.
   **b.** More likely to have health problems.
   **c.** Little or no health threat.
   **d.** Four or five drinks in a row.

**Paragraph 3**

There are four different dimensions of an arrest: legal, behavioral, subjective, and official. In **legal** terms, an arrest is made when someone lawfully deprives another person of liberty; in other words, that person is not free to go. The actual word _arrest_ need not be uttered, but the other person must be brought under the control of the arresting individual. The **behavioral** element in arrests is often nothing more than the phrase "You're under arrest." However, that statement is usually backed up by a tight grip on the arm or collar, or the drawing of an officer's handgun, or the use of handcuffs. The **subjective** dimension of arrest refers to whenever people believe they are not free to leave; to all intents and purposes, they are under arrest. In any case, the arrest lasts only as long as the person is in custody, which might be a matter of a few minutes or many hours. Many people are briefly detained on the street and then released. **Official** arrests are those detentions that the police record in an administrative record. When a suspect is "booked" at the police station, a record is made of the arrest.

—Barlow, *Criminal Justice in America*, p. 238

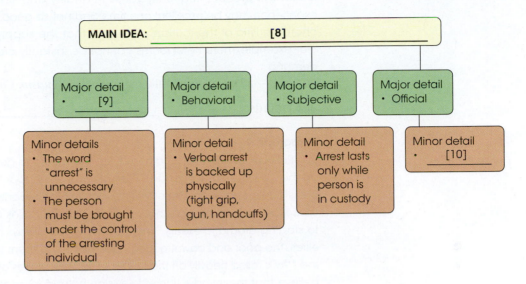

8. The correct sentence to fill in the blank labeled [8] is
   a. When a person is lawfully deprived of freedom, it is not necessary to use the word *arrest*.
   b. The four different dimensions of an arrest are legal, behavioral, subjective, and official.
   c. People can be subjectively under arrest even when they are not officially under arrest.
   d. The only official arrests are those that are recorded at the police station.

9. The correct word or phrase to fill in the blank labeled [9] is
   a. Dimensions.
   b. Liberty.
   c. Not free to go.
   d. Legal.

10. The correct word or phrase to fill in the blank labeled [10] is
    a. Arrest is recorded at police station.
    b. Detentions.
    c. Briefly detained.
    d. Booked.

## EXERCISE 6-2

# Identifying Major Details

**Directions:** Read each of the following paragraphs and write the numbers of the sentences that contain only the most important major details.

### Paragraph 1

There are four main characteristics of a tourism product. ²The first is service, which is intangible because it cannot be inspected physically. ³For example, a tourist cannot sample a Caribbean cruise or a European tour before purchasing one. [4]The second characteristic is that the tourism product is largely psychological in its attraction. [5]It is more than airline seats or car rentals; it is the temporary use of a different environment, its culture, heritage, and experiences. [6]A third characteristic is that the product frequently varies in quality and standards. [7]A tourist's hotel experience may be excellent one time and not so good at the next visit. [8]A fourth characteristic of the tourism product is that the supply of the product is fixed. [9]For example, more hotel rooms cannot be instantly created to meet increased demand.

—adapted from Walker and Walker, *Tourism: Concepts and Practices*, p. 11

Major Details: _____

### Paragraph 2

Political activists depend heavily on the media to get their ideas placed high on the governmental agenda. [2]Their arsenal of weapons includes press releases, press conferences, and letter writing; convincing reporters and columnists to tell their side; trading on personal contacts; and, in cases of desperation, resorting to staging dramatic events. [3]The media are not always monopolized by political elites; the poor and downtrodden have access to them too. [4]Civil rights groups in the 1960s relied heavily on the media to tell their stories of unjust treatment. [5]Many believe that the introduction of television helped to accelerate the movement by showing Americans just what the situation was. [6]Protest groups have learned that if they can stage an interesting event that attracts the media's attention, at least their point of view will be heard. [7]Radical activist Saul Alinsky once dramatized the plight of one neighborhood by having its residents collect rats and dump them on the mayor's front lawn. [8]The story was one that local reporters could hardly resist.

—adapted from Edwards et al., *Government in America*, p. 239

Major Details: _____

### Paragraph 3

To be patented, an invention must be novel, useful, and nonobvious. [2]An invention is *novel* if it is new and has not been invented and used in the past. [3]If the invention has been used before, it is not novel and cannot be patented. [4]An invention is *useful* if it has some practical purpose. [5]For example, an inventor received a patent for "forkchops," which are a set of chopsticks with a spoon at one handle-end and a fork on the other handle-end. [6]This invention is useful. [7]If the invention is *nonobvious*, it qualifies for a patent; if the invention is obvious, then it does not qualify for a patent. [8]For example, inventors received a patent for a cardboard sleeve that can be placed over a paper coffee cup so that the cup will not be as hot as if there were no sleeve. [9]This invention is novel, useful, and nonobvious.

—adapted from Goldman and Cheeseman, *The Paralegal Professional*, pp. 736–737

Major Details: _____

### Paragraph 4

People who exercise their mental abilities have been found to be far less likely to develop memory problems and even senile dementias such as Alzheimer's in old age. [2]"Use it or lose it" is the phrase to remember. [3]Working challenging crossword puzzles, for example, can be a major factor in maintaining a healthy level of cognitive functioning. [4]Reading, having an active social life, going to plays, taking classes, and staying physically active can all have a positive impact on the continued well-being of the brain.

—adapted from Ciccarelli and White, *Psychology: An Exploration*, p. 249

Major Details: _____

**Paragraph 5**

A general law practice is one that handles all types of cases. [2]This is what people usually think of as the small-town lawyer, the generalist to whom everyone in town comes for advice. [3]The reality is that the same generalists practice in cities as well as small towns throughout the country. [4]Their practices are as diverse as the law itself, handling everything from adoptions to zoning appeals. [5]As general practitioners, they serve the same function in the law as the general family practice doctor does in medicine. [6]Lawyers in this type of practice often work in several areas of law within the same day. [7]Their day may include attending a hearing in small-claims court in the morning, preparing a will before lunch, meeting with an opposing attorney to discuss settlement of an accident case, then helping someone who is forming a corporation, and finally appearing at a municipal government meeting in the evening to seek a zoning approval.

—adapted from Goldman and Cheeseman, *The Paralegal Professional*, p. 81

Major Details: _____

## Types of Supporting Details

There are many types of details that a writer can use to explain or support a main idea. As you read, be sure you look for the types of detail a writer uses to support his or her main idea: the way a writer explains and supports an idea may influence how readily you accept or agree with it. The most common types of supporting details are (1) examples, (2) facts or statistics, (3) reasons, (4) descriptions, and (5) steps or procedures. Each will be briefly discussed here.

### Examples

One way a writer may support an idea is by using examples. Examples make ideas and concepts real and understandable. In the following paragraph, an example is used to explain instantaneous speed.

The speed that a body has at any one instant is called instantaneous speed. It is the speed registered by the speedometer of a car. When we say that the speed of a car at some particular instant is 60 kilometers per hour, we are specifying its instantaneous speed, and we mean that if the car continued moving as fast for an hour, it would travel 60 kilometers. So the instantaneous speed, or speed at a particular instant, is often quite different from average speed.

—Hewitt, *Conceptual Physics*, p. 15

In this paragraph the author uses the speed of a car to explain instantaneous speed. As you read illustrations and examples, try to see the relationship between the examples and the concepts or ideas they illustrate.

### Facts or Statistics

Another way a writer supports an idea is by including facts and/or statistics. The facts and statistics may provide evidence that the main idea is correct.

Or the facts may further explain the main idea. For example, to prove that the divorce rate is high, the author may give statistics about the divorce rate and the percentage of the population that is divorced. Notice how, in the following paragraph, the main idea stated in the first sentence is explained using statistics.

The term **graying of America** refers to the increasing percentage of older people in the U.S. population. In 1900 only 4 percent of Americans were age 65 and older. Today almost 13 percent are. The average 65-year-old can expect to live another eighteen years. U.S. society has become so "gray" that the median age has doubled since 1850, and today there are seven million *more* elderly Americans than teenagers. Despite this change, on a global scale Americans rank fifteenth in life expectancy.

—Henslin, *Sociology*, p. 383

In this paragraph, the main idea that the number of older Americans is increasing is supported using statistics.

## Reasons

A writer may support an idea by giving reasons *why* a main idea is correct. A writer might explain *why* nuclear power is dangerous or give reasons *why* a new speed limit law should be passed by Congress. In the following paragraph, the author explains why warm air rises.

We all know that warm air rises. From our study of buoyancy we can understand why this is so. Warm air expands and becomes less dense than the surrounding air and is buoyed upward like a balloon. The buoyancy is in an upward direction because the air pressure below a region of warmed air is greater than the air pressure above. And the warmed air rises because the buoyant force is greater than its weight.

—Hewitt, *Conceptual Physics*, pp. 234–235

## Descriptions

When the topic of a paragraph is a person, object, place, or process, the writer may develop the paragraph by describing the object. Descriptions are details that help you create a mental picture of the object. In the following paragraph, the author describes a sacred book of the Islamic religion by telling what it contains.

The Koran is the sacred book of the Islamic religion. It was written during the lifetime of Mohammed (570–632) during the years in which he recorded divine revelations. The Koran includes rules for family relationships, including marriage and divorce. Rules for inheritance of wealth and property are specified. The status of women as subordinate to men is well defined.

## Steps or Procedures

When a paragraph explains how to do something, the paragraph details are often lists of steps or procedures to be followed. For example, if the main idea of a paragraph is how to prepare an outline for a speech, then the details would list or explain the steps in preparing an outline. In the following paragraph the author explains how fog is produced.

Warm breezes blow over the ocean. When the moist air moves from warmer to cooler waters or from warm water to cool land, it chills. As it chills, water vapor molecules begin coalescing rather than bouncing off one another upon glancing collisions. Condensation takes place, and we have fog.

—Hewitt, *Conceptual Physics*, p. 259

**EXERCISE 6-3**

# Identifying Types of Details

**Directions:** Each topic sentence is followed by a list of details that could be used to support it. Label each detail as *example, fact or statistic, reason, description,* or *step or procedure.*

1. *Topic sentence:* Every April 15th, millions of Americans make their way to the post office to mail their income tax forms.

   _____   Corporate taxes account for about 10 cents of every federal revenue dollar, compared with 47 cents from individual income taxes.

   _____   This year, the Burnette family filed a return that entitles them to a substantial refund on their state income taxes.

   _____   In order to submit an income tax return, you must first obtain the proper forms.

   —Edwards et al., *Government in America*, pp. 458–459

2. *Topic sentence:* Historical and cultural attractions can be found in a variety of shapes, sizes, and locations throughout the world.

   _____   In Europe, for every museum that existed in 1950, there are now more than four.

   _____   Living History Farms, located near Des Moines, Iowa, is an attraction that offers a "hands-on" experience for visitors.

   _____   More and more communities and countries are taking action to preserve historical sites because they attract visitors and generate income for local residents.

   —Cook, *Tourism*, p. 209

3. *Topic sentence:* Many Americans are obsessed with losing weight.

   _____   Weight loss obsession is often triggered by major events looming in the near future, such as a high school reunion or a "milestone" birthday.

   _____   The two ways to lose weight are to lower caloric intake (through improved eating habits) and to increase exercise (expending more calories).

_____ Studies show that on any given day in America, nearly 40 percent of women and 24 percent of men over the age of 20 are trying to lose weight.

_____ Juan, a college freshman from Raleigh, admits that he has been struggling with a weight problem since he reached puberty.
—Donatelle and Davis, *Access to Health*, pp. 358, 371

4. *Topic sentence:* In the 1920s, many young American writers and artists left their country behind and became expatriates.

_____ One of the most talented of the expatriates was Ernest Hemingway.

_____ The expatriates flocked to Rome, Berlin, and Paris, in order to live cheaply and escape what seemed to them the "conspiracy against the individual" in America.

_____ Some earned a living as journalists, translators, and editors, or made a few dollars by selling a poem to an American magazine or a painting to a tourist.
—Garraty and Carnes, *The American Nation*, p. 706

5. *Topic sentence:* The Anasazi Indians are best known for their artistic, architectural, and technological achievements.

_____ The Anasazi used all of the available materials to build their settlements; with wood, mud, and stone, they erected cliff dwellings and the equivalent of terraced apartment houses.

_____ The Anasazi built one structure with 500 living units; it was the largest residential building in North America until the completion of an apartment house in New York in 1772.

_____ One example of their technological genius was their use of irrigation: they constructed sand dunes at the base of hills to hold the runoff from the sometimes torrential rains.

_____ The Anasazi produced pottery that could rank in beauty with any in the world.
—Brummet et al., *Civilization*, p. 348

## EXERCISE 6-4   Identifying Types of Details

**Directions:** For each paragraph in Exercise 6-2 on pages 177–179, identify the type or types of details used to support the main idea. Write your answers below.

1. Type(s) of details: _____

2. Type(s) of details: _____

3. Type(s) of details: _____

4. Type(s) of details: _____

5. Type(s) of details: _____

# Think Critically About Details

■ GOAL 3
Think critically about details

Writers choose the details they provide to support a main idea. They rarely have the time, or the space, to list every available supporting detail. Consider the following paragraph:

> Cross-sex friendships [that is, friendships between a man and a woman] have many benefits. Befriending a person of the opposite sex can give one a unique perspective on the other sex, and gender roles become mitigated. Cross-sex friendships are even associated with higher self-esteem and self-confidence.
> —Kunz, *Think Marriages & Families*, p. 83

The author provides two details to support the topic sentence "Cross-sex friendships have many benefits." These are: (1) having a friend of the opposite sex can help you better understand the opposite sex, and (2) friends of the opposite sex can make you feel better about yourself. But the author could also have chosen other details. For example, some people believe that men become better listeners when they have female friends.

As you read, be aware of the details that the writer has chosen to include. Has the writer omitted any important details to make a stronger case? Has he or she used any specific words to influence you? For example, suppose you are looking to rent an apartment, and you see an ad that reads as follows:

> 1 bedroom, 1 bath apartment. Cozy and cute, very conveniently located. Monthly rent includes water and gas. Most appliances also included. On-street parking is available.

This apartment may seem appealing, but look carefully at the details. What exactly does "cozy" mean? Often, the word *cozy* really means "small." And "conveniently located" might mean the apartment is located at a busy intersection (which might be very noisy). The rent includes water and gas . . . but what about electricity? "Most" appliances are included—which ones aren't? (Maybe you'd have to buy a stove or a refrigerator.) And the fact that on-street parking is "available" doesn't guarantee that you'll always get a parking spot in front of the building.

**EXERCISE 6-5**

## Thinking Critically About Details

**Directions:** Read each paragraph and answer the questions that follow.

A lot of people are looking for a "magic pill" that will help them maintain weight loss, reduce their risk of diseases, make them feel better, and improve their quality of sleep. Although many people are not aware of it, regular physical activity is this "magic pill." That's because it promotes physical fitness: the ability to carry out daily tasks with vigor and alertness, without undue fatigue, and with ample energy to enjoy leisure-time pursuits and meet unforeseen emergencies.

—Thompson and Manore, *Nutrition for Life*, p. 302

1. What essential ingredient of good health/physical fitness is missing from this paragraph? _____

The world's most livable cities are not those with "perfect" auto access between all points. Instead, they are cities that have taken measures to reduce outward sprawl, diminish automobile traffic, and improve access by foot and bicycle in conjunction with mass transit. For example, Geneva, Switzerland, prohibits automobile parking at workplaces in the city's center, forcing commuters to use the excellent public transportation system. Copenhagen bans all on-street parking in the downtown core. Paris has removed 200,000 parking places in the downtown area. Curitiba, Brazil, is cited as the most livable city in all of Latin America. The achievement of Curitiba is due almost entirely to the efforts of Jaime Lerner, who, serving as mayor for many decades, guided development with an emphasis on mass transit rather than cars. The space saved by not building highways and parking lots has been put into parks and shady walkways, causing the amount of green area per inhabitant to increase from 4.5 square feet in 1970 to 450 square feet today.

—Wright and Boorse, *Environmental Science: Toward a Sustainable Future*, p. 604

2. What is the main idea of the paragraph?

_____

_____

3. Which four cities are offered as examples (supporting details) of livable cities?

_____

4. By not listing any U.S. examples of "livable cities," what might the author be implying (but not stating directly)?

_____

_____

5. What other cities might have been mentioned as having good systems of mass transit? (Hint: Think of U.S. cities that have reliable train and bus service.)

_____

_____

# Use Transitions to Guide Your Reading

■ **GOAL 4**
Use transitions to guide your reading

**Transitions** are linking words or phrases used to lead the reader from one idea to another. If you get in the habit of recognizing transitions, you will see that they often guide you through a paragraph, helping you to read it more easily.

In the following paragraph, notice how the circled transitions lead you from one important detail to the next.

The principle of rhythm and line also contributes to the overall unity of the landscape design. This principle is responsible for the sense of continuity between different areas of the landscape. One way in which this continuity can be developed is by extending planting beds from one area to another. For example, shrub beds developed around the entrance to the house can be continued around the sides and into the backyard. Such an arrangement helps to tie the front and rear areas of the property together. Another means by which rhythm is given to a design is to repeat shapes, angles, or lines between various areas and elements of the design.

—Reiley and Shry, *Introductory Horticulture*, p. 114

Not all paragraphs contain such obvious transitions, and not all transitions serve as such clear markers of major details. Transitions may be used to alert you to what will come next in the paragraph. If you see the phrase *for instance* at the beginning of a sentence, then you know that an example will follow. When you see the phrase *on the other hand*, you can predict that a different, opposing idea will follow. Table 6-1 lists some of the most common transitions used within a paragraph and indicates what they tell you.

## TABLE 6-1    COMMON TRANSITIONS

| Type of Transition | Example | What It Tells the Reader |
|---|---|---|
| Time Sequence | *first, later, next, finally* | The author is arranging ideas in the order in which they happened. |
| Example | *for example, for instance, to illustrate, such as* | An example will follow. |
| Enumeration | *first, second, third, last, one, another, next* | The author is marking or identifying each major point (sometimes these may be used to suggest order of importance). |
| Continuation | *also, in addition, and, further, another* | The author is continuing with the same idea and is going to provide additional information. |
| Contrast | *on the other hand, in contrast, however* | The author is switching to a different, opposite, or contrasting idea from that previously discussed. |
| Comparison | *like, likewise, similarly* | The writer will show how the previous idea is similar to what follows. |
| Cause/Effect | *because, thus, therefore, since, consequently* | The writer will show a connection between two or more things, how one thing caused another, or how something happened as a result of something else. |
| Summation | *to sum up, in conclusion* | The writer will draw his or her ideas together. |

**EXERCISE 6-6**

## Choosing Transitional Words

**Directions:** Read each of the following sentences. In each blank, write a transitional word or phrase from the list below that makes sense in the sentence.

| | | | | |
|---|---|---|---|---|
| next | however | for example | another | consequently |
| because | similarly | such as | to sum up | in addition |

1. After a heart attack, the heart muscle is permanently weakened; _____ its ability to pump blood throughout the body may be reduced.

2. Some metals, _____ gold and silver, are represented by symbols derived from their Latin names.

3. In order to sight-read music, you should begin by scanning it. _____, you should identify the key and tempo.

4. The *Oxford English Dictionary*, by giving all present and past definitions of words, shows how word definitions have changed with time. _____, it gives the date and written source where each word appears to have first been used.

5. Some scientists believe intelligence to be determined equally by heredity and environment. _____, other scientists believe heredity to account for about 60 percent of intelligence and environment for the other 40 percent.

6. Tigers tend to grow listless and unhappy in captivity. _____, pandas grow listless and have a difficult time reproducing in captivity.

7. _____, the most important ways to prevent heat stress are to (1) allow yourself time to get used to the heat, (2) wear the proper clothing, and (3) drink plenty of water.

8. Many people who are dissatisfied with the public school system send their children to private schools. _____ option that is gaining in popularity is homeschooling.

9. Studies have shown that it is important to "exercise" our brains as we age. _____, crossword puzzles are a good way to keep mentally fit.

10. Buying smaller-sized clothing generally will not give an overweight person the incentive to lose weight. People with weight problems tend to eat when they are upset or disturbed, and _____ wearing smaller clothing is frustrating and upsetting, overweight people will generally gain weight by doing so.

---

**EXERCISE 6-7**

*WORKING TOGETHER*

# Making Predictions

**Directions:** Each of the following beginnings of paragraphs uses a transitional word or phrase to tell the reader what will follow in the paragraph. Working in pairs, read each, paying particular attention to the underlined word or phrase. Then discuss what you would expect to find next in the paragraph. Summarize your findings in the space provided.

1. Price is not the only factor to consider in choosing a pharmacy. Many provide valuable services that should be considered. <u>For instance</u>, . . .

_____

2. There are a number of things you can do to prevent a home burglary. <u>First</u>, . . .

_____

3. Most mail order businesses are reliable and honest. <u>However</u>, . . .

_____

4. One advantage of a compact stereo system is that all the components are built into the unit. <u>Another</u> . . .

   _____

5. Taking medication can have an effect on your hormonal balance. <u>Therefore</u>, . . .

   _____

6. To select the presidential candidate you will vote for, you should examine his or her philosophy of government. <u>Next</u> . . .

   _____

7. Eating solely vegetables drastically reduces caloric and fat intake, two things on which most people overindulge. <u>On the other hand</u>, . . .

   _____

8. Asbestos, a common material found in many older buildings in which people have worked for decades, has been shown to cause cancer. <u>Consequently</u>, . . .

   _____

9. Cars and trucks are not designed randomly. They are designed individually for specific purposes. <u>For instance</u>, . . .

   _____

10. Jupiter is a planet surrounded by several moons. <u>Likewise</u>, . . .

   _____

# Identify Implied Main Ideas

■ **GOAL 5**
Find implied main ideas

As you know, when a writer leaves his or her main idea unstated, it is up to you, the reader, to look at the details in the paragraph and figure out the writer's main point.

The details, when taken together, will all point to a general and more important idea. You might want to think of such a paragraph as the pieces of a puzzle. You must put together the pieces or details to determine the meaning of the paragraph as a whole. Use the following steps as a guide to find implied main ideas.

1. **Find the topic.** As you know, the *topic* is the general subject of the entire paragraph. Ask yourself: "What is the one thing the author is discussing throughout the paragraph?"

2. **Figure out what is the most important idea the writer wants you to know about that topic.** Look at each detail and decide what larger idea is being explained.

3. **Express this main idea in your own words.** Make sure that the main idea is a reasonable one. Ask yourself: "Does it apply to all of the details in the paragraph?"

**Example**

Men's friendships are often built around shared activities—attending a ball game, playing cards, working on a project at the office. Women's friendships, on the other hand, are built more around a sharing of feelings, support, and "personalism." One study found that similarity in status, in willingness to protect one's friend in uncomfortable situations, in academic major, and even in proficiency in playing Password were significantly related to the relationship closeness of male-male friends but not of female-female or female-male friends.

—DeVito, *Messages: Building Interpersonal Communication Skills*, p. 290

The general topic of this paragraph is friendships. More specifically, the paragraph is about the differences between male and female friendships. Three details are given: (1) men's friendships are based on shared activities, (2) women's friendships are based on shared feelings, and (3) similarity is important in men's friendships but not in women's. Each of the three details is a difference between male and female friendships. The main point the writer is trying to make, then, is that men and women have different criteria for building friendships. You can figure out this writer's main idea even though no single sentence states this directly. You might visualize this paragraph as follows:

**VISUALIZE IT!**

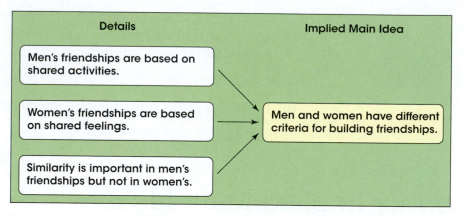

Here is another paragraph. Read it and then fill in the diagram that follows:

**Example**

By now most people know that the herb echinacea may help conquer the common cold. Herbal remedies that are less well known include flaxseed, for treating constipation, and fennel, for soothing an upset stomach. In addition, the herb chamomile may be brewed into a hot cup of tea for a good night's sleep.

**VISUALIZE IT!**

**Topic:** _____

| Details | Implied Main Idea |
|---|---|
| Echinacea— _____ | |
| Flaxseed— _____ | Different _____ may be used to treat a variety of ailments. |
| Fennel— _____ | |
| Chamomile— _____ | |

After you come up with a main idea, make sure it is broad enough. Every sentence in the paragraph should support the idea you have chosen. Work through the paragraph sentence by sentence. Check to see if each sentence explains or gives more information about the main idea. If some sentences do not explain your chosen idea, it probably is not broad enough. You may need to expand your idea and make it more general.

## EXERCISE 6-8  Locating Implied Meaning

**Directions:** For each of the following paragraphs, write a sentence that states its implied main idea.

1. As recently as 20 years ago, textbooks on child psychology seldom devoted more than a few paragraphs to the behaviors of the neonate—the newborn through the first 2 weeks of life. It seemed as if the neonate did not do much worth writing about. Today, most child psychology texts devote substantially more space to discussing the abilities of newborns. It is unlikely that over the past 20 years neonates have gotten smarter or more able. Rather, psychologists have. They have devised new and clever ways of measuring the abilities and capacities of neonates.

   —Gerow, *Psychology: An Introduction*, p. 319

   Implied main idea: _____

   _____

2. Severe punishment may generate such anxiety in children that they do not learn the lesson the punishment was designed to teach. Moreover, as a reaction to punishment that they regard as unfair, children may avoid punitive parents, who therefore will have fewer opportunities to teach and guide the child. In addition, parents who use physical punishment provide aggressive models. A child who is regularly slapped, spanked, shaken, or shouted at may learn to use these forms of aggression in interactions with peers.

   —Newcombe, *Child Development*, p. 354

   Implied main idea: _____

   _____

3. Most sporting goods manufacturers have long sold products for women, but this often meant simply creating an inferior version of the male product and slapping a pink label on it. Then the companies discovered that many women were buying products intended for boys because they wanted better quality, so some of them figured out that they needed to take this market segment seriously. Burton Snowboard Company was one of the early learners. When the company started to offer high-quality clothing and gear made specifically for women, female boarders snapped them up. Burton also changed the way it promotes these products and redesigned its Web site after getting feedback from female riders.

   —adapted from Solomon, *Consumer Behavior*, p. 189

   Implied main idea: _____

   _____

# Analyzing Paragraphs

**Directions:** Read each paragraph and answer the questions that follow.

**Paragraph 1**

Thanks to the Internet, you can shop 24 hours a day without leaving home, you can read today's newspaper without getting drenched picking up a hard copy in a rainstorm, and you don't have to wait for the 6:00 news to find out what the weather will be like tomorrow—at home or around the globe. And, with the increasing use of handheld devices and wireless communications, you can get that same information—from stock quotes to the weather—even when you're away from your computer.

—Solomon and Stuart, *The Brave New World of E-Commerce*, p. 13

1. What is the topic? _____

2. What is the implied main idea? _____

_____

**Paragraph 2**

Research suggests that women who are considered attractive are more effective in changing attitudes than are women thought to be less attractive. In addition, more attractive individuals are often considered to be more credible than less attractive people. They are also perceived to be happier, more popular, more sociable, and more successful than are those rated as being less attractive. With respect to shape and body size, people with fat, round silhouettes are consistently rated as older, more old-fashioned, less good-looking, more talkative, and more good-natured. Athletic, muscular people are rated as more mature, better looking, taller, and more adventurous. Tall and thin people are rated as more ambitious, more suspicious of others, more tense and nervous, more pessimistic, and quieter.

—Beebe and Masterson, *Communicating in Small Groups*, p. 150

3. What is the topic? _____

4. What is the implied main idea? _____

_____

**Paragraph 3**

Any zookeeper will tell you that the primate house is their most popular exhibit. People love apes and monkeys. It is easy to see why—primates are curious, playful, and agile. In short, they are fun to watch. But something else drives our fascination with these wonderful animals: We see ourselves reflected in them. The placement of their eyes and their small noses appear humanlike. They have hands with fingernails instead of paws with claws. Some can stand and walk on two legs for short periods. They can finely manipulate objects with their fingers and opposable thumbs. They show extensive parental care, and even their social relations are similar to ours—they tickle, caress, kiss, and pout.

—adapted from Belk and Maier, *Biology: Science for Life with Physiology*, p. 236

5. What is the topic? _____

6. What is the implied main idea? _____

_____

**Paragraph 4**

The Web has enabled people to work, "talk" to friends across town and across the ocean, and buy goods from online retailers without leaving their houses. It has also made some criminal enterprises and unethical behavior easier to accomplish and harder to trace—for example, people can scam others out of large sums of money, buy college term papers, and learn how to build a bomb.

—adapted from Divine et al., *America Past and Present*, p. 449

7. What is the topic? _____

8. What is the implied main idea? _____

**Paragraph 5**

Sleep conserves body energy so that we are rested and ready to perform during high-performance daylight hours. Sleep also restores the neurotransmitters that have been depleted during the waking hours. This process clears the brain of unimportant details as a means of preparing for a new day. Getting enough sleep to feel ready to meet daily challenges is a key factor in maintaining optimal physical and psychological status.

—Donatelle and Davis, *Access to Health*, p. 42

9. What is the topic? _____

10. What is the implied main idea? _____

_____

# WRITING

# Select and Organize Details to Support Your Topic Sentence

■ GOAL 6

Select and organize details to support your topic sentence

The details you choose to support your topic sentence must be both relevant and sufficient. **Relevant** means that the details directly explain and support your topic sentence. For example, if you were to write a paragraph for your employer explaining why you deserve a raise, it would not be relevant to mention that you plan to use the money to go to Florida next spring. A vacation has nothing to do with—is not relevant to—your job performance.

**Sufficient** means that you must provide enough information to make your topic sentence understandable and convincing. In your paragraph explaining why you deserve a raise, it would probably not be sufficient to say that you are always on time. You would need to provide more information about your job performance: for example, that you always volunteer to work holidays, that you've offered good suggestions for displaying new products, and that several customers have written letters praising your work.

In addition to choosing relevant and sufficient details, be sure to select a variety of details, use specific words, and organize your paragraph effectively.

## Selecting Relevant Details

Relevant details directly support your topic sentence. They help clarify and strengthen your ideas, whereas irrelevant details make your ideas unclear and confusing. Here is the first draft of a paragraph written by a student named Alex to explain why he decided to attend college. Can you locate the detail that is not relevant?

> [1]I decided to attend college to further my education and achieve my goals in life. [2]I am attempting to build a future for myself. [3]When I get married and have kids, I want to be able to offer them the same opportunities my parents gave me. [4]I want to have a comfortable style of living and a good job. [5]As for my wife, I don't want her to work because I believe a married woman should not work. [6]I believe college is the way to begin a successful life.

Sentence 5 does not belong in the paragraph. The fact that Alex does not want his wife to work is not a reason for attending college.

Use the following simple test to be sure each detail you include belongs in your paragraph:

## Test for Relevant Details

1. Read your topic sentence in combination with each of the other sentences in your paragraph. For example,

   read topic sentence + last sentence.

   read topic sentence + second-to-last sentence.

   read topic sentence + third-to-last sentence.

2. For each pair of sentences, ask yourself, "Do these two ideas fit together?" If your answer is "No," then you have found a detail that is not relevant to your topic. Delete it from your paragraph.

Another student wrote the following paragraph on the subject of the legal drinking age. As you read it, cross out the details that are not relevant.

> [1]The legal drinking age should be raised to 25. [2]Anyone who drinks should be old enough to determine whether or not it is safe to drive after drinking. [3]Bartenders and others who serve drinks should also have to be 25. [4]In general, teenagers and young adults are not responsible enough to limit how much they drink. [5]The party atmosphere enjoyed by so many young people encourages crazy acts, so we should limit who can drink. [6]Younger people think drinking is a game, but it is a dangerous game that affects the lives of others.

Which sentence did you delete? Why did you delete it? The third sentence does not belong in the paragraph because the age of those who bartend or serve drinks is not relevant to the topic. Sentence 5, about partying, should also be eliminated or explained because the connection between partying and drinking is not clear.

**EXERCISE 6-10**

# Identifying Relevant Details

**Directions:** Place a check mark by those statements that provide relevant supporting details.

1. Sales representatives need good interpersonal skills.

   _____ **a.** They need to be good listeners.

   _____ **b.** They should like helping people.

   _____ **c.** They should know their products well.

2. Water can exist in three forms, which vary with temperature.

_____ a. At a high temperature, water becomes steam; it is a gas.

_____ b. Drinking water often contains mineral traces.

_____ c. At cold temperatures, water becomes ice, a solid state.

3. Outlining is one of the easiest ways to organize facts.

_____ a. Formal outlines use Roman numerals and letters and Arabic numerals to show different levels of importance.

_____ b. Outlining emphasizes the relationships among facts.

_____ c. Outlines make it easier to focus on important points.

---

**EXERCISE 6-11**

**WRITING IN PROGRESS**

# Writing a Paragraph

**Directions:** Write a paragraph beginning with one of the topic sentences below. When you've finished, use the test described on p. 192 to make certain each detail is relevant.

1. Hunting is (is not) a cruel sport.
2. My hometown (city) has (has not) changed in the past five years.
3. Religion is (is not) important in my life.
4. White parents should (should not) be allowed to adopt African American children.
5. Most doctors are (are not) sensitive to their patients' feelings.

---

## Including Sufficient Detail

Including **sufficient detail** means that your paragraph contains an adequate amount of specific information for your readers to understand your main idea. Your supporting details must thoroughly and clearly explain why you believe your topic sentence is true. Be sure that your details are specific; do not provide summaries or unsupported statements of opinion.

Let's look at a paragraph a student wrote on the topic of billboard advertising.

> There is a national movement to oppose billboard advertising. Many people don't like billboards and are taking action to change what products are advertised on them and which companies use them. Community activists are destroying billboard advertisements at an increasing rate. As a result of their actions, numerous changes have been made.

This paragraph is filled with general statements. It does not explain who dislikes billboards or why they dislike them. It does not say what products are advertised or name the companies that make them. No detail is given about how the billboards are destroyed, and the resulting changes are not described. There is not sufficient support for the topic sentence. Here is the revised version:

> Among residents of inner-city neighborhoods, a national movement is growing to oppose billboard advertising. Residents oppose billboards that glamorize

*(continued)*

alcohol and target people of color as its consumers. Community activists have organized and are taking action. They carry paint, rollers, shovels, and brooms to an offending billboard. Within a few minutes the billboard is painted over, covering the damaging advertisement. Results have been dramatic. Many liquor companies have reduced their inner-city billboard advertising. In place of these ads, some billboard companies have placed public-service announcements and ads to improve community health.

If you have trouble thinking of enough details to include in a paragraph, try brainstorming or one of the other techniques for generating ideas described in Chapter 2. Write your topic sentence at the top of a sheet of paper. Then list everything that comes to mind about that topic. Include examples, events, incidents, facts, and reasons. You will be surprised at how many useful details you think of.

When you finish, read over your list and cross out details that are not relevant. (If you still don't have enough, your topic may be too specific. See pp. 158–159.) The section "Organize Details Effectively" on page 195 will help you decide in what order you will write about the details on your list.

## EXERCISE 6-12

**WRITING IN PROGRESS**

# Evaluating and Revising a Paragraph

**Directions:** Reread the paragraph you wrote for Exercise 6-11 to see if it includes sufficient detail. If necessary, revise your paragraph to include more detail, always making sure the details you add are relevant. Use a prewriting technique, if necessary, to generate additional details.

### Types of Supporting Details

There are many types of details that you can use to explain or support a topic sentence. As discussed earlier in this chapter (pp. 179–180), the most common types of supporting details are (1) examples, (2) facts or statistics, (3) reasons, (4) descriptions, and (5) steps or procedures. It is advisable to vary the types of details you use, and to choose those appropriate to your topic.

## EXERCISE 6-13

**WORKING TOGETHER**

# Writing Supporting Details

**Directions:** Working with a classmate, for each topic sentence, write at least three different types of details that could be used to support it. Label each detail as *example, fact or statistic, reason, description,* or *steps or procedure.*

1. People make inferences about you based on the way you dress.
2. Many retailers with traditional stores have decided to market their products through Web sites as well.
3. Many Americans are obsessed with losing weight.
4. Historical and cultural attractions can be found in a variety of shapes, sizes, and locations throughout the world.
5. Using a search engine is an effective, though not perfect, method of searching the Internet.

## Organize Details Effectively

Nan had an assignment to write a paragraph about travel. She drafted the paragraph and then revised it. As you read each version, pay particular attention to the order in which she arranged the details.

**FIRST DRAFT**

This summer I had the opportunity to travel extensively. Over Labor Day weekend I backpacked with a group of friends in the Allegheny Mountains. When spring semester was over, I visited my seven cousins in Florida. My friends and I went to New York City over the Fourth of July to see fireworks and explore the city. During June I worked as a wildlife-preservation volunteer in a Colorado state park. On July 15 I celebrated my twenty-fifth birthday by visiting my parents in Syracuse.

**REVISION**

This summer I had the opportunity to travel extensively in the United States. When the spring semester ended, I went to my cousins' home in Florida to relax. When I returned, I worked during the month of June as a wildlife-preservation volunteer in a Colorado state park. Then my friends and I went to New York City to see the fireworks and look around the city over the Fourth of July weekend. On July 15th, I celebrated my twenty-fifth birthday by visiting my parents in Syracuse. Finally, over Labor Day weekend, my friends and I backpacked in the Allegheny Mountains.

Did you find Nan's revision easier to read? In the first draft, Nan recorded details as she thought of them. There is no logical arrangement to them. In the second version, she arranged the details in the order in which they happened. Nan chose this arrangement because it fit her details logically. The three common methods for arranging details are as follows:

1. Time sequence
2. Spatial arrangement
3. Least/most arrangement

### Time Sequence

**Time sequence** means the order in which something happens. For example, if you were to write about a particularly bad day, you could describe the day in the order in which everything went wrong. You might begin with waking up in the morning and end with going to bed that night. If you were describing a busy or an exciting weekend, you might begin with what you did on Friday night and end with the last activity on Sunday.

When Su-ling gets ready to study at home, she follows a set routine. First of all, she tries to find a quiet place, far away from her kid sisters. This place might be her bedroom or the porch, or the basement, depending on the noise levels in her household. Next, she finds a snack to eat while she is studying, perhaps potato chips or a candy bar. If she is on a diet, she tries to find some healthy fruit. Finally, Su-ling tackles the most difficult assignment first because she knows her level of concentration is higher at the beginning of study sessions.

### Spatial Arrangement

Suppose you are asked to describe the room in which you are sitting. You want your reader, who has never been in the room, to visualize it. You need to describe, in an orderly way, where items are positioned. You could describe the room from left to right, from ceiling to floor, or from door to window. In other situations, your choices might include front to back, inside to outside, near to far, east to west, and so on. This method of presentation is called **spatial arrangement**. How are the details arranged in the following paragraph?

> Keith's antique car was gloriously decorated for the Fourth of July parade. Red, white, and blue streamers hung in front from the headlights and bumper. The hood was covered with small American flags. The windshield had gold stars pasted on it, arranged to form an outline of our state. On the sides, the doors displayed red plastic-tape stripes. The convertible top was down, and Mary sat on the trunk dressed up like the Statue of Liberty. In the rear, a neon sign blinked "God Bless America." His car was not only a show-stopper but the highlight of the parade.

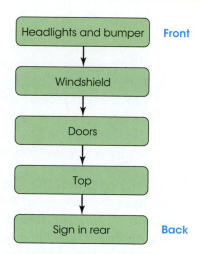

The topic you are writing about will often determine the arrangement you choose. In writing about a town, you might choose to begin with the center and then move to each surrounding area. In describing a building, you might go from bottom to top.

**EXERCISE 6-14**

## Using Spatial Arrangement

**Directions:** Indicate which spatial arrangement you would use to describe the following topics. Then write a paragraph on one of the topics.

1. A local market or favorite store
2. A photograph you value
3. A prized possession
4. A building in which you work
5. Your campus cafeteria, bookstore, or lounge

### The Least/Most Arrangement

Another method of arranging details is to present them in order from least to most or most to least, according to some quality or characteristic. For example, you might arrange details from least to most *expensive*, least to most *serious*, or least to most *important*.

The writer of the following paragraph uses a least-to-most arrangement.

> The entry level job in many industries today is administrative assistant. Just because it's a lower-level job, don't think it's an easy job. A good administrative assistant must have good computer skills. If you aren't proficient on a computer, you won't be able to handle your supervisor's correspondence and other paperwork. Even more important, an administrative assistant must be well organized. Every little task—from answering the phone to setting up meetings to making travel arrangements—lands on the administrative assistant's desk. If you can't juggle lots of loose ends, this is not the job for you. Most important of all, though, an administrative assistant needs a sense of humor. On the busiest days, when the office is in total chaos, the only way to keep your sanity—and your temper—is to take a deep breath, smile, and say "When all this is over, I'm going to have a well-earned nervous breakdown!"

VISUALIZE IT!

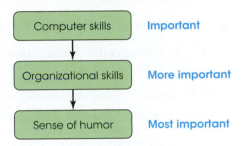

Notice that this writer wrote about a basic requirement for the job—computer skills—and then worked up to the most important requirement.

You can also arrange details from most to least. This structure allows you to present your strongest point first. Many writers use this method to construct a case or an argument. For example, if you were writing a business letter requesting a refund for damaged mail-order merchandise, you would want to begin with the most serious damage and put the minor complaints at the end, as follows:

> I am returning this merchandise because it is damaged. The white sneakers have dark streaks across both toes. One of the shoes has a red mark on the heel. The laces also have some specks of dirt on them. I trust you will refund my money promptly.

## EXERCISE 6-15    Using Least/Most Arrangement

**Directions:** Write a paragraph supporting one of the following topics. Organize your details using the most-to-least or least-to-most arrangement.

1. Reasons why you enjoy a particular sport or hobby
2. Five special items in your closet
3. Three favorite musicians or musical groups
4. Things to remember when renting an apartment
5. Why you like city (or small-town or country) living

## Use Specific Words

When you are writing a paragraph, use specific words to give your reader as much information as possible. You can think of words the way an artist thinks of colors on a palette. Vague words are brown and muddy; specific words are brightly colored and lively. Try to paint pictures for your reader with specific, vivid words. Here are a few examples of vague words along with more specific words or phrases for the same idea:

| | |
|---|---|
| VAGUE | fun |
| SPECIFIC | thrilling, relaxing, enjoyable, pleasurable |
| VAGUE | dark |
| SPECIFIC | hidden in gray-green shadows |
| VAGUE | experienced |
| SPECIFIC | five years in the job |
| VAGUE | tree |
| SPECIFIC | red maple |

The following suggestions will help you develop your details:

1. **Use specific verbs.** Choose verbs (action words) that help your reader picture the action.

| | |
|---|---|
| VAGUE | The woman left the restaurant. |
| SPECIFIC | The woman stormed out of the restaurant. |

2. **Give exact names.** Include the names of people, places, objects, and brands.

| | |
|---|---|
| VAGUE | A man was eating outside. |
| SPECIFIC | Anthony Hargeaves lounged on the deck of his yacht *Penelope*, spearing Heinz dill pickles out of a jar. |

3. **Use adjectives before nouns to convey details.**

| | |
|---|---|
| VAGUE | Juanita had a dog on a leash. |
| SPECIFIC | A short, bushy-tailed dog strained at the end of the leash in Juanita's hand. |

4. **Use words that appeal to the senses.** Choose words that suggest touch, taste, smell, sound, and sight.

| | |
|---|---|
| VAGUE | The florist shop was lovely. |
| SPECIFIC | Brilliant red, pink, and yellow roses filled the florist shop with their heady fragrance. |

To summarize, use words that help your readers create mental pictures.

| | |
|---|---|
| VAGUE | Al was handsome. |
| SPECIFIC | Al had a slim frame, curly brown hair, deep brown almond-shaped eyes, and perfectly straight, gleaming white teeth. |

**EXERCISE 6-16**

## Using Specific Words

**Directions:** Rewrite these vague sentences, using specific words.

1. The hair stylist used a gel on my hair.

   _____

2. Dress properly for an interview.

   _____

3. I found an interesting Web site on the Internet.

_____

4. The job fair was well attended.

_____

5. I'm going to barbecue something for dinner.

_____

## Revising a Paragraph

**WRITING IN PROGRESS**

**Directions:** Reread the paragraphs you revised in Exercise 6-12. As you read, underline any vague or general words. Then replace the underlined words with more specific ones.

# Use Transitional Words and Phrases to Connect Details

■ GOAL 7
Use transitional words and phrases to connect details

**Transitional words** allow readers to move easily from one detail to another; they show how details relate to one another. You might think of them as words that guide and signal. They guide the reader through the paragraph and signal what is to follow. As you read the following paragraph, notice the transitional words and phrases (highlighted in color) that this student used.

> I have so many things to do when I get home today. First, I have to take my dog, Othello, for a walk. Next, I should do my homework for history and study the chapter on franchises for business. After that I should do some laundry, since my drawers are empty. Then my brother is coming over to fix the tailpipe on my car. Afterward, we will probably order a pizza for a speedy dinner.

Table 6-2 shows some commonly used transitional words and phrases for each method of arranging details discussed on pages 196–197. To understand how these transitional words and phrases work, review the sample paragraph for each of these arrangements. Underline each transitional word or phrase.

| TABLE 6-2 | FREQUENTLY USED TRANSITIONS |
|---|---|
| **Arrangement** | **Transition** |
| **Time Sequence** | _first, next, during, eventually, finally, later, meanwhile, soon, when, then, suddenly, currently, after, afterward, before, now, until_ |
| **Spatial** | _above, below, behind, in front of, beside, next to, inside, outside, to the west (north, etc.) of, beneath, nearby, on the other side of_ |
| **Least/Most** | _most, above all, especially, even more_ |

## Revising a Paragraph

**WRITING IN PROGRESS**

**Directions:** Review the paragraphs you wrote for Exercise 6-17. Underline any transitions you used. Revise each paragraph by adding transitional words or phrases to clarify your details.

## NEED TO KNOW

### Important Terms

**Relevant details:** Details that directly explain the topic sentence.

**Sufficient details:** Details that provide adequate support of the topic sentence.

**Time sequence:** Arranging ideas in the order in which they happen.

**Spatial arrangement:** Arranging ideas according to their position in space.

**Least/most arrangement:** Presenting ideas from least to most or most to least according to some quality or characteristic.

**Specific words:** Words that provide a great deal of information.

**Transitional words and phrases:** Words that lead the reader from one detail to another.

## INTEGRATING READING AND WRITING

### READ AND RESPOND: A Student Essay

*James Sturm graduated from Kalamazoo College with a degree in International Studies. He is currently working as the Assistant for the Middlebury School in China and living in Beijing. His job entails introducing American students to China and facilitating their immersion in the language and culture of China.*

*Sturm wrote this essay to fulfill an assignment to write a personal essay for one of his classes at Kalamazoo College. As you read, notice Sturm's use of specific words and concrete detail.*

*Title: interest catching; suggests the writer's enthusiasm for China*

# The China Bug
## James Sturm

*Introduction: explanation of how China affected the writer; many details.*

*Descriptive adjectives*

1    I can't tell you the exact day it hit me. Perhaps it was the day I turned down computer games to play mahjong, or the time I chose green pea–flavored ice cream over chocolate, or maybe when I found myself haggling with a United Airlines representative—unsuccessfully—over the price of a ticket-change. I can't tell you when, but at some point I picked up the "China bug." The simple truth is that my ten months studying abroad in China had a profound effect on me. When I think back to my semesters spent in Beijing and Harbin, the words *epic, bizarre,* and *eye-opening* come to mind. I invested my time in learning Mandarin, seeking to understand the Chinese country and people, and having a blast while doing so. In the process, I developed a fervent affection for anything Chinese and a desire to share this affection with others.

**2**    Fortunately, I was provided with an appropriate outlet for this in serving as a China Education Tours CET Campus Ambassador. As a Campus Ambassador, I have had the privilege of helping create a rich environment at Kalamazoo College for the celebration and spread of Chinese culture. Also, I have interested curious underclassmen in cross-culturalism. I have accomplished this by using media technology, organizing cultural events, and providing direct venues for younger students to learn more about China.

*Thesis statement*

*Note details about how the writer shared information*

**3**    One way I spread Chinese culture and internationalism on my campus was by using media and technology. I made sure that every person studying Chinese at Kalamazoo College was exposed in some way to China from a CET perspective. For the freshman and sophomore Chinese classes, I prepared a PowerPoint presentation entitled "What Will I Encounter in China?" complete with photos and videos that I took while I was in China. I also printed 49 of these photos and posted them on the school's China bulletin board, which hangs in a place where it is seen by many students every day. Finally, I published three newspaper articles about my study abroad experience and shared them with my school. Of these three feature articles, one was selected by our Chinese professor to be reading material for an upcoming spring seminar on Chinese food culture.

*Topic sentence*

*Details about how photos were used*

**4**    Another way I spread internationalism on my campus was by organizing cultural events. I played a leading role in organizing the first annual Chinese New Year Party on campus, which was attended by 12% of the on-campus student population. The party featured jiaozi-making, a guzhen performance, and a showing of the recently released live-action film *Mulan*. At this event, it was obvious that all the attendees thoroughly enjoyed themselves.

*Topic sentence*

*Statistics show cause-effect*

*Inclusion of vivid details*

**5**    Finally, I created venues for underclass students of Chinese to learn more about China. In addition to presenting to both freshman- and sophomore-level classes and discussing China with various students one-on-one, I organized a "China Chat" pizza dinner which brought together 10 CET alumni and 15 underclassmen—two groups of students who rarely have the chance to mingle. This dinner allowed upperclassmen to share at great length with underclassmen about their experiences abroad, piquing the curiosity of the underclass students and fueling their desire to experience Asia. After dinner, I showed video footage about study abroad and explained a variety of interesting tidbits about life in China, such as transportation, street food, and even squat toilets. As I was cleaning up after the dinner, five particularly eager students waited afterwards to ask me even more questions about life in Beijing.

*Topic sentence*

*Specific details about information that was shared*

*Shows effect of the talk*

**6**    The school year is not yet finished, but I have already had countless conversations in which I have related my study abroad experience to those at Kalamazoo College. I am not shy about admitting to an infection of the China bug, and I'm pleased to report that I've managed to spread it to others.

*Conclusion: writer reflects on what he has accomplished*

## Examining Writing

1. Evaluate Sturm's use of detail. Which paragraphs have sufficient detail? Which, if any, paragraphs could use more detail?

2. Evaluate Sturm's use of transitions. How does he lead you from one example to another?

3. Look at Sturm's conclusion. How well does it summarize the essay?

## Writing Assignments

1. Write a paragraph evaluating the ways Jamie Sturm got students interested in studying in China. What methods appealed to you? What other methods could he have used?

2. Write a paragraph explaining why study abroad is or is not appealing to you.

3. Write an essay describing where you would study abroad (or elsewhere in this country) if you had the chance, why, and what you would hope to learn.

## READ AND RESPOND: A Professional Essay

### Thinking Before Reading

The following article, "The Most Hateful Words," taken from Amy Tan's book *The Opposite of Fate*, describes a daughter's relationship with her mother. As you read, notice how the author uses various types of detail to convey the main ideas of the essay.

1. Preview the reading, using the steps discussed in Chapter 1, page 15.

2. Connect the reading to your own experience by answering the following questions:

   a. In what situations have you heard "hateful words" being used?

   b. Have you ever regretted things that you have said?

3. Mark and annotate as you read.

# The Most Hateful Words

## Amy Tan

Amy Tan

1    The most hateful words I have ever said to another human being were to my mother. I was sixteen at the time. They rose from the storm in my chest and I let them fall in a fury of hailstones: "I hate you. I wish I were dead. . . ."

2    I waited for her to collapse, stricken by what I had just said. She was still standing upright, her chin tilted, her lips stretched in a crazy smile. "Okay, maybe I die too," she said between huffs. "Then I no longer be your mother!" We had many similar exchanges. Sometimes she actually tried to kill herself by running into the street, holding a knife to her throat. She too had storms in her chest. And what she aimed at me was as fast and deadly as a lightning bolt.

3    For days after our arguments, she would not speak to me. She tormented me, acted as if she had no feelings for me whatsoever. I was lost to her. And because of that, I lost, battle after battle, all of them: the times she criticized me, humiliated me in front of others, forbade me to do this or that without even listening to one good reason why it should be the other way. I swore to myself I would never forget these injustices. I would store them, harden my heart, make myself as impenetrable as she was.

4     I remember this now, because I am also remembering another time, just a few years ago. I was forty-seven, had become a different person by then, had become a fiction writer, someone who uses memory and imagination. In fact, I was writing a story about a girl and her mother, when the phone rang.

5     It was my mother, and this surprised me. Had someone helped her make the call? For a few years now, she had been losing her mind through Alzheimer's disease. Early on, she forgot to lock her door. Then she forgot where she lived. She forgot who many people were and what they had meant to her. Lately, she could no longer remember many of her worries and sorrows.

6     "Amy-ah," she said, and she began to speak quickly in Chinese. "Something is wrong with my mind. I think I'm going crazy."

7     I caught my breath. Usually she could barely speak more than two words at a time. "Don't worry," I started to say.

8     "It's true," she went on. "I feel like I can't remember many things. I can't remember what I did yesterday. I can't remember what happened a long time ago, what I did to you. . . ." She spoke as a drowning person might if she had bobbed to the surface with the force of will to live, only to see how far she had already drifted, how impossibly far she was from the shore.

9     She spoke frantically: "I know I did something to hurt you."

10     "You didn't," I said. "Don't worry."

11     "I did terrible things. But now I can't remember what. . . . And I just want to tell you . . . I hope you can forget, just as I've forgotten."

12     I tried to laugh so she would not notice the cracks in my voice. "Really, don't worry."

13     "Okay, I just wanted you to know."

14     After we hung up, I cried, both happy and sad. I was again that sixteen-year-old, but the storm in my chest was gone.

**bequeathed**
handed down, passed on

15     My mother died six months later. By then she had **bequeathed** to me her most healing words, as open and eternal as a clear blue sky. Together we knew in our hearts what we should remember, what we can forget.

# Getting Ready to Write

## Checking Your Comprehension

Answer each of the following questions using complete sentences.

1.  How did Tan's mother react to Amy's "most hateful words"?
2.  How did these arguments affect their relationship?
3.  What mental problems did Tan's mother face later in life?
4.  What healing words did Tan's mother offer?

## Strengthening Your Vocabulary

Using the word's context, word parts, or a dictionary, write a brief definition of each of the following words as it is used in the reading.

1.  humiliated (paragraph 3) _____

2.  injustices (paragraph 3) _____

3. impenetrable (paragraph 3) _____

4. bobbed (paragraph 8) _____

5. eternal (paragraph 15) _____

## Examining the Reading: Recognizing Types of Supporting Details

Before you can write about an author's ideas, you must understand how that author supports and explains his or her main points. Tan uses a variety of details. Specifically, she uses anecdotes (stories) and dialogue (conversation) to support her ideas. She also uses lively verbs and descriptive words and phrases to make her writing interesting.

Analyze Tan's use of supporting detail by indicating in which paragraphs she uses:

1. anecdotes _____

2. dialogue _____

3. specific verbs _____

4. adjectives to add detail _____

## Reacting to Ideas: Discussion and Journal Writing

Get ready to write about the reading by discussing the following:

1. Why do you think parents and children often have trouble getting along?

2. Discuss how the relationships between parents and children change as they get older.

3. What pressures do young people face today that they did not in the past? What do you see as the big challenges for the youth of the future?

**THINKING VISUALLY**

4. A photo of Amy Tan accompanies the reading. What other photos or visuals could accompany the reading that would contribute to its meaning?

## Thinking and Writing Critically

1. In paragraph 2, the author says her mother "had storms in her chest. And what she aimed at me was as fast and deadly as a lightning bolt." Write a paragraph explaining what Tan means by this statement.

2. Of all the hurts imposed by Amy Tan's mother, which is the worst in the author's eyes? Why?

3. Does Amy Tan ever apologize to her mother for saying the most hateful words? How much responsibility does Amy have for her troubled relationship with her mother? Write a paragraph in which you explore the answers to these questions.

MySkillsLab®

Complete
this
Exercise

# Writing About the Reading

## Paragraph Options

1. Tan describes what she felt were the most hateful words she has ever spoken. Write a paragraph describing words that you regret speaking.

2. Write a paragraph describing a difficult relationship you had with someone. What factors or circumstances made it so hard? Were you able to improve the relationship?

3. Tan and her mother had communication problems when Tan was a teenager. Write an essay about a communication problem you have experienced with a family member. Give details that make the problem clear. Try to identify the causes of the problem and describe how the problem was resolved.

4. Tan says she had become another person later in her life. Write a paragraph describing how you have changed, or become a different person, since you started college.

### Essay Options

5. The author felt that her mother treated her unfairly. Write an essay about a time when you felt you were being treated unfairly. Describe the situation and explain how you dealt with it.

6. Tan's mother's healing words were a gift, but it was an intangible one—one that she could not touch or see. Write an essay about an intangible gift someone has given you.

7. Tan describes her words as being "hateful." Write an essay about the most hateful words you have heard. You might write about a personal experience or you might write about words you have seen or heard in local, national, or international events or news.

8. Tan and her mother knew what they should remember and what they should forget. Write an essay explaining what you hope people will remember about you.

9. Everyone has faults, and it is sometimes necessary to overlook them to build or maintain a relationship. Write about characteristics you have tried to forget or overlook in a person you care about.

# SELF-TEST SUMMARY

To test yourself, cover the Answer column with a sheet of paper and answer each question in the left column. Evaluate each of your answers as you work by sliding the paper down and comparing your answer with what is printed in the Answer column.

| QUESTION | ANSWER |
| --- | --- |
| ■ GOAL 1 Understand details, transitions, and implied main ideas<br><br>What are details, transitions, and implied main ideas? | Supporting details are facts and ideas that prove or explain a paragraph's main idea. Transitions are linking words and phrases that pull the paragraph together by connecting the details. Implied main ideas are thoughts suggested but not directly stated in a topic sentence. |

*(continued)*

(*continued*)

| QUESTION | ANSWER |
|---|---|
| ■ GOAL 2 **Identify supporting details**<br><br>What is the difference between major and minor details?<br><br>What are the most common types of supporting details? | Major details directly explain a paragraph's main idea. Minor details provide additional information, offer an example, or further explain a major detail.<br><br>The most common types of supporting details are *examples, facts or statistics, reasons, descriptions,* and *steps or procedures.* |
| ■ GOAL 3 **Think critically about details**<br><br>How can you think critically about details? | Analyze the details the writer has chosen to include. Consider whether the writer has omitted important details or used specific words to influence you. |
| ■ GOAL 4 **Use transitions to guide your reading**<br><br>How do transitions guide your reading? | Transitions lead you from one idea to another. See Table 6-1 for a list of common transitions used within a paragraph and what they tell you. |
| ■ GOAL 5 **Find implied main ideas**<br><br>How do you find an implied main idea? | To find an implied main idea, first find the topic. Next, figure out what is the most important idea the writer wants you to know about that topic. Finally, express this main idea in your own words. |
| ■ GOAL 6 **Select and organize details to support your topic sentence**<br><br>How do you select and organize details? | ■ Use relevant details that directly explain and support the topic sentence.<br>■ Use *sufficient* (enough) details to make your topic sentence understandable and convincing.<br>■ Use a variety of details to develop your topic sentence: *time sequence, spatial,* and *least-to-most arrangements.*<br>■ Use specific words and phrases to help your readers create a mental picture of the place, person, or event you are describing. Choose action words, give exact names, include adjectives, and choose words that appeal to the senses. |
| ■ GOAL 7 **Use transitional words and phrases to connect details**<br><br>How do transitional words and phrases signal what is to follow? | Transitional words and phrases indicate the arrangement of ideas in a paragraph. See Table 6-2 for a list of common transitions for each method of arranging details. |

For more help with **Details, Transitions, and Implied Main Ideas**, go to your learning path in MySkillsLab at www.myskillslab.com.

# Organization: Basic Patterns

## 7

LEARNING
### GOALS
Learn how to . . .

■ **GOAL 1**
Identify patterns
of organization

■ **GOAL 2**
Read and write using
time sequence: chrono-
logical order, process,
and narration

■ **GOAL 3**
Read and write using
description

■ **GOAL 4**
Read and write using
example

■ **GOAL 5**
Think critically
about patterns
of organization

## THINK About It!

Study the photograph above. Assume it appeared on an animal rights activism Web site. Write a sentence explaining what impression or feeling the photograph creates.

Suppose you volunteer for an activist group that opposes keeping wild animals in captivity solely for human entertainment. You have been asked to help draft an article to submit to the local newspaper explaining the group's mission. In order to write an effective article, you might first read about animals in captivity, learning how they are treated and the problems they face. Next, you would plan how to write the article, considering various effective ways to develop it. One way you might develop the article would be to narrate—or tell the story— of a particular animal, following it from capture through captivity. Another method would be to describe animals in captivity, focusing on their living conditions, behavioral problems, and health issues. A third approach might be to make a statement that wild animals have a poor quality of life in captivity and support this statement with examples of particular animals. These three methods, *narration*, *description*, and *example*, are effective ways to develop your ideas. These methods could also be used to write an essay from the oppos-ing viewpoint—that keeping animals in captivity preserves species, saves lives, and builds public awareness and appreciation. You will learn how to read and write each of these methods in this chapter.

# Reading and Writing Connections

### EVERYDAY CONNECTIONS

- **Reading** You read a review of a new restaurant in which the reviewer vividly describes the restaurant's warm and inviting atmosphere and recommends several delicious-sounding items on the menu.
- **Writing** You write an e-mail to a friend explaining that the new restaurant is pricey by giving examples of the costs of specific menu items such as fried shrimp and Caesar salad.

### ACADEMIC CONNECTIONS

- **Reading** You read a section of an American government text called "The Presidency" that describes the process of impeachment as written in the Constitution.
- **Writing** For an assignment in American government, you write a summary of the series of events leading up to the impeachment and acquittal of President Bill Clinton.

### WORKPLACE CONNECTIONS

- **Writing** As an EMT (emergency medical technician), you write a report detailing your response to a 911 call involving a gas leak at a home near an elementary school.
- **Reading** Your supervisor reads the memo and suggests alternative measures you could have taken to evacuate students more quickly.

## FOCUSING ON READING AND WRITING

# What Are Patterns of Organization?

■ **GOAL 1**
Identify patterns
of organization

There are several ways to organize a paragraph or essay, and writers use a variety of **patterns of organization**, depending on what they want to accomplish. These patterns, then, are the different ways that writers present their ideas.

To help you think a bit about patterns, complete each of the following steps:

1. Study each of the drawings on the following page for a few seconds (count to ten as you look at each one).
2. Cover up the drawings and try to draw each from memory.
3. Check to see how many you had exactly correct.

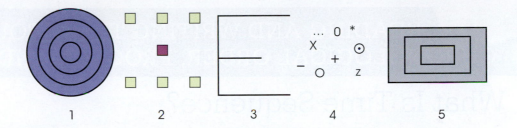

You probably drew all but the fourth correctly. Why do you think you got that one wrong? How does it differ from the others?

Drawings 1, 2, 3, and 5 have patterns. Drawing 4, however, has no pattern; it is just a group of randomly arranged symbols.

From this experiment you can see that it is easier to remember drawings that have a pattern—a clear form of organization. The same is true of written material. If you can see how a paragraph or essay is organized, it is easier to understand and remember. In this chapter you will learn about some of the common patterns writers use and how to recognize them: (1) time sequence (chronological order, process, and narration), (2) description, and (3) example.

Separate sections of this chapter are devoted to reading and writing using each of the following patterns of organization:

| METHOD OF DEVELOPMENT | WHAT IT DOES | AN EXAMPLE OF ITS USE |
|---|---|---|
| Chronological order | Explains events in the order in which they occurred | Telling the history of cake making since ancient times |
| Process | Explains how something is done or how something works | Explaining how to make a cake |
| Narration | Tells a story that makes a point | Telling a story that involves cake |
| Description | Uses sensory details to help the reader visualize a topic | Describing the look, taste, texture, or flavor of cake |
| Example | Explains a concept by giving concrete instances that demonstrate what it is | Giving examples of celebrations in which cake is served |

Patterns of organization are useful to both readers and writers. They help writers pull together their ideas and present them in a clear and logical manner. They help readers by enabling them to see how information is related, making it easier to understand and remember.

Additional patterns of organization will be covered in Chapter 8. By learning to identify and use each pattern, you will develop a variety of new approaches to reading and writing paragraphs.

## READING AND WRITING TIME SEQUENCE: CHRONOLOGICAL ORDER, PROCESS, AND NARRATION

# What Is Time Sequence?

■ **GOAL 2**
Read and write using time sequence: chronological order, process, and narration

The terms chronological order and process both refer to the order in which something occurs or is done. When writers tell a story, they usually present events in **chronological order**. In other words, they start with the first event, continue with the second, and so on. For example, if you were telling a friend about finding a new part-time job, you would probably start by explaining how you found out about the job, continue by describing your interview, and end with the result—the manager was impressed with you and hired you on the spot. You would put events in order according to the *time* they occurred, beginning with the first event. **Process** is a pattern used to explain how something is done or how something works. For example, a writer might explain how to change a flat tire or describe how a tornado is formed. **Narration** is another pattern that uses time sequence to tell a story. Whether you are reading or writing, time sequence is used whenever ideas are organized according to the order in which they occurred.

You can visualize and draw the chronological order and process patterns as follows:

**VISUALIZE IT!**

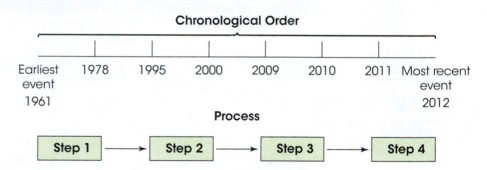

**Chronological Order**

| Earliest event 1961 | 1978 | 1995 | 2000 | 2009 | 2010 | 2011 | Most recent event 2012 |

**Process**

Step 1 → Step 2 → Step 3 → Step 4

# Reading Chronological Order and Process

When you read stories for an English class or material in a history or political science text, you will often encounter chronological order. When writers use this pattern, they often include time transitions, such as *first*, *next*, and *finally* (see box on p. 211). They may also use actual dates to help readers keep track of the sequence of events.

> Organized baseball teams first emerged in the 1840s, but the game only became truly popular during the Civil War, when it was a major form of camp recreation for the troops. After the war professional teams began to appear, and in 1876 teams in eight cities formed the National League. The American League followed in 1901. After a brief period of rivalry, the two leagues made peace in 1903, the year of the first World Series.
>
> —adapted from Garraty and Carnes, *The American Nation*, p. 518

As you can see in this paragraph from a history text, the writers use chronological order to discuss the evolution of organized baseball. They use several phrases to show the reader the time sequence—*in the 1840s, during the Civil War, After the war, in 1876, in 1901,* and *in 1903.* As you read, look for such phrases as well as for time transitions.

Writers also follow a time sequence when they use the **process pattern**—when they explain how something is done or made. When writers explain how to put together a bookcase, how to knit a sweater, or how bees make honey, they use steps to show the appropriate order.

> To make a basic white sauce, follow a few easy steps. First, melt two tablespoons of butter over low heat. Next, add two tablespoons of flour and stir until the flour and butter are combined. Then add one cup of milk and continue stirring over low heat. Finally, when the mixture has thickened, add salt and pepper, or other seasonings, to taste.

This writer uses four time transitions—*first, next, then,* and *finally*—to make the order clear for the reader. Note that she also uses the word *steps* in the topic sentence. In the process pattern and in other patterns as well, the topic sentence often provides a clue as to the kind of pattern that will be used.

### Common Time Sequence Transitions

| | | | | | |
|---|---|---|---|---|---|
| *after* | *as soon as* | *finally* | *in addition* | *meanwhile* | *then* |
| *also* | *before* | *first* | *last* | *next* | *until* |
| *another* | *during* | *following* | *later* | *second* | *when* |

**EXERCISE 7-1**

## Understanding Chronological Order and Process

**Directions:** Using either chronological order or process, put each of the following groups of sentences in the correct order. For each sentence, write a number from 1 to 4 in the space provided, beginning with the topic sentence.

1. _____ Rail travel originated in Europe in 1825, and four years later, North America welcomed the advent of passenger rail service.

   _____ Transcontinental service began in the United States in 1869 and in Canada in 1885.

   _____ Passenger rail service has been an important form of domestic transportation for more than 175 years.

   _____ In 1875 Fred Harvey introduced the golden age of passenger railroad service in the U.S., with the addition of dining cars and lodging facilities.
   —adapted from Cook, Yale, and Marqua, *Tourism: The Business of Travel*, p. 102

2. _____    Next, chemicals are released that attract even more platelets to the site.

   _____    Basically, once damage has occurred, blood elements called platelets immediately begin to cling to the injured site.

   _____    This rapidly growing pile-up of platelets initiates the sequence of events that finally forms a clot.

   _____    Blood clotting is a normal response to a break in the lining of a blood vessel.
   —adapted from Marieb, *Human Anatomy & Physiology*, p. 13

3. _____    A gold rush into Colorado in 1859 sent thousands of greedy prospectors across the Plains to drive the Cheyenne and Arapaho from land guaranteed them in 1851.

   _____    Thus it happened that in 1862, most of the Plains Indians rose up against the whites.

   _____    The American government showed no interest in honoring agreements with Indians.

   _____    By 1860 most of Kansas and Nebraska had been cleared, while other trouble developed in the Sioux country.
   —adapted from Garraty and Carnes, *The American Nation*, p. 455

4. _____    Once the defendant appears at the trial, the bail bond is refunded.

   _____    When a person is arrested for a crime, he or she is taken to court and bail is set.

   _____    The defendant is required to appear in person for the trial date, or the court keeps the entire bond that was posted.

   _____    The person who is arrested (defendant) can pay the bail herself or himself, or a bail bondsperson can be paid a fee to post the bond, and the defendant is then released until trial.

5. _____    In the final stage, disorientation is often complete, and the person becomes completely dependent on others for eating, dressing, and other activities.

   _____    These symptoms accelerate in the second stage, which also includes agitation and restlessness, loss of sensory perceptions, muscle twitching, and repetitive actions.

   _____    During the first stage, symptoms include forgetfulness, memory loss, impaired judgment, increasing inability to handle routine tasks, disorientation, and depression.

   _____    Alzheimer's disease is characteristically diagnosed in three stages.
   —adapted from Donatelle and Davis, *Access to Health*, p. 533

# Writing Process Paragraphs

A process is a series of steps or actions that one follows in a particular order to accomplish something. When you assemble a toy, bake a cake, rebuild an engine, or put up a tent, you do things in a specific order. A **process paragraph** explains the steps to follow in completing a process. The steps are given in the order in which they are done. Here is a sample process paragraph. In it, the student writer explains how copyediting is done at his college's student newspaper.

The Fourth Estate's copyediting process is not very complicated. First, articles are submitted in electronic format and are read by Merren, the copy editor. Next, she makes changes and ensures all the articles are in their proper place. Then, section editors have a day to read the stories for their sections and make changes. Finally, all articles, photographs, cartoons, and anything else to be included in the upcoming issue is read and fact-checked by the editor-in-chief.

In this paragraph the writer identifies four steps. Notice that they are presented in the order in which they happen. You can visualize a process paragraph as follows. Study the model and the map that are given below for the paragraph above.

**VISUALIZE IT!**

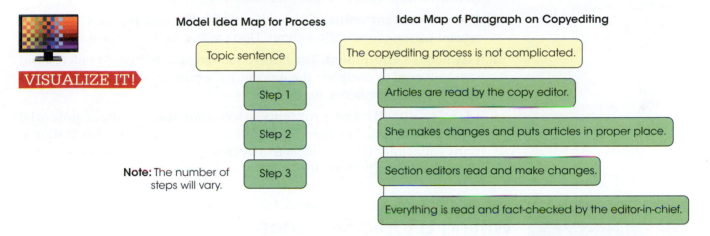

**Model Idea Map for Process**

Topic sentence

Step 1

Step 2

**Note:** The number of steps will vary.

Step 3

**Idea Map of Paragraph on Copyediting**

The copyediting process is not complicated.

Articles are read by the copy editor.

She makes changes and puts articles in proper place.

Section editors read and make changes.

Everything is read and fact-checked by the editor-in-chief.

There are two types of process paragraphs—a "how-to" paragraph and a "how-it-works" paragraph:

- **A "how-to" paragraph explains how something is done.** For example, it may explain how to change a flat tire, aid a choking victim, or locate a reference source in the library.
- **A "how-it-works" paragraph explains how something operates or happens.** For example, it may explain the operation of a pump, how the human body regulates temperature, or how children acquire speech.

Developing a process paragraph involves writing a topic sentence and explaining each step clearly and thoroughly.

## Writing a Topic Sentence

For a process paragraph, your topic sentence should accomplish two things:

1. **It should identify the process or procedure.**
2. **It should explain to your reader why familiarity with it is useful, interesting, or important (*why* he or she should learn about the process).** Your topic sentence should state a goal, offer a reason, or indicate what can be accomplished by using the process.

Here are a few examples of topic sentences that contain both of these important elements:

Reading maps, a vital skill if you are taking vacations by car, is a simple process, except for the final refolding.

Because reading is an essential skill, all parents should know how to interest their children in recreational reading.

To locate information on the Internet, you must know how to use a search engine.

## Explaining the Steps

Use the following tips when explaining each step in a process:

1. **Include only essential, necessary steps.** Avoid comments, opinions, and unnecessary information because they may confuse your reader.

2. **Assume that your reader is unfamiliar with your topic** (unless you know otherwise). Be sure to define unfamiliar terms and describe clearly any technical or specialized tools, procedures, or objects.

3. **Use a consistent point of view.** Use either the first person ("I") or the second person ("you") throughout. Don't switch between them.

4. **List needed equipment.** For how-to paragraphs, tell your readers what they will need to complete the process. For a how-to paragraph on making chili, list the ingredients, for example.

5. **Identify pitfalls and problems.** Alert your readers about potential problems and places where confusion or error may occur. For instance, warn your chili-making readers to add chili peppers gradually and to taste the chili frequently along the way.

### EXERCISE 7-2

**WRITING IN PROGRESS**

## Writing a Topic Sentence

**Directions:** Write a topic sentence for one of the topics listed below. Then write a paragraph using the tips listed above.

1. How to have an exciting vacation
2. How to cure an illness
3. How to shop on the Internet
4. How to build or repair _____
5. How _____ works

## How to Organize a Process Paragraph

Process paragraphs should be organized sequentially according to the order in which the steps are done or occur. It is usually a good idea to place your topic sentence first. Placing it in this position provides your reader with a purpose for reading. Be sure to use transitional words and phrases to signal your readers that you are moving from one step to another. Common transitions are listed in the box on page 211.

### EXERCISE 7-3

**WRITING IN PROGRESS**

## Adding Transitions

**Directions:** Revise the draft you wrote for Exercise 7-3. Check transitional words and phrases and add more, if necessary, to make your ideas clearer.

# Reading Narration

**Narration** is similar to chronological order and process but it differs in one respect—it shapes events to make a point. Chronological order and process are used in textbooks and other types of writing intended to explain, but narration is used in essays where the purpose is to present a viewpoint or tell a story. For example, in a paralegal textbook the writer may discuss the process of mediation, in which a neutral third party (the mediator) helps settle a dispute. In a narrative essay, the writer might describe his family's use of mediation in resolving a dispute with a neighbor and make the point that mediation is a valuable alternative to filing a lawsuit.

**EXERCISE 7-4**

## Understanding Narration

**Directions:** For each paragraph below, identify the main point of the writer's narrative and write it in the space provided.

1.  At one time, passenger pigeons were the most numerous species of birds in North America and perhaps in the world. They nested and migrated in huge flocks and probably numbered in the billions. When flocks passed overhead, the sky would be dark with pigeons for days at a time. Although the Native Americans had long hunted these birds, the demise of the passenger pigeon is usually tied to the arrival of the Europeans, who increased the demand for pigeons as a source of food and sport. The birds were shot and netted in vast numbers; by the end of the nineteenth century, an animal species that had been looked on as almost indestructible because of its enormous numbers had almost completely disappeared. The last known passenger pigeon died in the Cincinnati Zoo in 1914.

    —Miller et al., *The Economics of Public Issues*, pp. 163–164

    Main point: _____

2.  After Arun Bharat Ram returned to India with a degree from the University of Michigan, his mother announced that she wanted to find him a wife. Arun would be a good catch anywhere: 27 years old, educated, well mannered, intelligent, handsome—and, not incidentally, heir to a huge fortune. Arun's mother already had someone in mind. Manju came from a middle-class family and was a college graduate. Arun and Manju met in a coffee shop at a luxury hotel—along with both sets of parents. He found her pretty and quiet. He liked that. She was impressed that he didn't boast about his background. After four more meetings, including one at which the two young people met by themselves, the parents asked their children whether they were willing to marry. Neither had any major objections.

    —Henslin, *Essentials of Sociology*, p. 337

    Main point: _____

3.  Coffee is one drink that people enjoy the world over. Coffee was first used by nomads in Ethiopia, where, according to legend, it was discovered by a goatherd who noticed that goats exhibited unusual energy after eating the red berries. The goatherd, named Kaldi, tried the berries himself and experienced an energy surge. A monk from a nearby monastery boiled the berries to make a drink, the

ancestor of coffee as we know it today. Sometime between 1000 and 1300, coffee was made into a beverage. And although some authorities date coffee's earliest cultivation to late-sixth-century Yemen, coffee isn't mentioned in literature until the end of the first millennium.

—Benton and DiYanni, *Arts and Culture*, p. 576

Main point: _____

# Writing Narration Paragraphs

The technique of making a point by telling a story is called **narration**. Narration is *not* simply listing a series of events—"this happened, then that happened." Narration shapes and interprets events to make a point. Notice the difference between the two paragraphs below.

> **Paragraph 1: Series of Events**
>
> Last Sunday we visited the National Zoo in Washington, D.C. As we entered, we decided to see the panda bear, the elephants, and the giraffes. All were outside enjoying the springlike weather. Then we visited the bat cave. I was amazed at how closely bats pack together in a small space. Finally, we went into the monkey house. There we spent time watching the giant apes watch us.

> **Paragraph 2: Narrative**
>
> Last Sunday's visit to the National Zoo in Washington, D.C., was a lesson to me about animals in captivity. First, we visited the panda, the elephants, and the giraffes. All seemed slow moving and locked into a dull routine—pacing around their yards. Then we watched the seals. Their trainer had them perform stunts for their food; they would never do these stunts in the wild. Finally, we stopped at the monkey house, where sad, old apes stared at us and watched kids point at them. The animals did not seem happy or content with their lives.

The first paragraph retells events in the order in which they happened, but with no shaping of the story. The second paragraph, a narrative, also presents events in the order in which they happened, but uses these events to make a point: animals kept in captivity are unhappy. Thus, all details and events work together to support that point. You can visualize a narrative paragraph as follows. Study the model and the map for paragraph 2.

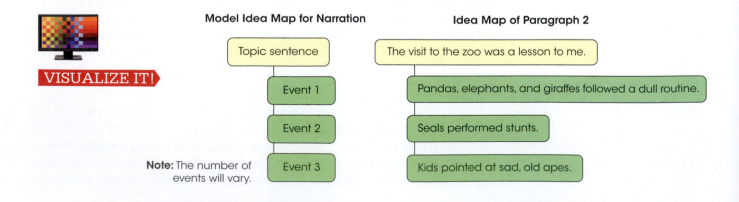

**VISUALIZE IT!**

**Model Idea Map for Narration**

Topic sentence

Event 1

Event 2

**Note:** The number of events will vary.

Event 3

**Idea Map of Paragraph 2**

The visit to the zoo was a lesson to me.

Pandas, elephants, and giraffes followed a dull routine.

Seals performed stunts.

Kids pointed at sad, old apes.

Developing a narrative paragraph involves writing a topic sentence and presenting sufficient details to support it.

## Writing a Clear Topic Sentence

Your topic sentence should accomplish two things:

1. **It should identify your topic.**
2. **It should reveal your attitude toward your topic.**

For example, suppose you are writing about visiting a zoo. Your topic sentence could take your narrative in a variety of directions, each of which would reveal a very different attitude toward the experience.

- During my recent visit to the zoo, I was saddened by the animals' behavior in captivity.
- A recent visit to the zoo gave my children a lesson in geography.
- My recent visit to the zoo taught me more about human nature than about animals.

**EXERCISE 7-5**

**WRITING IN PROGRESS**

## Writing Topic Sentences

**Directions:** Complete three of the following topic sentences by adding information that describes an experience you have had related to the topic.

**Example**   **My first job** *was an experience I would rather forget.*

1. Holidays _____

2. A frightening event _____

3. My first day on campus _____

4. Cell phones _____

5. My advisor/instructor _____

## Including Sufficient Details

A narrative paragraph should include enough detail to support your topic sentence and allow your reader to understand fully the experience you are writing about. Be sure you have answered most of the following questions:

- *What* events occurred?
- *Where* did they happen?
- *When* did they happen?
- *Who* was involved?
- *Why* did they happen?
- *How* did they happen?

## EXERCISE 7-6
**WRITING IN PROGRESS**

# Brainstorming Details

**Directions:** Using one of the topic sentences you wrote in Exercise 7-5, brainstorm a list of relevant and sufficient details to support it.

## How to Organize a Narrative Paragraph

The events in a narrative are usually arranged in the order in which they happened. Transitions are especially important in narrative paragraphs because they identify and separate events from one another. Useful transitions are shown in the box on page 211.

## EXERCISE 7-7
**WRITING IN PROGRESS**

# Using Time Sequence Transitions

**Directions:** Using the topic sentence you wrote in Exercise 7-5, and the relevant and sufficient details you generated in Exercise 7-6, present your details in time sequence order, using transitions as needed.

# READING AND WRITING DESCRIPTION

# What Is Description?

■ **GOAL 3**
Read and write using description

**Descriptive writing** involves using words and phrases that appeal to the senses—taste, touch, smell, sight, and hearing. As a writer, your task is to use language to help your readers visualize or imagine an object, person, place, or experience. As a reader, your task is to pay attention to these descriptive details, examine what they reveal, and take away an impression or overall feeling of the item being described. Below is a sample paragraph on the preparation of chili.

> My favorite chili recipe requires a trip to the grocery store and a day to hang around the kitchen stirring, but it is well worth the expense and time. Canned, shiny red kidney beans and fat, great white northern beans simmer in the big pot, while ground beef and kielbasa sizzle and spit in a cast-iron skillet. Raw white onions bring tears to one's eyes, and they are quickly chopped. Plump yellow and orange peppers are chopped to add fiber and flavor, while six cloves of garlic, smashed, make simmering all day a necessity. When it cooks, this chili makes the whole house smell mouthwateringly good. When eaten, chunks of kielbasa stand out in a spicy, garlicky sauce with small nuggets of ground beef.

You can visualize and draw the descriptive pattern as shown on the next page.

**VISUALIZE IT!**

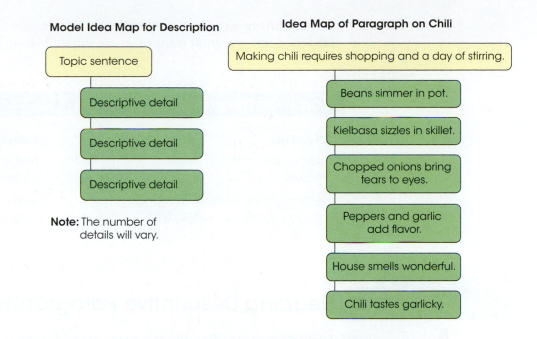

The writer of this paragraph described sights, sounds, smells, and colors of the chili-making process. As you read the paragraph what did you sense and feel? Could you almost smell the onions yourself, for example? And did it leave you with an impression that chili making is worth the work it involves?

# Reading Description

A descriptive paragraph has three key features—an *overall impression, sensory details*, and *descriptive language*. As you read descriptive writing, pay attention to each of these features.

1. **The overall impression**. The **overall impression** is the one central idea the piece of writing presents. It is the single, main point that all of the details prove or support. To find the overall impression, ask yourself, "What do all these details and descriptions, taken together, mean or suggest?" Often, this dominant impression is unstated; it is left for you to infer.

2. **Sensory details**. Each detail is important, but the details, when added together, create the overall impression. Be careful not to skip details, and for each, consider what it contributes to the overall meaning. For example, in the description of a man, the detail that his hair was uncombed by itself does not mean much. However, when added together with details that his nails were dirty, his shirt unevenly buttoned, and his shoes untied, the writer creates the impression of the person as careless and unkempt.

3. **Descriptive language**. **Descriptive language** uses words that create a visual or imaginary picture of the topic. Descriptive language brings the topic to life, so to speak. As you read, be sure to read slowly enough to allow the language to "sink in." Mark and annotate particularly striking or unusual words and phrases, too. Stop and reflect, too, about why a particularly descriptive phrase was chosen.

When writing a descriptive paragraph, writers use transitions to orient their readers. Some common transitions are shown below.

---

### Common Description: Transitions

| Spatial | Least/Most |
|---|---|
| *above, below, beside, inside, outside* | *first, primarily, second, secondarily* |
| *across, facing, in front of, nearby, next to, to the left, to the right* | *also important, most important* |

---

### EXERCISE 7-8

## Reading Descriptive Paragraphs

**Directions:** Underline the topic sentence in each of the following paragraphs and highlight particularly descriptive details.

1.     Michelangelo's restless, unceasing quest for perfection helps explain why he was not content to stay only with the art of sculpture. He also aspired to be the greatest painter the world had ever known. His biggest challenge—even greater than that of the seventeen-foot block of marble that became *David*—was a task given him by Pope Julius II: to paint the ceiling of the Sistine Chapel inside the Vatican. Michelangelo's imagination was immediately stirred. There was the height itself, as close to heaven as his art was ever likely to take him. There was the huge expanse of the ceiling, allowing for a series of paintings on religious themes that would at the same time present to the viewer a totally unified effect. And there was the challenge that fresco posed, for the plaster had to be applied to the ceiling and painted before it was completely dry. Legend has it that the artist worked almost single-handedly for four long years, lying on his back for hours at a time while plaster continually dripped down on his face. But Michelangelo was both passionate and businesslike in his work. He had assistants, and the project was carefully planned—and kept secret even from the pope until the gasp-filled unveiling.
   —Janaro and Altshuler, *The Art of Being Human*, p. 136

2.     Desert landscapes frequently appear stark. Their profiles are not softened by a carpet of soil and abundant plant life. Instead, barren rocky outcrops with steep, angular slopes are common. At some places the rocks are tinted orange and red. At others they are gray and brown and streaked with black. For many visitors, desert scenery exhibits a striking beauty; to others the terrain seems bleak. No matter which feeling is elicited, it is clear that deserts are very different from the more humid places where most people live.
   —Lutgens et al., *Essentials of Geology*, p. 272

3.     "Love of the good life" seems to be the creed of many Italians, although the bursts of song from Venetian gondoliers and the cheers from opera-goers may be just a bit

more muted today than in earlier years. Still, the highlight of Italian daily life has to be the food! The tantalizing aromas that waft from dishes created with wonderful olive oil, garlic, tomato, balsamic vinegar, mushrooms, and perhaps a bit of pesto simply entice the lucky diner. Don't forget the wonderful Italian breads, often washed down with a hearty red wine. Then, if there is still a bit of room for it, a gelato (ice cream) may be the perfect ending to a leisurely and sensually gratifying dining experience.

—adapted from McWilliams, *Food Around the World*, p. 149

# Writing a Descriptive Paragraphs

A descriptive paragraph has three key features, an overall impression, sensory details, and descriptive language.

1. **Create an overall impression.** The **overall impression** is the *one* central idea you want to present to your reader. It is the single, main point that all of your details prove or support. For example, if you are writing a paragraph about your math instructor's sense of humor, then all of your details should be about amusing things he or she has said or done. Your overall impression should be expressed in your topic sentence, usually at the beginning of the paragraph. Notice that each of the following topic sentences expresses a different overall impression of Niagara Falls:

   > Niagara Falls is stunningly beautiful and majestic.
   >
   > The beauty of Niagara Falls is hidden by its tourist-oriented, commercial surroundings.
   >
   > Niagara Falls would be beautiful to visit if I could be there alone, without the crowds of tourists.

   Your overall impression is often your first reaction to a topic. Suppose you are writing about your college snack bar. Think of a word or two that sums up how you feel about it. Is it noisy? Smelly? Relaxing? Messy? You could develop any one of these descriptive words into a paragraph. For example, your topic sentence might be:

   > The snack bar is a noisy place that I try to avoid.

   The details that follow would then describe the noise—the clatter of plates, loud conversations, chairs scraping the floor, and music blaring.

2. **Include sensory details. Sensory details** appeal to your senses—your sense of touch, taste, sight, sound, and smell. Try to imagine your topic—the person, place, thing, or experience. Depending on what your topic is, write down what it makes you see, hear, smell, taste, or feel.

3. **Use descriptive language. Descriptive language** uses words that help your readers imagine your topic and make it exciting and vivid to them. Consider the following sentences. The first is dull and lifeless; the second describes what the writer sees and feels.

| NONDESCRIPTIVE | The beach was crowded with people. |
|---|---|
| DESCRIPTIVE | The beach was overrun with teenage bodies wearing neon Lycra suits and slicked with sweet-smelling oil. |

Making your details more descriptive is not difficult. Use the guidelines below.

---

> **! NEED TO KNOW**
>
> ### Using Descriptive Details
>
> 1. **Use verbs that help your reader picture the action.**
>
>    NONDESCRIPTIVE    The boy walked down the beach.
>
>    DESCRIPTIVE    The boy ambled down the beach.
>
> 2. **Use exact names.** Include the names of people, places, brands, animals, flowers, stores, streets, products—whatever will make your description more precise.
>
>    NONDESCRIPTIVE    Kevin parked his car near the deserted beach.
>
>    DESCRIPTIVE    Kevin parked his maroon Saturn convertible at Burke's Garage next to the deserted beach.
>
> 3. **Use adjectives to describe.** Adjectives are words that describe nouns. Place them before or after nouns to add detail.
>
>    NONDESCRIPTIVE    The beach was deserted.
>
>    DESCRIPTIVE    The remote, rocky, windswept beach was deserted.
>
> 4. **Use words that appeal to the senses.** Use words that convey touch, taste, smell, sound, and sight.
>
>    NONDESCRIPTIVE    I saw big waves roll on the beach.
>
>    DESCRIPTIVE    Immense black waves rammed the shore, releasing with each crash the salty, fishy smell of the deep ocean.

---

**EXERCISE 7-9**

WRITING IN PROGRESS

## Brainstorming, Reacting, and Writing Topic Sentences

**Directions:** Brainstorm a list of words that sum up your reaction to each of the following topics. Then develop each list of words into a topic sentence that expresses an overall impression and could lead to a descriptive paragraph.

**Example**

TOPIC    A parent or guardian

REACTION    *Dad: loving, accepting, smart, helpful, calm, generous*

TOPIC SENTENCE    *My whole life, my father has been generous and helpful in the way he let me be myself.*

**1.** TOPIC            A library, gym, or other public place that you have used

   REACTION        _____

   TOPIC SENTENCE  _____

                        _____

**2.** TOPIC            A part-time job, past or present

   REACTION        _____

   TOPIC SENTENCE  _____

                        _____

**3.** TOPIC            A small shop or a shopkeeper familiar to you

   REACTION        _____

   TOPIC SENTENCE  _____

                        _____

**4.** TOPIC            A music video, movie, or song

   REACTION        _____

   TOPIC SENTENCE  _____

                        _____

**5.** TOPIC            A person in the news

   REACTION        _____

   TOPIC SENTENCE  _____

                        _____

**EXERCISE 7-10**

**WRITING IN PROGRESS**

# Brainstorming Details

**Directions:** Using one of the topic sentences you wrote in Exercise 7-9, brainstorm details that support the overall impression it conveys.

## How to Organize a Descriptive Paragraph

Among the common methods of ordering details in descriptive writing are

■ **Spatial arrangement.** You organize details according to their physical location. (See Chapter 6, p. 196, for a discussion of this method.) For example, you could describe a favorite newsstand by arranging your details from right to left or from front to back.

■ **Least/most arrangement.** You organize details in increasing or decreasing order, according to some quality or characteristic, such as importance. (See Chapter 6, p. 197, for a discussion of this method.) Suppose your overall impression of a person is that she is disorganized. You might start with some minor traits (she can never find a pen) and move to more serious and important characteristics of disorganization (she misses classes and forgets appointments).

Whatever method you choose to arrange your details, you will want to use good transitional words and phrases between details. Useful transitions are shown in the box on page 220.

**EXERCISE 7-11**

**WRITING IN PROGRESS**

## Writing a Descriptive Paragraph

**Directions:** Using the details you developed in Exercise 7-10, write a paragraph. Assume that your reader is unfamiliar with what you are describing. Use descriptive language and organize your paragraph using a spatial or least/most arrangement, and use transitions as needed.

## READING AND WRITING EXAMPLE

# What Is an Example?

■ **GOAL 4**
Read and write using example

An **example** is a specific instance or situation that explains a general idea or statement. Apples and grapes are examples of fruit. Martin Luther King Day and Thanksgiving Day are examples of national holidays. Here are a few sample general statements along with specific examples that illustrate them:

| GENERAL STATEMENT | EXAMPLES |
|---|---|
| 1. I had an exciting day. | a. My sister had her first baby. |
| | b. I got a bonus check at work. |
| | c. I reached my goal of 20 laps in the pool. |
| 2. Joe has annoying habits. | a. He interrupts me when I am talking. |
| | b. He is often late and makes no apologies. |
| | c. He talks with his mouth full. |

Here is a sample paragraph that uses examples to explain the general idea of superstitious beliefs:

> Superstition affects many people on a daily basis. For example, some people think it is very unlucky if a black cat crosses their path, so they go to great lengths to avoid one. Also, according to another superstitious belief, walking under a ladder brings bad luck. Putting shoes on a bed is thought to be a sign that a death will occur in the family. People tend either to take superstitions very seriously or to reject them out of hand as fanciful imagination; regardless, they play an important part in our culture.

Notice that the paragraph gives three examples of superstitions. You can visualize an example paragraph as follows. Study the model and the map for the paragraph on superstitions.

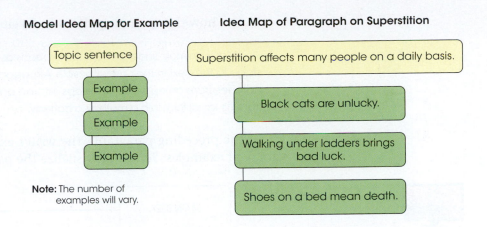

**Model Idea Map for Example**

Topic sentence → Example → Example → Example

**Note:** The number of examples will vary.

**Idea Map of Paragraph on Superstition**

Superstition affects many people on a daily basis.
- Black cats are unlucky.
- Walking under ladders brings bad luck.
- Shoes on a bed mean death.

As a writer you can use examples to make unfamiliar, difficult, or complicated ideas clear or make abstract ideas more concrete and understandable for your reader. Depending on the knowledge and sophistication of your audience, you may include more or fewer examples, depending on what is needed to be sure the message is understood. As a reader, you can use examples to make what you are reading come alive and seem more real. You can also use them to see how the topic connects to real-world situations. Examples often help you realize the use or importance of the idea being illustrated. To test your understanding of the idea being illustrated, try to think of additional examples that illustrate it. If you cannot, it is possible that you may not yet fully understand the idea. If so, rereading may be helpful.

# Reading Example

One of the clearest ways to explain something is to give an example. This is especially true when a subject is unfamiliar. Suppose, for instance, you are taking a course in child psychology and your sister asks you to explain what aggressive behavior is in children. You might explain by giving examples of aggressive behavior, such as biting other children, striking playmates, and throwing objects at others. Through examples, your sister would get a fairly good idea of what aggressive behavior is.

When organizing a paragraph, a writer often states the main idea first and then follows it with one or more examples. The main idea is expressed in a topic sentence and a detailed example makes up the supporting details of the paragraph. In some paragraphs, of course, a writer might use several examples. And in a longer piece of writing, a separate paragraph may be used for each example.

Here is one way to visualize the example pattern in a paragraph:

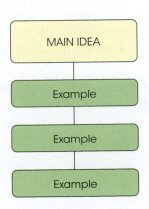

MAIN IDEA → Example → Example → Example

Notice how this example pattern is developed in the following paragraph.

> Many animals undergo a metamorphosis as they move from one developmental stage to the next in their growth cycle. A maggot transforms into a fly. A tadpole hatches from an egg and develops into an adult frog. A caterpillar changes from its larval form into a moth or a butterfly.

In the preceding paragraph, the writer explains metamorphosis through a variety of examples. You could visualize the paragraph as follows:

**VISUALIZE IT!**

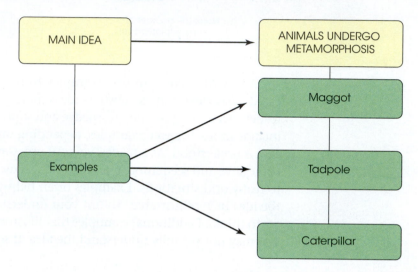

Sometimes writers use transitional words—*for example, for instance*, or *such as*—to signal the reader that an example is to follow. The writer of the following paragraph uses transitions in this way:

> New technologies are helping to make alternative sources of energy cost-effective. In Pennsylvania and Connecticut, *for example*, the waste from landfills is loaded into furnaces and burned to generate electricity for thousands of homes. Natural sources of energy, *such as* the sun and the wind, are also becoming more attractive. The electricity produced by 300 wind turbines in northern California, *for instance*, has resulted in a savings of approximately 60,000 barrels of oil per year. Solar energy also has many applications, from pocket calculators to public telephones to entire homes, and is even used in spacecraft, where conventional power is unavailable.
>
> —adapted from Bergman and Renwick, *Introduction to Geography*, p. 356 and Carnes and Garraty, *The American Nation*, p. 916

By using examples and transitions, the writer describes alternative sources of energy. Although writers don't always use transitions with examples, be on the lookout for them as you read.

## Common Transitions

| | | |
|---|---|---|
| also | to illustrate | one example |
| another example | for instance | such as |
| for example | | |

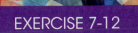

## EXERCISE 7-12    Understanding the Example Pattern

**Directions:** The following paragraphs, both of which are about animal habitats, use the example pattern. Read each paragraph and answer the questions that follow.

**Paragraph 1**

**HABITAT AND NICHE**

**Habitat** refers to the kind of place—defined by the plant community and the physical environment—where a species is biologically adapted to live. For example, a deciduous forest, a swamp, and a grassy field are types of habitats. Different types of forests (for instance, coniferous versus tropical) provide markedly different habitats and support different species of wildlife. Because some organisms operate on very small scales, we use the term *microhabitat* for things like puddles, sheltered spaces by rocks, and holes in tree trunks that might house their own small community.

—Wright, *Environmental Science*, pp. 56–57

1. What transition does the author use to introduce the examples of types of habitats?

   _____

2. List the three examples of habitats in the diagram below.

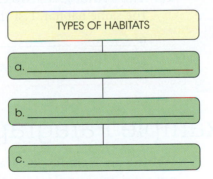

3. Does the topic sentence occur first, second, or last?

   _____

4. What transition does the author use to introduce an example of a type of forest?

   _____

5. What transition does the author use to introduce examples of microhabitats?

   _____

6. List the three examples of microhabitats.

   a. _____

   b. _____

   c. _____

**Paragraph 2**

Even when different species occupy the same habitat, competition may be slight or nonexistent because each species has its own niche. An animal's ecological **niche** refers to what the animal feeds on, where it feeds, when it feeds, where it finds shelter, how it responds to abiotic factors, and where it nests. Basically, the niche is the sum of all of the conditions and resources under which a species can live. Similar species can coexist in the same habitat, but have separate niches. Competition is minimized because potential competitors are using different resources. For example, woodpeckers, which feed on insects in deadwood, do not compete with birds that feed on seeds. Bats and swallows both feed on flying insects, but they do not compete because bats feed on night-flying insects and swallows feed during the day.

—Wright, *Environmental Science*, p. 57

7.  Does the topic sentence of this paragraph occur first, second, or last?

_____

8.  What transition does the author use to introduce species that are not competing within a habitat?

_____

9.  Why is competition minimized between species that have different niches?

_____

10. The author gives two examples of pairs of species that do not compete in the same habitat. List the pairs.

a. _____

b. _____

# Writing Example Paragraphs

Writing an example paragraph involves writing a topic sentence and selecting appropriate examples to support it.

## Writing a Topic Sentence

Your topic sentence should accomplish two things:

1.  **It should identify your topic.**
2.  **It should make a general statement that the examples support.**

Here are a few examples of topic sentences. Can you predict the types of examples each paragraph would contain?

Consumers often purchase brand names they have seen advertised in the media.

Advertisers use attention-getting devices to make a lasting impression in the minds of their consumers.

Some teenagers are obsessed with instant messaging, using it to the extreme and forsaking other forms of communication.

## Choosing Appropriate Examples

Make sure the examples you choose directly support your topic sentence. Use the following guidelines in choosing examples:

1. **Choose clear examples.** Do not choose an example that is complicated or has too many parts; your readers may not be able to see the connection to your topic sentence clearly.

2. **Use a sufficient number of examples to make your point understandable.** The number you need depends on the complexity of the topic and your readers' familiarity with it. One example is sufficient only if it is well developed. The more difficult and unfamiliar the topic, the more examples you will need. For instance, if you are writing about how purchasing books at the college bookstore can be viewed as an exercise in patience, two examples may be sufficient. However, if you are writing about religious intolerance, you probably will need more than two examples.

3. **Include examples that your readers are familiar with and understand.** If you choose an example that is out of the realm of your readers' experience, the example will not help them understand your main point.

4. **Vary your examples.** If you are giving several examples, choose a wide range from different times, places, people, etc.

5. **Choose typical examples.** Avoid outrageous or exaggerated examples that do not accurately represent the situation you are discussing.

6. **Each example should be as specific and vivid as possible, accurately describing an incident or situation.** Include as much detail as is necessary for your readers to understand how the situation illustrates your topic sentence.

7. **Make sure the connection between your example and your main point is clear to your readers.** If the connection is not obvious, include an explanation. For instance, if it is not clear that poor time management is an example of poor study habits, explain how the two relate.

**EXERCISE 7-13**

**WRITING IN PROGRESS**

# Brainstorming Examples

**Directions:** Select one of the topics listed below, narrow it, and write a topic sentence for it. Then brainstorm a list of examples that support it.

1. The behavior of professional athletes
2. The value of travel or a vacation
3. People's eating habits
4. Television commercials
5. Restaurant dining

## How to Organize an Example Paragraph

Be sure to arrange your examples logically. You might arrange them from most to least important or least to most important. (See Chapter 6, p. 197.) You might also arrange them chronologically, if the examples are events in the past.

For example, if you are reporting on how early educational experiences influenced you, you might begin with the earliest situation and progress to the most recent.

Regardless of the order you use, be sure to connect your examples with transitional words and phrases like those shown in the box on page 226.

## Writing an Example Paragraph

**Directions:** Using the topic sentence and examples you generated in Exercise 7-13, write an example paragraph. Present your details in a logical order, using transitions as needed.

# Thinking Critically About Patterns of Organization

■ GOAL 5
Think critically about patterns of organization

Patterns of organization are useful ways for writers to organize ideas, but they also give writers leeway in choosing the types of details to include or exclude in their writing. Like any other feature of writing, be sure to think critically about how a writer employs a specific pattern and why he or she chose it. Use the following guidelines to critically evaluate each of the patterns covered in this chapter.

## Time Sequence

When recounting an event or explaining a process, writers have the choice of which events to include and which to omit. When recounting an event, such as Occupy Wall Street, the details the writer chooses to include shape the readers' impression of the event. Reporting events as disorderly and disruptive will create one impression, while recounting events as filled with action-oriented individuals who attempt to get their message across by peaceful demonstration creates an entirely different impression.

For a process, a writer may choose to include a caution about pitfalls or problems, such as "be sure not to overbake the cookies or they will be dry and hard." Other writers may not be as helpful or as forthcoming, making a process seem easy and simple when it is actually quite complex. Be sure to check other sources to determine whether you are getting a fair and objective view of an event or process.

## Description

The descriptive details that a writer chooses to include shape your attitude toward the subject. A writer can create different impressions of a restaurant by giving details that make it seem pleasant and enjoyable or by selecting details that make it seem unappealing and undesirable. A restaurant described as "overcrowded, filled with noisy people and unruly children" does not create the same response as it would if it were described as being "busy, filled with fun-loving people and families enjoying their dining experience and sharing it with others."

Also consider what descriptive details or facts the writer omitted, if any. Does the writer give you a complete picture of the subject or has he or she selected details that will sway you in one direction or another? For example, a newspaper ad from a local animal shelter may describe a cat that is up for adoption as fun-loving, cuddly, and playful. But did the writer mention that it cannot get along with other cats and is terrified of other small pets?

## Example

Study the nature and types of examples a writer chooses. Pay particular attention to what feature or features of the topic he or she decides to show. If all the examples in an essay about the use of video games by teenagers demonstrate negative effects, then the writer may have an intentional or unintentional bias against video games. Also consider whether the examples are typical and representative of what the writer is trying to explain. For example, are the examples typical of how most teenagers play and use the games?

Also consider whether the examples create an emotional response. If so, the writer may be using the example to sway you to accept a particular viewpoint toward the topic. For instance, a detailed example of a greyhound dog suffering from neglect, locked in a tiny kennel, may be included in an essay intended to persuade you to oppose greyhound racing.

# INTEGRATING READING AND WRITING

## READ AND RESPOND: A Student Essay

*Yesenia De Jesus is in her junior year at Palm Beach State College. Her essay is a true story. She was hesitant to write about her experience initially, but her teacher convinced her to do so, and De Jesus felt that if telling her story influenced or inspired even one student to take chances and be successful, it was worth sharing such a personal story.*

*De Jesus submitted this essay to Writing Rewards, a Pearson-sponsored essay contest open to students in college writing classes. Her essay was selected for use in this book because it is a strong example of a narrative essay. Study the annotations as you read to note her use of narrative techniques.*

Title: Suggests the positive outcome of the essay

# From Bullet to Blue Sky

## Yesenia De Jesus

Introduction      1      The sun was in the process of its morning stretch. While the residents of gated communities came alive to be greeted by the tropical heat of south Florida, the stragglers of the universe awoke to the sounds of a 9 mm dispersing its gun powder to the blue sky. The ghetto houses that sheltered these citizens were painted different colors; some exposed faded paint, and others told stories in graffiti, inspired by gang artists marking their territories. Roll bars protected

Background information about the neighborhood

the windows covered with filthy bed sheets that not even dogs would lie on.

Broken toy pieces scattered over the dead grass in the yard outside. The lanky, dark-haired girl lay in her bed twisting and turning, trying to catch a cool wave from the ceiling fan that spun and thumped overhead all night. She always heard the same dogs barking; her ears still rang from the sound of that gun. She still felt the warm, thin blood that stained her hands. She still felt a sharp, pounding pain along her left side; for every breath she took, the pain reminded her she was human. She had witnessed many shootings before; she had seen more blood in her days. Why was this shooting any different? It was because for the first time she was the victim. I understood her pain, for I was that girl.

2     It all started with Mr. Tangye in the fall of 2004. He was an inspiring math teacher, who convinced me that I had more to offer this world than I had thought. As the bell rang at Conniston Middle School, we marched like zombies to our classes. I passed through dark hallways of vandalized lockers with torn papers and ripped books scattered over the ground like a dump. I made my way past the miserable teachers and devilish students. The administrators surrounded the hallways like a S.W.A.T. team, commanding everyone to go to class, I walked into Mr. Tangye's math class; he had a bright, white smile that hurt my eyes every time I looked at him. Before I could make it to my seat, Mr. Tangye handed me a paper that itched my fingers; it was a math test. I stared at that test, and I begged my brain to wake up! The other kids shuffled the paper back and forth on top of their desks or used it as a pillow on which to lay their heads. I secretly tried my best at every problem and flippantly turned it in.

3     As the bell rang, I dashed for the exit. I swiftly dropped off my homework, but Mr. Tangye caught me and pulled me aside to show me my test. He said, "You are the only one who has passed the test." Then as Mr. Tangye showed my grade to me, he said, "You are on the borderline of failing or passing this class, I'd like to see you pass!" I listened to every word he said because I was tired of being perceived as an idiot.

4     As I finished out the rest of that day, all I could think about was whether to study or not to study. I hated being stuck between a world that offered happiness and stability, whose proverb was "anything is possible" and a world that followed the theory of Charles Darwin's "survival of the fittest." People in my world struggled for everything—money, power, respect, even the last piece of fried chicken. My world had an underground feudal system to follow with rules to be respected, lines not to be crossed. Although this world was violent, senseless, crazy, it was my world. This unmerciful, savage world . . . I was comfortable in it. I felt super-glued to this world; I felt guilty leaving it behind, like a crack head quitting dope. I silenced that inner voice that begged me to stay. I was going to make it out of my world of hardship and struggle and bullets.

5     When I got home, I was greeted by a warm aroma from the kitchen, where I always found my mother. We greeted each other in our usual exchange. After I gave my mother a brief overview of how school went, I rushed to my room to study. I was tired of the struggles, fights, problems, which by birth, I did not deserve. I was going to be somebody; I was going to do something with my life. I was not going to be another Al Capone or Bonnie with a Clyde.

Descriptive detail about the victim

A dramatic and interest-catching thesis

Topic sentence

Details about the school and her math class

Transition

Dialogue adds interest and detail to the story

Topic sentence

Transition
Topic sentence

Topic sentence

I was going to be somebody the way God intended. I was going to earn a living the right, clean way, but in order to be somebody, I needed an education. I would have to get an "A" on my chapter test in Mr. Tangye's math class. I had to do it. I would!

**Transition**    6    Four gruesome weeks passed. I slept, ate, and studied. The morning of the test, I woke up early. I studied some more, for I wanted to be alert in case an unusual math problem was on the test. I left early that day to ask a few questions. Usually, I took a longer route to school to avoid crossing enemy lines, but I rushed through a shortcut. The shortcut led me to the back of the school, where boys played basketball and girls double-dutched after school, but the recess court was empty. No one stood in the courtyard but me. My eyes locked on the formula sheet I memorized. Suddenly, I heard a familiar sound as gunshots sliced the morning air; tires screeched. As I walked toward the school building, I

**Descriptive details add suspense**    felt something drizzle down the side of my torso. I grabbed my shirt; something slightly tickled me. It was wet. It was not sweat; it was blood. Three small holes

**Topic sentence**    pierced my skin, leaving bloody trails racing down my hip. I had been shot. It happened so quickly. I threw my paper and books, bloody from my handprint, on the ground. I screamed at top of my lungs, not because I had been shot, but because I knew I could not take my math test, the test I had studied so damn hard for. My memory faded before I collapsed. A former fire rescuer spotted me on the ground and got help.

**Transition**    7    As I lay in my bed at home, I tried to crawl around my brain; I wanted a reason why God led me to this path. I was not connected to these savages, who shot me. These thugs just wandered around the neighborhood trying to find an ordinary person to become a victim, whose fate would carry a dark message.

**Topic sentence**    8    When I was shot, it did not overpower my life; it empowered my spirit. As I got out of bed, I tried to convince myself I should stay there, but I could not find any good reason. My injuries were three-days fresh, but I was determined to

**Vivid details**    take that math test. I reached to find the strength from deep within my soul to move. The pain gripped my side like 500 needles repeatedly stabbing my ribs. I grabbed a chair so deeply that I bent my nails backwards. My arms and legs shook. I screamed with every movement I made, yet the agonizing pain only intensified. I gripped my book as I walked out the door. Slow steps minimized the pain. I gave my mother a kiss as the bus approached the curb. She touched my arm and reassured me that I could make up the test after I healed completely. I objected because I was ready for this test now. I told my mom that morning that I tried to better myself. This neighborhood, this ghetto, hardship-world I lived in tried to bring me down; it tried to kill me. I refused to allow it.

9    On a sunny day with blue sky above, I dropped my coins into the bus depositor, found a seat, and quietly, painfully moaned along the ride. My mother waved to me as the bus drove off. She was staring at me with a satisfied expression upon

**Conclusion: The story ends on a positive self-affirming note**    her face, for she knew she was raising a fighter, a winner, and a believer. She was raising a somebody.

## Examining Writing

1. Draw an idea map of De Jesus's essay, placing the events she describes in chronological order.

2. Was the essay interesting and engaging? Why or why not?

3. Evaluate the level and type of detail included in this essay. Was there too much or too little detail, or a sufficient amount?

4. Did De Jesus include sufficient introductory and background information? If not, what further information was needed?

5. Did De Jesus use details related to all five senses? Circle examples of each sense she used.

## Writing Assignments

1. De Jesus made a decision to study hard and pass the math test. Write a paragraph describing your response to a difficult academic or workplace challenge.

2. Write a narrative essay describing a frightening or life-threatening event you experienced. Explain how it happened and describe its effect on you.

3. De Jesus was inspired by her math instructor, Mr. Tangye. Write an essay describing someone who has inspired you. Explain how and why he or she inspired you and give examples showing how that person has changed your life.

## READ AND RESPOND: A Professional Essay

### Thinking Before Reading

In the following essay, the author describes her experience as an American women taking the subway to work in a foreign country. As you read, pay particular attention to the author's descriptive details.

1. Preview the reading using the steps discussed in Chapter 1 on page 15.

2. Connect the reading to your own experience by answering the following questions:

   a. If you have ever traveled to another country, how comfortable were you as a foreigner in a strange land? How did the locals react to you?

   b. What qualities do you think people around the world share or have in common?

3. Mark and annotate as you read.

# Cairo Tunnel

## Amanda Fields

1    I nudge through the turnstile, putting the stiff yellow ticket in my pocket and crossing a footbridge to the other side of the tracks, where I head toward the cluster of women on the platform. It's rush hour. Morning salutations compete with beehive intensity. I scoot forward and back. Soon, the Metro barrels up, and the women's car, painted with a red stick-lady in a triangle skirt, sighs open.

2    I shove and fold in with a throng of women heading to low-paying public sector jobs, or to clean expatriates' houses such as mine, or to public school. Once inside, there is no need to hold onto the metal bars, already bombarded with curled hands, wrapped over and bullying each other. We are like books on a shelf, supporting each other's weight.

3    A short woman, eyes looming behind a black mask, presses her gloved hands flat against my chest. I only see the eyes, dark and liquid—she is without a mouth or nose or ears or cheekbones or eyebrows. I look down the length of my buttoned blouse, to her fingertips, to my skin. Still, I can smell her sour breath, and she can probably smell mine. I find my hands and legs in immovable positions. Someone tentatively touches my hair, probably a little girl.

4    It is April, and hot. A single fan rotates. I can see the dust on itsblades, and the windows are dingy and cracked, and through them the slums of Cairo whip by, the crumbling grey buildings, the jumbled sand and trash.

5    The back of my shirt grows slick. At each stop, more women force themselves in, and I begin to feel the pressure on my ribs, the itchy cloth of the woman in **niqab** against my bare arms. Even schoolgirls, writhing with giggles, are a burden to the rest of us. All is gravity and physicality. The Metro rattles into a dark tunnel, one weak bulb lighting the car. We might squeeze each other to death.

6    I was warned about taking the Metro in Cairo. My upper-class students had warned that there would be staring, pushing, insults. And that was just in the women's car. I had heard stories of women taunting each other for the tint of their skin, of women in niqab shouting about Allah and bared flesh. Desperate women would sneak on the Metro without a ticket and peddle tissues and crumbling cosmetics for a few **pounds**. Cover your arms, said my students. Deny the American University, they advised.

7    I try to breathe deeply, my chest barely moving beneath the woman's hands. I once heard a rumor about a study of Cairo's traffic patterns. The Japanese scientists couldn't figure out how it worked, how there weren't multiple car accidents every second. I have learned to put faith in this inscrutability.

8    Some of the women look at me with frankness, but I cannot sense what they see. They cling to each other in something more than physical necessity. Most of them look tired.

**niqab**
a veil that covers a woman's head and face

**pounds**
unit of currency in Egypt, equivalent to about 17 U.S. cents

**hijab**

a headscarf that covers a woman's hair but leaves her face bare

9    Behind me, a fleeting space opens. I grapple for a handhold, clenching a breast, then a stomach. "Sorry," I mutter.

10    Then a woman in lime-colored **hijab** says, "Welcome." Her makeup is minimal, like mine. She wears a pantsuit, an oversized purse against her hip. She smiles.

11    When I respond in stilted Arabic, other women smile, eyes crinkling. The woman in niqab looks up. As we near Sadat station, a schoolgirl taps my shoulder to let me know it is time to start shoving toward the door, assuming, rightly, that I'm going to the university.

12    The car slows to the blur of hundreds of faces, hundreds of clamoring women. I try to stick with the schoolgirl as we push through women staying, women going, women trying to get on before others can depart. The woman with the lime-colored hijab prods me forward. As we pass, a Sudanese girl gets spun in a circle as easily as a rack of clothes, her braids flying.

13    A sea of women—we crest, then topple out, gripping each other, pressing, patting in a womanly empathy so familiar in Cairo. I can't understand how I'm not falling, how I'm not getting trampled. I can't understand how we carry each other in such smooth uncertainty. And all the while, women are laughing, I am laughing. We have this in common.

# Getting Reading to Write

## Checking Your Comprehension

Answer each of the following questions using complete sentences.

1. Where is the author going and how is she getting there?

2. What warnings did the author's students give her about taking the subway?

3. Describe the author's experience on the Metro. What happens toward the end of the ride to change the author's initial impression?

4. What does the author say she has in common with the women on the Metro?

## Strengthening Your Vocabulary

Using the word's context, word parts, or a dictionary, write a brief definition of each of the following words as it is used in the reading:

1. salutations (paragraph 1) _____

2. expatriates (paragraph 2) _____

3. writhing (paragraph 5) _____

4. inscrutability (paragraph 7) _____

5. stilted (paragraph 11) _____

## Examining the Reading: Marking Revealing Actions, Descriptions, and Statements

Writers often reveal how they feel and what they think through description rather than through direct statements. For example, the author never directly says that it is crowded on the subway, but the details make it clear that the women's car is unpleasantly full of people.

As you read descriptive writing, it is helpful to highlight words, phrases, or bits of conversation that are particularly revealing about the writer's attitude toward the subject. For example, in paragraph 5 the following passages reveal the writer's attitude toward being on the crowded subway: "The back of my shirt grows slick . . . I begin to feel the pressure on my ribs, the itchy cloth of the woman in niqab against my bare arms . . . We might squeeze each other to death."

Actions, too, may reveal an author's feelings. In paragraph 7, the author describes trying to breathe deeply on the crowded subway. This action suggests that she is trying to remain calm while feeling uncomfortably close to the people around her.

To enhance your understanding of descriptive writing, review the reading and underline particularly revealing actions, descriptions, and statements.

## Reacting to Ideas: Discussion and Journal Writing

Get ready to write about the reading by discussing the following:

1. Why do you think the author chooses to ride the subway despite the warnings? Do you think she is ultimately glad she did?

2. Explain what the author means when she says "all is gravity and physicality."

3. What does the author say about the other women riding the subway with her? What part of Cairo does she observe through the subway windows? Explain how her observations and descriptions help create a dominant impression.

4. Explain what the author's students mean when they advise her to "deny the American University."

5. Compare the author's tone in the first paragraph to that in the last paragraph. How does the last paragraph leave you feeling about the author's experience?

**THINKING VISUALLY**

6. How does the photograph reflect what the author has described in the reading? What other photographs might be used to illustrate this essay?

## Thinking and Writing Critically

1. What do you think the author's purpose is for writing this article? Who is her intended audience?

2. Interestingly, "Cairo Tunnel" does not have a clearly expressed thesis statement. Write one as part of an introductory paragraph to add to the start of the selection.

3. What dominant impression does the author, Amanda Fields, create regarding the women's car of the Cairo Metro?

---

**MySkillsLab®**

⚙
**Complete** this Exercise

## Writing About the Reading

### Paragraph Options

⚙ 1. How does the author help the reader to visualize what she has seen? Identify examples of vivid language in the reading that help the reader see what the author is describing.

2. In this essay, the author takes the reader along on her journey to work. Think about a journey you take each day, either to class or your job, and write a "how-to" paragraph explaining the steps you take to get from Point A (your home or dorm) to Point B (your class or job).

3. The author clearly stands out as a foreigner among her fellow passengers. Write a paragraph about an experience in which you were clearly different from the people around you. How did you feel about being different? How did people respond to you?

## Essay Options

4. A kind word and a smile from a stranger dramatically changed the author's unpleasant subway ride to a memorable, cross-cultural experience. When has a seemingly small gesture from someone made a dramatic difference in your day (or your life)? Write an essay describing your experience.

5. How might one of the other people on the subway have described the same subway ride? Rewrite the essay from another person's point of view. You may choose the woman in niqab, the woman in lime-colored hijab, or the schoolgirl who tapped the author on the shoulder, or you may imagine another person not mentioned in the original essay.

6. Write an essay describing your own experience in an unfamiliar place. Begin with a topic sentence such as "My experience in _____ was memorable in many ways." Support your topic sentence with specific examples and include sensory details and descriptive language to make your experience vivid for readers.

# SELF-TEST SUMMARY

To test yourself, cover the Answer column with a sheet of paper and answer each question in the left column. Evaluate each of your answers as you work by sliding the paper down and comparing your answer with what is printed in the Answer column.

| QUESTION | ANSWER |
|---|---|
| ■ GOAL 1  Identify patterns of organization<br><br>What are patterns of organization and how do they help readers and writers? | Some common patterns of organization are *chronological order, process, narration, description,* and *example.* Patterns help writers present ideas in a clear and logical manner and help readers see how information is related. |
| ■ GOAL 2  Read and write using time sequence<br><br>Which patterns use time sequence and how? | *Chronological order* presents events in the order in which they happened. *Process* explains how something is done or how something works, in a particular order. *Narration* uses time sequence to tell a story or make a point. |

| QUESTION | ANSWER |
|---|---|
| ■ GOAL 3  Read and write using description  <br><br>What is description? | *Description* uses words and phrases that appeal to the senses—taste, touch, smell, sight, hearing—to help readers imagine an object, person, place, or experience. |
| ■ GOAL 4  Read and write using example  <br><br>What is an example and how do you develop an example paragraph? | An *example* is a specific instance or situation that explains a general idea or statement. Developing an example paragraph involves writing a topic sentence and choosing appropriate examples to illustrate it. |
| ■ GOAL 5  Think critically about patterns of organization  <br><br>How can you think critically about patterns of organization? | Consider the types of details the writer has chosen to include or exclude, as well as how the writer uses the pattern and why he or she chose it. |

 For more help with **Basic Patterns of Organization**, go to your learning path in MySkillsLab at www.myskillslab.com.

# 8 Organization: Additional Patterns

## LEARNING GOALS

Learn how to . . .

- **GOAL 1**
  Identify additional patterns of organization

- **GOAL 2**
  Read and write using definition

- **GOAL 3**
  Read and write using classification

- **GOAL 4**
  Read and write using comparison and contrast

- **GOAL 5**
  Read and write using cause and effect

- **GOAL 6**
  Read and write using other patterns of organization

- **GOAL 7**
  Think critically about patterns of organization

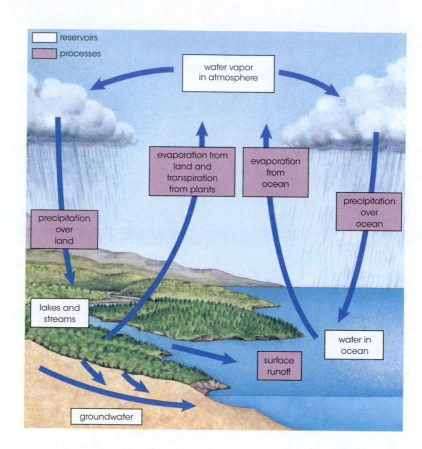

## THINK About It!

Suppose you are taking a biology course and the chapter you are studying this week contains the diagram on this page. Write a sentence describing what it shows or explains.

To figure out the diagram, you used a number of different thought patterns. You had to focus on cause and effect relationships; you could see that water vapor in the atmosphere passes through clouds and creates precipitation over land, for instance. Definitions were also useful and important; you had to pay attention to terminology—*transpiration, surface runoff,* and *evaporation,* for example. Perhaps you compared how evaporation occurs over land with how it occurs over ocean water, thus using the comparison and contrast pattern. You might also have classified the types of water—groundwater, ocean water, and surface runoff. You can see that regardless of whether you are reading the diagram, drawing your own diagram to test your recall for study and review purposes, or writing about evaporation for an in-class paper or exam, these patterns are very useful in helping you organize information. In this chapter you will learn to both read and write using these four patterns.

# Reading and Writing Connections

### EVERYDAY CONNECTIONS

- **Reading** You read an online movie review comparing and contrasting two films: the original, which was released in 1970, and a 2011 remake of the film.
- **Writing** You write an e-mail to a friend summarizing the plot of the recently released film to help her decide whether it is suitable for her ten-year-old to see.

### ACADEMIC CONNECTIONS

- **Reading** You read an assignment for geology in which you must learn the twelve broad categories for classifying types of soil.
- **Writing** For an exam in geology, you write an answer explaining the effects of three factors—time, climate, and topography—on the formation of different types of soil.

### WORKPLACE CONNECTIONS

- **Reading** You read an article in a veterinary journal about the causes and effects of laryngeal trauma in dogs. The article includes a brief description of where the larynx is situated relative to the pharynx, the trachea, and the esophagus in a dog's throat.
- **Writing** As a veterinary technician, you write a report for a dog owner explaining the definition of the term *laryngeal trauma* based on the article you read.

# FOCUSING ON READING AND WRITING

# What Are Additional Patterns of Organization?

■ **GOAL 1**
Identify additional patterns of organization

In addition to the patterns discussed in Chapter 7, there are several other patterns that help readers grasp ideas and help writers develop and organize their writing, which you will learn about in this chapter: *definition, classification, comparison and contrast*, and *cause and effect*.

| PATTERN OF ORGANIZATION | WHAT IT DOES | AN EXAMPLE OF ITS USE |
|---|---|---|
| Definition | Explains a topic by discussing its characteristics | Defining wind power as a form of renewable energy and including some of its important characteristics |
| Classification | Explains a topic by organizing it into categories or parts | Discussing the use of wind power in different countries |
| Comparison and Contrast | Shows how things are similar and/or different | Comparing and contrasting wind power with other forms of renewable energy |
| Cause and Effect | Explains why things happen or what happens as a result of an event or action | Explaining the positive and negative effects of wind power |

Other useful patterns covered briefly in this chapter include *statement and clarification, summary, addition,* and *spatial order.* You will also become familiar with the transitions that will help you read and write using each of these patterns.

## READING AND WRITING DEFINITION

# What Is Definition?

■ GOAL 2
Read and write using definition

A **definition** is an explanation of what something is. It has three essential parts:

1. The term being defined
2. The group, or category, to which the term belongs
3. Its distinguishing characteristics

Suppose you had to define the term *cheetah.* If you said it was a cat, then you would be stating the group to which it belongs. **Group** means the general category of which something is a part. If you said a cheetah lives in Africa and southwest Asia, has black-spotted fur, is long-legged, and is the fastest animal on land, you would be giving some of its distinguishing characteristics. **Distinguishing characteristics** are those details that allow you to tell an item apart from others in its same group. The details about the cheetah's fur, long legs, and speed enable a reader to distinguish it from other large cats in Africa and southwest Asia. Here are a few more examples:

| TERM | GROUP | DISTINGUISHING CHARACTERISTICS |
|---|---|---|
| opal | gemstone | greenish blue colors |
| comedian | entertainer | makes people laugh |
| fear | emotion | occurs when a person feels threatened or in danger |

Here is a sample definition paragraph written by a student.

Sushi is a Japanese food consisting of small cakes of cooked rice wrapped in seaweed. While it is commonly thought of as raw fish on rice, it is actually any preparation of vinegared rice. Sushi can also take the form of conical hand rolls and the more popular sushi roll. The roll is topped or stuffed with slices of raw or cooked fish, egg, or vegetables. Slices of raw fish served by themselves are commonly mistaken for sushi but are properly referred to as *sashimi.*

In the paragraph above, the term being defined is *sushi.* Its group is *Japanese food,* and its distinguishing characteristics are detailed. You can visualize a definition paragraph as follows. Study the model and the map for the paragraph on sushi shown on the next page.

**Model Idea Map for Definition**          **Idea Map of Paragraph on Sushi**

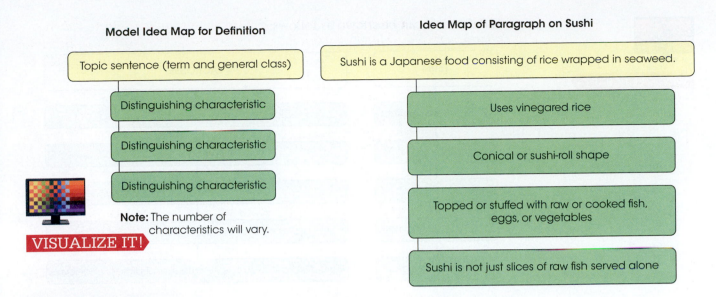

**Model Idea Map for Definition**

Topic sentence (term and general class)

Distinguishing characteristic

Distinguishing characteristic

Distinguishing characteristic

**Note:** The number of characteristics will vary.

**Idea Map of Paragraph on Sushi**

Sushi is a Japanese food consisting of rice wrapped in seaweed.

Uses vinegared rice

Conical or sushi-roll shape

Topped or stuffed with raw or cooked fish, eggs, or vegetables

Sushi is not just slices of raw fish served alone

**VISUALIZE IT!**

---

**EXERCISE 8-1**

# Classifying Terms

**Directions:** For each term listed below, give the group it belongs to and at least two of its distinguishing characteristics.

| Term | Group | Distinguishing Characteristics |
|---|---|---|
| 1. baseball | | |
| 2. a role model | | |
| 3. blogging | | |
| 4. terrorism | | |
| 5. facial expressions | | |

---

# Reading Definition

You commonly encounter the definition pattern. Let's say that you see a game of lacrosse being played in your neighborhood and you mention this to a friend. Since your friend does not know what lacrosse is, you have to define it. Your definition should describe the sport's characteristics or features, explaining how it is different from other sports. Thus, you might define lacrosse as follows:

> Lacrosse was first played by Native Americans, making it the oldest sport in North America. Modern lacrosse is a fast-paced game played on a field by two teams of ten players each. During the game, players use the crosse—a long-handled stick with a webbed pouch—to maneuver a ball into the opposing team's goal. There are youth lacrosse teams for boys and girls, college and amateur teams for men and women, and professional teams for men.

This definition can be shown as follows:

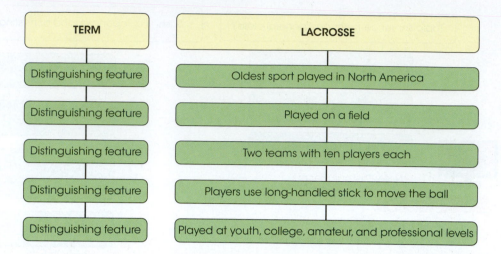

| TERM | LACROSSE |
|------|----------|
| Distinguishing feature | Oldest sport played in North America |
| Distinguishing feature | Played on a field |
| Distinguishing feature | Two teams with ten players each |
| Distinguishing feature | Players use long-handled stick to move the ball |
| Distinguishing feature | Played at youth, college, amateur, and professional levels |

As you read passages that use the definition pattern, keep these questions in mind:

1. What is being defined?
2. What makes it different from other items or ideas?

Apply these questions to the following paragraph:

> **Humid subtropical climates** have several defining characteristics. They occur in latitudes between about 25 and 40 degrees on the eastern sides of continents and between about 35 and 50 degrees on the western sides. These climates are relatively warm most of the year but have at least occasional freezing temperatures during the winter. Most humid subtropical climates have deciduous species of vegetation that lose their leaves in autumn and become dormant in winter. Eastern China, the southeastern U.S., and parts of Brazil and Argentina are the largest areas of humid subtropical climates.
> —adapted from Bergman and Renwick, *Introduction to Geography*, p. 280

When you ask yourself the preceding questions, you can see, first of all, that the term being defined is *humid subtropical climates*. In addition, the definition lists four ways that humid subtropical climates are different from other climates: (1) they occur in latitudes between 25 and 40 degrees on the eastern sides of continents and between 35 and 50 degrees on the western sides, (2) they are warm most of the year but have some freezing temperatures during the winter, (3) they have deciduous species of vegetation that lose their leaves in autumn and become dormant in winter, and (4) the largest areas of humid subtropical climates are in eastern China, the southeastern United States, Brazil, and Argentina.

## Combining Definition and Example

It is important to note that definitions are often combined with examples. For instance, if someone asks you to define the term *fiction writer*, you might begin by saying that a fiction writer is someone who creates novels and stories that describe imaginary people or events. You might also give some examples of well-known fiction writers, such as Ernest Hemingway or Stephen King. When definition and example are used together in this way, you can visualize the pattern as follows:

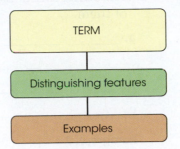

You will often encounter the definition and example pattern in your textbooks. An author will define a term and then use examples to explain it further, as shown in this passage from a health text:

> Generally, positive stress, or stress that presents the opportunity for personal growth and satisfaction, is called **eustress**. Getting married, starting school, beginning a career, developing new friendships, and learning a new physical skill all give rise to eustress.
>
> —Donatelle and Davis, *Access to Health*, p. 65

First the authors define *eustress,* and then they provide several examples to make the definition more understandable. You have probably already noticed that textbook authors often put an important term in **boldfaced** type when they define it. This makes it easier for students to find definitions as they read or study for tests. They also use transitional words and phrases to signal that a definition is being presented (see box below).

## Common Definition Transitions

| | | |
|---|---|---|
| *are those that* | *involves* | *is literally* |
| *can be defined as* | *is* | *means* |
| *consists of* | *is a term that* | *occurs when* |
| *corresponds to* | *is called* | *refers to* |
| *entails* | *is characterized by* | |

 **EXERCISE 8-2**

## Understanding the Definition Pattern

**Directions:** Read each paragraph and answer the questions that follow.

### Paragraph 1

No time to socialize? Surely you can spare six minutes. That's how long potential couples usually spend getting acquainted while **speed dating**—an accelerated form of dating in which men and women choose whether to see each other again based on a very short interaction. Originally created for young Jewish singles in 1999, speed dating now provides homosexuals, heterosexuals, and a number of religious and ethnic groups with an opportunity to participate in quick, one-on-one dates with like-minded singles. Individuals spend six minutes talking to each date. If both individuals are interested, they are provided with each other's e-mail addresses.

—Kunz, *Think Marriages & Families*, p. 119

1. What term is being defined? _____

2. The writer mentions several distinguishing features of this term. List three of them.

   a. _____

   _____

   b. _____

   c. _____

### Paragraph 2

The patterns of stars seen in the sky are usually called constellations. In astronomy, however, the term **constellation** refers to a region of the sky. Any place you point in the sky belongs to some constellation; familiar patterns of stars merely help locate particular constellations. For example, the constellation Orion includes all the stars in the familiar pattern of the hunter, along with the region of the sky in which these stars are found.

—Bennett, *The Cosmic Perspective, Brief Edition,* p. 28

3. What term is being defined? _____

4. What example is given to illustrate the term being defined? _____

5. What transitional phrase does the writer use? _____

### Paragraph 3

The name "tale" is sometimes applied to any story, whether short or long, true or fictitious. But defined in a more limited sense, a **tale** is a story, usually short, that sets forth strange and wonderful events in more or less bare summary, without detailed character-drawing. "Tale" implies a story in which the goal is to reveal something marvelous rather than to reveal the character of someone. In the English folk tale "Jack and the Beanstalk," for instance, we take away a more vivid impression of the miraculous beanstalk and the giant who dwells at its top than of Jack's mind or personality.

—adapted from Kennedy and Gioia, *Literature,* p. 7

6. What term is being defined? _____

7. What example is given to illustrate the term being defined?

   _____

8. What transitional phrase do the writers use? _____

### Paragraph 4

The **nervous system**, the master controlling and communicating system of the body, has three overlapping functions: (1) It uses millions of sensory receptors to monitor changes occurring both inside and outside the body. These changes are called stimuli and the gathered information is called *sensory input.* (2) It processes and interprets the sensory input and decides what should be done at each moment—a process called *integration.* (3) It causes a response by activating our muscles or glands; the response is called *motor output.* An example will illustrate how these functions work together. When you are driving and see a red light ahead (sensory input), your nervous system integrates this information (red light means "stop"), and your foot goes for the brake (motor output).

—Marieb, *Human Anatomy & Physiology,* p. 387

9. What term is being defined? Enter it in the diagram below.

10. In defining this term, the writer mentions three distinguishing features. List them in the diagram.

# Writing Definition Paragraphs

Developing a definition paragraph involves writing a topic sentence and adding explanatory details.

## Writing a Topic Sentence

The topic sentence of a definition paragraph should accomplish two things:

1. **It should identify the term you are explaining.**
2. **It should place the term in a general group. It may also provide one or more distinguishing characteristics.**

In the topic sentence below, the term being defined is *psychiatry*, the general group is "a branch of medicine," and its distinguishing feature is that it "deals with mental and emotional disorders."

Psychiatry is a branch of medicine that deals with mental and emotional disorders.

**EXERCISE 8-3**

**WRITING IN PROGRESS**

## Writing a Topic Sentence

**Directions:** Write a topic sentence that includes a group and a distinguishing characteristic for each of the following items.

1. shirt _____

2. horror _____

3. hip-hop _____

4. age discrimination _____

5. ballroom dancing _____

## Adding Explanatory Details

Your topic sentence will usually *not* be sufficient to give your reader a complete understanding of the term you are defining. You will need to explain it further in one or more of the following ways:

1. **Give examples.** Examples can make a definition more vivid and interesting to your reader. (To learn more about using examples, see Chapter 7, p. 225)

2. **Break the term into subcategories.** Breaking your subject down into sub-categories helps to organize your definition. For example, you might explain the term *discrimination* by listing some of its types: *racial, gender,* and *age.*

3. **Explain what the term is not.** To bring the meaning of a term into focus for your reader, it is sometimes helpful to give counterexamples, or to discuss in what ways the term means something different from what one might expect. Notice that this is done in the paragraph on sushi.

4. **Trace the term's meaning over time.** If the term has changed or expanded in meaning over time, it may be useful to trace this development as a way of explaining the term's current meaning.

5. **Compare an unfamiliar term to one that is familiar to your readers.** If you are writing about rugby, you might compare it to football, a more familiar sport. Be sure to make the connection clear to your readers by pointing out characteristics that the two sports share.

## How to Organize a Definition Paragraph

You should logically arrange the distinguishing characteristics of a term. You might arrange them from most to least familiar or from more to less obvious, for example. Be sure to use strong transitional words and phrases to help your readers follow your presentation of ideas, guiding them from one distinguishing characteristic to another. Useful transitional words and phrases are shown in the box on page 245.

**EXERCISE 8-4**

**WRITING IN PROGRESS**

## Writing a Definition Paragraph

**Directions:** Select one of the topic sentences you wrote for Exercise 8-3. Write a paragraph defining that topic, using transitions as needed.

# READING AND WRITING CLASSIFICATION

# What Is Classification?

■ GOAL 3
Read and write using
classification

**Classification** explains a subject by identifying and describing its types or categories. For instance, a good way to discuss medical personnel is to arrange them into categories: doctors, nurse practitioners, physician's assistants, nurses, technicians, and nurse's aides. If you wanted to explain who makes up your college faculty, you could classify the faculty members by the disciplines they teach (or, alternatively, by age, level of skill, or some other factor).

Here is a sample classification paragraph:

> If you are interested in entering your pedigreed pet in the upcoming cat show, make sure you check with the Cat Fanciers' Association first. The CFA, sponsor of the show, has strict rules regarding eligibility. You must enter your cat in the right category. Only cats in the Championship Class, the Provisional Class, or the Miscellaneous Class will be allowed to participate. The first category in every cat show is the Championship Class. There are 37 pedigreed breeds eligible for showing in this class, some of which may sound familiar, such as the Abyssinian, the Maine Coon, the Siamese, and the Russian Blue. The Provisional Class allows only three breeds: the American Bobtail, a breed that looks like a wildcat but acts like a pussycat; the LaPerm, a curly-haired cutie that's descended from early American barn cats; and the semi-longhaired Siberian, a breed that was first imported from Russia in 1990. The Miscellaneous Class allows only one breed—the big Ragamuffin with its silky, rabbitlike coat. So, before you rush out and pay the entry fee, make sure you have something fancy enough for the Cat Fanciers' Association.

This paragraph explains the eligibility for a cat show by describing the three categories of cats allowed to enter the show.

You can visualize the process of classification as follows. Study the model and the map for the paragraph on cats below.

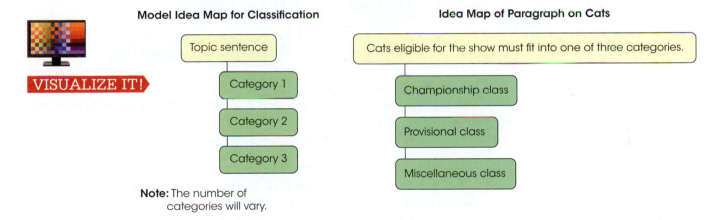

**VISUALIZE IT!**

**Model Idea Map for Classification**

Topic sentence

Category 1

Category 2

Category 3

**Note:** The number of categories will vary.

**Idea Map of Paragraph on Cats**

Cats eligible for the show must fit into one of three categories.

Championship class

Provisional class

Miscellaneous class

# Reading Classification

**Classification** is a process of sorting people, things, or ideas into groups or categories to make them more understandable. Your dresser drawers are probably organized by categories, with t-shirts and socks in different drawers. Convenience stores, phone directories, and restaurant menus arrange items in groups according to similar or shared characteristics. In reading and writing, the classification pattern is used to explain a topic by describing its types or parts. It is often used when a topic is difficult or complex.

Textbook writers often use the classification pattern to explain an unfamiliar or complicated topic by dividing it into more easily understood parts. These parts are selected on the basis of common characteristics. For example, a psychology textbook writer might explain human needs by classifying them into two categories, primary and secondary. Or in a chemistry textbook, various compounds may be grouped or classified according to common characteristics, such as the presence of hydrogen or oxygen.

The following paragraph explains horticulture. As you read, try to identify the categories into which the topic of horticulture is divided.

Horticulture, the study and cultivation of garden plants, is a large industry. Recently it has become a popular area of study. The horticulture field consists of four major divisions. First, there is pomology, the science and practice of growing and handling fruit trees. Then there is olericulture, which is concerned with growing and storing vegetables. A third field, floriculture, is the science of growing, storing, and designing flowering plants. The last category, ornamental and landscape horticulture, is concerned with using grasses, plants, and shrubs in landscaping.

This paragraph approaches the topic of horticulture by describing its four areas or fields of study. You could diagram the paragraph as follows:

**VISUALIZE IT!**

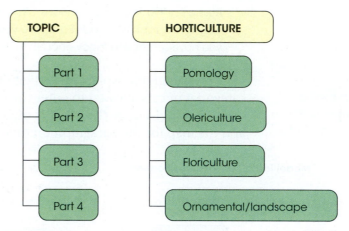

When reading textbook material that uses the classification pattern, be sure you understand *how* and *why* the topic was divided as it was. This technique will help you remember the most important parts of the topic.

Here is another example of the classification pattern:

A newspaper is published primarily to present current news and information. For large city newspapers, more than 2,000 people may be involved in the distribution of this information. The staff of large city papers, headed by a publisher, is organized into departments: editorial, business, and mechanical. The editorial department, headed by an editor-in-chief, is responsible for the collection of news and preparation of written copy. The business department, headed by a business manager, handles circulation, sales, and advertising. The mechanical department is run by a production manager. This department deals with the actual production of the paper, including typesetting, layout, and printing.

You could diagram this paragraph as follows:

**VISUALIZE IT!**

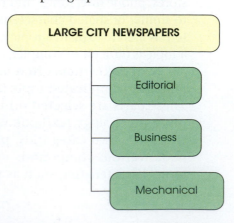

Paragraphs and passages that are organized using classification frequently use transitional words and phrases to guide the reader. These include:

## Common Classification Transistions

| | | |
|---|---|---|
| another | different stages of | last |
| another kind | finally | one |
| classified as | first | second |
| comprises | include | types of |
| different groups that | is composed of | varieties of |

**EXERCISE 8-5**

# Analyzing Classification Paragraphs

**Directions:** Read each of the following passages. Then identify the topic and the parts into which each topic is divided.

1.    We can separate the members of the plant kingdom into a mere four types. These are the *bryophytes*, which include mosses; the *seedless vascular plants*, which include ferns; the *gymnosperms*, which include coniferous ("cone-bearing") trees; and the *angiosperms*, a vast division of flowering plants—by far the most dominant on Earth today—that includes not only flowers such as orchids, but also oak trees, rice, and cactus.

—adapted from Krogh, *Biology: A Guide to the Natural World*, p. 429

Topic: _____

Parts: _____

2.    The name of the cancer is derived from the type of tissue in which it develops. Carcinoma (carc = cancer; omo = tumor) refers to a malignant tumor consisting of epithelial cells. A tumor that develops from a gland is called an adenosarcoma (adeno = gland). Sarcoma is a general term for any cancer arising from connective tissue. Osteogenic sarcomas (osteo = bone; genic = origin), the most frequent type of childhood cancer, destroy normal bone tissue and eventually spread to other areas of the body. Myelomas (myelos = marrow) are malignant tumors, occurring in middle-aged and older people, that interfere with the blood-cell-producing function of bone marrow and cause anemia. Chondrosarcomas (chondro = cartilage) are cancerous growths of cartilage.

—Tortora, *Introduction to the Human Body*, p. 56

Topic: _____

Parts: _____

3.    The amount of space that people prefer varies from one culture to another. North Americans use four different "distance zones." *Intimate distance* extends to about 18 inches from our bodies. We reserve this space for comforting, protecting, hugging, intimate touching, and love-making. *Personal distance* extends from 18 inches to 4 feet. We reserve it for friends and acquaintances and ordinary

conversations. *Social distance*, extending out from us about 4 to 12 feet, marks impersonal or formal relationships. We use this zone for such things as job interviews. *Public distance*, extending beyond 12 feet, marks even more formal relationships. It is used to separate dignitaries and public speakers from the general public.

—adapted from Henslin, *Sociology: A Down-to-Earth Approach*, pp. 109, 111

Topic: _____

Parts: _____

# Writing Classification Paragraphs

Developing a **classification paragraph** involves deciding on a basis of classification for the subject you are discussing, writing a topic sentence, and explaining each subgroup.

## Deciding on What Basis to Classify Information

To write a paper using classification, you must first decide on a basis for breaking your subject into subgroups. Suppose you are given an assignment to write about some aspect of campus life. You decide to classify the campus services into groups. You could classify them by benefit, location, or type of facility, depending on what you wanted the focus of your writing to be.

The best way to plan your classification paragraph is to find a good general topic and then brainstorm different ways to break it into subgroups or categories.

EXERCISE 8-6

WORKING TOGETHER

## Using Brainstorming

**Directions:** For each of the following topics, brainstorm to discover different ways you might classify them. Compare your work with that of a classmate and select the two or three most effective classifications.

1. **Topic** Crimes

   Ways to Classify _____

   _____

   _____

2. **Topic** Movies

   Ways to Classify _____

   _____

   _____

3. **Topic** Web sites

   Ways to Classify _____

   _____

   _____

Most topics can be classified in a number of different ways. Stores can be classified by types of merchandise, prices, size, or customer service provided, for example. Use the following tips for choosing an appropriate basis of classification:

- **Consider your audience.** Choose a basis of classification that will interest them. Classifying stores by size may not be as interesting as classifying them by merchandise, for example.

- **Choose a basis that is uncomplicated.** If you choose a basis that is complicated or lengthy, your topic may be difficult to write about. Categorizing stores by prices may be unwieldy, since there are thousands of products sold at various prices.

- **Choose a basis with which you are familiar.** While it is possible to classify stores by the types of customer service they provide, you may have to do some research or learn more about available services in order to write about them.

**EXERCISE 8-7**

**WRITING IN PROGRESS**

## Using Brainstorming

**Directions:** Choose one of the following topics. Brainstorm a list of possible ways to classify the topic.

1. professional athletes or their fans

2. bad drivers

3. diets

4. cell phone users

5. friends

## Writing a Topic Sentence

Once you have chosen a way to classify a topic and have identified the subgroups you will use, you are ready to write a topic sentence. Your topic sentence should accomplish two things:

1. **It should identify your topic.**
2. **It should indicate how you will classify items within your topic.**

The topic sentence may also mention the number of subgroups you will use. Here are a few examples:

> Three relatively new types of family structures are single-parent families, blended families, and families without children.

> Since working as a waiter, I've discovered that there are three main types of customer complaints.

**EXERCISE 8-8**

WRITING IN PROGRESS

## Writing a Topic Sentence

**Directions:** For one of the topics in Exercise 8-7, write a topic sentence that identifies the topic and explains your method of classification.

### Explaining Each Subgroup

The details in your paragraph should explain and provide further information about each subgroup. Depending on your topic and/or your audience, it may be necessary to define each subgroup. If possible, provide an equal amount of detail for each subgroup. If you define or offer an example for one subgroup, you should do the same for each of the others.

### How to Organize a Classification Paragraph

The order in which you present your categories depends on your topic. Possible ways to organize the categories include from familiar to unfamiliar, from oldest to newest, or from simpler to more complex. Be sure to use transitions to signal your readers that you are moving from one category to another. Useful transitions are shown in the box on page 251.

**EXERCISE 8-9**

WRITING IN PROGRESS

## Writing a Classification Paragraph

**Directions:** For the topic sentence you wrote in Exercise 8-8, write a classification paragraph. Be sure to identify and explain each group. Use transitions as needed.

# READING AND WRITING COMPARISON AND CONTRAST

# What Are Comparison and Contrast?

■ **GOAL 4**
Read and write using comparison and contrast

Comparison and contrast are two ways of organizing information about two or more subjects. **Comparison** focuses on similarities; **contrast** focuses on differences. When writing paragraphs, it is often best to focus either on similarities or on differences, instead of trying to cover both in a short piece of writing. Essay-length pieces can focus on both similarities and differences, but it is often easier to concentrate on one or the other. Here is a sample contrast paragraph:

> Every time I go out for Mexican food, I have to choose between tacos de carne asada and tacos al pastor—they are tasty, but different. The tacos de carne asada are three small tortillas stuffed with chopped steak, served with a dish each of cilantro, onion, tomato, and fiery salsa. The tacos al pastor are similar, but chorizo is added to the chopped steak. While the tacos al pastor are a little greasier, they also have more spice and heat. Tacos de carne asada are drier with less flavor, but there's more room to add the vegetables, and that often makes for more dynamic flavor possibilities.

In this paragraph, the writer discusses the differences between two types of tacos. He examines their ingredients, their spiciness, and their overall flavor. You can visualize a comparison or contrast paragraph as follows. Study the models and the map for the paragraph on tacos.

**VISUALIZE IT!**

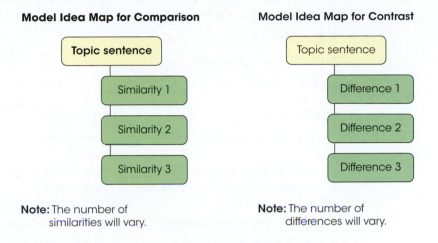

**Model Idea Map for Comparison**

Topic sentence

Similarity 1

Similarity 2

Similarity 3

**Note:** The number of similarities will vary.

**Model Idea Map for Contrast**

Topic sentence

Difference 1

Difference 2

Difference 3

**Note:** The number of differences will vary.

**Idea Map of Contrast Paragraph on Tacos**

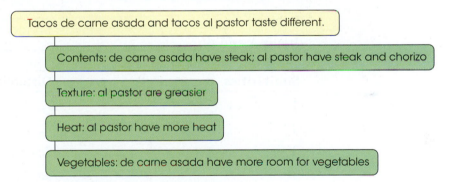

Tacos de carne asada and tacos al pastor taste different.

Contents: de carne asada have steak; al pastor have steak and chorizo

Texture: al pastor are greasier

Heat: al pastor have more heat

Vegetables: de carne asada have more room for vegetables

# Reading Comparison and Contrast

You use comparison and contrast every day. For example, when you decide which pair of shoes to buy, where to apply for a part-time job, or what topic to choose for a research paper, you are thinking about similarities and differences.

Writers use comparison or contrast to explain how something is similar to or different from something else. **Comparison** treats similarities, whereas **contrast** emphasizes differences. For example, a writer who is *comparing* two U.S. presidents would focus on their shared features: experience in politics, leadership characteristics, and commitment to fulfill the duties of the office. But a writer who is *contrasting* the two presidents would discuss how they differ in foreign policy, education, family background, and so forth.

As you read, you will find passages that only compare, some that only contrast, and some that do both.

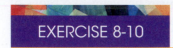

## Understanding Comparison and Contrast Patterns

EXERCISE 8-10

**Directions:** Choose one of the following subjects: two musical groups, two jobs, two professors, or two cities. Then, using the box below as a guide, make a list of five similarities and five differences.

**Example**

**Subject:** two restaurants

**Items A and B:** Blue Mesa and Chico's

| Similarities | Differences |
|---|---|
| 1. Both specialize in Mexican food. | 1. Blue Mesa is much more expensive than Chico's. |
| 2. Both serve lunch and dinner. | 2. Chico's is a chain, while Blue Mesa is a single restaurant. |
| 3. Both are located on the east side of town. | 3. Only Chico's offers takeout. |
| 4. Both employ college students. | 4. Blue Mesa is closed on Mondays, while Chico's is open every day. |
| 5. Both have a special menu for children. | 5. Only Blue Mesa accepts reservations. |

**Subject:** _____

**Items A and B:** _____

| Similarities | Differences |
|---|---|
| 1. | 1. |
| 2. | 2. |
| 3. | 3. |
| 4. | 4. |
| 5. | 5. |

## Comparison

A writer who is concerned only with similarities may identify the items to be compared and then list the ways they are alike. The following paragraph describes apparent similarities between two planets, Earth and Mars.

Early telescopic observations of Mars revealed several uncanny resemblances to Earth. The Martian rotation axis is tilted about the same amount as Earth's, and on both planets a day lasts about 24 hours. In addition, Mars has polar caps, which we now know to be composed primarily of frozen carbon dioxide, with smaller amounts of water ice. Telescopic observations also showed seasonal variations in surface coloration over the course of the Martian year (about 1.9 Earth years). All these discoveries led to the perception that Mars and Earth were at least cousins, if not twins. By the early 1900s, many astronomers—as well as the public—envisioned Mars as nearly Earth-like, possessing water, vegetation that changed with the seasons, and possibly intelligent life.

—adapted from Bennett et al., *The Cosmic Perspective*, p. 249

Such a pattern can be diagrammed as follows:

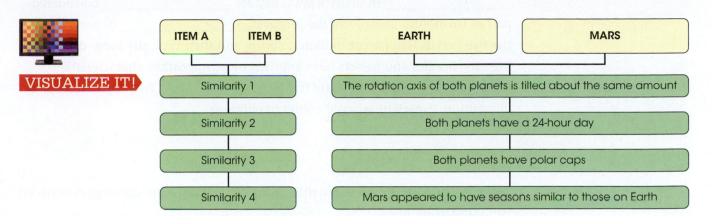

| ITEM A | ITEM B | | EARTH | MARS |
|--------|--------|--|-------|------|
| Similarity 1 | | | The rotation axis of both planets is tilted about the same amount | |
| Similarity 2 | | | Both planets have a 24-hour day | |
| Similarity 3 | | | Both planets have polar caps | |
| Similarity 4 | | | Mars appeared to have seasons similar to those on Earth | |

Look at the paragraph again, and notice the clues the writers provide about what kind of pattern they are following. In the first sentence—the topic sentence—the phrase *several uncanny resemblances* tells you that the paragraph will be about the similarities between Earth and Mars. The writers also use the words *same* and *both,* which signal that a comparison is being made. As you read, be on the lookout for words that indicate comparison or contrast.

When writers use comparison or contrast, sometimes they also include transitions to introduce each important point they are making. In the paragraph about Earth and Mars, for example, the writers use the transitions *in addition* and *also* to help the reader follow the main points of the comparison. Although such transitions are not always used in comparison and contrast, you will often find them in longer selections.

## Common Comparison and Contrast Transitions

| To show similarities | | To show differences | |
|----------------------|--|---------------------|--|
| *alike* | *just as* | *although* | *in spite of* |
| *also* | *like* | *as opposed to* | *instead* |
| *as well as* | *likewise* | *despite* | *nevertheless* |
| *both* | *resembles* | *differs from* | *on the other hand* |
| *correspondingly* | *share* | *however* | *unlike* |
| *in common* | *similarly* | *in contrast* | *whereas* |
| *in comparison* | *to compare* | | |
| *in the same way* | *too* | | |

## EXERCISE 8-11    Using Comparison Transitions

**Directions:** Select the comparison word or phrase from the box below that best completes each sentence in the paragraph. Write each answer in the space provided. Use each choice only once.

| same | in common | both | similarities | alike |
|------|-----------|------|--------------|-------|

Although beagles and basset hounds are different breeds, they are _____ in many ways. They are _____ considered part of the hound group, and the physical _____ between the two breeds is apparent in their coloring and their typically long, drooping ears. Beagles and bassets have another, more important characteristic _____: they share the _____ friendly and sociable disposition, especially when it comes to children.

## Contrast

The following paragraph was written to point out only the differences between two types of tumors:

> Not all tumors are **malignant** (cancerous); in fact, most are **benign** (noncancerous). Benign and malignant tumors differ in several key ways. Benign tumors are generally composed of ordinary-looking cells enclosed in a fibrous shell or capsule that prevents their spreading to other body areas. Malignant tumors, in contrast, are usually not enclosed in a protective capsule and can therefore spread to other organs. Unlike benign tumors, which merely expand to take over a given space, malignant cells invade surrounding tissue, emitting clawlike protrusions that disrupt chemical processes within healthy cells.
> —adapted from Donatelle, *Health: The Basics*, p. 324

Such a pattern can be diagrammed as follows:

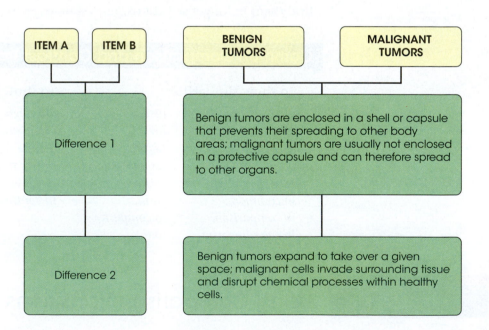

Look at the preceding paragraph again, and circle the contrast clues you can find (use the box on page 257 to help you). Did you circle the following words and phrases: *differ, in contrast,* and *unlike*?

# Writing Comparison or Contrast Paragraphs

Developing a comparison or contrast paragraph involves writing a topic sentence and developing points of comparison or contrast.

## Writing a Topic Sentence

Your topic sentence should do two things:

1. **It should identify the two subjects that you will compare or contrast.**
2. **It should state whether you will focus on similarities, differences, or both.**

Here are a few sample topic sentences that meet the requirements above:

> Judaism is one of the smallest of the world's religions; Hinduism is one of the largest.
>
> Neither Judaism nor Hinduism limits worship to a single location, although both hold services in temples.
>
> Unlike Hinduism, Judaism teaches belief in only one God.

Be sure to avoid topic sentences that announce what you plan to do. Here's an example: "I'll compare network news and local news and show why I prefer local news."

## Developing Points of Comparison or Contrast

The first thing you have to decide in writing a comparison or contrast paragraph is on what bases you will compare or contrast your two subjects. These bases are called **points of comparison** or **contrast.** Suppose you are comparing two different jobs that you have held. Points of comparison could be your salary, work schedule, required tasks, responsibilities, relationships with other employees, relationship with your boss, and so forth. The points of comparison you choose should depend on what you want your paragraph to show—your purpose for writing. If your purpose is to show what you learned from the jobs, then you might compare the tasks you completed and your responsibilities. If you want to make a case that working conditions in entry level jobs are poor, then you might use responsibilities, work schedule, and relationship with your boss as points of comparison.

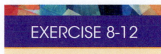

EXERCISE 8-12

**WRITING IN PROGRESS**

## Brainstorming and Writing Topic Sentences

**Directions:** For two of the topics below, brainstorm lists of similarities or differences. Review your lists and choose points of comparison. Then write topic sentences for them.

1. two special places
2. two favorite pastimes
3. two styles of dress
4. two cars

5. two public figures
6. two sports
7. two college classes
8. two relatives

## How to Organize a Comparison or Contrast Paragraph

Once you have identified similarities or differences between two items and drafted a topic sentence, you are ready to organize your paragraph. There are two ways you can organize a comparison or contrast paragraph:

- subject by subject
- point by point

### Subject-by-Subject Organization

In the **subject-by-subject method**, you write first about one of your subjects, covering it completely, and then about the other, covering it completely. Ideally, you cover the same points of comparison or contrast for both and in the same order. With subject-by-subject organization, you begin by discussing your first job—its salary, working conditions, and responsibilities. Then you discuss your second job—its salary, working conditions, and responsibilities. You can visualize the arrangement with the idea map shown below.

To develop each subject, focus on the same kinds of details and discuss the same points of comparison in the same order. Organize your points within each topic, using a most-to-least or least-to-most arrangement.

**VISUALIZE IT!**

**Model Idea Map for Subject-by-Subject Organization**

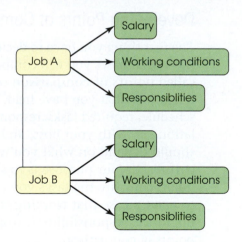

Job A → Salary
Job A → Working conditions
Job A → Responsiblities

Job B → Salary
Job B → Working conditions
Job B → Responsiblities

---

**EXERCISE 8-13**

WRITING IN PROGRESS

## Writing a Paragraph

**Directions:** Using the subject-by-subject method of organization, write a comparison or contrast paragraph on one of the topics you worked with in Exercise 8-12.

### Point-by-Point Organization

In the **point-by-point method of organization**, you discuss both of your subjects together for each point of comparison or contrast. For the paragraph on jobs, you would write about the salary for Job A and Job B, and then you would write about working conditions for Job A and Job B, and so on.

You can visualize the organization this way:

**VISUALIZE IT!**

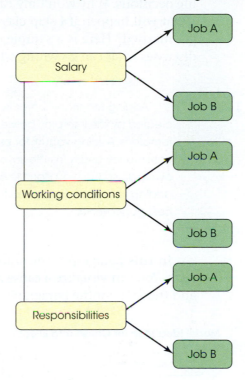

**Model Idea Map for Point-by-Point Organization**

When using this organization, maintain consistency by discussing the same subject first for each point. (For example, always discuss Job A first and Job B second.)

If your paragraph focuses only on similarities or only on differences, arrange your points in a least-to-most or most-to-least pattern.

Transitions are particularly important in comparison and contrast writing. Because you are discussing two subjects and covering similar points for each, your readers can easily become confused. Useful transitions are shown in the box on page 257.

**EXERCISE 8-14**

**WRITING IN PROGRESS**

## Using Transitions

**Directions:** Review the paragraph you wrote for Exercise 8-13. Add transitions as needed.

## READING AND WRITING CAUSE AND EFFECT

# What Are Cause and Effect?

■ GOAL 5
Read and write using cause and effect

**Causes** are explanations of why things happen. **Effects** are explanations of what happens as a result of an action or event. Each day we face situations that require cause and effect analysis. Some are daily events; others mark important life decisions. Why won't my car start? Why didn't I get my student loan check? What will happen if I skip class today? How will my family react if I decide to get married? Here is a sample cause and effect paragraph. The student writer discusses what can go wrong when preparing guacamole.

> Adding too many ingredients to guacamole will ruin the delicate flavor created by the interplay between fatty avocado, spicy peppers, and sweet tomatoes. Adding yogurt, for example, dilutes the dip to an almost souplike consistency and ruins the flavor. Dumping in salsa overpowers the delicate avocado so that you don't know what you are eating. Another common error, adding too much salt, masks the luxurious flavor of the avocado found in the best guacamole.

In this paragraph, the student writer identifies three causes and three effects. You can visualize a cause and effect paragraph as follows. Study the model and the map for the paragraph.

**VISUALIZE IT!**

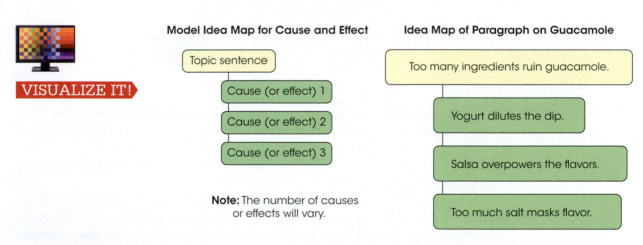

**Model Idea Map for Cause and Effect**

Topic sentence
→ Cause (or effect) 1
→ Cause (or effect) 2
→ Cause (or effect) 3

**Note:** The number of causes or effects will vary.

**Idea Map of Paragraph on Guacamole**

Too many ingredients ruin guacamole.
→ Yogurt dilutes the dip.
→ Salsa overpowers the flavors.
→ Too much salt masks flavor.

# Reading Cause and Effect

Writers use the **cause and effect** pattern to explain why an event or action causes another event or action. For example, if you are describing a skiing accident to a friend, you would probably follow a cause and effect pattern. You would tell what caused the accident and what happened as a result.

When a single cause has multiple effects, it can be visualized as follows:

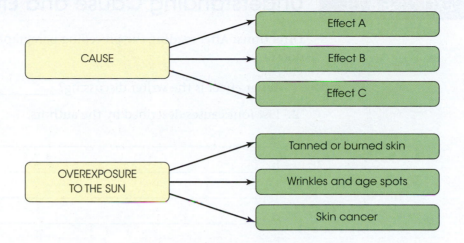

Sometimes, however, multiple causes result in a single effect. This kind of cause and effect pattern can be visualized this way:

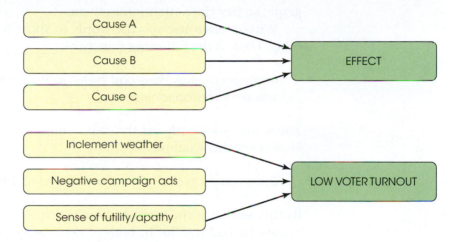

Read the following paragraph, which discusses the multiple causes of a single effect.

Although ulcers are commonly associated with stress, they can be brought on by other risk factors. Chronic use of aspirin and other nonsteroidal anti-inflammatory drugs increases the risk of ulcer because these agents suppress the secretion of both mucus and bicarbonate, which normally protect the lining of the GI tract from the effects of acid and pepsin. The risk of ulcer is also increased by chronic alcohol use or the leakage of bile from the duodenum into the stomach, both of which can disrupt the mucus barrier. Surprisingly, ulcers are usually not associated with abnormally high rates of stomach-acid secretion; more often than not, acid secretion is normal or even below normal in most people with ulcers.

—adapted from Germann and Stanfield, *Principles of Human Physiology*, p. 622

| EXERCISE 8-15 | Understanding Cause and Effect Patterns |
|---|---|

**Directions:** After reading the preceding paragraph, answer each of the following questions.

1. What effect is the writer discussing? _____

2. List four causes described by the authors.

    a. _____

    b. _____

    c. _____

    d. _____

As you worked on Exercise 8-15, did you notice that the topic sentence tells the reader that the paragraph will be about causes, referred to as *risk factors*? Topic sentences often provide this important clue in a cause and effect paragraph, so pay close attention to them.

Writers often use specific words to show why one event is caused by another. Look at the following statement:

> Shirley accidentally drove past the exit for her dentist's office. Consequently, she was late for her appointment.

The word *consequently* ties the cause—missed the exit—to the effect—being late. Here is another example:

> Deion was not in class all week because he had the flu.

In this sentence the word *because* ties the effect—Deion was absent—to the cause—he had the flu. In both of these examples, the cause and effect words help explain the relationship between two events. As you read, watch for words that show cause and effect; some common ones are listed in the box below.

## Common Cause and Effect Transitions

| For causes | For effects |
|---|---|
| *because* | *as a result* |
| *because of* | *consequently* |
| *cause is* | *hence* |
| *due to* | *one result is* |
| *for* | *results in* |
| *for this reason* | *therefore* |
| *one cause is* | *thus* |
| *one reason is* | |
| *since* | |
| *stems from* | |

**EXERCISE 8-16**     # Using Cause and Effect Transitions

**A. Directions:** After reading the following paragraph, select the cause and effect word in the box below that best completes each sentence in the paragraph. Write your answer in the space provided. Not all words will be used.

| consequently | effects | reasons |
|---|---|---|
| because of | cause | result |

Although it was a frightening experience, Bill's heart attack last year has had several positive _____. First, Bill realized that his diet had to change. He has eliminated the high-fat, high-sodium foods that were a major _____ of his health problems, replacing them with healthy, low-fat foods that he can prepare at home. Another aspect of Bill's life that has changed _____ his heart attack is his attitude toward exercise. He used to drive everywhere; now he walks whenever possible. In addition, he has started an exercise program approved by his doctor. As a _____, he looks and feels better than he has in years. Finally, Bill's heart attack served as a powerful reminder of the importance of his family. _____, he has adjusted his work schedule so that he is able to spend more time with the people he loves.

**B. Directions:** After reading the preceding paragraph, answer the following questions.

1. What cause is being discussed? _____

2. What three effects does the writer mention?

    a. _____

    b. _____

    c. _____

3. Does the topic sentence tell you that this will be a cause and effect paragraph? _____

4. Aside from the cause and effect words, list four transitions that the writer uses to lead the reader through the information.

    a. _____    b. _____    c. _____    d. _____

# Writing Cause and Effect Paragraphs

Developing a **cause and effect paragraph** involves distinguishing between causes and effects, writing a topic sentence, and providing relevant and sufficient details.

## Distinguishing Between Cause and Effect

How can you distinguish between causes and effects?

■ To determine causes, ask: "Why did this happen?"

■ To identify effects, ask: "What happened because of this?"

Let's consider an everyday situation: you lost your set of keys, so you are locked out of your apartment. This is a simple case in which one cause produces one effect. You can diagram this situation as follows:

Most situations, however, are much more complicated than the one shown above. Sometimes cause and effect work like a chain reaction: one cause triggers an effect, which in turn becomes the cause of another effect. In a chain reaction, each event in a series influences the next, as shown in the following example:

At other times, many causes may contribute to a single effect, as shown in the following diagram.

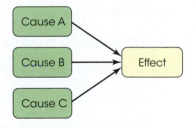

For example, there may be several reasons why you decided to become a veterinarian:

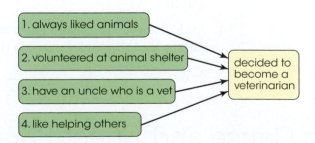

At other times, a single cause can have multiple effects, as shown below:

**VISUALIZE IT!**

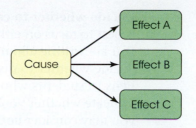

Suppose, for example, you decide to take a second part-time job:

**VISUALIZE IT!**

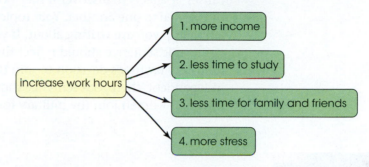

When analyzing a cause and effect situation that you plan to write about, ask yourself the following questions:

1. What are the causes? What are the effects? (To help answer these questions, draw a diagram of the situation.)

2. Which should be emphasized—cause or effect?

3. Are there single or multiple causes? Single or multiple effects?

4. Is a chain reaction involved?

---

**EXERCISE 8-17**

**WRITING IN PROGRESS**

## Identifying Causes and Effects

**Directions:** Identify possible causes and effects for three of the following topics:

1. Spending too much time surfing the Internet

2. Academic cheating or dishonesty

3. An important decision you made

4. The popularity of cell phones

5. Earning good grades

---

## Writing a Topic Sentence

To write effective topic sentences for cause and effect paragraphs, do the following:

1. **Clarify the cause and effect relationship.** Before you write, carefully identify the causes and the effects. If you are uncertain, divide a sheet of paper into two columns. Label one column "Causes" and the other "Effects." Brainstorm about your topic, placing your ideas in the appropriate column.

2. **Decide whether to emphasize causes or effects.** In a single paragraph, it is best to focus on either causes or effects—not both. For example, suppose you are writing about students who work two part-time jobs. You need to decide whether to discuss why they work two jobs (causes) or what happens to students who work two jobs (effects). Your topic sentence should indicate whether you are going to emphasize causes or effects. (In essays, you may consider both causes and effects.)

3. **Determine whether the events are related or independent.** Analyze the causes or effects to discover if they occurred as part of a chain reaction or are not related to one another. Your topic sentence should suggest the type of relationship you are writing about. If you are writing about a chain of events, your topic sentence should reflect this—for example, "A series of events led up to my brother's decision to join the military." If the causes or effects are independent, then your sentence should indicate that—for example, "Young men and women join the military for a number of different reasons."

## EXERCISE 8-18

**WRITING IN PROGRESS**

# Writing a Topic Sentence

**Directions:** For one of the topics you chose in Exercise 8-17, decide whether you will focus on causes or effects. Then write a topic sentence for a paragraph that will explain either causes *or* effects.

## Providing Relevant and Sufficient Details

Each cause or effect you describe must be relevant to the situation introduced in your topic sentence. Each cause or reason requires explanation, particularly if it is *not* obvious. Jot down a list of the causes or reasons you plan to include. This process may help you think of additional ones and will give you a chance to consider how to explain or support each cause or reason. You might decide to eliminate one or to combine several.

## How to Organize a Cause and Effect Paragraph

There are several ways to arrange the details in a cause and effect paragraph. The method you choose depends on your purpose in writing, as well as on your topic. Suppose you are writing a paragraph about the effects of a hurricane on a coastal town. Several different arrangements of details are possible:

1. **Chronological.** A chronological organization arranges your details in the order in which situations or events happened. For example, the order in which damage occurs during the course of a hurricane would become the order in which you present your details about the event. This arrangement is similar to the arrangement you learned about in Chapter 7, page 210. A chronological arrangement works for situations and events that occurred in a specific order.

2. **Order of importance.** In an order-of-importance organization, the details are arranged from least to most important or from most to least important. In describing the effects of a hurricane, you could discuss the most severe damage first and then describe lesser damage. Alternatively, you could build up to the most important damage for dramatic effect.

3. **Spatial.** Spatial arrangement of details uses physical or geographical position as a means of organization. In recounting the hurricane damage, you could start by describing damage to the beach and then work toward the center of town.

4. **Categorical.** This method of arrangement divides the topic into parts or categories. Using this arrangement to describe hurricane damage, you could recount what the storm did to businesses, roads, city services, and homes.

Because cause and effect relationships can be complicated, be sure to use transitional words and phrases to signal your reader which are causes and which are effects. Useful transitions are shown in the box on page 264.

## READING AND WRITING OTHER PATTERNS OF ORGANIZATION

■ GOAL 6
Read and write using other patterns of organization

The patterns presented in the preceding section are the most common. Table 8-1 presents a brief review of those patterns and their corresponding transitional words. However, writers do not limit themselves to these patterns or those described in Chapter 7. Especially in academic writing, you may find one or more of the patterns listed in Table 8-2 (page 271), as well.

**TABLE 8-1   A REVIEW OF PATTERNS AND TRANSITIONAL WORDS**

| Pattern | Characteristics | Transitional Words |
|---|---|---|
| **Definition** | Explains the meaning of a word or phrase | *are those that, can be defined as, consists of, corresponds to, entails, involves, is, is a term that, is called, is characterized by, is literally, means, occurs when, refers to* |
| **Classification** | Divides a topic into parts based on shared characteristics | *another, another kind, classified as, comprises, different groups that, different stages of, finally, first, include, is composed of, last, one, second, types of, varieties of* |
| **Comparison and Contrast** | Discusses similarities and/or differences among ideas, theories, concepts, objects, or persons | Similarities: *alike, also, as well as, both, correspondingly, in common, in comparison, in the same way, just as, like, likewise, resembles, share, similarly, to compare, too* |
| | | Differences: *although, as opposed to, despite, differs from, however, in contrast, in spite of, instead, nevertheless, on the other hand, unlike, whereas* |
| **Cause and Effect** | Describes how one or more things cause or are related to another | Causes: *because, because of, cause is, due to, for, for this reason, one cause is, one reason is, since, stems from* |
| | | Effects: *as a result, consequently, hence, one result is, results in, therefore, thus* |

# Statement and Clarification

Many writers make a statement of fact and then proceed to clarify or explain that statement. For instance, a writer may open a paragraph by stating that "The best education for you may not be the best education for someone else."

The remainder of the paragraph would then discuss that statement and make its meaning clear by explaining how educational needs are individual and based on one's talents, skills, and goals. Here is another example:

> The Constitution of the United States of America is the *supreme law of the land.* This means that any law—federal, state, or local—that conflicts with the U.S. Constitution is unconstitutional and, therefore, unenforceable. The principles enumerated in the Constitution are extremely broad, because the founding fathers intended them to be applied to evolving social, technological, and economic conditions. The U.S. Constitution often is referred to as a "living document" because it is so adaptable. States also have their own constitutions, often patterned after the U.S. Constitution. Provisions of state constitutions are valid unless they conflict with the U.S. Constitution or any valid federal law.
>
> —adapted from Goldman and Cheeseman, *The Paralegal Professional*, p. 183

Transitional words associated with this pattern are listed in Table 8-2.

# Summary

A **summary** is a condensed statement that recaps the key points of a larger idea or piece of writing. The summaries at the end of each chapter of this text provide a quick review of the chapter's contents. Often writers summarize what they have already said or what someone else has said. For example, in a psychology textbook you will find many summaries of research. Instead of asking you to read an entire research study, the textbook author will summarize the study's findings. Other times a writer may repeat in condensed form what he or she has already said as a means of emphasis or clarification. Here is a sample paragraph:

> To sum up, the minimax strategy is a general principle of human behavior that suggests that humans try to minimize costs and maximize rewards. The fewer costs and the more rewards we anticipate from something, the more likely we are to do it. If we believe that others will approve an act, the likelihood increases that we will do it. In short, whether people are playing cards with a few friends or are part of a mob, the principles of human behavior remain the same.
>
> —Henslin, *Sociology*, p. 637

Transitional words associated with this pattern are listed in Table 8-2.

# Addition

Writers often introduce an idea or make a statement and then supply additional information about that idea or statement. For instance, an education textbook may introduce the concept of homeschooling and then provide in-depth information about its benefits. This pattern is often used to expand, elaborate, or discuss an idea in greater detail. Here is an example:

> Millions of people work at home on computers connected to an office, an arrangement known as **telecommuting.** Telecommuting eases the pressure on transport facilities, saves fuel, and reduces air pollution. Moreover, it has been shown to increase workers' productivity and reduce absenteeism. It also allows employers to accommodate employees who want flexible work arrangements,

thus opening employment opportunity to more people, such as women who are still homemakers.

—Bergman and Renwick, *Introduction to Geography*, p. 430

Transitional words associated with this pattern are listed in Table 8-2.

# Spatial Order

Spatial order is concerned with the physical location or position in space. Spatial order is used in disciplines in which physical descriptions are important. A photography textbook may use spatial order to describe the parts of a camera. An automotive technology textbook may use spatial order to describe disk brake operation. Here is a sample paragraph:

We can taste food because chemoreceptors in the mouth respond to certain chemicals in food. The chemoreceptors for taste are located in structures called **taste buds**, each of which contains 50–150 receptor cells and numerous support cells. At the top of each bud is a pore that allows receptor cells to be exposed to saliva and dissolved food molecules. Each person has over 10,000 taste buds, located primarily on the tongue and the roof of the mouth, but also located in the pharynx.

—Germann and Stanfield, *Principles of Human Physiology*, pp. 303–304

Transitional words associated with this pattern are listed in Table 8-2.

| TABLE 8-2 A REVIEW OF ADDITIONAL PATTERNS AND TRANSITIONAL WORDS | | |
|---|---|---|
| **Pattern** | **Characteristics** | **Transitional Words** |
| **Statement and Clarification** | Gives information explaining an idea or concept | *clearly, evidently, in fact, in other words, obviously* |
| **Summary** | Provides a condensed review of an idea or piece of writing | *in brief, in conclusion, in short, in summary, on the whole, to sum up, to summarize* |
| **Addition** | Provides additional information | *additionally, again, also, besides, further, furthermore, in addition, moreover* |
| **Spatial Order** | Describes physical location or position in space | *above, behind, below, beside, in front of, inside, nearby, next to, opposite, outside, within* |

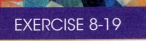

EXERCISE 8-19

# Identifying Patterns of Organization

**Directions:** For each of the following statements, identify the pattern that is evident and indicate it in the space provided. Choose from among the following patterns:

    **a.** statement and clarification
    **b.** summary
    **c.** addition
    **d.** spatial order

_____ 1. Short fibers, dendrites, branch out around the cell body and a single long fiber, the axon, extends from the cell body.

_____ 2. Aspirin is not as harmless as people think. It may cause allergic reactions and stomach irritation. In addition, aspirin has been linked to an often fatal condition known as Reye's syndrome.

_____ 3. If our criminal justice system works, the recidivism rate—the percentage of people released from prison who return—should decrease. In other words, in a successful system, there should be a decrease in the number of criminals who are released from prison and then become repeat offenders.

_____ 4. Students who are informed about drugs tend to use them in greater moderation. Furthermore, they tend to help educate others.

_____ 5. To sum up, a successful drug addiction treatment program would offer free or very cheap drugs to addicts.

_____ 6. Sociologists study how we are socialized into sex roles—the attitudes expected of males and females. Sex roles, in fact, identify some activities and behaviors as clearly male and others as clearly female.

_____ 7. The pollutants we have just discussed all involve chemicals; we can conclude that they threaten our environment and our well-being.

_____ 8. A residual check valve that maintains slight pressure on the hydraulic system is located in the master cylinder at the outlet for the drum brakes.

_____ 9. In conclusion, it is safe to say that crime by women is likely to increase as greater numbers of women assume roles traditionally held by men.

_____ 10. The meninges are three membranes that lie just outside the organs of the central nervous system.

# Thinking Critically About Patterns of Organization

■ GOAL 7
Think critically about patterns of organization

As explained in Chapter 7, patterns of organization are useful ways for writers to organize ideas, but they also give writers leeway in choosing the types of details to include or exclude in their writing. Like any other feature of writing, be sure to think critically about how the writer employs the pattern and why he or she chose it. Use the following guidelines to critically evaluate each of the primary patterns covered in this chapter.

## Definition

Depending on the topic, some definitions are objective and straightforward. A biology textbook chapter that defines photosynthesis is an example. Other definitions tend to be more subjective, involving interpretation, bias, and opinion. An essay defining reality television shows, for instance, is likely to reveal, directly or indirectly, whether the writer likes or dislikes them. So when reading definitions that are subjective, be sure to ask yourself whether you agree or disagree with the author's stance. Also determine whether the author provides sufficient evidence to support his or her opinion.

## Classification

When reading classification paragraphs and essays, be sure to examine the categories the writer has chosen. Are the categories complete? That is, do the categories cover most or all of the subject? For example, if you are reading an essay about the types of Facebook users, does the article cover most types of users, or are some left out? Also consider whether each category is treated in equal and sufficient detail. If some categories are treated in depth and others are not fully explained, you might wonder if the author has a bias against or special interest toward some of the categories. Finally, be sure to examine whether the principle of classification is appropriate and reasonable and suited to the author's purpose. For instance, if you are reading about unhealthy fast-food restaurants, it would be appropriate to classify the restaurants by the amounts of high-calorie food they serve, but it would not be useful to categorize them according the type of clientele they serve.

## Comparison and Contrast

A comparison or contrast always involves two or more topics. As a critical reader, check to see whether the author treats both or all topics equally and fairly. The amount of coverage should usually be approximately the same and each should be approached with the same level of objectivity or subjectivity. The same points of comparison should be covered for each, as well. For example, if a writer is comparing two- and four-year colleges, the writer should cover the same points of comparison for each, such as degrees offered, class size, faculty accessibility, and so forth. It would be unfair to use points of comparison that reveal all the advantages of two-year colleges and only the disadvantages of four-year schools.

## Cause and Effect

The cause and effect pattern is open to many logical errors. (See Chapter 16 for more about logical fallacies.) One of the most common reasoning errors is to assume that a cause and effect relationship exists between two events that occurred at the same time. If you take an aspirin and then feel dizzy, you might reason that the aspirin caused the dizziness. But, if you took the aspirin because you have the flu, the dizziness may be unrelated to the aspirin, although both occurred at the same time. As you read cause and effect writing, then, be sure to evaluate whether the author has provided sufficient evidence to support one event causing another.

Also evaluate whether the author's description of the cause and effect relationship is complete and objective. Has the author identified all relevant causes and/or effects? For example, a writer may argue that the death penalty causes undue pain and suffering to the prisoner and his or her family. To be objective, however, the writer should consider other effects of the death penalty as well, such as retribution for crimes committed, and so forth. Certainly writers are free to be subjective and present only reasons supporting their opinions, but they should do so openly. It is the reader's responsibility to recognize and evaluate the opposing viewpoints.

# INTEGRATING READING AND WRITING

## READ AND RESPOND: A Student Essay

*Jessica Nantka is a student at the State University College at Buffalo where she is majoring in elementary education.*

*For her writing class, Nantka was asked to write a cause-and-effect essay; she chose to write about the benefits of joining the military. As you read, notice that she devotes one paragraph to each benefit.*

Straightforward title

# Benefits of Joining the Military
## Jessica Nantka

1    The military has been around for many centuries in one form or another. It has been the basis for many societies, but today joining the military is a controversial issue. Throughout the many wars our world has seen, people have begun to realize the negative outcomes war and military service can have. Despite these

Thesis statement

negative effects, there are many reasons why joining the military is appealing and beneficial.

Effect 1: travel opportunities    2    Joining the military is a great way to see the world. Through various assignments and deployments, people can travel all around the world at the government's expense. They may not have a great deal of free time while in another country as they would if they were on vacation; however, just being there and experiencing life is gratifying enough. For example, my father traveled a lot when he was in the Navy; he traveled to Europe, Asia, and the Middle East and in the limited time he had, he briefly visited many of the worlds' most scenic and historical areas.

Effect 2: educational benefits    3    Educational benefits are another reason for joining the military. Schooling is offered and the military may even pay for a large portion of the tuition bill, depending on a number of factors such as length of service, rank, and so forth.

Enlistees can often get loans from the military for the rest, too. The military is very supportive of soldiers obtaining degrees, and encourages enlisted men and women to begin their studies while enlisted.

Effect 3: job training  4    <mark>Military enlistment offers great job training and many career options.</mark> Many enlistees are encouraged to select jobs in categories they are interested in, and they receive valuable job training and experience. When they leave the military, they find themselves ready to step into a job in the real world. Having served in the military is a great thing to have on a resume too.

Effect 4: health care coverage  5    <mark>Soldiers can obtain excellent health care for themselves and their dependents.</mark> Active duty soldiers receive free medical and dental care. Other services, such as counseling, are available depending on need. As veterans, retired soldiers and their families may be eligible for benefits which include hospital care, outpatient care, and medical supplies, again depending on the length of their service and other factors. Enlistees have to stay in for many years, though, to qualify for lifetime healthcare.

Effect 5: financial benefits  6    <mark>Enlisting in the military also makes financial sense in a lot of ways; there are many benefits.</mark> Military personnel can shop at the commissary and save a lot of money because things are sold there at a discount to military members and their families. The military pays a salary as well as offering free accommodation on base or providing a housing allowance, depending on factors such as a person's rank, location, and number of dependents. It may pay for food too. If you serve for 20 years, you get a pension for life.

Effect 6: builds character  7    <mark>Another reason many people, including myself, think about joining the armed forces is to build strength: strength for now, strength for later.</mark> Due to the fact that I am a female, many people treat me as though I am weak—but I am not. I want to prove to myself and others that I can do whatever I set my mind to do. The military offers training that will help me become a stronger person.

Effect 7: personal pride and public recognition  8    <mark>Honor and respect is obtained by serving in the military: pride for one's country is another reason why people join the military.</mark> Military personnel are respected and looked up to because they love their country so much that they will do anything for it. They fight to keep the rights that were set in place many years ago, to protect their country, and seek revenge on those that threaten it. President John F. Kennedy once said, "Ask not what your country can do for you, ask what you can do for your country." I remember that quote every time I think of joining the military. There are many things one can do to serve one's country such as volunteering with the Red Cross or Habitat for Humanity, but there is only one place in which one can actually protect one's country—the military.

Conclusion: refers back to the idea of joining the military being controversial  9    Most parents fear their children joining the armed forces; they do not want them to die in times of war. However, what they have to understand is the strength and pride that their children have. Every time I look at a soldier, I see respect and honor. To me, soldiers are the best; they are my heroes.

## Examining Academic Writing

1. How does Nantka introduce the subject?

2. Nantka refers to the negative effects of joining the military, but does not enumerate them. Should she have? How would this have affected the essay?

3. Suggest ways Nantka could make the introduction more lively and engaging.

4. What parts of the essay did you find the most persuasive?

## Academic Writing Assignments

1. You are taking a course in computer basics. Your instructor has asked the class to write a paragraph explaining why spamming—the process of sending advertisements to a large number of e-mail addresses—is a wasteful practice. Write a paragraph giving reasons why spamming is wasteful.

2. In your criminal justice class you are studying white-collar crimes—nonviolent crimes that are carried out in one's place of employment. Write a paragraph exploring reasons why an employee might commit a crime against his or her company.

3. For a health and wellness class, you have been asked to choose an unhealthy practice or habit and to write an essay defining it and explaining why it is unhealthy. (You might choose smoking, binge drinking, or overeating, for example.)

## READ AND RESPOND: A Professional Essay

### Thinking Before Reading

In this reading, from a textbook titled *Environment: The Science Behind the Stories*, the authors examine the consequences of the growing amount of electronic waste in our world. As you read, identify the effects of e-waste and of e-waste recycling.

1. Preview the reading using the steps discussed in Chapter 1, p. 15.

2. Connect the reading to your own experience by answering the following questions:

   a. What kinds of things do you recycle on a regular basis?

   b. What new electronic devices—cell phone, laptop, MP3 player, and so forth—have you bought in the past year? What happened to the old electronic devices you replaced?

3. Mark and annotate as you read.

# E-Waste and E-Waste Recycling

## Jay Withgott and Scott Brennan

**incinerators**
furnaces designed to burn waste completely
**EPA**
Environmental Protection Agency
**leach**
leak or seep out

1    Today's proliferation of computers, printers, cell phones, handheld devices, TVs, DVD players, fax machines, MP3 players, and other electronic technology has created a substantial new source of waste (see **ENVISION IT**, below). These products have short lifetimes before people judge them obsolete, and most are discarded after only a few years. The amount of this **electronic waste**—often called **e-waste**—is growing rapidly, and now comprises 2% of the U.S. solid waste stream. Over 3 billion electronic devices have been sold in the United States since 1980. Of these, half have been disposed of, about 40% are still being used (or reused), and 10% are in storage. American households discard close to 400 million electronic devices per year—two-thirds of them still in working order.

2    Of the electronic items we discard, roughly four of five go to landfills and **incinerators**, where they have traditionally been treated as conventional solid waste. However, most electronic products contain heavy metals and toxic flame retardants, and recent research suggests that e-waste should instead be treated as hazardous waste. The **EPA** and a number of states are now taking steps to keep e-waste out of conventional sanitary landfills and incinerators and instead treat it as hazardous waste.

3    More and more e-waste today is being recycled. The devices are taken apart, and parts and materials are refurbished and reused in new products. According to EPA estimates, Americans were recycling 15% of e-waste in 1999, and this rose to 18% by 2007. However, so many more items have been manufactured each year that the amount of e-waste we sent to landfills and incinerators in that time period increased by a greater amount. Disposal has risen faster than recycling: In 2007 we recycled 45 million more tons of e-waste than in 1999, but we also disposed of 169 million more tons of e-waste in landfills and incinerators.

4    Besides keeping toxic substances out of our environment, e-waste recycling is beneficial because a number of trace metals used in electronics are globally rare, so they can be lucrative to recover. A typical cell phone contains close to a dollar's worth of precious metals. Every bit of metal we can recycle from a manufactured item is a bit of metal we don't need to mine from the ground, so "mining" e-waste for precious metals helps reduce the environmental impacts that mining exerts. By one estimate,

**ENVISION IT**

Every five minutes, Americans throw away the number of cell phones shown on this page.

The 426,000 cell phones entering the U.S. waste stream daily can **leach** toxic heavy metals into the environment . . .

. . . or they can be recycled for reuse and for the recovery of valuable metals.

**YOU CAN MAKE A DIFFERENCE**
- Recycle your old phone with an approved e-waste recycling service.
- Donate your phone to a person or a charity that can reuse it.
- Think twice before buying yet another new electronic gadget that you don't really need.

1 ton of computer scrap contains more gold than 16 tons of mined ore from a gold mine. In one of the more intriguing efforts to promote sustainability through such recycling, the 2010 Winter Olympic Games in Vancouver produced its stylish gold, silver, and bronze medals from metals recovered from recycled and processed e-waste!

5    There are serious concerns, however, about the health risks that recycling may pose to workers doing the disassembly. Wealthy nations ship much of their e-waste to developing countries, where low-income workers disassemble the devices and handle toxic materials with minimal safety regulations. These environmental justice concerns need to be resolved, but if electronics recycling can be done responsibly, it seems likely to be the way of the future.

6    In many North American cities, used electronics are collected by businesses, nonprofit organizations, or municipal services, and are processed for reuse or recycling. So next time you upgrade to a new computer, TV, DVD player, cell phone, or handheld device, find out what opportunities exist in your area to recycle your old ones.

# Getting Ready to Write

## Checking Your Comprehension

Answer each of the following questions using complete sentences.

1. How much of the U.S. solid-waste stream is made up of electronic waste?
2. Of the more than 3 billion electronic devices sold in the United States since 1980, list the percentages of those that have been disposed of, are still being used, and are in storage.
3. How many electronic devices do American households discard per year?
4. Describe three benefits of e-waste recycling.
5. What are the environmental justice concerns associated with e-waste recycling?

## Strengthening Your Vocabulary

Using the word's context, word parts, or a dictionary, write a brief definition of each of the following words as it is used in the reading:

1. obsolete (paragraph 1) _____
2. comprises (paragraph 1) _____
3. toxic (paragraph 2) _____
4. lucrative (paragraph 4) _____
5. exerts (paragraph 4) _____
6. disassembly (paragraph 5) _____

### Examining the Reading: Using an Idea Map to Grasp Cause and Effect Relationships

In "E-Waste and E-Waste Recycling," the authors describe some positive and negative effects of e-waste recycling. Create an idea map that starts with the title and thesis of the essay and then lists the positive and negative effects of e-waste recycling.

### Reacting to Ideas: Discussion and Journal Writing

Get ready to write about the reading by discussing the following:

1. What is the thesis of this selection? Write a journal entry stating the thesis in your own words.

2. Discuss the e-waste statistics cited in this selection. Which statistics were most surprising to you and why?

3. Discuss the benefits of e-waste recycling. In your opinion, which benefit described in the selection was most compelling? Why?

4. What does *environmental justice* mean to you? Write a journal entry giving your definition of the term.

5. Three suggestions are listed within the photograph for how to make a difference. Evaluate each suggestion. Are they realistic and practical? Can you think of other ways to make a difference?

### Thinking and Writing Critically

1. List at least three sets of causes and effects that are discussed in this reading, carefully separating the causes from the effects.

2. Which method has the author used to organize details: chronological, order of importance, spatial, or categorical?

3. What is the purpose of the photograph that accompanies the reading? How does it reflect the content of the reading?

**THINKING VISUALLY**

MySkillsLab®

**Complete** this Exercise

## Writing About the Reading

### Paragraph Options

1. Did this article influence your opinion about donating or recycling your old electronics? Will it make you "think twice" before buying a new electronic gadget? Write a paragraph explaining your answers.

2. Write a paragraph describing how you can reduce the amount of waste that you generate in your own life. Include electronic waste as well as other types of waste, such as plastic, paper, glass, and so forth.

3. Think about the recyclable items you use on a regular basis. What items do you always recycle? Sometimes recycle? Never recycle? Write a paragraph classifying the recyclable items you use into these three categories and explaining why.

4. Write a paragraph describing the last time you bought an electronic gadget such as a cell phone or MP3 player. Did you comparison shop among two or more items that met the same basic requirements? Explain how you chose

between the different ones you considered purchasing. After reading this article, would you have been willing to pay more if the price included the cost of recycling?

### Essay Options

5. Imagine that you must convince your college administration, your dorm, or a campus group to begin an e-waste recycling program. Write a persuasive essay in which you discuss the consequences of electronic waste and the importance of an e-waste recycling program.

6. Write an essay addressing the environmental justice concerns mentioned in this selection. How might such concerns be resolved? What responsibility do the manufacturers of electronic devices have to the environment and to the workers handling e-waste?

7. The use of recycled metals to create Olympic medals is cited as one effort to promote sustainability through e-waste recycling. Can you think of other uses or applications for recycled metals? Write an essay exploring the possibilities.

# SELF-TEST SUMMARY

To test yourself, cover the Answer column with a sheet of paper and answer each question in the left column. Evaluate each of your answers as you work by sliding the paper down and companing your anwers with what is printed in the Answer column.

| QUESTION | ANSWER |
| --- | --- |
| ■ GOAL 1 Identify additional patterns of organization<br><br>What are some additional patterns of organization? | Additional patterns of organization are *definition, classification, comparison and contrast,* and *cause and effect.* See Table 8-1 (p. 269) for a review of characteristics and transitions for each of these patterns. |
| ■ GOAL 2 Read and write using definition<br><br>What are the three essential parts of a definition? | The three essential parts are:<br>1. The term being defined<br>2. The group or category to which the term belongs<br>3. Its distinguishing characteristics |
| ■ GOAL 3 Read and write using classification<br><br>How does classification explain a subject? | Classification explains a subject by identifying and describing its types or categories. |

| QUESTION | ANSWER |
|---|---|
| ■ GOAL 4 Read and write using comparison and contrast<br><br>What are comparison and contrast? What are two ways to organize a comparison or contrast paragraph? | Comparison treats similarities, whereas contrast emphasizes differences. You may organize a comparison or contrast paragraph either subject by subject or point by point. |
| ■ GOAL 5 Read and write using cause and effect<br><br>What are causes and effects? What are four ways to organize cause and effect paragraphs? | Causes are explanations of why things happen, whereas effects are explanations of what happens as a result of an action or event. Cause and effect paragraphs may be organized chronologically, in order of importance, spatially, or in categories. |
| ■ GOAL 6 Read and write using other patterns of organization<br><br>What are some other useful patterns of organization? | Other useful patterns include statement and clarification, summary, addition, and spatial order. See Table 8-2 (p. 271) for a review of characteristics and transitions for each of these patterns. |
| ■ GOAL 7 Think critically about patterns of organization<br><br>How can you think critically about patterns of organization? | When considering the details the writer has chosen to include, evaluate whether the details are complete and relevant, and whether topics are treated equally and sufficiently. Consider how the writer uses the pattern and why he or she chose it. |

**MySkillsLab**®  For more help with **Additional Patterns of Organization**, go to your learning path in MySkillsLab at www.myskillslab.com.

# Strategies for Revising Paragraphs

## THINK About It!

The two photographs above show the same room in two different conditions. Write a sentence describing what was done in order to make the room more livable.

The person who lived there obviously looked around the room, assessed what needed to be done, and then made a plan for reorganizing and cleaning up the room. The same process occurs in writing. First, the writer looks over a draft, perhaps reading it three or four times, assessing what needs to be done and creating a plan to improve it. Next, the writer carries out the plan for revision. The changes may involve reorganization, adding material to strengthen the paragraph, and deleting material that is not useful. Finally the writer edits or cleans up the paragraph, clarifying any confusions, choosing more effective wording, and checking grammar, spelling, punctuation, and mechanics. All of the changes a writer makes are made with his or her readers in mind. Changes are made to make the message clear, easy to understand, and free of distracting errors. In this chapter, you will learn how to assess a draft and effectively revise and edit it.

# Reading and Writing Connections

### EVERYDAY CONNECTIONS

- **Reading** After repeatedly rereading the user's manual that accompanies new software you purchased, you draw an idea map to help you understand and organize the information so you can figure out why the software will not install properly.
- **Writing** You write a complaint letter to the company that sold you the defective software, and then revise it when your friend says you should explain more about how the problem has inconvenienced you and why you should receive your money back.

### ACADEMIC CONNECTIONS

- **Writing** You reread and revise an outline for a speech because you realize the speech needs to appeal more directly to your audience.
- **Reading** You read the draft of a classmate's speech and decide to revise your own speech to include more details.

### WORKPLACE CONNECTIONS

- **Writing** You revise a memo you are sending to your boss after you reread it and realize it only focuses on your complaints about a situation and does not include your suggestions for how to remedy it.
- **Reading** You read about a job opening for applicants bilingual in Spanish and English, and you revise your cover letter to tailor it to the job and to reflect changes you have made to your résumé.

## FOCUSING ON READING AND WRITING

# What Is Revision?

■ **GOAL 1**
Understand the purpose
of revising

**Revising** a paragraph involves examining your ideas by rereading, most likely several times, every idea and sentence you have written and often making major changes to them. You might add ideas, delete details, or rearrange parts. **Editing** is a part of the revision process that focuses on clarity and correctness. It involves adding or deleting words and phrases, as well as correcting your grammar, spelling, punctuation, and mechanics. Before you go on, you may want to review the material in "Revise and Rewrite Drafts" in Chapter 2 (p. 69), and "Proofread Your Final Draft (p. 70) including the paragraph on peer review, and Reading and Writing Success Tip #5, "Collaborate for Success" on page 11.

## READING

# Read Critically to Revise

■ GOAL 2
Read critically to revise

The first step in preparing to revise a paragraph is to read it critically with the purpose of finding out what works and what doesn't. Use the following suggestions, in addition to those listed in Chapter 2.

It is easy to like your own work and feel you have done a great job, so mentally prepare yourself to look at your writing from afar, as if someone else wrote it. Right after you finish a paragraph, it is especially difficult to see how to improve it. Whenever possible, let your draft sit a day or two before returning to it to revise.

Allow enough time to read your paragraph several times, each for a different purpose. It is difficult to check for all aspects of writing at the same time. Instead, use the following strategy:

■ **Read the paragraph once, examining content**. Does it say what you want it to say? If it doesn't, make the necessary changes, and then read it again. If you aren't sure if your meaning is clear, ask a friend or classmate to review your draft (see "Collaborate for Success," p. 11, for suggestions on how to make peer review work effectively).

■ **Read the paragraph again, evaluating how effectively you have expressed your ideas**, again making changes to improve the draft. Reread to make sure your changes work.

■ **Read the paragraph a third time, checking for correctness**. You might want to read the draft several times, looking for one common error at a time.

## WRITING

# Consider Your Purpose and Audience

■ GOAL 3
Consider your purpose and audience

As was mentioned in Chapter 2, good writing should achieve your purpose and be directed toward a specific audience. When you are ready to revise, read your draft through once or twice to get an overall impression of it. Then decide whether the paragraph accomplishes what you want it to. If it doesn't, try to identify what went wrong, using the Revision Checklist on page 290. If it is difficult to identify the reasons a draft doesn't achieve its purpose, ask a friend or classmate to read your writing and summarize what it does accomplish. This information will often give you clues about how to improve the piece.

To evaluate whether your writing is suited to your audience, read it from the audience's viewpoint. Try to anticipate what ideas your audience might find unclear, what additional information might be needed, and whether the overall reaction will be positive or negative. Imagine that someone else wrote the piece and you are reading it for the first time. Does it keep your interest and make some fresh and original points? Could you treat your subject in a more engaging way?

# Examine Your Ideas

■ **GOAL 4**
Examine your ideas

The most important part of revision is reevaluating your ideas. Think of revision as an opportunity to reassess your ideas in order to make what you are writing as effective as possible.

Often simply reading and rereading your writing do not help you to recognize what to change or improve. One of the best ways to discover what to revise is to use an idea map. An **idea map** is a visual display of the ideas you have written about in a paragraph or essay. Think of it as similar to a road map. A road map allows you to see how towns and cities connect to one another. An idea map allows you to see how ideas relate and connect to one another. An idea map can help you check two important features of your writing:

■ your use of relevant and sufficient detail

■ the logical organization of your ideas

To draw a paragraph idea map, follow these steps:

1. Write a shortened topic sentence at the top of your paper.

2. Then go through your paragraph sentence by sentence and list each detail that directly supports the topic sentence.

3. If you spot an example of one of the details already listed, or a further explanation of a detail, write it underneath the detail it relates to and indent it.

4. If you spot a detail that does not support or is not related to anything else, write it to the right of your list, as in the sample below.

**VISUALIZE IT!**

**Sample Revision Map**

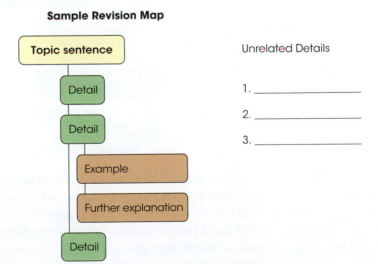

## Relevant and Sufficient Detail

As you revise, you want to be sure you have provided enough information about your subject and that all your details directly support your topic sentence. Drawing an idea map allows you to see if you have explained each detail adequately. You will also see immediately any details that are not relevant.

Here is the first draft of a paragraph written by a student named Joe. His idea map follows.

*Draft 1*

Currently, Herbalife is one of the top companies in the world for rate of growth and also for leading the industry in research and development of nutritional products. You may begin your own distributorship as I did with as little as 50 dollars. Your income potential depends on the effort you put forth. Herbalife makes health products. It is backed by a team of doctors and scientists who are the leaders in weight-loss research and maintenance on a daily basis. Herbalife will continue to be a leader because its products are of high quality and it cares about the health of the entire world. My involvement with Herbalife is just beginning, and I look forward to a profitable future.

**VISUALIZE IT!**

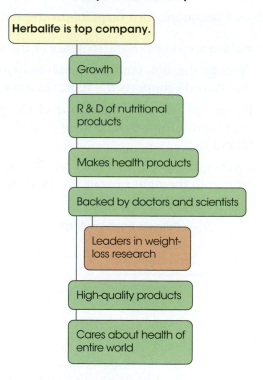

**Sample Revision Map**

Herbalife is top company.

Growth

R & D of nutritional products

Makes health products

Backed by doctors and scientists

Leaders in weight-loss research

High-quality products

Cares about health of entire world

Unrelated Details

1. Begin distributorship—$50
2. Income potential depends on effort
3. Involvement is just beginning

Joe's map shows him how he structured his paragraph. It allows him to see whether his ideas connect and whether he has enough detail to support his main ideas. By studying this map, he can spot details that do not fit and ideas that need further development or explanation. Joe found three details (see right side of map) that did not support his original topic sentence. He realized that these details related instead to why he felt Herbalife was a good company with which to begin his own business. Joe rewrote his topic sentence to include this idea and added more explanation in his revised paragraph.

*Draft 2*

Because Herbalife is one of the top companies in the world for nutrition and health, it is a good opportunity for me to start my own business. It is a company that is not only growing rapidly but also becoming a leader in the research and development of nutritional products. Herbalife products are easy to sell because they are backed by medical doctors and scientists. The products are appealing because they are high quality and because the company demonstrates its concern for worldwide health through its advertising. You can start your own distributorship for only 50 dollars. There are no hidden costs, and you are not required to maintain a large inventory. I'm expecting my Herbalife distributorship to be the start of a business that will help me pay for college.

This second draft focuses more directly on the newly sharpened topic and includes relevant and sufficient detail. Further decisions might focus on improving sentence structure, strengthening the connection among details, and adding transitional words and phrases.

## Drawing an Idea Map

**Directions:** Read the following student paragraph and draw an idea map for it. Compare your map with that of a classmate. Select the more effective map and use it to identify details that are not relevant to the topic. When you find details that are not relevant, underline them.

Employees of large companies benefit from labor unions. Labor unions protect workers' rights. Union leaders organize employees so that they can't be exploited by company management. Being a union leader is a difficult but important job. Unions are also important because they make sure that all employees are treated equally and fairly. Before unions were created, each employee had to make his or her own deal with an employer, and some workers ended up doing the same job as others but for less pay. Employers listen to unions because unions can organize strikes and contact federal agencies about violations. Sometimes strikes fail and people are out of work for long periods. Many times this is on the news. Labor unions also make sure that work sites are safe and that there are no health hazards.

## Writing a Paragraph and Drawing an Idea Map

**Directions:** Assume that you are taking a course in communication and that your instructor has given you a choice of the following topics as your first assignment. Choose a topic and write a first draft. Then draw an idea map that will help you evaluate whether you have relevant and sufficient detail.

1. Describe one important convenience or service you would miss if the Internet did not exist, and imagine life without it.

2. Give three reasons the Internet is useful.

3. Make a list of everyday products, activities, or services that do not require a computer in any way. Write a paragraph summarizing your findings.

4. How can computers and the personal information stored in them jeopardize our right to privacy? Give your views.

5. A computer-controlled robot has been developed to perform specialized types of surgery. Discuss the advantages and disadvantages of this innovation.

## Logical Organization of Ideas

Another major issue to consider as you revise is whether you have arranged your ideas in a way your readers can follow. As we saw in Chapter 6, even if you have plenty of detail, the wrong organization can throw your readers off track. In addition, you need to make sure you use transitional words and phrases to help readers follow your thoughts.

Revision maps are also useful for checking your organization. By listing the ideas in the order in which they appear in your paragraph, you can see if they are arranged logically. Study the following student paragraph and then its revision map.

*Draft 1*

The women's movement has produced important changes in women's lifestyles. Women started the movement with rallies and marches. The Nineteenth Amendment to the Constitution gave women the vote. A lot of men were not happy about that. Women never used to be able to vote and they were not supposed to drink or swear or wear pants. That was ridiculous. Women now have more rights and freedoms. But women still don't get paid as much as men. Many women have jobs in addition to taking care of their families. Women do a lot more than men. Women now have a choice about what they want to do for a career but are not rewarded as much as men.

VISUALIZE IT!

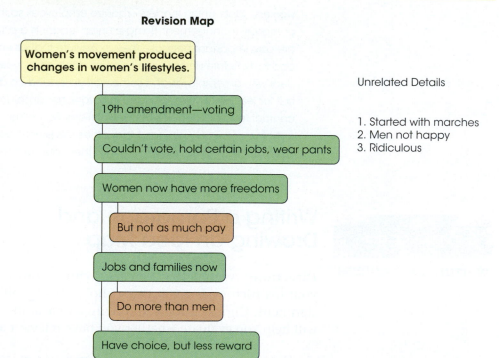

**Revision Map**

Women's movement produced changes in women's lifestyles.

19th amendment—voting

Couldn't vote, hold certain jobs, wear pants

Women now have more freedoms

But not as much pay

Jobs and families now

Do more than men

Have choice, but less reward

Unrelated Details

1. Started with marches
2. Men not happy
3. Ridiculous

The map shows that the details are not arranged in any specific order. Since most of them relate to changes in women's rights, these details could be arranged from past to present. The writer arranged the details in chronological order in her second draft.

*Draft 2*

The women's movement has produced important changes in women's lifestyles. Before 1900, women could not vote, hold certain jobs, or wear pants. They were oppressed. The Nineteenth Amendment to the Constitution, passed in 1920, allowed women to vote. Other rights have come gradually over the years.

> Now women have a wide variety of job possibilities, and they certainly are not forbidden to wear pants. Women have more freedom now, but they still do not earn as much as men. Today women have more choices, but they are still short on rewards.

Notice the added transitional words and phrases in Draft 2. The writer added the phrase "Before 1900" to signal the reader that she was going to review the early status of women.

Idea maps are also useful for identifying several other common writing problems.

- If you strayed from your topic, you will see it happening on your idea map.

- If your paragraph is repetitious, you will realize as you study your idea map that you are saying the same thing more than once.

- If your paragraph is unbalanced because you have emphasized some ideas and not others that are equally important, your idea map will show it.

## Using an Idea Map

**Directions:** Study the idea map of the paragraph you wrote for Exercise 9-2. Evaluate your arrangement of details. If they are not arranged logically, number them on your map and revise your paragraph. After you have examined your ideas, you should make sure that you have expressed them effectively and appropriately. That is, you should determine whether the language you have chosen is specific and vivid, whether it is suited to your audience, and whether it achieves your purpose for writing.

### Revise for Specific and Vivid Language

In Chapter 6, we discussed using specific and vivid words and phrases to provide accurate and interesting detail. As you revise, look for drab, nondescriptive words and phrases. Replace them with lively words that enable your reader to create a mental picture of your topic.

Here is a paragraph, with revisions, that a student wrote on the topic of aerobic dancing. Notice how she changed and replaced words to make her details more specific and vivid.

> Aerobic dancing is ~~great~~ *energizing and enjoyable* exercise. It makes you ~~use a lot of~~ *stretch and exert* muscles *from nearly all muscle groups*. It also gives your cardiovascular system a good workout because ~~it gets~~ *starts* your heart pumping and (increases) your rate of breathing. You maintain the pace for ~~awhile~~ *20 or 30 minutes*, which is also beneficial. Aerobic dancing builds endurance and stamina, which make you ~~feel as if you are in good physical condition~~ *r body come alive and scream, "I'm in shape!"*. In aerobics the risk of injury is slight since there is no intense strain on any one part of the body.

## Revising a Paragraph

**Directions:** Evaluate your use of specific and vivid language in the paragraph you wrote for Exercise 9-2. Revise the paragraph to make your language livelier and more descriptive.

During revision, there is a lot to think about. This Revision Checklist will help you keep in mind important questions to ask about your writing.

## Revision Checklist

1. Who is your audience? How interested are they in your subject and how much do they know about it? Is your paragraph suited to your audience?

2. What is your purpose? Does your paragraph accomplish your purpose?

3. Is your main point clearly expressed in your topic sentence?

4. Is each detail relevant? Does each explain or support the topic sentence directly?

5. Have you supported your topic sentence with sufficient detail to make it understandable and believable?

6. Do you use specific and vivid words to explain each detail?

7. Do you connect your ideas with transitional words and phrases?

# Edit for Correctness

■ **GOAL 5**
Correct errors in grammar, spelling, and punctuation

Errors (mistakes) in grammar, spelling, and punctuation make your writing less effective. A writer who seems careless loses the reader's confidence. **Editing** is a process of making corrections. It is an important *final step* to writing a good paragraph. Of course, if you notice an error while you are drafting or revising, you should correct it. In general, however, focus on looking for errors only after you are satisfied with the content and organization of your paragraph.

## What Errors to Look For

Many students wonder how they will ever learn enough to spot all the errors in their writing. The job is easier than you think! Most students make certain types of errors. The Handbook (p. 511) addresses the most common errors students make:

- sentence fragments (p. 547)
- run-on sentences (p. 552)
- subject-verb agreement (p. 563)
- pronoun-antecedent agreement (p. 566)
- pronoun reference (p. 568)
- shifts and mixed constructions (p. 578)

- dangling modifiers (p. 577)
- misplaced modifiers (p. 576)
- verb tense (p. 518)
- coordinate sentences (p. 580)
- subordinate clauses (p. 582)
- parallelism (p. 584)
- when to use commas (p. 594)
- using colons and semicolons (p. 597)

The following Proofreading Checklist will remind you to check for spelling, punctuation, and other mechanical errors.

## Proofreading Checklist

1. Does each sentence end with an appropriate punctuation mark (period, question mark, exclamation point, or quotation mark)?
2. Is all punctuation within each sentence correct (commas, colons, semicolons, apostrophes, dashes, and quotation marks)?
3. Is each word spelled correctly?
4. Are capital letters used where needed?
5. Are numbers and abbreviations used correctly?
6. Are any words left out?
7. Have all typographical errors been corrected?
8. Are the pages in the correct order and numbered?

## Keeping an Error Log

Many students consistently make certain types of errors and not others. You can identify and learn to avoid yours by keeping a record of your mistakes. Use an error log like the sample shown below. Each time your instructor returns a paper, count how many errors you made of each type, and enter that number in the log. Soon you will see a pattern. You can then review your final drafts to locate these specific errors.

If you make frequent spelling errors, be sure to use the spell-checker on your computer. Also, keep a separate list of the words you misspell. Study them and practice writing them correctly.

**EXERCISE 9-5**

**WRITING IN PROGRESS**

## Using an Error Log

**Directions:** Check the paragraph you wrote for Exercise 9-2 for errors and correct any you find. Enter them in an error log (see sample).

| | A | B | C | D | E | F |
|---|---|---|---|---|---|---|
| 1 | | | | Sample Error Log | | |
| 2 | ASSIGNMENT | | | TYPES OF ERRORS | | |
| 3 | | Sentences | | Grammar | Punctuation | Misspelled Words |
| 4 | | run-on | fragments | | | |
| 5 | 1 | one | one | subject-verb agreement | comma | favorite |
| 6 | | | | verb tense | | relies |
| 7 | | | | pronoun ref. | | knowledge |
| 8 | 2 | two | – | verb tense | comma | chemicals |
| 9 | | | | | quotation | majority |
| 10 | | | | | | especially |
| 11 | 3 | one | – | subject-verb agreement | comma | necessary |
| 12 | | | | verb tense | semicolon | hoping |
| 13 | | | | pronoun ref. | | definitely |
| 14 | 4 | | | | | |
| 15 | | | | | | |
| 16 | | | | | | |
| 17 | 5 | | | | | |
| 18 | | | | | | |
| 19 | | | | | | |
| 20 | 6 | | | | | |

# INTEGRATING READING AND WRITING

## READ AND RESPOND: A Student Essay

*Elizabeth Lawson (she requested that we change her name to reprint her essay) is a student at an Illinois college. She is working on her bachelor's degree in psychology and hopes to become a high school guidance counselor. In her writing class, Elizabeth was given the following assignment: Write an essay describing a difficult or challenging situation that you faced.*

*Three versions of her essay are shown below. The first is her first draft. Elizabeth asked a classmate to review this draft and make suggestions. These are shown in handwriting on and at the end of the first draft. The second draft shows the changes Elizabeth made in the content of the essay. You will see that she deleted some ideas and added others. The third draft shows the editing corrections Elizabeth made in sentence structure, grammar, punctuation, and spelling. Study each draft carefully to learn how the revision process works.*

## FIRST DRAFT

It seems that everyday on the news you hear about some Hollywood celebrity or sports star having an addiction problem whether it's steroids or alcohol or pain-killers or something even worse like crystal meth. You think it can never happen to you because your life is fine and you can deal with your issues, no problem. But now I understand it more. For example who can blame a baseball player for juicing up on steroids? ① They make a boatload of money to hit home runs and steroids make them stronger. If they don't hit homeruns, they get knocked off the team and who wants to lose all that money?

*1. This is an interesting introduction, but I don't understand why you go into detail on steroids. They're not part of the experience you are describing in your essay.*

But the main reason I understand it more is because I went through an addiction myself. It wasn't steroids, as a woman who is 5 feet tall I would look pretty silly being all muscular like that, but it was tranquilizers.

*2. I don't see a clear thesis statement anywhere in the first two paragraphs.*

I can't really complain about my life because I know how good I had it. I was ② raised by a single mom and she did a great job. She was the youngest of six children who were all born in different cities, and she was the only girl with five brothers. Her mother and father moved around a lot because her father was a traveling salesman. We were always so close, I remember when my father died (I was 8) we made a deal that we were going to be a team and stick together. It was just the two of us and she worked super hard to put food on the table and buy me things I wanted but she couldn't really afford (which makes me feel selfish now, but that's another story). Of course we had our fights especially when I was a teenager but she was always like a mixture of a good friend that I liked to talk to, plus a parent who tried to teach me the right things to do. I made mistakes, everyone does, but at the end of the day we watched out for each other. One time I heard some neighbor women gossiping about her, I marched right up to them and told them to knock it off because they had no idea what she went through. She actually punished me for being rude to the neighbors but when she was dying several years later she told me how proud of me she was when I did that.

Because that's what happened, she died. I was 22 years old and in college and you would think a grown woman would be able to handle it. But I fell apart, I was crying all the time. I just kept thinking about what a great person she was and how much I missed her, and luckily I didn't feel guilty about mistreating her because I was with her til the end (she died of cancer), so as we promised each other, we were a team. But the weeks went by and I couldn't get over it. I couldn't study, I couldn't eat, and worst of all I couldn't sleep. I was exhausted and having panic attacks, I even hallucinated once or twice. I was a total mess and I refused to go to a counselor because I thought I could deal with it on my own. Well I was wrong about that.

Then my uncle, my mother's brother, came to visit me and he took one look at me and said how awful I looked. He had a prescription for tranquilizers and he gave some to me because I felt like if I didn't get some sleep I was going to die. So I took one and it worked so incredibly well, it relaxed me and I fell asleep and I woke up the next day after sleeping about 15 hours. I also felt super relaxed and much, much less upset so I went to the doctor and asked for a prescription and he gave it to me but said he would do it only if I went to a grief counselor also so I took those pills twice a day for 3 months and they helped me sleep and get over all my upset. The problem was they also took away my energy. And talking about everything with the counselor (Jane) was a huge load off my mind, so at the end of the 3 months I thought, OK, I don't need these pills anymore, so I stopped taking them.

_3. The essay does not have a concluding paragraph that summarizes what you learned from your experience._

And that is when the trouble started. My heart started racing like crazy after ③ a couple of days without the pills. My vision got blurry and I started getting weird cramps. I could not sleep a wink and went 72 hours without sleep. I would just lay there with my heart racing a mile a minute. Then something happened that really scared me, I started feeling zaps of electricity in my brain, like my brain was short circuiting. That really scared me, I was terrified and thought I was having a stroke. So I went to the emergency room and they figured out what was happening, I was having withdrawal symptoms from going off the meds too fast. It turns out that the type of medication I was on, you have to stop taking it gradually otherwise you get these terrible effects. They gave me one of the tranquilizers I was taking and the problems stopped almost immediately. And then this is the part you would not believe. It took me almost six months to stop taking those pills. I had to reduce the dose by a tiny amount, take that dose for a week, then reduce the dose a little more, take that for a week, then reduce it again and again and so on until I could stop taking it. Finally I got off it and I feel better. I still miss my Mom though.

### Peer Review Comments

Elizabeth,

    Your essay really made me understand what you went through and how addictions can happen without a person realizing it. I was also touched by how you describe your relationship with your mother. Here are a few changes you could make:

1. What point are you trying to make in the whole essay? You describe what you went through, but I would like to know how the experience changed your life or how you feel different as a result of it.
2. Did your friends know what you were going through, or did you hide it from them? Why were you afraid to ask for help?
3. It is hard to find topic sentences in some of the paragraphs. Some of the paragraphs seem long and unfocused. Can you split them up and deal with just one main idea at a time, and maybe eliminate some of the unnecessary details?

You didn't mention which tranquilizer you were taking. I think it would be a good idea to name it, so that people who read your essay will know the dangers of it when they see it.

## FIRST REVISION—SHOWING CHANGES IN IDEAS

# My Unexpected Addiction
### Elizabeth Lawson

1    It seems that everyday on the news you hear about some Hollywood celebrity or sports star having an addiction problem whether it's steroids or alcohol or painkillers or something even worse like crystal meth. You think it can never happen to you because your life is fine and you can deal with your issues, no problem. **But now I understand it more because I developed an addiction of my own, and I had to struggle to free myself from it. In the process I learned a few things about myself and what makes me tick.** It all happened so fast that I didn't know what was happening at the time, but looking back now I understand it better.

*Added thesis statement, which is actually two sentences here*

2    There's no reason I should have developed an addiction, because I had a basically good life with a stable, loving mother. I was raised by a single mom and she did a great job. We were always so close I remember when my father died (I was 8) we made a deal that we were going to be a team and stick together. It was just the two of us and she worked super hard to put food on the table and buy me things I wanted but she couldn't really afford. Of course we had our fights especially when I was a teenager but she was always like a mixture of a good friend that I liked to talk to, plus a parent who tried to teach me the right things to do. I made mistakes, everyone does, but at the end of the day we watched out for each other. One time I heard some neighbor women gossiping about her, I marched right up to them and told them to knock it off because they had no idea what she went through. She actually punished me for being rude to the neighbors but when she was dying several years later she told me how proud of me she was when I did that.

*Added strong topic sentence*

*Eliminated some detail to keep the paragraph focused*

3    It was when she died that I fell apart and started having all sorts of problems I never had before. I was 22 years old and in college and you would think a grown

*Added strong topic sentence*

woman would be able to handle it. But I fell apart, I was crying all the time. I just kept thinking about what a great person she was and how much I missed her. But the weeks went by and I couldn't get over it. I couldn't study, I couldn't eat, and worst of all I couldn't sleep. I was exhausted and having panic attacks, I even hallucinated once or twice. I was a total mess and I refused to go to a counselor because I thought I could deal with it on my own. Well I was wrong about that.

4    Then my uncle, my mother's brother, came to visit me and he took one look at me and said how awful I looked. He had a prescription for a tranquilizer called Ativan (also called lorazepam) and he gave some to me because I felt like if I didn't get some sleep I was going to die. So I took one and it worked so incredibly well, it relaxed me and I fell asleep and I woke up the next day after sleeping about 15 hours. I also felt super relaxed and much, much less upset so I went to the doctor and asked for a prescription and he gave it to me but said he would do it only if I went to a grief counselor also so I took those pills twice a day for 3 months and they really helped me. The problem was they also took away my energy. And talking about everything with the counselor at my college (Jane) was a really big help. She helped me see something I didn't see on my own: that I would feel like I was betraying my mother if I went to someone other than her for help and advice. Jane also asked, Wouldn't my mother want me to be happy instead of crying all the time? Of course it made complete sense! So at the end of the 3 months I thought, OK, I don't need these pills anymore, so I stopped taking them.

5    And that is when the trouble started. My heart started racing like crazy after a couple of days without the pills. My vision got blurry and I started getting weird cramps. I went 72 hours without sleep. I would just lay there with my heart racing a mile a minute. Then something happened that really scared me, I started feeling zaps of electricity in my brain, like my brain was short circuiting. I was terrified and thought I was having a stroke. So I went to the emergency room and they figured out what was happening, I was having withdrawal symptoms from going off the meds too fast. It turns out that the type of medication (called a benzodiazepine, or benzo for short) I was on, you have to stop taking it gradually otherwise you get these terrible effects. They gave me an Ativan and the problems stopped almost immediately. And then this is the part you would not believe. I had to reduce the dose by a tiny amount, take that dose for a month, then reduce the dose a little more, take that for a month, then reduce it again and again and so on until I could stop taking it.

6    It took me almost six months to reduce my dose to zero. And I learned a few things about myself and the world through the experience. First, maybe all the celebrities you read about with their addiction problems actually deserve a little sympathy instead of scorn. Maybe they, like me, had a problem they were trying to deal with, and things got out of control without them ever realizing it. Second, people with addictions are not bad people or even low class people. They are trying to cope with their problems but don't know the right way to do it. Third, and probably most important, I realized that it is OK to ask for help when you need it. If I had gone to grief counseling early, or even if I went to a support group while Mom was sick, I would have had more support and more understanding of what people go through and how to cope with it. I still miss Mom, but I know she's up there, proud that I overcame my addiction and smiling proudly the way she did when she reminded me about the time I told off those stupid neighbors.

Added the name of the tranquilizer

Explained why she did not ask for help earlier

Added concluding paragraph that summarizes experiences and lessons learned

## SECOND REVISION—SHOWING EDITING AND PROOFREADING

# An Unexpected Addiction

### Elizabeth Lawson

It seems that everyday on the news you hear about some Hollywood celebrity or ~~sports star~~ **athlete** having an addiction problem, whether ~~it's~~ steroids ~~or~~ alcohol, or painkillers ~~or something even worse like crystal meth~~. You think it can never happen to you because your life is fine and you can deal with your **own** issues, ~~no problem~~. But now I understand ~~it~~ **addiction** more because I developed ~~an addiction~~ **one** of my own, and I had to struggle to free myself from it. In the process I learned a few things about myself, ~~and what makes me tick. It all happened so fast that I didn't know what was happening at the time, but looking back now I understand it better.~~

There's no reason I should have developed an addiction, because I had a basically good life with a stable, loving mother. I was raised by a single mom and she did a great job. We were always so close **.** I remember when my father died (I was ~~8~~ **eight years old**) we made a deal that we were going to be a team and stick together. It was just the two of us and she worked ~~super~~ **very** hard to put food on the table and buy me things I wanted but she couldn't ~~really~~ afford. Of course we had our fights, especially when I was a teenager, but she was always ~~like~~ a mixture of a good friend that I liked to talk to, plus a parent who ~~tried to teach~~ **taught** me the right things to do. I made mistakes **(** everyone does **)** but at the end of the day we watched out for each other. One time I heard some neighbor**s** ~~women~~ gossiping about her **and** I marched ~~right~~ up to them and told them to ~~knock it off~~ **stop** because they had no idea what she went through. She actually punished me for being rude to the neighbors but when she was dying ~~several~~ **ten** years later she told me ~~how~~ **she was** proud of me ~~she was when I did~~ **for doing** that.

It was when she died that I fell apart and started having ~~all sorts of~~ problems I never ~~had~~ **had** before. I was 22 years old and in college, and ~~you would think a grown woman would be able to~~ **I thought I could** handle ~~it~~ **my mother's death**. But I fell apart **;** I was crying all the time. I ~~just~~ kept thinking about what a great person she was and how much I missed her. ~~But the weeks went by and I couldn't get over it.~~ I couldn't study, I couldn't eat, and worst of all I couldn't sleep. I was exhausted and having panic attacks **.** I even hallucinated once or twice. I was a total mess **but** ~~and~~ I refused to go to a counselor because I thought I could deal with ~~it~~ **my problems** on my own. Well **,** I was wrong about that.

Then my uncle, my mother's brother, came to visit me **.** ~~and~~ **H**e took one look at me and said how awful I looked. He had a prescription for a tranquilizer called Ativan (also called lorazepam) and he gave **me** some ~~to me because I felt like if I didn't get some sleep I was going to die.~~ **pills to help me sleep.** So I took one and it worked ~~so~~ incredibly

---

1. Eliminated comma splice

2. Fixed fused sentence

3. Added commas to set off parenthetical phrase

4. Eliminated unnecessary word to make essay sound more formal

5. Added parentheses

6. Eliminated sexist language

7. Made change to keep narrative voice consistent (I instead of you)

8. Fixed unclear pronoun reference

**9. Eliminated redundancy**

**10. Fixed run-on sentence**

**11. Eliminated cliché**

**12. Eliminated slang**

well, ~~I~~ it relaxed me and I fell asleep and I woke up the next day after sleeping about 15 hours. I also felt ~~super relaxed and much,~~ much less upset so I went to the doctor and asked for a prescription ~~and~~ He gave it to me but said he would do it only if I went to a grief counselor also. So I took those pills twice a day for ③ *three* months, and they really helped me. The problem was they also took away my energy. And talking about everything with ~~the~~ *my* counselor ~~at my college~~ (Jane) was a ~~really~~ big help. She helped me see something I didn't see on my own: that I would feel like I was betraying my mother if I went to someone other than ~~her~~ *Mom* for help and advice. Jane also asked, "Wouldn't ~~my~~ *your* mother want ~~me~~ *you* to be happy instead of crying all the time? Of course, ~~it~~ *Jane's advice* made complete sense! So at the end of the ~~③ months~~ *three months* I thought, "OK, I don't need these pills anymore, so I stopped taking them.

And that is when the trouble started. My heart started racing ~~like crazy after~~ *wildly* *after I stopped taking* a couple of days ~~without~~ the pills. My vision got blurry and I started getting ~~weird~~ *unexpected* *all over my body* cramps. I went 72 hours without sleep. I would just ~~lay~~ *lie* there with my heart racing ~~a mile a minute.~~ Then something happened that really scared me. I started feeling zaps of electricity in my brain, like my brain was short circuiting. I was terrified and thought I was having a stroke. So I went to the emergency room and they figured out what was happening. I was having withdrawal symptoms from going off the ~~meds~~ *medication* too ~~fast~~ *quickly*. It turns out that ~~the~~ *with* the type of medication I was on, (called a benzodiazepine, or benzo for short) you have to stop taking it gradually. ~~otherwise~~ *If you try to stop cold turkey,* you ~~get these~~ *experience side* terrible effects. ~~They~~ *emergency room doctor* gave me an Ativan, and the problems stopped almost immediately. ~~And then this is the part you would not believe~~ *To get off the Ativan,* I had to reduce the dose by a tiny amount, take that dose for a week, then reduce the dose a little more, take that for a week, ~~then reduce it again and again~~ and so on ~~until I could stop taking it.~~

It took me almost six months to reduce my dose to zero. And I learned a few things about myself and the world through the experience. First, maybe all the celebrities ~~you~~ *we* read about with their addiction problems ~~actually~~ deserve a little sympathy instead of scorn. Maybe they, like me, had a problem they were trying to deal with, and things got out of control without them ever realizing it. Second, people with addictions are not *necessarily* bad people ~~or even low class people~~. They are trying to cope with their problems but don't know the right way to do it. Third, and probably most important, I realized that it is ~~OK~~ *acceptable* to ask for help when ~~you~~ *I* need it. If I had gone to grief counseling ~~early~~ *earlier* or even if I went to a support group while Mom was sick, I would have had more support and more understanding of what people go through and how to cope with ~~it~~ *a loved one dying of cancer*. I still miss Mom, but I know she's up there *in heaven*, proud that I overcame my addiction and smiling ~~proudly~~ the way she did when she reminded me about the time I ~~told off~~ *confronted* those ~~stupid~~ *nosy* neighbors.

## Examining Writing

1. Highlight the topic sentences in Lawson's second revision and evaluate their use. Does each announce the main point of the paragraph? Do any need further revision?

2. Evaluate Lawson's use of detail. Did she provide sufficient detail? In what paragraphs could greater detail have been provided?

3. What did you learn about the revision process from Lawson's two drafts?

## Writing Assignments

1. Did this essay change your attitude toward people with addictions? Write a paragraph explaining whether you agree or disagree with Lawson that celebrities and other people with addictions deserve sympathy rather than scorn.

2. Have you ever confronted a nosy or gossipy person? Write a paragraph describing your experience, including why you decided to confront the person, how the person reacted, and what you learned from the experience.

3. Complete the same assignment that Lawson did by writing an essay about a difficult or challenging event or experience.

## READ AND RESPOND: A Professional Reading

### Thinking Before Reading

The following reading appeared in a sociology textbook. In the reading, the author explores the issue of rationing medical treatment in the United States. As you read, notice the author's use of detail to support his thesis.

1. Preview the reading, using the steps discussed in Chapter 1, page 15.

2. Connect the reading to your own experience by answering the following questions:

   a. If you have ever faced a medical problem, were you able to get treatment for it? Was the treatment affordable?

   b. Do you think the rationing of health care is a reasonable response to limited medical resources and expensive technology? Would you support or oppose health care rationing?

3. Mark and annotate as you read.

# Who Should Live, and Who Should Die? The Dilemma of Rationing Medical Care

## James M. Henslin

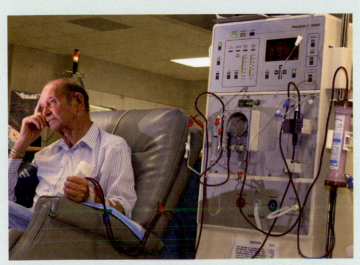

The high cost of some medical treatments, such as dialysis, shown here, has led to the issue of rationing medical care.

1    A 75-year-old woman enters the emergency room, screaming and in tears from severe pain. She is suffering from metastatic cancer (cancer that has spread through her body). She has only weeks to live, and she needs immediate admittance to the intensive care unit.

2    At this same time, a 20-year-old woman, severely injured in a car wreck, is wheeled into the emergency room. To survive, she must be admitted to the intensive care unit.

3    As you probably guessed, there is only one unoccupied bed left in intensive care. What do the doctors do?

4    This story, not as far-fetched as you might think, distills a pressing situation that faces U.S. medical health care. Even though a particular treatment is essential to care for a medical problem, there isn't enough of it to go around to everyone who needs it. Other treatments are so costly that they could bankrupt society if they were made available to everyone who had a particular medical problem. Who, then, should receive the benefits of our new medical technology?

5    In the situation above, medical care would be rationed. The young woman would be admitted to intensive care, and the elderly person would be directed into some ward in the hospital. But what if the elderly woman had already been admitted to intensive care? Would physicians pull her out? That is not as easily done, but probably.

6    Consider the much less dramatic, more routine case of dialysis, the use of machines to cleanse the blood of people who are suffering from kidney disease. Dialysis is currently available to anyone who needs it, and the cost runs several billion dollars a year. Many wonder how the nation can afford to continue to pay this medical bill. Physicians in Great Britain act much like doctors would in our opening example. They ration dialysis informally, making bedside assessments of patients' chances of survival and excluding most older patients from this treatment.

7    Modern medical technology is marvelous. People walk around with the hearts, kidneys, livers, lungs, and faces of deceased people. Eventually, perhaps, surgeons will be able to transplant brains. The costs are similarly astounding. Our

national medical bill runs more than $2 trillion a year. Frankly, I can't understand what a trillion of anything is. I've tried, but the number is just too high for me to grasp. Now there are two of these trillions to pay each year. Where can we get such fantastic amounts? How long can we continue to pay them? These questions haunt our medical system, making the question of medical rationing urgent.

8    The nation's medical bill will not flatten out. Rather, it is destined to increase. Medical technology, including new drugs, continues to advance—and to be costly. And we all want the latest, most advanced treatment. Then there is the matter that people are living longer and the number of elderly is growing rapidly. It is the elderly who need the most medical care, especially during their last months of life.

9    The dilemma is harsh: If we ration medical treatment, many sick people will die. If we don't, we will indebt future generations even further.

# Getting Ready to Write

## Checking Your Comprehension

Answer each of the following questions using complete sentences.

1.  What are the two aspects of modern medical care that create a dilemma?
2.  What is dialysis? What does the author say is the cost of dialysis per year?
3.  Explain how physicians in Great Britain apply rationing to dialysis patients.
4.  How much is the national annual medical bill for the United States?
5.  According to the author, who needs the most medical care?
6.  What does the author say will happen if we ration medical treatment? What does he say will happen if we do not?

## Strengthening Your Vocabulary

Using the word's context, word parts, or a dictionary, write a brief definition of each of the following words as it is used in the reading:

1.  distills (paragraph 4) _____

2.  bankrupt (paragraph 4) _____

3.  rationed (paragraph 5) _____

4.  assessments (paragraph 6) _____

5.  haunt (paragraph 7) _____

## Examining the Reading: Drawing Idea Maps

Earlier in this chapter, you learned to draw revision maps to check the content and organization of your own writing. Maps can also help you analyze someone else's writing. They can help you understand how the writer's ideas relate to one another and how the piece is organized. You will also find that by expressing the writer's ideas briefly in your own words, you'll better remember the material you read. Create an idea map of "Who Should Live, and Who Should Die?" Start with the title and thesis and include the main ideas and major supporting details.

## Reacting to Ideas: Discussion and Journal Writing

Get ready to write about the reading by discussing the following:

1. Discuss what makes medical care rationing a dilemma.

2. Evaluate the opening paragraph of the reading. How well does the story of two women arriving in the same emergency room reflect the subject of the reading and capture your interest?

3. Do you perceive medical rationing as positive or negative? Discuss factors that may affect your opinion such as your age and general health. For example, would you feel differently about rationing if you were elderly or in poor health?

4. Consider the author's purpose in writing this. Does he achieve his purpose? Who is his intended audience? Write a journal entry explaining your answers.

5. What type of medical treatment is illustrated by the photograph? Which paragraph in the reading contains information describing this treatment?

**THINKING VISUALLY**

## Thinking and Writing Critically

1. What assumptions does the author make in this reading? Are the details he includes convincing and relevant?

2. What would you consider the author's purpose for writing this essay? Who do you think his intended audience is?

3. Which paragraph do you think contains the most vivid language? Write a paragraph explaining your answer.

**MySkillsLab®**

**Complete** this Exercise

# Writing About the Reading

## Paragraph Options

1. Do you think rationing is the best solution to the medical care dilemma identified by the author? Write a paragraph explaining why or why not.

2. What do you think of the criteria used by physicians in Great Britain to ration dialysis treatment? Write a paragraph describing your answer.

3. Do you agree that the concept of "a trillion of anything" is difficult to grasp? How might you break this huge number down so that it is understandable? Write a paragraph giving your ideas.

## Essay Options

4. According to the author, there are dire consequences to rationing or not rationing medical treatment. Choose one side and write a persuasive essay either supporting or opposing the rationing of medical care. Include any other suggestions you might have for dealing with limited resources and expensive treatments.

5. The author describes modern medical technology as "marvelous" and mentions different organ transplants as examples. In your opinion, what are the three most remarkable developments in medical technology? Write an essay explaining your answer.

6. Have you faced a harsh dilemma in your own life? Consider a time when you had to struggle to set priorities, make a difficult decision, or choose between two equally good (or bad) options. Write an essay describing your experience, including whether you were able to resolve the dilemma.

# SELF-TEST SUMMARY

To test yourself, cover the Answer column with a sheet of paper and answer each question in the left column. Evaluate each of your answers as you work by sliding the paper down and comparing your answer with what is printed in the Answer column.

| QUESTION | ANSWER |
|---|---|
| ■ **GOAL 1 Understand the purpose of revising**<br><br>What is involved in revising and editing? | Revising involves rereading every idea and sentence in a paragraph you have written and making changes to them as needed. Editing involves adding or deleting words and sentences, as well as correcting errors in grammar, spelling, and punctuation. |
| ■ **GOAL 2 Read critically to revise**<br><br>Why and how do you read a paragraph critically to revise? | Read your paragraph critically in order to find out what works and what doesn't. Read it several times, examining content, evaluating how effectively you have expressed your ideas, and checking for correctness. Use the Revision Checklist on page 290. |
| ■ **GOAL 3 Consider your purpose and audience**<br><br>How do you evaluate your purpose and audience? | To evaluate purpose, reread your draft and decide whether it accomplishes what you want it to. Ask a peer to read and summarize what your writing does accomplish. To evaluate audience, read your paragraph from the audience's viewpoint or imagine that someone else wrote it and you are reading it for the first time. |

| QUESTION | ANSWER |
|---|---|
| ■ GOAL 4 Examine your ideas<br><br>How can an idea map help you examine your ideas? | An idea map can help you check your use of relevant and sufficient detail as well as the logical organization of your ideas. |
| ■ GOAL 5 Correct errors in grammar, spelling, and punctuation<br><br>Why is it important to edit for correctness, and what tools can you use to do so? | Errors in grammar, spelling, and punctuation make your writing less effective and decrease the reader's confidence in what you write. Use an error log to help you avoid errors you make consistently, and refer to the Proofreading Checklist on page 291 for a list of questions to help you spot errors. |

For more help with **Strategies for Revising Paragraphs,** go to your learning path in MySkillsLab at www.myskillslab.com.

# 10

# Reading, Planning, and Organizing Essays

## THINK About It!

The above photograph shows the Tibet Railway, a $4.2 billion investment, passing through rural countryside. It was included in an essay discussing changes occurring within the country. Suppose you were asked to write a paragraph describing the point the above photograph illustrates. Before beginning to write, what would you do? First you would have to read the essay and understand the point it makes. Then, you would study, analyze, and interpret the photograph. You would study the scene and think about the value and impact of the railway in the rural countryside. You would also read and reread the essay, searching for clues from the writer as to why this particular photograph is included and what it is intended to illustrate. If you felt you needed more information, you might Google the Tibet Railway to read and learn more about it. Once you felt you had adequate information, you might make notes or use brainstorming to generate ideas to write about. Once you had ideas to work with, you would begin to think about how to organize and fit them together. Reading, planning, and organization are important in most writing that you do, and this chapter will guide you through the process.

# Reading and Writing Connections

### EVERYDAY CONNECTIONS

- **Reading** You read a newspaper article about a group of cycling enthusiasts who want to improve and expand the bike trail system in your state. The group is hoping to gain funding through a transportation bill in Congress.
- **Writing** In response to the newspaper article, you write a letter to your state senators and ask for their support in developing and funding the bike trail system.

### ACADEMIC CONNECTIONS

- **Reading** In your Introduction to Literature class, you read an essay by Alice Walker on what it is like to be a black female writer in America.
- **Writing** You write an essay for a literature exam in which you refer to Alice Walker's essay in discussing her novel *The Color Purple.*

### WORKPLACE CONNECTIONS

- **Reading** You read an article online in *Fortune* magazine about small businesses that have started using cell phones and credit card swipers to process credit card transactions at locations outside of the business office.
- **Writing** As the owner of a lawn care business, you write a proposal to obtain a small business loan to buy the credit card software and equipment you read about in the online article.

## FOCUSING ON READING AND WRITING

# Why Read and Write Essays?

■ **GOAL 1**
Understand the purpose of an essay

An **essay** is a group of paragraphs that are all about one subject. Reading essays enables you to learn about a topic and discover the author's perspective, viewpoint, or approach toward the topic. Writing an essay allows you the opportunity to present your ideas on a topic and explain and support those ideas. Throughout college you will have many occasions to read and write essays. If you know how essays are structured, you will be able to read them more easily and write them more effectively.

## READING

# Read Essays to Build Comprehension and Recall

■ **GOAL 2**
Read essays effectively

Reading an essay involves understanding what the writer says and remembering what you read so you can discuss and write about it. To understand the writer's ideas, it is helpful to analyze the essay's essential parts.

Essays usually have a different structure from articles. Understanding how they are organized and recognizing the different types will help you read them more effectively and efficiently.

## Understand the Structure of an Essay

**Essays** are short pieces of writing that examine a single topic and focus on a single idea about that topic. They may be encountered in anthologies, newspapers, and magazines of all types. Essays follow a standard organization and usually have the following parts:

- **title**
- **introduction**
- **thesis statement**
- **supporting information in body paragraphs**
- **conclusion**

The structure of an essay is similar to that of a paragraph. Like a paragraph, an essay has a topic. It also explores a single idea about the topic; in an essay this is called the **thesis statement**. Like a paragraph, an essay provides ideas and details that support the thesis statement, each main idea discussed in a body paragraph. However, unlike a paragraph, an essay deals with a broader topic and the idea that it explores is often more complex. You can visualize the structure of an essay as follows:

**VISUALIZE IT!**

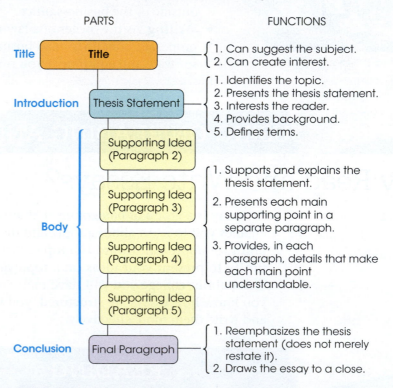

**Note:** There is no set number of paragraphs that an essay should contain. This model shows six paragraphs, but in actual essays, the number will vary greatly.

Let's examine the function of each of these parts of an essay in greater detail by referring to an essay titled "To Catch a Liar." It was written by Sandra Parshall and first appeared in a blog titled *Poe's Deadly Daughters*.

Title · **TO CATCH A LIAR**

Author · Sandra Parshall

Source Information

**From *Poe's Deadly Daughters,* A Blog for Mystery Lovers**
*The author of this article is a journalist and author of four mystery novels. You can find more information about her at her Web page http://www.sandraparshall.com/.*

Introduction: interest-catching question

1    Do you think you're pretty good at spotting when somebody's lying? Sorry, but I'll bet you're not as sharp as you think you are.

2    Researchers have found that most people have a dismally low success rate, even in a lab setting where they know for certain that some of those they're studying are lying. If we're especially vigilant, we might spot half of all lies—which means we'll miss half. Police officers aren't much better than the rest of us, although they improve with experience. Those super-cops who can always detect a lie, like the fictional Special Agent Gibbs on the TV show *NCIS,* do exist in reality, but they're extremely rare and psychologists have yet to determine how they do it. Since the detective's ability to spot lies is crucial to crime-solving, some scientists are finding ways to teach the skill to cops.

Thesis Statement

3    *Scientific American Mind* magazine's September/October issue reports on experiments conducted by one of them, social psychologist Aldert Vrij of the University of Portsmouth in England. Vrij's work is based on the human mind's inability to think along multiple tracks simultaneously. Lying is more demanding than simply telling the truth, so if the interrogator gives the suspect's mind too much to process at one time, the person being questioned is likely to slip up if he's trying to sell a phony story.

Details about Vrig's research study

Body

4    Here's the premise: The liar has to worry about keeping his story consistent and believable, first of all—which means suppressing all thought of the truth so it doesn't inadvertently slip out—but he also has to "look honest" by controlling his expression and body movements. And he's constantly monitoring the cop's reaction to what he's saying. All that is exhausting, and if the interrogator adds even a little more pressure, that may be enough to trip up a liar.

5    Vrij and his colleagues have found several useful strategies for applying that extra pressure.

- First, discount sweating and general nervousness. Even an honest person will be nervous under police scrutiny.
- One way to trip up a liar is to ask the suspect to tell his or her story backward, beginning at the end. Devising a false story and keeping it straight is hard enough without the burden of having to recount phony events in reverse. In lab tests, this greatly increased mistakes and the likelihood of catching a liar.
- Interrogators can also rattle a suspect by insisting that he maintain eye contact. Liars have trouble concentrating on their stories if they're looking directly into the eyes of the people they're lying to.

- Asking suspects to draw pictures of what they're describing can also reveal the liars. Their pictures will show fewer details than those drawn by truth-tellers, and often the pictures won't be consistent with verbal descriptions.

Conclusion

6 These easy techniques have proven highly effective in the lab and should help police in the real world do their work more efficiently. Best of all, they're simple enough to be used by fictional cops who aren't endowed with the special mental powers of Special Agent Gibbs.

Final comment on the usefulness of the strategies

### The Title

The title usually suggests the subject of the essay and is intended to capture the reader's interest. Some titles are highly descriptive and announce exactly what the essay will be about. For example, the essay titled "To Catch a Liar" announces the subject of the essay. Other titles are less directly informative.

Some essays have both a title and a subtitle. In these essays, the subtitle usually suggests the subject matter more directly. In an essay titled "Citizenship or Slavery?" the title is mainly intended to capture your interest rather than to directly announce the subject. The subtitle, "How Schools Take the Volunteer Out of Volunteering," focuses you more clearly on what the essay will be about.

EXERCISE 10-1

WORKING TOGETHER

## Analyzing Titles

**Directions:** Working with a classmate, decide what you expect to be discussed in essays with each of the following titles.

1. Animal Rights: Right or Wrong

   _____

2. Firearms, Violence, and Public Policy

   _____

3. The Price of Power: Living in the Nuclear Age

   _____

   _____

4. The Nature and Significance of Play

   _____

5. Uncivil Rights—The Cultural Rules of Anger

   _____

   _____

### The Introduction

The introduction, usually one or two paragraphs long, sets the scene for the essay and places the subject within a framework or context. The introduction may

- present the thesis statement of the essay
- offer background information (explain television addiction as an issue, for example)
- define technical or unfamiliar terms (define *addiction,* for example)
- build your interest (give an instance of an extreme case of television addiction)

Notice how in the sample essay "To Catch a Liar" these goals are accomplished in its first two paragraphs.

---

**EXERCISE 10-2**

## Analyzing an Introduction

**Directions:** Read only the first two paragraphs of the essay "Mind Your Own Browser" by Simson L. Garfinkel below. What types of information do they provide?

_____

_____

**MIND YOUR OWN BROWSER**

Simson L. Garfinkel

1    Most of us depend on free web services, from Google to Facebook, but unless you're careful, using them has a price: your privacy. Web advertisers, who keep these sites in business, track what you do online in order to deliver targeted, attention-grabbing ads. Your web browser reveals a surprising amount about you, and advertisers are keen to find out even more.

2    A new draft report from the Federal Trade Commission (FTC) recommends the creation of a "Do Not Track" mechanism that would let Internet users choose, with the click of a button, whether to allow advertisers to track them. While this would offer better privacy controls than exist currently, the FTC's approach falls short, because tracking technology is interwoven into our most popular websites and mobile services (without tracking, they simply don't work) and businesses are opposed to reform.

3    Few people realize that many web ads are tailored using huge amounts of personal data collected, combined, and cross-referenced from multiple sources—an approach known as "behavioral advertising." Advertisers ferret out clues to where you live, where you work, what you buy, and which TV shows you watch, then refine their ads accordingly.

4    Behavioral advertising works. A study conducted by Microsoft Research Asia found that users were up to seven times likelier to click on targeted ads than on nontargeted ones. Targeted ads earn much more for websites—an average of $4.12 per thousand views versus $1.98 per thousand for regular ads, according to a study commissioned by the Network Advertising Initiative, a trade group that promotes self-regulation.

5    While many people are simply opposed on principle to unrestricted tracking, there are real risks involved. Without safeguards, tracking techniques could be exploited to steal identities or to hack into computers. And the big databases that advertisers are building could be misused by unscrupulous employers or malicious governments.

6    Over the past 15 years the United States has developed a peculiar approach to protecting consumer privacy. Companies publish detailed "privacy policies" that are supposed to explain what information they collect and what they plan to do with it. Consumers can then choose whether they want to participate.

7    The FTC report says that this model no longer works (if it ever did). "Many companies are not disclosing their practices," FTC chairman Jon Leibowitz says. "And even if companies do disclose them, they do so in long, incomprehensible privacy policies and user agreements that consumers don't read, let alone understand."

8    The FTC is trying to rein this in. It recommends, for example, that companies collect information only when there is a legitimate business need to do so, and asks them to destroy that information when they no longer need it. It also wants companies to do a better job of explaining their policies to consumers.

9    Of course, real choice requires more than clear information—it requires options. At the moment, that means activating the "private browsing" mode built into modern web browsers (which prevents sites from accessing cookies) or using browser plug-ins that automatically block ads and certain tracking technologies.

10   But there is no rule prohibiting advertisers from circumventing private-browsing modes, and many are doing so. The FTC's solution to this problem is "Do Not Track," loosely modeled on the agency's popular "Do Not Call" list. Instead of a centralized list of consumers who don't want to be tracked, however, they envision a browser setting that would transmit an anonymity request to web advertisers. If behaviorally targeted ads really are beneficial to consumers, most

people will leave the feature switched off. Otherwise, websites better get used to $1.98 per thousand ads viewed.

11    Browser makers have started building tracking controls for their software. Google recently released an add-on for Chrome called Keep My Opt-Outs, and Microsoft has announced a similar feature for Internet Explorer 9 called Tracking Protection. These features tell websites when someone doesn't want to be tracked. But it's still up to companies to honor this request. And, unsurprisingly, the advertising industry fiercely opposes tracking restrictions, especially if they are enabled in browsers by default.

12    The real problem with "Do Not Track" is that it derives from an earlier understanding of web advertising—that ads are distributed to news sites, search engines, and other destinations that don't necessarily need to know who you are. Nowadays many popular websites are unusable unless you let them track you.

13    Take Facebook: The website has seen explosive ad-revenue growth precisely because it tracks users' interests in great detail. There's no way to turn off tracking and still use the site. Thanks to Facebook Connect, which lets you log on to other websites with your Facebook credentials, and the "Like" button, which sends links from external pages back to your profile, Facebook now tracks you across the web. Or, more accurately, you tell Facebook where you are.

14    Smartphones will accelerate this trend. Already, many phones deliver ads based on your GPS-determined position. Future ads might depend on the applications you've installed, whom you've called, even the contents of your address book.

15    There is a way to resolve this conundrum: Create simple and enforceable policies that limit companies' retention and use of consumer data. These could be dictated by the government or, conceivably, built into browsers and customized by users. For example, you could tell Google to archive your searches forever, but make them anonymous after six months. You could tell Facebook to keep your posts indefinitely, but use them for advertising purposes only for a year.

16    Unfortunately, any kind of reform will face stiff opposition from vested interests. But if the government wants to defend us from privacy-trampling advertising, it needs more than "Do Not Track."

*Simson L. Garfinkel is a contributing editor to the world's oldest technology magazine.* Technology Review, *an independent biomonthly published by MIT. Excerpted from* Technology Review *(March–April 2011).*

## The Thesis Statement

The **thesis statement** of an essay is its main point. All other ideas and paragraphs in the essay support this idea. Once you identify an essay's thesis, you have discovered the key to its meaning. The thesis is usually stated in a single sentence and this sentence appears in the introductory paragraphs. It often follows the background information and the attention-getter. In the sample essay "To Catch a Liar" the thesis is stated at the end of the second paragraph. Occasionally, an author will first present evidence in support of the thesis and finally state the thesis at the end of the essay. This organization is most common in argumentative essays (see Chapter 15).

You may also find, on occasion, that an author implies rather than directly states the thesis; the thesis is revealed through the supporting paragraphs. When you cannot find a clear statement of the thesis, ask yourself this question: "What is the one main point the author is making?" Your answer is the implied thesis statement.

Here are a few sample thesis statements.

> Due to its negative health effects, cigarette smoking is once again being regarded as a form of deviant behavior.
>
> Career choice is influenced by numerous factors including skills and abilities, attitudes, and life goals.
>
> Year-round school will provide children with a better education that is more cost-effective.

## EXERCISE 10-3    Identifying a Thesis Statement

**Directions:** Read the entire essay "Mind Your Own Browser" (p. 309) and identify its thesis statement.

_____

_____

### The Body

The body of the essay contains sentences and paragraphs that explain or support the thesis statement. This support may be in the form of

- examples
- descriptions
- facts
- statistics
- reasons
- anecdotes (stories that illustrate a point)
- personal experiences and observations
- quotations from or references to authorities and experts
- comparisons

Most writers use various types of supporting information. In the sample essay "To Catch a Liar" (pp. 307–309) the author uses several types of information in her supporting paragraphs. Notice how she gives an example of a super cop in paragraph 2 and offers reasons why lying is complex in paragraph 4. Paragraph 5 presents facts and description.

## Analyzing Supporting Information

**EXERCISE 10-4**

**Directions:** Review the essay "Mind Your Own Browser" and mark where the body begins and ends. Then, in the margin beside each supporting paragraph, label the type(s) of supporting information the author used.

### The Conclusion

An essay is brought to a close with a brief conclusion, not a summary. (A summary provides a review of the key ideas presented in an article. Think of a summary as an outline in paragraph form. The order in which the information appears in the summary reflects the order in which it appears in the article itself.) A **conclusion** is a final statement about the subject of the essay. A conclusion does not review content as a summary does. Instead, a conclusion often refers back to, but does not repeat, the thesis statement. It may also suggest a direction for further thought or introduce a new way of looking at what has already been said. The sample essay "To Catch a Liar" (pp. 307–309) ends with a conclusion that comments on the usefulness of the strategies presented.

## Analyzing a Conclusion

**EXERCISE 10-5**

**Directions:** Explain how the conclusion of "Mind Your Own Browser" draws the essay to a close.

_____

_____

## Read for Retention, Recall, and Response

Once you understand what the author of an essay is saying, your task is to remember what you read so you can react and respond to it. Use the following strategies to build your retention and response skills.

- **Highlight as you read.** Sorting ideas that are important to remember from those that are not will strengthen your recall and identify ideas to which to respond. (See Chapter 3 for highlighting techniques.)
- **Annotate as you read.** It is helpful to record your thinking as you read, so you do not lose track of your reactions as you encounter other new ideas. Writing your ideas will help cement them in your mind, and your annotations will be a good starting point for review. (See Chapter 3 for annotating techniques.)
- **Connect ideas to your background experience.** By connecting what you have read to your own experiences, you create memory links that will help you recall the information. These connections are also useful when finding ideas to write about in response to the essay.

- **Identify the organization pattern(s) used.** Patterns help guide your reading and help you see how ideas fit together. Once you see how ideas fit together, you will be able to remember them more easily. (See Chapters 7–9 for more about patterns.)

- **Review and write after reading.** When you have finished reading an essay, quickly review its major points by rereading your highlighting and annotations. Review will give you the big picture: it will help you see the essay as a whole, rather than as single paragraphs, which is an important step for both retention and response.

**EXERCISE 10-6**

## Strengthening Recall

**Directions:** Highlight, annotate, and identify the pattern(s) used in the essay "Mind Your Own Browser" (pp. 307–309). Then write a sentence or two connecting the reading to your own experience. How well did these strategies work to strengthen your recall? Write a few sentences evaluating each as a method of helping you remember what you read.

# Think Critically About Essays

■ GOAL 3
Analyze and evaluate essays

Essays require close examination. In order to be able to discuss and write about an essay you have read, be sure to evaluate and analyze it using all the critical reading skills presented in Chapters 13–15, and the "Thinking Critically About . . ." sections in previous chapters. Important critical thinking questions to ask about essays include

- **Who is the author and is he/she qualified to write about the topic of the essay?** For professional essays, check to see if it is a name you recognize. Try to learn something about the author and his or her qualifications to write. For "To Catch a Liar," there is information about the author at the beginning of the essay that suggests she would be knowledgeable about lying.

- **What is the author's purpose?** Is the writer trying to present information, convince you of something, entertain you, or express an attitude or opinion? For "To Catch a Liar," the author's purpose is to inform.

- **Does the author provide adequate support for his or her ideas?** Is a variety of supporting information provided? An essay that relies entirely upon the author's personal experiences, for example, to support a thesis, may be of limited use for research purposes. In "To Catch a Liar," the author provides research evidence, reasons and strategies.

- **Did the author supply sources, references, and citations for ideas not his or her own?** You should be able to verify the information presented and turn to those sources should you wish to read more about the topic. As is common practice for essays published in popular sources, full citation and source information is not included for "To Catch a Liar."

- **Analyze any visuals that accompany the essay.** Determine their purpose and how they relate to the essay.

## WRITING

# Choose a Topic

■ **GOAL 4**
Choose a topic

In some situations, your instructor will assign a topic; other times you will be free to choose your own topic. Below you will find suggestions for handling either situation. In both situations, however, be sure to

- **Find out about the expected length of the paper.** If your instructor does not give a page or word count, be sure to ask. Knowing his or her expectations will help you know how much information to include.

- **Pay attention to due dates and specific requirements.** Keep track of when your essay is due. Some instructors may also require that a preliminary draft or a working thesis statement be submitted before the final deadline. Many instructors penalize late papers or may even refuse to accept them.

- **Find out what format you should follow in submitting your paper.** You need to know what is expected in terms of a cover sheet, margins, double or single spacing, and so forth. Some instructors may prefer essays submitted electronically, while others may require a paper copy.

## Working with Assigned Topics

In many situations, your instructor will either assign a topic or give you a choice of several topics. Be sure to read and study the assignment carefully before you begin. (If your instructor gives the assignment orally, record as much as you can of what he or she says so you can review it later.) Usually your instructor will offer clues as to what is expected, and you can use these to guide you as you plan and draft your essay. Use the following tips:

- **Determine the purpose of the assignment.** Identify, as precisely as you can, what your instructor wants you to do. Is the purpose of the essay to inform (present information), express your feelings, explore an issue, or persuade? Here is a sample assignment:

    **Assignment:** Define what a bully is and explain how to deal with one.

    This is a two-part assignment. First you should define, or explain, what a bully is, and then you should offer advice on how to cope with bullying behavior.

- **Connect the assignment to classroom instruction.** What skills taught recently in class does your instructor want you to apply as you write? For the above assignment, for example, you might have been learning how to define terms or exploring how to use examples to support a thesis (for instance, you could give examples of situations in which a bully was handled).

- **Watch for clue words that suggest how to write and organize your essay.** Instructors often use words that suggest what you should write about and how to organize the information. In the sample assignment, there are two important clue words—*define* and *explain.* These indicate the instructor expects the essay to include a definition of the term *bully* as well as a discussion, with examples, of how to deal with one. Refer to Table 10-1 for a list of clue words and how to use them as you respond to assigned topics.

| TABLE 10-1 | CLUE WORDS AND HOW TO USE THEM | |
| --- | --- | --- |
| **Clue Word** | **Example** | **Information to Include** |
| **Describe** | Describe the process of tattooing or another form of body art. | Tell how something happened, including how, who, where, and why. |
| **Compare** | Compare the levels of violence in two forms of public entertainment. | Show how items are similar as well as different; include details or examples. |
| **Contrast (differentiate)** | Contrast the health care system in the United States with that in England. | Show how the items are different; include details or examples. |
| **Argue** | Argue that pets are valuable for human therapy. | Give reasons or evidence, or establish that a concept or theory is correct, logical, or valid. |
| **Justify** | Justify the decision to keep the names of rape victims private. | Give reasons that support an action, event, or policy. |
| **Criticize** | Criticize the campus policy on Internet usage. | Make judgments about quality or worth; include both positive and negative aspects, explaining or giving reasons for your judgments. |
| **Evaluate** | Evaluate the strategies our society has used to control drunk driving. | React to the topic in a logical way. Discuss the merit, strengths, weaknesses, advantages, or limitations of the topic, explaining your reasons. |
| **Discuss** | Discuss the effectiveness of gun control laws. | Consider important characteristics and main points. |
| **Summarize** | Summarize the arguments for and against offering sex education courses in public schools. | Cover the major points in brief form. |
| **Define** | Define sexist language and include several examples. | Give an accurate meaning of the term with enough detail to show that you really understand it. |

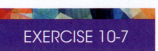

**EXERCISE 10-7**

## Analyzing Writing Assignments

**Directions:** For each of the following writing assignments, underline key words that suggest the purpose of the assignment.

1. Discuss the issue of sex education in public schools.

2. Evaluate the level of violence on two or more popular television shows.

3. Explore the problems of living at home with parents.

4. Write an essay arguing for or against the testing of cosmetic beauty products on animals.

5. Compare two television commercials, examining their purpose and the persuasive devices that they use.

## Choosing Your Own Topic

When your instructor gives you an assignment, you may not like the topic, but at least a good part of the preliminary work has been done for you. When your instructor allows you to choose your own topic, you have to brainstorm for ideas and explore possible topics using the prewriting techniques described in Chapter 2 (pp. 59–66). Use the following suggestions to help you choose an appropriate, effective, and workable topic:

- **Take time to think about your choice.** Don't grab the first topic you come upon. Instead think it through, and weigh its pros and cons. It is often helpful to think of several topics and then choose the one you feel you are best prepared to write about.

- **Choose a topic that interests you.** You will feel more like writing about it and will find you have more to say.

- **Write about something familiar.** Select a topic you know a fair amount about. Otherwise, you will have to research your topic in the library or online. Your experience and knowledge of a familiar topic will provide the content of your essay.

- **Use your writing journal as a source for ideas.** For more on journal writing, see Success Tip #4 on page 9.

- **Discuss possible topics with a friend or classmate.** These conversations may help you discover worthwhile topics.

Table 10-2 lists additional sources of ideas for essay topics.

### TABLE 10-2    SOURCES OF IDEAS FOR ESSAY TOPICS

| Sources of Ideas | Examples |
|---|---|
| **Your daily life.** Pay attention to events you attend, activities you participate in, and routines you follow. | Attending a sporting event may suggest topics about professional athletes' salaries, sports injuries, or violence in sports. |
| **Your college classes.** Both class lectures and discussions as well as reading assignments may give you ideas for topics. | A class discussion in sociology about prejudice and discrimination may suggest you write about racial or ethnic identities, stereotypes, or types of discrimination (age, gender, weight, etc.). |
| **Your job.** Your responsibilities, your boss, your co-workers, and your customers are all sources of ideas. | Watching a family with wild, misbehaving children throwing food and annoying other customers in a restaurant may prompt you to write about restaurant policies, child rearing, or rude and annoying behavior. |
| **The media.** Radio, television, movies, newspapers, magazines, and online sources all contain hundreds of ideas for a topic each day. | A commercial for a weight-loss product may suggest an essay on society's emphasis on thinness or the unrealistic expectations for body image presented in commercials. |

EXERCISE 10-8

WRITING IN PROGRESS

## Brainstorming Topics

**Directions:** Using the suggestions listed in Table 10-2, make a list of five possible topics you could use to write a two- to three-page, double-spaced essay.

# Generate Ideas About Your Topic

■ **GOAL 5**
Generate ideas about your topic

Once you have chosen a working topic, the next step is to generate ideas about it. This step will help you determine whether the topic you have selected is usable. It will also provide you with a list of ideas you can use in planning and developing your essay. If you have trouble generating ideas about a topic, consider changing topics. Here are four methods for generating ideas. (See pp. 59–66 in Chapter 2 for a detailed review of each.)

1. **Freewriting.** Write nonstop for a specified time, recording all the ideas that come to mind on the topic.

2. **Brainstorming.** Write a list of all ideas that come to mind about a specific topic.

3. **Questioning.** Write a list of questions about a given topic.

4. **Branching.** Draw a diagram showing possible subtopics into which your topic could be divided.

When a student named Ted was assigned a two-page paper on a topic of his choice, he decided to write about online social networking sites. To generate ideas, Ted used brainstorming and wrote the following list of ideas:

> **SOCIAL NETWORKING SITES**
>
> Keep tabs on and connect with friends
> Create your own profile—describe yourself as you like
> Profiles aren't necessarily true or accurate
> Receive requests from people who want to friend you
> People date online
> People cheat on spouses through online relationships
> Employers check applicants' Facebook sites
> Unless blocked, private information can be seen by strangers
> High school students use them too
> Facebook and MySpace are popular ones
> What did people do before these sites were available?

You can follow the progress of Ted's essay through the remainder of this chapter, where you can examine how he develops a topic, freewrites to generate ideas, and creates a working thesis.

EXERCISE 10-9

WRITING IN PROGRESS

## Generating Ideas

**Directions:** Select one of the topics you listed in Exercise 10-8. Use freewriting, brainstorming, questioning, or branching to generate ideas about the topic.

## Narrowing Your Topic Further

Avoid working with a topic that is either too broad or too narrow. If your topic is too narrow, you will find you don't have enough to write about. If it is too broad, you will have too much to say, which will create several related problems:

- You will tend to write in generalities.
- You will not be able to explore each idea in detail.
- You will probably wander from topic to topic.
- You will become unfocused.

It is difficult to know if your topic is too broad, but here are a few warning signals:

- You feel overwhelmed when you try to think about the topic.
- You don't know where to start.
- You feel as if you are going in circles with ideas.
- You don't know where to stop.

You can use the ideas you generate during brainstorming, freewriting, questioning, or branching to help narrow your topic. One or more of those ideas may be a more manageable topic.

Often, more than one round of narrowing is necessary. You may need to reduce a topic several times by dividing it into smaller and smaller subtopics. You can do this by using one of the prewriting techniques again, or you can use a simple diagram to help you. After studying his brainstorming, Ted decided to write about online relationships. The following diagram shows how Ted further narrowed the topic of online relationships.

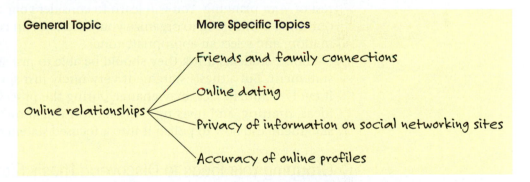

In this way, he wound up with several manageable topics related to online relationships to choose from. Finally, he decided to write about online dating relationships.

A question many students ask is, "How do I know when to stop narrowing?" For an essay, you will need at least three or four main points to support your thesis. Make sure that you have at least this number and that you can support each one with adequate detail. If you cannot do this, you'll know you have narrowed too far.

**EXERCISE 10-10**

*WORKING TOGETHER*

## Narrowing Topics

**Directions:** Working with a classmate, narrow three of the following topics. Continue narrowing each one until you find a topic about which you could write a five- to seven-paragraph essay. Circle your final topic choice for each.

1. advertisements
2. junk mail
3. colleges
4. news reporting

5. politicians
6. wildlife preservation
7. parenting

**EXERCISE 10-11**

**WRITING IN PROGRESS**

## Narrowing a Topic

**Directions:** Use the topic you generated ideas about in Exercise 10-9 and narrow it to a workable topic about which you could write a five- to seven-paragraph essay.

# Plan Your Essay

■ **GOAL 6**
Plan your essay

Planning pays off when it comes to essay writing. The more you think through your essay before you write it, the easier the actual writing will be. This section will show you how to develop a working thesis statement and use it to guide the rest of your planning. You will learn to consider your audience and purpose, use outlining or mapping to organize your ideas, obtain complete and correct information, and select an appropriate tone.

Some students think they should be able to just sit down and write a thesis statement. But a thesis statement very rarely just springs into a writer's mind: it evolves and, in fact, may change during the process of prewriting, grouping ideas, drafting, and revising. This section will show you how to draft a thesis statement and how to polish it into a focused statement.

## Grouping Your Ideas to Discover a Thesis Statement

Once you have narrowed your topic and you know what you want to write about, the next step is to group or connect your ideas to form a thesis. Let's see how Ted produced a thesis following these steps.

First, Ted chose to do freewriting about his topic of online dating to discover more ideas about it. This freewriting is shown on page 327. Read his freewriting now before you continue with this section. As you will see, Ted tends to write many ideas, far more than he needs, and then sorts them out afterward.

Once he completed his freewriting, Ted reviewed what he had written and decided to limit his essay to one social network—Facebook. He highlighted usable ideas and tried to group or organize them logically. In his freewriting Ted saw three main groups of ideas: finding someone to date, dating, and breaking up, so he sorted his ideas into those categories. Once Ted had grouped his ideas into these three categories, he wrote a working thesis statement.

**Working Thesis Statement:** The dating process using Facebook involves screening, dating, and breaking up.

This working thesis statement identifies his topic—dating online using Facebook—and suggests that he will examine how the dating process works. You can see that this thesis statement grew out of his idea groupings. Furthermore, this thesis statement gives readers clues as to how the essay will be organized. A reader knows from this preview the order in which steps in the dating process will be discussed.

How do you know which ideas to group? Look for connections and relationships among the ideas that you generate during prewriting. Here are some suggestions:

1. **Look for categories.** Try to discover ways your ideas can be classified or subdivided. Think of categories as titles or slots in which ideas can be placed. Look for a general term that is broad enough to cover several of your ideas. For example, suppose you are writing a paper on where sexual discrimination occurs. You could break down the topic by location.

   SAMPLE THESIS STATEMENT | Sexual discrimination exists in the workplace, in social situations, and in politics.

2. **Try organizing your ideas chronologically.** Group your ideas according to the clock or calendar. Ted organized the dating process in the order in which it happens, from start to finish.

   SAMPLE THESIS STATEMENT | Tracing metal working from its early beginnings in history to modern times reveals certain social and economic patterns.

3. **Look for similarities and differences.** When working with two or more topics, see if they can be approached by looking at how similar or different they are.

   SAMPLE THESIS STATEMENT | Two early biologists, Darwin and Mendel, held similar views about evolution.

4. **Separate your ideas into causes and effects or problems and solutions.** Events and issues can often be analyzed in this way.

   SAMPLE THESIS STATEMENT | Both employer and employees must work together to improve low morale in an office.

5. **Divide your ideas into advantages and disadvantages or pros and cons.** When you are evaluating a proposal, product, or service, this approach may work.

   SAMPLE THESIS STATEMENT | Playing on a college sports team has many advantages but also several serious drawbacks.

6. **Consider several different ways to approach your topic or organize and develop your ideas.** As you consider what your thesis statement is going

to be, push yourself to see your topic from a number of different angles or a fresh perspective.

For example, Ted could have considered how online dating differs from traditional dating, or he could have examined his freewriting and decided to focus on his personal history using Facebook to date.

In Chapter 11 you will learn how to refine your thesis statement as you draft and revise your essay.

## Writing a Working Thesis Statement

**Directions:** For the topic you chose in Exercise 10-11, write a working thesis statement.

## Considering Your Audience

A student wrote the following paragraph as part of an essay for a class assignment. His audience was his classmates.

> When the small, long-iron clubhead is behind the ball, it's hard to stop tension from creeping into your arms. When this happens, your takeaway becomes fast and jerky. Your backswing becomes shorter and you lose your rhythm. Even worse, this tension causes your right hand to uncock too early. One result is that the clubhead reaches its peak speed before it hits the ball. Another result is the clubhead goes outside the line of play and cuts across the ball steeply from outside to in. A slice or pull results.

His classmates found the paragraph confusing. Why? This writer made a serious error: he failed to analyze his audience. He assumed they knew as much about golf as he did. Readers who do not play golf would need more background information. Terms specific to golf should have been defined.

Analyzing your audience is always the first step when writing any essay. It will help you decide what to say and what type of detail to include. Here are some key questions to begin your analysis:

- Is my reader familiar with the topic?
- How much background or history does my reader need to understand the information?
- Do I need to define any unfamiliar terms?
- Do I need to explain any unfamiliar people, places, events, parts, or processes?

Suppose you are writing an essay on how to find an apartment to rent. As you plan your essay, you need to decide how much information to present. This decision involves analyzing both your audience and your purpose.

First, consider how much your audience already knows about the topic. If you think your readers know a lot about renting apartments, briefly review in your essay what they already know and then move on to a more detailed explanation of new information.

On the other hand, if your topic is probably brand new to your readers, capture their interest without intimidating them. Try to relate the topic to their own experiences. Show them how renting an apartment resembles something they already know how to do. For example, you might compare renting an apartment to other types of shopping for something with certain desired features and an established price range.

If you are uncertain about your audience's background, it is safer to include information they may already know rather than to assume that they know it. Readers can skim or skip over information they know, but they cannot fill in gaps in their understanding without your help.

Once you have made these decisions about your audience, you will want to identify your purpose. Is your purpose to give your readers an overview of a topic or do you want to give your readers specific, practical information about it? You would need much more detail for the second purpose than you would for the first.

### Considering Your Purpose

A well-written essay should have a goal, or purpose. That is, it should be written to accomplish something. The three main purposes for writing are:

- **To express yourself.** In expressive essays, you focus on your feelings and experiences. You might, for example, write an expressive essay about the value of friendship.

- **To inform.** Informative essays are written to present information. An essay on how to cook chili is an informative essay.

- **To persuade.** Persuasive essays attempt to convince readers to accept a particular viewpoint or take a particular action. A persuasive essay might attempt to convince you that zoos are inhumane.

When planning your essay, keep your essay focused on its purpose. Decide what you want your essay to accomplish, and focus on how to meet that goal.

---

**EXERCISE 10-13**

## Defining Audience and Purpose and Generating Ideas

**Directions:** For each of the following topics, define at least two different audiences and purposes. Explain how your essays would differ.

1. The lack of privacy in our society
2. The value of sports
3. Balancing job and school
4. Choosing a career
5. How to make new friends

---

**EXERCISE 10-14**

WRITING IN PROGRESS

## Defining Audience and Purpose

**Directions:** For the thesis statement you wrote on Exercise 10-12, define your purpose and audience.

---

**EXERCISE 10-15**

WRITING IN PROGRESS

## Generating Ideas

**Directions:** For the thesis statement you wrote in Exercise 10-14, generate additional ideas to include in your essay.

## Using Outlining and Idea Mapping

Outlining is one good way to organize your ideas, discover the relationships and connections between them, and show their relative importance. As you learned in Chapter 3, an outline generally follows a format that begins with your first major idea, followed by supporting details, your second major idea followed by supporting details, and so on.

Now read the following partial outline of the essay, "To Catch A Liar," pages 307–308.

---

I. Scientists want to teach cops to detect lies.
   A. Social psychologist Aldert Vrij's research on lying
      1. The mind cannot think along multiple tracks at once.
      2. Lying is harder than telling the truth.
         a. Keep story consistent and believable.
         b. Look honest.
         c. Monitor cops' reactions.
      3. Vrij's strategies for catching liars
         a. Disregard sweating and general nervousness.
         b. Ask suspects to tell story in reverse.
         c. Make suspects maintain eye contact.
         d. Have suspects draw a picture of what they're describing.

---

Another way to write a solid, effective essay is to plan its development using an idea map, a list of the ideas you will discuss in the order you will present them. Here is a sample idea map for Ted's essay on online dating.

**VISUALIZE IT!**

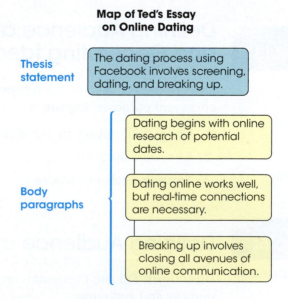

**Map of Ted's Essay on Online Dating**

**Thesis statement**
The dating process using Facebook involves screening, dating, and breaking up.

**Body paragraphs**
Dating begins with online research of potential dates.

Dating online works well, but real-time connections are necessary.

Breaking up involves closing all avenues of online communication.

## EXERCISE 10-16

# Drawing a Map or Outline

**WRITING IN PROGRESS**

**Directions:** For the ideas you generated in Exercise 10-15, draw a map or outline connecting your ideas.

## Obtaining Complete and Correct Information

At times, you know enough about your topic to explain it clearly and completely. At other times, however, you need additional information. For ideas on how to locate, use, and document sources, consult Chapter 16, "Writing Essays Using Sources."

## Deciding on an Appropriate Tone

Since the purpose of an essay is to present information, your tone should reflect your seriousness about the topic. **Tone** means how you sound to your readers and how you feel about your topic. An essay can have a serious, argumentative, or informative tone, for example. A humorous, sarcastic, flip, or very informal tone can detract from your essay and suggest that what you say should not be taken seriously.

As a general rule, your tone should reflect your relationship to your audience. The less familiar you are with your audience, the more formal your tone should be.

Here are a few examples of sentences in which the tone is inappropriate for most academic and career writing and how they could be revised to be appropriate for an academic audience.

| | |
|---|---|
| **INAPPROPRIATE** | I think Taylor would be so amazing for the assistant manager job. She works really hard, she is super nice to customers, and she always shows up when she says she will. |
| **REVISED** | I highly recommend Taylor for the assistant manager job. She is reliable and hardworking, and she has excellent customer service skills. |
| **INAPPROPRIATE** | It would be great if you'd let me know about the work-study program. I'm mainly wanting to know how I'd go about working as a tutor at the community outreach center. |
| **REVISED** | Please advise me about the requirements for the work-study program. I am especially interested in becoming a tutor at the community outreach center. |
| **INAPPROPRIATE** | I freaked out when I found out my brother blew off class to go shoot hoops. |
| **REVISED** | I was upset to learn that my brother missed class to play basketball. |

Follow these suggestions to help keep your tone appropriate:

1. Avoid slang expressions.
2. Use first-person pronouns (*I, me*) sparingly.
3. Make your writing sound more formal than casual conversation or a letter to a close friend.
4. To achieve a more formal tone, avoid informal or everyday words. For example:

Use *met* instead of *ran into*.

Use *children* instead of *kids*.

Use *annoying* instead of *bugging*.

**EXERCISE 10-17** | **Revising Tone**

**Directions:** Revise each of the following statements to give it a more formal tone.

1. The new cafeteria manager changed up the menu so it's way better than it was last year.

2. The guy who runs the gym I go to is old school; he is all about weights, push-ups, and jump ropes.

3. For spring break this year, I mostly just hung out with my bros.

4. Lots of people were hating on the band at first, but by the third song everyone was out there dancing.

5. Emily Dickinson is an awesome poet; her poems are sick.

**EXERCISE 10-18** | **Deciding on the Tone of Your Essay**

**WRITING IN PROGRESS**

**Directions:** For the essay you are working on, decide upon a tone that suits your audience and purpose. Try to describe it in a few words.

_____

_____

# Organize Your Essay

■ GOAL 7
Organize your essay

Analyzing your audience and purpose will also help you choose which pattern or patterns of organization to use. Essays use the patterns of organization that you learned about in Chapters 7 and 8: *chronological order, process, narration, description, example, definition, classification, comparison and contrast,* and *cause and effect.* You can select the one that suits your audience and purpose best.

Ted's draft essay on online dating uses the chronological order pattern. Your pattern of organization depends on your purpose. See Table 10-3 for examples. You may also use more than one of these patterns of organization. You might define a behavior and then offer examples to explain it. Or you might explain how a group of people are classified and then discuss similarities and differences between the classifications.

**TABLE 10-3  CHOOSING A PATTERN OF ORGANIZATION**

| If Your Purpose Is To . . . | Use . . . |
|---|---|
| Explain events in the order they occurred | Chronological order (see Chapter 7) |
| Tell a story that makes a point | Narration (see Chapter 7) |
| Present a visual or sensory image | Description (see Chapter 7) |
| Explain how something works or how to perform a specific task | Process (see Chapter 7) |
| Explain a topic, using specific examples | Example (see Chapter 7) |
| Explain what something is | Definition (see Chapter 8) |
| Explain a topic by showing the parts into which it can be divided or the group to which it belongs | Classification (see Chapter 8) |
| Emphasize similarities or differences between two topics or explain something by comparing it to something already familiar | Comparison and Contrast (see Chapter 8) |
| Explain why something happened | Cause and Effect (see Chapter 8) |

# INTEGRATING READING AND WRITING

## READ AND RESPOND: Student Freewriting

*Ted Sawchuck was a student at the University of Maryland, where he majored in journalism. He was the editor of the student newspaper. Ted decided to write an essay for the college newspaper about social networking sites and narrowed his topic to online dating relationships, as shown earlier in the chapter. Shown here is the freewriting Ted did to discover more ideas about online dating.*

**Uses of Facebook**

1    I use Facebook, a popular social networking site, to keep tabs on what my friends do, buy, and feel. Facebook showed me when my friend who'd launched a Facebook crusade to get back his girlfriend left her for good, that my sociology of gender prof is still up at 3 a.m. and the journalism student I'm still crushing on is also a fan of Green Day. I upload videos and post links. It's become an essential part of my life and an essential part of my relationships.

**Background on Facebook**

2    Facebook owns the college crowd because from its September 2004 launch in a Harvard dorm room until September 2006, you needed a .edu address to join. College students made the site their own community, and there was a sense that this was our world even though there's no real way to prevent nonstudents with .edu addresses from joining. The first sign of nonstudents entering what was increasingly seen as a walled community occurred in May 2006 when employers were added as available networks, followed by Facebook opening to the public in September that year.

**Overview of online dating process**

3    At the University of Maryland, the dating process goes like this:

1. Get someone's name.

2. Look the person up on Facebook.

3. Use that information to decide how to proceed.

**Facebook searches**

4    A Facebook search is the first thing I do when I meet someone and she sets off those neurons that make me hum "Maybe it's love." A Facebook page will tell me age, indicate whether or not she's taken, and give me a decent idea (if the profile is not locked) of what image she's trying to present. Note that I don't trust Facebook to tell me who people are—merely who they want to show people they are. I look through photos and see what they value enough to show me. I check posted links, because what someone thinks is worth sharing is another window into who she is.

5    Facebook pokes can be used for many purposes, but a friend who has a boyfriend uses them to let me know when she's thinking about me. It amounts to several pokes a day, and she receives one when she crosses my mind. She does it to let me know she's thinking about me frequently, which is great for me and not so hot for her boyfriend.

6    My first high school girlfriend couldn't even type when we started dating. She eventually got used to instant messaging, but was really slow for a year or two.

First girlfriend used IM

After that, every relationship I had was conducted at least partially over instant messaging and e-mail at first, and then via text message later.

7    I e-mailed and instant messaged with romantic interests, eventually meeting a girl named Sunshine in a public chat room, which then were full of actual people instead of the ad-bots that populate them today. We talked via instant messaging for five years with the complete truthfulness you save for someone you're never going to meet in person, and fell in love. We tried to do distance, which is like feeding your heart a subsistence diet, and managed to hold it together with phone calls, instant messages, webcam chats and the occasional bus trip—17 hours one way. The relationship didn't work out, but technology made it possible. Although for most of our relationship Sunshine was pixels on a screen, she's still the standard by which I judge everyone I date.

Online relationship with Sunshine

Online relationship with Maggie

8    I met Maggie at a campus newspaper meeting. After we took a liking to each other, we had a nice moment in her living room, sitting side-by-side in matching black armchairs with our laptops, as I updated my relationship status and she con-firmed that we were in a relationship—although it was clear, there's something to be said for your partner being eager to share it with her friends. When we broke up, I defriended her on Facebook because I couldn't bear to read her status updates (or honestly, even realize she existed—the first week is tough), blocked her on my instant messenger, and took her e-mail address out of my contacts list. I deleted her LiveJournal from my bookmarks and finished by updating my relationship status to single. The next day, ten people asked how I was doing before I told anyone about it. Breaking up was hard to do before the Internet. Now my list after leaving someone includes blocking her on instant messaging, taking her e-mail address out of my quick contacts list and out of my e-mail's autocomplete list, avoiding her blog/LiveJournal/MySpace, and defriending her on Facebook.

## Examining Writing

1. What other ideas do you see in Ted's freewriting that might be used to write an essay with a different focus?

2. What pattern of organization could Ted use to organize his essay?

## Writing Assignments

Assume you are taking the course "Interpersonal Communication Skills." In addition to tests and quizzes, your instructor requires two papers. For your first paper, choose one of the assignments below, and use one method of prewriting to generate ideas about it. Then review your prewriting, try to group your ideas, and write a working thesis statement.

1. Watch a portion of a television program with the sound turned off. If you could understand what was happening, write a paper explaining how you knew.

2. Suppose you are applying for a full-time job today and your prospec-tive employer asks you to describe your "people skills." Write an essay answering the employer's question.

3. We encounter conflict in our daily lives. Write a paper describing a recent conflict you had and how you and the other person handled the situation.

4. Describe a communication breakdown between you and another person. Why did it happen? Could it possibly have been prevented? How?

5. Describe a situation in which a person's body language (gestures, posture, facial expressions) allowed you to understand what he or she was really saying. Describe the body language and what it told you.

## READ AND RESPOND: A Professional Essay

### Thinking Before Reading

The following reading, "Measuring Success by Access to Gadgets," first appeared in *Salon* magazine in March 2011. As you read, notice how the author presents and develops his thesis statement, how he organizes his essay, and how he introduces and concludes his essay.

1. Preview the reading, using the steps discussed in Chapter 1, p. 15.

2. Connect the reading to your own experience by answering the following questions:

   a. How important to you are your "gadgets" (cell phone, laptop computer, etc.)?

   b. What types of things represent progress to you, both in the world and in your own community?

3. Mark and annotate as you read.

# Measuring Success by Access to Gadgets

## Patrick Smith

1    "Is there not something desperately wrong," I wondered, writing from Thailand in a column a few weeks ago, "in a world where everybody has a mobile telephone but nobody has clean drinking water?"

2    I was using hyperbole to make a point, but this isn't quite the exaggeration it might seem. Those who've traveled know what I'm talking about, and have seen the ways in which technology—the mobile phone being the most ubiquitous example—has crept into every corner of the planet. It has cut across every class line, into the tiniest rural village and the most fetid urban slum.

3    There are those who mark this as progress, but I am not seeing it that way. Not when the most elementary human needs—water, healthcare, education and basic sanitation—go ignored at every level. What exactly is the benefit—to society or to the individual—of owning a cellular telephone when you're illiterate and knee-deep in sewage? I understand the benefits of electronic connectivity—the values of the Internet and wireless communications. But in certain contexts they are somewhere between overrated and irrelevant, and I fail to see the upward mobilization, the "empowerment," that is either the symptom or the cause of a growing addiction to phones and computers.

4    I recently read how the standard of living in Egypt has doubled in the past 20 years. Is that the same Egypt in which I saw a makeshift traffic circle constructed entirely of garbage, with its vast neighborhoods of crumbling apartments and smothering blankets of air pollution? You can cite all the statistics you want. My eyes show me that the world is as filthy and desperate as it's ever been. Meanwhile there is something wholly upside-down about a system that measures success in terms of access to gadgets.

**subsidize**
provide financial support

5    Granted, any individual, wealthy or poor, is entitled to buy a phone if he or she desires one, but it's especially distressing when governments foster and **subsidize** an inverted sense of priorities. I was in Guyana recently—one of the poorest countries in the Western Hemisphere. The government there is planning to spend $30 million over the next three years giving away laptop computers to children and families—part of the One Laptop per Child initiative. Praise humanity, for now the children of Guyana can have their own Facebook pages. Meanwhile, in the capital city of Georgetown, people urinate into sidewalk gutters, and the drinking water is so polluted that it actually runs brown from the tap. This is progress?

6    Poor kids in poor countries do not need laptop computers. Or if they do, they need other things *first*.

**conflation**
combining two items or ideas into one

7    Is there some tenet of economics that I'm failing to grasp? Am I guilty of some naive **conflation**? Was the advent of the microprocessor *really* an important step toward empowerment and development?

8    A key to profits, it has been, if nothing else. Profits for the likes of Microsoft and Apple, Nokia and Motorola. This explains much.

9    Profits explain lots of things, including the reasons that governments in developing nations are lazy to enact critical but expensive improvements in public works. Why spend the money when investors and corporations can take care of it, reaping billions while pretending to fix the problem? Take something as crucial as safe drinking water, access to which ought to be a basic human right. In much of the developing world, drinking water no longer comes from the tap, it comes from a plastic bottle, sold and distributed by **conglomerates** like Nestle and Coca-Cola. Across the U.S. and Europe we've seen a backlash against the conspicuous consumption of bottled water. But in much of the Third World, for rich and poor alike, bottled water isn't just a luxury for tourists, it's the only viable option.

**conglomerates**
large corporations consisting of a group of companies in a variety of unrelated industries

10    Globally, the production and transportation of bottled water uses millions of barrels of petroleum every year, and only a small fraction of bottles are ever recycled. Many are tossed into the street or into the ocean. They are used for five minutes, then spend centuries polluting the earth.

11    I digress, I know. This column is called "Ask the Pilot" and I'm supposed to be talking about airplanes and the airline business.

12    Though in many ways, that is what I'm talking about. For a pilot, international flying has its privileges, for sure: long layovers in exotic cities, luxurious hotels, five-course crew meals. But it also has its downsides, not the least of which is a firsthand view of some of this planet's more unfortunate realities. The depressing, demoralizing aspects of travel are something I've described before, but the world never ceases to suffocate one's optimism.

# Getting Ready to Write

## Checking your Comprehension

Answer each of the following questions using complete sentences.

1. According to the author, what four basic human needs are being ignored?
2. What has happened to the standard of living in Egypt in the past 20 years? What three aspects of Egypt does the author describe to contradict that statistic?
3. What is the government in Guyana planning to do as part of the One Laptop per Child initiative?
4. What does the author say explains why governments in developing nations do not make improvements in public works?
5. What is the author supposed to be talking about in this essay?
6. List three privileges and one negative aspect of international flying as described by the author.

## Strengthening Your Vocabulary

Using the word's context, word parts, or a dictionary, write a brief definition of each of the following words as it is used in the reading:

1. hyperbole (paragraph 2) _____
2. ubiquitous (paragraph 2) _____
3. fetid (paragraph 2) _____
4. foster (paragraph 5) _____
5. inverted (paragraph 5) _____
6. tenet (paragraph 7) _____
7. viable (paragraph 9) _____

## Examining the Reading: Using an Idea Map to Understand a Reading

In this reading, the author argues that access to cell phones and computers is not an accurate measurement of progress in the world. Create an idea map of "Measuring Success by Access to Gadgets" that starts with the title and thesis of the essay and then lists the main points of the author's argument.

### Reacting to Ideas: Discussion and Journal Writing

Get ready to write about the reading by discussing the following:

1. Evaluate the opening paragraph of the reading. How does it reveal both what the essay is about and how the author feels about the subject?

2. What is the author's purpose in writing this essay? In your opinion, does he achieve his purpose? Write a journal entry explaining your answers.

3. What types of evidence does the author use to support his thesis? How effective or convincing is it? What other evidence might he have included?

4. Discuss the author's tone and how he reveals his feelings about his subject. For example, when he writes "Praise humanity" in paragraph 5, what is he really saying?

5. Define the term *empowerment*. Do you think technology leads to empowerment? Why or why not?

6. Explain the purpose of the photograph that accompanies the reading. Why is a water faucet shown on the screen of a laptop?

**THINKING VISUALLY**

### Thinking and Writing Critically

1. In the list of suggestions for choosing your own topic for an essay (p. 317), "choose a topic that interests you" and "write about something familiar" are listed. How can you tell that the topic of this essay—the massive increase in gadgets while more basic human needs are left unfulfilled—interests the author? How is the author familiar with his topic?

2. What is the author's purpose in this essay? Who is his intended audience?

3. How would you describe the tone of "Measuring Success by Access to Gadgets"?

---

**MySkillsLab®**

Complete this Exercise

## Writing About the Reading

### Paragraph Options

1. Write a paragraph giving your own answer to the question posed by the author at the beginning of this essay.

2. Consider the author's statement: "My eyes show me that the world is as filthy and desperate as it's ever been." Write a paragraph describing what your eyes show you about the world.

3. Do you agree that profits explain why some governments are lazy about making critical improvements? What other reasons might there be? Write a paragraph explaining your answers.

### Essay Options

4. Think about how you would define the term *progress*. Is access to technology (or "gadgets") a mark of progress? Or do you agree with the author that the benefits of electronic connectivity fall "somewhere between overrated and irrelevant"? Write an essay defining *progress* and giving your answers to these questions.

5. When you have traveled, what kinds of things have you observed about our planet? Write an essay describing your observations.

6. The author says that "the world never ceases to suffocate one's optimism." Have you ever felt that the world was suffocating your optimism? In general, do you tend to be hopeful or pessimistic about the world? Write an essay explaining your answers.

# SELF-TEST SUMMARY

To test yourself, cover up the Answer column with a sheet of paper and answer each question listed in the left column, Evaluate each of your answers as you work by sliding the paper down and comparing your answer with what is printed in the Answer column.

| QUESTION | ANSWER |
|---|---|
| ■ GOAL 1 Understand the purpose of an essay<br><br>What do essays do, and how are essays organized? | An essay introduces an idea, states it, explains it, and draws a conclusion about it. Essays include an introductory paragraph and thesis statement, supporting paragraphs, and a conclusion. |
| ■ GOAL 2 Read essays effectively<br><br>How can you read essays effectively? | Examine each part of the essay closely, assess the author's credentials, consider any background information that is provided, express the thesis in your own words, and identify the organizational pattern. |
| ■ GOAL 3 Analyze and evaluate essays<br><br>Why and how should you analyze essays? | Essays often express opinions or viewpoints, so it is important to read them critically. You should determine who the author is and whether he or she is qualified to write about the topic; the author's purpose; the adequacy of the support provided; if sources are provided, whether they verify the information in the essay; and analyze any visuals. (see Chapters 13–15 for additional critical reading skills.) |
| ■ GOAL 4 Choose a topic<br><br>How do you develop an assigned topic? How do you choose your own topic? | For an assigned topic, determine the purpose of the assignment, connect it to classroom instruction, and watch for clue words suggesting how to write and organize your essay. For your own topic, take your time choosing a topic that interests you and is familiar, and use sources of ideas listed in Table 10-2 on p. 317. |

*(continued)*

*(continued)*

| QUESTION | ANSWER |
|---|---|
| ■ GOAL 5 Generate ideas about your topic<br><br>How do you generate ideas and narrow your topic? | Generate ideas by freewriting, brainstorming, questioning, and branching. Narrow your topic into subtopics until you find one that is manageable. A diagram can help you reduce a topic as well. |
| ■ GOAL 6 Plan your essay<br><br>What is involved in planning your essay? | Planning your essay involves grouping ideas to form a thesis statement, considering audience and purpose, using outlining and mapping, obtaining information, and choosing an appropriate tone. |
| ■ GOAL 7 Organize your essay<br><br>How should you organize your essay? | Analyze your audience and purpose to help you choose the most appropriate pattern of organization for your essay. See Table 10-3 on p. 326 for a list of patterns of organization. |

**MySkillsLab®**  For more help with **Reading, Planning, and Organizing Essays**, go to your learning path in MySkillsLab at www.myskillslab.com.

# Drafting and Revising Essays

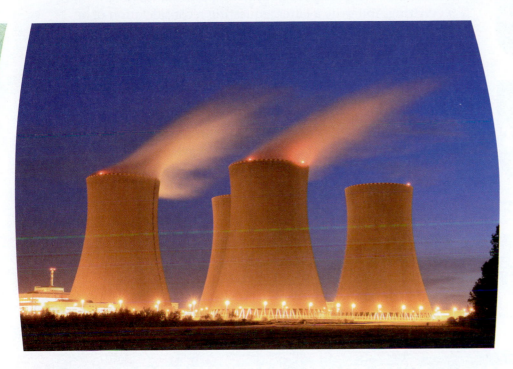

## 11

## THINK About It!

Study the photograph above, showing nuclear power plants in operation. Write a sentence that states your view on whether nuclear power plants are a safe energy source.

The sentence you have written could be the thesis statement for an essay on nuclear power. You might have written that nuclear power is an important alternative energy source and more plants should be built. Or you might have stated that nuclear power is risky and nuclear plants should be phased out. Or perhaps you felt you did not know enough about nuclear power, its risks or its benefits, and decided you needed to research the topic. After reading about the issue, maybe you decided that nuclear power plants present dangers and wrote a thesis statement saying that although nuclear power has obvious risks, its benefits far outweigh its risks so it should be a continuing source of energy.

Regardless of the thesis statement you wrote, you usually need to read, reread, evaluate, and revise it to make it as clear and effective as possible. This chapter will focus on writing and evaluating thesis statements and drafting an essay that supports a thesis. You will also learn how to revise, edit, and proofread your essay.

## LEARNING GOALS

Learn how to . . .

- **GOAL 1**
  Draft an essay

- **GOAL 2**
  Read while drafting an essay

- **GOAL 3**
  Write and revise a thesis statement

- **GOAL 4**
  Support your thesis with substantial evidence

- **GOAL 5**
  Use transitions to make connections

- **GOAL 6**
  Write introductions, conclusions, and titles

- **GOAL 7**
  Think critically as you revise your draft

- **GOAL 8**
  Edit and proofread

# Reading and Writing Connections

### EVERYDAY CONNECTIONS

- **Reading** You read a letter from your insurance agent suggesting adding coverage to your homeowner's insurance policy.
- **Writing** You write a letter requesting reconsideration of an insurance claim that was denied.

### ACADEMIC CONNECTIONS

- **Reading** You read a section of your art history textbook describing American folk art, craft, and design.
- **Writing** You write an essay for your art history course describing your visit to a folk art exhibit at a local gallery.

### WORKPLACE CONNECTIONS

- **Reading** You read the prospectus, or business plan, of a company you are planning to visit as part of a sales trip.
- **Writing** You write a report summarizing activities and outcomes of a recent sales trip.

# FOCUSING ON READING AND WRITING

# What Is a Draft?

■ GOAL 1
Draft an essay

A **draft** is a tentative or preliminary version of your essay. You should plan to write several drafts before you end up with an essay you are satisfied with. Use the following general suggestions for getting started; then work on drafting each paragraph as described on the following pages.

## General Suggestions

Here are some tips for writing essay drafts. Also refer to the tips for drafting in Chapter 2 on pages 68–69.

- ■ **Leave time between your drafts**. If you try to write too many drafts in one sitting, you may find it difficult to sort them all out and see the strengths and weaknesses of each one.
- ■ **Think of drafting as a chance to experiment**. Find out what works and what does not. You might want to write your essay several different ways, trying out different approaches, different content, and different ways of organizing the information.

■ **Focus on ideas, not correctness.** Especially for the first few drafts, concentrate on recording your ideas. Do not worry yet about grammatical errors or sentence structure, for example.

■ **Be prepared to make major changes.** Often as your essay develops, you may realize that you want to change direction or that you should further limit your topic. Do not hesitate to do so.

Reading, rereading, analyzing, and evaluating are all important parts of drafting an essay and preparing to revise it. To be an effective writer, you have to read and think critically about your draft, considering whether your draft says what you want it to say and whether it does so clearly and effectively.

## READING

# Read While Drafting

■ **GOAL 2**
Read while drafting an essay

Most students think of drafting as a writing process, but it is also a reading process. While drafting an essay, it is important to frequently read and reread what you have already written. Going back is helpful for several reasons. Rereading will help you

■ Stay focused on the topic
■ Realize where you need to add further explanation or support
■ Decide when to start a new paragraph
■ Know when transitions are needed to connect your ideas
■ Recognize when you repeat yourself
■ Recognize that you need to think more about organization

## WRITING

# Write and Revise Your Thesis Statement

■ **GOAL 3**
Write and revise a thesis statement and support it with evidence

Drafting involves expressing your thesis statement and supporting it with evidence. At various stages in the drafting process, you may decide to rewrite, revise, or completely change your thesis statement. Remember, a thesis statement should explain what your essay is about and also give your readers clues about its organization. You may not know, for example, how your essay will be organized until you have written one or more drafts. Use the following suggestions to make sure your thesis statement is clear and effective.

## How to Write an Effective Thesis Statement

Think of your thesis statement as a promise; it promises your reader what your paper will deliver. Here are some guidelines to follow for writing an effective thesis statement:

1. **It should state the main point of your essay**. It should not focus on details; it should give an overview of your approach to your topic.

   | | |
   |---|---|
   | **TOO DETAILED** | A well-written business letter has no errors in spelling. |
   | **REVISED** | To write a grammatically correct business letter, follow three simple rules. |

2. **It should assert an idea about your topic**. Your thesis should express a viewpoint or state an approach to the topic.

   | | |
   |---|---|
   | **LACKS AN ASSERTION** | Advertising contains images of both men and women. |
   | **REVISED** | In general, advertising presents men more favorably than women. |

3. **It should be as specific and detailed as possible**. For this reason, it is important to review and rework your thesis *after* you have written and revised drafts.

   | | |
   |---|---|
   | **TOO GENERAL** | Advertisers can influence readers' attitudes toward competing products. |
   | **REVISED** | Athletic-shoe advertisers focus more on attitude and image than on the actual physical differences between their product and those of their competitors. |

4. **It may suggest the organization of your essay**. Mentioning key points that will be discussed in the essay is one way to do this. The order in which you mention them should be the order in which you discuss them in your essay.

   | | |
   |---|---|
   | **DOES NOT SUGGEST ORGANIZATION** | Public-school budget cuts will negatively affect education. |
   | **REVISED** | Public-school budget cuts will negatively affect academic achievement, student motivation, and the drop-out rate. |

5. **It should not be a direct announcement**. Do not begin with phrases such as "In this paper I will" or "My assignment was to discuss."

   | | |
   |---|---|
   | **DIRECT ANNOUNCEMENT** | The purpose of my paper is to show that businesses lose money due to inefficiency, competition, and inflated labor costs. |
   | **REVISED** | Businesses lose money due to inefficiency, competition, and inflated labor costs. |

6. **It should offer a fresh, interesting, and original perspective on the topic.** A thesis statement can follow the guidelines above, but if it seems dull or predictable, it needs more work.

| | |
|---|---|
| PREDICTABLE | Circus acts fall into three categories: animal, clown, and acrobatic. |
| REVISED | Each of the three categories of circus acts—animal, clown, and acrobatic—is exciting because of the risks it involves. |

## Drafting Body Paragraphs

Once you have a working thesis statement, you are ready to start planning and writing the individual paragraphs of your essay. It is often best to start with the body of the essay, those paragraphs that provide the support for your thesis statement. There are a number of different ways you can begin drafting the body of your essay. Some students write an outline; others draw a graphic organizer; still others write a list of topic sentences that support the thesis. Don't worry too much about the order of the items in your draft. At this point it is more important to get your ideas down in writing. In later drafts you can rearrange your ideas.

Once you have identified topics or topic sentences that support your thesis, you are ready to write first-draft paragraphs. These, too, may change, so concentrate primarily on making sure that each topic sentence supports the thesis and that each paragraph has a clear topic sentence (see Chapter 5), supporting details (see Chapter 6), and transitions (see Chapter 6).

Here is the initial list of topic sentences Ted wrote for the first draft of his online dating essay.

> Facebook owns the college crowd and is widely popular for dating.
> Here's how the dating process works at the U. of Maryland.
> On Facebook everyone is reduced to a set of bullets.
> I use Facebook to stalk a potential date.
> When dating begins it is nice to change our status on Facebook together.
> Facebook can encourage infidelity.
> Breaking up was hard to do before the Internet.

You will see that he changed, added, and expanded these topic sentences as he wrote his first draft, which appears on pp. 342–343.

## How to Revise Your Thesis Statement

The best time to evaluate and, if necessary, revise your thesis statement is after you have written a first draft. When evaluating your thesis statement, ask the following questions:

1. **Does my essay develop and explain my thesis statement?** As you write an essay, its focus and direction may change. Revise your thesis statement to reflect any changes. If you discover that you drifted away from your original thesis and want to maintain it, work on revising so that your paper delivers what your thesis promises.

2. **Is my thesis statement broad enough to cover all the points made in the essay?** As you develop your first draft, you may find that one idea leads naturally to another. Both must be covered by the thesis statement. For example, suppose your thesis statement is "Media coverage of national political events shapes public attitudes toward politicians." If, in your essay, you discuss media coverage of international events as well as national ones, then you need to broaden your thesis statement.

3. **Does my thesis statement use vague or unclear words that do not clearly focus the topic?** For example, in the thesis statement "The possibility of animal-organ transplants for humans is interesting," the word *interesting* is vague and does not suggest how your essay will approach the topic. Instead, if your paper discusses both the risks and benefits of these transplants, this approach should be reflected in your thesis: "Animal-organ transplants for humans offer both risks and potential benefits."

**EXERCISE 11-1**

*WORKING TOGETHER*

## Evaluating Thesis Statements

**Directions:** Working with a classmate, identify what is wrong with the following thesis statements, and revise each one to make it more effective:

1. Jogging has a lot of benefits.
2. Counseling can help people with problems.
3. Getting involved in campus activities has really helped me.
4. Budgeting your time is important.
5. Commuting to college presents problems.
6. The movie is about parenting.
7. Violence on television must be brought to an end.
8. Divorce laws are unfair and favor women.
9. Fad diets are losing their appeal.
10. Automobile air bags save lives.

# Support Your Thesis with Substantial Evidence

■ GOAL 4
Support your thesis with substantial evidence

Every essay you write should offer substantial evidence in support of your thesis statement. This evidence makes up the body of your essay. **Evidence** can consist of personal experience, anecdotes (stories that illustrate a point), examples, reasons, descriptions, facts, statistics, and quotations (taken from sources).

Many students have trouble locating concrete, specific evidence to support their thesis. Though prewriting yields plenty of good ideas and helps you focus your thesis, prewriting ideas may not always provide sufficient evidence. Often you need to brainstorm again for additional ideas. At other times, you may need to consult one or more sources to obtain further information on your topic (see in Chapter 16, p. 488).

Ted realized that he did not have enough ideas for his essay on online dating. Table 11-1 lists ways to explain a thesis statement and gives an example of how Ted could use each in his essay.

## TABLE 11-1  WAYS TO ADD EVIDENCE

### Topic: Online Dating

| Explain Your Thesis by . . . | Example |
| --- | --- |
| Telling a story (narration) | Relate a story about an online dating experience. |
| Adding descriptive detail (description) | Add a description of a social network profile. |
| Explaining how something works (process) | Explain how a person can change his or her relationship status on Facebook. |
| Giving an example | Discuss specific instances of prescreening a potential date using Google. |
| Discussing types or kinds (classification) | Discuss types of profiles people create of themselves. |
| Giving a definition | Explain the meaning of terms such as *profile, poking,* or *defriending.* |
| Making distinctions | Contrast prescreening a date online and without the use of a computer. |
| Making comparisons | Compare two social networking sites. |
| Giving reasons | Explain why breaking up is difficult when so many online connections exist. |
| Analyzing effects | Explain how online profiles can be misleading. |

Table 11-1 offers a variety of ways Ted could add evidence to his essay. But he does not need to use all of them; instead, he should choose the ones that are most appropriate for his audience and purpose. Ted could also use different types of evidence in combination. For example, he could *tell a story* that illustrates the *effects* of misleading online profiles.

Use the following guidelines in selecting evidence to support your thesis:

1. **Be sure your evidence is relevant.** That is, it must directly support or explain your thesis.

2. **Make your evidence as specific as possible.** Help your readers see the point you are making by offering detailed, concrete information. For example, if you are explaining the effects of right-to-privacy violations on an individual, include details that make the situation come alive: names of people and places, types of violations, and so forth.

3. **Be sure your information is accurate.** It may be necessary to check facts, verify stories you have heard, and ask questions of individuals who have provided information.

4. **Locate sources that provide evidence.** Because you may not know enough about your topic and lack personal experience, you may be unable to provide strong evidence. When this happens, locate several sources on your topic. Consult Chapter 16 for information on synthesizing sources.

5. **Be sure to document any information that you borrow from other sources.** See Chapter 16, page 493, for further information on crediting sources.

Now let's take a look at how Ted developed his essay on online dating. As you read, notice, in particular, the types of evidence he uses and how his thesis statement promises what his essay delivers. In this first draft he uses his free-writing from pages 327–328 and his list of topic sentences on page 339.

Facebook is a social networking Internet site. It allows a user to connect with people, make friends, and join interest groups using the convenience of their own computer. It also allows a user to learn more information about said friends, as well as post text, photos, video, links, and information.

Facebook owns the college crowd, because from its September 2004 launch in a Harvard dorm room until September 2006, a user needed a .edu e-mail address to join. College students made the site their own community, and there was a sense that this was our world even though there's no real way to prevent non-students with .edu addresses from joining. The first sign of non-students entering what was our walled community occurred in May 2006 when employers were admitted, followed by Facebook opening to the public in September of that year.

Facebook has become widely popular. Much has been written about it in my student newspaper, but no one has yet dug into what the site has done to change our relationships, and specifically the dating process. The dating process has changed dramatically since Facebook came on the scene. Not all the changes have been positive.

I know when Facebook friends break up, fail tests, and hate their parents, but I don't really know them as people, just **infobits** on an **LCD**. The dating process works well initially over this medium, but real connections are only formed with substantial time-spending, preferably in person. Online talks, even via Skype or webcam, are still only a fraction of the experience and do not convey as high a percentage of the information one can glean during an in-person encounter.

At the University of Maryland, the dating process begins like this: get someone's name; look him or her up on Facebook; use that information to decide how to proceed. When I meet someone and she sets off those neurons that make me hum "Maybe it's love," I do a Facebook search. A profile page will tell me her age, indicate whether or not she's taken, and give me a decent idea (if the profile is not privacy protected) of what image she's trying to present. Note that I don't trust Facebook to tell me who people are—merely who they want to show people they are. I look through photos and see what they value enough to show me. I check posted links because what someone thinks is worth sharing is another window into who she is.

On Facebook, everyone seems reduced to a set of bullet points—"goth, tall, cat person"—that we rely on before even meeting someone. In real life, careful observation can reveal truths about people they won't discuss, especially things they don't want known.

However, a fidgety, nervous guy who sweats when he sees a pretty girl may have a better chance sending a Facebook message, which can be drafted and redrafted and edited and rewritten and shown to friends before sending, than approaching her in real life, so it does have its benefits.

After using Facebook to research the person, I have a decent idea of whether she's a probable friend or romantic interest. Next I hit Google—first searching with her e-mail address, then with her name, then with her nickname if I have reason to believe the person I'm into uses the Internet for more than e-mail. This turns up message boards, possibly her blog, and maybe even a Flickr site, all worth plumbing for details about my new fascination.

I have serious doubts as to whether being able to download someone's self with a little searching on Facebook and Google is actually a good thing for beginning relationships. For one, online searches result in tons of information with absolutely no context. Judging what you learn without cross-referencing it with the person him- or herself is a recipe for misinterpretative disaster, yet checking means admitting you've been snooping. I **snoop** anyway.

---

**infobits**
small amounts of information

**LCD**
liquid crystal display used in computer monitors

**snoop**
to try to get private information by looking somewhere you're not supposed to look

When I start dating someone new, it's usually a nice moment to change our relationship status on Facebook. After the last time I did that, we communicated more via messages on Facebook, posted on each other's walls, and even updated our statuses at the same time. I'm glad we never committed the ultimate act of Facebook couplehood, however.

I knew my housemate was in deep when her profile picture changed from just her to her being held by her girlfriend. I knew it was even worse when her girlfriend's photo changed the same way. The face they'd chosen to show couldn't be just theirs—it was sweet but creeped me out.

Internet access means access to your romantic interest, even during work in many cases. E-mail replaces IM for quick messages because many jobs require e-mail use. The Internet lets you do couples things like play Scrabble or check up on each other regardless of distance.

Time spent communicating with someone, especially just one person, can build connections that lead to relationships or strengthen current ones. Although Skyping someone is **about as emotionally satisfying as being courteously deferential**, you still get to hear his or her voice. Tone, pauses, **nuance**, and volume are all stripped from instant messages—at least Skype gives you those back. Human laughter beats "LOL" in pixels any day, but holding her while she tells you about her day wins whenever possible.

Facebook can also provoke new frontiers of infidelity. One way is through chatting online. It's very poor form to chat up someone else's girlfriend in a bar, but when chatting online there's no boyfriend looming over you to enforce her morality. Combine that freedom with the very personal qualities of online relationships and the large amount of time most people spend online and you've got a formula anyone who's dating anyone who gets online should worry about.

The poke feature is another way Facebook can promote infidelity. One of my friends who has a boyfriend uses it to let me know when she's thinking about me. It amounts to several pokes a day, and she receives one when she crosses my mind. She does it to let me know she's thinking about me frequently, which is great for me and not so hot for her boyfriend.

Breaking up is hard to do, but the Internet makes it easier. You don't want to get a continually updated feed of information about that person. Knowing someone's getting over you and trying to date is one thing; knowing they're doing it at seven-thirty at Club Kozmo with someone they met last weekend is another.

After I leave someone, he or she disappears from instant messaging, my e-mail contacts, Facebook friends, and my web bookmarks. Forget one step and the "getting over her" process becomes that much harder. There's a measure of comfort to be found in thinking someone's fallen off the face of the earth romantically, especially if your return to dating hasn't been as successful. After the relationship ends, I like the flood of data the Internet provides much less than in my prescreening stage.

That level of cutting someone off requires an amount of effort commonly reserved for reporters on deadline or college students who fell asleep before they got to the all-nighter. You become like a recovering alcoholic, not just avoiding them in person. Certain sites take on new meaning. Any bit of forgotten information is another **barb**, another **pang**, another realization. Invariably, you'll miss something and see a status update or a text message or a voice mail. It helps at times, when missing someone so badly means wishing the person were dead. Once you get over it, refriend the person if you can do it without going crazy. Sometimes a little bit of ignorance can be blissful indeed, but most connections are worth preserving.

---

**"About as emotionally satisfying as being courteously deferential"**

a comparison meaning that it's not at all satisfying. Being *courteously deferential* means being polite and respectful

**nuance**

small difference in tone

**barb and pang**

words that refer to the mental pain of being reminded of a lost love

## EXERCISE 11-2 — Evaluating a Draft

WORKING TOGETHER

**Directions:** Working with a classmate, evaluate Ted's first draft. What problems do you see? What revisions does he need to make? Assume you are working together as peer reviewers (see Chapter 2, p. 69). Write a response to Ted, explaining both the strengths and weaknesses of his first draft.

## EXERCISE 11-3 — Writing a First Draft

WRITING IN PROGRESS

**Directions:** Write a first draft of an essay for the working thesis statement you wrote in Exercise 10-12 (p. 322). Support your thesis statement with at least three types of evidence.

# Use Transitions to Make Connections

■ GOAL 5
Use transitions to make connections

To produce a well-written essay, be sure to make it clear how your ideas relate to one another. There are several ways to do this:

1. **Use transitional words and phrases.** Transitional words and phrases are helpful for making your essay flow smoothly and communicate clearly. Table 11-2 lists useful transitions for each method of organization. Notice the use of these transitional words and phrases in Ted's first draft: *however, next, for one, although, another, after.*

2. **Write a transitional sentence.** This sentence is usually the first sentence in the paragraph. It might come before the topic sentence or it might *be* the topic sentence. Its purpose is to link the paragraph in which it appears with the paragraph before it.

3. **Repeat key words.** Repeating key words also enables your reader to stay on track. Key words often appear in your thesis statement, and, by repeating some of them, you remind your reader of your thesis and how each new idea is connected to it.

You need not repeat the word or phrase exactly as long as the meaning stays the same. You could substitute "keeps your audience on target" for "enables your reader to stay on track," for example. The following excerpt from an essay on clothing illustrates the use of key-word repetition.

> ### The Real Functions of Clothing
>
> Just as a product's packaging tells us a lot about the product, so does a person's clothing reveal a lot about the person. Clothing reflects the way we choose to present ourselves and reveals how we feel about ourselves.
>
> Clothing reveals our emotions. We tend to dress according to how we feel. If we feel relaxed and comfortable, we tend to dress in comfortable, relaxed clothing. For instance, some people wear sweatshirts and sweatpants for a relaxed evening at home. If we feel happy and carefree, our clothing often reflects it. Think of how fans dress at a football game, for example. Their dress reflects casual comfort, and their team-supporting hats, T-shirts, etc., reveal their emotional support for the team. Clothing also reveals our expectations and perceptions.

**TABLE 11-2　USEFUL TRANSITIONAL WORDS AND PHRASES**

| Type of Connection | Transitional Words and Phrases |
| --- | --- |
| Importance | *most important, above all, especially, particularly important* |
| Spatial relationships | *above, below, behind, beside, next to, inside, outside, to the west (north, etc.), beneath, near, nearby, next to, under, over* |
| Time sequences | *first, next, now, before, during, after, eventually, finally, at last, later, meanwhile, soon, then, suddenly, currently, after, afterward, after a while, as soon as, until* |
| Recounting events or steps | *first, second, then, later, in the beginning, when, while, after, following, next, during, again, after that, at last, finally* |
| Examples | *for example, for instance, to illustrate, in one case* |
| Types | *one, another, second, third* |
| Definitions | *means, can be defined as, refers to, is* |
| Similarities | *likewise, similarly, in the same way, too, also* |
| Differences | *however, on the contrary, unlike, on the other hand, although, even though, but, in contrast, yet* |
| Causes or results | *because, consequently, since, as a result, for this reason, therefore, thus* |
| Restatement | *in other words, that is* |
| Summary or conclusion | *finally, to sum up, all in all, evidently, in conclusion* |

## EXERCISE 11-4

**WRITING IN PROGRESS**

## Analyzing a Draft

**Directions:** Review the draft you wrote for Exercise 11-3. Analyze how effectively you have connected your ideas. Add key words or transitional words, phrases, or sentences, as needed.

# Write the Introduction, Conclusion, and Title

- **GOAL 6**
  Write introductions, conclusions, and titles

The introduction, conclusion, and title each serve a specific function. Each strengthens your essay and helps your reader understand your ideas.

## Writing the Introduction

An **introductory paragraph** has three main purposes:

- It presents your thesis statement.
- It interests your reader in your topic.
- It provides any necessary background information.

Although your introductory paragraph appears first in your essay, it does *not* need to be written first. In fact, it is sometimes best to write it last, after you have developed your ideas, written your thesis statement, and drafted your essay.

We have already discussed writing thesis statements earlier in the chapter (see p. 338). Here are some suggestions on how to interest your readers in your topic:

## Techniques for Writing Introductions

| TECHNIQUE | EXAMPLE |
|---|---|
| Ask a provocative or controversial question. | *What would you do if you were sound asleep and woke to find a burglar in your bedroom?* |
| State a startling fact or statistic. | *Did you know that the federal government recently spent $687,000 on a research project that studied the effect of Valium on monkeys?* |
| Begin with a story or an anecdote. | *Mark Brown, a social worker, has spent several evenings riding in a police cruiser to learn about neighborhood problems.* |
| Use a quotation. | *Oscar Wilde once said, "Always forgive your enemies—nothing annoys them so much."* |
| State a little-known fact, a myth, or a misconception. | *It's hard to lose weight and even harder to keep it off. Right? Wrong! A sensible eating program will help you lose weight.* |

A straightforward, dramatic thesis statement can also capture your reader's interest, as in the following example:

> The dream job that I'd wanted all my life turned out to be a complete disaster.

An introduction should also provide the reader with any necessary background information. Consider what information your reader needs to understand your essay. You may, for example, need to define the term *genetic engineering* for a paper on that topic. At other times, you might need to provide a brief history or give an overview of a controversial issue.

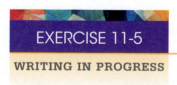

**EXERCISE 11-5**

**WRITING IN PROGRESS**

# Writing/Revising the Introduction

**Directions:** Revise your introduction to the essay you wrote for Exercise 11-3.

## Writing the Conclusion

The final, **concluding paragraph** of your essay has two functions: It should re-emphasize your thesis statement and draw the essay to a close. It should not be a direct announcement, such as "This essay has been about" or "In this paper I hoped to show that."

It's usually best to revise your essay at least once *before* working on the conclusion. During your first or second revision, you often make numerous changes in both content and organization, which may, in turn, affect your conclusion.

Here are a few effective ways to write a conclusion. Choose one that will work for your essay:

1. **Suggest a new direction for further thought**. Raise a related issue that you did not address in your essay, or ask a series of questions.

2. **Look ahead**. Project into the future. Consider outcomes or effects.

3. **Return to your thesis**. If your essay is written to prove a point or convince your reader of the need for action, it may be effective to end with a sentence that recalls your main point or calls for action. If you choose this way to conclude, don't merely repeat your first paragraph. Be sure to reflect on the thoughts you developed in the body of your essay.

4. **Summarize key points**. Especially for longer essays, briefly review your key supporting ideas. In shorter essays, this tends to be unnecessary.

If you have trouble writing your conclusion, you may need to work further on your thesis or organization.

**EXERCISE 11-6**

**WRITING IN PROGRESS**

# Writing/Revising the Conclusion

**Directions:** Write or revise a conclusion for the essay you wrote for Exercise 11-3.

## Selecting a Title

Although the title appears first in your essay, it is often the last thing you should write. The **title** should identify the topic in an interesting way, and it may also suggest the focus. To select a title, reread your final draft, paying particular attention to your thesis statement and your overall method of development. Here are a few examples of effective titles:

> "Surprise in the Vegetable Bin" (for an essay on vegetables and their effects on cholesterol and cancer)
>
> "Denim Goes High Fashion" (for an essay describing the uses of denim for clothing other than jeans)
>
> "Babies Go to Work" (for an essay on corporate-sponsored day-care centers)

To write accurate and interesting titles, try the following tips:

1. **Write a question that your essay answers**. For example: "Why Change the Minimum Wage?"

2. **Use key words that appear in your thesis statement**. If your thesis statement is "The new international trade ruling threatens the safety of the dolphin, one of our most intelligent mammals," your title could be "New Threat to Dolphins."

3. **Use brainstorming techniques to generate options**. Don't necessarily use the first title that pops into your mind. If in doubt, try out some options on friends to see which is most effective.

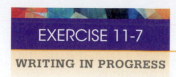

## Selecting a Title

**Directions:** Come up with a good title for the essay you wrote for Exercise 11-3.

# Think Critically About and Revise Your Draft

■ GOAL 7
Think critically as you revise your draft

As you learned in Chapter 9, the first step in preparing to revise a draft is to read it critically to find out what works and what doesn't. Thinking critically about your draft involves examining, evaluating, and revising your ideas as well as the content and structure of your draft.

## Examining Your Ideas

Revising is a process of closely evaluating your draft to determine if it accomplishes what you want it to. This is the time to be sure the essay says what you want it to say and that it does so in a clear and effective way. Later, once you are confident that your ideas are expressed clearly, you can move to editing, in which you make sure your essay is error free.

### General Essay Revision Strategies

Here are some general suggestions for revising your final essay draft. Also refer to the Tips for Revising box in Chapter 2, page 70, and the strategies for revising paragraphs presented in Chapter 9.

- **Allow time between finishing your last draft and revising, until the next day, if possible**. When you return to the draft, you will have a clear mind and a new perspective.

- **Look for common problems**. If you usually have trouble, for example, with writing thesis statements or with using transitions, then evaluate these features closely each time you revise.

- **Read the draft aloud**. You may hear ideas that are unclear or realize they are not fully explained.

- **Ask a friend to read your paper aloud to you**. If the person hesitates or seems confused or misreads, the person may be having trouble grasping your ideas. Reread and revise any trouble spots.

- **Read a print copy**. Although you may be used to writing on a computer, your essay may read differently when you see a paper copy.

### Using Revision Maps to Revise

In Chapter 9, "Strategies for Revising Paragraphs," pages 285–289, you learned to draw revision maps to evaluate paragraphs. The same strategy works well for essays, too. A revision map will help you evaluate the overall flow of ideas as well as the effectiveness of individual paragraphs.

To draw an essay revision map, work through each paragraph, recording your ideas in abbreviated form, as shown on the following page. Then write the key words of your conclusion. If you find details that do not support the topic sentence, record those details to the right of the map.

**VISUALIZE IT!**

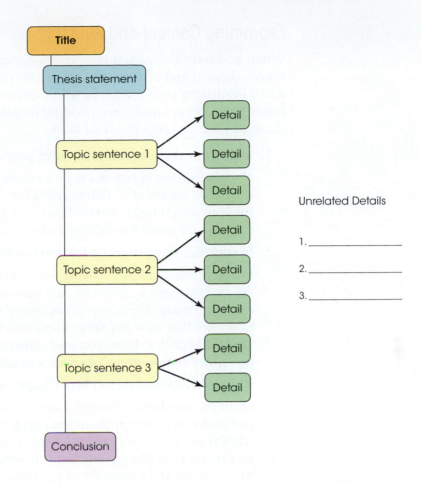

When you've completed your revision map, conduct the following tests:

1. **Read your thesis statement along with your first topic sentence.** Does the topic sentence clearly support your thesis? If not, revise to make the relationship clearer. Repeat this step for each topic sentence.

2. **Read your topic sentences, one after the other, without corresponding details.** Is there a logical connection between them? Are they arranged in the most effective way? If not, revise to make the connection clearer or to improve your organization.

3. **Examine each individual paragraph.** Are there enough relevant, specific details to support the topic sentence?

4. **Read your introduction and then look at your topic sentences.** Does the essay deliver what the introduction promises?

5. **Read your thesis statement and then your conclusion.** Are they compatible and consistent? Does the conclusion agree with and support the thesis statement?

**EXERCISE 11-8**

**WRITING IN PROGRESS**

## Drawing a Revision Map

**Directions:** Draw a revison map of the essay you wrote for Exercise 11-3 and make necessary revisions.

## Examining Content and Structure

When you have completed your revision map, you are ready to evaluate your essay's content and organization. If you do not ask yourself the right questions when evaluating your draft, you won't discover how to improve it. Each of the following questions and corresponding revision strategies will guide you in producing a clear and effective final essay.

1. **Does your essay accomplish your purpose?**

   *If you are writing in response to an assignment, reread it and make sure you have covered all aspects of it.* Delete any sentences or paragraphs that do not fulfill your assignment or stated purpose. Do you have enough ideas left? If not, do additional freewriting to discover new ideas.

2. **Is your essay appropriate for your audience?**

   *Visualize your audience reading your essay.* How will they respond? If you are not sure, ask a classmate or a person who is part of your audience to read your essay. Then, revise your essay with your audience in mind. Add examples that may appeal to them; delete those that would not. Examine your word choice. Have you used language that is understandable and will not either confuse them or create a negative impression?

3. **Is your thesis statement clearly expressed?**

   *Highlight your thesis statement.* Does it state the main point of your essay and make an assertion about your topic? If not, write one sentence stating what your essay is intended to explain or show. Use this sentence to help you revise your thesis statement. If you revise your thesis statement, be sure to revise the remainder of your essay to reflect your changes.

4. **Does each paragraph support your thesis?**

   *Reread each topic sentence.* Does each clearly and specifically explain some aspect of your thesis statement? If not, revise or drop the paragraph. Does the essay contain enough information to fully explain your thesis and make it understandable to your reader? If not, do additional prewriting to help you discover more ideas. If you are stuck, your thesis statement may be too narrow or you may need to read more about your topic. Be sure to give credit for any ideas you borrow from print or online sources. (Refer to Chapter 16 for information on how to give credit to sources you use.)

5. **Is your essay logically organized?**

   *Examine your revision map to be sure your paragraphs are in the right order.* If not, rearrange them. Be sure to add sentences or transitions to connect your ideas and show your new organization. Use Table 10-3, "Choosing a Pattern of Organization," on page 326 to consider different ways you might rearrange your ideas.

6. **Have you used transitions to connect your ideas?**

   *Circle all transitional words, phrases, and sentences.* Do you use transitions to move from each main point to another? If not, add transitions, referring to Table 11-2, page 345, as needed.

7. **Are your introduction, conclusion, and title effective?**

   *Reread your introduction.* If it does not lead your reader into the essay and/or does not offer needed background information, it needs revision. Revise by assuming your reader knows little about the topic and has shown little interest. Decide what to add to help this uninterested reader get involved with your essay. *Next, reread your conclusion.* Does it draw the essay to a close and remind the reader of your thesis statement? If not, revise it using the suggestions on page 347. *Finally, reconsider your title.* Is it an appropriate label for your essay? If it does not draw your reader into the essay, try to think of a snappier, more interesting title.

## Revising Paragraphs

Once you are satisfied with the overall content and structure of your essay, next evaluate each paragraph. Ask yourself each of the following questions about each paragraph. For any items for which you answer no, refer to the pages listed for revision help.

- Is the topic of the paragraph specific enough so that it can be adequately covered in a single paragraph? (Chapter 5, p. 158)
- Does the topic sentence clearly identify the topic and express a point of view about it? (Chapter 5, p. 160)
- Are there enough relevant details to support the topic sentence? (Chapter 6, pp. 191–194)
- Are the details arranged in a logical order? (Chapter 6, p. 195)
- Are transitional words and phrases used to connect my ideas? (Chapter 6, p. 199)

## Revising Sentences and Words

Once you are satisfied with your paragraphs, examine each sentence by asking the following questions:

- **Are your sentences wordy?** Do they express your meaning in as few words as possible? Here is an example of a wordy sentence, along with a possible revision. Notice that the first sentence contains empty words that do not contribute to its meaning.

| | |
|---|---|
| **WORDY** | In light of the fact that cell phone technology changes every year or so, upgrading your cell phone is what everybody has to do |
| **REVISED** | Cell phone technology changes yearly, so regular upgrades are necessary. |

For information on how to write more concise sentences, refer to Reviewing the Basics, Section D.7, page 589.

- **Do your sentences repeat the same idea in slightly different words?** Here is an example of a sentence that is redundant.

| | |
|---|---|
| **REDUNDANT** | My decision to choose to attend college was the best decision I have made in a long time |
| **REVISED** | Choosing to attend college was one of my best decisions. |

- **Do all of your sentences follow the same pattern?** That is, are they all short, or do they all start the same way? Do they seem choppy or monotonous?

Sentences that are too similar make your writing seem mechanical and uninteresting. Try to vary your sentences using the four sentence patterns explained in Reviewing the Basics, Section B.4, page 535, and the classifications shown in Section B.8. Also try to expand short sentences using the suggestions shown in Sections B.6 and B.7.

■ **Do you use strong active verbs?** These make your writing seem lively and interesting. Which of the following sentences is more interesting?

> The puppy was afraid of a laundry basket.
>
> The puppy whimpered, quivered, and scampered away when my sister carried a laundry basket into the room.

The second sentence helps you visualize the situation, while the first is simply factual. Reread your essay looking for verbs that seem dull or convey very little meaning. Replace them, using a dictionary or thesaurus, as needed.

■ **Have you used concrete, specific language?** Your words should convey as much meaning as possible. Which phrase in each of the following pairs provides more meaning?

> a fun vacation            white-water rafting trip
>
> many flowers              lavender, petunias, and white begonias

Reread your essay and highlight words that seem dull and ordinary. Use a dictionary or thesaurus to help you find more concrete and specific replacements.

■ **Have you used words with appropriate connotations?** A word's connotative meaning is the collection of feelings and attitudes that come along with the word. The words *strolled*, *swaggered*, and *lumbered* all mean walking in a forward direction, but only *swaggered* would be appropriate when describing someone walking in a bold and arrogant manner. To be sure you have used words with appropriate connotations, check any you are unsure of in a dictionary.

■ **Have you avoided clichés?** A cliché is a tired, overused expression that carries little meaning. Here are a few examples.

> better later than never          shoulder to cry on
>
> light as a feather               hard as a rock
>
> green with envy                  bite the bullet

Reread your essay and replace clichés with more exact and descriptive information. You could, for example, replace *shoulder to cry on* with *sympathetic and understanding best friend* or *bite the bullet* with *accept responsibility*.

■ **Have you avoided sexist language?** Sexist language expresses narrow or unfair assumptions about men's and women's roles, positions, or value. Here are a few examples of sexist language:

> SEXIST     A compassionate nurse reassures her patients before surgery.
>
> REVISED    Compassionate nurses reassure their patients before surgery.
>
> SEXIST     Many policemen hold college degrees.
>
> REVISED    Many police officers hold college degrees.

■ **Have you used standard American English and avoided using nonstandard dialect?** While dialects such as Black English, Spanglish, and Creole are acceptable in many situations, they are not acceptable when writing essays for college classes. If you speak a dialect of English in addition to standard American English, be sure to reread your essay and replace any dialect words or expressions.

**EXERCISE 11-9**

**WRITING IN PROGRESS**

## Evaluating and Revising a Draft

**Directions:** Evaluate your draft of the essay you revised in Exercise 11-8, using the questions in the preceding section. Make revisions as needed.

# Edit and Proofread

■ **GOAL 8**
Edit and proofread

Once you are satisfied that your essay expresses your ideas as you intended and is organized in a logical way, you are ready to make sure your essay is clear, error free, and presented in acceptable manuscript form. At this stage, you should try to correct errors in spelling, punctuation, and grammar, as well as typographical errors.

## General Suggestions

Here are ways to edit and proofread effectively:

■ **Work with a double-spaced print copy of your essay.** You are likely to see more errors when working with a print copy than you do with an electronic version.

■ **Use your Error Log (see p. 291).** Read your paper once looking for the errors you make the most often.

■ **Read your essay backward, starting with the last sentence and working toward the first.** Reading this way will help you focus on errors without the distraction of the flow of ideas.

■ **Read your essay aloud.** You may catch errors in agreement, use of dialect, or punctuation.

■ **Ask a classmate to proofread your paper.**

## Common Errors to Watch For

Table 11-3 (p. 354) lists the most common errors students make in their writing. The table also includes a reference to Part VI, "Reviewing the Basics," which explains these errors in detail.

## Using Spell-Checkers and Grammar Checkers

Many students mistakenly rely on a computer's spell-check program to catch their misspellings. While a spell-checker can help you spot some spelling and keyboarding errors, you cannot trust the program to catch all of your errors. Although it can detect misspelled words, it cannot detect when a word is used inappropriately. For example, it cannot distinguish whether you should use *there* or *their* in a particular sentence.

When the spell-checker finds a misspelled word, it may suggest a list of alternatives and highlight the one it considers most likely to be correct. Be sure to verify the suggested spelling with a dictionary, since some of the suggestions may be wrong.

Grammar and style checkers may identify some incorrect grammar and awkward or incomplete sentences. However, you cannot count on them to find all the problems. They may also identify sentences that are correct and need no editing. Therefore use these checkers cautiously.

| TABLE 11-3 | COMMON ERRORS AND WHERE TO FIND HELP CORRECTING THEM |
| --- | --- |
| **Error** | **Part VI, "Reviewing the Basics"** |
| Sentence fragments | p. 547 |
| Run-on sentences | p. 552 |
| Subject-verb agreement | p. 563 |
| Pronoun-antecedent agreement | p. 566 |
| Pronoun reference | p. 568 |
| Shifts and mixed constructions | p. 578 |
| Dangling modifiers | p. 577 |
| Misplaced modifiers | p. 576 |
| Verb tense | p. 518 |
| Coordinate sentences | p. 580 |
| Subordinate clauses | p. 582 |
| Parallelism | p. 584 |
| Comma usage | p. 594 |
| Colon and semicolon usage | p. 597 |

## Using a Proofreading Checklist

Use the proofreading checklist on p. 356, also shown in Chapter 9, to remind you of the types of errors to look for when proofreading.

## Presenting Your Essay

Before your instructor even begins to read your essay, he or she forms a first impression of it. A paper that is carelessly assembled, rumpled, or has handwritten corrections creates a negative first impression. Use the following suggestions to present your paper positively. Always follow carefully any guidelines or requests that your instructor makes on format, method of submission, and so forth.

- Make sure your name, course and section number, and date appear at the top of your essay (unless otherwise specified by your instructor).
- Type and double-space your essay.
- Number the pages and staple or paperclip them together.
- Present a neat, clean copy. (Carry it in a manila folder or envelope until you turn it in so it does not get rumpled or dirty.)
- If you need to make last-minute corrections, reprint your essay; do not make hand corrections.

- Avoid adjusting the margins to meet a page-length limit.
- If submitting your paper online, be sure to use an appropriate subject line identifying the submission.

## Revision and Proofreading Checklists

### Revision Checklist for PARAGRAPHS

1. Who is your audience? How interested are they in your subject, and how much do they know about it? Is your paragraph suited to your audience?
2. What is your purpose? Does your paragraph accomplish your purpose?
3. Is your main point clearly expressed in your topic sentence?
4. Is each detail relevant? Does each explain or support the topic sentence effectively?
5. Have you supported your topic sentence with sufficient detail to make it understandable and believable?
6. Do you use specific and vivid words to explain each detail?
7. Do you connect your ideas with transitional words and phrases?

### Revision Checklist for ESSAYS

1. Is your essay appropriate for your audience?
2. Does your essay accomplish your purpose?
3. Is your thesis statement clearly expressed?
4. Does each paragraph support your thesis?
5. Is your essay logically organized?
6. Have you used transitions to connect your ideas?
7. Are your introduction, conclusion, and title effective?

### Proofreading Checklist

1. Does each sentence end with an appropriate punctuation mark (period, question mark, exclamation point, or quotation marks)?
2. Is all punctuation within each sentence correct (commas, colons, semicolons, apostrophes, dashes, and quotation marks)?
3. Is each word spelled correctly?
4. Are capital letters used where needed?
5. Are numbers and abbreviations used correctly?
6. Are any words left out?
7. Have all typographical errors been corrected?
8. Are the pages in the correct order and numbered?

# INTEGRATING READING AND WRITING

## READ AND RESPOND: A Student Essay

*Ted Sawchuck is the author of the essay on online dating that we have been following in this chapter and in the preceding one.*

*In order to prepare his essay for publication, Ted made extensive revisions to his first draft (shown on p. 327) and produced the final version shown below.*

*Descriptive title: identifies the essay's subject*

# Relationships 2.0: Dating and Relating in the Internet Age
## Ted Sawchuck

*Introduction: background on Facebook*

1    Facebook is a social networking Internet site. It allows a user to conveniently connect online with people, make friends, and join interest groups via his or her computer. It also allows a user to learn more about his or her friends, as well as post text, photos, video links, and information. Facebook has become widely popular. Much has been written about it in my student newspaper, but no one has yet dug into how the site affects relationships on our campus, and specifically the dating process. *Each stage of the dating process is influenced by Facebook; on our campus, not all the changes have been positive.*

*Thesis statement*

*Topic sentence: identifies first stage of online dating*

2    At the University of Maryland, the dating process begins like this: get someone's name; look him or her up on Facebook; then use that information to decide how to proceed. When I meet someone and she sets off those neurons that make me hum "Maybe it's love," I do a Facebook search. A profile page will tell me her age, indicate whether or not she is taken, and give me a decent idea (if the profile is not privacy protected) of what image she is trying to present. Note that I do not trust Facebook to tell me who people are—merely who they want to show other people they are. I look through photos and see what the person values enough to show me. I check posted links because what someone thinks is worth sharing is another window into who she is.

*Transitional sentence*

*Topic sentence: identifies second stage of online dating*

3    After using Facebook to check out someone, I have a decent idea of whether she is a probable friend or possible romantic interest. Next I hit Google—searching first with her e-mail address, then with her name, and next with her nickname. This search turns up message boards, possibly her blog, and maybe even a Flickr site, all worth plumbing for details about my new fascination.

*Topic sentence: states first drawback of online dating*

4    I have serious doubts as to whether being able to download someone's self with a little searching on Facebook and Google is actually a good thing for beginning a relationship. For one thing, online searches result in tons of information with absolutely no context. Judging what you learn without cross-referencing it with the

person is a recipe for misinterpretative disaster, yet checking means admitting you have been snooping. I snoop anyway.

Transitional word

Topic sentence: identifies second drawback of online dating

5    Also, on Facebook, everyone seems reduced to a set of bullet points—"goth, tall, cat person"—that you rely on before even meeting the person. In real life, careful observation can reveal truths about people they will not discuss online, especially things they do not want generally known. However, a fidgety, nervous guy who sweats when he sees a pretty girl may have a better chance sending a Facebook message, which can be drafted and redrafted and edited and rewritten and shown to friends before sending, than approaching her in real life, so it does have its benefits.

Topic sentence: identifies third drawback of online dating

6    The dating process works well online initially, but real connections are only formed by spending substantial time together in person. Online talks, even via Skype or webcam, are still only a fraction of the real experience and convey only a fraction of the information one can glean during an in-person encounter. Time spent online communicating with someone can build connections that lead to a relationship or strengthen a current one. However, tone, pauses, nuance, and volume are all stripped from instant messages. Human laughter beats "LOL" any day, and holding her while she tells you about her day wins whenever possible.

Topic sentence: identifies fourth drawback of online dating

7    Facebook can also provide new avenues for infidelity. One way is through chatting online. It is very poor form to chat up someone else's girlfriend in a bar, but when chatting online there is no boyfriend looming over you to enforce boundaries. Combine that freedom with the very personal qualities of online relationships and the large amount of time most people spend online and you have a situation that anyone who's dating anyone who goes online a lot should worry about. The poke feature—a virtual way to let someone know you are thinking about him or her without actually saying anything—is another way Facebook can promote infidelity. One of my friends who has a boyfriend uses them to let me know when she is thinking about me. It amounts to several pokes a day, and she receives ones from me whenever she crosses my mind. She does it to let me know she is thinking about me frequently, which is great for me and not so hot for her boyfriend.

8    Breaking up is hard to do but the Internet makes it easier. Once a relationship ends, you do not want to get a continually updated feed of information about the other person from any source. Knowing someone is getting over you and trying to date is one thing; knowing she is doing it at seven-thirty at Club Kozmo with someone she met last weekend is another. So now my list for after leaving someone includes blocking her on instant messaging, taking her e-mail address out of my quick contacts list and out of my e-mail's auto-complete list, avoiding her blog and defriending her on Facebook. Forget one step and the "getting over her" process becomes that much harder. There is a measure of comfort to be found in thinking someone has fallen off the face of the earth romantically, especially if your return to dating has not been as successful as hers.

Topic sentence: describes break-up stage of online dating

Conclusion: Sawchuck offers advice on online dating breakups

9    Cutting someone off requires effort. Any bit of forgotten information is another barb, another pang, another realization of what you have lost. Invariably, you will miss something and see a status update or a text message or a voice mail. It helps at times, when missing someone so badly means wishing she were dead. Once you get over it yourself, refriend the person if you can do it without going crazy. Sometimes a little bit of ignorance can be blissful indeed, but most connections are worth preserving.

## Examining Writing

1. Compare Ted's thesis with his working thesis shown on page 321. How did he change it?

2. Compare his first draft on page 327 with his final draft above. What content did he delete? What did he add? Why do you think he made these decisions?

3. How did his organization change?

4. Evaluate his title, introduction, and conclusion.

5. What other changes would you recommend to further improve the essay?

## Writing Assignments

1. For an education class, write an essay examining the trend toward online college courses. Do research to discover what is offered at your college and other nearby colleges. Summarize your findings in a short essay.

2. For a health class, you are asked to write an essay comparing two popular diets. Choose two diets, such as the South Beach Diet and the Protein Power diet, research what is involved in each, and report your findings in an essay.

3. For a business management class, your instructor has given the following assigment. Choose two local business franchises that sell the same products. You might choose two fast-food restaurants, two shoe stores, or two drugstores, for example. Visit both businesses and research each on the Internet. Write an essay comparing the two businesses. Indicate which you feel is likely to be more profitable over the course of the next year.

# READ AND RESPOND: A Professional Essay

## Thinking Before Reading

This essay, which originally appeared in *The Chronicle of Higher Education*, was written by a 2009 graduate of Stanford University. Read the selection to find out what he believes is most important for college students to focus on when choosing a major. As you read, identify the author's topic, his thesis, and the types of details he includes to support his point.

1. Preview the reading, using the steps discussed in Chapter 1, p. 15.

2. Connect the reading to your own experience by answering the following questions:

   a. Have you chosen a major?

   b. Do you feel it is important for college students to choose a major during their first year or before beginning college?

3. Mark and annotate as you read.

# Stop Asking Me My Major

## Scott Keyes

*Scott Keyes, a recent college graduate, advises against
gearing one's study concentration to fickle job prospects.
Instead, he says, follow your intellectual passion.*

1    One of my best friends from high school, Andrew, changed majors during his first semester at college. He and I had been fascinated by politics for years, sharing every news story we could find and participating in the Internet activism that was exploding into a new political force. Even though he was still passionate about politics, that was no longer enough. "I have to get practical," he messaged me one day, "think about getting a job after graduation. I mean, it's like my mom keeps asking me: What can you do with a degree in political science anyway?"

2    I heard the same question from my friend Jesse when students across campus were agonizing about which major was right for them. He wasn't quite sure what he wanted to study, but every time a field sparked his interest, his father would pepper him with questions about what jobs were available for people in that discipline. Before long, Jesse's dad had convinced him that the only way he could get a job and be successful after college was to major in pre-med.

3    My friends' experiences were not atypical.

4    Choosing a major is one of the most difficult things students face in college. There are two main factors that most students consider when making this decision. First is their desire to study what interests them. Second is the fear that a particular major will render them penniless after graduation and result in that dreaded postcollege possibility: moving back in with their parents.

5    All too often, the concern about a major's practical prospects are pushed upon students by well-intentioned parents. If our goal is to cultivate students who are happy and successful, both in college as well as in the job market, I have this piece of advice for parents: Stop asking, "What can you do with a degree in (fill in the blank)?" You're doing your children no favors by asking them to focus on the job prospects of different academic disciplines, rather than studying what interests them.

6    It is my experience, both through picking a major myself and witnessing many others endure the process, that there are three reasons why parents (and everyone else) should be encouraging students to focus on what they enjoy studying most, rather than questioning what jobs are supposedly available for different academic concentrations.

7    The first is psychological. For his first two years of college, Jesse followed his dad's wishes and remained a pre-med student. The only problem was that he hated it. With no passion for the subject, his grades slipped, hindering his chances of getting into medical school. As a result his employability, the supposed reason he was studying medicine in the first place, suffered.

8    The second reason to stop asking students what they can do with a major is that it perpetuates the false notion that certain majors don't prepare students for the workplace. The belief that technical majors such as computer science are more

likely to lead to a job than a major such as sociology or English is certainly understandable. It's also questionable. "The problem," as my friend Jose explained to me, "is that even as a computer-science major, what I learned in the classroom was outdated by the time I hit the job market." He thought instead that the main benefit of his education, rather than learning specific skills, was gaining a better way of thinking about the challenges he faced. "What's more," he told me, "no amount of education could match the specific on-the-job training I've received working different positions."

9    Finally, it is counterproductive to demand that students justify their choice of study with potential job prospects because that ignores the lesson we were all taught in kindergarten (and shouldn't ignore the closer we get to employment): You can grow up to be whatever you want to be. The jobs people work at often fall within the realm of their studies, but they don't have to. One need look no further than some of the most prominent figures in our society to see illustrations. The TV chef Julia Child studied English in college. Author Michael Lewis, whose best sellers focus on sports and the financial industry, majored in art history. Matt Groening, creator of *The Simpsons*, got his degree in philosophy, as did the former Hewlett Packard chief executive Carly Fiorina. Jeff Immelt, chief executive of General Electric, focused on mathematics. Indeed, with the Department of Labor estimating that on average people switch careers (not just jobs) two or three times in their lives, relying on a college major as career preparation is misguided.

10    I'm not saying any applicant can get any job. Job seekers still need marketable skills if they hope to be hired. However, in a rapidly changing economy, which majors lead to what jobs is not so clear cut. Many employers look for applicants from a diverse background—including my friend who has a degree in biochemistry but was just hired at an investment consulting firm.

11    That doesn't mean that majors no longer matter. It is still an important decision, and students are right to seek outside counsel when figuring out what they want to study. But questioning how a particular major will affect their employability is not necessarily the best approach. Although parents' intentions may be pure—after all, who doesn't want to see their children succeed after graduation?—that question can hold tremendous power over impressionable freshmen. Far too many of my classmates let it steer them away from what they enjoyed studying to a major they believed would help them get a job after graduation.

12    One of those friends was Andrew. He opted against pursuing a degree in political science, choosing instead to study finance because "that's where the jobs

13      Jesse, on the other hand, realized that if he stayed on the pre-med track, he would burn out before ever getting his degree. During his junior year he changed tracks and began to study engineering. Not only did Jesse's grades improve markedly, but his enthusiasm for the subject recently earned him a lucrative job offer and admission to a top engineering master's program.

14      Andrew and Jesse both got jobs. But who do you think feels more successful?

# Getting Ready to Write

## Checking Your Comprehension

Answer each of the following questions using complete sentences.

1. What are the two main factors students consider when choosing a major, according to the author?

2. According to the author, why should people stop asking students about the job prospects of different majors?

3. What kindergarten lesson does the author believe should not be ignored?

4. What point do the examples Julia Child, Matt Groening, and Carly Fiorina help prove?

5. What does the author believe his two friends, Jesse and Andrew, demonstrate?

## Strengthening Your Vocabulary

Using the word's context, word parts, or a dictionary, write a brief definition of each of the following words as it is used in the reading.

1. atypical (paragraph 3) _____

2. render (paragraph 4) _____

3. perpetuates (paragraph 8) _____

4. misguided (paragraph 9) _____

5. lucrative (paragraph 13) _____

## Examining the Reading: Using an Idea Map

Create an idea map of "Stop Asking Me My Major." Start with the title and thesis and include the main ideas and conclusions.

## Reacting to Ideas: Discussion and Journal Writing

Get ready to write about the reading by discussing the following:

1. How does the author try to influence your opinions in this selection? Is he successful?

2. What arguments could you make against the author's assertion that people should study only what interests them?

3. How did you decide what your major will be? What factors influenced your decision? What did your parents have to say?

4. The author points to his friend Jesse as support for his argument, but why might he not be a good example?

5. Explain the purpose of the photograph included with the selection. Is the photograph effective?

## Thinking and Writing Critically

1. What is the author's purpose in writing this essay? Who is his intended audience?

2. Evaluate the introduction and conclusion. Does the introduction lead you into the essay? Does the conclusion draw the essay to a close and remind you of the author's thesis statement?

3. Evaluate the title, "Stop Asking Me My Major." What does it suggest about the author's tone? What other titles would be appropriate and effective for this essay?

# Writing About the Reading

## Paragraph Options

1. Reread Jose's statements in paragraph 8. Write a paragraph presenting your response to Jose's point of view.

2. Replace the underlined words in the following quote from paragraph 5 so the statement reflects your own philosophy: "If our goal is to cultivate students who are happy and successful, both in college as well as in the job market, I have this piece of advice for parents: Stop asking 'What can you do with a degree in (fill in the blank)?'" Write a paragraph explaining your revised statement.

3. The author gives examples of well-known people who got jobs outside of their major. Choose one of these people and write a paragraph explaining how the person's major may have been useful or contributed to their career success.

## Essay Options

4. Write an essay describing your ideal job. Include at least three or four characteristics that would be important to you, for example, type of work, working conditions, pay, or opportunities for promotion.

5. Write an essay explaining how you would give advice to a younger friend or relative about choosing a major. Rely on your personal experience and that of people you know.

6. According to the author, parents' opinions heavily influence students' choices in college. How have your parents influenced your choices in college and in life? Write an essay exploring this.

7. Write an essay explaining what communication or interpersonal skills are necessary for career success, regardless of the specific job chosen.

# SELF-TEST SUMMARY

To test yourself, cover the Answer column with a sheet of paper and answer each question in the left column. Evaluate each of your answers as you work by sliding the paper down and comparing your answer with what is printed in the Answer column.

| QUESTION | ANSWER |
| --- | --- |
| ■ GOAL 1  Draft an essay <br><br> What are four suggestions for drafting an essay? | (1) Leave time between drafts. (2) Experiment with different approaches, content, and ways of organizing information. (3) Focus on ideas, not correctness. (4) Be prepared to make major changes. |
| ■ GOAL 2  Read while drafting an essay <br><br> Why is it important to read while you are drafting an essay? | Reading your draft helps you stay focused on the topic, decide where to add information or transitions or start a new paragraph, think more about organization, and realize when you are repeating information. |
| ■ GOAL 3  Write and revise a thesis statement and support it with evidence <br><br> What makes a thesis statement effective and what constitutes substantial evidence? | An effective thesis statement: <br> ■ states the main point of your essay <br> ■ expresses an idea about your topic <br> ■ is specific and detailed <br> ■ may suggest the organization of the essay <br> ■ is not a direct announcement <br> ■ offers a fresh perspective on your topic <br> Evidence can consist of personal experience, anecdotes, examples, reasons, descriptions, facts, statistics, and quotations. Evidence should be relevant, specific, and accurate, and sources should be documented. For a list of ways to add evidence, see Table 11-1 on page 341. |
| ■ GOAL 4  Support your thesis with substantial evidence <br><br> What constitutes substantial evidence? | Evidence can consist of personal experience, anecdotes, examples, reasons, descriptions, facts, statistics, and quotations. Evidence should be relevant, specific, and accurate, and sources should be documented. For a list of ways to add evidence, see Table 11-1 on page 341. |

*(continued)*

*(continued)*

| QUESTION | ANSWER |
|---|---|
| ■ GOAL 5 Use transitions to make connections<br><br>How do you use transitions to make connections among your ideas? | Use transitional words and phrases, write transitional sentences, and repeat key words. See Table 11-2 on page 345 for useful transitional words and phrases. |
| ■ GOAL 6 Write introductions, conclusions, and titles<br><br>What should an introduction, conclusion, and title do? | An introduction should present your thesis, interest your reader, and provide background information. A conclusion should reemphasize your thesis statement and draw the essay to a close. A title should identify the topic in an interesting way. |
| ■ GOAL 7 Think critically about your draft<br>How do you think critically about your draft? | Think critically by revising your ideas and by examining your essay's content and structure. Use the Revision Checklists on page 355. |
| ■ GOAL 8 Edit and proofread<br>What do editing and proofreading involve? | Editing and proofreading involve making sure your essay is clear, error free, and presented in an acceptable form. Use the Proofreading Checklist on page 356 to remind you of what to look for when proofreading. |

**MySkillsLab** ®    For more help with **Drafting and Revising Essays**, go to your learning path in MySkillsLab at www.myskillslab.com.

# Reading and Writing Essays with Multiple Patterns

LEARNING
## GOALS

Learn how to . . .

- **GOAL 1**
  Define a multi-pattern essay

- **GOAL 2**
  Recognize multiple patterns of organization in readings

- **GOAL 3**
  Choose a primary pattern of organization for your essay

- **GOAL 4**
  Use secondary patterns of organization in your essay

- **GOAL 5**
  Plan and write a multi-pattern essay

- **GOAL 6**
  Write multi-pattern introductions, body paragraphs, and conclusions

## 12

## THINK About It!

Pictured above is one of the world's most famous paintings, the *Mona Lisa*. How much do you know about this masterpiece, which was painted by Leonardo da Vinci in the 1500s? To learn more about the image, you might consult an art appreciation textbook or a biography about the artist. Each reading would provide different types of information. For example, the art appreciation textbook would likely provide a good deal of description about the *Mona Lisa*, while a biography would provide a narrative of Leonardo's life. Other sources might contain more than one pattern of organization. For instance, an article in the art journal *ArtForum* might compare and contrast Leonardo with another famous Italian artist, Michelangelo, and argue that Leonardo was the more accomplished painter. As you read various sources, you will use the techniques you've learned earlier in this text, including previewing, writing guide questions, highlighting, annotating, and summarizing.

In Chapters 7 and 8 you learned to recognize the pattern of organization used in a reading. Many sources, including textbooks and other college-oriented materials, use more than one pattern of organization. Multiple patterns permit richer, deeper analysis of a topic. This chapter focuses on reading and writing essays that use more than one pattern. You will learn how to recognize the use of multiple patterns in an essay. You will also learn how to use multiple patterns when writing your own essays.

# Reading and Writing Connections

## EVERYDAY CONNECTIONS

- **Reading** You are having trouble sleeping, so you search the Internet for insomnia cures. You read an article that *defines* the term insomnia, *describes* the symptoms, and offers a list of suggestions to help you fall asleep (*process, examples*).
- **Writing** On the comments section of the Web page, you post a note about your own experiences with insomnia (*narration*) and how a lack of sleep is affecting your life (*cause and effect*).

## ACADEMIC CONNECTIONS

- **Reading** You read a chapter titled "Personal Communication" in a communications textbook. The reading not only *classifies* the different types of communication, it also teaches you how to be a more effective communicator (*process*).
- **Writing** On an essay exam for your communications class, your instructor asks you to define the three types of personal distance (*definition, classification*) and to explore the similarities and differences among them (*comparison and contrast*).

## WORKPLACE CONNECTIONS

- **Reading** You work in a hospital. Your co-workers want to unionize in order to receive better pay and working conditions. You read the union pamphlet, which *describes* and provides *examples* of good working conditions at other hospitals and lists the benefits of joining a union (*cause and effect*).
- **Writing** The hospital's managers ask you to write a report on problems with employee motivation and morale. Your report will identify the *causes* of the problem and propose a step-by-step solution (*process, argument*). The report may describe the experiences of several workers (*narrative*).

# FOCUSING ON READING AND WRITING

Patterns of organization are sometimes called **development patterns** or **rhetorical modes.** For this reason, readings and essays that combine the patterns of organization are often called **multi-pattern**, or **multimodal**, readings and essays.

# What Is a Multi-Pattern Essay?

■ **GOAL 1**
Define a multi-pattern essay

A **multi-pattern reading or essay** is one that uses more than one pattern of organization. Think back to the image that opens this chapter, the *Mona Lisa.* If you were asked to write an essay about it, you might find yourself thinking, "This painting is so famous and so complicated, using just one pattern of organization won't do justice to the topic." As a result, you may choose to write an essay that combines *definition*—by explaining who the real Mona Lisa was (the wife of Francesco del Giocondo, an Italian nobleman)—along with a *description* of Mona Lisa's famous smile or the scenery behind her.

## READING

# Recognize Multiple Patterns

■ **GOAL 2**
Recognize multiple patterns of organization in readings

Recognizing multiple patterns in a reading has several benefits for you as a reader:

- ■ It helps you better understand the reading's overall organization and its key points.
- ■ It helps you develop a fuller understanding of the topic.
- ■ It helps you prepare for essay examinations, which often require the use of these patterns in your answers.

Most multi-pattern readings have one dominant, or **primary**, pattern. (Here, the words *dominant* and *primary* mean "main" or "most important.") The primary pattern is the reading's key organizing principle. It provides the framework on which the writer builds support for the thesis statement or central thought. Additional, or **secondary**, patterns provide further explanation, details, clarification, and information.

### Identifying the Primary Pattern

Table 12-1 provides a summary of the key organizational patterns, as well as an example of how each pattern might be used with the topic of skateboarding. (For more detail on each pattern, see Chapters 7, 8 and 15.)

| TABLE 12-1 | PATTERNS OF ORGANIZATION | |
|---|---|---|
| **Pattern** | **What It Does** | **An Example of Its Use** |
| Chronological Order/Process | Chronological order presents details in the order in which they occur. Process explains how something is done or how it works, usually step by step. | An explanation of the steps to follow in preparing for a skateboarding competition. If the reading is arranged chronologically, the reader would follow these steps in sequence. |
| Narration | Tells a story that makes a point. | A story of how a particular skateboarder became interested in skateboarding |
| Description | Uses sensory details to help readers visualize a topic. | A description of a particular skateboard or skateboarder |
| Example | Explains a concept by providing concrete instances or illustrations. | A discussion of several ways skateboarding can increase physical fitness and build stamina |
| Definition | Explains a topic by discussing its characteristics. | Defining skateboarding as a boarding sport, including some of its unique characteristics |
| Classification | Explains a topic by organizing it into categories or parts. | A discussion of the types of people who typically enjoy skateboarding |
| Comparison and Contrast | Shows how things are similar and/or different. | Comparing or contrasting two sports: skateboarding and snow skiing |
| Cause and Effect | Explains why things happen or what happens as a result of them. | Explaining why skateboarding is an enjoyable and popular sport and the sport's effects on the lives of skateboarders |
| Argument | Presents a line of reasoning intended to persuade readers to accept a viewpoint or take a specific action. | Arguing for or against a ban prohibiting skateboarding in busy, populated public places |

## Argument and Secondary Patterns

An **argument** is the presentation of logical reasons and evidence in support of a particular viewpoint. An effective argument deals with an issue, makes a claim (takes a stand) on the issue, and provides support for that claim. For example, for the *issue* of graphic coverage of accidents and other human tragedies by journalists, you might make the *claim* that restrictions should apply that preserve human dignity. You would then *support* your claim by offering reasons why restrictions are needed. Support might consist of examples of graphic reporting, quotations from experts about the effects of such coverage, statistics documenting the nature and degree of coverage, or the story of a particular victim who suffered stress and humiliation from the coverage. You can see, then, that argument, when used as a primary pattern, often involves the use of numerous secondary patterns to support its claim. For more detail on the argument pattern, consult Chapter 15, "Reading and Writing Arguments."

Here are some suggestions for how to determine a multi-pattern reading's primary pattern of organization:

### NEED TO KNOW

#### How to Identify the Primary Pattern in a Multi-Pattern Reading

- **Look for the thesis statement or central thought.** Examine it closely to identify which pattern it signals. For example, the following thesis statement signals a comparison and contrast pattern: "Even though skiing and skateboarding both pose great risks, each sport is unique in several ways."

- **Look for transition words that signal the primary pattern.** In the skiing/skateboarding thesis statement, the transitions *even though* and *both* signal the comparison and contrast pattern.

- **If you cannot determine the primary pattern from the thesis statement or central thought, examine the supporting details.** Ask yourself what the reading does (its overall purpose) and refer to the second column of Table 12-1 to help you determine the primary pattern.

- **In an essay, check the concluding paragraph.** Often, the closing paragraph summarizes the essay, reviewing the writer's key point and primary organizational pattern.

EXERCISE 12-1

## Identifying Primary Patterns of Organization

**Directions:** Identify the primary pattern of organization signaled by each of the following thesis statements.

1. The life of Marilyn Monroe was glamorous, shocking, and ultimately tragic.

_____

2. As a developed nation and world leader, the United States must ban the death penalty, which is both unjust and inhuman.

_____

3. To get a novel published, you must first write the manuscript. You must then find an agent, make the changes he or she requests, and then wait while the agent submits your work to various editors.

## Identifying Secondary Patterns

Within a reading, **secondary patterns** provide additional support, explanation, details, and information. While understanding the primary pattern will give you a good overall sense of the reading, recognizing the information in the secondary patterns will provide you with a greater understanding of the topic.

After you've analyzed the thesis statement or central thought and identified the primary pattern, use the tips in the following Need to Know box to identify the reading's secondary patterns.

---

### NEED TO KNOW

#### Identifying Secondary Patterns

- **Keep the length of the reading in mind.** The longer the reading, the more likely it uses multiple patterns.

- **In an essay, examine the topic sentences of the body paragraphs.** These may point to secondary patterns.

- **Throughout the reading, look for transition words that signal secondary patterns.** Annotate the reading, making notes about the patterns in the margins.

- **Watch for single sentences that use secondary patterns.** In many readings, it's common to find a definition, description, and example within a single sentence.

---

The following reading, "Picking Partners," comes from a health textbook. It describes the criteria that people use to choose their romantic partners. Review the annotations and look for the primary and secondary patterns as you read.

## Picking Partners

First sentence implies a → comparison, but this is not the primary pattern

Topic sentence mentions the word *process*, but process isn't the primary pattern. The reading is talking about the ways people pick their partners. The primary pattern is therefore cause and effect.

Just as males and females may find different ways to express emotions themselves, the process of partner selection also* shows distinctly different patterns. For both males and females, more than just chemical and psychological processes influence the choice of partners. One of these factors is *proximity,* or being in the same place at the same time. The more you see a person in your hometown, at social gatherings, or at work, the more likely that an interaction will occur. Thus, if you live in New York, you'll probably end up with another New Yorker. If you live in northern Wisconsin, you'll probably end up with another Wisconsinite.

\* Transition word for comparison pattern

Italics signal a ← secondary pattern: definition

← This sentence is a mini-statement of cause and effect

← Another secondary pattern: example

The old adage that "opposites attract" usually isn't true. You also pick a partner based on *similarities* (attitudes, values, intellect, interests). If your potential partner expresses interest or liking, you may react with mutual regard known as *reciprocity*. The more you express interest, the safer it is for someone else to return the regard, and the cycle spirals onward.

Another factor that apparently plays a significant role in selecting a partner is *physical attraction*. Whether such attraction is caused by a chemical reaction or a socially learned behavior, males and females appear to have different attraction criteria. Men tend to select their mates primarily on the basis of youth and physical attractiveness. Although physical attractiveness is an important criterion for women in mate selection, they tend to place higher emphasis on partners who are somewhat older, have good financial prospects, and are dependable and industrious.

—Donatelle, *Health: The Basics*, p. 105

*Sometimes definitions appear in parentheses, but the words in parentheses here aren't definitions. What are they?*

*The author raises a question here, but she does not answer it. Why do you think this question is left unanswered?* →

*Secondary pattern:* → *Comparison and Contrast (contrasting men and women)*

*← Another definition. Notice that this definition implies a process!*

*← Here, a key idea is placed in italics but it is not defined. How would you define physical attraction?*

## EXERCISE 12-2

# Identifying Primary and Secondary Patterns of Organization

**Directions:** Read the following multi-pattern essay and answer the questions that follow.

## Guerrilla Marketing

1. Historically, one of the most successful alternative media marketing programs is guerrilla marketing, as first developed by marketing guru Jay Conrad Levinson. **Guerrilla marketing** programs are designed to obtain instant results while using limited resources. The tactics rely on creativity, quality relationships, and the willingness to try unusual approaches. These programs were originally aimed at small businesses; however, now guerrilla marketing tactics are found in a wide array of firms. Guerrilla marketing emphasizes a combination of media, advertising, public relations, and surprise tactics to reach consumers.

FIGURE A
Traditional vs. Guerrilla
Marketing

| Traditional Marketing | Guerrilla Marketing |
| --- | --- |
| • Requires money | • Requires energy and imagination |
| • Geared to large businesses with big budgets | • Geared to small businesses and big dreams |
| • Results measured by sales | • Results measured by profits |
| • Based on experience and guesswork | • Based on psychology and human behavior |
| • Increases production and diversity | • Grows through existing customers and referrals |
| • Grows by adding customers | • Cooperates with other businesses |
| • Obliterates the competition | • Aims messages at individuals and small groups |
| • Aims messages at large groups | • Uses marketing to gain customer consent |
| • Uses marketing to generate sales | • "You Marketing" that looks at how can we help "You" |
| • "Me Marketing" that looks at "My" company | |

2. Figure A compares guerrilla marketing to traditional marketing. Guerrilla marketing tends to focus on specific regions or areas. It is not a national or international campaign, and instead features personal communication. The idea is to create

excitement that will spread to others by word-of-mouth. Guerrilla marketing often involves interacting with consumers, not just sending out a message. The idea is to build relationships with customers. By getting consumers to react or to do something, the program enhances the chance that the message will hit home. Advertisements are made accessible to consumers, where they live, play, and work in a way that it is noticed. The eventual relationships that evolve help create brand loyalty and positive recommendations to other consumers.

3.    A notable example of guerrilla marketing was used by the Harley-Davidson franchise in Gloversville, New York. The company advertised a "cat shoot," to be held at the store. Local police, the Humane Society, the mayor, and the Society for Prevention of Cruelty to Animals all inquired, and the event generated front-page stories for 3 straight days in local papers. The event was actually a three-for-a-dollar paintball shoot at a 6-foot-high cartoon cat, with proceeds benefiting the local Humane Society. It was tremendously successful in helping customers find their way to the store. Although bizarre, the approach used by Van's Harley-Davidson illustrates the concept of guerrilla marketing.

4.    Guerrilla marketing not only utilizes alternative media tactics and venues; the program focuses on finding creative ways of doing things. The objective is to change the thinking process in the marketing department itself. The first step is to discover "touch points" with customers. In other words, where do the customers eat, drink, shop, hang out, and sleep? This makes it possible to reach customers at the points the product interconnects with their lives in creative and imaginative ways. Figure B identifies six reasons to use guerrilla marketing.

FIGURE B
Reasons for Using
Guerrilla Marketing

- To find a new way to communicate with consumers
- To interact with consumers
- To make advertising accessible to consumers
- To impact a spot market
- To create buzz
- To build relationships with consumers

—Clow and Baack, *Integrated Advertising, Promotion, and Marketing Communications*, pp. 274–276

1. What is the primary pattern of each of the first three paragraphs?

_____

_____

2. Which pattern is used in Figure A? In Figure B?

_____

_____

3. What is the reading's primary pattern? What are its secondary patterns?

_____

_____

4. Which pattern is hinted at in the fourth paragraph but not developed fully? Which transitional word or phrase signals this pattern?

_____

_____

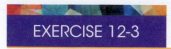

**EXERCISE 12-3**

# Identifying Secondary Patterns of Organization

**Directions:** In addition to the primary pattern you identified for each of the thesis statements in Exercise 12-1, choose a secondary pattern that would provide you with a greater understanding of the topic.

## WRITING

Individual patterns of organization provide a clear method for organizing and presenting your thoughts. Each of these patterns, from narration and description through cause and effect and argument, allows you to focus on one important aspect of the topic. Specifically, when you're writing an essay, the organization pattern supports your thesis statement.

But as you write, you may find yourself tempted to stray from the pattern you've chosen. For example, let's return to the image that opens this chapter. Suppose you're writing a narrative essay about the *Mona Lisa*'s history, explaining that the artist left it unfinished for more than a decade and how he finally completed the work after moving from Italy to France. You may decide that your paragraph would benefit from additional examples of other famous works by Leonardo, such as *The Last Supper*. To discuss these additional works, you may find yourself using the illustration pattern within your narrative essay.

Combining patterns of organization is often effective when

- **You are writing a longer essay or term paper.** It can sometimes be difficult to sustain one pattern for several pages.

- **You want to explore multiple facets of a topic.** Using multiple patterns can help you examine the topic from a variety of perspectives.

- **An essay examination requires you to demonstrate your analytical abilities.** For example, a history exam may ask the following question: "How did the American Civil War differ from the American Revolution? How were the two wars similar? Describe the effects of each war on the structure of the U.S. government." This question is asking you to combine two patterns: comparison and contrast and cause and effect.

As you think about combining patterns, remember that your essay should always have one primary pattern. The main pattern provides the framework on which you build support for your thesis statement. Additional patterns provide further details and information but should not distract your reader from the main pattern.

As a writer, using multiple patterns will help you write effectively and thoughtfully across all the college disciplines, as well as prepare you for workplace writing.

# Choose a Primary Pattern of Organization for Your Essay

■ GOAL 3
Choose a primary pattern of organization for your essay

Suppose you have been given a writing assignment. Your instructor specifies that your paper must be at least five pages long. You know you want to use multiple patterns of organization, but how do you choose the primary pattern? You will want to consider five main factors:

- The assignment
- Your purpose
- Your audience
- The complexity of your topic
- The course for which you are writing

## The Assignment

In some cases, your instructor will ask you to choose a topic and write about it. However, instructors often provide specific writing assignments or writing prompts. Analyzing the assignment will help you determine the primary pattern of organization for your essay. Look in the assignment for key words and phrases that offer clues.

Suppose, for example, you receive the following assignment in your hotel and restaurant management class:

> Choose one of the following beverages and write an essay describing how it is made: espresso, beer, or soda.

The assignment makes it clear that a process essay is required. The key phrase "how it is made" is your clue. The key word *describing* also appears in the assignment, so be sure to include some description. Suppose you choose to write about soda. Your key goal, then, is to organize your essay to focus on the *process* of soda making. Your essay might also include examples of specific types of soda (cola, ginger ale, club soda) or a narrative about John Pemberton, who created Coca-Cola.

**EXERCISE 12-4**

*WORKING TOGETHER*

## Choosing Primary and Secondary Patterns of Organization

**Directions:** Working with a classmate or in small groups, brainstorm a thesis statement for an essay on each of the following topics. List the primary pattern of organization your essay will use and two additional patterns that will help make the essay more interesting.

1. Gangs: An Urban Family

2. Reality TV: An Embarrassment to America

3. Studying for Exams: Do's and Don'ts

4. Oprah Winfrey: A One-Woman Industry

5. My City: Its People and Neighborhoods

**EXERCISE 12-5** | Choosing Multiple Patterns of Organization

**Directions:** Choose a primary pattern of organization for each of the following writing assignments. Indicate what other patterns you might use and why.

1. Lovers of mystery novels often separate them into different categories: hard-boiled, cozy, caper, private detective, and police procedural. Define and provide examples of each category.

   _____

   _____

2. Those who don't travel on airplanes are often unprepared for the demands of air travel. What steps can an inexperienced traveler take to ensure a comfortable airline flight?

   _____

   _____

3. Two of the most famous American poets are Emily Dickinson and T.S. Eliot. How did each poet approach the writing of poetry? In what ways are the poems of Dickinson and Eliot similar? In what ways are they different?

   _____

   _____

## Your Purpose

When an instructor gives you a specific writing assignment, your purpose for writing is quite clear: to answer the question that has been raised. You simply need to follow the directions, write a good essay, and collect a good grade!

However, when you must choose your own topic, you need to determine your purpose for writing. You can clarify your purpose by asking yourself the questions in the following Need to Know box.

 **NEED TO KNOW**

### Considering Your Purpose

■ What am I trying to accomplish?
■ What do I want my readers to understand after they've read my essay?

Suppose you are a vegetarian and you want to write about vegetarianism. If you think most people don't truly understand what a vegetarian is, you might choose *definition* as your main pattern, because your goal is to clearly define what a vegetarian is and how a vegetarian eats. If you think most people understand the basic definition of a vegetarian, you might choose instead to write a *classification* essay describing the different types of vegetarians (for example, ovo-lacto vegetarians, fruitarians, vegans). Within your primary pattern, you will likely find opportunities to use other patterns. For example, your definition essay might include the *effects* of a vegetarian diet on the human body. Your classification essay might *compare and contrast* the different types of vegetarians.

## Your Audience

All good writing takes the audience into account. To help determine the primary pattern of organization for your essay, ask yourself the questions in the following Need to Know box.

> ## NEED TO KNOW
>
> ### Considering Your Audience
>
> - How much do my readers know about the topic?
> - What can I assume about my readers' backgrounds and experiences?
> - Who is most likely to read what I've written?

Consider the controversial topic of steroids and professional athletes. If your audience is composed of readers who don't know or care much about sports, you might choose to write a *definition* essay, explaining what steroids are and why some athletes use them. You might then provide additional information about the *effects* of steroid use on the body and on athletic performance. Working with both these patterns of organization, you will provide your readers with a basic understanding of steroids and the controversies surrounding them.

Now suppose you are a college baseball coach. You have heard of players dying due to liver failure as a result of steroid usage. You are tired of hearing people say athletes have the right to use steroids to improve their performance. If your audience is composed of devoted sports fans, your purpose might be to convince them that steroids (a) are harmful to the human body and (b) provide unfair advantages to the players who use them. In this case, you may choose to write an essay that is predominantly *argument* based while also including *narratives* about the lives of the young athletes who died as a result of steroid use.

## The Complexity of Your Topic

Some topics are simply more complex or more multifaceted than others. Consider the following essay topics:

- The range of human emotions
- The three branches of the U.S. government: executive, legislative, judicial
- Your bedroom

Which of these topics is the simplest? Which is the most complicated? Most likely you would agree that your bedroom is the simplest topic, and the range of human emotions is the most complicated.

For an essay about your bedroom, you could write effectively using one of the less complicated patterns, such as *description* or *example*, because your bedroom is most likely a fairly small room with limited contents: a bed, a television, a bookshelf, a closet. However, for an essay on the much more complicated topic of human emotions, you will want to choose a pattern that allows for greater depth of analysis, such as *comparison and contrast* (How do conscious feelings differ from subconscious feelings?), *classification* (What are the different kinds of emotions?), or *cause and effect* (What causes depression? What are effects of depression?).

## The Course for Which You Are Writing

Each college discipline makes heavy use of specific types of analysis and writing patterns. For instance, literature classes often focus on *narrative* because stories and novels are generally written with the narrative pattern. The Need to Know box below outlines the patterns most commonly used in a variety of college disciplines. When you receive a writing assignment in each of these courses, consider using one of the patterns listed as your primary pattern. Doing so will usually fulfill your instructor's expectations and help you get the best grade.

 **NEED TO KNOW**

### Academic Thought Patterns

| DISCIPLINE | COMMON THOUGHT PATTERNS | SAMPLE WRITING ASSIGNMENT OR ESSAY EXAM QUESTION |
|---|---|---|
| **Business** (accounting, economics, finance, human resources, management, marketing, operations, organizational behavior) | Classification | Explain the various types of payroll taxes and how each affects an employee's paycheck. |
| | Process | Describe the process by which a consumer-goods company test-markets a new product. |
| | Example | Provide three examples of viral YouTube videos that have led to overnight success for a person or product. |
| **Liberal Arts, Humanities, and Education** (art history, communication, education, English, foreign languages, history/government) | Process | Describe Leo Tolstoy's method for writing a novel. |
| | Cause and Effect | Evaluate the effects of Vincent van Gogh's thick paint strokes on the viewer. |
| | Comparison and Contrast | Compare William Wordsworth's "The Prelude" to Samuel Taylor Coleridge's "Kubla Khan." |
| **Life and Physical Sciences** (anatomy, astronomy, botany, chemistry, geology, nursing, physics, zoology) | Process, Cause and Effect | Explain how plate tectonics have created the continents we see on Earth today. |
| | Classification | Define and describe the three types of animal eggs. |
| **Mathematics** (banking, biotechnology, cryptography, finance, mathematics education) | Process | Describe how to solve an equation that contains parentheses, brackets, addition, multiplication, and exponents. |
| | Comparison and Contrast | What do addition and multiplication have in common? What do subtraction and division have in common? |
| **Social Sciences** (anthropology, criminal justice, economics, geography, psychology, sociology) | Comparison and Contrast | Explain the difference between relative and chronometric dating methods. |
| | Cause and Effect | Describe the factors that influence consumer spending and saving, and explain the effects of spending and saving on the economy. |
| | Example | List three myths about old age. |
| | Definition | Define the term *communism* and list three nations with a communist system. |
| **Technical and Applied Fields** (automotive, child care, computer information systems, hotel and restaurant management, HVAC) | Process | Provide a detailed summary of *fracking*. |
| | Cause and Effect | Explain how acid rain develops, spreads, and destroys. |

**EXERCISE 12-6**

# Considering Audience and Purpose When Choosing Patterns

**Directions:** Analyze the following writing assignment and answer the questions that follow.

> **Writing assignment:** You are a volunteer for a charitable foundation that "rescues" golden retrievers. People who can no longer take care of their pets contact your foundation, and volunteers provide foster homes for the animals until a permanent home can be found. The president of the foundation has asked you to prepare a letter asking people to donate $10 to the organization.

1. Describe your intended audience.

2. What is your purpose for writing?

3. Brainstorm a list of ideas your readers might find helpful or illuminating.

4. Determine a primary pattern of organization for the assignment. Which secondary patterns will you use?

5. Write the letter, and then share it with a classmate. Revise and finalize based on the feedback you receive.

# Common Secondary Patterns of Organization

■ **GOAL 4**
Use secondary patterns of organization in your essay

Three patterns are particularly useful for supporting your thesis statement:

- Example
- Definition
- Description

The following sections offer tips for using each of these secondary patterns effectively.

## Example

Examples are common in almost all written materials because they help readers tie concepts or ideas to the real world. They also help fix key ideas in readers' minds. Including examples makes it easier to understand abstract or difficult ideas.

Below is a *classification* paragraph about the biological concept of asexual reproduction. The inclusion of three examples helps the reader better visualize and understand the process.

Definition →
Classification →
(primary pattern)

Example #1 →

Example #2 →

Example #3 →

Asexual reproduction occurs when offspring arise from a single parent rather than from two parents. Three common forms of asexual reproduction are fission, budding, and fragmentation. In fission, the parent literally splits into two separate organisms of approximately the same size. The single-celled blobs called amoebas that we learned about in our early science classes reproduce by fission. In budding, the parent splits into one larger organism and one smaller organism (called the bud). The yeast used to make bread reproduces through budding. In fragmentation, a new organism grows from a fragment of the parent. Starfish reproduce this way. The arm of a starfish can split off from the parent and then grow into its own organism.

An idea map showing the organization of this paragraph appears below.

**VISUALIZE IT!**

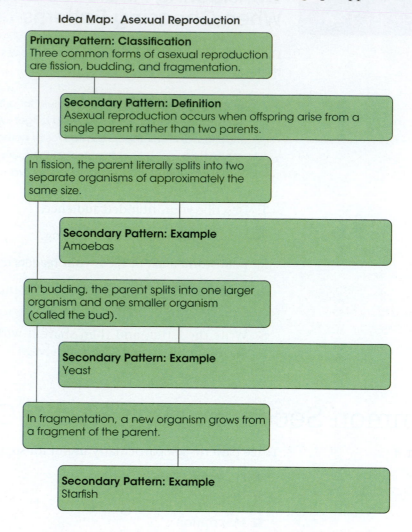

**Idea Map:  Asexual Reproduction**

**Primary Pattern: Classification**
Three common forms of asexual reproduction are fission, budding, and fragmentation.

**Secondary Pattern: Definition**
Asexual reproduction occurs when offspring arise from a single parent rather than two parents.

In fission, the parent literally splits into two separate organisms of approximately the same size.

**Secondary Pattern: Example**
Amoebas

In budding, the parent splits into one larger organism and one smaller organism (called the bud).

**Secondary Pattern: Example**
Yeast

In fragmentation, a new organism grows from a fragment of the parent.

**Secondary Pattern: Example**
Starfish

## Definition

Because so much writing requires readers to have a basic understanding of the terms used, writers often use definition as a secondary pattern. Often the definition is provided in a single sentence, as in the definition of asexual reproduction in the paragraph on the previous page.

However, in longer pieces of writing, the author may take a full paragraph (or even several paragraphs) to discuss a definition. For example, a writer who is comparing and contrasting the cultures of China and the United States may choose to write several paragraphs defining *culture*, which is a complicated concept that includes learned similarities in speech, livelihood, perceptions, traditions, and religion. A reader needs to understand what *culture* means before he or she can fully appreciate a comparison between American culture and Chinese culture.

## Description

Certain kinds of writing call for heavy levels of description. For example, novels often describe characters and settings in detail. Art historians will describe great artworks (like the *Mona Lisa*) in detail. Travel writers are paid to provide vivid descriptions of exotic destinations.

However, description is not the main goal of many types of academic writing. Why? Most college instructors believe that *describing* something is not as important as *understanding* and *analyzing* it. For example, you may be able to describe Mona Lisa's smile, but that doesn't mean you understand that Leonardo da Vinci painted the smile using a technique called *sfumato*, which the artist defined as "without lines or borders, in the manner of smoke."

For this reason, description is often used as a secondary pattern in academic writing. When used with a primary pattern, description can offer additional sensory details and help the reader form a dominant impression. Just a bit of extra description can make an essay much more visual, memorable, or vivid. Consider the following paragraph, which *contrasts* a central business district with a master-planned community.

Definition #1 →

Contrast (primary pattern) →
Definition #2 →

Example and Description →

> A city's central business district, or CBD, grows around the city's most accessible point, and it typically contains a dense concentration of offices and stores. CBDs grow with the needs of the community; they expand and contract organically as the city grows and changes. In contrast, a master-planned community is a residential suburban development. In master-planned developments, houses are designed to look alike and "match," and the community also offers private recreational facilities (such as tennis courts and swimming pools) for its residents. Often, the community is gated to prevent non-residents from entering. Weston is a master-planned community that covers 10,000 acres in Florida. In Weston, almost all aspects of the community are controlled and regulated. Shrubs are planted to shield residents from having to look at the interstate highway. Road signs have a uniform style, each in a stylish frame. Weston offers different areas to cater to different incomes and lifestyles. The houses in the Tequesta Point section come with Roman bathtubs, while an even wealthier section provides larger plots of land for people who own horses.

Note that the paragraph concludes with a description of Weston, a large master-planned community in Florida. The writer could simply have listed Weston as an example, but he chose to describe the community in detail. As a result, the reader has a much better sense of the design of, and life in, a master-planned community.

## EXERCISE 12-7    Using Multiple Patterns of Organization

**Directions:** Analyze the following writing assignment and answer the questions that follow.

> **Writing assignment:** Compare and contrast the high school experience with the college experience. Some topics you might consider: social life, interaction with instructors, costs, and demands on your time.

1. According to the assignment, which primary pattern of organization should you use?

2. Provide at least one term and definition you might use in the assignment.

3. Provide at least two examples you might use in the assignment.

4. What kinds of descriptions might you use in the assignment?

5. Write an essay based on the assignment.

# Plan and Write a Multi-Pattern Essay

■ GOAL 5
Plan and write a
multi-pattern essay

As you begin your brainstorming and prewriting activities, review the patterns of organization in Table 12-1 (p. 367). Then develop your essay using the following steps.

**How to Write a Multi-Pattern Essay**

■ Narrow the topic and select primary and secondary patterns.

■ Write a thesis statement that reflects your primary pattern.

■ Draft your introduction, body paragraphs, and conclusion. When using secondary patterns, include topic sentences that reflect those patterns.

■ Throughout the essay, use transitions to help readers follow your thought patterns.

■ Check to make sure your conclusion revisits your thesis statement and primary pattern.

Each of these steps is explained in detail below

## Narrowing the Topic and Selecting Primary and Secondary Patterns

When thinking about your assignment, use your experiences with the various patterns of organization to brainstorm approaches to the topic. For example, suppose you are given this assignment:

> *Write an essay about gardening.*

The topic "gardening" is quite broad, so think about how you can use different patterns of organization to focus your essay. Using narration, you could tell the story of a family member who is an avid gardener. Using process, you could explain how to prepare soil for planting or describe the best techniques for caring for seedlings. Using argument, you could argue that home gardening is both organic and healthy, and urge your readers to grow more of the foods they eat.

Once you have narrowed the topic, you can choose your primary pattern of organization. After you've made that choice, think about other patterns that will help bring your essay to life. Suppose that you are particularly interested in tomatoes. Within the context of gardening, some of your body paragraphs might focus on tomatoes as an example of a plant that is particularly easy to grow and has many uses. Within your discussion of tomatoes, you might decide to classify the various types of tomatoes so that your readers will know which types best suit their tastes.

## Writing a Thesis Statement that Reflects Your Primary Pattern

Once you have narrowed your topic, write a thesis statement that will serve as the organizing principle for your essay. The thesis statement should reflect your primary pattern. For example, the following thesis statement clearly states that the essay will be organized primarily around the *process* pattern:

> To grow healthy tomato plants that yield many tomatoes by mid-summer, the gardener has to take several steps: start the seeds at the appropriate time, keep the soil fertilized with manure, and protect the growing tomatoes from wildlife and diseases.

## Planning a Multi-Pattern

**WRITING IN PROGRESS**

**Directions:** You have received an assignment to write an essay on the topic of music. Narrow your topic and select your primary and secondary patterns. Then write a thesis statement that reflects your primary pattern.

### Drafting Your Introduction, Body Paragraphs, and Conclusion

Include your thesis statement in the introduction of your essay. Then draft the body paragraphs to support your thesis statement. Make sure everything in your essay, regardless of the pattern you use, supports your thesis.

When using secondary patterns in the body of your essay, make sure each paragraph has a topic sentence that signals the secondary pattern. Each sentence in the paragraph should then provide support for the topic sentence. Within your essay about growing tomatoes, for example, you might have a paragraph that includes the following topic sentence (underlined):

> Before you ever sow your first batch of tomato seeds, however, you'll need to determine which type of tomato you want to grow. Many people do not know that many different types of tomatoes can be grown, and each is used for different types of cooking and eating: beefsteak tomatoes for sandwiches, plum tomatoes for sauce, and cherry tomatoes for salad.

This topic sentence signals that you will use *classification* as the organizing pattern for the rest of this body paragraph.

## Writing Using Secondary Patterns

**WRITING IN PROGRESS**

**Directions:** Draft the music essay you planned in Exercise 12-8, using topic sentences in body paragraphs to signal secondary patterns.

### Using Transitions to Help Readers Follow Your Thought Patterns

Use the transitional words and phrases you learned in Chapters 7 and 8 to help readers follow your thought patterns throughout your essay. Refer to the tables of transitional words and phrases often used with each pattern of development in those chapters.

The following paragraph provides an effective topic sentence, support, and transitions:

Transition →
Topic sentence indicates classification pattern →
Category #1 with description →

Category #2 with description →

Category #3 with description →

> Before you ever sow your first batch of tomato seeds, however, you'll need to determine which type of tomato you want to grow. Many people do not know that many different types of tomatoes can be grown, and each is used for different types of cooking and eating. Beefsteak tomatoes are large, juicy tomatoes with a thin skin and a short shelf life. Their juiciness makes them popular in sandwiches. Plum tomatoes (which are shaped like small plums or pears) are more solid and less juicy, which makes them perfect for creating tomato sauces and pastes. Cherry tomatoes and grape tomatoes, named for the fruits they resemble, are small, bite-sized tomatoes that are often used in salads or as garnishes.

**WRITING IN PROGRESS**

## Writing Using Transitions

**Directions:** Read the draft you wrote for Exercise 12-9 to ensure that you have used transitional words and phrases when necessary. You might ask a classmate to read your draft and indicate where "choppiness" indicates a need for a transition.

### Checking to Make Sure Your Conclusion Revisits Your Thesis Statement and Primary Pattern

A good concluding paragraph both summarizes the essay and reminds readers of its key organizing principles. In your essay's final paragraph, be sure you have restated your thesis and primary pattern of organization. Doing so will ensure that your readers understand your purpose and main points.

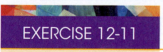

**WRITING IN PROGRESS**

## Writing Conclusions and Revising Essays

**Directions:** Check the essay you wrote for Exercise 12-9 to ensure the concluding paragraph revisits the thesis statement and your essay's primary pattern. Then revise the essay, ensuring that it flows smoothly and that your primary pattern of organization is obvious. Eliminate sentences or paragraphs that do not support your thesis statement, and proofread your work for grammar and accuracy.

# Use Multiple Patterns in Introductions, Body Paragraphs, and Conclusions

■ **GOAL 6**
Write multi-pattern introductions, body paragraphs, and conclusions

Following are some suggestions for using multiple patterns in specific parts of your essay.

## Using Multiple Patterns in the Introduction

In a typical essay, the introductory paragraph accomplishes three goals:

- ■ It introduces the topic and provides any necessary background information.
- ■ It stimulates the reader's interest.
- ■ It provides a thesis statement as the essay's main point and key organizing principle.

Using multiple patterns in your essay's introduction can help you accomplish all these goals, allowing you to specify your primary method and hint at your secondary methods. Let's look at a specific example written by a college student, Dejohn Harris.

Dejohn's instructor gave his class the following writing assignment:

> A *subculture* is a group within a larger, more mainstream culture, often with its own set of rules, beliefs, and expected behaviors. Often, members of the subculture reject larger society and choose to live in their own world. For example, fans of the Japanese art called *anime* or *manga* compose a subculture, as do punk rockers, bikers, and Goths. Write an essay about a subculture to which you belong. If you do not belong to a subculture, identify a subculture that you have observed, encountered, or experienced and write an essay about it.

Dejohn was arrested for crimes he committed when he belonged to an infamous Los Angeles street gang, the Crips. In prison, he converted to Islam and decided to pursue an education and a career as a music producer when he was released from jail. At the time he received this assignment, he was a student at a southern California community college.

Dejohn had lived deeply within the street gang subculture for many years, so he decided to write about gangs. Because he had so much to say about the topic, he decided to list his ideas to focus his thoughts and determine the best content and organization for his essay. This is the list he generated:

| | | | |
|---|---|---|---|
| ① | Crips' intense rivalry with another gang, the Bloods | ⑧ | things most people don't know about gangs |
| ② | how I got involved in the gang | ⑨ | how we're different from motorcycle gangs like the Hell's Angels |
| ③ | why people join gangs | ⑩ | the code of the street, "respect," and "street cred" |
| ④ | what I had to do to prove myself | ⑪ | gang leaders |
| ⑤ | the hierarchy and types of gang members | ⑫ | "decent families" (less likely to join a gang) vs. "street families" (more likely to join a gang) |
| ⑥ | the crimes I committed: theft, vandalism, turf wars, drug dealing (other crimes I didn't commit: murder, drive-by shootings) | ⑬ | how a gang is like a big family |
| ⑦ | my time in prison | ⑭ | the "rules" |
| | | ⑮ | gangs' love of guns |

After thinking about the best way to organize his essay, Dejohn decided to focus on point #8 on his list: *things most people don't know about gangs*. He believed that many of the other points on his list would fit within that category. Therefore, he chose *example* as his primary pattern of organization.

Dejohn felt his experience as a gang member was important to establishing the truthfulness of his essay. He didn't want his essay to read like a textbook on gangs; rather, he wanted to emphasize that he had witnessed and lived everything he was going to write about. For this reason, he decided to begin his essay with an introductory *narrative* paragraph about his life and how he got involved in the Crips:

Introductory paragraph opens as a narrative →

Definitions of the Crips and Bloods included →

Thesis statement signals the primary pattern of organization (example) →

Closing sentence of introductory paragraph suggests that comparison and contrast will also be used in the essay →

> When I was 12 years old, my favorite cousin, Sean, who was 16 at the time, was shot and killed in a drive-by shooting. He was a good student and a fantastic basketball player. His high school coach was talking to a bunch of colleges about getting a scholarship for him. Sean wasn't a gang member, but his girlfriend's brother belonged to the Crips, one of L.A.'s biggest and most dangerous gangs. Sean was hanging out with his girlfriend and her brother, and someone from the Bloods, a rival gang, drove past and took a shot at the brother. He missed the brother and killed my cousin instead. I can still remember how angry I felt when I got the news. Two days later, a Crip stopped me when I was walking home from school. He asked me if I wanted to let the Bloods get away with what they did. I said no, I wanted them to pay. And that's how I became a gang member at the age of 12. A lot of people are shocked when someone tells them that gangs recruit kids who aren't even teenagers yet, but there's a lot more to being in a gang than any outsider realizes or hears about. For example, many people don't understand the difference between a "street family" and a "decent family," and the fact that coming from a street family makes you much more likely to join a gang.

Note that this introductory paragraph accomplishes all the goals listed above. It stimulates readers' interest in the topic, provides a thesis statement signaling the primary pattern of organization, and offers information about the writer's background.

## EXERCISE 12-12 — Choosing Patterns of Organization

**Directions:** Review Dejohn Harris's brainstorming list. Identify which primary pattern of organization he would likely have chosen for his essay if he had decided to focus on each of the following points.

1. Point #2 (how I got involved in the gang):

   _____

2. Point #5 (the hierarchy and types of gang members):

   _____

3. Point #9 (how we're different from motorcycle gangs like the Hell's Angels):

   _____

4. Point #12 ("decent families" vs. "street families"):

   _____

**EXERCISE 12-13**

# Using Secondary Patterns in an Introduction

**Directions:** Explain which secondary patterns (other than definition and comparison and contrast) Dejohn could have used effectively in his introduction. Why would these patterns be effective?

## Using Multiple Patterns in the Body

Once Dejohn made the decision to use example as his primary pattern of organization, he organized his thoughts and decided to focus on three key examples. The following list summarizes Dejohn's ideas for topic sentences and explains his strategy for supporting them.

1. *Most gangs have female members.* I'm going to tell the story of Tamika and Jocelyn, who were tougher than many of the guys I knew. (narration, description)

2. *People think all city kids come from street families, because the media never report on decent families.* I have to explain the difference between a "street family" and a "decent family." I also want to point out that most people never hear about all the honest, hard-working people who live in the inner city. (comparison and contrast, argument)

3. *Most gang members <u>want</u> to get out of the gang and/or have <u>tried</u> to get out of the gang.* I need to explain why people join gangs and then why they want to leave. (cause and effect)

With his topic sentences and introductory paragraph drafted, Dejohn drafted the body of his essay. (What follows is a part of his final essay, after he revised and proofread it.)

Example #1 Topic Sentence ➔

Comparison: Guys and girls ➔
Cause and Effect: Why people join gangs ➔

Narrative ➔
Transitional phrase ➔

Example #2 Topic Sentence (includes Cause and Effect) ➔

Definitions of *decent family* and *street family* ➔

Comparison and Contrast ➔

<u>Though most people don't realize it, most gangs have plenty of female members.</u> Looking back to my days as a Crip, I would guess that about one out of every ten Crips was female. Like the guys, the girls who join gangs are looking for support and a family, because their mothers are junkies and their fathers are gone. Sometimes they are the girlfriends of Crips, and they end up joining the gang because they want to be a part of their boyfriend's life and also part of a group. Something these girls never talk about is the way they were sexually molested when they were younger, but I know this is true about a lot of them. Two of the female Crips I was closest to, Tamika and Jocelyn, both told me that their mothers' boyfriends had taken advantage of them and mistreated them. But even though many gang members are female, they are never in charge. In other words, they are never the gang leader.

<u>Because the media focuses on the "ghetto" and the "hood" and all the negative stereotypes that go with them, many people don't realize how family life leads young people to join a gang.</u> If you come from a decent family, you probably won't join a gang, but if you come from a street family, you probably will. What do these terms mean? A "decent family" is a family that tries to support itself honestly. Usually they go to church and work their social lives around church activities. So the church becomes their extended family, and they don't have to look to gangs for support. In contrast, a "street family" is one that is focused on public respect and an emphasis on physical strength, the idea being that

Cause and Effect →
Argument →

a man should do whatever it takes to protect his family. Coming from a street family leads to thug life, and thug life leads to joining a gang, which is just one big street family. Maybe if the media showed more positive role models for inner-city kids, and told stories of all the hard-working mothers and fathers who try to protect their kids from crime and drugs, street life wouldn't seem so glamorous to 12-year-olds.

Transitional word →
Example #3 →

Another little-known piece of information is the fact that many, many gang members try to leave the gang. They look around at the drugs, and the violence, and the murders, and the fact they may end up dead, and they decide gang life isn't right for them. But by that point it is too late. Once you're in, the leaders usu-

Definition →
Cause and Effect →

ally won't let you out. Some gangs have a practice called "jumping out," where people who want to leave get beaten mercilessly. If they live through it, they can leave the gang. If they die, well, they also get their wish to leave the gang.

## Using Multiple Patterns in the Conclusion

Recall from Chapter 11 that an essay's concluding paragraph has two main functions:

- It reemphasizes the thesis statement.
- It draws the essay to a close.

As a former gang member, Dejohn thought the best way to close his essay would be to discourage young people from joining a gang. To accomplish that goal, he revisited his thesis statement, once again pointing to the essay's primary pattern of organization, and he closed his essay with a strong cause-and-effect statement and a strong argument.

Closing paragraph refers to essay's primary method of organization (example) →

I could write many more pages providing additional examples of little-known facts about life in a gang. I could talk about the weekly meetings we had to attend, the monetary dues we had to pay, the crimes we had to commit, the way we got our nicknames, and the types of graffiti we used to tag our territory. All of it would be interesting to people who don't know anything about gangs, and a lot of it would be shocking. But let me tell you: I can write this essay because I

The effects of gang member-ship on the individual →

Closing argument based on the author's experiences →

lived as a gang member. And it's not as glamorous or fun as rap music makes it sound. It drains your individuality, your soul, and your morality. It's much better for your life, your happiness, your friends, and your family if you read about gangs instead of joining one.

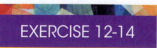

EXERCISE 12-14

## Writing Using Multiple Patterns of Organizations

**Directions:** Write a multi-pattern essay on one of the following topics.

1. junk food
2. fashion
3. friendship
4. social media
5. presidential campaigns

6. exercise
7. single parenthood
8. addiction
9. gay marriage

# INTEGRATING READING AND WRITING

## READ AND RESPOND: A Student Essay

*Dejohn Harris (not his real name) is a former gang member who is currently attending community college in the Los Angeles area. Dejohn's instructor assigned a multi-pattern essay as the semester's final project. The assignment was as follows:*

A *subculture* is a group within a larger, more mainstream culture, often with its own set of rules, beliefs, and expected behaviors. Often, members of the subculture reject larger society and choose to live in their own world. For example, fans of the Japanese art called *anime* or *manga* compose a subculture, as do punk rockers, bikers, and Goths. Write an essay about a subculture to which you belong. If you do not belong to a subculture, identify a subculture that you have observed, encountered, or experienced and write an essay about it.

*Now that you have seen Dejohn's essay in process, read it as a whole and answer the questions that follow.*

# Gang Life: Better from the Outside
## Dejohn Harris

When I was 12 years old, my favorite cousin, Sean, who was 16 at the time, was shot and killed in a drive-by shooting. He was a good student and a fantastic basketball player. His high school coach was talking to a bunch of colleges about getting a scholarship for him. Sean wasn't a gang member, but his girlfriend's brother belonged to the Crips, one of L.A.'s biggest and most dangerous gangs. Sean was hanging out with his girlfriend and her brother, and someone from the Bloods, a rival gang, drove past and took a shot at the brother. He missed the brother and killed my cousin instead. I can still remember how angry I felt when I got the news. Two days later, a Crip stopped me when I was walking home from school. He asked me if I wanted to let the Bloods get away with what they did. I said no, I wanted them to pay. And that's how I became a gang member at the age of 12. A lot of people are shocked when someone tells them that gangs recruit kids who aren't even teenagers yet, but there's a lot more to being in a gang than any outsider realizes or hears about. For example, many people don't understand the difference between a "street family" and a "decent family," and the fact that coming from a street family makes you much more likely to join a gang.

Though most people don't realize it, most gangs have plenty of female members. Looking back to my days as a Crip, I would guess that about one out of every ten Crips was female. Like the guys, the girls who join gangs are looking for support and a family, because their mothers are junkies and their fathers are gone. Sometimes they are the girlfriends of Crips, and they end up joining the gang because they want to be a part of their boyfriend's life and also part of a group. Something these girls never talk about is the way they were sexually molested when they were younger, but I know this is true about a lot of them. Two of the female Crips I was closest to, Tamika and Jocelyn, both confided in me that their mothers' boyfriends had taken advantage of them and mistreated them. But even though many gang members are female, they are never in charge. In other words, they are never the gang leader.

Because the media focuses on the "ghetto" and the "hood" and all the negative stereotypes that go with them, many people don't realize how family life leads young people to join a gang. If you come from a decent family, you probably won't join a gang, but if you come from a street family, you probably will. What do these terms mean? A "decent family" is a family that tries to support itself honestly. Usually they go to church and work their social lives around church activities. So the church becomes their extended family, and they don't have to look to gangs for support. In contrast, a "street family" is one that is focused on public respect and an emphasis on physical strength, the idea being that a man should do whatever it takes to protect his family. Coming from a street family leads to thug life, and thug life leads to joining a gang, which is just one big street family. Maybe if the media showed more positive role models for inner-city kids, and told stories of all the hard-working mothers and fathers who try to protect their kids from crime and drugs, street life wouldn't seem so glamorous to 12-year-olds.

Another little-known piece of information is the fact that many, many gang members try to leave the gang. They look around at the drugs, and the violence, and the murders, and the fact they may end up dead, and they decide gang life isn't right for them. But by that point it is too late. Once you're in, the leaders usually won't let you out. Some gangs have a practice called "jumping out," where people who want to leave get beaten mercilessly. If they live through it, they can leave the gang. If they die, well, they also get their wish to leave the gang.

I could write many more pages providing additional examples of little-known facts about life in a gang. I could talk about the weekly meetings we had to attend, the monetary dues we had to pay, the crimes we had to commit, the way we got our nicknames, and the types of graffiti we used to tag our territory. All of it would be interesting to people who don't know anything about gangs, and a lot of it would be shocking. But let me tell you: I can write this essay because I lived as a gang member. And it's not as glamorous or fun as rap music makes it sound. It drains your individuality, your soul, and your morality. It's much better for your life, your happiness, your friends, and your family if you read about gangs instead of joining one.

## Examining Writing

1. Describe Dejohn's purpose for writing the essay and his intended audience.

2. Can you suggest an alternative title for the essay?

3. Evaluate Dejohn's use of multiple patterns of organization. Is his primary pattern clearly stated? Which other development methods could he have used effectively in his essay?

4. Suppose Dejohn wants to turn his essay into a five-page term paper for his sociology class. What advice would you give him? Which topics from his brainstorming list or from his concluding paragraph would you find most interesting?

5. Create an idea map for "Gang Life: Better from the Outside."

## Writing Assignments

For one of the following assignments, use the process described in this chapter to narrow your topic and outline a multi-pattern essay, specifying your primary pattern as well as the secondary patterns you will use. Then draft, revise, and proofread your paper.

1. For a business class, you are asked to write an essay about advertising. You can choose to write about any aspect of the topic. For example, you might write about one brand's specific advertising strategy (Coca-Cola, Levi's, or any other company you find interesting) or about the advertisements you have found most entertaining or annoying.

2. For a communications class, you are assigned an essay on the topic of social media. In the assignment, your instructor specifies that you can explore any aspect of the topic that you find interesting. So, for example, you might compare and contrast two popular forms of social media (such as Facebook and Twitter), or you might talk about the effects of social media on your life or on the lives of today's teenagers.

3. You are taking a biology class, and your instructor assigns an essay on the general topic of the common cold. He provides no further details. How would you go about narrowing the topic to one you find interesting? Which patterns of organization would you use? How would you get your reader interested in the topic in the opening paragraph? Draft your essay and share it with two classmates. Then incorporate their feedback into your revised, final, proofread essay.

## Read and Respond: A Professional Essay

### Thinking Before Reading

The following reading is taken from a Web site, WebMD Health News. As you read, notice how the author uses multiple patterns of organization.

1. Preview the reading, using the steps discussed in Chapter 1, p. 15.

2. Connect the reading to your own experiences by answering the following questions:

   a. What do you know about cyberbullying?

   b. What episodes or effects of cyberbullying have you seen, heard, or read about?

3. Mark and annotate as you read.

# Emotional Troubles for 'Cyberbullies' and Victims

## Denise Mann

*Study Shows Mental and Physical Impact of Cyberbullying on Victims and Bullies*

### WebMD Health News Reviewed by Louise Chang, MD

1   New research sheds important light on the prevalence, extent, and consequences of "cyberbullying" as well as some of the emotional and physical characteristics of cyberbullies and their victims. Both the cyberbullies and those they bully online are more likely to report a host of physical and mental problems, according to a new study in the July issue of the *Archives of General Psychiatry.*

2   A relatively new phenomenon, cyberbullying is defined as "an aggressive intentional act carried out by a group or individual using electronic forms of contact repeatedly and over time against a victim who cannot easily defend him or herself," according to the study. The increase in cyberbullying **dovetails** with the explosion in the use of computers, cell phones, and other electronic devices by children. Unlike traditional bullying, which largely relies on physical threats, rumors, and exclusion, cyberbullies can reach larger audiences via social media and other technology, making it difficult for the intended victim to escape their bullies. Cyberbullies can also do so relatively anonymously.

**dovetails**
fits together closely

3   The new study included information on 2,215 Finnish teens aged 13 to 16. Overall, 4.8% of the teens said that they were victimized by cyberbullies, 7.4% admitted to being cyberbullies, and 5.4% said they were both cyberbullies and had been cyberbullied. Most of the cyberbullying was done via computer instant messages and discussion groups, the study showed. Cyberbullies often harassed peers of the same age. Sixteen percent of girls surveyed said they were bullied by boys, whereas just 5% of boys said they were cyberbullied by girls.

### Emotional and Physical Issues

4   Victims of cyberbullying reported emotional, concentration, and behavioral issues, as well as trouble getting along with their peers. These teens were also more likely to report frequent headaches, recurrent stomach pain, and difficulty sleeping; one in four said they felt unsafe at school. What's more, those teens who were victimized by cyberbullies were less likely to be living with both biological parents, the researchers report.

5   Cyberbullies also reported emotional difficulties, concentration and behavior issues, and difficulty getting along with others. They were also more likely to be hyperactive, have conduct problems, abuse alcohol, and smoke cigarettes. In addition, cyberbullies also reported frequent headaches and feeling unsafe at school. Those teens who were both

cyberbullies and victims reported all of these physical and mental health issues, the study found.

6    "Policy makers, educators, parents, and adolescents themselves should be aware of the potentially harmful effects of cyberbullying," conclude the researchers, who were led by Andre Sourander, MD, PhD, a child psychiatrist at Turku University in Finland. "Future research is needed on whether anti-bullying policies, materials, interventions, and mobile telephone and Internet user guidelines are effective for reducing cyberbullying."

## Staying Safe Online

7    Parry Aftab's life mission is to keep children and teens safe online. An Internet privacy and security lawyer in Fort Lee, N.J., Aftab is the executive director of wiredsafety.org, an online safety and educational site that is the parent group for a charity called stopcyberbullying.org. "Cyberbullying is when a minor uses technology as a weapon to hurt another," she says. It can take many forms such as stealing another kid's password or his or her points in an online game or digitally adding a peer's face to a photo of a naked body and then posting it online (where it can quickly go viral), she says. "There are millions of different ways to [cyberbully]; it is limited only by the bandwidth and creativity of kids."

8    Cyberbullying changes the typical playground or schoolyard social structure. "It brings a whole different group of kids into the problem," she says. "Real-life victims can become online bullies because it is rarely a matter of size," she explains. "It gets the girls and geeks involved and they are normally the ones being bullied." There is no escape from cyberbullies, she says. If a child was bullied at school, home was often a safe haven. But "teens are always connected, and technology follows you everywhere you are, 24-7," she says. "Cyberbullying can have devastating consequences, and parents need to understand that most kids have been cyberbullied at least once."

9    The question becomes what to do about it. Aftab's advice to teens who are victims of cyberbullies? "Stop, block, and tell," she says. "Do not reply. Block the message and then tell a trusted adult," she says. Other tips include using non-obvious passwords and changing them after breakups to discourage hackers. Parents of children who are bullied online need to take a deep breath before they overreact and make things worse, she says. "If there is a teacher or guidance counselor with whom you have a good relationship, call that person first so your child won't be blamed as a tattletale," she advises. But "if there is a threat, you have to call the police."

10    Aftab's group is planning to release a free stop cyberbullying toolkit for schools in August. Child psychoanalyst Leon Hoffman, MD, the executive director of the Bernard L. Pacella Parent Child Center in New York City, agrees with Aftab. "This [research] paper stresses the importance of a no-tolerance policy that the adults have to enforce vigorously." "This paper verifies that cyberbullying is a significant problem," Aftab tells WebMD. "More importantly, it promotes the idea that school and mental health personnel need to be aware of its existence."

11    More research is needed to get a better handle on some of the physical and mental characteristics of cyberbullies and their victims, he says. "Whether

**perpetrator**
one who commits a wrong action

cyberbullying [victim or **perpetrator** or both] is the cause of a variety of problems or whether kids with a variety of psychosocial and medical problems are prone to bullying, victimization or both is a question that has to be studied."

Sources: Sourander, A. Archives of General Psychiatry, 2010; vol 67: pp. 720–727.
Parry Aftab, Internet privacy and security lawyer, Fort Lee, N.J.; executive director, wiredsafety.org.
Leon Hoffman, MD, executive director, Bernard L. Pacella Parent Child Center, New York City.

# Getting Ready to Write

## Checking Your Comprehension

Answer each of the following questions using complete sentences.

1. How is cyberbullying different from traditional bullying?
2. What effects do victims of cyberbullying commonly report?
3. How does cyberbullying change the typical playground or schoolyard structure?
4. According to this article, what should adults do about cyberbullying?
5. In which country was the study conducted?

## Strengthening Your Vocabulary

Using the word's context, word parts, or a dictionary, write a brief definition of each of the following words as it is used in the reading.

1. prevalence (paragraph 1) _____
2. phenomenon (paragraph 2) _____
3. harassed (paragraph 3) _____
4. hyperactive (paragraph 5) _____

## Examining the Reading: Using an Idea Map

Create an idea map of "Emotional Troubles for 'Cyberbullies' and Victims." Start with the title and thesis and include the main points of the essay.

## Reacting to Ideas: Discussion and Journal Writing

Get ready to write about the reading by discussing the following:

1. Why do you think cyberbullies experience negative emotional and physical consequences?
2. Why do you think people engage in cyberbullying?
3. How is cyberbullying different from regular bullying?
4. Why is the photograph a useful addition to the reading?

**THINKING VISUALLY**

## Thinking and Writing Critically

1. How does the definition of cyberbullying in the *Archives of General Psychiatry* differ from the definition provided by Parry Aftab?

2. What primary method of development does the reading use? Which secondary methods are used? Point to specific paragraphs, sentences, or transitions that signal each method.

3. List three questions that the reading suggests or raises but does not answer.

**MySkillsLab®**

**Complete** this Exercise

# Writing About the Reading

## Paragraph Options

1. Write a paragraph describing cyberbullying that you or someone you know experienced.

2. In your opinion, what rules should a school's zero-tolerance cyberbullying policy include? Describe the no-tolerance policy in a paragraph.

3. How can parents prevent cyberbullying? Write a paragraph offering some suggestions beyond those listed in the reading.

## Essay Options

4. How has modern technology changed the way teens deal with one another? Write a multi-pattern essay explaining how technology has changed teen behavior.

5. Playground bullies terrorized schoolyards long before cyberbullies began using the Internet as a weapon. Why do you think some kids and teens become bullies? From the bully's perspective, what are the "benefits" of bullying? Write a multi-pattern essay explaining your thoughts.

# SELF-TEST SUMMARY

To test yourself, cover the Answer column with a sheet of paper and answer each question in the left column. Evaluate each of your answers as you work by sliding the paper down and comparing your answer with what is printed in the Answer column.

| QUESTION | ANSWER |
| --- | --- |
| ■ **GOAL 1** Define a multi-pattern essay <br><br> What is a multi-pattern essay? | A multi-pattern essay is one that uses more than one pattern of organization. |

*(continued)*

*(continued)*

| QUESTION | ANSWER |
|---|---|
| ■ **GOAL 2** Recognize multiple patterns of organization in readings<br><br>Why is it important to recognize multiple patterns within a reading? How do you recognize primary and secondary patterns? | Recognizing multiple patterns helps you understand the reading's overall organization and key points, develop a deeper understanding of the topic, and prepare for essay exams. The primary pattern is the reading's key organizing principle and provides the framework on which the writer builds support for the thesis statement. Secondary patterns provide further explanation, details, clarification, and information. |
| ■ **GOAL 3** Choose a primary pattern of organization for your essay<br><br>How do you choose a primary pattern of organization for your essay? | To choose a primary pattern, consider the assignment, your purpose, your audience, the complexity of your topic, and the course for which you are writing. |
| ■ **GOAL 4** Use secondary patterns of organization in your essay<br><br>What three secondary patterns of organization can help you support your thesis statement? | Example, definition, and description can help you support your thesis statement. |
| ■ **GOAL 5** Plan and write a multi-pattern essay<br><br>What process should you follow to write a multi-pattern essay? | To write a multi-pattern essay, first narrow the topic and select primary and secondary patterns. Next, write a thesis statement that reflects your primary pattern. Draft your introduction, body paragraphs, and conclusion. Include topic sentences that reflect secondary patterns and use transitions to help readers follow your thought patterns. Make sure your conclusion revisits your thesis statement and primary pattern. |
| ■ **GOAL 6** Write multi-pattern introductions, body paragraphs, and conclusions<br><br>Why should you use multiple patterns in introductions, body paragraphs, and conclusions? | In introductions, multiple patterns can help introduce the topic, provide background information, stimulate the reader's interest, and provide the essay's key organizing principle. In body paragraphs, multiple patterns can help support the thesis statement. In conclusions, multiple patterns can help reemphasize the thesis statement and provide additional food for thought. |

**MySkillsLab**®  For more help with **Reading and Writing Essays with Multiple Patterns,** go to your learning path in MySkillsLab at www.myskillslab.com.

# Critical Thinking: Making Inferences and Analyzing the Author's Message

# 13

## THINK About It!

The newspapers and tabloids shown in this photograph contain a wide variety of information. Some of these sources make sensational claims and report implausible events, while others report factual information in a clear and straightforward manner. How can you know which stories report factual information and which offer opinions and misleading information? How would you know which sources are trustworthy and able to be used as sources when writing essays? Write a few sentences summarizing what factors you would consider in evaluating a source.

This chapter will teach you a number of critical thinking skills that are important for both reading and writing. Topics include making inferences, evaluating evidence, and analyzing tone.

## Reading and Writing Connections

### EVERYDAY CONNECTIONS

- **Reading** You read an opinion piece in your newspaper about the importance of technology in elementary schools. To support this viewpoint, the writer cites a survey of more than 1,000 teachers and school administrators in the United States.
- **Writing** As a volunteer at your child's school, you are asked to draft a letter for the school's fund-raising campaign to buy new computers. In your letter, you refer to the survey cited in the newspaper article, keeping the tone of your letter informative as well as positive and energetic.

### ACADEMIC CONNECTIONS

- **Reading** You read an article assigned in your political science class that criticizes candidates for accepting money from political action committees (PACs). You notice that the writer uses negative words such as *destructive* and *outrageous*.
- **Writing** In response to the article, you write an essay arguing for campaign finance reform. You support your argument with facts, reasons, and examples, and you use in-text citations to give credit to your sources.

### WORKPLACE CONNECTIONS

- **Reading** You read an e-mail from a co-worker asking you to serve as a reference in her application for a job in another city. You know that she recently became a grandmother and you make an inference that she will be relocating to be closer to her new grandchild.
- **Writing** You write a reference for your co-worker, sincerely recommending her for the job and including examples of her professionalism and strong work ethic.

# FOCUSING ON READING AND WRITING

# What Is Critical Thinking?

■ **GOAL 1**
Understand the benefits of critical thinking

College reading assignments are not just about reading and memorization. They are also about *thinking*. You may have noticed that annotation skills require you not only to identify key material, but also to *analyze* what you are reading. **Critical thinking** is another term for analytical thinking.

In this context, *critical* does not mean "negative." Critical thinking requires you to evaluate what you read, rather than to accept everything as the truth. Thinking critically sometimes requires you to disagree with the author or express a different opinion.

The ability to think and read critically offers many benefits to writers. Specifically, critical thinking allows you to:

- Distinguish good information from incomplete, inaccurate, or misleading information.
- Write paragraphs, essays, term papers, and essay exams that exhibit a strong understanding of what you've read.

Critical thinking should take place at all times, no matter what you read or write. For example:

- **When reading a college textbook**, you might ask yourself if the author is trying to influence your opinions.
- **When reading a newspaper**, you might ask yourself if the journalist is telling the full story or if she is leaving something out.
- **When writing an essay**, you might consider whether you have fully explained your ideas or omitted important points or essential information.
- **When writing a research paper**, you should be certain that you use reliable sources and that you support your ideas with strong factual evidence.

# READING

# Make Inferences

- GOAL 2
  Make inferences

Reading involves much more than just understanding what an author says. You also have to figure out what an author is suggesting or implying. To do so, you need to make inferences and predictions.

## What Is an Inference?

Just as you use inference when you study a photograph, you also use it when you try to figure out why a friend is sad or what an author's message is in a particular piece of writing. An **inference** is an educated guess or prediction about something unknown based on available facts and information. It is the logical connection that you draw between what you observe or know and what you do not know.

Here are a few everyday situations. Make an inference for each.

A well-dressed man walks toward the front of your lecture hall on the first day of class.

You see a young woman in a shopping mall wearing a wedding ring pushing a baby in a stroller with two young children following her.

In the first situation, a good inference might be that the man is the instructor because he is not dressed like the average student. However, it is possible that the man is a student who has an important appointment right after class. In the second situation, one inference is that the woman was married very young and had three children in a row; another possibility is that she is married but is just babysitting the children.

When you make inferences about what you read, you go beyond what a writer says and consider what he or she *means*. Writers may directly state some ideas but hint at others. It is left to the reader, then, to pick up on the clues or suggestions and to figure out the writer's unstated message. This chapter will show you how to do so.

## How to Make Inferences

Making an inference is a thinking process. As you read, you are following the writer's thoughts. You are also alert for ideas that are suggested but not directly stated. Because inference is a logical thought process, there is no simple, step-by-step procedure to follow. Each inference depends on the situation, the facts provided, and the reader's knowledge and experience.

However, here are a few guidelines to keep in mind as you read. These will help you get in the habit of looking beyond the factual level.

1. **Be sure you understand the literal meaning.** Before you can make inferences, you need a clear grasp of the facts, the writer's main ideas, and the supporting details.

2. **Notice details.** Often a particular detail provides a clue that will help you make an inference. When you spot a striking or unusual detail, ask yourself: Why did the writer include this piece of information? Remember that there are many kinds of details, such as descriptions, actions, and conversations.

3. **Add up the facts.** Consider all the facts taken together. Ask yourself: What is the writer trying to suggest with this set of facts? What do all these facts and ideas point toward?

4. **Look at the writer's choice of words.** A writer's word choice often suggests his or her attitude toward the subject. Notice, in particular, descriptive words, emotionally charged words, and words that are very positive or negative.

5. **Understand the writer's purpose.** An author's purpose, which is discussed later in this chapter, affects many aspects of a piece of writing. Ask yourself: Why did the author write this?

6. **Be sure your inference is supportable.** An inference must be based on fact. Make sure there is sufficient evidence to justify any inference you make.

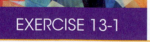
**EXERCISE 13-1**

# Understanding Inferences

**Directions:** Read each of the following passages. Based on the information contained in each passage, use inference to determine whether the statements that follow it are likely to be true (T) or false (F). Write your answer in the space provided.

### A. Targeting Inner-City Consumers

Cigarette, beer, and fast-food marketers have generated controversy in recent years by their attempts to target inner-city minority consumers. For example, McDonald's and other chains have drawn criticism for pitching their high-fat, salt-laden fare to low-income, urban residents. Similarly, R.J. Reynolds took heavy

flak in the early 1990s when it announced plans to market Uptown, a menthol cigarette targeted toward low-income blacks. It quickly dropped the brand in the face of a loud public outcry and heavy pressure from African-American leaders.
—Adapted from Armstrong and Kotler, *Marketing: An Introduction*, p. 192

_____ 1. R.J. Reynolds withdrew its ads because it was concerned about the risk of lung cancer among low-income blacks.

_____ 2. Low-income urban consumers are fast-food consumers.

_____ 3. McDonald's salt-laden foods include burgers and fries.

_____ 4. These companies have never in the past targeted any specialized groups.

_____ 5. Due to the outcry, McDonald's began offering healthier choices.

**B. Is Laughter the Best Medicine?**

Lucy went to the hospital to visit Emma, a neighbor who had broken her hip. The first thing Lucy saw when the elevator door opened at the third floor was a clown, with an enormous orange nose, dancing down the hall, pushing a colorfully decorated cart. The clown stopped in front of Lucy, bowed, and then somersaulted to the nurses' station. A cluster of patients cheered. Most of them were in wheelchairs or on crutches. Upon asking for directions, Lucy learned that Emma was in the "humor room," where the film *Blazing Saddles* was about to start.

Since writer Norman Cousins's widely publicized recovery from a debilitating and usually incurable disease of the connective tissue, humor has gained new respectability in hospital wards around the country. Cousins, the long-time editor of the *Saturday Review*, with the cooperation of his physician, supplemented his regular medical therapy with a steady diet of Marx brothers movies and *Candid Camera* film clips. Although he never claimed that laughter alone effected his cure, Cousins is best remembered for his passionate support of the notion that, if negative emotions can cause distress, then humor and positive emotions can enhance the healing process.
—Zimbardo and Gerrig, *Psychology and Life*, p. 501

_____ 6. The clown was at the hospital to celebrate a patient's birthday.

_____ 7. *Blazing Saddles* and Marx brothers movies would be classified as comedy films.

_____ 8. Cousins believed that humor should be only a part of a person's health-care plan.

_____ 9. Lucy watched the movie with Emma.

_____10. Emma probably used a wheelchair or crutches to reach the humor room.

**EXERCISE 13-2**    # Using Inferences

**Directions:** After reading the following selection, select the choice that best completes each of the statements that follow.

### Avatar Fantasy Life: The Blurring Lines of Reality

Dissatisfied with your current life? Would you like to become someone else? Maybe someone rich? Maybe someone with no responsibilities? You can. Join a world populated with virtual people and live out your fantasy.

For some, the appeal is strong. *Second Life*, one of several Internet sites that offer an alternative virtual reality, has exploded in popularity. Of its 8 million "residents," 450,000 spend twenty to forty hours a week in their second life.

To start your second life, you select your avatar, a kind of digital hand puppet, to be your persona in this virtual world. Your avatar comes in just a basic form, although you can control its movements just fine. But that bare body certainly won't do. You will want to clothe it. For this, you have your choice of outfits for every occasion. Although you buy them from other avatars in virtual stores, you have to spend real dollars. You might want some hair, too. For that, too, you'll have your choice of designers. And again, you'll spend real dollars. And you might want to have a sex organ. There is even a specialty store for that.

All equipped the way you want to be?

Then it is time to meet other avatars, the virtual personas of real-life people. In this virtual world, they buy property, open businesses, and interact with one another. They share stories, talk about their desires in life, and have drinks in virtual bars.

Avatars flirt, too. Some even date and marry.

For most people, this second life is just an interesting game. They come and go, as if playing *Tomb Raider* or *World of Warcraft* now and then. Some people, though, get so caught up in their virtual world that their real world shrinks in appeal, and they neglect friends and family. That is, they neglect their real friends and family, but remain attentive to their virtual friends and family. As the virtual replaces the real, the virtual becomes real and the real fades into nonreality.

—Henslin, *Sociology: A Down-to-Earth Approach*, p. 153

_____ **1.** It is likely that people turn to avatars in order to
  **a.** cheat on their spouses.
  **b.** commit crimes without the consequences.
  **c.** improve their computer skills.
  **d.** live a life they couldn't experience otherwise.

_____ **2.** Starting an avatar first involves
  **a.** building its personality.
  **b.** designing its bodily features.
  **c.** choosing its friends.
  **d.** establishing its budget.

_____ **3.** The name of the Internet site *Second Life* suggests that leading a virtual life through an avatar
  **a.** is more complicated than real life.
  **b.** offers users a chance to be successful.
  **c.** is an opportunity to avoid stressful relationships.
  **d.** is second to real life.

_____ **4.** Which fact from the selection supports the idea that some people become too caught up with the virtual world?
  **a.** *Second Life* is an interesting game to most people.
  **b.** You buy avatar clothes from avatars in virtual stores.
  **c.** 450,000 people spend 20 to 40 hours a week on *Second Life*.
  **d.** Avatars flirt.

_____ **5.** What can you infer about people who spend a lot of time on *Second Life*?

    **a.** They are neglecting their real life.

    **b.** They can afford the costs involved.

    **c.** Their virtual connections may be more real than connections with actual people.

    **d.** all of the above

# Assess the Source and Author Qualifications

■ GOAL 3
Assess sources and
author qualifications

Two very important considerations in evaluating any written material are the source in which it was printed and the authority, or qualifications, of the author.

## Considering the Source

Your reaction to and evaluation of printed or online material should take into account its source. Be sure to assess whether or not the writer has carefully researched and accurately reported the subject. Although many writers are careful and accurate, some are not. Often the source of a piece of writing can indicate how accurate, detailed, and well documented the article is.

    Let's consider an example. Suppose you are in the library trying to find information on sleepwalking for a term paper. You locate the following sources, each of which contains an article on sleepwalking. Which would you expect to be the most factual, detailed, and scientific?

■ an encyclopedia entry on sleepwalking

■ an article titled "Strange Things Happen While You Are Sleeping" in *Woman's Day*

■ an article titled "An Examination of Research on Sleepwalking" in *Psychological Review*

You can see that from the source alone you can make predictions about the content and approach used. You would expect the encyclopedia entry to provide only a general overview of the topic. You might expect the article in *Woman's Day* to discuss various abnormalities that occur during sleep; sleepwalking might be only one of several topics discussed. Also, you might expect the article to relate several unusual or extreme cases of sleepwalking, rather than to present a factual analysis of the topic. The article in *Psychological Review,* a journal that reports research in psychology, is the one that would contain a factual, authoritative discussion of sleepwalking.

    Ask the questions in the following Need to Know box to evaluate a source:

## NEED TO KNOW

### How to Evaluate a Source

1. **What reputation does the source have?**

2. **What is the audience for whom the source is intended?**

3. **Are references or documentation provided?**

### Considering the Author's Credentials

To evaluate printed or online material, you must also consider the competency of the author. Use the following guidelines:

- **In textbooks, the author's credentials may be described in one of two places.** The author's college or university affiliation, and possibly his or her title, may appear on the title page beneath the author's name.

- **In nonfiction books and general market paperbacks, a synopsis of the author's credentials and experiences may be included on the book jacket or the back cover.**

- **In newspapers, magazines, and reference books, you are given little or no information about the writer.** You are forced to rely on the judgment of the editors or publishers to assess an author's authority.

EXERCISE 13-3

WORKING TOGETHER

## Evaluating Sources

**Directions:** Working with a classmate, predict and discuss how useful and appropriate each of the following sources would be for the situation described.

1. Using an article from *Working Women* on family aggression for a term paper for your sociology class

   _____

2. Quoting an article in *The New York Times* on recent events in China for a speech titled "Innovation and Change in China"

   _____

3. Reading an article titled "Bilingual Education in the Twenty-First Century" printed in the *Educational Research Quarterly* for a paper arguing for increased federal aid for bilingual education

   _____

4. Using an article in *TV Guide* on television's coverage of crime and violence for a term paper on the effects of television on society

   _____

5. Using information from a book written by former First Lady Nancy Reagan in a class discussion on use and abuse of presidential power

   _____

# Evaluate Internet Sources

■ GOAL 4
Evaluate Internet sources

Although the Internet contains a great deal of valuable information and resources, it also contains rumor, gossip, hoaxes, and misinformation. In other words, not all Internet sources are trustworthy. You must evaluate a source before accepting it. Here are some guidelines to follow when evaluating Internet sources.

## Evaluate the Content of a Web Site

When evaluating the content of a Web site, evaluate its appropriateness, its source, its level of technical detail, its presentation, its completeness, and its links.

**Evaluate Appropriateness**   To be worthwhile a Web site should contain the information you need. That is, it should answer one or more of your search questions. If the site only touches upon answers to your questions but does not address them in detail, check the links on the site to see if they lead you to more detailed information. If they do not, search for a more useful site.

**Evaluate the Source**   Another important step in evaluating a Web site is to determine its source. Ask yourself "Who is the sponsor?" and "Why was this site put up on the Web?" The sponsor of a Web site is the person or organization who paid for its creation and placement on the Web. The sponsor will often suggest the purpose of a Web site. For example, a Web site sponsored by Nike is designed to promote its products, while a site sponsored by a university library is designed to help students learn to use its resources more effectively.

If you are uncertain who sponsors a Web site, check its URL, its copyright, and the links it offers. Another way to check the ownership of a Web site is to try to locate the site's home page.

**Evaluate the Level of Technical Detail**   A Web site's level of technical detail should be suited to your purpose. Some sites may provide information that is too sketchy for your search purposes; others assume a level of background knowledge or technical sophistication that you lack. For example, if you are writing a short, introductory-level paper on global warming, information on the University of New Hampshire's NASA Earth Observing System site (http://www.eos-ids.sr.unh.edu/) may be too technical and contain more information than you need, unless you have some previous knowledge in that field.

**Evaluate the Presentation**   Information on a Web site should be presented clearly; it should be well written. If you find a site that is not clear and well written, you should be suspicious of it. If the author did not take time to present ideas clearly and correctly, he or she may not have taken time to collect accurate information, either.

**Evaluate Completeness**   Determine whether the site provides complete information on its topic. Does it address all aspects of the topic that you feel it should? For example, if a Web site on important twentieth-century American poets does not mention Robert Frost, then the site is incomplete. If you discover that a site is incomplete, search for sites that provide a more thorough treatment of the topic.

**Evaluate the Links**   Many reputable sites supply links to other related sites. Make sure that the links are current. Also check to see if the sites to which you are sent are reliable sources of information. If the links do not work or the sources appear unreliable, you should question the reliability of the site itself. Also determine whether the links provided are comprehensive or only present a representative sample. Either is acceptable, but the site should make clear the nature of the links it is providing.

**EXERCISE 13-4**

# Evaluating Content

**Directions:** Evaluate the content of two of the following sites. Explain why you would either trust or distrust each site as a source of reliable content.

1.  http://www.innercircleofpoets.com

2.  http://www.earlham.edu/~peters/knotlink.htm

3.  http://www.age-of-the-sage.org/psychology/

## Evaluate the Accuracy and Timeliness of a Web Site

When using information on a Web site for an academic paper, it is important to be sure that you have found accurate and up-to-date information. One way to determine the accuracy of a Web site is to compare it with print sources (periodicals and books) on the same topic. If you find a wide discrepancy between the Web site and the printed sources, do not trust the Web site. Another way to determine a site's accuracy is to compare it with other Web sites that address the same topic. If discrepancies exist, further research is needed to determine which site is more accurate.

The site itself will also provide clues about the accuracy of its information. Ask yourself the following questions:

- **Are the author's name and credentials provided?** A well-known writer with established credentials is likely to author only reliable, accurate information. If no author is given, you should question whether the information is accurate.

- **Is contact information for the author included on the site?** Sites often provide an e-mail address where the author may be contacted.

- **Is the information complete or in summary form?** If it is a summary, use the site to find the original source. Original information has less chance of error and is usually preferred in academic papers.

- **If opinions are offered, are they presented clearly as opinions?** Authors who disguise their opinions as facts are not trustworthy.

- **Does the writer make unsubstantiated assumptions or base his or her ideas on misconceptions?** If so, the information presented may not be accurate.

- **Does the site provide a list of works cited?** As with any form of research, sources used to put information up on a Web site must be documented. If sources are not credited, you should question the accuracy of the Web site.

It may be helpful to determine whether the information is available in print form. If it is, try to obtain the print version. Errors may occur when an article or essay is put up on the Web. Web sites move, change, and delete information, so it may be difficult for a reader of an academic paper to locate the Web site that you used in writing it. Also, page numbers are easier to cite in print sources than in electronic ones.

Although the Web is well known for providing up-to-the-minute information, not all Web sites are current. Evaluate a site's timeliness by checking the following dates:

- The date on which the Web site was published (put up on the Web)
- The date when the document you are using was added

- The date when the site was last revised
- The date when the links were last checked

This information is usually provided at the end of the site's home page or at the end of the document you are using.

## EXERCISE 13-5  Evaluating Accuracy and Timeliness

**Directions:** Complete each of the following items.

1. Evaluate the accuracy of two of the following Web sites:

    **a.** http://www.nlf.net/

    **b.** http://www.krysstal.com/democracy.html

    **c.** http://www.idausa.org/facts/pg.html

2. Evaluate the timeliness of two of the following Web sites, using the directions given for each site.

    **a.** http://www.hwg.org/resources/?cid=30
    See when these links were last checked. Find out the consequences by checking the links yourself.

    **b.** http://www.chebucto.ns.ca/Urbancap/
    Evaluate whether this site contains up-to-date information and links for the Community Access Program in Nova Scotia.

    **c.** http://conference.journalists.org/2004conference/
    Explain what information on this site might be useful even though the event is over. How would you find out current information for this conference?

# Distinguish Between Fact and Opinion

■ GOAL 5
Distinguish between fact and opinion

Facts are statements that can be verified—that is, proven to be true. Opinions are statements that express feelings, attitudes, or beliefs and are neither true nor false.

> ### Facts
>
> Martin Luther King, Jr., was assassinated in 1968.
>
> The main source of food for Native Americans was the buffalo.
>
> ### Opinions
>
> Americans should give up their cars and take public transportation instead.
>
> By the year 2025, food shortages will be a major problem in most Asian countries.

Opinions are sometimes signaled by the use of such key words or phrases as *apparently, this suggests, some believe, it is likely that, seemingly, in my view,* and *one explanation is.*

Opinions can be divided into two categories. **Informed opinions** are made by people whose learning and experience qualify them to offer expert opinions. **Uninformed opinions** are made by those who have few qualifications. To determine whether an opinion is informed or not, ask these questions:

■ What experience does this person have regarding the subject matter?

■ What do other respected authorities think of this person?

■ Is the opinion expressed in a respectful way? Or is it expressed in a manner that is disrespectful or intolerant?

■ Does the opinion appear in a respected publication, or is it found on a Web site where people can say whatever they want?

Be sure to read the directions to your writing assignments carefully. If the assignment calls for strictly factual reporting, do not offer your opinion.

## EXERCISE 13-6   Identifying Facts and Opinions

**Directions:** Indicate whether each of the following statements is a fact (F) or an opinion (O).

_____ 1. Alligators provide no physical care for their young.

_____ 2. Humans should be concerned about the use of pesticides that kill insects at the bottom of the food chain.

_____ 3. There are 28 more humans living on Earth now than there were 10 seconds ago.

_____ 4. We must bear greater responsibility for the environment than our ancestors did.

_____ 5. Nuclear power is the only viable solution to our dwindling natural resources.

_____ 6. Between 1850 and 1900 the death rate in Europe decreased due to industrial growth and advances in medicine.

_____ 7. Dogs make the best pets because they can be trained to obey.

_____ 8. Solar energy is available wherever sunlight reaches Earth.

_____ 9. By the year 2020, many diseases, including cancer, will be preventable.

_____ 10. Hormones are produced in one part of the body and carried by the blood to another part of the body where they influence some process or activity.

## EXERCISE 13-7   Distinguishing Between Fact and Opinion

**Directions:** Each of the following paragraphs contains both fact and opinion. Read each paragraph and label each sentence as fact or opinion.

**A.**     [1]Flowering plants that are native to the South include purple coneflower and rose verbena. [2]In the view of many longtime gardeners, these two plants are an essential part of the Southern landscape. [3]Trees that are native to the South include a variety of oaks, as well as flowering dogwoods and redbuds. [4]Dogwoods are especially lovely, with their white, pink, or coral blossoms announcing the arrival of spring. [5]For fall color, the deep red of the Virginia willow makes a spectacular show in the native Southern garden.

1. _____    2. _____    3. _____

4. _____    5. _____

**B.**     [1]Today, many companies provide child-care assistance, either on- or off-site, for their employees. [2]This suggests that employers are becoming aware that their workers' family concerns can affect the company's bottom line. [3]The Eli Lilly pharmaceutical company, for example, has built two child-development centers with a total capacity of more than 400 children. [4]In addition to assistance with daily child care, Bank of America reimburses employees for child-care expenses related to business travel. [5]It seems clear that other, less progressive employers will have to follow these companies' leads in order to attract and retain the best employees.

1. _____    2. _____    3. _____

4. _____    5. _____

**C.**     [1]Preparing a will is an important task that people ignore because they prefer not to think about their own death. [2]However, if you die without a will, the courts will determine how your assets should be distributed, as directed by state law. [3]Even more important than establishing a will, in my opinion, is expressing your willingness to be an organ donor upon your death. [4]Each year, twenty-five thousand new patients are added to the waiting list for organ transplants. [5]The legacy of an organ donor is far more valuable than any material assets put in a will.

1. _____    2. _____    3. _____

4. _____    5. _____

# Evaluate Evidence and Omissions

■ **GOAL 6**

Evaluate data, evidence, and omissions

Many writers who express their opinions, state viewpoints, or make generalizations provide evidence to support their ideas. Your task as a critical reader is to examine this evidence and assess its quality and its adequacy. In addition to evaluating the evidence the author has provided, you must also consider what the author has chosen to leave out. Writers may mislead their readers by omitting important information.

## What Evidence Has the Author Provided?

You should be concerned with two factors: the type of evidence being presented and the relevance of that evidence. Various types of evidence include the following:

■ personal experience or observation

■ statistical data

■ examples, descriptions of particular events, or illustrative situations

- analogies (comparisons with similar situations)
- historical documentation
- experimental evidence
- reasons

Each type of evidence must be weighed in relation to the statement it supports. Acceptable evidence should directly, clearly, and indisputably support the case or issue in question.

## Identifying Evidence

**Directions:** For each of the following statements, discuss the type or types of evidence that you would need in order to support and evaluate the statement with a classmate.

1. Individuals must accept primary responsibility for the health and safety of their babies.

    _____

2. Apologizing is often seen as a sign of weakness, especially among men.

    _____

3. There has been a steady increase in illegal immigration over the past 50 years.

    _____

4. More college women than college men agree that abortions should be legal.

    _____

5. Car advertisements sell fantasy experiences, not means of transportation.

    _____

## What Information Has the Author Omitted?

Writers can mislead their readers by omission. Here are five common ways writers mislead their readers:

1. **Omitting essential details.** The writer may deliberately leave out details that are relevant and important to understanding the topic. Consider whether the writer presents a complete picture of the topic.

2. **Ignoring contradictory evidence or selectively reporting details.** To be fair, a writer should report all of the evidence, not just evidence that he or she wants the reader to know. Does the writer leave out certain details or evidence that contradicts his or her conclusions?

3. **Making an incomplete comparison.** A writer may claim that something is "better" without explaining what it is better *than*. Consider whether the writer has completed the comparison.

4. **Using passive voice.** Writers may avoid revealing information by using a sentence structure that does not identify who performed a specified action.

5. **Using unspecified nouns and pronouns.** Writers may also avoid revealing information by using nouns and pronouns (such as *they* or *it*) that do not refer to a specific person or thing.

**EXERCISE 13-9**

## Analyzing Omissions

**Directions:** For each of the following statements, indicate what information is missing.

1. Our neighborhood was ruined by the water treatment plant.

   _____

2. They raised test scores in that state.

   _____

3. People were hurt by welfare reform.

   _____

4. Some animal testing has been banned in other countries.

   _____

5. Athletes are overpaid.

   _____

6. They say the Columbia River has too many dams.

   _____

7. Anyone can get on the Internet.

   _____

8. They filed charges.

   _____

9. Orchestras in many cities have gone out of business.

   _____

   _____

10. The check was probably forged.

    _____

# Analyze Tone

■ **GOAL 7**
Analyze tone

The tone of a speaker's voice helps you interpret what he or she is saying. If a friend says to you, "Would you mind closing the door?" you can tell by her tone of voice whether she is being polite, insistent, or angry. Or if your brother asks, "Where did you get that coat?" he may mean that he wants to know where you bought it, or maybe he is being sarcastic and really dislikes it. You can tell by his tone of voice. The speaker's tone of voice, then, reveals the intended meaning. Writers also convey a tone, or feeling, through writing. **Tone** refers to the attitude or feeling a writer expresses about his or her subject. Think of tone as the feelings, mood, or emotions that a writer expresses through a piece of writing.

A writer can express a variety of different tones. In the following example, notice how each writer reveals a different attitude toward the same subject:

> We cannot trust our police chief; he is corrupt and completely ignorant of our community's problems.
>
> Our feelings of disappointment over the police chief's actions are overwhelming; we truly believed he would be the one to turn our community around, but he has betrayed us just like his predecessor.
>
> Is anyone really surprised by the scandal surrounding our police chief? Trusting a city official is like trusting a fox in a hen house.

In the first example, the writer is angry, in the second the writer is sad and disappointed, and in the third the writer is cynical. As you can see, writers can express a wide range of tones:

- **An instructive tone.** The writer values his or her subject and thinks it is important for the reader to know about it. Information about the subject is presented in a straightforward, helpful manner.

> When purchasing a piece of clothing, one must be concerned with quality as well as with price. Be certain to check for the following: double-stitched seams, matched patterns, and ample linings.

- **A sympathetic tone.** The writer reveals sympathy or sorrow toward the subject.

> The forlorn, frightened-looking child wandered through the streets alone, searching for someone who would show an interest in helping her find her parents.

- **A convincing tone.** The writer feels his or her ideas are correct and urges readers to accept them.

> Child abuse is a tragic occurrence in our society. Strong legislation is needed to control the abuse of innocent victims and to punish those who are insensitive to the rights and feelings of others. Write to your congressional representative today.

- **An entertaining tone.** The writer finds the subject light and amusing and wishes to share this with his or her readers.

> Gas prices are climbing again, which means some super-hard driving decisions in our family. Driving to the gym is definitely out—besides, walking builds character as well as muscle. And when Cousin Stanley comes to town, I hope he does not expect to be chauffeured around; walking may help him lose a couple of pounds that need to go. Of course, the 50-mile trek to Edgar's Easter Egg Extravaganza is a no-go this spring. Tough times = tough choices!

■ **A nostalgic tone.** The writer is thinking about past times or events. The writer is often sentimental, recalling the past with happiness, sadness, or longing.

> Television is not what it used to be. There was a time when TV shows were truly entertaining and worthwhile. Wouldn't it be wonderful to see shows like *I Love Lucy* or *Batman* again?

■ **An outraged tone.** The writer expresses anger and indignation toward something he or she finds offensive.

> It is appalling that people sit on bus seats talking loudly on their cell phones and expecting me to listen to their ignorant conversations. I'd like to grab their cell phones and throw them out the window.

A writer's tone is intended to rub off on you, so to speak. Tone is also directly tied to the author's purpose (see Chapter 2). A writer whose tone is humorous hopes you will be amused. A writer whose tone is convincing hopes you will accept his or her viewpoint.

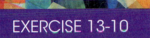

**EXERCISE 13-10**

## Recognizing Tone

**Directions:** Select the word from the box that best describes the tone of each of the following statements. Not all of the words will be used.

| | |
|---|---|
| **optimistic:** hopeful, positive | **disapproving:** disliking, condemning |
| **angry:** extremely annoyed, mad | **formal:** serious, official |
| **admiring:** approving, holding a high opinion | **informative:** factual |
| **cynical:** distrustful, doubting | **sarcastic:** saying the opposite of what is meant |
| **excited:** feeling enjoyment and pleasure | **apathetic:** lacking enthusiasm, energy, or interest |
| **humorous:** amusing, making people laugh | |

1. Taking a young child to a PG-13 movie is inappropriate and shows poor judgment on the part of the parents. _____

2. The brown recluse spider has a dark, violin-shaped marking on the upper section of its body. _____

3. The dedication and determination of the young men and women participating in the Special Olympics were an inspiration to everyone there. _____

4. It does not matter to me which mayoral candidate wins the election, so I won't bother to vote. _____

5. Nobody is ever a complete failure; he or she can always serve as a bad example. _____

6. The councilman once again demonstrated his sensitivity toward the environment when he voted to allow commercial development in an area set aside as a nature preserve. _____

7. The success of the company's youth mentoring program will inspire other business groups to establish similar programs. _____

8. Professional athletes have no loyalty toward their teams or their fans anymore, just their own wallets. _____

9. We were thrilled to learn that next year's convention will be held in San Antonio—we've always wanted to see the Alamo! _____

10. To be considered for the president's student-of-the-year award, an individual must demonstrate academic excellence as well as outstanding community service, and the individual must furnish no fewer than four letters of reference from faculty members. _____

**EXERCISE 13-11**

# Reading Critically

**Directions:** Read the following paragraph, and think analytically and critically when you answer the questions that follow.

> In survey after survey, 60 to 80 percent of food shoppers say they read food labels before selecting products; they consume more vegetables, fruits, and lower-fat foods; and they are cutting down on portion sizes and total calories. Diet-book sales are at an all-time high as millions of people make the leap toward what they think is healthy eating. But we still have a long way to go. In fact, although reports indicate that increasing numbers of us read labels and are trying to eat more healthfully, nearly 78% of all adults indicate that they are not eating the recommended servings of fruits and vegetables and that they are still eating too many refined carbohydrates and high-fat foods.
>
> —Donatelle, *Health*, p. 255

1. The passage talks about surveys, which is another word for *questionnaires*. Why might the survey results not truly reflect reality?

   _____

   _____

2. Does the fact that diet-book sales are at an all-time high mean that more people are going on diets and/or eating more healthfully? In a sentence or two, explain why or why not.

   _____

   _____

3. Write a sentence or two summarizing the author's opinion regarding a good way to eat more healthfully. Do you agree or disagree with this opinion?

_____

_____

4. Have you ever watched a friend, co-worker, or family member start a diet? On a separate sheet of paper, write a paragraph describing that person's approach to dieting. For example, did he or she decide to start exercising every morning? Did his or her approach work?

## WRITING

# Think Critically When Writing

■ GOAL 8
Think critically when writing

It is important for writers, as well as readers, to think critically—to examine their ideas and make sure they are logical and reasonable. Use the following suggestions to apply the critical thinking skills taught earlier in the chapter to your own writing.

## Inferences

If you want to be completely sure that your readers understand your message, state it directly. If you only imply an idea and do not directly state it, there is a chance your reader may miss your point. Worse yet, there is a possibility that less than careful readers may infer an idea you had not intended, creating a misunderstanding or miscommunication.

There are occasions on which you may deliberately leave an idea unstated. You may want to lead you readers to an idea, but let them figure it out for themselves, thinking it was their idea. Especially in argument, you may want to lead your readers to take action or accept a particular viewpoint, but you may prefer not to make a direct plea. When doing so, be sure to supply enough detail and evidence so your readers make the desired inference.

## Source and Authority

As critical thinkers, your readers will assess your qualifications and knowledge of the subject you are writing about. Many factors can create an image of you as a serious, competent writer, qualified to write on your topic. These include

■ **A correct, error-free essay that is neatly presented**. Readers may assume that if you haven't taken the time to present your paper carefully, you may not have taken the time to research or think through your ideas, either.

■ **A well-documented paper**. If you use sources, be sure to give your sources credit using in-text citations and a Works Cited list. See Chapter 17 for more detailed information on how to do this. Failure to credit sources is dishonest, and your readers may realize it.

■ **An honest approach to your topic**. If you are not an expert on your topic, don't present yourself as one. Avoid using an authoritative tone. If you do have expertise on your topic, you might build mention of your expertise into the essay for the purpose of establishing your credibility. For example, if you are a first-responder for your community volunteer fire company and are writing about accidents that occur when drivers are texting, you might acknowledge your experience responding to accidents.

## Fact and Opinion

Facts are the building blocks of many paragraphs and are essential to good writing. Opinions, however, may or may not be appropriate, depending on your purpose and the nature of the writing task or assignment. If you are writing a summary, for instance, your opinion of the material does not belong in it. If you are writing a research paper, your personal opinions are not useful or appropriate.

In some other types of assignments, the use of personal opinion may be appropriate, as long as you substantiate or provide evidence to support it. In writing a response to a poem for a literature class, for example, it is certainly appropriate to express your reactions and feelings about it, as long as you support your opinions with references to the poem. Or in writing an essay about Super Bowl advertising, you may express a viewpoint that the commercials are the best part of the show or that they are extravagant wastes of money. Again, you should give reasons, examples, and so forth to support your viewpoint. Never just offer opinions without explanation and justification.

## Data and Evidence

As you draft essays, one of your main tasks is to provide adequate, reliable, and appropriate data and evidence to support your thesis statement. (For more on using evidence to support your thesis, see Chapter 11, p. 340.) Good writers try to vary the data they choose to suit their audience and their purpose. Examples may be appropriate for one audience, but facts and statistics may be more appealing to another. To achieve your purpose, select your evidence carefully. If your purpose is to persuade your readers to take action, such as to vote for a particular political candidate, reasons are needed. But you may also want to include descriptions of the candidate's achievements or draw comparisons to other successful political figures.

Be sure not to omit details that are relevant and important to the topic. Doing so will make your readers distrust you and question your ideas.

## Tone

The tone you use contributes to or detracts from meaning. Be sure to use a tone that is appropriate for your readers. Consider the following factors about your readers.

■ **Knowledge of the topic**. If your readers are not knowledgeable about the topic, you might use a supportive, helpful tone. If they are familiar with the topic, the same helpful, supportive tone may be insulting.

■ **Background and experience of your readers.** Consider the education level, training, professional position, and factors such as age and gender when adopting a tone. A letter written to a panel of community leaders might use a deferential tone because they expect to be treated with respect, while a letter to an editor might use a less formal, but informative tone.

■ **Attitudes and beliefs of your readers.** If your readers are likely to agree with your ideas, using a strongly emotional tone may seem inappropriate and unnecessary. If your readers are likely to disagree with your ideas, an energetic, positive, convincing tone may help sway your readers.

## Applying Critical Thinking Skills to Writing

**Directions:** Assume that you have been assigned to write an essay on one of the topics below. On a separate sheet of paper, describe how you would approach the assignment, including what sources you would use, whether your paragraph would include opinion as well as fact, what data and evidence you would use to support your thesis, and what tone you would use.

1. the health benefits of coffee (or another food of your choice)

2. the qualities of a good teacher or coach

3. the value of volunteer work

## Analyzing an Essay

**Directions:** Choose an essay you have written for this class or for another college class. Evaluate your essay using each of the following questions and make any revisions that are needed.

1. Highlight any paragraphs that require your reader to make inferences. Have you supplied sufficient detail and evidence for any inferences you expect your readers to make?

2. Examine how your essay is presented. Have you presented yourself as a serious, competent writer?

3. Underline any statement of opinion. Have you provided reasons, examples, or other evidence for any opinions you offer?

4. Evaluate whether you have provided sufficient evidence to support your thesis.

5. Choose a word or phrase that describes your tone. Is it suitable for your purpose or audience?

# INTEGRATING READING AND WRITING

## READ AND RESPOND: A Student Essay

*Santiago Quintana Garcia will be a sophomore at Beloit College this fall, where he plans to major in Literature.*

**Title captures reader's interest and suggests the topic**

# Life Between the Tropics
## Quintana Garcia

**Introduction provides background information about the author**

1    In elementary school, I was taught that the earth moves through four seasons. I was born in the mountains of Mexico City, and currently live in Beloit, Wisconsin, where what I learnt in school finally matches what I see outside my window. Summer, for most people around the world, means the bright sun and thick, humid air. Sometimes this is freshened by rains and mountain, sea or plain breezes. Nearer to the equator, between the tropics of Cancer and Capricorn, the seasons are different. Life between the tropics looks like June paid February a visit, and stayed for too long. **Thesis** I didn't take well to monthly changes in the weather when I came to Beloit: between the tropics, trees lose leaves because kids pluck them in the middle of January, not because winter takes them away.

**Topic sentence**

2    My childhood and adolescence revolved around *Desierto de los Leones National Park*. Here, I took a break from smog and car exhaust and breathed fresh forest air. This park was a place where my family would go on the weekends when I was seven, where my mother took me to collect leaves for my collection when I was ten, where I went to find peace and quiet when I needed it as a teenager, and where I had my first encounter with ecology in my late teens. I would swing from branch to branch like a **Descripative details and quotation support topic sentence** monkey, and the branches would still hold me, no matter my age. In the park, among the trees and the moss, "I was green and carefree," in the words of Dylan Thomas. I would be woken up by the songs of owlets and swallows from the mountains. This was January, or November, or June, or anything you want. This, of course, would change along with many parts of my life when I decided to attend college in Wisconsin.

3    Beloit College is located in Beloit, Wisconsin. It is a small liberal arts school where you can have tea with your teachers and twenty in a classroom is way too **Topic sentence** many. I was to learn first appearances can be deceptive. Upon arriving at Beloit, I met The United States in the summer. It was similar to the mountain summer that **Vivid details** I knew so well, more extreme. The cicadas screamed so loud that my ears buzzed even when I slept. Breathing was hard and heavy. The birds sang cries for help, breeding for survival. Summer in this country, far from the tropics, had a cutting

Descriptive language

edge to it. I could not distinguish between the air's moisture and my own sweat. It felt like I was in nature's stomach, and it was digesting me, breaking me up into little pieces. This, like many things in life, did not last very long. Before I could make sense of any of it, nature changed and displayed the most beautiful red, gold and brown colors I have ever seen. In nature, the prettiest creatures are often the most poisonous. Sure enough, as I fell in love with beautiful colored leaves, nature took them away from me too. Then snow covered everything my eye could see.

Transition

I noticed the air was thin and sharp, and there was no echo any more, like a room with many carpets. Where are the cicadas?

Descriptive details leading up to topic sentence

4    From my science courses, I knew this was happening because of the placement of our planet in relation to the sun and the moon. The novelty of the situation crept into every cell of my body and raised every hair in my back. Polar bears know how to glide through the frozen tundras they call home. Penguins' webbed feet allow them to swim at incredible speeds and their specialized feathers keep them warm enough among icy crystals and snow. In arctic Wisconsin tundras, I feel like an African lion. I don't know how to avoid the ice blocks and the snow storms and wish I had webbed feet and a gliding belly to catch the seal I need

Topic sentence

due tomorrow at ten in the morning. Winter was not my home.

Vivid details

5    I dreamed of shorts and tank tops in the hazy city downtown. I could almost smell the pine needles in my beloved forest miles away. Winter, instead of pine needles, had air that made my skin dry. Afternoon tea heated my body after class and kept alive the memories of the forest and the streams. I was trapped be-

Topic sentence

tween homework assignment and homework assignment. All I could do was read about summer and forests and dream. Then, the dream began coming true.

Descriptive language

6    My roommate woke me one morning by calling, "It's warm outside!" My mind was too asleep to take a joke like this one so early in the morning. Like ice, it had to be warmed up back to life slowly, not with a hit of a hammer. I dressed up for winter like I had done every day; covering my sleepy self with three or four layers of clothes. My roommate kept laughing at me, but I didn't pay any attention and continued. Then, in a crack in the pavement I saw a bud of a dandelion, and its bright yellow petals finally woke me up completely. I ran back to my room into my summer clothes and back outside, smiling widely. I was born in the mountains of

The conclusion restates the thesis

Mexico City and in my first year at Beloit College, I didn't take very well to seasons

The essay ends on a positive note

and life outside the tropics. But a yellow dandelion left one thing very clear; it all depends on where you stand and where you look.

## Examining Writing

1.  What types of evidence does the author use throughout the essay? Can you find examples of facts and opinions in this essay?

2.  What inferences can you make based on this essay? What details support your inferences?

3.  How would you describe the author's tone in this essay? Identify words and sentences that reveal his attitude toward his subject.

4.  Explain the meaning of the title and evaluate its effectiveness.

## Writing Assignments

1. In parts of the essay, the author longs for his home in the tropics. Write a paragraph describing a time when you were homesick, or longing to be in another place.

2. The author concludes his essay by saying, "it all depends on where you stand and where you look." Write a paragraph explaining what the author means and how you might apply this philosophy to a situation in your own life.

3. What types of adjustments did you have to make in your first year of college? Write an essay describing your experience and explaining how you coped with the changes you faced.

## READ AND RESPOND: A Professional Essay

### Thinking Before Reading

The following reading, "Are Latinos Different?" was written by Sandra Márquez, a Los Angeles–based journalist. In this article, which appeared on Hispanic-Magazine.com, Márquez addresses the health differences between Hispanics and non-Hispanic whites in the United States, as well as the implications for medical research, in the context of Proposition 54. This was a California ballot initiative that would have banned state officials from gathering information on race and ethnicity; it was defeated in September 2003.

1. Preview the reading, using the steps discussed in Chapter 1, page 15.
2. Connect the reading to your own experience by answering the following questions:
    a. What is racial or ethnic profiling?
    b. Do health issues vary among different ethnic groups?
3. Mark and annotate as you read.

# Are Latinos Different?

## Sandra Márquez

**taboo**
forbidden

1    Profiling, the practice of compiling data for the purpose of making generalizations about a particular race or ethnic group, is considered taboo, or at least politically incorrect, when it comes to criminal behavior or traffic stops. In terms of science, most anyone who received a U.S. public school education was taught that, despite different skin colors, all human bodies were created equally. There was no genetic difference among races.

2    So why the growing trend toward "medical profiling"? Why the need to do medical research that specifically looks at health patterns of Hispanics? The answer is simple, according to Dr. David Hayes-Bautista, director of the Center for the Study of Latino Health and Culture at the University of California Los Angeles. The more than 38 million Latinos living in the United States represent an

**epidemiological**

referring to the branch of medicine that studies the causes, distribution, and control of diseases in populations

**paradox**

a statement that seems contradictory but is true

**cultura**

culture

"**epidemiological paradox**." Despite popular conceptions, Latinos live longer and have a lower incidence of heart attacks, the leading forms of cancer and strokes than the general public, and it is important to know why.

3    The difference isn't a genetic one, according to the doctor. His research on the topic has convinced him that the generally good health of Hispanics is rooted in **cultura**, and by studying Latino health patterns, he believes that the general public will benefit.

4    "Although Latino populations may generally be described as low-income and low-education with little access to care, Latino health outcomes are generally far better than those of non-Hispanic whites," Hayes-Bautista writes in *Latinos: Remaking America*, published in 2002 by Harvard University and the University of California Press. "This paradox has been observed in so many Latino populations in so many regions over so many years that its existence cries out to be explained," states Hayes-Bautista.

5    The flip side of his research also merits further inquiry. Hispanics have a high incidence of diabetes—64 percent higher than white Americans—AIDS and cirrhosis of the liver, the latter of which is higher among Hispanics than any other group. Recent studies looking specifically at Hispanic health patterns have been conducted by the American Cancer Society, the American Heart Association and the National Alliance of State and Territorial AIDS Directors.

6    The Cancer Society study found that Hispanics are less likely than white Americans to develop and die from lung, breast, prostate and colon cancer—while being more prone to the less common cancer of the cervix, liver and gall bladder. The Heart Association study found that Type 2 diabetes has reached epidemic proportions among Hispanics. And the AIDS study found that Hispanics, who comprise 13 percent of the U.S. population, account for 20 percent of those living with AIDS.

7    But the issue of medical profiling is not without controversy. The debate is reflected in a California ballot measure to be decided Oct. 7, 2003. Proposition 54, dubbed the Racial Privacy Act, would bar state officials from gathering data on race and ethnicity. The initiative's website (www.racialprivacy.org) claims the measure is a step toward creating a "colorblind society." "As the most ethnically diverse state in the Union, California has the most to gain by compelling its government to treat all citizens equally and without regard to race. The latest U.S. Census divides Americans into a whopping 126 different ethnic/racial categories. How many categories should Californians put up with?" it asks.

8    Although Proposition 54's backers say the new law would include an exemption for medical research, prominent groups, such as Kaiser Permanente and the California Health Association, appear unconvinced and have opposed the measure.

9    Oscar Cisneros, a policy analyst for the Latino Issues Forum, a public policy and advocacy institute in San Francisco, said the medical research exemption would only apply to clinical settings. If approved, he said the measure would make it harder

for public health officials who rely on government data to tailor messages to specific risk groups. It would also have implications for tracking a public health threat such as SARS, which originated in China, Cisneros says. "It's not like they force people to reveal their race," Cisneros says of government demographic data. "It's all voluntary information that allows them to get a better picture of what is really going on."

10      Lorenzo Abundiz, 50, a retired Santa Ana, California, firefighter who was told he had just weeks to live after being diagnosed with a rare form of sarcoma cancer five years ago, said he would like to see medical research focus on one thing—finding a cure for all cancers. "Cancer has no preference. It will get everyone: black, white, Mexican. It will nail you. I want to see where everybody bonds together, like cancer survivors like me, and says, 'Let's find a cure,'" says Abundiz, who in July underwent a CAT scan indicating he was in full remission.

11      Abundiz received a state firefighter medal of valor for rescuing two fellow firefighters from a tire shop fire by single-handedly lifting a 500-pound wall without wearing protective breathing gear. He has also been lauded for rescuing pets from burning homes and in June 2001, he married his sweetheart, Peggy, in New York's Times Square in front of millions of viewers on ABC's *Good Morning America*. He believes toxic exposure on the job made him susceptible to cancer. Nonetheless, it does run in his family. His father died of prostate cancer. He credits the love of his wife, a vegetarian diet, and learning to live more with nature by "letting butterflies land on my fingers and seeing God in nature" for his survival.

12      Dr. Hayes-Bautista says a "Latino norm" is apparent in all of his medical research. He believes "something that Latinos do each day" explains Hispanic health patterns and further study could lead to a reduction of heart disease, cancer and strokes in the population at large. "At the larger level, it has to be culture, which would include what people eat. It probably has to include family or social networks, and it [even] might have something to do with spirituality, the mind-body connection," he says.

## Getting Ready to Write

### Checking Your Comprehension

Answer each of the following questions using complete sentences.

1. Define the term *profiling*.

2. Briefly compare Latinos with non-Hispanic whites on the following health issues discussed in the article. (The first one is done for you.)

   **a.** length of life: Latinos live longer. _____

   **b.** heart attacks: _____

   **c.** diabetes: _____

   **d.** AIDS: _____

   **e.** cirrhosis of the liver: _____

   **f.** lung, breast, prostate, and colon cancer: _____

   _____

3. What does Dr. Hayes-Bautista believe is at the root of Hispanics' generally good health?

4. What is the purpose of California's Proposition 54?

5. Why was Lorenzo Abundiz awarded a medal of valor?

6. What does Lorenzo Abundiz believe made him susceptible to cancer?

## Strengthening Your Vocabulary

Using the word's context, word parts, or a dictionary, write a brief definition of each of the following words as it is used in the reading.

1. epidemic (paragraph 6) _____

2. controversy (paragraph 7) _____

3. exemption (paragraph 8) _____

4. remission (paragraph 10) _____

   _____

5. valor (paragraph 11) _____

6. lauded (paragraph 11) _____

7. susceptible (paragraph 11) _____

## Examining the Reading: Using an Idea Map

Draw an idea map of the reading, starting with the title and thesis and listing the main ideas.

## Reacting to Ideas: Discussion and Journal Writing

Get ready to write about the reading by discussing the following:

1. What is controversial about medical profiling?

2. Why does the good health of Hispanics present a paradox?

3. Explain what is meant by the phrase "a colorblind society" (paragraph 7).

4. Evaluate the quality of the supporting evidence in this article. What sources does the author draw upon for information? How credible are they?

## Thinking and Writing Critically

1. What is the author's purpose for writing this article? Who is her intended audience?

2. What inferences can you make based on the material in this article? Be sure your inferences are supported by facts.

3. Describe the author's tone and explain why her use of the Spanish word *cultura* (paragraph 3) was appropriate in this article.

4. How does the photo support the thesis of the article?

**THINKING VISUALLY**

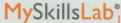

MySkillsLab®

Complete
this
Exercise

## Writing About the Reading

### Paragraph Options

1. Why do you think the author wrote about Lorenzo Abundiz in this article? Write a paragraph explaining who he is and why his story is significant.

2. Have you ever felt that you were stereotyped—or even profiled—based on some aspect of your identity (for example, age, ethnicity, or gender)? Write a paragraph describing your experience.

3. Do you think Proposition 54 should have been passed? Write a paragraph explaining why or why not.

### Essay Options

4. In the context of Dr. Hayes-Bautista's research, *culture* includes what people eat, their family or social networks, and spirituality. Write an essay describing these aspects of your culture and how they could affect your own health. Feel free to include other aspects of your culture that may be relevant to your health.

5. In addition to medical profiling, many other medical issues provoke debate and/or controversy. Choose an issue, such as stem-cell research or medicinal marijuana, and write an essay taking a stand on one side of the issue. Be sure to include evidence to support your argument and to persuade your readers to accept your point of view.

6. According to the article, supporters of Proposition 54 object to the U.S. census's "whopping 126 different ethnic/racial categories" for Americans. How do you feel about being asked to place yourself in a particular category? Write an essay describing your response to requests for personal information about yourself, whether in a national census or on a college application or some other type of form. Are you ever concerned about how the information will be used?

## SELF-TEST SUMMARY

To test yourself, cover the Answer column with a sheet of paper and answer each question in the left column. Evaluate each of your answers as you work by sliding the paper down and comparing your answer with what is printed in the Answer column.

| QUESTION | ANSWER |
| --- | --- |
| ■ GOAL 1 Understand the benefits of thinking critically <br><br> What are the benefits of critical thinking? | Critical thinking allows you to distinguish good information from inaccurate or incomplete information and to show in your writing a strong understanding of what you've read. |

| QUESTION | ANSWER |
|---|---|
| ■ **GOAL 2** Make inferences<br><br>What is an inference and how do you make inferences? | An inference is an educated guess about something unknown based on available information. To make an inference, understand the literal meaning first, notice details, add up the facts, notice the writer's choice of words, understand the writer's purpose, and be sure your inference is supportable. |
| ■ **GOAL 3** Assess sources and author qualifications<br><br>How do you evaluate the source of material and the qualifications of the author? | To evaluate a source, consider the source's reputation, the audience for whom the source is intended, and whether documentation or references are provided. Look for a textbook author's credentials on the title page; for nonfiction books and general market paperbacks, look on the book jacket or back cover. |
| ■ **GOAL 4** Evaluate Internet sources<br><br>What factors should be considered when evaluating Internet sources? | Evaluate content by considering appropriateness, source, level of technical detail, and presentation. Also evaluate the accuracy and timeliness of the site. |
| ■ **GOAL 5** Distinguish between fact and opinion<br><br>What is the difference between facts and opinions? | Facts are statements that can be verified, or proven to be true. Opinions are statements that express feelings, attitudes, or beliefs and are neither true nor false. |
| ■ **GOAL 6** Evaluate data, evidence, and omissions<br><br>How do you evaluate evidence? How do writers mislead by omission? | Consider the type of evidence being presented and the relevance of that evidence. Writers mislead by omitting essential details, ignoring contradictory evidence, making incomplete comparisons, using the passive voice, and using unspecified nouns and pronouns. |
| ■ **GOAL 7** Analyze tone<br><br>What is tone and what are some examples of tone? | Tone refers to the attitude or feeling a writer expresses about his or her subject. Six words commonly used to describe tone are *instructive, sympathetic, convincing, entertaining, nostalgic,* and *outraged.* |
| ■ **GOAL 8** Think critically when writing<br><br>What is involved in thinking critically when writing? | Think critically when writing by stating ideas directly; presenting work that is correct, neat, well documented, and honest; considering whether opinions are appropriate; providing adequate and reliable evidence; and using the appropriate tone for your readers. |

For more help with **Making Inferences and Analyzing the Author's Message**, go to your learning path in MySkillsLab at www.myskillslab.com.

## 14

# Critical Thinking: Evaluating the Author's Techniques

## THINK About It!

How would you describe the person in the photo? Words like *modern*, *individualistic*, and *unique* may come to mind. However, no matter how you would describe her, one thing is clear: she expresses herself very clearly through her sense of style. The same way that people express individual style through hair, clothing, and jewelry choices, authors express themselves with a variety of techniques that move beyond simple words on a page. In this chapter you will see how writers can persuade using colorful language, make assumptions and generalizations that may or may not be based on facts, and reveal their biases. Thinking critically about an author's techniques will improve your reading skills and help you write more effectively.

# Reading and Writing Connections

## EVERYDAY CONNECTIONS

- **Reading** You read a parenting blog that addresses the question of when children are old enough to be left at home alone. One writer makes a generalization that all children over 12 are old enough, while another makes an assumption that the parents of "latch-key kids" don't want to pay for child care.
- **Writing** You write a response based on your experience as a elementary school teacher (and as a parent), suggesting ways to determine when a child is ready to be left at home alone. You make it clear that you are expressing a bias by beginning your comments with the phrase, "In my opinion."

## ACADEMIC CONNECTIONS

- **Reading** You read an article assigned in your economics class in which the writer compares the U.S. housing market to a roller coaster on which many "riders" started out excited and thrilled but were sick to their stomachs by the time the ride ended.
- **Writing** For an exam in economics, you write an essay discussing the factors that led to the mortgage crisis. You are careful to provide adequate and sufficient evidence, and you decide to revise your word choice for describing mortgage brokers from "greedy con artists" to "unscrupulous lenders."

## WORKPLACE CONNECTIONS

- **Reading** In your part-time job at a discount retail store, you read an inventory bulletin indicating that toy trucks and foam dart guns are to be stocked under "Boys' Activities" and arts-and-crafts items are to be stocked under "Girls' Interests."
- **Writing** You write an e-mail to your manager proposing that the inventory categories be revised so that toys are stocked in aisles according to age or type of activity rather than according to assumptions based on gender.

# FOCUSING ON READING AND WRITING

# Why Evaluate the Author's Techniques?

■ **GOAL 1**
Evaluate the author's techniques

Critical thinking, reading, and writing involve examining not only *what* is said but *how* it is said. Readers need to consider what an author is trying to accomplish and what techniques he or she uses to do so. Writers need to carefully choose techniques that will help them achieve their purpose, convey their message, and reach their audience.

In this chapter you will learn to look at language and discover how word choice affects meaning. You will learn to be alert for assumptions and generalizations—beliefs held by writers that are not necessarily stated but underlie their assertions—which have an impact on the strength or validity of their stated ideas. You will also be asked to consider your assumptions and to use them appropriately as you write. Finally, you will learn to look for bias in what you read and become aware of bias in your own writing.

## READING

# Understand Connotative and Figurative Language

■ GOAL 2
Understand connotative and figurative language

Writers know that words influence a reader greatly, and they choose their words carefully. For this reason, reading critically involves understanding the connotative meanings of words and how they affect the reader, as well as understanding and evaluating figurative language.

## Connotative Language

If you were wearing a jacket that looked like leather but was made out of man-made fibers, would you prefer it be called *fake* or *synthetic*? Would you rather be part of a *crowd* or a *mob*?

Each word in the pairs above has basically the same meaning. A *crowd* and a *mob* are both groups of people. Both *fake* and *synthetic* refer to something man-made. If the words have similar meanings, why did you choose *crowd* rather than *mob* and *synthetic* rather than *fake*? While the pairs of words have similar primary meanings, they carry different shades of meaning called connotative meanings.

All words have one or more standard meanings. These meanings are called **denotative meanings.** Think of them as dictionary meanings. They tell us what the words name. Many words also have connotative meanings. **Connotative meanings** include the feelings and associations that may accompany a word. For example, the denotative meaning of *sister* is a female sibling. However, the word carries many connotations. For some, *sister* suggests a playmate with whom they shared their childhood. For others, the term may suggest an older sibling who watched over them.

Connotations can vary from individual to individual. The denotative meaning for the word *flag* is a piece of cloth used as a national emblem. To many, the American flag is a symbol of patriotism and love of one's country. To some people, though, it may mean an interesting decoration to place on their clothing.

Writers use connotative meanings to stir your emotions or to bring to mind positive or negative associations. Suppose a writer is describing how someone drinks. The writer could choose words such as *gulp, sip, slurp,* or *guzzle*. Each creates a different image of the person. Connotative meanings, then, are powerful tools of language. When you read, be alert for meanings suggested by the author's word choice. When writing, be sure to choose words with appropriate connotations.

## EXERCISE 14-1

# Recognizing Connotative Meanings

**Directions:** For each of the following pairs of words, underline the word with the more positive connotation.

1. dent        dimple
2. bold        brash
3. cheap       frugal
4. displease   repel
5. tipsy       drunk

6. agony       ache
7. untidy      grubby
8. haughty     proud
9. deckhand    sailor
10. job        chore

## EXERCISE 14-2

# Using Connotative Meanings

**Directions:** For each word listed, write a word that has a similar denotative meaning but a negative connotation. Then write a word that has a positive or neutral connotation.

| Word | Negative Connotation | Positive or Neutral Connotation |
|------|----------------------|---------------------------------|
| Example: costly | extravagant | expensive |
| 1. leisurely | | |
| 2. small | | |
| 3. take | | |
| 4. talk | | |
| 5. satirize | | |
| 6. farmer | | |
| 7. choosy | | |
| 8. delay | | |
| 9. desire | | |
| 10. famous | | |

## EXERCISE 14-3

*WORKING TOGETHER*

# Analyzing Connotative Meanings

**Directions:** With two of your classmates, discuss the differences in connotative meaning of each of the following sets of words. Consult a dictionary, if necessary.

1. **painful:** hurtful—sore—excruciating
2. **aware:** familiar—alert—privy
3. **room:** chamber—study—cubicle

4. **someone who travels:** globe-trotter—tourist—pilgrim

5. **understanding:** mastery—insight—comprehension

6. **harmony:** agreement—conformity—order

7. **education:** literacy—schooling—learning

8. **proper:** correct—appropriate—demure

9. **seclusion:** isolation—privacy—withdrawal

10. **lovable:** adorable—attractive—winning

## Figurative Language

**Figurative language** makes a comparison between two unlike things that share one common characteristic. If you say that your apartment looked as if it had been struck by a tornado, you are comparing two unlike things—your apartment and the effects of a tornado. Figurative language makes sense creatively or imaginatively, but not literally. You mean that the apartment is messy and disheveled. Figurative language is a powerful tool that allows writers to create images or paint pictures in the reader's mind. Figurative language also allows writers to suggest an idea without directly stating it. If you say the councilman bellowed like a bear, you are suggesting that the councilman was animal-like, loud, and forceful, but you have not said so directly. By planting the image of bear-like behavior, you have communicated your message to your reader.

There are three primary types of figurative language—*similes*, *metaphors*, and *personification*. A **simile** uses the words *like* or *as* to make the comparison:

> The computer hums like a beehive.
>
> After 5:00 P.M. our downtown is as quiet as a ghost town.

A **metaphor** states or implies the relationship between the two unlike items. Metaphors often use the word *is*.

> The computer lab is a beehive.
>
> After 5:00 P.M. our downtown is a ghost town.

**Personification** compares humans and nonhumans according to one characteristic, attributing human characteristics to ideas or objects. If you say "the wind screamed its angry message," you are giving the wind the humanlike characteristics of screaming, being angry, and communicating a message. Here are two more examples:

> The sun mocked us with its relentless stare.
>
> After two days of writer's block, her pen started dancing across the page.

Be sure to analyze the author's motive for using figurative language. Often, a writer uses it as a way of describing rather than telling. A writer could say "The woman blushed" (telling) or "The woman's cheeks filled with the glow of a fire" (describing).

## NEED TO KNOW

### How to Evaluate Figurative Language

When evaluating figurative language, ask the following questions:

1. Why did the writer make the comparison?
2. What is the basis of the comparison, that is, the shared characteristic?
3. Is the comparison accurate?
4. What images do you have in your mind? How do these images make you feel?
5. Is the comparison positive or negative?
6. Are several different interpretations possible?

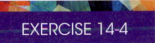

## EXERCISE 14-4    Understanding Figurative Language

**Directions:** Explain the comparison in each of the following examples of figurative language.

1. The view from the summit was like a painting.
2. Her memory was a blank tablet.
3. The library renovation project was an uncontrollable beast.
4. During the morning commute, the lanes of cars were snarled like a nest of snakes.
5. As the tide rolled in, the waves roared at her to escape quickly.

## EXERCISE 14-5    Analyzing Figurative Language

*WORKING TOGETHER*

**Directions:** With a classmate, discuss how the writer of each of the following passages uses figurative language to create a specific impression. Then compare your analysis with those of your classmates.

1.  As a vacation port of call, Southern California has got it all. It's like a giant geographic theme park. Want to lap up glistening waves and bury your feet in the sand? The beach beckons. How about thick forests with fir- and pine-covered mountains? The majestic Angeles National Forest is a quick drive from Los Angeles. I prefer to use Dante's "Inferno" as my Baedeker [a guidebook for travelers]. Every summer, whenever I get the itch for a little rest and relaxation, I venture deep into the inner circle of hell—otherwise known as Palm Springs.
    —Mark Weingarten, "Palm Springs in August: The Ducks Use Sunblock,"
    *The New York Times,* August 9, 2002

2. Thick as a truck at its base, the Brazil-nut tree rises 10 stories to an opulent crown, lord of the Amazon jungle. It takes the tree a century to grow to maturity; it takes a man with a chain saw an hour to cut it down. "It's a beautiful thing," nods Acelino Cardoso da Silva, a 57-year-old farmer. "But I have six hungry people at home. If the lumberman turns up, I'll sell."

—Margolis, "A Plot of Their Own," *Newsweek*

3. If parenting is like an endurance race, senior year should be the section where parents triumphantly glide toward the finish line with a smiling graduate-to-be alongside. Instead, it's often more like heartbreak hill at the 20-mile mark of the Boston marathon, the bump that leaves parents exhausted and wondering what they were thinking 17 years ago.

—Dunnewind, "Launching Kids to Independence," *Seattle Times*

---

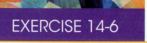
**EXERCISE 14-6**

## Writing Figurative Expressions

**Directions:** Convert each of the following statements into a sentence using figurative language.

Example: I am nervous. _I feel as if I have a thousand butterflies fluttering in my stomach._

1. He was hungry. _____

_____

2. The clouds were beautiful. _____

_____

3. Everyone argued. _____

_____

4. The test was hard. _____

_____

5. My friend laughed. _____

_____

---

# Analyze Assumptions

■ **GOAL 3**
Analyze assumptions

Suppose a friend asked you, "Have you stopped cheating on your girlfriend?" This person, perhaps not a friend after all, is making an assumption. He or she is assuming that you already have been cheating. An **assumption** is an idea or principle the writer accepts as true and makes no effort to prove or substantiate. Assumptions often use words such as *since, if,* or *when.* Here are a few more examples:

> You're going to make that mistake again, are you? (The assumption is that you have already made the mistake at least once.)
>
> When you're mature, you'll realize you made a mistake. (The assumption is that you are not mature now.)

> You are as arrogant as your sister. (The assumption is that your sister is arrogant.)
>
> My dog is angry. (The assumption is that dogs have and can express emotions.)

Each of the statements above makes no attempt to prove or support the hidden assumption; it is assumed to be true.

Writers often make assumptions and make no effort to prove or support them. For example, an author may assume that television encourages violent behavior in children and proceed to argue for restrictions on TV viewing. If a writer's assumption is wrong or unsubstantiated, then the statements that follow from the assumption should be questioned. If television does not encourage violent behavior, for example, then the suggestion to restrict viewing should not be accepted unless other reasons are offered to support it.

## EXERCISE 14-7 | Identifying Assumptions

**Directions:** Read each of the following statements and then place a check mark before those choices that are assumptions made by the writer of the statement.

1. Cosmetics should not be tested on animals, since they may cause pain, injury, or even death.

    _____ a. Animals have the right to avoid pain and suffering.

    _____ b. Cosmetics should be tested on people.

    _____ c. Animals should be anesthetized before research is conducted.

2. Teacher's aides lack advanced college degrees: therefore, they are unable to teach children effectively.

    _____ a. Teacher's aides should obtain advanced degrees.

    _____ b. Advanced college degrees are needed in order to teach effectively.

    _____ c. Teachers who hold advanced degrees are not necessarily effective teachers.

3. Border states in the United States must take action to curb illegal immigration; otherwise, state funds will be quickly exhausted.

    _____ a. State funds should not be used to help illegal immigrants.

    _____ b. Immigrants must enter the United States legally to receive state aid.

    _____ c. State funding guidelines should be revised.

## EXERCISE 14-8 | Identifying Assumptions

**Directions:** For each statement listed below, identify at least one underlying assumption.

1. Grocery stores should reduce the number of weekly sale items and lower overall prices.

_____

2. Eliminating essay exams in psychology courses would diminish students' writing abilities.

_____

3. More public transit should be added to our cities to reduce traffic and pollution.

_____

4. Endangered species should be bred in captivity to ensure their survival.

_____

5. Artists do not need grants from the government because they sell their works for such high prices.

_____

6. Hunters serve their communities by keeping down the deer population.

_____

7. Lobbyists hinder the work of our elected officials; these groups should be banned from Washington, D.C.

_____

8. Doing away with unions would increase productivity in our country.

_____

9. Learning a foreign language is a waste of time; Americans can get by anywhere.

_____

_____

10. Violence in sports affects everyone. Such brutality corrupts play, a form of free expression.

_____

**EXERCISE 14-9**

*WORKING TOGETHER*

# Identifying and Evaluating Assumptions

**Directions:** Working in pairs, identify the assumption(s) in each of the following passages. Then, discuss whether the authors have provided valid support for their assumptions.

1.    Most kids, of course, listen barely if at all to what adults say. Instead they watch what adults do. And, for better or worse, there may be no lesson we impart to them so efficiently as how we adults react to events that upset us, from a fender-bender to a threatening new era of conflict.
        —Editorial, "Raising the Sept. 11 Generation," *Chicago Tribune*

2.    Speaking from developments in my own family, there are way too many young students out there whose focus centers on partying, dress competition,

music, souped-up cars and sex. Goal-setting and accomplishment in their studies as they prepare themselves for what is a highly competitive world do not figure too prominently in their day-to-day lives.

—Editorial, "School's First Week Provides a Few Bright Exceptions,"
*Toronto Star*

3.    Most products—from cigarette lighters to medicine bottles—have to be designed to protect against foreseeable misuse. But there is no regulator to help the plaintiffs: guns and tobacco are the only products that the Consumer Product Safety Commission does not oversee. And even though lawsuits have often helped push up safety standards elsewhere, there are plenty of conservative judges who do not think it is the courts' job to create gun laws.

—Editorial, "From the hip; Gun control," *The Economist* (U.S.)

4.    In the meantime, a disturbing message is being sent to the guys and girls in the little leagues. Practice hard, work out, eat nutritiously—and sneak illegal steroids because, after all, winning and setting records are everything. And besides, if you make it big, you'll have enough money to care for your broken body.

—Editorial, "Steroids Should Be Tagged Out," *San Jose Mercury News*

5.    Britain on Wednesday marked the 150th anniversary of its public toilets. This reminds us of the barbaric lack of such facilities in the United States. Along with an increasingly chaotic and unfair health system, sparse public transportation and a paucity of neighborhood parks, the absence of public loos here evokes America's depressing distance from the perfect place that pathological patriots assert that it is.

—Editorial, "Sign of Civilization," *Providence Journal*

# Evaluate Generalizations

■ GOAL 4
Evaluate generalizations

Suppose you are reading an article that states, "Musicians are temperamental people." Do you think that every musician who ever wrote or performed a song or played a musical instrument is temperamental? Can you think of exceptions? This statement is an example of a generalization. A **generalization** is a reasoned statement about an entire group (musicians) based on known information about part of the group (musicians the writer has met or observed). A generalization requires a leap from what is known to a conclusion about what is unknown. Generalizations may be expressed using words such as *all, always, none,* or *never.* Some statements may imply but not directly state that the writer is referring to the entire group or class. The statement "Musicians are temperamental people" suggests but does not directly state that all musicians are temperamental. Here are a few more generalizations:

> Rich people are snobs.
>
> Chinese food is never filling.
>
> Pets are always troublesome.

The key to evaluating generalizations is to evaluate the type, quality, and amount of evidence given to support them.

## NEED TO KNOW

### How to Evaluate Generalizations

A critical reader should do the following:

1. **Evaluate types of evidence.** Here are a few more generalizations. What type of evidence would you need to convince you that each is or is not true?

   > College students are undecided about future career goals.
   >
   > Fast food lacks nutritional value.
   >
   > Foreign cars outperform similar American models.

2. **Evaluate the quality of evidence.** For the generalization about college students, you might need to see research studies about college students' career goals, for example. And, then, even if the studies did conclude that many college students are undecided, it would not be fair to conclude that every single student is undecided. If no evidence is given, then the generalization is not trustworthy and should be questioned.

3. **Evaluate the specifics.** For the statement "Pets are always troublesome," ask what kind of pets the author is referring to—a pet potbellied pig, an iguana, or a cat? Then ask what is meant by troublesome—does it mean the animal is time-consuming, requires special care, or behaves poorly?

4. **Think of exceptions.** For the generalization *Medical doctors are aloof and inaccessible*, can you think of a doctor you have met or heard about who was caring and available to his or her patients? If so, the generalization is not accurate in all cases.

---

### EXERCISE 14-10

## Identifying Generalizations

**Directions:** Read each of the following statements and place a check mark before each generalization.

_____ 1. The Internet is changing America.

_____ 2. Influenza causes severe epidemics in different parts of the world each year.

_____ 3. Most drug cases start with busts of small, local dealers and move to a search of their suppliers.

_____ 4. Attending college is essential for economic success and advancement.

_____ 5. Colds are caused by viruses, not bacteria, not cold weather, and not improper diet.

## EXERCISE 14-11 | Identifying Generalizations

**Directions:** Read each of the following items and underline each generalization.

1. Child care workers are undereducated in relation to the importance of their jobs. A whole generation of children is being left day after day in the hands of women with little more than high-school-level education. These children will suffer in the future for our inattention to the child care employment pool.

2. Americans have had enough of libraries providing Internet pornography to children. They want filtering on all computers or computers used in libraries. When will librarians listen to their customers (who also pay their salaries)?

3. For the past few years, drivers have been getting worse. Especially guilty of poor driving are the oldest and youngest drivers. There should be stricter tests and more classes for new drivers and yearly eye exams and road tests for drivers once they hit age 60. This is the only way to ensure the safety of our roads.

## EXERCISE 14-12 | Evaluating Generalizations

WORKING TOGETHER

**Directions:** Working with a classmate, indicate what questions you would ask and what types of information you would need to evaluate each of the following generalizations.

1. Vegetarians are pacifists and they do not own guns.
2. Most crimes are committed by high school dropouts.
3. It always rains in Seattle.
4. Private school students get a better education than public school students.
5. Scientists don't believe in any kind of higher power.

# Identify Bias

■ GOAL 5
Identify bias

Think of a television commercial you have seen recently, perhaps for a particular model of car. The ad tells you the car's advantages—why you want to buy it—but does it tell you its disadvantages? Does it describe ways in which the model compares unfavorably with competitors? Certainly not. Do you feel the ad writer is being unfair? We expect advertisers to present a one-sided view of their products. We expect other forms of writing, however, to be honest and forthright; otherwise they present a biased point of view. You can think of **bias** as a writer's prejudice; if an author is biased, then, he or she is partial to one point of view or one side of a controversial issue.

In the following excerpt from a biology text, the author's choice of words (see highlighting) and sarcastic comment in parentheses reveal his attitude toward seal hunters.

Greenpeace is an organization dedicated to the preservation of the sea and its great mammals, notably whales, dolphins, and seals. Its ethic is nonviolent but its aggressiveness in protecting our oceans and the life in them is becoming legendary.

Greenpeace volunteers routinely place their lives in danger in many ways, such as by riding along the backs of whales in inflatable zodiacs, keeping themselves between the animal and the harpoons of ships giving chase. They have pulled alongside Dutch ships to stop the dumping of dangerous toxins into the sea. They have confronted hostile sealers on northern ice floes to try to stop them from bludgeoning the baby seals in the birthing grounds, skinning them on the spot, and leaving the mother sniffing at the glistening red corpse of her baby as its skin is stacked aboard the ship on the way to warm the backs of very fashionable people who gather where the bartender knows their favorite drink. (The mother seal would be proud to know that her dead baby had nearly impressed some bartender.) They have petitioned the International Whaling Commission to establish rules and enact bans.

—Wallace, *Biology: The World of Life*, p. 754

# NEED TO KNOW

### Identifying Bias

To identify bias, ask the following questions:

1. Is the author acting as a reporter—presenting facts—or as salesperson—providing only favorable information?
2. Does the author feel strongly about or favor one side of the issue?
3. Does the author use connotative or figurative language to create a positive or negative image?
4. Does the author seem emotional about the issue?
5. Are there other views toward the subject that the writer does not recognize or discuss?

---

**EXERCISE 14-13**    ## Identifying Bias

**Directions:** Read each of the following statements, and place a check mark in front of the ones that reveal bias.

_____ 1. Cities should be designed for the pedestrian, not the automobile.

_____ 2. There are more channels than ever before on cable television.

_____ 3. The current system of voter registration is a sham.

_____ 4. Professional sports have become elitist.

_____ 5. Space exploration costs millions of dollars each year.

---

**EXERCISE 14-14**    ## Identifying Bias

**Directions:** After reading each passage, select the choice that best answers each of the questions that follow.

**A.**    The fact that different climate studies reach widely different conclusions is not surprising. Much of the global warming debate centers on the output of highly questionable computer models that conjure figures from scarcely understood variables, dubious raw data and gaping holes filled with assumptions that usually confirm the researchers' biases. No wonder that even as reliable temperature measurements show global temperatures have flatlined or been falling for the past decade, claims of imminent catastrophe have grown more shrill. Garbage in, warming out.

—Editorial, "A Climate of Fraud," *The Washington Times*, November 30, 2011, p. 2

_____ 1. The author seems biased against
    **a.** all computer models
    **b.** global warming advocates
    **c.** global warming measurement
    **d.** climate study

_____ 2. Which of the following phrases best reveals the author's bias?
    **a.** "widely different conclusions"
    **b.** "temperatures have flatlined"
    **c.** "gaping holes filled with assumptions"
    **d.** "global warming debate centers on"

**B.**    Plenty of statistics show a large number of offenders should never go to prison for nonviolent offenses. I, too, believe that the record should be expunged when the sentence is served. It is bad enough to have to pay back fines and court costs and perhaps child support that has accumulated during years in prison. To not be able to rent an apartment or get a job only ensures the person will soon return to prison. Criminologists have known for years that harsh punishments do not prevent crime. The plain fact is prisons are money-makers. Nothing is done for rehabilitation in the prisons, especially the private ones, which are only interested in the money. Frequently, the media, written and broadcast, are responsible for stirring up fear of being "soft on crime." Oklahomans should be thoroughly ashamed to have more women in prison than any other state. Rehabilitation programs work, as do monitoring and community service.

—Morrow, "Letter to the Editor: Life After Prison," *Tulsa World*, April 2010, p. A16

_____ 3. The author's primary bias concerns the
    **a.** length of criminal sentences in general.
    **b.** imprisonment of nonviolent criminals.
    **c.** media portrayal of crime.
    **d.** cost of imprisonment.

_____ 4. Which of the following phrases expresses the author's bias?
    **a.** "offenders should never go to prison for nonviolent offenses"
    **b.** "soft on crime"
    **c.** "Oklahomans should be thoroughly ashamed"
    **d.** "more women in prison"

**C.**    More than half of all video games are rated as containing violence, including more than 90% of games rated as appropriate for children 10 years or older. These games "provide an ideal environment in which to learn violence and use many of the strategies that are most effective for learning." The player is in the role of the aggressor and is rewarded for successful violent behavior. The games encourage repetitive and long playing to improve scores and advance to higher levels, and in some children and adolescents, promote addiction and an acceptance of violence as an appropriate means of solving problems and achieving goals.

—Masters, "Playing at War," *Women Against Military Madness Newsletter,*
March 2010

_____ 5. The author is biased concerning
   **a.** the learning strategies children are exposed to.
   **b.** the violence in video games.
   **c.** how much time children spend playing video games.
   **d.** the way video games target young children.

_____ 6. Which phrase best suggests the author's bias?
   **a.** "ideal environment in which to learn violence"
   **b.** "encourage repetitive and long playing"
   **c.** "advance to higher levels"
   **d.** "promote addiction"

**EXERCISE 14-15**

*WORKING TOGETHER*

# Analyzing Bias

**Directions:** Working with a classmate, identify the author's bias in each of the following statements. Then discuss how you determined the author's biases.

1.   Now that Americans are vulnerable to attack in the United States by terrorists, gun control should no longer be an issue for our politicians to waste time debating. Law-abiding, innocent citizens need the means to protect themselves from foreign enemies right here in their homeland. We must reduce the risk of losing more lives to extremists by allowing our people to carry weapons for defense.

2.   I have expressed in the past that police officers should refrain from enforcing immigration laws so that police departments can maintain good relations with Hispanics. If Latinos fear that police will report them or their family members to the immigration service, they might fear coming forward to help solve crimes.

   —Salinas, "Will All Hispanic Men Be Suspect?" *Seattle Post-Intelligencer*

3.   Parents trust their children less and less these days. Convinced beyond a doubt that violent video games will turn their sons and daughters into criminals, parents go to the extreme by banning all forms of electronic entertainment from their homes. Instead of seizing the opportunity to teach a child about limits, self-regulation, and good taste, moms and dads all over America are unwittingly increasing the desire for taboo entertainment. Today's kids are not being allowed to experiment and test themselves while under their parents' supervision. This parental disservice can only lead to a backlash in the future when young men and women experiment with risky behaviors as soon as they leave their parents' tight hold.

4.   Those clamoring to shut down the farmers, however, should look hard at the prospect of a prairie full of subdivisions and suburban pollution: car exhaust, lawn and garden fertilizers, wood stoves, sewage. Certainly, the smoke from field burning is an annoyance, particularly to the hard-hit Sandpoint area, and to some it's a health hazard. But the benefits the sturdy farmers produce 50 weeks of the year shouldn't be dismissed casually.

   —Oliveria, "Burning Will Go; That's Not All Good," *Spokesman Review*

5.   Money doesn't grow on trees, but some trees might as well be pure gold. The world's voracious (and growing) appetite for wood, paper, and other forest products is driving a stampede to mow down forests. Much of this logging is illegal.

—Haugen, "Logging Illogic," *World Watch*

# WRITING

# Write Effectively and Fairly

- **GOAL 6**
  Write effectively and fairly

To write effectively, you need to think critically about what you write and how you express it. Try to express your ideas openly in order to build a trusting, open relationship with your reader.

## Using Connotative Language Carefully

Word meanings are very powerful. You can shape your readers' attitudes and responses to your topic in part by the connotative meanings of words you choose. Use the following strategies to evaluate your word choice:

- **Reread drafts.** Once you have written a draft and revised so that you are satisfied with the overall content and organization of the essay, reread it once looking only at your choice of words and phrases.
- **Circle any words with emotional impact.**
- **Examine the connotative meaning of the words you circled.** Ask yourself: "What emotion does this word or phrase suggest?" and "Is this the meaning I really want to convey?"
- **Revise, if necessary.**

## Making Fair Comparisons Using Figurative Language

Figurative language can make your writing lively, interesting, and engaging. It is also a creative way to describe and explain. To use it effectively, use the following suggestions.

- **Use fresh, interesting figures of speech.** Avoid using tired, overused expressions that have become clichés.
- **Make clear comparisons.** Because figurative language makes a comparison between two unlike things, be sure that you create figurative expressions that compare items for which the likeness is obvious and that do not suggest similarities to aspects you do not intend. For example, if you say, "Monty eats like a horse," it is clear that you are comparing only eating qualities and not suggesting that Monty is horselike in other respects. However, if you say "Monty is a horse, and everyone in the restaurant recognized it," it is unclear what characteristics Monty and the horse share.
- **Avoid figurative expressions when you want to be precise, exact, and direct.** Figurative expressions leave room for interpretation and can lead to misinterpretation.

## Making Reasonable Assumptions

Be sure the assumptions on which you base your ideas are logical and consistent. Also be aware of whether your readers may agree or disagree with your assumptions. If they are likely to disagree, then you may need to explain them in detail and demonstrate why they are valid.

## Making Generalizations Based on Sufficient Evidence

A topic sentence is a generalization that you support in the remainder of your paragraph. Likewise, a thesis statement is a generalization that you explain throughout the remainder of your essay. Always be sure to provide adequate and sufficient evidence in support of these and other generalizations you make. (For more on adequate and sufficient evidence, see Chapter 6, p. 191, and Chapter 11, p. 340.)

## Handling Bias Openly

Readers appreciate the open and straightforward expression of ideas and mistrust writers who pretend to be objective while actually presenting a one-sided viewpoint. There are writing situations in which you will want to express your opinions and reveal your bias. When these occur, be sure to do so openly. One way to make it clear that you are expressing a bias is to include phrases such as "in my opinion," "one viewpoint is," or "one way of looking at." It is also helpful to mention opposing viewpoints by referring to or summarizing them, and by refuting them, if you choose.

---

**EXERCISE 14-16**

# Thinking Critically About an Essay

**Directions:** Select an essay you have written recently, either for this class or for another college course. For the essay you chose, complete the following tasks:

1. Highlight words with strong connotative meanings. Examine each and determine if the word conveys your meaning accurately. If not, revise.

2. Evaluate any figurative expressions you have used. Do they make fair comparisons? Could the essay be improved by the use of figurative expressions? If so, add them.

3. Upon what assumptions is your essay based? Write a sentence stating them. Evaluate each assumption and determine if it is reasonable.

4. Underline generalizations, if any, that you make in the essay. Examine your essay: does it provide sufficient evidence to support each generalization? If not, revise to add additional supporting evidence.

5. Have you expressed bias in your essay? If so, have you done so openly? If not, revise.

# INTEGRATING READING AND WRITING

## READ AND RESPOND: A Student Essay

*Aurora Gilbert is a sophomore at Columbia University, studying Business Management and Hispanic Studies. She hopes to attend graduate school for public health and go on to work for global health in Latin America.*

*Gilbert wrote this essay as part of her application process to Columbia University. She was careful to write a coherent, correct essay that also demonstrated that she is a serious, intellectually capable student with diverse interests and goals.*

**Title suggests thesis**

# From Ignorant Bliss to Painful Awareness
## Aurora Gilbert

**Introduction: Gilbert describes an engaging scene to interest her readers**

1   Warmth and sunlight washed over me as I cracked open my eyes, still trapped in the serenity between sleep and consciousness. I smelled the smoky warmth of the cooking fire and I heard what sounded like a million voices chattering in Spanish on the other side of my bedroom wall. A gaggle of young children came bouncing into my room and swarmed my bed, jumping up and down, yelling "¡Aurora, Aurora!" I pretended to still be asleep, yet the enthusiasm in their voices overwhelmed my emotions and forced a smile to my face, and I could no longer lie in bed. Pushing through my mosquito net, I yelled "¡Buenos días!" to anyone who could hear me, and I was ready to take on the day that awaited.

**Topic sentence**

**Background information on living in DR**

2   For one month, I followed this same routine as I stayed with a family in the small village of Gualete in the Dominican Republic (DR). I held daily English classes for the locals and attempted to immerse myself in a culture completely different from my own. Though I had been doing service work at food banks and shelters around Seattle for years, I was new to the experience of immersion. For the first time, I lived the lives of the people I served. The concept of complete isolation from my world in the United States was terrifying at first, but I soon found myself infatuated with the DR.

**Topic sentence**

3   The love, the music, and the dancing of this culture overtook and enveloped me, but not for long. They swept me into a place where suffering is obscured from view, and I forgot that the world around me was anything but a perfect dream. Then one day, I saw the boy across the street come home late, carrying a familiar-looking wooden box. I realized that he was one of the shoeshine boys who begged me for money in the larger towns and who are often forced into prostitution. I learned that some of the local children had just been abandoned

by their mother for four days, left alone in their house, starving and dirty. I noticed that food was running short because my family barely had enough money for three meals a day.

**Thesis statement** 4    What once was ignorant bliss became painful awareness. I was furious that these Dominicans must live in such undeserved despair, and frustrated with myself for not realizing earlier the dark truth behind the veil of carefree customs. Every act of generosity shown to me by these people made me feel sick with guilt. I felt discouraged and lost in the face of such a severe situation, yet a glint of hope revealed itself in my clouded perspective. Although the people of Gualete are the most impoverished people I've ever met, they are also the most compassionate and grateful, which inspired me like nothing ever had before.

**Conclusion: Gilbert reflects on her experience and its meaning** 5    As I stood outside of my house on the last day of my trip with my sisters in my arms and tears streaming down my cheeks, I promised myself that I would never forget these people. The feeling that pervaded my senses was no longer one of blind happiness or anger, but one of understanding and determination. Now home in Seattle, when I help the Latinos at the food bank or work with Spanish-speaking kids at the local elementary school, I am momentarily transported back to that land of love and life, poverty and despair; the flame of passion in my heart flares even higher as I am reminded that my work is completely worth it, but only just beginning.

## Examining Writing

1. What does the title suggest about the thesis of this essay? Evaluate the effectiveness of the title, introduction, and conclusion.

2. Identify examples of connotative and figurative language in this essay. Highlight three places where Gilbert uses descriptive details effectively.

3. What assumptions does Gilbert make at the beginning of her experience? Try to identify at least two in the essay, and describe how these assumptions changed.

4. Evaluate bias in this essay by examining what facts or other aspects of the author's experience were omitted.

## Writing Assignments

1. How would this essay be different if it were written as a factual report? Write a summary of the essay using facts only.

2. Gilbert describes how her experience and perceptions brought her from happiness to anger to eventual understanding and determination. Write a paragraph describing an experience in which your initial feelings (of joy or pain) were transformed into something very different.

3. When Gilbert describes her last day in Gualete, she refers to her "sisters." Are there people in your life whom you consider family even though they are not related to you? Write a short essay explaining who they are and why you consider them family.

## READ AND RESPOND: A Professional Essay

### Thinking Before Reading

In the following reading, the author discusses the difficult working conditions faced by workers in the seafood industry in Santa Rosalia, Mexico. Before you read:

1. Preview the reading, using the steps discussed in Chapter 1, page 15.
2. Connect the reading to your own experience by answering the following questions:
   a. What were working conditions like at your most recent job?
   b. How important is it for you to know the source of the food that you eat?
3. Mark and annotate as you read.

# Sweatshops at Sea

## Virginia Sole-Smith

1    It was a little after eight in the evening, and the sun was just beginning to set over the Gulf of California. Our small motorboat, known here in Santa Rosalia, Mexico, as a *panga*, sped out over the shimmering water. The breezy sea air felt good and clean after the heat of the day, and soon Delmar, the 26-year-old squid fisherman who had agreed to take us out for his night's work, was cracking open cans of Tecate. When we reached Delmar's fishing spot, he cut the engine and flipped on a tiny lightbulb duct-taped to a pole on the middle bench of the *panga*. Floating all around us were dozens of other *pangas*, and as night fell, the dots of light twinkled like a hundred fallen stars. It was beautiful and peaceful. Then we began to fish.

2    Delmar unraveled a glow-in-the-dark plastic tube fitted with sharp metal hooks that was attached to a thousand feet of clear fishing line. He tossed it overboard, wrapping the other end around a piece of scrap wood. When the line went tight after a few minutes, he began to pull, bare hand over bare hand, hauling the line back up through hundreds of feet of water. Seconds later, a 40-pound Humboldt squid splashed up from the depths with an enormous spray of salt water and sticky black ink. From tentacles to tail, it was almost as long as the *panga* was wide.

3    In one fluid movement, Delmar yanked the squid out of the water, slapped it down, grabbed a rusty machete, and chopped off its head. Four hours later, the piles of red squid bodies and heads had grown so large that we had to balance with our feet braced awkwardly against the slick benches. When we had to move around the boat, we'd slip on spare eyeballs and black slime, and occasionally a spastic tentacle would wrap itself around the odd ankle. To make matters even worse, there were no life vests, radios, or emergency lights on board Delmar's *panga*.

**Tecate**
a brand of Mexican beer

**machete**
a large, heavy knife

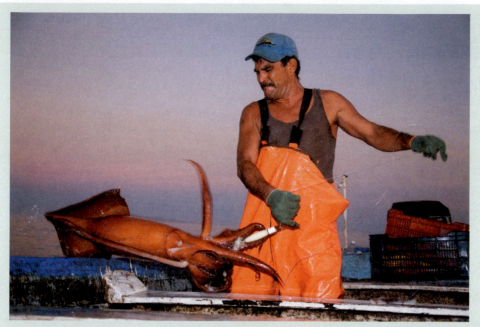

Tightening U.S. seafood regulations could improve human rights in Mexico.

4    It's no wonder that, every season, at least two or three fishermen like Delmar die at sea. The unsafe, grotesque working conditions on the water are just one of the many problems facing the working people of Santa Rosalia, a town of around 10,000 that is located in Baja California Sur. There are no spring break parties here. The dirty waterfront is devoted to three squid factories and the *panga* docks, because fishing the millions of Humboldt squid swimming in 25 square miles of Santa Rosalia's waters is the only game in town.

5    The squid processing plants—Korean-owned Brumar de San Bruno, Korean-owned Hanjin Mexico, and Chinese-owned Pesquera de Longing, SA—buy each day's catch from middlemen who have frozen the price the fishermen receive for their squid at just two pesos per kilo. That means most consider a $50 paycheck for a 10-hour fishing trip to be a good night. And it is, at least when you compare those wages to what the fishermen's wives, mothers, and daughters make working in the plants themselves, which—far from the federal labor offices in Mexico City—operate Wild West style.

6    Rosa Ceseña Ramirez began working in the Hanjin Mexico factory in 1994. She never knew when a shift was going to start or how long it would last. "You can either drink coffee for hours to stay awake, or sleep on the factory floor like an animal," Rosa explains. "Once the squid arrives, we have to work until it's all processed, even if it takes until the next afternoon. Then we go home for a few hours to sleep and see our kids, and have to come right back that evening."

7    The breaking point for Rosa came in November 2002, when Hanjin Mexico allegedly failed to pay its workers a federally mandated annual bonus and short-changed their weekly paychecks. Rosa gathered signatures and filed a complaint with the Santa Rosalia labor office. Rosa says Hanjin Mexico responded by firing her and more than 90 workers. Eight years later, the former Hanjin Mexico workers are still waiting for the labor office to resolve their dispute, and conditions at all three Santa Rosalia factories have worsened.

8    At the neighboring Pesquera de Longing, workers report that only two toilets are available for more than 80 workers. Conditions at Brumar de San Bruno are no better. Most of the workers are migrant laborers who come from other Mexican states and live at the plant in a long, barracks-style dorm. "There are six of us sleeping in one room and whenever it's time to go back to work, the Koreans just open the door and yell, 'Let's go,'" worker Sonia Sanchez says. "They don't care if you're undressed or sleeping. We're treated like slaves."

9    The owners of the Santa Rosalia factories vehemently deny all of their workers' complaints, which is why Enlace International, a coalition of unions and worker centers in Mexico and the United States, is now approaching year eight of a campaign to create better working conditions for Santa Rosalia's labor force. "There will never be any enforcement of the labor laws in Mexico because this is a country with $212 billion in foreign debts," says Garrett Brown, coordinator of the Maquiladora Health and Safety Support Network. "If Americans want to help these workers, getting our government and banks to forgive Mexico's debt would be a big first step."

10    Another big step would be to tighten U.S. regulation of imported seafood. According to U.S. Department of Agriculture data, imports of processed squid from China totaled more than 1.1 million pounds in 2009 (along with 120 million pounds of unprocessed squid). But figuring out which U.S. retailers to hold accountable for the dire conditions in Santa Rosalia is all but impossible. "Seafood is often shipped from port to port before it reaches the United States, and it can be relabeled upon entry and exit, so we have no way of telling where it originally came from," explains Patrick Woodall of Food and Water Watch, a nonprofit consumer advocacy organization in Washington, D.C. "Companies can catch squid in Mexico, then ship it back to China for processing so they can take advantage of even cheaper labor markets and lower food safety regulations, then send it back to the United States. . . . There's just no way to trace it all."

11    Meanwhile Rosa balances her day job at a local supermarket with raising funds for the local union. She holds meetings for interested workers in the playground of the local school and writes letters to government officials. The process is slow, and more workers suffer every day. But Rosa is not deterred. "We know that one day it will be our daughters working in those factories," she says. "One part of my heart is sad for all the bad things that have happened. But the other part of my heart is happy because I know we are supporting one another."

# Getting Ready to Write

## Checking Your Comprehension

Answer each of the following questions using complete sentences.

1. Explain what a *panga* is and briefly describe the work that occurs on it. What makes this work dangerous?

2. Who owns the squid processing plants described in this essay?

3. Describe conditions at the Hanjin Mexico factory. What caused Rosa Ceseña Ramirez to reach her breaking point and how did her employer respond?

4. What is Enlace International and what is it trying to accomplish?

5. According to the essay, what are two big steps that would help the Mexican workers?

## Strengthening Your Vocabulary

Using the word's context, word parts, or a dictionary, write a brief definition of each of the following words as it is used in the reading.

1. grotesque (paragraph 4) _____

2. allegedly (paragraph 7) _____

3. mandated (paragraph 7) _____

4. vehemently (paragraph 9) _____

5. coalition (paragraph 9) _____

6. dire (paragraph 10) _____

7. deterred (paragraph 11) _____

## Examining the Reading: Using an Idea Map

Review the reading by creating an idea map of "Sweatshops at Sea," starting with the title and thesis and listing the main ideas and supporting details.

## Reacting to Ideas: Discussion and Journal Writing

Get ready to write about the reading by discussing the following:

1. Evaluate the introductory paragraphs of the essay. How does the initial description of the fishing trip contrast with the work that takes place on the boat and in the factories?

2. Discuss why this essay is called "Sweatshops at Sea."

3. Explain what the author means when she says that the seafood processing plants operate "Wild West style."

4. What aspects of the essay are illustrated by the photograph? Discuss details in the photograph that correspond to descriptions in the essay.

**THINKING VISUALLY**

## Thinking and Writing Critically

1. What is the author's purpose for writing this article? Who is her intended audience?

2. Identify descriptive words in the essay and indicate which words have positive or negative connotations. What is the author's purpose in using these words?

3. Can you identify any bias in this piece? Consider whether facts or opposing viewpoints were omitted.

4. Examine the essay for assumptions and generalizations.

MySkillsLab®

Complete
this
Exercise

# Writing About the Reading

## Paragraph Options

1. What is the most difficult work you have ever done? Write a paragraph describing your experience and what made it difficult.

2. Did this essay make you sympathetic to the plight of these workers? Write a paragraph explaining your answer.

3. Were you surprised to learn about the business practices surrounding imported seafood? Write a paragraph explaining your answer and whether this information will affect your consumption of seafood or other imported foods.

### Essay Options

4. What can you tell from this reading about the author's attitude toward the workers and the owners of the factories? Write an essay examining the ways in which the author reveals her feelings toward each.

5. Why do you think Rosa Ceseña Ramirez is undeterred after eight years? Write an essay from her point of view explaining her motivations and her commitment to this cause.

6. Consider the two steps that are suggested as ways to improve conditions for the labor force. Do you agree or disagree that these actions should be taken? Can you think of other steps that might be effective? Write an essay explaining your answers.

# SELF-TEST SUMMARY

To test yourself, cover the Answer column with a sheet of paper and answer each question in the left column. Evaluate each of your answers as you work by sliding the paper down and comparing your answer with what is printed in the Answer column.

| QUESTION | ANSWER |
| --- | --- |
| **GOAL 1 Evaluate the author's techniques**<br>What is involved in evaluating an author's techniques? | Evaluating an author's techniques involves examining the author's word choice, assumptions, generalizations, and bias. |
| **GOAL 2 Understand connotative and figurative language**<br>What are denotative and connotative meanings? What does figurative language do, and what are the three primary types of figurative language? | Denotative meanings are the standard, dictionary meanings of words; connotative meanings include the feelings and associations that accompany a word. Figurative language makes a comparison between two unlike things that share a common characteristic. The three primary types of figurative language are similes, metaphors, and personification. |
| **GOAL 3 Analyze assumptions**<br>What is an assumption? | An assumption is an idea or principle the writer accepts as true and makes no effort to prove or substantiate. |

*(continued)*

*(continued)*

| QUESTION | ANSWER |
|---|---|
| ■ GOAL 4 **Evaluate generalizations**<br><br>What is a generalization? How do you evaluate generalizations? | A generalization is a statement made about a large group based on observation or experience with a portion of that group. To evaluate generalizations, consider whether the author provides evidence to support the generalization and what the author has based the generalization on. |
| ■ GOAL 5 **Identify bias**<br><br>What is bias and how do you identify it? | Bias is a preference for or prejudice against a person, object, or idea; biased material is one-sided. To identify bias, ask yourself what facts were omitted and what impression you would have if different words were used. |
| ■ GOAL 6 **Write effectively and fairly**<br><br>How do you write effectively and fairly? | Write effectively and fairly by using connotative language carefully, by making fair comparisons using figurative language, by making reasonable assumptions, by supporting generalizations with adequate and sufficient evidence, and by handling bias openly. |

**MySkillsLab**®

For more help with **Evaluating the Author's Techniques**, go to your learning path in MySkillsLab at www.myskillslab.com.

# Critical Thinking: Reading and Writing Arguments

LEARNING
## GOALS

Learn how to . . .

- **GOAL 1**
  Understand the use of argument

- **GOAL 2**
  Recognize the parts of an argument

- **GOAL 3**
  Read an argument effectively

- **GOAL 4**
  Think critically about arguments

- **GOAL 5**
  Write argument paragraphs

- **GOAL 6**
  Write argument essays

## THINK About It!

Study the above photograph. What issues do the bumper stickers address? Choose one issue. Write a paragraph that answers the following questions: What position (pro or con) does the bumper sticker take on the issue? What are some of the possible reasons for agreeing with this position?

The paragraph you have just written is a brief argument. An argument presents logical reasons and evidence to support a point of view on an issue. In this chapter you will learn how to read arguments effectively, think critically about arguments, and write arguments that persuade readers to support your point of view.

# Reading and Writing Connections

## EVERYDAY CONNECTIONS

- **Reading** You read an essay in the student newspaper calling on students to boycott the campus cafeteria because of a lack of appetizing and nutritional foods. The writer offers several examples and quotes other students in support of his claim.
- **Writing** As a student council member, you write a letter to school administrators and the cafeteria manager, urging them to revise the menu. You argue that more students will use the cafeteria while benefiting from healthier, more appealing options.

## ACADEMIC CONNECTIONS

- **Reading** For a business management class, you read an article that argues against the "open office" concept, in which managers work alongside employees rather than in private offices.
- **Writing** You write an essay for business management arguing in favor of the "open office" concept. You include facts and statistics that indicate higher levels of efficiency, productivity, and morale in open offices as compared with traditional office arrangements.

## WORKPLACE CONNECTIONS

- **Reading** In your job at a grocery store, you read a memo from your manager defending the store's decision to stop giving free samples to customers.
- **Writing** You write an e-mail to your manager arguing that the free sample policy be continued. You acknowledge your manager's claim that it is expensive, but you argue that the expense is offset by the number of customers who purchase a product after receiving a free sample.

# FOCUSING ON READING AND WRITING

# What Is an Argument?

■ **GOAL 1**
Understand the use of argument

An **argument** is a line of reasoning intended to persuade the reader or listener to agree with a particular viewpoint or take a particular action. If you turn on the television or radio, or open a magazine or newspaper, you are sure to encounter the most common form of argument—advertising. Commercials and ads are attempts to persuade you to buy a particular product or service.

Here are a few examples of arguments:

> Many students have part-time jobs that require them to work late afternoons and evenings during the week. These students are unable to use the library during the week. Therefore, library hours should be extended to weekends.

> Because parents have the right to determine their children's sexual attitudes, sex education should take place in the home, not at school.

No one should be forced to inhale unpleasant or harmful substances. That's why the ban on cigarette smoking in public places was put into effect in our state. Why shouldn't there be a law to prevent people from wearing strong colognes or perfumes, especially in restaurants, since sense of smell is important to taste?

## READING

# The Parts of an Argument

■ **GOAL 2**
Recognize the parts of an argument

An **argument** presents reasons for accepting a belief or position or for taking a specific action. It has three essential parts:

- ■ **An issue.** This is the problem or controversy that the argument addresses. It is also the topic of an argument paragraph or essay.

- ■ **A claim.** A claim is the particular point of view a writer has on an issue. There are always at least two points of view on an issue—pro and con. For example, you may be for or against gun control. You may favor or oppose lowering the legal drinking age. Often, there are several points of view about an issue.

- ■ **Support.** Support consists of the details that demonstrate a claim is correct and should be accepted. There are three types of support: *reasons*, *evidence*, and *emotional appeals*.

Here are a few examples:

| Issue | Claim | Support |
|-------|-------|---------|
| Welfare system | The welfare system is unjust and needs reform. | People cheat, deserving people cannot get benefits, and it costs taxpayers too much money. |
| Plus-minus grading system | The plus-minus grading system is confusing and unnecessary. | It costs instructors extra time, employers do not understand it, and it complicates the computation of GPA. |

You can visualize an argument paragraph as follows:

**VISUALIZE IT!**

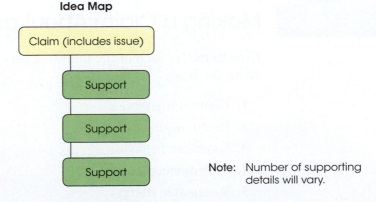

**Idea Map**

Claim (includes issue)

Support

Support

Support

**Note:** Number of supporting details will vary.

Here is a sample argument paragraph:

> Year-round school is advantageous to both parents and children, and more school districts should adopt a full-year calendar. Most parents work year round and find child care and supervision troublesome and expensive during the summer months when their children are not in school. Further, continuous year-round application of skills will prevent forgetting and strengthen students' academic preparation. Finally, children themselves admit they are bored in the summer and end up hanging out in malls, staying up late, and sleeping in the mornings to kill time. A well-rounded school year will produce well-rounded children and happy parents.

You can visualize this paragraph as follows:

**VISUALIZE IT!**

**Idea Map**

**Claim (includes issue)**

Year-round school is advantageous, and school districts should adopt a full-year calendar.

Parents work year round and find supervision troublesome and expensive.

Year-round school will prevent forgetting and strengthen skills.

Children get bored with summers off.

An argument sometimes includes a fourth part—a **refutation**. A refutation considers opposing viewpoints and attempts to disprove or discredit them. For example, a claim could be made that baseball players' use of steroids is unhealthy and unfair. An opposing viewpoint may be that steroid use enhances performance, which makes the game more fun for fans. This opposing viewpoint could be refuted by providing evidence that fans would prefer to see the game played without the use of performance-enhancing drugs or providing facts about the serious side effects of steroid use.

**EXERCISE 15-1**

## Making a Claim About an Issue

**Directions:** For each of the following issues, write a sentence that makes a claim about the issue.

1. Community service
2. Health insurance
3. Sports fan behavior
4. Violent video games
5. Sustainable energy

**EXERCISE 15-2**

# Understanding Issues

**Directions:** For each of the following issues, place a check mark in front of the statement that makes a claim about the issue.

1. Issue: Community service

   _____ a. Twenty hours of community service is required at Dodgeville High School.

   _____ b. Community service should be required of all high school students.

   _____ c. Some students voluntarily perform many hours of community service yearly.

2. Issue: State-required vaccinations

   _____ a. Parents who wish to opt out of vaccine requirements for their children should be given that right.

   _____ b. Vaccinations prevent children dying from many communicable diseases.

   _____ c. States issue lists of vaccines that are required in order for children to attend public school.

3. Issue: Public libraries and the Internet

   _____ a. People should be able to view whatever sites they choose at the public library.

   _____ b. Filtering software cannot block all offensive Web sites.

   _____ c. Many public libraries filter their Internet access.

4. Issue: Sports fan behavior

   _____ a. Many football stadiums now have alcohol-free seating areas.

   _____ b. Tickets to athletic events are expensive, so fans should be free to act however they choose.

   _____ c. Sports arena security forces eject unruly fans.

5. Issue: Wikipedia as a research source.

   _____ a. Faculty at some colleges ban the use of Wikipedia in academic papers.

   _____ b. Anyone can write entries or correct those written by others.

   _____ c. Because Wikipedia lacks quality control, it should be used with caution.

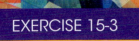

**EXERCISE 15-3**

# Understanding Claims

**Directions:** For each of the following issues, write a statement that takes a position on the issue. Write your claim in the space provided.

1.  Issue: Minimum wage

    Claim: _____

    _____

2.  Issue: Global climate changes

    Claim: _____

    _____

3.  Issue: Air travel safety

    Claim: _____

    _____

4.  Issue: Alternative medicine

    Claim: _____

5.  Issue: Pop music

    Claim: _____

# Read an Argument Effectively

■ **GOAL 3**
Read an argument
effectively

Arguments need to be read slowly and carefully. Count on reading an argument more than once. The first time you read it, try to get an overview of its three essential elements: *issue, claim*, and *support*. Then reread it more carefully to closely follow the author's line of reasoning and to identify and evaluate the evidence provided.

## Recognizing Types of Supporting Evidence

A writer supports a claim by offering reasons and evidence that the claim should be accepted. A **reason** is a general statement that backs up a claim. Here are a few reasons that support an argument in favor of parental Internet controls:

> The Internet contains millions of sites that are not appropriate for children, so parents must accept responsibility for controlling what their children see.
>
> Parental controls are needed because the Internet can be a place for sexual predators to find victims.
>
> Parental controls are needed because the Internet is not controlled by any other entity.

However, for any of these reasons to be believable and convincing, they need to be supported with evidence. **Evidence** consists of facts, statistics, quotations, examples, personal experience, and comparisons that demonstrate why the claim is valid.

■ **Facts.** Facts are true statements. Writers may use facts to lead readers to a conclusion. However, the conclusion does not always follow from the facts presented. For example, a writer may state that you will not get a cold if you eat a lot of oranges because oranges have vitamin C. It is true that oranges have vitamin C, but that does not necessarily mean that eating them will keep you cold free.

■ **Statistics.** Statistics—the reporting of figures, percentages, averages, and so forth—is a common method of support. For example, in an argument about the overuse of elective surgery in hospitals, a writer may present statistics showing the increase in Caesarean sections over the past few years. However, this increase could be due to other factors such as physicians' assessment of risk during childbirth or patients' physical conditions. Statistics can be misused, misinterpreted, or used selectively to give other than the most objective, accurate picture of a situation.

■ **Quotations and citations.** Writers often substantiate or confirm their ideas by including quotations or citations from experts or authorities on the subject. For instance, a writer may quote or cite an oncologist to support the view that overuse of alcohol increases one's risk of certain types of cancers.

■ **Examples.** Examples are descriptions of particular situations that are used to illustrate or explain a principle, concept, or idea. In supporting the statement that people would rather drive their own cars than use public transportation, a writer may give the example that almost no one in his office takes the bus to work. Examples should not be used by themselves to prove the concept or idea they illustrate. The writer's experience may be atypical, or not representative, of what is common.

■ **Personal experience.** A writer may use his or her own personal account or observation of a situation. For example, in supporting the claim that Internet controls are useful, a writer may report that she has put a filter on her child's computer and her child has never come across a pornographic Web site. Although a writer's personal experience may provide an interesting perspective on an issue, personal experience should not be accepted as proof.

■ **Comparisons and analogies.** Comparisons or analogies (extended comparisons) serve as illustrations. Their reliability depends on how closely the comparison corresponds or how similar it is to the situation to which it is being compared. For example, Martin Luther King Jr., in his famous letter from the Birmingham jail, compared nonviolent protesters to a robbed man. To evaluate this comparison, you would need to consider how the two are similar and how they are different.

| EXERCISE 15-4 | Recognizing Support for Claims |

**Directions:** Read each of the following sets of statements. Identify the statement that is a claim and label it *C*. Label the one statement that supports the claim as *S*.

1. _____  Year-round school is advantageous for both parents and children.

 _____  Continuous, year-round application of skills will prevent forgetting and strengthen students' academic preparation.

 _____  Year-round school may be costly to school districts.

2. _____ Many celebrities have been in trouble with the law lately because of their involvement with theft, drunk driving, violence, and even murder.

_____ Celebrities do not act as positive role models for the people who admire them.

_____ Acquiring fame and fortune does not automatically relieve a person of stress and suffering.

3. _____ Millions of students cannot afford to attend college because tuition costs and fees are so high.

_____ States should find ways to control tuition costs at public colleges and universities.

_____ Officials at private institutions of higher learning do not have to worry about budget issues since they have huge endowments.

4. _____ Drug companies should not be allowed to advertise on television.

_____ My grandparents are easily persuaded to buy expensive medications they do not need.

_____ Physicians do not provide all the necessary information patients need.

5. _____ Today's artists receive more media attention than in previous decades.

_____ Modern art is confusing.

_____ I am never sure what an abstract painting represents.

### EXERCISE 15-5 Understanding Types of Evidence

**Directions:** Each item below begins with a claim, followed by supporting statements. Identify the type(s) of evidence used to support each claim. Choose from among the following types: personal experience (PE), examples (E), statistics (S), facts (F), quotations and citations (Q), and comparisons (C).

_____ 1. Library hours should be extended to weekends to make the library more accessible. My sisters have part-time jobs that require them to work late afternoons and evenings during the week. They are unable to use the library during the week.

_____ 2. Because parents have the right to determine their children's sexual attitudes, sex education should take place in the home, not at school. Teaching children about sex in school is like teaching them to sit in assigned seats and walk around quietly in single file at home.

_____ 3. It is more expensive to own a dog than a cat. According to the American Veterinary Medical Association, a dog visits the vet twice as many times as a cat.

_____ 4. Many married couples find that they need to set aside special times to be together. Some married couples find that planning a weekend retreat helps them focus on their special relationship.

_____ 5. Parents should read to their children to promote literacy skills. Children who were read to as preschoolers learned to read earlier than children who were not read to.

_____ 6. Dr. Samuel Rodriguez, a child psychologist, urges parents to read several books to their children daily (McGraw 71).

Use the following specific strategies for reading arguments:

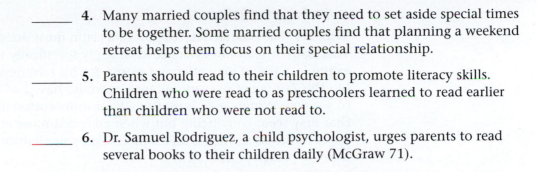

## NEED TO KNOW

### Tips for Reading Arguments Effectively

1. **Read once for an initial impression.** Do not focus on specifics; instead, try to get a general feel for the argument.

2. **Read the argument several more times.** First identify the specific claim the writer is making and start to identify the reasons and evidence that support it. Read the argument again to examine whether the writer acknowledges or refutes opposing viewpoints.

3. **Annotate as you read.** Record your thoughts; note ideas you agree with, those you disagree with, questions that come to mind, additional reasons or evidence overlooked by the author, and the counterarguments not addressed by the author.

4. **Highlight key terms.** Often, an argument depends on how certain terms are defined. In an argument on the destruction of forests, for example, what does "destruction" mean? Does it mean building homes within a forest, or does it refer to clearing the land for timber or to create a housing subdivision? Highlight both the key terms and the definitions the author provides.

5. **Diagram or map to analyze structure.** Because many arguments are complex, you may find it helpful to diagram or map them. By mapping the argument, you may discover unsubstantiated ideas, reasons for which evidence is not provided, or an imbalance between reasons and emotional appeals.

# Think Critically About Arguments

■ GOAL 4
Think critically about arguments

Not all arguments are reasonable and not all arguments are sound and logical. Thinking critically about arguments involves evaluating evidence, examining opposing viewpoints, considering emotional appeals, and identifying errors in reasoning.

## Evaluating Evidence

When you evaluate evidence, consider whether the evidence provided is relevant—in other words, does it directly support the claim?—and whether sufficient evidence has been provided.

### Is the Evidence Relevant?

Evidence that is offered in support of a claim must directly relate to that claim. That is, to be relevant, evidence must apply specifically to the issue at hand. For example, a friend may offer as a reason for his tardiness that he had a flat tire, but this fact is not relevant because he would have had to walk only one block to see you. Writers may intentionally or unintentionally include information that may seem convincing but when analyzed more closely does not directly apply to the issue. Here is an example. Can you identify the irrelevant information the paragraph contains?

> Business students, especially those in MBA programs, need to take more classes in ethics. Stricter requirements in this area will ensure that tomorrow's corporate executives will be more responsible and honest than they have been in the past. More women should be admitted to the top business schools. The trust and confidence that employees and investors have lost can be built back if today's professors commit to teaching right and wrong. Future businesspeople will then move the economy forward without the setbacks created by corporate scandal and bankruptcy.

In this paragraph, the sentence about women being admitted to business school is not relevant because the argument is not about whether women are more honest than men or whether higher numbers of women would make a difference in the climate of business ethics.

To decide whether a statement is relevant, reread the claim and then immediately afterward reread the statement in question. Ask yourself, "Are the two logically connected?"

**EXERCISE 15-6**

# Identifying Relevant Evidence

**Directions:** For each claim listed below, place a check mark in front of those statements that provide relevant supporting evidence. The number of relevant statements varies, but there are always at least two.

1. Claim: Alcohol abuse is common among teenagers and needs to be curtailed.

   _____ **a.** Thousands of young people die each year in alcohol-related crashes.

   _____ **b.** According to the National Institute on Alcohol Abuse and Alcoholism, young people who drink have an increased chance of developing problems with alcohol later in life.

   _____ **c.** People who take medication need to limit or cease their alcohol intake.

   _____ **d.** Many teens who drink have a parent who is an alcoholic.

2. Claim: Fish populations are decreasing because of overfishing.

   _____ **a.** The UN Food and Agriculture Organization reports that because of overharvesting, four of the fifteen main fishing areas in the world are depleted and another nine are declining.

   _____ **b.** Regulations to save fish populations will hurt fishermen.

   _____ **c.** The fish cannot reproduce fast enough to keep up with the rate they are harvested.

   _____ **d.** These days people are eating less red meat for health reasons.

3. Claim: Recycling helps the environment.

 _____ a. Products made from recycled materials are expensive.

 _____ b. Buying items in bulk reduces the need for extra packaging.

 _____ c. Recycling keeps reusable materials out of landfills.

 _____ d. It takes less energy to make a new product from recycled material.

4. Claim: Controversial art should not be exhibited in public places.

 _____ a. Children might see disturbing images, causing them to develop behavioral problems.

 _____ b. Taxpayers do not want their money going to fund what they consider to be obscene art.

 _____ c. Public funds have to be used for security if there are protesters.

 _____ d. Art is covered under the "Freedom of Speech" amendment.

5. Claim: Any stock or bond investment is risky and must be researched before money exchanges hands.

 _____ a. The Securities and Exchange Commission collects financial data on public companies.

 _____ b. Day traders sometimes use borrowed money for their activities.

 _____ c. Stocks and bonds may lose their value.

 _____ d. Not all brokers are responsible with their clients' money.

### Is the Evidence Sufficient?

There must be a sufficient number of reasons or pieces of evidence to support a claim. The amount and degree of detail of supporting evidence will vary with the issue, its complexity, and its importance. For any serious issue, it is not usually sufficient to offer a single reason or piece of evidence. For example, to say that our oceans are dying due to coastal development is not convincing because only a portion of the world's oceans are affected by coastal development. Other evidence to support this claim could include industrial waste dumping, oil drilling, ecosystem imbalance, and rising water temperatures.

The evidence a writer offers must also be sufficiently detailed to be convincing and believable. For instance, the statement "A parrot is an ideal pet because it can be taught to mimic language" does not provide sufficient information to persuade anyone to choose a parrot as a pet. To be convincing, more details would be needed about the habits, personality, longevity, and beauty of parrots.

**EXERCISE 15-7**

# Understanding Types of Evidence

**Directions:** For each of the claims listed, find three pieces of evidence in the box on the next page that support it. Write the letters of the evidence in the space provided. Not all pieces of evidence will be used.

**Claims**

 _____ 1. People are becoming ruder in our country.

 _____ 2. Many children who receive special education services do not really need them.

        **3.** Parents and teachers should fight to keep art and music in the schools.

        **4.** Standardized tests do not accurately represent what American students know.

### Evidence

A. Research shows that children need a variety of ways to express themselves.

B. The media bombard our children with images of violence.

C. Telemarketers just will not take no for an answer.

D. Celebrities live public lives of immorality, making promiscuity, drugs, reckless behavior, and divorce seem normal and even glamorous.

E. Incidents of road rage are increasing every year.

F. Not all teachers realize that every child has a different learning style.

G. Teachers are quick to label any child who needs extra help with a learning disorder.

H. Our society puts pressure on children to be consumers at a young age.

I. Learning to play an instrument helps with math skills.

J. Many students experience test anxiety, which can have a negative impact on their scores.

K. Many people have been storming out of stores because of insulting customer service.

L. In some schools there is tremendous pressure on teachers to boost test scores, forcing teachers to "teach to the test."

M. Studies have shown that learning to read music helps students with their regular reading skills.

N. Special education teachers are too aggressive in identifying students who need their services just so they can keep their jobs.

O. Test writers understand education only in theory and do not write questions that are relevant to today's students.

## Examining Opposing Viewpoints

Many arguments recognize opposing viewpoints. For example, an author may argue that gay people should be allowed to marry. However, the author may recognize or admit that opponents believe marriage should only be allowed between a man and a woman.

    Many arguments also attempt to refute the opposing viewpoint (explain why it is wrong, flawed, or unacceptable). For example, a writer may refute the notion that gay people will compromise cohesiveness in the military by stating that soldiers are unified against the enemy, not each other. Basically, then, refutation is a process of finding weaknesses in the opponent's argument.

    When reading arguments that address opposing viewpoints, ask yourself the following questions.

- Does the author address opposing viewpoints clearly and fairly?
- Does the author refute the opposing viewpoint with logic and relevant evidence?

## Considering Emotional Appeals

**Emotional appeals** are ideas that are targeted toward needs or values that readers are likely to care about. Needs include physiological needs (food, drink, shelter) and psychological needs (sense of belonging, sense of accomplishment, sense of self-worth). An argument on gun control, for example, may appeal to a reader's need for safety, while an argument favoring restrictions on banks sharing personal or financial information may appeal to a reader's need for privacy and financial security.

Unfair emotional appeals attempt to involve or excite readers by appealing to their emotions, thereby controlling the reader's attitude toward the subject. Several types of emotional appeals are described below.

1. **Emotionally charged or biased language.** By using words that create an emotional response, writers establish positive or negative feelings. For example, an advertisement for a new line of fragrances promises to "indulge," "refresh," "nourish," and "pamper" the user. An ad for an automobile uses phrases such as "limousine comfort," "European styling," and "animal sleekness" to interest and excite readers.

2. **False authority.** False authority involves using the opinion or action of a well-known or famous person. We have all seen athletes endorsing underwear or movie stars selling shampoo. This type of appeal works on the notion that people admire celebrities and strive to be like them, respect their opinion, and are willing to accept their viewpoint.

3. **Association.** An emotional appeal also is made by associating a product, idea, or position with others that are already accepted or highly regarded. Patriotism is already valued, so to call a product All-American in an advertisement is an appeal to the emotions. A car being named a Cougar to remind you of a fast, sleek animal, a cigarette ad picturing a scenic waterfall, or a speaker standing in front of an American flag are other examples.

4. **Appeal to "common folk."** Some people distrust those who are well educated, wealthy, highly artistic, or in other ways distinctly different from the average person. An emotional appeal to this group is made by indicating that a product or idea originated from, is held by, or is bought by ordinary citizens. A commercial may advertise a product by showing its use in an average household. A politician may describe her background and education to suggest that she is like everyone else; a salesperson may dress in styles similar to his clients.

5. *Ad hominem*. An argument that attacks the holder of an opposing viewpoint rather than his or her viewpoint is known as *ad hominem,* or an attack on the man. For example, the statement, "How could a woman who does not even hold a college degree criticize a judicial decision?" attacks the woman's level of education, not her viewpoint.

6. **"Join the crowd" appeal**. The appeal to do, believe, or buy what everyone else is doing, believing, or buying is known as *crowd appeal* or the *bandwagon appeal*. Commercials that proclaim their product the "#1 best-selling car in America" are appealing to this motive. Essays in support of a position that cite opinion polls on a controversial issue—"68 percent of Americans favor capital punishment"—are also using this appeal.

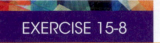

# Understanding Emotional Appeals

**Directions:** Indicate the type of emotional appeal each of the following statements represents.

a. emotionally charged or biased language
b. false authority
c. association

d. appeal to common folk
e. *ad hominem*
f. join the crowd

_____ 1. Michelle Obama recommends the book *Beloved*, by Toni Morrison; it must be very good.

_____ 2. We must preserve our historic neighborhoods in order to save the memories of the hardworking men and women who built our cities with their sweat and blood.

_____ 3. Don't go to that restaurant; the owner can't even keep her garden growing.

_____ 4. Everyone who cares about education is voting for Proposition E.

_____ 5. The mayor eats Mrs. Baker's pecan sandies; they must be the best.

_____ 6. Mandatory collection of DNA samples from all criminals will stop brutal sexual assaults on our helpless women and innocent children.

_____ 7. We provide quality service just like in the good old days.

_____ 8. Join together with your brothers and sisters in the union; don't let rich managers and executives oppress you any longer.

_____ 9. No one dresses like that anymore.

_____ 10. My dentist is awful; he drives a Dodge Dart.

## Errors in Identifying Reasoning

**Errors in reasoning**, often called *logical fallacies*, are common in arguments and they can invalidate arguments or render them flawed. Several common errors in logic are described next.

### Circular Reasoning

Also known as *begging the question*, this error involves using part of the conclusion as evidence to support the argument. Here are two examples.

> Cruel medical experimentation on defenseless animals is inhumane.
>
> Female police officers should not be sent to crime scenes because apprehending criminals is a man's job.

In circular reasoning, because no evidence is given to support the claim—it is simply restated—there is no reason to accept the argument.

### Hasty Generalization

This fallacy means that the conclusion has been derived from insufficient evidence. Here is one example: You taste three tangerines and each is sour, so you conclude that all tangerines are sour. Here is another: After observing one performance of a musical group, you conclude the group will never be a success.

### Non Sequitur ("It Does Not Follow")

The false establishment of cause and effect is known as a *non sequitur.* To say, for example, that "Because my doctor is young, I'm sure she'll be a good doctor" is a *non sequitur* because youth does not cause good medical practice. Here is another example: "Arturio Alvarez is the best choice for state senator because he is an ordinary citizen." Being an ordinary citizen does not necessarily mean someone will be an effective state senator.

### False Cause

The **false cause fallacy** is the incorrect assumption that two events that occur close to each other in time are causally related. Suppose you walked under a ladder and then lost your wallet. If you said you lost your wallet because you walked under a ladder, you would be assuming false cause.

### Either-Or Fallacy

This fallacy assumes that an issue is only two sided, or that there are only two choices or alternatives for a particular situation. In other words, there is no middle ground. Consider the issue of censorship of violence on television. An either-or fallacy is to assume that violence on TV must be either allowed or banned. This fallacy does not recognize other alternatives such as only showing violent material after 10 PM, restricting certain types of violence from being shown on TV, and so forth.

**EXERCISE 15-9**

## Identifying Fallacies

**Directions:** Identify the logical fallacy in each of the following statements.

**a.** circular reasoning      **d.** false cause
**b.** hasty generalization      **e.** either-or fallacy
**c.** *non sequitur*

_____ 1. All African-American students in my biology class earned A grades, so African-Americans must excel in life sciences.

_____ 2. If you are not for nuclear arms control, then you're against protecting our future.

_____ 3. My sister gets nervous when asked to do mathematical computations or balance her checkbook because she has math anxiety.

_____ 4. A well-known mayor, noting a decline in the crime rate in the four largest cities in his state, quickly announced that his new "get-tough on criminals" publicity campaign was successful and took credit for the decline.

_____ 5. Carlos lives in a large house, so his father must have a high-paying job.

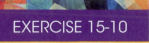

**EXERCISE 15-10**

# Evaluating an Argument

**Directions:** This editorial, originally published in *The Buffalo News*, explores the issue of sports hunting. Read the essay, and then answer the questions that follow.

**FROM A VEGETARIAN:**

**LOOKING AT HUNTING FROM BOTH SIDES NOW**

Timothy Denesha

1    Deer hunting season opened Nov. 18, and as the gunfire resumes in our woodlands and fields so will the perennial sniping between hunters and animal rights supporters. I always feel caught in the cross-fire on this matter, because I have been a vegetarian and animal rights advocate for over 25 years, but I also have friends I respect who are hunters. I've learned the issue is not as black-and-white as I once believed.

2    Growing up with many beloved pets and no hunters in my life, I assumed these people were bloodthirsty animal haters. When, in my 20s, I read the great humanitarian Albert Schweitzer's writings on reverence for life, I became a vegetarian and even more contemptuous of hunters.

3    But I had to revise my opinion after seeing the classic 1981 African film, "The Gods Must Be Crazy." The hero, a good-hearted bushman, slays a small gazelle, then tenderly strokes her, apologizing for taking her life. He explains his family is hungry and thanks her for providing food. I was stunned: a hunter practicing reverence for life! Later, I learned that Native American tradition has the same compassionate awareness about life lost so another life may be sustained.

4    My position softened further several years ago when Alex Pacheco, a leading animals-rights activist, spoke here. Detailing inhumane practices at meat-packing plants and factory farms, he said the most important thing anyone could do to lessen animal suffering was to stop eating meat. I decided to work toward being vegan (eating no animal products) and reluctantly admitted that hunters were not the animal kingdom's worst enemies. However, I still disliked them.

5    What really changed my perspective was getting to know some hunters personally, through my job at a Red Cross blood-donation center. Some of my co-workers and a number of our donors are civic-minded people who donate blood (which most people don't) but also shed animal blood with their guns and arrows. Confronting this paradox brought me some realizations.

6    First, hunters are like any group that differs from me: lacking personal experience of them made it easier to demonize them. They aren't monsters. I don't know if any of them apologizes to or thanks his kill as the hungry bushman did, but I do know they aren't cruel, sadistic or bloodthirsty—quite the opposite, as I later discovered.

7    Second, these people aren't just amusing themselves by ending a life; they are acquiring food. This death that sustains another life has a meaning that, for

example, fox hunting does not. To the animal, this distinction may mean little. But it is significant when considering a person's intentions.

8     Also, I was informed that hunters don't "like to kill." They enjoy the outdoors, the camaraderie and the various skills involved. (One of these skills, the "clean kill," is prized precisely because it minimizes suffering.) Like vegetable garden-ers, they enjoy providing food [for] themselves and their families with their own hands. Like those who fish, they enjoy a process of food acquisition that involves an animal's death, but not because it does. Again, this may seem a small point (especially to the prey), but I feel it is meaningful from the standpoint of the hunt-er's humanity.

9     In addition, I've come to see a certain integrity in hunters as meat-eaters who "do their own dirty work." Packaged cold-cuts and fast-food burgers mask the fact of lives bled out on the killing floor. Hunters never forget this, for they accept per-sonal responsibility for it.

10     Furthermore, were I an animal that had to die to feed a human, I'd rather it happen one-on-one, at the hands of that person in the woods that were my home, than amidst the impersonal mass-production machinery of a meat factory. Either way is death, but one way has more dignity, less fear and less suffering.

11     There are bad hunters who trespass, shoot domestic animals, hunt intoxicated or disregard that cardinal rule of hunting's unwritten code of ethics: wounded prey must not be allowed to suffer. Last Thanksgiving morning in Chestnut Ridge Park, I found a fresh trail of deer tracks in the snow, heavily splashed with blood. It was horrible.

12     One of my hunter co-workers was also upset when I told him about it, and had this story. He himself was able to hunt only one day last season and sighted a small, wounded doe. As a student on a tight budget with a family, he hunts for food and would have preferred to ignore the doe's plight and meet his license limit with a large buck. Instead, he devoted a long, difficult day to trailing her until he was close enough to end her suffering. This was an act of mercy and even self-sacrifice, not the action of a heartless person insensitive to animals. It was reverence for life. He claims many hunters would do and have done the same.

13     And I realized that compassion has many faces, some of the truest the most unexpected.

**1.** With what issue is the argument concerned?

_____

**2.** What is the author's claim?

_____

_____

_____

**3.** What types of evidence does the author offer to support the claim? What other types of evidence could have been used?

_____

_____

4. Does the author recognize or refute opposing viewpoints? If so, how?

_____

_____

5. How does the attempt to win the readers over to his viewpoint?

_____

_____

6. Evaluate the overall effectiveness of the argument. Was it convincing?

_____

_____

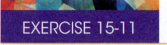

## Evaluating an Argument

**Directions:** From among the reading assignments you have completed this semester, choose one that involved persuasive or argumentative writing. Review this piece of writing and then complete the following.

1. Summarize what is being argued for.

2. List the key points of the argument.

3. Indicate what type of evidence the writer uses.

4. Determine whether the evidence is adequate and sufficient to support the author's point.

5. Identify any counterarguments the author recognizes or refutes.

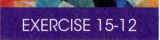

## Evaluating Techniques and Emotional Appeals

**Directions:** Visit a newsgroup that focuses on a controversial issue and either follow or participate in the discussion. What persuasive techniques or emotional appeals (see p. 460) did you observe?

## WRITING

# Write Argument Paragraphs

■ **GOAL 5**
Write argument
paragraphs

Writing an argument paragraph involves the same paragraph-writing skills you have been learning and practicing throughout this book. You may want to review the techniques covered in Chapters 5 and 6, and then use the following guidelines to write an effective argument paragraph.

## Writing Your Topic Sentence

Your topic sentence should do the following:

- identify the issue
- state your claim about the issue

In a lengthy argument, it may also suggest the major reasons you will offer to support your position. The following topic sentence makes it clear that the writer will argue against the use of animals for medical research:

> The use of animals in medical research should be outlawed because it is cruel, unnecessary, and disrespectful of animals' place in the chain of life.

Notice that this topic sentence identifies the issue and makes it clear that the writer opposes animal research. It also suggests the three major reasons she will present: (1) it is cruel, (2) it is unnecessary, and (3) it is disrespectful. You do not always have to include the major points of your argument in your topic sentence, but including them does help the reader to know what to expect. This topic sentence also makes clear what action the author thinks is appropriate: *using animals in medical research should be outlawed.*

Here are a few more topic sentences. Notice that they use the verbs *should*, *would*, and *must*.

> If we expect industries to dispose of their wastes properly, then we **should** provide tax breaks to cover the extra expense.
>
> It **would** be a mistake to assume racial discrimination has been eliminated or even reduced significantly over the past 20 years.
>
> The proportion of tenured women and minority faculty on our campus **must** be increased.

**EXERCISE 15-13**

**WRITING IN PROGRESS**

# Writing Topic Sentences

**Directions:** For three of the following issues, take a position and write a topic sentence.

1. Employee health care benefits

2. The right of insurance companies to deny medical coverage to certain individuals

3. Banning smoking in public places

4. Outlawing sport hunting of wild animals

5. Mandatory counseling for drunken drivers

6. Buying American-made products

7. Volunteer work

8. Athletes and the use of steroids

## Supporting Your Position

As discussed on pages 454–455, there are two primary types of support that can be used to explain why your position should be accepted: **reasons**—general statements that back up a position—and **evidence**, which includes facts and statistics, quotations from authorities, examples, and personal experience. Each is discussed in more detail in the section on writing argument essays.

# Write Argument Essays

■ GOAL 6
Write argument essays

The skills you learned for writing an argument paragraph apply to essay writing as well. See Chapters 10 and 11 for detailed coverage of essay-writing techniques. Use these guidelines to write an effective argument essay.

## Writing a Thesis Statement

Your thesis statement should identify the issue and state your claim about it. It may also suggest the primary reasons for accepting the claim. Place your thesis statement where it will be most effective. There are three common placements:

**a.** Thesis statement in the beginning

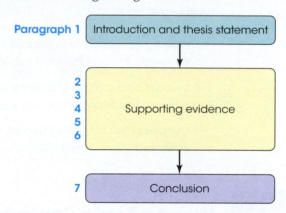

**b.** Thesis statement after responding to objections

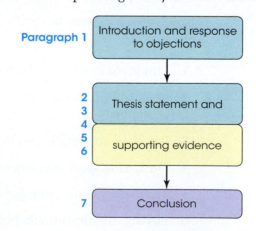

c. Thesis statement at the end

VISUALIZE IT!

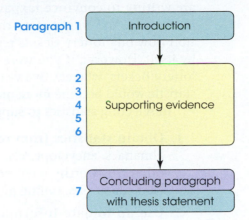

In general, placing the thesis in the beginning is best when addressing an audience in agreement with your claim or one that is neutral about the topic under discussion. For an audience that does not agree with your argument, a later placement gives you the opportunity to respond to the audience's objections before you present your thesis.

## Providing Adequate Supporting Evidence

Here are five types of supporting evidence you can use to develop your thesis.

### Facts and Statistics

As in writing any other type of paragraph or essay, you must choose facts that directly support the position you express in your topic sentence. Here is an excerpt that uses facts and statistics as evidence to argue that the population of the United States is aging:

**Population Aging and the "Graying" of the Globe**

The United Nations categorizes countries in which 7 percent or more of the population is over age 65 as "aged." Although many developing nations still have short life expectancies and young populations, the United States and most industrialized and postindustrial nations meet the criterion for "aged," and by 2020 almost all nations will (Novak, 2009). The United State is experiencing a "senior boom" due to the rapid growth of its elderly population. In 1900, people over age 65 made up only about 4 percent of the U.S. population (about 1 in 25 people); by 2010 over 14 percent, or more than 1 in 7 Americans (34.8 million), were over age 65. Today, that figure is approximately 44 million (U.S. Bureau of Census, 2009). Demographic projections indicate that by the year 2050, approximately 82 million Americans (over twice as many as today) will be over the age of 65. The 85 and older population in the United States stands at approximately 5.5 million and is also increasing dramatically. Currently, people over the age of 100 (centenarians) are the fastest-growing segment of the U.S. population, numbering over 72,000 (Huffington Post 4/26/11).

—Thompson and Vickey, *Society in Focus*, pp. 328–329

It is usually more effective to present more than one statistic. Suppose you are writing to convince taxpayers that state lotteries have become profitable businesses. You might state that more than 60 percent of the adult population now buy lottery tickets regularly. This statistic would have little meaning by itself. However, if you were to state that 60 percent of adults now purchase lottery tickets, whereas five years ago only 30 percent purchased them, the first statistic would become more meaningful.

In selecting statistics to support your position, be sure to:

1. **Obtain statistics from reliable print or online sources.** These include almanacs, encyclopedias, articles in reputable journals and magazines, or other trustworthy reference material from your library. Online sources include databases, online journals, and scholarly Web sites.

2. **Use up-to-date information, preferably from the past year or two.** Dated statistics may be incorrect or misleading.

3. **Make sure you define terms and units of measurement.** For example, if you say that 60 percent of adults regularly play the lottery, you should define what "regularly" means. Does it mean daily, weekly, or monthly?

4. **Verify that the statistics you obtain from more than one source are comparable.** For example, if you compare the crime rates in New York City and Los Angeles, be sure that each crime rate was computed the same way, that each represents the same types of crimes, and that report sources were similar.

### Quotations or Citations from Authorities

You can also support your claim by using expert or authoritative statements of opinion or conclusions. **Experts or authorities** are those who have studied a subject extensively, conducted research on it, or written widely about it. For example, if you are writing an essay calling for stricter preschool-monitoring requirements to prevent child abuse, the opinion of a psychiatrist who works extensively with abused children would provide convincing support.

### Examples

Refer to Chapter 6 for a review of how to use examples as supporting details. In a persuasive essay, your examples must represent your claim and should illustrate as many aspects of your claim as possible. Suppose your claim is that a particular movie should have been X-rated because it contains excessive violence. The evidence you choose to support this claim should be clear, vivid examples of violent scenes.

The examples you choose should also, if possible, relate to your audience's experience. Familiar examples are more appealing, convincing, and understandable. Suppose you are taking a position on abortion. You're audience consists of career women between 30 and 40 years old. It would be most effective to use as examples women of the same age and occupational status.

### Personal Experience

If you are knowledgeable about a subject, your personal experiences can be convincing evidence. For example, if you were writing an essay supporting the position that physical separation from parents encourages a teenager or young adult to mature, you could discuss your own experiencees with leaving home and assuming new responsibilities.

### Comparisons and Analogies

Comparison and analogies (extended comparisons) are useful especially when writing for an audience that lacks background and experience with your subject. By comparing something unknown to something that is known and familiar, you can make your readers comfortable, non-threatened. For example, you could explain a new dance step by likening it dance steps that are traditional and familiar to most readers. Be sure to make it clear what characteristics or features are similar and which are not.

### EXERCISE 15-14

WRITING IN PROGRESS

# Supporting a Topic Sentence

**Directions:** Generate reasons and evidence to support one of the topic sentences you wrote for Exercise 15-13.

### Researching Your Topic

An **argument essay** must provide specific and convincing evidence that supports the topic sentence. Often it is necessary to go beyond your own knowledge and experience. You may need to research your topic. For example, if you were writing to urge the creation of an environmentally protected wetland area, you would need to find out what types of wildlife live there, which are endangered, and how successful other protected wetland sites have been in protecting wildlife.

At other times, you may need to interview people who are experts on your topic or directly involved with it. Suppose you are writing a memo urging other employees in your department to participate in a walk-a-thon. It is being held to benefit a local shelter for homeless men and women. The director of the shelter or one of her employees could offer useful statistics, share personal experiences, and provide specific details about the clientele the shelter serves that would help you make a convincing case.

### EXERCISE 15-15

WRITING IN PROGRESS

# Evaluating Evidence

**Directions:** Evaluate the evidence you collected in Exercise 15-14, and research your topic further if needed. Write the first draft of the paragraph. Exchange paragraghs with a classmate and critique each other's paragraph. Revise using your classmate's suggestion.

Here is a sample argument written by one student. Note how he presents reasons and evidence for taking a specific action.

### Buckle Up

As a paramedic, I am the first to arrive at the scene of many grim and tragic accidents. One awful accident last month involved four women in one car. The front-seat passenger died instantly, another died during a mercy flight to the nearest hospital, one lost both legs, and one walked away from the accident without serious injury. Only one woman was wearing a seat belt. Guess which one? Though many people protest and offer excuses, seat belts do save lives.

Many people avoid wearing seat belts and say they'd rather be thrown free from an accident. Yet they seldom realize that the rate at which they will be thrown is the same rate at which the car is moving. Others fear being trapped inside by their seat belt in case of a fire. However, if not ejected, those without a belt are likely to be stunned or knocked unconscious on impact and will not be alert enough to escape uninjured.

Seat belts save lives by protecting passengers from impact. During a crash, a body slams against the windshield or steering wheel with tremendous force if unbelted. The seat belt secures the passenger in place and protects vital organs from injury.

Recent statistics demonstrate that a passenger is five times more likely to survive a crash if a seat belt is worn. Life is a gamble, but those are good odds. Buckle up!

This writer introduces the topic with a startling example from his personal experience. The thesis statement occurs at the end of the first paragraph. The second and third paragraphs offer evidence that supports the writer's thesis. The last paragraph concludes the essay by offering a convincing statistic and reminding the reader of the thesis "Buckle up." You can visualize this short argument as follows:

**VISUALIZE IT!**

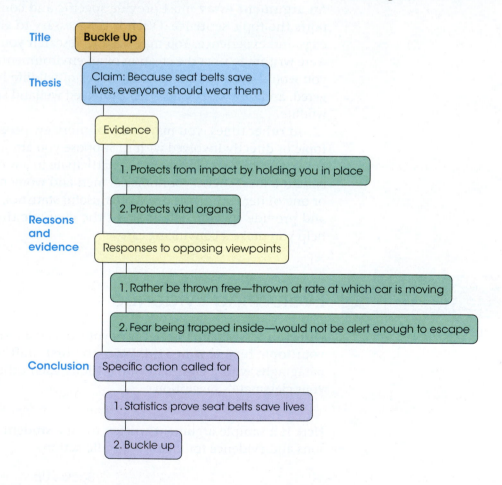

| | |
|---|---|
| **Title** | **Buckle Up** |
| **Thesis** | Claim: Because seat belts save lives, everyone should wear them |
| | Evidence |
| | 1. Protects from impact by holding you in place |
| | 2. Protects vital organs |
| **Reasons and evidence** | Responses to opposing viewpoints |
| | 1. Rather be thrown free—thrown at rate at which car is moving |
| | 2. Fear being trapped inside—would not be alert enough to escape |
| **Conclusion** | Specific action called for |
| | 1. Statistics prove seat belts save lives |
| | 2. Buckle up |

## Analyzing Your Audience

Analyzing your audience is a crucial step in planning a convincing argument. There are three types of audiences:

■ **Audiences who agree with your claim.** These are the easiest to write for because they already accept most of what you will say. Audiences in agreement with you are likely to have positive feelings toward you because you think the way they do about the issue. For this audience, state your claim and explain why you think it is correct.

- **Neutral audiences.** These readers have not made up their minds or have not given much thought to the issue. They may have questions, they may misunderstand the issue, or they may have heard arguments supporting the opposing viewpoint. An essay written for a neutral audience should be direct and straightforward, like those written for an audience in agreement with your point of view. However, a fuller explanation of the issue is necessary to answer questions, clear up misunderstandings, and respond to opposing arguments.

- **Audiences who disagree with your claim.** These are the most difficult to address. Some members will have thought about the issue and taken a position that opposes yours. Others who disagree may not have examined the issue at all and are making superficial judgments or are relying on misinformation. Both types think their position is correct, so they will not be eager to change their minds. They may also distrust you, because you think differently from them. For such an audience, your biggest challenge is to build trust and confidence. Before writing, carefully analyze this audience and try to answer these questions:

  - Why does your audience disagree with your claim?
  - Is their position based on real facts and sound evidence, or on personal opinion? If it is based on evidence, what type?
  - What type of arguments or reasons are most likely to appeal to your audience? For example, will they be convinced by facts and statistics, or by statements made by authorities? Would personal anecdotes and examples work well?

Once you understand how your audience thinks, you can plan your essay more effectively.

## INTEGRATING READING AND WRITING

## READ AND RESPOND: A Student Essay

*Quinne Sember is a student at the State University of New York at Buffalo where she is a pre-medical student majoring in political science and biomedical science.*

*Sember wrote this essay for a political science class. She was asked to choose an issue discussed in class and write an essay taking a position on the issue.*

Quinne Sember

Dr. McCombs

ENG 112

18 March 2012

Marijuana: An Argument for Legalization

Marijuana is a commonly used drug in the United States. It is not as dangerous or addictive as alcohol or tobacco. Yet alcohol and tobacco are legal in the United States, while marijuana is not. It costs the United States millions of dollars to prosecute and detain people who possess marijuana when the government could be making money taxing the substance. The argument for the legalization of marijuana is a strong one and many people support a law that would take this action.

The economic effect of the criminalization of marijuana in the U.S. is astounding. We create a large number of criminals by sentencing people for non-violent acts, including possession of marijuana. The United States holds 25% of the world's prisoners, but has only 5% of its total population. We also spend $68 billion dollars just on corrections and one third of that money is spent on people serving time for drug crimes that are non-violent. In addition to that money, another $150 billion is spent on courts and police activity. The majority (47.5%) is spent on marijuana activity (Klein). For a nation that is in so much debt, that is a large amount of money that could be spent elsewhere. Shouldn't we improve the roads or healthcare before we spend so much money on people who are not committing violent crimes?

Legalization of marijuana, besides saving the country money, could also help us to make money. Taxation of the drug would produce considerable profits. In a report sent to the president, authored by Jeffrey Miron, it is estimated that the taxation of marijuana could produce $2.4 billion in revenue if it were taxed like most other consumer drugs. If it were taxed like alcohol, however, it could produce up to $6.2 billion per year (Moffatt). With the combined savings, the country could

**Title**

**Introduction: Makes a comparison of alcohol and tobacco**

**Thesis statement**

**Reason 1**

**Statistical evidence**

**Reason 2**

be over $200 billion richer with the legalization of marijuana. The government could make even more money if licenses were required to grow the plant. That is an astonishing amount of money that could be spent on healthcare, schools, or infrastructure. Miron's report was signed by over 500 economists who ensured its accuracy (Moffatt). Obviously, regulation and education about marijuana are more logical than the criminalization of its users.

Marijuana can have an effect on health and it is not always a negative one. Many people utilize the drug to assist them with medical conditions. Cannabis can help to alleviate the symptoms of multiple sclerosis, Crohn's disease, and other inflammatory diseases. It can also increase appetite in people who are struggling with chemotherapy. In a handful of states, doctors can prescribe medical marijuana for these conditions. However, people in states where medical marijuana is illegal are out of luck. It is also very difficult for people without a specific disease who have other problems for which marijuana could be helpful to get medical marijuana. Nathan Seppa says "people smoke the drug to alleviate pain, sleep easier and deal with nausea, lack of appetite and mood disorders such as anxiety, stress and depression" (Seppa). The American Medical Association has recognized that marijuana can have a positive effect on nausea, glaucoma, extreme muscle tension, and pain (Cloud). With the legalization of marijuana, people could buy the drug on their own accord to treat whatever symptoms they may have without having to battle with a doctor to get a prescription.

Maybe the most convincing evidence for the legalization of marijuana is that people support it. A Gallup poll from 2009 shows that 44% of Americans favored legalizing the drug, while 54% opposed it. This was the highest rate since the poll started in 1970. The rate has continued to grow by one to two percent each year (Saad). Therefore, by 2012, the legalization of marijuana could be supported by a majority of the population. This was already the case in the West in 2009, where 53% of people favored legalization.

*Margin annotations:*

Statistical evidence

Reason 3

Facts as evidence

Citation of expert opinion as evidence

Reason 4

Statistical evidence

Sember 3

Reason 5

Quotation by authority

Recognition and refutation of opposing viewpoint

Conclusion: Sember recaps her reasons and makes a final statement

If this is not enough evidence, even the former U.S. Surgeon General, Joycelyn Elders, supports legalization. She told CNN, "'What I think is horrible about all of this, is that we criminalize young people. And we use so many of our excellent resources . . . for things that aren't really causing any problems. It's not a toxic substance.'" Elders says that we have the "'highest number of people in the world being criminalized, many for non-violent crimes related to marijuana'" (CNN). She strongly believes that our resources can be put to better use.

Marijuana legalization is opposed by some who claim it has a negative impact on health; however, marijuana is actually much healthier than tobacco or alcohol. No one has ever died of THC (the active chemical in the marijuana) poisoning or overdose (Cloud). People die every day from the effects of tobacco and alcohol and these drugs are legal. Tobacco is proven to cause cancer and while there has not been any evidence to show that smoking marijuana does cause cancer, there have not been any conclusive studies to show that it does not. Others argue that marijuana is an addictive substance. However, while one-third of tobacco users get hooked and fifteen percent of drinkers become addicted to alcohol, only nine percent of people using marijuana become addicted.

The legalization of marijuana would help a lot of people. It would directly help people who suffer from symptoms of illnesses that can be treated with the drug. It would also indirectly affect children who go to poor schools or people who can't afford healthcare because of the amount of money that is tied up in the courts, prisons, and police activity regarding marijuana. This money could be used by the government for much more serious and useful things. Many people believe that the legalization and use of marijuana is risky. With education and regulation, this practice would not be any more risky (probably less risky, in fact) than the use of tobacco and alcohol, legal substances in our country.

Sember 4

Works Cited

Cloud, John. "Is Pot Good For You?" *TIME*. Time Inc., 4 Nov. 2002. Web. 15
    Apr. 2011.

"Former surgeon general calls for marijuana legalization." *CNN*. Turner Broadcasting
    System, Inc., 18 Oct. 2010. Web. 17 Apr. 2011.

Klein, Joe. "Why Legalizing Marijuana Makes Sense." *TIME*. Time Inc., 16 Apr. 2009.
    Web. 15 Apr. 2011.

Moffatt, Mike. "Time to Legalize Marijuana?—500+ Economists Endorse Marijuana
    Legalization." *About.com*. New York Times Company, 2011. Web. 15 Apr. 2011.

Saad, Lydia. "U.S. Support for Legalizing Marijuana Reaches New High." *Gallup*.
    Gallup, Inc., 19 Oct. 2009. Web. 15 Apr. 2011.

Seppa, Nathan. "Not Just a High." *Science News* 177.13 (2010): 16–20. MasterFILE
    Premier. Web. 15 Apr. 2011.

## Examining Writing

1. For what type of audience does Sember seem to be writing—neutral, in agreement, or not in agreement?
2. Did you find her argument convincing? Why or why not?
3. What other reasons could Sember have included?
4. Does Sember rely too heavily on statistics? Why or why not? What other types of evidence could she have included?

## Writing Assignments

1. You are taking an ecology class. You have been asked to select a type of environmental pollution and develop an argument urging steps be taken to control it in your community.
2. You are taking a political science class and you are studying voter registration and participation. Your instructor has asked you to write an editorial for your local newspaper urging that either more citizens become registered voters or more voters use their voting privilege.
3. You are taking a zoology class and are studying the function of zoos. You are considering such questions as: Do zoos protect animals or put them on display? Do they preserve endangered species or do they sacrifice animal needs for those of humans? Write an essay that takes a position on zoos. Develop an argument that supports your position.

## READ AND RESPOND: Paired Professional Essays

In the following pair of readings, the authors address the same question from a different viewpoint. As you read each essay, identify the parts of an argument and the types of evidence used to support the authors' claims.

### Thinking Before Reading

**Reading 1: Pro Argument from Sen. Joseph Lieberman, I-Conn**

1. Preview the reading, using the steps discussed in Chapter 1, page 15.
2. Connect the reading to your own experience by answering the following questions:
   a. Do you think online sites should ban postings by groups identified as terrorists?
   b. Should the Internet be subject to more censorship?
3. Mark and annotate as you read.

# Pro: Should Online Sites Ban Postings by Groups the Government Identifies as Terrorists?

## Sen. Joseph I. Lieberman, I-Conn.

*Chairman, Senate Committee on Homeland Security and Governmental Affairs. From the Committee Web site, May 19 and May 20, 2008, http://hsgac.senate.gov.*

1 Islamist terrorist organizations rely extensively on the Internet to attract supporters and advance their cause. This Internet campaign is described in a bipartisan staff report by the Senate Committee on Homeland Security and Governmental Affairs. . . . The report explains how al-Qaeda manages an online media operation intended to enlist followers. Central to it is the branding of content with an icon to guarantee that the content was produced by al-Qaeda or allied organizations like al-Qaeda in Iraq. All of these groups have been designated Foreign Terrorist Organizations by the Department of State.

2 Searches on YouTube return dozens of videos branded with an icon or logo identifying the videos as the work of one of these Islamist terrorist organizations. A great majority document horrific attacks on American soldiers in Iraq and Afghanistan. Others provide weapons training, speeches by al-Qaeda leadership and general material intended to radicalize potential recruits.

3 In other words, Islamist terrorist organizations use YouTube to disseminate propaganda, enlist followers and provide weapons training—activities that are all essential to terrorist activity. The online content produced by al-Qaeda and other

Islamist terrorist organizations can play a significant role in the process of radicalization, the end point of which is the planning and execution of a terrorist attack. YouTube also, unwittingly, permits Islamist terrorist groups to maintain an active, pervasive and amplified voice, despite military setbacks or successful operations by the law-enforcement and intelligence communities.

4    Protecting our citizens from terrorist attacks is a top priority for our government. The private sector can help us do that. By taking action to curtail the use of YouTube to disseminate the goals and methods of those who wish to kill innocent civilians, Google will make a singularly important contribution to this effort.

5    Google apparently has taken 80 videos off YouTube that violated the company's own guidelines against gratuitous violence. That is a start, but it is not enough. Videos produced by al-Qaeda and al-Qaeda affiliates showing attacks on American troops remain on YouTube's Web site and violate YouTube's own community guidelines. Those should be taken down immediately. Furthermore, Google continues to allow the posting of videos by organizations the State Department has designated as foreign terrorist organizations. No matter what their content, videos produced by terrorist organizations like al-Qaeda, that are committed to attacking America and killing Americans, should not be tolerated. Google must reconsider its policy.

# Getting Ready to Write

## Checking Your Comprehension

Answer each of the following questions using complete sentences.

1. According to the reading, for what two purposes do Islamist terrorist organizations rely on the Internet?

2. Describe the content of the YouTube videos identified as the work of Islamist terrorist organizations.

3. What activities are described as essential to terrorist activity?

4. According to Sen. Lieberman, what is the "end point" of the process of radicalization?

5. What does Sen. Lieberman want Google to do?

## Strengthening Your Vocabulary

Using the word's context, word parts, or a dictionary, write a brief definition of each of the following words as it is used in the reading.

1. bipartisan (paragraph 1) _____

2. radicalize (paragraph 2) _____

3. disseminate (paragraph 3) _____

4. unwittingly (paragraph 3) _____

5. pervasive (paragraph 3) _____

6. curtail (paragraph 4) _____

7. gratuitous (paragraph 5) _____

## Thinking Before Reading

**Reading 2: Con Argument from Leslie Harris and John Morris**

1. Preview the reading, using the steps discussed in Chapter 1, page 15.

2. Connect the reading to your own experience by answering the following questions:

   a. Do you think online sites should be allowed to host postings by groups identified as terrorists?

   b. Should the Internet be subject to less censorship?

3. Mark and annotate as you read.

# Con: Should Online Sites Ban Postings by Groups the Government Identifies as Terrorists?

## Leslie Harris, John Morris

*President and CEO, Center for Democracy & Technology. General Counsel, Center for Democracy & Technology. From The Huffington Post, May 28, 2008, http://www.huffingtonpost.com*

1 Sen. Joe Lieberman took a step backward in America's "war on terrorism," by demanding that YouTube censor hundreds of videos allegedly posted by Islamic terrorist groups. And when the Google-owned site responded by promptly removing a large number of videos, which violated its guidelines against hate speech and violence, he insisted that action was "not enough."

2    What would be "enough" in the senator's estimation? The removal of all tainted videos, even those that were plainly constitutionally protected advocacy, albeit abhorrent, and a plan "to prevent the content from reappearing"?

3    Civil liberties continue to be a casualty in our efforts against terrorism. So far, broad Internet censorship has not taken root, but censorship is the path we would take if Google acceded to Lieberman's demand.

4    The system we have devised, in which online services establish rigorous terms of service and enforce them, is a wise one. Users help police the system, and sites that are notified of potentially offensive content generally take down content that violates their rules. In the spirit of self-policing, Lieberman's request to review specific videos is fair, but demanding ongoing review of all videos, and removal of those that don't meet with self-selected criteria, crosses the line. . . .

5    For the last year, Congress has made the Internet a focus of anti-terrorism activities. The Violent Radicalization and Homegrown Terrorism Prevention Act, which has already passed the House, specifically finds that the Internet "aided in facilitating violent radicalization, ideologically based violence and the homegrown terrorism process in the United States by providing access to broad and constant streams of terrorist-related propaganda."

6    Congress can take away two diametrically opposed lessons from this finding. The first is that the Internet is an essential communications tool that America should learn to better use to counter terrorism and tout our values. The other is to fight terrorism by censoring the Internet and destroying our first freedom.

7    Ironically, while Lieberman's letter was being delivered to Google a Senate panel on human rights was hearing testimony on threats to Internet freedom from repressive regimes. Some, like China, have built a network of gatekeepers to block content that challenges the government's official messages. Congress cannot [advocate] Internet freedom with one voice and [call] for censorship with another.

## Getting Ready to Write

### Checking Your Comprehension

Answer each of the following questions using complete sentences.

1. Why did YouTube remove videos allegedly posted by Islamist terrorist groups?
2. What do the authors refer to as a "casualty" of antiterrorism efforts?
3. How does the current system work to control online content?
4. According to the authors, what two possible lessons can Congress take away from the findings of the Violent Radicalization and Homegrown Terrorism Prevention Act?

### Strengthening Your Vocabulary

Using the word's context, word parts, or a dictionary, write a brief definition of each of the following words as it is used in the reading.

1. allegedly (paragraph 1) _____
2. abhorrent (paragraph 2) _____
3. acceded (paragraph 3) _____
4. rigorous (paragraph 4) _____
5. facilitating (paragraph 5) _____
6. tout (paragraph 6) _____
7. repressive (paragraph 7) _____

## Getting Ready to Write About Both Readings

### Examining the Readings: Using Idea Maps

Create an idea map for each reading showing the structure of each argument. Begin by stating the issue that both readings address ("Should Online Sites Ban Postings by Groups the Government Identifies as Terrorists?"), then list the claim and the evidence presented in each reading.

## Reacting to Ideas: Discussion and Journal Writing

Get ready to write about the readings by discussing the following:

1. Do you think Google and other online sites should ban postings by groups identified as terrorists? Why or why not?

2. What does *censorship* mean to you? In your opinion, when is censorship necessary or acceptable?

3. Do you think the current level of online censorship is generally appropriate, too restrictive, or not restrictive enough?

## Thinking and Writing Critically

1. Compare the authors' credentials. How qualified are they to write about the issue?

2. Highlight words in each reading that have strong positive or negative connotations. How do these words enhance or detract from the authors' arguments?

3. Compare the tones of the two readings.

4. Which argument attempts to refute the other? How successful is it?

5. Which reading is more persuasive? Explain your answer.

6. In what ways do the authors support their arguments? Evaluate the types of evidence used in each reading.

---

**MySkillsLab®**

Complete this Exercise

## Writing About Both Readings

### Paragraph Options

1. Assume you will be participating in a debate on the topic of censoring Internet content the government considers to be the work of terrorist groups. Write a "pro" paragraph and a "con" paragraph that summarizes each side of the argument.

2. Write a paragraph in which you agree or disagree with this statement from paragraph 3 of Reading 2: "Civil liberties continue to be a casualty in our efforts against terrorism."

3. Have you ever encountered censorship, either on the Internet or elsewhere? Write a paragraph describing your experience with censorship, including your response.

### Essay Options

4. In your opinion, what responsibility or obligation does the private sector have in helping fight terrorism? Do individual citizens have a responsibility as well, and if so, to what extent? Write an essay exploring the answers to these questions.

5. If you were on a panel developing guidelines for an Internet site such as YouTube, what standards would you suggest? What type of content would you prohibit? Write an essay describing your guidelines and how you would enforce them (for example, would you rely on users to help police the system?).

# SELF-TEST SUMMARY

To test yourself, cover the Answer column with a sheet of paper and answer each question in the left column. Evaluate each of your answers as you work by sliding the paper down and comparing your answer with what is printed in the Answer column.

| QUESTION | ANSWER |
| --- | --- |
| ■ GOAL 1 **Understand the use of argument**<br><br>What is an argument? | An argument is a line of reasoning intended to persuade the reader or listener to agree with a particular viewpoint or take a particular action. |
| ■ GOAL 2 **Recognize the parts of an argument**<br><br>What are the essential parts of an argument? | An argument has three essential parts: an issue (the problem or controversy that the argument addresses); a claim (the writer's viewpoint on an issue); and support (the details that demonstrate a claim is correct and should be accepted). Some arguments may also include a refutation, which attempts to disprove opposing viewpoints. |
| ■ GOAL 3 **Read an argument effectively**<br><br>How do writers support a claim? What types of evidence are used to support a claim? | Writers support a claim by offering reasons and evidence that the claim should be accepted. A reason is a general statement that backs up a claim. Evidence consists of facts, statistics, quotations, examples, personal experience, and comparisons that demonstrate why a claim is valid. |
| ■ GOAL 4 **Think critically about arguments**<br><br>How do you think critically about arguments? | Think critically about arguments by evaluating evidence, examining opposing viewpoints, considering emotional appeals, and identifying errors in reasoning. |
| ■ GOAL 5 **Write argument paragraphs**<br><br>How do you write argument paragraphs? | Write a topic sentence that identifies the issue and states your claim, and support your claim with reasons and/or evidence. |
| ■ GOAL 6 **Write argument essays**<br><br>How do you write argument essays? | Write a thesis statement that identifies the issue and states your claim. Place the thesis statement in the beginning, at the end, or after responding to objections. Determine what type of audience you have and provide adequate support for your claim. |

For more help with **Reading and Writing Arguments**, go to your learning path in MySkillsLab at www.myskillslab.com.

# 16

# Writing Essays Using Sources

## THINK About It!

Study the photo above, and then write a sentence explaining how writing an essay is like learning a sport. You might write about the sport shown in the photograph or another sport of your choice.

Although both learning a sport and writing an essay take effort, each can be broken down into manageable parts. Both require a systematic approach, as well. In order to become a good athlete, you learn and practice skills; you listen to your coach, read books about your sport, and talk with peers; and you synthesize (combine) everything you hear and read and decide what steps you need to take in order to improve your performance. To write an essay, you begin by reading about the topic, systematically choosing and evaluating sources, selecting appropriate parts to read carefully, making notes, and pulling together the information from various sources. Then, as you begin writing, you also follow a process. You plan and organize your ideas, draft, revise, and edit. In this chapter you will learn the steps in writing essays using sources and how to correctly credit your sources.

## Reading and Writing Connections

### EVERYDAY CONNECTIONS

- **Reading** As part of your vacation planning, you read reviews of several hotels in the city that you are going to visit. You also consult the hotels' Web sites to find out about their vacation packages, room options, and proximity to local attractions.
- **Writing** After your vacation, you write a letter to the editor of a local travel magazine telling readers about your trip, explaining the process you went through in order to have a successful vacation, and the different sources they could access to plan their own trip.

### ACADEMIC CONNECTIONS

- **Reading** You read a chapter in your American history textbook discussing the responsibilities of the president as commander-in-chief of the U.S. armed forces as well as several articles about how recent presidents have acted in this role.
- **Writing** You write an essay in which you compare and contrast the actions of two presidents as commanders-in-chief during times of war citing the sources you used.

### WORKPLACE CONNECTIONS

- **Reading** You read about expanding populations in three cities so you conduct a market analysis to determine which city would be best for a new branch of your company.
- **Writing** You write a summary of your research and provide detailed support for your recommendation for the city to be considered for a new company branch.

## INTEGRATING READING AND WRITING

# What Is an Essay That Uses Sources?

■ GOAL 1
Use sources to write essays

Many assignments in college require you to integrate your reading and writing skills by locating and reading several sources of information on a topic and then using them to support your ideas in an essay or report. At other times you may be asked to integrate your skills by examining print and online sources and coming up with a new idea or thesis about them in the form of a research paper. In this chapter you will integrate your reading and writing skills by selecting and narrowing a topic, developing a thesis, using sources to find information on your topic, pulling together ideas from the sources to support your thesis, writing an essay, and documenting your sources.

# Find and Record Appropriate Sources

■ GOAL 2
Find and record appropriate sources

Libraries are filled with sources—print, electronic, and more. They house thousands of books, journals, videos, DVDs, pamphlets, tapes, and newspapers, as well as computers that enable you to access the World Wide Web. Yet this very abundance of sources means that one of the hardest parts of doing research is locating the sources that will be the most help to you.

Many books have been written on how to do research and how to use and document print and electronic sources. Therefore, this section gives only a brief overview of the research process and offers advice on how to get started.

## Tips for Finding Appropriate Sources

Suppose you are writing an essay about differences in men's and women's communication styles. Although you will find many sources on your topic, not all will be appropriate for your particular assignment.

Some sources may be too technical; others may be too sketchy. Some may be outdated, others too opinionated. Your task is to find sources that will give you good, solid, current information or points of view. Use the following tips:

1. **Consult a reference librarian.** If you are unsure of where to begin, ask a reference librarian for advice. It is a reference librarian's job to suggest useful sources. He or she can be very helpful to you.

2. **Use a systematic approach.** Start by using general sources, either print or electronic, such as general reference books. Then, as needed, move to more specific sources such as periodicals and journals (scholarly magazines written for people focused on a particular area of study).

3. **Use current sources.** For many topics, such as controversial issues or scientific or medical advances, only the most up-to-date sources are useful. For other topics, such as the moral issues involved in abortion or euthanasia, older sources can be used. Before you begin, decide on a cut-off date—a date before which you feel information will be outdated and therefore not useful to you.

4. **Sample a variety of viewpoints.** Try to find sources that present differing viewpoints on the same subject rather than counting on one source to contain everything you need. Various authors take different approaches and have different opinions on the same topic, all of which can increase your understanding of the topic.

5. **Preview articles by reading abstracts or summaries.** Many sources begin with an abstract or end with a summary. Before using the source, check the abstract or summary to determine whether the source is going to be helpful.

6. **Read sources selectively.** Many students spend time needlessly reading entire books and articles thoroughly when they should be reading selectively—skimming to avoid parts that are not on the subject and to locate portions that relate directly to their topic. To read selectively,

   ■ use indexes and tables of contents to locate the portions of books that are useful and appropriate. In articles, use abstracts or summaries as a guide to the material's organization: the order in which ideas appear in the summary or abstract is the order in which they appear in the source itself.

   ■ after you have identified useful sections, preview (see p. 15) to get an overview of the material.

   ■ use headings to select sections to read thoroughly.

7. **Choose reliable, trustworthy sources.** The Internet contains a great deal of valuable information, but it also contains rumor, gossip, hoaxes, and misinformation. Before using a source, evaluate it by checking the author's

credentials, considering the sponsor or publisher of the site, checking the date of posting, and verifying links. If you are uncertain about the information presented on a site, verify the information by cross-checking it with another source.

8. **Look for sources that lead to other sources.** Some sources include a bibliography, which provides leads to other works related to your topic. Follow links included in electronic sources.

## Recording Sources to Avoid Plagiarism

Keep track of all the sources you use. There are important reasons for doing this:

■ **You are more likely to avoid plagiarism if you keep accurate records of your sources. Plagiarism** is using an author's words or ideas without acknowledging that you have done so. It is a serious ethical error and legal violation. In some colleges, plagiarism is sufficient cause for failing a course or even being dismissed from the college. You can easily avoid plagiarism by properly acknowledging your sources within your paper.

■ **All sources you use must be cited.** When you use sources in an essay, you must acknowledge them all at the end of your paper in a bibliography, or "Works Cited" or "References" list. Providing your reader with information on your sources is called **documentation**.

■ **You may want to refer to the source again.**

Be sure to record all publication information about each print and electronic source you decide to use.

■ **For print sources,** record the title, author(s), volume, edition, place and date of publication, publisher, and page number(s).

■ **For online sites,** record the author, title of the work, title of the Web site, version or edition used, the publisher of the site, and the date of publication.

You may want to use index cards or a small bound notebook to record source information, using a separate card or page for each source. Other options are photocopying pages from print sources, downloading and/or printing information from Web site sources, and bookmarking sites that might be useful for future reference. (You will learn how to document sources you use later in this chapter.)

Also, keep in mind that a good essay does not just consist of a series of quotations strung together. Instead, you should combine information you find in sources to come up with new ideas, perspectives, and responses to your topic. Annotating, outlining, paraphrasing, and summarizing are all important skills for doing this and are covered in Chapter 3:

■ annotating (p. 92)          ■ paraphrasing (p. 102)
■ outlining (p. 99)           ■ summarizing (p. 104)

**EXERCISE 16-1**

**WRITING IN PROGRESS**

## Narrowing a Topic and Developing a Thesis Statement

**Directions:** Choose one of the following broad topics. Use a prewriting strategy to narrow the topic and develop a working thesis statement (see p. 338). Locate at least three reference sources that are useful and appropriate for writing an essay of two to three pages on the topic you have developed. Make a photocopy of the pages you consulted in each source. Print copies of Web sites used. Be sure to record all the bibliographic information for each source.

1. Privacy on social media sites
2. Date rape
3. Gay marriage
4. The history of trade unions
5. The spread, control, or treatment of "bird flu"
6. The Great Depression of the 1930s
7. Controversy over college athletic scholarships
8. Legalized gambling (or lotteries)

# Use Sources to Support Your Thesis and Develop Your Essay

■ **GOAL 3**
Use sources to support your thesis and develop your essay

Suppose you are writing an essay on one aspect of the homeless situation in America. Your thesis states that more social programs should be funded to help homeless people regain control of their lives. In order to present a convincing argument, you need facts, statistics, and evidence to support your opinions. For example, you might need

■ statistics on the numbers of homeless and the increase in homelessness in recent years.

■ statistics on the amount of money spent on programs for the homeless.

■ facts on the types of social programs currently in operation.

■ evidence from experts in the field about which programs work and which do not.

■ statistics on the costs of existing programs.

To gather this information, you would need to consult one or more sources. Follow these guidelines to use sources you find properly:

1. **Write a first draft of your essay.** Before consulting sources to support your ideas, work through the first three steps of the writing process: *prewriting, organizing,* and *drafting.* Decide on a working thesis statement and write your own ideas about the topic down on paper. Once you have drafted your essay, you will be able to see what types of supporting information are necessary. If you research first, you might get flooded with facts and with other writers' voices and viewpoints, and lose your own.

2. **Analyze your draft to identify where you need additional information.** Study your draft and look for statements that require supporting information in order to be believable. For example, suppose you have written

> The number of homeless people is increasing in Chicago each year, and nothing is being done about the increase.

To support the first part of this statement, you need statistics on the increase in homelessness in Chicago. To support the second part, you need evidence that there has not been an increase in federal, state, or local funding for the homeless in Chicago.

The following types of statements benefit from supporting information:

- **Opinions**

| | |
|---|---|
| **EXAMPLE** | Homeless people do not know how to help themselves. |
| **NEEDED INFORMATION** | Why? What evidence supports that opinion? |

- **Broad, general ideas**

| | |
|---|---|
| **EXAMPLE** | Social programs for the homeless don't work as well as they should. |
| **NEEDED INFORMATION** | What programs are available? What evidence suggests they don't work? |

- **Cause and effect statements**

| | |
|---|---|
| **EXAMPLE** | Most homeless people are on the street because they lost their jobs. |
| **NEEDED INFORMATION** | How many are homeless because they lost their jobs? How many are homeless for other reasons? |

- **Statements that assert what should be done**

| | |
|---|---|
| **EXAMPLE** | The homeless should be given more assistance in obtaining jobs. |
| **NEEDED INFORMATION** | How much are they given now? How many are helped? For how many is assistance not available? |

3. **Write questions.** Read your draft looking for unsupported statements, underlining them as you find them. Then make a list of needed information, and form questions that need to be answered. Some students find it effective to write each question on a separate index card.

4. **Record information and note sources.** As you locate needed information, make a decision about the best way to record it. Should you photocopy or make a printout of the source and annotate it? Should you paraphrase? Should you write a summary? Your answer will depend on the type of information you are using as well as the requirements of your assignment. Always include complete bibliographic information for each source.

   As you consult sources, you will probably discover new ideas and perhaps even a new approach to your topic. For example, you may learn that the homeless are not all the same: some are well educated and employable, some are down on their luck, and others are burdened with problems that would make holding a job difficult. Record each of these new ideas on a separate index card along with its source.

5. **Revise your paper.** Begin by re-evaluating your thesis based on your research. You may need to fine tune or revise it as a result of what you have learned. Add new supporting information (the next section of this chapter discusses how to add and document information from other sources), and then re-evaluate your draft, eliminating statements for which you could not locate supporting information, statements you found to be inaccurate, and statements for which you found contradictory evidence.

## Writing a First Draft

**Directions:** Write a first draft of an essay on the topic you chose in Exercise 16-1. To support your ideas, use the three sources you located. If any of these sources are dated or not focused enough for your thesis, you may need to locate additional ones.

# Synthesize Sources

■ GOAL 4
Synthesize sources

**Synthesis** is a process of using information from two or more sources in order to develop new ideas about a topic or to draw conclusions about it. Many college assignments require you to synthesize material—that is, to locate and read several sources on a topic and use them to write an essay. Synthesizing in the college setting, then, is a process of putting ideas together to create new ideas or insights based on what you have learned from the sources you consulted. For example, in a sociology course, you may be asked to consult several sources on the topic of organized crime and then write an essay describing the relationship between organized crime and illegal-drug sales. In a marketing class, your instructor may direct you to consult several sources on advertising strategies and on the gullibility of young children, and write an essay weighing the effects of television commercials on young children. Both of these assignments involve synthesizing ideas from sources.

Did you notice that, in each of the above examples, you were asked to come up with a new idea, one that did not appear in any of the sources but was *based* on all the sources? Creating something new from what you read is one of the most basic, important, and satisfying skills you will learn in college.

Synthesis is also often required in the workplace:

■ As a sales executive for an Internet service provider company, you may be asked to synthesize what you have learned about customer hardware problems.

■ As a medical office assistant, you may have extensive problems with a new computer system. The office manager asks you to write a memo to the company that installed the system, categorizing the types of problems you have experienced.

■ As an environmental engineer, you must synthesize years of research in order to make a proposal for local river and stream cleanup.

## How to Compare Sources to Synthesize

Comparing sources is part of synthesizing. Comparing involves placing them side by side and examining how they are the same and how they are different. However, before you begin to compare two or more sources, be sure you understand each fully. Depending on how detailed and difficult each source is, use annotating, paraphrasing, and summarizing (see Chapter 3) or underline, outline, or draw idea maps to make sure that you have a good grasp of your source material.

Let's assume you are taking a speech course in which you are studying non-verbal communication, or body language. You have chosen to study one aspect of body language: eye contact. Among your sources are the following excerpts:

*Source A*

> Eye contact, or *gaze*, is also a common form of nonverbal communication. Eyes have been called the "windows of the soul." In many cultures, people tend to assume that someone who avoids eye contact is evasive, cold, fearful, shy, or indifferent; that frequent gazing signals intimacy, sincerity, self-confidence, and respect; and that the person who stares is tense, angry, and unfriendly. Typically, however, eye contact is interpreted in light of a pre-existing relationship. If a relationship is friendly, frequent eye contact elicits a positive impression. If a relationship is not friendly, eye contact is seen in negative terms. It has been said that if two people lock eyes for more than a few seconds, they are either going to make love or kill each other (Kleinke, 1986; Patterson, 1983).
>
> —Brehm and Kassin, *Social Psychology*

*Source B*

> Eye contact often indicates the nature of the relationship between two people. One research study showed that eye contact is moderate when one is addressing a very high-status person, maximized when addressing a moderately high-status person, and only minimal when talking to a low-status person. There are also predictable differences in eye contact when one person likes another or when there may be rewards involved.
>
> Increased eye contact is also associated with increased liking between the people who are communicating. In an interview, for example, you are likely to make judgments about the interviewer's friendliness according to the amount of eye contact shown. The less eye contact, the less friendliness. In a courtship relationship, more eye contact can be observed among those seeking to develop a more intimate relationship. One research study (Saperston, 2003) suggests that the intimacy is a function of the amount of eye gazing, physical proximity, intimacy of topic, and amount of smiling. This model best relates to established relationships.
>
> —Weaver, *Understanding Interpersonal Communication*

To compare these sources, ask the following questions:

1. **On what do the sources agree?** Sources A and B recognize eye contact as an important communication tool. Both agree that there is a connection between eye contact and the relationship between the people involved. Both also agree that more frequent eye contact occurs among people who are friendly or intimate.

2. **On what do the sources disagree?** Sources A and B do not disagree, though they do present different information about eye contact (see the next item).

3. **How do they differ?** Sources A and B differ in the information they present. Source A states that in some cultures the frequency of eye contact suggests certain personality traits (someone who avoids eye contact is considered to be cold, for example), but Source B does not discuss cultural interpretations. Source B discusses how eye contact is related to

status—the level of importance of the person being addressed—while Source A does not.

4. **Are the viewpoints toward the subject similar or different?** Sources A and B both take a serious approach to the subject of eye contact.

5. **Does each source provide supporting evidence for major points?** Source A cites two references. Source B cites a research study.

After comparing your sources, the next step is to form your own ideas based on what you have discovered.

## How to Develop Ideas about Sources

Developing your own ideas is a process of drawing conclusions. Your goal is to decide what both sources, taken together, suggest. Together, Sources A and B recognize that eye contact is an important part of body language. However, they focus on different aspects of how eye contact can be interpreted. You can conclude that studying eye contact can be useful in understanding the relationship between two individuals: you can judge the relative status, the degree of friendship, and the level of intimacy between the people.

Once you decide what major idea to work with, you are ready to develop an essay. Use your newly discovered idea as your thesis statement. Then use details, documented properly, from each source to develop and support your thesis statement.

**EXERCISE 16-3**

# Synthesizing Sources

**Directions:** Read each of the following excerpts from sources on the topic of lost and endangered species. Synthesize these two sources, using the steps listed above, and develop a thesis statement about the causes of the decline and loss of plant and animal species.

### Source A

#### What Causes Extinction?

Every living organism must eventually die, and the same is true of species. Just like individuals, species are "born" (through the process of speciation), persist for some period of time, and then perish. The ultimate fate of any species is **extinction,** the death of the last of its members. In fact, at least 99.9% of all the species that have ever existed are now extinct. The natural course of evolution, as revealed by fossils, is continual turnover of species as new ones arise and old ones become extinct.

The immediate cause of extinction is probably always environmental change, in either the living or the nonliving parts of the environment. Two major environmental factors that may drive a species to extinction are competition among species and habitat destruction.

#### Interactions with Other Species May Drive a Species to Extinction

Interactions such as competition and predation serve as agents of natural selection. In some cases, these same interactions can lead to extinction rather than to adaptation. Organisms compete for limited resources in all environments. If a species' competitors evolve superior adaptations and the species doesn't evolve fast enough to keep up, it may become extinct.

**Habitat Change and Destruction Are the Leading Causes of Extinction**

Habitat change, both contemporary and prehistoric, is the single greatest cause of extinctions. Present-day habitat destruction due to human activities is proceeding at a rapid pace. Many biologists believe that we are presently in the midst of the fastest-paced and most widespread episode of species extinction in the history of life on Earth. Loss of tropical forests is especially devastating to species diversity. As many as half the species presently on Earth may be lost during the next 50 years as the tropical forests that contain them are cut for timber and to clear land for cattle and crops.

### Source B

The driving force behind today's alarming decline in species is the destruction, degradation and fragmentation of habitat due to our increasing human population and wasteful consumption of resources. Human populations virtually all around the globe are on the rise. . . . Because Americans consume so much more energy, food and raw material than our counterparts in other developed countries, our impact on our environment is proportionally much greater. As a result, wildlife and wild places in the United States are being pushed to the brink of extinction.

While the United States does not currently face as significant an increase in population as other countries, the movement of our population to new areas and the ensuing development has resulted in the destruction of species and their habitat. Thus, not surprisingly, there is a high correlation between human population and economic development trends in the United States and species decline and ecosystem destruction.

—http://www.sierraclub.org/habitat/habitatloss.asp

**EXERCISE 16-4**

**WRITING IN PROGRESS**

# Recording Sources

**Directions:** List source information for the essay you drafted in Exercise 16-2 to use in your Works Cited or References list. See page 487 for tips on what information to include.

# Document Sources

■ GOAL 5
Document sources

You can incorporate researched information into your paper in one of two ways: (1) summarize or paraphrase the information or (2) quote directly from it. In both cases, you must give credit to the authors from whom you borrowed the information by documenting your sources in a list of references so your reader can locate it easily. Failure to provide documentation of a source is called plagiarism: using an author's words or ideas without acknowledging that you have done so (see p. 487 for how to avoid plagiarism).

## Documentation

There are a number of different documentation formats (these are often called *styles*) that are used by scholars and researchers. Members of a particular academic discipline usually use the same format. For example, biologists follow a format described in *Scientific Style and Format: A Manual for Authors, Editors, and Publishers.*

Two of the most common methods of documenting and citing sources are those used by the Modern Language Association (MLA) and the American Psychological Association (APA). Both use a system of in-text citation: a brief note in the body of the text that refers to a source that is fully described in the Works Cited list (MLA) or References (APA) at the end of the paper, where sources are listed in alphabetical order.

The MLA format is typically used in English and humanities papers, while the APA format is commonly used in social science papers. Use the following guidelines for providing correct in-text citations using the MLA and APA documentation styles.

# An Overview of the MLA Style

■ GOAL 6
Use MLA style

For a comprehensive review of MLA style, consult the *MLA Handbook for Writers of Research Papers*, 7th edition, by Joseph Gibaldi.

## MLA In-Text Citations

When you refer to, summarize, paraphrase, quote, or in any other way use another author's words or ideas, you must indicate the source from which you took them by inserting an **in-text citation** that refers your reader to your "**Works Cited" list**, a complete alphabetized list of all the sources you have used.

Place your citation at the end of the sentence in which you refer to, summarize, paraphrase, or quote a source. It should follow a quotation mark, but come before punctuation that ends the sentence. If a question mark ends the sentence, place the question mark before the citation and a period after the citation.

Here are some guidelines about what to include in your in-text citations and how to incorporate quotations into your essay:

1. **If the source is introduced by a phrase that names the author, the citation need only include the page number.**

   > Miller poses the idea that if a good story is supposed to be a condensed version of life, then life should be lived like a good story in the first place (39).

2. **If the author is not named in the sentence, then include both the author's name and the page number in the citation.**

   > If a good story is supposed to be a condensed version of life, then life should be lived like a good story in the first place (Miller 39).

3. **If there are two or three authors, include the last names of all of them.**

   > Business ethics are important: "Many companies also have codes of ethics that guide buyers and sellers" (Lamb, Hair, and McDaniel 95).

4. **If there are four or more, include only the first author's last name and follow it with "et al.," which means "and others."**

   > Therefore, impalas "illustrate the connections between animal behavior, evolution, and ecology" (Campbell et al. 703).

5. **If you have used two or more works by the same author, either include the relevant title in your sentence or include the title, if brief, or an abbreviated version in your citation.**

   > In *Stealing MySpace: The Battle to Control the Most Popular Website in America*, Angwin concludes . . . (126).
   >
   > Or
   >
   > Angwin concludes . . . (*MySpace* 120).

6. **When you include a quotation in your essay, you should signal your reader that one is to follow.** For example, use such introductory phrases as the following:

   > According to Miller, "[quotation]."
   >
   > As Miller notes, "[quotation]."
   >
   > In the words of Miller, "[quotation]."

7. **To use a direct quotation, copy the author's words exactly and put them in quotation marks.** You do not always have to quote the full sentences; you can borrow phrases or clauses as long as they fit into your sentence, both logically and grammatically.

   > Miller comments that he "wondered whether a person could plan a story for his life and live it intentionally" (39).

8. **If the quotation is lengthy (four sentences or longer), set it apart from the rest of your essay.** Indent the entire quotation one inch from the margin, double-space the lines, and do not use quotation marks. Include an in-text citation after the final punctuation mark at the end of the quotation.

   > When discussing adapting a screenplay from his memoir, Miller noted the following:
   >
   > > It didn't occur to me at the time, but it's obvious now that in creating the fictional Don, I was creating the person I wanted to be, the person worth telling stories about. It never occurred to me that I could re-create my own story, my real life story, but in an evolution, I had moved toward a better me. I was creating someone I could live through, the person I'd be if I redrew the world, a character that was me but flesh and soul other. And flesh and soul better too. (29)

## MLA Works Cited List

Your list of works cited should include all the sources you referred to, summarized, paraphrased, or quoted in your paper. Start the list on a separate page at the end of your paper and title it "Works Cited." Arrange the entries alphabetically by each author's last name. If an author is not named (as in an editorial), then alphabetize the item by title. Double-space between and within entries. Start entries flush left, and if they run more than one line, indent subsequent lines half an inch.

1. **The basic format for a book can be illustrated as follows:**

> | Author | Title | Place of Publication | Publisher | Date | Medium of Publication |
> 
> Lin, Marvin. *Kid A*. New York: Continuum, 2011. Print.

Special cases are handled as follows:

a. **Two or more authors.** If there are two or three authors, include all their names in the order in which they appear in the source. If there are four or more, give the first author's name only and follow it with "et al."

> Authors       Title
> 
> Spicer, Mark S., and John R. Covach. *Sounding Out Pop: Analytical Essays in Popular Music*. Ann Arbor: Michigan UP, 2010. Print.
> 
> Place of Publication    Publisher    Date Medium of Publication

b. **Two or more works by the same author.** If your list contains two or more works by the same author, list the author's name only once. For additional entries, substitute three hyphens followed by a period in place of the name.

> Miller, Donald. *A Million Miles in a Thousand Years: What I Learned While Editing My Life*. Nashville: Nelson, 2009. Print.
> 
> ---. *Searching for God Knows What*. Nashville: Nelson, 2004. Print.

c. **Editor.** If the book has an editor instead of an author, list the editor's name at the beginning of the entry and follow it with "ed."

> McDannell, Colleen, ed. *Catholics in the Movies*. Oxford: Oxford UP, 2008. Print.

d. **Edition.** If the book has an edition number, include it after the title.

> DeVito, Joseph A. *Human Communication: The Basic Course*. 11th ed. Boston: Pearson, 2009. Print.

e. **Publisher.** The entire name of the publisher is not used. For example, the Houghton Mifflin Company is listed as "Houghton."

2. **What format is used for articles?** The basic format for a periodical can be illustrated as follows:

> | Author | Article Title | Name of Periodical | Volume/Issue No. |
> 
> Wilentz, Sean. "Bob Dylan in America." *The New York Review of Books* 57.18 (2010): 34. Print.
> 
> Date Page Medium of No. Publication

Special cases are handled as follows:

a. **Newspaper articles.** Include the author, article title, name of the newspaper, date, section letter or number, page(s), and medium of publication. Abbreviate all months except May, June, and July, and place the day before the month.

> Weiner, Jonah. "Shaggy, Yes, but Finessed Just So." *New York Times* 25 Oct. 2009, New York ed.: AR20. Print.

b. **An article in a weekly magazine.** List the author, article title, name of the magazine, date, page(s), and medium of publication. Abbreviate months as indicated above.

> Lilla, Mark. "The President and the Passions." *New York Times Magazine* 19 Dec. 2010: MM13. Print.

## Internet Sources

Information on the Internet comes from a wide variety of sources. For example, there are journals that are online versions of print publications, but there are also journals that are published only online. There are online books, articles from online databases, government publications, government Web sites, and more. Therefore, it is not sufficient merely to state that you got something from the Web. Citations for Internet resources must adequately reflect the exact type of document or publication that was used.

Include enough information to allow your readers to locate your sources. For some Internet sources, it may not be possible to locate all the required information; provide the information that is available. For sources that appear only online, include the following information: the name(s) of the author, editor, translator, narrator, compiler, performer, or producer of the material; the title of the work; the title of the Web site (if different); the version or edition used; the publisher or sponsor of the site (if unknown, write n.p.); the date of publication (day, month, year; write n.d. if not known); the medium of publication (Web); and the date of access (day, month, year). *Do not* include the URL unless the site cannot be found without using it.

1. **The basic format for an Internet source is as follows:**

> Breihan, Tom. "My Morning Jacket Ready New Album." *Pitchfork.* Pitchfork Media Inc. 3, Mar. 2011. Web. 6 Mar. 2011.

2. **The basic format for an Internet source that originally appeared in print is as follows:** Start your entry with the same information you would for a print source. Then add the title of the Web site or database (in italics) followed by a period, the medium of publication (Web) followed by a period, and the date you accessed the source (day, month, year) followed by a period. *Do not* include the URL unless the site cannot be found without using it.

> Wald, Mathew L. "Study Details How U. S. Could Cut 28% of Greenhouse Gases." *New York Times* 30 Nov. 2007: Business. *nytimes.com.* Web. 12 Aug. 2012.

**a. Online book**—If you consulted an entire online book, use this format:

> Woolf, Virginia. *Monday or Tuesday*. New York: Harcourt, 1921. *Bartleby.com.*
>    Web. 6 Aug. 2012.

**b. Online book**—If you consulted part of an online book, use this format:

> Seifert, Kelvin, and David Zinger. "Effective Nonverbal Communication."
>    *Educational Psychology*. Boston: Houghton, 2009. *The Online Books Page.*
>    Web. 6 Feb. 2011.

**c. Article from an online periodical**—If you accessed the article *directly* from an online journal, magazine, or newspaper, use this format:

> Sommers, Jeffrey. "Historical Arabesques: Patterns of History." *World History*
>    *Connected* 5.3. University of Illinois at Urbana-Champaign, June 2008. Web.
>    15 May 2011.

**d. Article from an online database**—If you accessed an article using an online database, and a Digital Object Locator (DOI) was provided for the article, include it. If not, include the name of the database and the document number, if available.

> Barnard, Neal D., et al. "Vegetarian and Vegan Diets in Type 2 Diabetes
>    Management." *Nutrition Reviews*, 67(5), 255–263. Web. 21 Apr. 2011.
>    doi:10.1111/j.1753-4887.2009.00198.x
>
> Bivins, Corey. "A Soy-free, Nut-free Vegan Meal Plan." *Vegetarian Journal*, 30(1),
>    14–17. *AltHealth Watch*. Web. 21 Apr. 2011. (2010918153)

**e. Online government publication**—If you consulted a document published by a government entity:

> United States. Financial Crisis Inquiry Commission. *The Financial Crisis Inquiry*
>    *Report: Final Report of the National Commission on the Causes of the*
>    *Financial and Economic Crisis in the United States*. Washington: Financial
>    Crisis Inquiry Commission, 2010. *FDLP Desktop*. Web. 20 Mar. 2011.

### *Other Electronic Sources*

1. **CD-ROM nonperiodical publication.**

> Beck, Mark. F. *Theory & Practice of Therapeutic Massage: Student CD-ROM*. Clifton Park,
>    NY: Milady, 2011. CD-ROM.

2. **Interview from a radio Web site.**

> Merritt, Stephin. Interview. *The Strange Powers of Stephin Merritt & the Magnetic Fields.*
>    KEXP, 10 Dec. 2011. Web. 13 Apr. 2011.

3. **Television documentary viewed on the Internet.**

   Lacy, Susan, prod. "Troubadours." *American Masters.* PBS, 2 Mar. 2011. Web. 16 Apr. 2011.

4. **Photograph viewed on the Internet.**

   Warhol, Andy. *Self-Portrait.* 1963–1964. Photograph. *The Warhol.* The Andy Warhol
   Museum. Web. 17 Aug. 2011.

## Writing a Works Cited List

**EXERCISE 16-5**

**WRITING IN PROGRESS**

**Directions:** Using MLA style, add two quotations to the essay you drafted in Exercise 16-2. Add in-text citations and write a Works Cited list for your essay that includes entries for all your sources.

# An Overview of the APA Style

■ **GOAL 7**
Use APA style

For a comprehensive overview of APA style, refer to the *Publication Manual of the American Psychological Association* (6th ed.).

## APA In-Text Citations

When you use the APA style, if you refer to, summarize, paraphrase, quote, or in any other way use another author's words or ideas, you indicate the source by inserting an **in-text citation** that refers your reader to your source list, called "**References**," which you include at the end of your essay. The in-text citation identifies the page number of your source and the author(s) last name if you do not include it in your introduction to the quotation.

Place the publication year in parentheses after the author's name when introducing the material. Include the page number after a quotation. Citations should come after quotation marks but before the punctuation. If a question mark ends the sentence, place the question mark before the citation and a period after the citation.

Here are some guidelines about what to include in your in-text citations and how to incorporate quotations into your essay:

1. **When the author is named in the sentence or phrase, insert the publication date in parentheses after the author's name.**

   In his book *A Million Miles in a Thousand Years: What I Learned While Editing My Life,* Donald Miller (2009) poses the idea that if a good story is supposed to be a condensed version of life, then life should be lived like a good story in the first place (p. 39).

2. **If the author is not named in the sentence, then include both the author's name and the publication date in the citation.**

   If a good story is supposed to be a condensed version of life, then life should be lived like a good story in the first place (Miller, 2009, p. 39).

3. **If you have used two or more works by the same author, include the last name of the author and year of each publication with each citation.**

> Miller (2004) was still developing his style with his earlier memoir *Searching for God Knows What*, but Miller (2009) refined his voice with *A Million Miles in a Thousand Years: What I Learned While Editing My Life*.

4. **The first time a source with multiple authors is cited, include all of the last names in the parentheses and the year of publication.** In subsequent citations of the same source, only the first author's last name followed by "et al." and the year are needed. (Note, however, that when a source has six or more authors, list only the last name of the first author followed by "et al." for the first and subsequent citations.)

> The mainstream pop music focuses on . . . (Spicer & Kovach, 2010).
>
> Or
>
> In conclusion . . . (Spicer et al., 2010).

5. **When you include a quotation in your paper, you should use an introductory phrase that includes the author's last name followed by the date of publication in parentheses.**

> Miller (2009) comments that he "wondered whether a person could plan a story for his life and live it intentionally" (p. 39).

If you do not name the author in your introductory phrase, include the author's last name and date of publication in parentheses after the quotation.

> He said that he "wondered whether a person could plan a story for his life and live it intentionally" (Miller, 2009, p. 39).

6. **If the quotation is lengthy (longer than 40 words), start the quotation on a new line, indent the entire quotation half an inch from the left margin and double-space it.** The parenthetical citation should be placed after the final punctuation mark at the end of the quotation.

> When discussing adapting a screenplay from his memoir, Miller (2009) noted the following:
>
> > It didn't occur to me at the time, but it's obvious now that in creating
> >
> > the fictional Don, I was creating the person I wanted to be, the person
> >
> > worth telling stories about. It never occurred to me that I could re-create
> >
> > my own story, my real life story, but in an evolution, I had moved toward a
> >
> > better me. I was creating someone I could live through, the person I'd be
> >
> > if I redrew the world, a character that was me but flesh and soul other. And
> >
> > flesh and soul better too. (p. 29)

## APA References

Your list of works cited should include all the sources you referred to, summarized, paraphrased, or quoted in your essay. It appears on a separate page at the end of your essay and is titled "References." Arrange the entries alphabetically by each author's last name. If an author is not named (as in an editorial), then alphabetize the item by title. Double-space between and within entries. Start entries flush left, and if they run more than one line, indent subsequent lines half an inch.

When referring to books, chapters, articles, or Web pages, capitalize only the first letter of the first word of a title and subtitle, the first word after a colon or a dash in the title, and proper nouns. Use italics for titles of longer works, do not italicize or use quotation marks for shorter works, and capitalize all major words in journal titles.

1. **The basic format for a book can be illustrated as follows:**

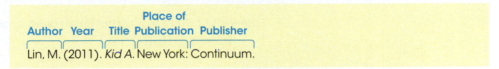

Lin, M. (2011). *Kid A.* New York: Continuum.

Special cases are handled as follows:

a. **Two to six authors.** If your list contains works by two to six authors, separate the names with commas and use an ampersand (&) before the last name.

Spicer, M. S., & Covach, J. R. (2010). *Sounding out pop: Analytical essays in popular music.* Ann Arbor: University of Michigan Press.

b. **Two or more works by the same author.** If your list contains two or more works by the same author, list each source separately and place the earliest source first.

Miller, D. (2004). *Searching for God knows what.* Nashville, TN: Nelson Books.

Miller, D. (2009). *A million miles in a thousand years: What I learned while editing my life.* Nashville, TN: Thomas Nelson.

c. **Editor.** If the book has an editor instead of an author, list the editor in place of the author and add (Ed.) after his or her name.

McDannell, C. (Ed.). (2008). *Catholics in the movies.* Oxford, England: Oxford University Press.

d. **Edition.** If the book has an edition number, then include the edition number after the title in parentheses.

Tempel, E. R., Seiler, T. L., Aldrich, E. E., & Rosso, H. A. (2011). *Achieving excellence in fundraising* (3rd ed.). San Francisco, CA: Jossey-Bass.

2. **The basic format for a periodical can be illustrated as follows:**

| Author | Date | Title | Publication |
|---|---|---|---|

Harvey, G. (2010, January 1). Bob Dylan in America. *The New York Review of Books,* *57* (18), 34.

**Volume  Pages**
**Number**

3. **Special cases are handled as follows:**

   a. **Newspaper articles.** When citing newspaper articles, place "p." or "pp." before the page number.

   Goldman, M. (2011). Something magic. *Buffalo News,* p. C1.

   b. **An article in a weekly magazine.**

   Enserink, M. (2011). Making her life an open book to promote expanded care. *Science* 331(6024), 1549.

### Internet Sources

Most electronic references are formatted the same as print ones, starting with the author name, date, and title. These are followed by either a Digital Object identifier (DOI) or URL. In addition, APA does not require an access date if there is a publication date or edition or version number or if the source is stable. If you have to break a URL or DOI, do so before a period or slash and do not use a hyphen.

Weiner, J. (2009, October 25). Shaggy, yes, but finessed just so. *The New York Times.* Retrieved from http://www.nytimes.com

1. **Online book**—If you consulted the whole book:

   Seifert, K., & Zinger, D. (2009) *Educational psychology.* Boston: Houghton. Retrieved from: http://docs.globaltext.terry.uga.edu:8095/anonymous/webdav /Educational%20Psychology/Educational%20Psychology.pdf

2. **Online book**—If you consulted part of an online book:

   Seifert, K., & Zinger, D. (2009). Effective nonverbal communication. *Educational psychology* (Chap. 2). Boston: Houghton. Retrieved from: http://docs .globaltext.terry.uga.edu:8095/anonymous/webdav/Educational%20 Psychology/Educational%20Psychology.pdf

3. **Article from an online periodical.**

   Sifton, S. (2011, March 29). Crosstown tour of India. *The New York Times.* Retrieved from: http://www.nytimes.com/

4. **Article from an online database.** If a Digital Object Locator (DOI) is provided for the article, include it. If not, include the name of the database and the document number, if available.

Barnard, N. D., Katcher, H. I., Jenkins, D. A., Cohen, J., & Turner-McGrievy, G. (2009). Vegetarian and vegan diets in type 2 diabetes management. *Nutrition Reviews, 67*(5), 255–263. doi:10.1111/j.1753-4887.2009.00198.x

Bivins, C. (2011). A soy-free, nut-free vegan meal plan. *Vegetarian Journal, 30*(1), 14–17. Retrieved from AltHealth Watch. (2010918153)

### 5. Government publication.

United States. (2010). *The financial crisis inquiry report: Final report of the National Commission on the Causes of the Financial and Economic Crisis in the United States.* Washington, DC: Financial Crisis Inquiry Commission. Retrieved from http://www.fdlp.gov/

### 6. CD-ROM nonperiodical publication.

Beck, M. F. (2011). *Theory & practice of therapeutic massage: Student CD-ROM.* Clifton Park, NY: Milady.

### 7. Interview from a radio Web site.

Merritt, S. (2011, December 10). *The strange powers of Stephin Merritt & the magnetic fields.* KEXP.

### 8. Television documentary viewed on the Internet.

Lacy, S. (Producer). (2011, March 2). *American Masters* (Troubadours). New York, NY: PBS. Retrieved from: http://www.pbs.org/wnet/americanmasters

### 9. Photograph viewed on the Internet.

Warhol, A. (1963–1964). *Self-portrait* [Photograph]. The Warhol. Retrieved from: http://www.warhol.org

---

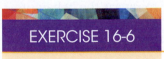

**EXERCISE 16-6**

**WRITING IN PROGRESS**

## Writing a References List

**Directions:** Using APA style, add two quotations to the essay you drafted in Exercise 16-2. Add in-text citations and write a References list for your essay that includes entries for all your sources.

---

## READ AND RESPOND: A Student Essay in MLA Format

*Adam Simmons is a first-year student at a local state university where he is majoring in criminal justice. For his sociology class, Simmons was asked to write an essay that examined the pros and cons of a social problem or issue.*

Adam Simmons

Professor Martin

Sociology 101

4 April 2012

Weighing the Consequences of Censorship in Media

There are different opinions about censorship in the media. Each side has good intentions; one side is saying censorship is protecting people or the country and the other is saying censorship limits the Constitutional right to freedom of speech.

People in favor of censorship of the media often talk about the morality of the content. A common argument is that some media contain inappropriate material that could unintentionally be seen by young children. In this case, inappropriate material is defined as pornographic, violent, vulgar, or sexual in any way. The argument is that it could lead kids to try and repeat what they are seeing on the television or what they are hearing about in music (Pillai). By censoring such materials, children would hypothetically be less likely to repeat the behavior and would not be exposed to things that might not be appropriate for their age, so censorship would protect children.

Some people also believe that censorship is important when it is used to protect military information and "helps preserve the secrets of a nation being revealed" ("Pros of Censorship"). With the government monitoring what information the media offers, it is less likely that information the government does not want leaked out will be made public. This could mean keeping troops safe and protecting domestic and foreign policy, especially in wartime when enemies can track news sources to find out about U.S. strategy. It can also help keep dangerous information, such as details about weaponry, from getting into the wrong hands.

Simmons 2

Censorship has some dangers though. It can be viewed as directly violating the First Amendment of the Constitution and taking away freedom of speech. The amendment states "Congress shall make no law . . . abridging the freedom of speech, or of the press . . ." There are some who say the First Amendment acts as a "complete barrier to government censorship" (Pember 43); since the Constitution creates this ban, censorship is in effect unlawful. However, there are Supreme Court cases that have modified the interpretation of this amendment, such as the Smith Act which makes it "a crime to advocate the violent overthrow of the government" (Pember 52).

There are other reasons that people object to censorship. Some people argue that censorship can also be abused by the government and in the wrong hands it can lead to a loss of freedom of speech and halt a flow of ideas in a society, as seen under various dictatorships (Neuharth). It can also be said that censorship stifles creativity. Saying that some works are immoral or unsuitable is making a legal statement that some art is good and some art is bad ("What Is Censorship?"). Art, in itself, is subjective and cannot really be labeled that way. If art has to be made to meet the requirements of the censors, then it will never be able to be completely creative and free.

Both viewpoints about censorship approach the topic with the hope of doing what is best for society, but come at it from completely different angles. One hopes to make things better by removing immoral or dangerous speech and the other seeks to let every person have the ability to say what they want regardless of whether it is seen moral by others.

Simmons 3

Works Cited

Neuharth, Al. "Google Is Gutsy to Spit in China's Eye." *USA Today* 26 Mar. 2010:

15a. Print.

Pember, Don R., and Clay Calvert. *Mass Media Law*. Boston: McGraw-Hill, 2009. Print.

Pillai, Prabhakar. "Pros and Cons of Censorship." *Buzzle Web Portal: Intelligent Life on*

*the Web*. Buzzle.com, n.d. Web. 8 Apr. 2012.

"Pros of Censorship." *Laws.com*. n.d. Web. 8 Apr. 2012.

"What Is Censorship?" American Civil Liberties Union. 30 Aug. 2006. Web. 08 Apr. 2012.

## Examining Writing

1. How is this essay organized?
2. Examine Simmons's use of sources. What does each reference to a source contribute to this essay?
3. Suggest an introduction that could be more interesting.
4. For what audience does Simmons seem to be writing?
5. Are there any details that do not seem relevant to the thesis?
6. Does the author provide adequate support for the two sides of the argument that he presents? If not, what additional details could he have included (facts, statistics, informed opimion, etc.)?

## Writing Assignments

1. For an education class, write an essay examining the trend toward online college courses. Do research to discover what is offered at your college and other nearby colleges. Summarize your findings in a short essay.
2. For a health class, you are asked to write an essay comparing two popular diets. Choose two diets, such as the South Beach Diet and the Mediterranean diet, research what is involved in each, and report your findings in an essay.
3. For a business management class, your instructor has given the following assignment: Choose two local business franchises that sell the same products. You might choose two fast-food restaurants, two shoe stores, or two drugstores, for example. Visit both businesses and research each on the Internet. Write an essay comparing the two businesses. Indicate which you feel is likely to be more profitable over the course of the next year.

## Revision Checklist

1. Does your paragraph or essay accomplish your purpose?

2. Does your paragraph or essay provide your audience with the background information they need?

3. Is your main point clearly expressed?

4. Have you supported your main point with sufficient detail from sources to make it understandable and believable?

5. Is each detail relevant? Does each one explain or support your main point?

6. Is your paragraph or essay logically arranged?

7. Have you used transitions to connect your ideas within and between paragraphs?

8. Have you credited each source from which you paraphrased, summarized, or directly quoted?

9. Have you used an appropriate documentation style?

10. Does your concluding sentence or paragraph reemphasize your topic sentence or thesis statement?

# SELF-TEST SUMMARY

To test yourself, cover the Answer column with a sheet of paper and answer each question in the left column. Evaluate each of your answers as you work by sliding the paper down and comparing your answer with what is printed in the Answer column.

| QUESTION | ANSWER |
| --- | --- |
| ■ GOAL 1 Use sources to write essays<br><br>What is involved when you write essays using sources? | Using sources for essays involves finding appropriate sources, recording information from them, and organizing and synthesizing the information to support your thesis. |
| ■ GOAL 2 Find and record appropriate sources<br><br>How do you find appropriate sources? | To find sources, consult a reference librarian; use a systematic approach, starting with general sources; use current and reliable sources; sample different viewpoints; preview by reading abstracts or summaries; read selectively; and follow leads to additional sources. |
| How do you record sources? | Use note cards or a small notebook to record critical source information; photocopy print sources, download and/or print and bookmark online sources. |

*(continued)*

*(continued)*

| QUESTION | ANSWER |
|---|---|
| ■ GOAL 3 Use sources to support your thesis and develop your essay<br><br>How do you use sources to support your thesis and develop your essay? | Use sources to find facts, statistics, and other evidence that support your thesis. Write a first draft, analyze where you need support, revise your thesis if necessary based on new information, research sources to find relevant facts, opinions, and other evidence, and record the sources you use. |
| ■ GOAL 4 Synthesize sources<br><br>What does it mean to synthesize sources? | Synthesizing means locating several sources on a topic and putting together the ideas you discover to create new ideas and insights about the topic. |
| ■ GOAL 5 Document sources<br><br>Why is it important to document your sources? How do you document sources? | When you quote, paraphrase, or summarize a source, you must credit the author in order to avoid plagiarism. Two common methods for citing and documenting sources are the MLA and APA styles. |
| ■ GOAL 6 Use MLA style<br><br>What is MLA style, and when is it used? | The Modern Language Association (MLA) style is typically used for documenting sources in English and the humanities and consists of in-text citations that refer readers to a Works Cited list of all sources used organized alphabetically by authors' last names. |
| ■ GOAL 7 Use APA style<br><br>What is APA style, and when is it used? | The American Psychological Association (APA) style is used for documenting sources in psychology and other social sciences and consists of in-text citations that refer readers to a References list of all sources used organized alphabetically by authors' last names. |

**MySkillsLab®**

For more help with **Writing Essays Using Sources**, go to your learning path in MySkillsLab at www.myskillslab.com.

# Reviewing the Basics

## PART VI

# OVERVIEW

Most of us know how to communicate in our language. When we talk or write, we put our thoughts into words and, by and large, we make ourselves understood. But many of us do not know the specific terms and rules of grammar. Grammar is a system that describes how language is put together. Grammar must be learned, almost as if it were a foreign language.

Why is it important to study grammar, to understand grammatical terms like *verb*, *participle*, and *gerund* and concepts like *agreement* and *subordination*? There are several good reasons. Knowing grammar will allow you to

- **recognize an error in your writing and correct it.** Your papers will read more smoothly and communicate more effectively when they are error free.

- **understand the comments of your teachers and peers.** People who read and critique your writing may point out a "fragment" or a "dangling modifier." You will be able to revise and correct the problems.

- **write with more impact.** Grammatically correct sentences are signs of clear thinking. Your readers will get your message without distraction or confusion.

As you will see in this part of the text, "Reviewing the Basics," the different areas of grammatical study are highly interconnected. The sections on parts of speech, sentences, punctuation, mechanics, and spelling fit together into a logical whole. To recognize and correct a run-on sentence, for example, you need to know both sentence structure *and* punctuation. To avoid errors in capitalization, you need to know parts of speech *and* mechanics. If grammar is to do you any good, your knowledge of it must be thorough. As you review the following "basics," be alert to the interconnections that make language study so interesting.

Grammatical terms and rules demand your serious attention. Mastering them will pay handsome dividends: error-free papers, clear thinking, and effective writing.

# Understanding the Parts of Speech

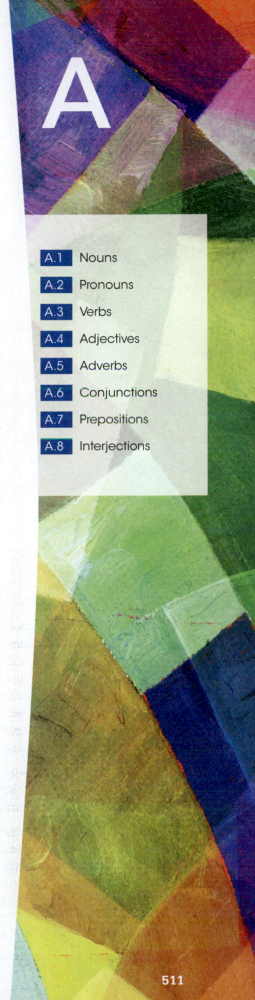

The eight parts of speech are **nouns**, **pronouns**, **verbs**, **adjectives**, **adverbs**, **conjunctions**, **prepositions**, and **interjections**. Each word in a sentence functions as one of these parts of speech. Being able to identify the parts of speech in sentences allows you to analyze and improve your writing and to understand grammatical principles discussed later in this section.

It is important to keep in mind that *how* a word functions in a sentence determines *what* part of speech it is. Thus, the same word can be a noun, a verb, or an adjective, depending on how it is used.

| A.1 | Nouns |
| A.2 | Pronouns |
| A.3 | Verbs |
| A.4 | Adjectives |
| A.5 | Adverbs |
| A.6 | Conjunctions |
| A.7 | Prepositions |
| A.8 | Interjections |

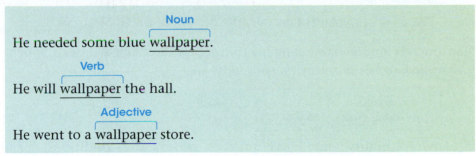

**Noun**

He needed some blue <u>wallpaper</u>.

**Verb**

He will <u>wallpaper</u> the hall.

**Adjective**

He went to a <u>wallpaper</u> store.

## A.1 Nouns

A **noun** names a person, place, thing, or idea.

| People | *woman, winner, Maria Alvarez* |
| Places | *mall, hill, Indiana* |
| Things | *lamp, ship, air* |
| Ideas | *goodness, perfection, harmony* |

The form of many nouns changes to express **number** (**singular** for one, **plural** for more than one): *one bird, two birds; one child, five children*. Most nouns can also be made **possessive** to show ownership by the addition of *-'s*: *city's, Allison's*.

Sometimes a noun is used to modify another noun:

**Noun modifying diploma**

Her goal had always been to earn a <u>college</u> diploma.

Nouns are classified as proper, common, collective, concrete, abstract, count, and noncount.

1. **Proper nouns** name specific people, places, or things and are always capitalized: *Martin Luther King Jr.; East Lansing; Ford Taurus*. Days of the week and months are considered proper nouns and are capitalized.

> Proper noun    Proper noun                Proper noun
> In September Allen will attend Loyola University.

2. **Common nouns** name one or more of a general class or type of person, place, thing, or idea and are not capitalized: *president, city, car, wisdom*.

> Common noun   Common noun   Common noun            Common noun
> Next fall the students will enter college to receive an education.

3. **Collective nouns** name a whole group or collection of people, places, or things: *committee, team, jury*. They are usually singular in form.

> Collective noun                    Collective noun
> The flock of mallards flew over the herd of bison.

4. **Concrete nouns** name tangible things that can be tasted, seen, touched, smelled, or heard: *sandwich, radio, pen*.

> Concrete noun           Concrete noun
> The frozen pizza was stuck in the freezer.

5. **Abstract nouns** name ideas, qualities, beliefs, and conditions: *honesty, goodness, poverty*.

> Abstract nouns  Abstract noun
> Their marriage was based on love, honor, and trust.

6. **Count nouns** name items that can be counted. Count nouns can be made plural, usually by adding *-s* or *-es*: *one river, three rivers; one box, ten boxes*. Some count nouns form their plural in an irregular way: *man, men; goose, geese*.

> Count noun        Count noun       Count noun
> The salespeople put the invoices in their files.

7. **Noncount nouns** name ideas or qualities that cannot be counted. Noncount nouns almost always have no plural form: *air, knowledge, unhappiness*.

> Noncount noun                                Noncount noun
> As the rain pounded on the windows, she tried to find the courage to walk home from work.

# A.2 Pronouns

A **pronoun** is a word that substitutes for or refers to a noun or another pronoun. The noun or pronoun to which a pronoun refers is called the pronoun's **antecedent**. A pronoun must agree with its antecedent in person, number, and gender (these terms are discussed later in this section).

After the campers discovered the cave, they mapped it for the next group, which was arriving next week. [The pronoun *they* refers to its antecedent, *campers*; the pronoun *it* refers to its antecedent, *cave*; the pronoun *which* refers to its antecedent, *group*.]

The eight kinds of pronouns are **personal**, **demonstrative**, **reflexive**, **intensive**, **interrogative**, **relative**, **indefinite**, and **reciprocal**.

1. **Personal pronouns** take the place of nouns or pronouns that name people or things. A personal pronoun changes form to indicate **person**, **gender**, **number**, and **case**.

   **Person** is the grammatical term used to distinguish the speaker (**first person**: *I, we*); the person spoken to (**second person**: *you*); and the person or thing spoken about (**third person**: *he, she, it, they*). **Gender** is the term used to classify pronouns as **masculine** (*he, him*); **feminine** (*she, her*); or **neuter** (*it*). **Number** classifies pronouns as **singular** (one) or **plural** (more than one). Some personal pronouns also function as adjectives modifying nouns (*our house*).

|  | *Singular* | *Plural* |
|---|---|---|
| First person | I, me, my, mine | we, us, our, ours |
| Second person | you, your, yours | you, your, yours |
| Third person |  |  |
|     Masculine | he, him, his |  |
|     Feminine | she, her, hers | they, them, their, theirs |
|     Neuter | it, its |  |

First-person singular / First-person singular (pronoun/adjective) / Third-person singular / Third-person plural

I called my manager about my new clients. She wanted to know as soon as they placed their first orders. "Your new clients are important to us," she said.

Third-person plural (pronoun/adjective) / Second-person singular (pronoun/adjective) / First-person plural / Third-person singular

A pronoun's **case** is determined by its function as a subject (**subjective** or **nominative case**) or an object (**objective case**) in a sentence. A pronoun that shows ownership is in the **possessive** case. (See p. 570 for a discussion of pronoun case.)

2. **Demonstrative pronouns** refer to particular people or things. The demonstrative pronouns are *this* and *that* (singular) and *these* and *those* (plural). (*This, that, these,* and *those* can also be demonstrative adjectives when they modify a noun.)

   This is more thorough than that.

   The red shuttle buses stop here. These go to the airport every hour.

3. **Reflexive pronouns** indicate that the subject performs actions to, for, or upon itself. Reflexive pronouns end in -*self* or -*selves*.

---

**Tip for Writers**

*This, that, these,* and *those* all refer to a thing, a person, things, or people within the speaker's sight, but *that* and *those* refer to things farther away. *This* and *these* refer to what is close to the speaker or writer.

| Distance | Singular | Plural |
|---|---|---|
| near | this | these |
| far | that | those |

|              | *Singular* | *Plural*   |
|--------------|------------|------------|
| First person | myself     | ourselves  |
| Second person| yourself   | yourselves |
| Third person | himself<br>herself<br>itself | themselves |

We excused <u>ourselves</u> from the table and left.

4. An **intensive pronoun** emphasizes the word that comes before it in a sentence. Like reflexive pronouns, intensive pronouns end in *-self* or *-selves*.

> The filmmaker <u>herself</u> could not explain the ending.
>
> They <u>themselves</u> repaired the copy machine.

*Note:* A reflexive or intensive pronoun should not be used as a subject of a sentence. An antecedent for the reflexive pronoun must appear in the same sentence.

> INCORRECT   <u>Myself</u> create colorful sculpture.
>
> CORRECT     I <u>myself</u> create colorful sculpture.

5. **Interrogative pronouns** are used to introduce questions: *who, whom, whoever, whomever, what, which, whose.* The correct use of *who* and *whom* depends on the role the interrogative pronoun plays in a sentence or clause. When the pronoun functions as the subject of the sentence or clause, use *who.* When the pronoun functions as an object in the sentence or clause, use *whom* (see p. 572).

> <u>What</u> happened?
>
> <u>Which</u> is your street?
>
> <u>Who</u> wrote *Ragtime*? [*Who* is the subject of the sentence.]
>
> <u>Whom</u> should I notify? [*Whom* is the object of the verb *notify*: *I should notify whom?*]

6. **Relative pronouns** relate groups of words to nouns or other pronouns and often introduce adjective clauses or noun clauses (see p. 543). The relative pronouns are *who, whom, whoever, whomever,* and *whose* (referring to people) and *that, what, whatever,* and *which* (referring to things).

> In 1836 Charles Dickens met John Forster, <u>who</u> became his friend and biographer.
>
> Jason did not understand <u>what</u> the consultant recommended.
>
> We read some articles <u>that</u> were written by former astronauts.

7. **Indefinite pronouns** are pronouns without specific antecedents. They refer to people, places, or things in general.

> <u>Someone</u> has been rearranging my papers.
>
> <u>Many</u> knew the woman, but <u>few</u> could say they knew her well.

### Tip for Writers

Be sure to use a *singular verb* after the *indefinite pronouns* that are grammatically singular: <u>Everybody</u> is here now. Let's eat! (Even though *everybody* means at least three people, it's grammatically singular.)

Here are some frequently used <u>indefinite pronouns</u>:

| SINGULAR | | PLURAL |
|---|---|---|
| another | nobody | all |
| anybody | none | both |
| anyone | no one | few |
| anything | nothing | many |
| each | one | more |
| either | other | most |
| everybody | somebody | others |
| everyone | someone | several |
| everything | something | some |
| neither | | |

8. The **reciprocal pronouns** *each other* and *one another* indicate a mutual relationship between two or more parts of a plural antecedent.

> Armando and Sharon congratulated <u>each other</u> on their high grades.

---

EXERCISE 1

## Identifying Nouns and Pronouns

**Directions:** In each of the following sentences, (a) circle each noun and (b) underline each pronoun.

EXAMPLE (Jamila) parked <u>her</u> (car) in the (lot) <u>that</u> is reserved for (commuters) like her.

1. Shakespeare wrote many plays that have become famous and important.

2. Everyone who has visited Disneyland wishes to return.

3. Jonathan himself wrote the report that the president of the company presented to the press.

4. That desk used to belong to my boss.

5. My integrity was never questioned by my co-workers.

6. The class always laughed at jokes told by the professor, even though they were usually corny.

7. When will humankind be able to travel to Mars?

8. Whoever wins the lottery this week will become quite wealthy.

9. As the plane landed at the airport, many of the passengers began to gather their carry-on luggage.

10. This week we are studying gravity; next week we will study heat.

---

# A.3 Verbs

Verbs express action or state of being. A grammatically complete sentence has at least one verb in it.

There are three kinds of verbs: **action verbs**, **linking verbs**, and **helping verbs** (also known as **auxiliary verbs**).

1. **Action verbs** express physical and mental activities.

> Mr. Royce dashed for the bus.
>
> The incinerator burns garbage at high temperatures.
>
> I think that seat is taken.
>
> The programmer worked until 3:00 A.M.

Action verbs are either **transitive** or **intransitive**. The action of a **transitive verb** is directed toward someone or something, called the **direct object** of the verb. Direct objects receive the action of the verb. Transitive verbs require direct objects to complete the meaning of the sentence.

> Transitive  Direct
> Subject    verb    object
> Amalia made clocks.

An **intransitive verb** does not need a direct object to complete the meaning of the sentence.

> Intransitive
> Subject    verb
> The traffic stopped.

Some verbs can be both transitive and intransitive, depending on their meaning and use in a sentence.

> INTRANSITIVE   The traffic stopped. [No direct object]
>
>                              Direct object
> TRANSITIVE   The driver stopped the bus at the corner.

2. A **linking verb** expresses a state of being or a condition. A linking verb connects a noun or pronoun to words that describe the noun or pronoun. Common linking verbs are forms of the verb *be* (*is, are, was, were, being, been*), *become, feel, grow, look, remain, seem, smell, sound, stay,* and *taste.*

> Their child grew tall.
>
> The office looks messy.
>
> Mr. Davenport is our accountant.

3. A **helping (auxiliary) verb** helps another verb, called the **main verb**, to convey when the action occurred (through verb tense) and to form questions. One or more helping verbs and the main verb together form a **verb phrase**. Some helping verbs, called **modals**, are always helping verbs:

> can, could          shall, should
>
> may, might          will, would
>
> must, ought to

The other helping verbs can sometimes function as main verbs as well:

> am, are, be, been, being, did, do, does
>
> had, has, have
>
> is, was, were

**Tip for Writers**

A *direct object* answers the question *Who?* or *What?* about the verb.

**Tip for Writers**

Be sure to use an adjective, not an adverb, after a *linking verb*. Use adverbs to describe other verbs: He seems nice. (but) He paints nicely.

The verb *be* is a very irregular verb, with eight forms instead of the usual five: *am, are, be, being, been, is, was, were*.

Helping  Main
verb    verb

The store will close early on holidays.

Helping           Main
verb              verb

Will the store close early on New Year's Eve?

## Forms of the Verb

All verbs except *be* have five forms: the **base form** (or dictionary form), the **past tense**, the **past participle**, the **present participle**, and the **-s form**. The first three forms are called the verb's **principal parts**. The infinitive consists of "to" plus a base form: *to go, to study, to talk*. For **regular verbs**, the past tense and past participle are formed by adding *-d* or *-ed* to the base form. **Irregular verbs** follow no set pattern to form their past tense and past participle.

|  | *Regular* | *Irregular* |
|---|---|---|
| Infinitive | work | eat |
| Past tense | worked | ate |
| Past participle | worked | eaten |
| Present participle | working | eating |
| *-s* form | works | eats |

Verbs change form to agree with their subjects in person and number (see p. 563); to express the time of their action (**tense**); to express whether the action is a fact, command, or wish (**mood**); and to indicate whether the subject is the doer or the receiver of the action (**voice**).

## Principal Parts of Irregular Verbs

Consult the following list and your dictionary for the principal parts of irregular verbs.

| BASE FORM | PAST TENSE | PAST PARTICIPLE |
|---|---|---|
| be | was | been |
| become | became | become |
| begin | began | begun |
| bite | bit | bitten |
| blow | blew | blown |
| burst | burst | burst |
| catch | caught | caught |
| choose | chose | chosen |
| come | came | come |
| dive | dived, dove | dived |
| do | did | done |
| draw | drew | drawn |
| drive | drove | driven |
| eat | ate | eaten |
| fall | fell | fallen |
| find | found | found |

*(continued)*

A. Parts of Speech

| BASE FORM | PAST TENSE | PAST PARTICIPLE |
|-----------|-----------|-----------------|
| fling | flung | flung |
| fly | flew | flown |
| get | got | gotten |
| give | gave | given |
| go | went | gone |
| grow | grew | grown |
| have | had | had |
| know | knew | known |
| lay | laid | laid |
| lead | led | led |
| leave | left | left |
| lie | lay | lain |
| lose | lost | lost |
| ride | rode | ridden |
| ring | rang | rung |
| rise | rose | risen |
| say | said | said |
| set | set | set |
| sit | sat | sat |
| speak | spoke | spoken |
| swear | swore | sworn |
| swim | swam | swum |
| tear | tore | torn |
| tell | told | told |
| throw | threw | thrown |
| wear | wore | worn |
| write | wrote | written |

## Tense

The **tenses** of a verb express time. They convey whether an action, process, or event takes place in the present, past, or future.

The three **simple tenses** are **present, past,** and **future**. The **simple present** tense is the base form of the verb (and the *-s* form of third-person singular subjects; see p. 556); the **simple past** tense is the past-tense form; and the **simple future** tense consists of the helping verb *will* plus the base form.

The **perfect tenses**, which indicate completed action, are **present perfect, past perfect,** and **future perfect**. They are formed by adding the helping verbs *have* (or *has*), *had,* and *will have* to the past participle.

In addition to the simple and perfect tenses, there are six progressive tenses. The **simple progressive tenses** are the **present progressive**, the **past progressive**, and the **future progressive**. The progressive tenses are used for continuing actions or actions in progress. These progressive tenses are formed by adding the present, past, and future forms of the verb *be* to the present participle. The **perfect progressive tenses** are the **present perfect progressive**, the **past perfect progressive**, and the **future perfect progressive**. They are formed by adding the present perfect, past perfect, and future perfect forms of the verb *be* to the present participle.

The following chart shows all the tenses for a regular verb and an irregular verb in the first person. (For more on tenses, see p. 556.)

| | REGULAR | IRREGULAR |
|---|---|---|
| Simple present | I talk | I go |
| Simple past | I talked | I went |
| Simple future | I will talk | I will go |
| Present perfect | I have talked | I have gone |
| Past perfect | I had talked | I had gone |
| Future perfect | I will have talked | I will have gone |
| Present progressive | I am talking | I am going |
| Past progressive | I was talking | I was going |
| Future progressive | I will be talking | I will be going |
| Present perfect progressive | I have been talking | I have been going |
| Past perfect progressive | I had been talking | I had been going |
| Future perfect progressive | I will have been talking | I will have been going |

## Mood

The **mood** of a verb indicates the writer's attitude toward the action. There are three moods in English: **indicative**, **imperative**, and **subjunctive**.

1. The **indicative mood** is used for ordinary statements of fact or questions.

   > The light flashed on and off all night.
   >
   > Did you check the batteries?

2. The **imperative mood** is used for commands, suggestions, or directions. The subject of a verb in the imperative mood is *you*, though it is not always included.

   > Stop shouting!
   >
   > Come to New York for a visit.
   >
   > Turn right at the next corner.

3. The **subjunctive mood** is used for wishes, requirements, recommendations, and statements contrary to fact. For statements contrary to fact or for wishes, the past tense of the verb is used. For the verb *be*, only the past-tense form *were* is used.

   > If I had a million dollars, I'd take a trip around the world.
   >
   > If my supervisor were promoted, I would be eligible for her job.

To express suggestions, recommendations, or requirements, the infinitive form is used for all verbs.

   > I recommend that the houses be sold after the landscaping is done.
   >
   > The registrar required that Maureen pay her bill before attending class.

## Voice

Transitive verbs (those that take objects) may be in either the active voice or the passive voice (see p. 560). In an **active-voice** sentence, the subject performs the action described by the verb; that is, the subject is the actor. In a **passive-voice** sentence, the subject is the receiver of the action. The passive voice of a verb is formed by using an appropriate form of the helping verb *be* and the past participle of the main verb.

> Subject   Active
> is actor   voice
>
> Dr. Hillel delivered the report on global warming.
>
> Subject is receiver                    Passive voice
>
> The report on global warming was delivered by Dr. Hillel.

---

**EXERCISE 2**

## Changing Tenses

**Directions:** Revise the following sentences, changing each verb from the present tense to the tense indicated.

EXAMPLE   I <u>know</u> the right answer.

PAST TENSE    I knew the right answer.

1. Allison <u>loses</u> the sales to competitors.

   SIMPLE PAST _____

2. Malcolm <u>begins</u> classes at the community college.

   PAST PERFECT _____

3. The microscope <u>enlarges</u> the cell.

   PRESENT PERFECT _____

4. Reports <u>follow</u> a standard format.

   SIMPLE FUTURE _____

5. Meg Ryan <u>receives</u> excellent evaluations.

   FUTURE PERFECT _____

6. Juanita <u>writes</u> a computer program.

   PRESENT PERFECT _____

7. The movie <u>stars</u> Brad Pitt.

   SIMPLE FUTURE _____

8. Dave <u>wins</u> medals at the Special Olympics.

   SIMPLE PAST _____

9. Many celebrities <u>donate</u> money to AIDS research.

   PRESENT PERFECT _____

10. My nephew <u>travels</u> to Michigan's Upper Peninsula on business.

    PAST PERFECT _____

# A.4 Adjectives

**Adjectives** modify nouns and pronouns. That is, they describe, identify, qualify, or limit the meaning of nouns and pronouns. An adjective answers the question *Which one? What kind?* or *How many?* about the word it modifies.

| | |
|---|---|
| **WHICH ONE?** | The twisted, torn umbrella was of no use to its owner. |
| **WHAT KIND?** | The spotted owl has caused heated arguments in the Northwest. |
| **HOW MANY?** | Many customers waited for four days for telephone service to be restored. |

In form, adjectives can be **positive** (implying no comparison), **comparative** (comparing two items), or **superlative** (comparing three or more items). (See p. 572 for more on the forms of adjectives.)

**Positive**
The computer is fast.

**Comparative**
Your computer is faster than mine.

**Superlative**
This is the fastest computer I have ever used.

There are two general categories of adjectives. **Descriptive adjectives** name a quality of the person, place, thing, or idea they describe: *mysterious man, green pond, healthy complexion*. **Limiting adjectives** narrow the scope of the person, place, or thing they describe: *my computer, this tool, second try*.

## Descriptive Adjectives

A **regular** (or **attributive**) adjective appears next to (usually before) the word it modifies. Several adjectives can modify the same word.

The enthusiastic new hair stylist gave short, lopsided haircuts.
The wealthy dealer bought an immense blue vase.

Sometimes nouns function as adjectives modifying other nouns:

*tree house, hamburger bun*

A **predicate adjective** follows a linking verb and modifies or describes the subject of the sentence or clause (see p. 532; see p. 537 on clauses).

**Predicate adjective**
The meeting was long. [Modifies the subject, *meeting*]

## Limiting Adjectives

1. The **definite article**, *the,* and the **indefinite articles**, *a* and *an,* are classified as adjectives. *A* and *an* are used when it is not important to specify a

particular noun or when the object named is not known to the reader (*A radish adds color to a salad*). *The* is used when it is important to specify one or more of a particular noun or when the object named is known to the reader or has already been mentioned (*The radishes from the garden are on the table*).

> A squirrel visited <u>the</u> feeder that I just built. <u>The</u> squirrel tried to eat some bird food.

2. When the possessive pronouns *my, your, his, her, its, our,* and *their* are used as modifiers before nouns, they are considered **possessive adjectives** (see p. 521).

> <u>Your</u> friend borrowed <u>my</u> laptop for <u>his</u> trip.

3. When the demonstrative pronouns *this, that, these,* and *those* are used as modifiers before nouns, they are called **demonstrative adjectives** (see p. 512). *This* and *these* modify nouns close to the writer; *that* and *those* modify nouns more distant from the writer.

> Buy <u>these</u> formatted disks, not <u>those</u> unformatted ones.
>
> <u>This</u> freshman course is a prerequisite for <u>those</u> advanced courses.

4. **Cardinal adjectives** are words used in counting: *one, two, twenty,* and so on.

> I read <u>four</u> biographies of Jack Kerouac and <u>seven</u> articles about his work.

5. **Ordinal adjectives** note position in a series.

> The <u>first</u> biography was too sketchy; whereas the <u>second</u> one was too detailed.

6. **Indefinite adjectives** provide nonspecific, general information about the quantities and amounts of the nouns they modify. Some common indefinite adjectives are *another, any, enough, few, less, little, many, more, much, several,* and *some.*

> <u>Several</u> people asked me if I had <u>enough</u> blankets or if I wanted the thermostat turned up a <u>few</u> degrees.

7. The **interrogative adjectives** *what, which,* and *whose* modify nouns and pronouns used in questions.

> <u>Which</u> radio station do you like? <u>Whose</u> music do you prefer?

8. The words *which* and *what,* along with *whichever* and *whatever,* are **relative adjectives** when they modify nouns and introduce subordinate clauses.

> She couldn't decide <u>which</u> job she wanted to take.

9. **Proper adjectives** are adjectives derived from proper nouns: *Spain* (noun), *Spanish* (adjective); *Freud* (noun), *Freudian* (adjective); see p. 511. Most proper adjectives are capitalized.

> Shakespeare lived in <u>Elizabethan</u> England.
>
> The speaker used many <u>French</u> expressions.

**EXERCISE 3**

# Adding Adjectives

**Directions:** Revise each of the following sentences by adding at least three adjectives.

EXAMPLE     The cat slept on the pillow.

REVISED     The old yellow cat slept on the expensive pillow.

1. Before leaving on a trip, the couple packed their suitcases.

 

2. The tree dropped leaves all over the lawn.

 

3. While riding the train, the passengers read newspapers.

 

4. The antiques dealer said that the desk was more valuable than the chair.

 

5. As the play was ending, the audience clapped their hands and tossed roses onstage.

 

6. Stew is served nightly at the shelter.

 

7. The engine roared as the car stubbornly jerked into gear.

 

8. The tourists tossed pennies into the fountain.

 

9. Folders were stacked on the desk next to the monitor.

 

10. Marina's belt and shoes were made of the same material and complemented her dress.

_____

_____

# A.5 Adverbs

**Adverbs** modify verbs, adjectives, other adverbs, or entire sentences or clauses (see p. 542 on clauses). Like adjectives, adverbs describe, qualify, or limit the meaning of the words they modify.

An adverb answers the question *How? When? Where? How often?* or *To what extent?* about the word it modifies.

| | |
|---|---|
| **HOW?** | Lian moved <u>awkwardly</u> because of her stiff neck. |
| **WHEN?** | I arrived <u>yesterday</u>. |
| **WHERE?** | They searched <u>everywhere</u>. |
| **HOW OFTEN?** | He telephoned <u>repeatedly</u>. |
| **TO WHAT EXTENT?** | Simon was <u>rather</u> slow to answer his e-mail. |

Many adverbs end in *-ly* (*lazily, happily*), but some adverbs do not (*fast, here, much, well, rather, everywhere, never, so*), and some words that end in *-ly* are not adverbs (*lively, friendly, lonely*). Like all other parts of speech, an adverb may be best identified by examining its function within a sentence.

I <u>quickly</u> skimmed the book. [Modifies the verb *skimmed*]

<u>Very</u> angry customers crowded the service desk. [Modifies the adjective *angry*]

He was injured <u>quite</u> seriously. [Modifies the adverb *seriously*]

<u>Apparently</u>, the job was bungled. [Modifies the whole sentence]

Like adjectives, adverbs have three forms: **positive** (does not suggest any comparison), **comparative** (compares two actions or conditions), and **superlative** (compares three or more actions or conditions; see also p. 572).

**Positive**                    **Positive**
Julian rose <u>early</u> and crept downstairs <u>quietly</u>.

**Comparative**                                    **Comparative**
Isaiah rose <u>earlier</u> than Julian and crept downstairs <u>more quietly</u>.

**Superlative**                                    **Superlative**
Cody rose <u>earliest</u> of anyone in the house and crept downstairs <u>most quietly</u>.

Some adverbs, called **conjunctive adverbs** (or **adverbial conjunctions**)—such as *however, therefore,* and *besides*—connect the ideas of one sentence or clause to those of a previous sentence or clause. They can appear anywhere in a sentence. (See p. 553 for how to punctuate sentences containing conjunctive adverbs.)

> Conjunctive adverb
>
> James did not want to go to the library on Saturday; <u>however</u>, he knew the books were overdue.
>
> Conjunctive adverb
>
> The sporting goods store was crowded because of the sale. Leila, <u>therefore</u>, was asked to work extra hours.

Some common conjunctive adverbs are listed below, including several phrases that function as conjunctive adverbs.

| | | | |
|---|---|---|---|
| accordingly | for example | meanwhile | otherwise |
| also | further | moreover | similarly |
| anyway | furthermore | namely | still |
| as a result | hence | nevertheless | then |
| at the same time | however | next | thereafter |
| besides | incidentally | nonetheless | therefore |
| certainly | indeed | now | thus |
| consequently | instead | on the contrary | undoubtedly |
| finally | likewise | on the other hand | |

## EXERCISE 4    Using Adverbs

**Directions:** Write a sentence using each of the following comparative or superlative adverbs.

> EXAMPLE    better: _My car runs better now than ever before._

1. farther: _____

   _____

2. most: _____

   _____

3. more: _____

   _____

4. best: _____

   _____

5. least neatly: _____

   _____

6. louder: _____

   _____

7. worse: _____

   _____

**A. Parts of Speech**

8. less angrily: _____

_____

9. later: _____

_____

10. earliest: _____

_____

# A.6 Conjunctions

**Conjunctions** connect words, phrases, and clauses. There are three kinds of conjunctions: **coordinating**, **correlative**, and **subordinating**. **Coordinating** and **correlative conjunctions** connect words, phrases, or clauses of equal grammatical rank. (A **phrase** is a group of related words lacking a subject, a predicate, or both. A **clause** is a group of words containing a subject and a predicate; see pp. 531 and 532.)

1. The **coordinating conjunctions** are *and, but, nor, or, for, so,* and *yet.* These words must connect words or word groups of the same kind. Therefore, two nouns may be connected by *and,* but a noun and a clause cannot be. *For* and *so* can connect only independent clauses.

   Coordinating
   Noun   conjunction   Noun
   We studied the novels of Toni Morrison and Alice Walker.

   Coordinating
   conjunction
   Verb        Verb
   The copilot successfully flew and landed the disabled plane.

   Coordinating   Independent
   Independent clause                    conjunction   clause
   The carpentry course sounded interesting, so Meg enrolled.

   Coordinating   Subordinate
   Subordinate clause                    conjunction   clause
   We hoped that the mail would come soon and that it would contain our bonus check.

2. **Correlative conjunctions** are pairs of words that link and relate grammatically equivalent parts of a sentence. Some common correlative conjunctions are *either/or, neither/nor, both/and, not/but, not only/but also,* and *whether/or.* Correlative conjunctions are always used in pairs.

   Correlative conjunctions
   Either the electricity was off, or the bulb had burned out.

3. **Subordinating conjunctions** connect dependent, or subordinate, clauses to independent clauses (see p. 553). Some common subordinating conjunctions are *although, because, if, since, until, when, where,* and *while.*

Subordinating conjunction

<u>Although</u> the movie got bad reviews, it drew big crowds.

Subordinating conjunction

She received a lot of mail <u>because</u> she was a reliable correspondent.

# A.7 Prepositions

A **preposition** links and relates its **object** (a noun or a pronoun) to the rest of the sentence. Prepositions often show relationships of time, place, direction, and manner.

Preposition    Object of preposition

I walked <u>around</u> the <u>block</u>.

Preposition    Object of preposition

She called <u>during</u> our <u>meeting</u>.

## Common Prepositions

| | | | | |
|---|---|---|---|---|
| along | besides | from | past | up |
| among | between | in | since | upon |
| around | beyond | near | through | with |
| at | by | off | till | within |
| before | despite | on | to | without |
| behind | down | onto | toward | |
| below | during | out | under | |
| beneath | except | outside | underneath | |
| beside | for | over | until | |

Some prepositions consist of more than one word; they are called **phrasal prepositions** or **compound prepositions**.

Phrasal preposition  Object of preposition

<u>According to</u> our <u>records</u>, you have enough credits to graduate.

Phrasal preposition    Object of preposition

We decided to make the trip <u>in spite of</u> the <u>snowstorm</u>.

## Common Compound Prepositions

| | | |
|---|---|---|
| according to | in addition to | on account of |
| aside from | in front of | out of |
| as of | in place of | prior to |
| as well as | in regard to | with regard to |
| because of | in spite of | with respect to |
| by means of | instead of | |

The object of the preposition often has modifiers.

|  | | Obj. of | | | Obj. of |
|---|---|---|---|---|---|
| Prep. | Modifier | prep. | Prep. | Modifier | prep. |

Not a sound came <u>from</u> the <u>child's</u> <u>room</u> <u>except</u> a <u>gentle</u> <u>snoring</u>.

**A. Parts of Speech**

Sometimes a preposition has more than one object (a **compound object**).

Compound object of preposition
Preposition

The laundromat was between campus and home.

Usually the preposition comes before its object. In interrogative sentences, however, the preposition sometimes follows its object.

Object of preposition          Preposition

What did your supervisor ask you about?

The preposition, the object or objects of the preposition, and the object's modifiers all form a **prepositional phrase**.

Prepositional phrase

The scientist conducted her experiment throughout the afternoon and early evening.

There may be many prepositional phrases in a sentence.

Prepositional phrase          Prepositional phrase

The water from the open hydrant flowed into the street.

The noisy kennel was underneath the beauty salon, despite the complaints of customers.

Alongside the weedy railroad tracks, an old hotel with faded grandeur stood near the abandoned brick station on the edge of town.

> **Tip for Writers**
>
> *Throughout* means "all through." *Alongside* means "next to."

Prepositional phrases frequently function as adjectives or adverbs. If a prepositional phrase modifies a noun or pronoun, it functions as an adjective. If it modifies a verb, adjective, or adverb, it functions as an adverb.

The auditorium inside the conference center has a special sound system. [Adjective modifying the noun *auditorium*]

The doctor looked cheerfully at the patient and handed the lab results across the desk. [Adverbs modifying the verbs *looked* and *handed*]

## EXERCISE 5

# Expanding Sentences Using Prepositional Phrases

**Directions:** Expand each of the following sentences by adding a prepositional phrase in the blank.

EXAMPLE          A cat hid **under the car** when the garage door opened.

1. Fish nibbled _____ as the fisherman waited.

   _____

2. The librarian explained that the books about Africa are located _____.

   _____

3. When the bullet hit the window, shards flew _____.

_____

4. _____, there is a restaurant that serves alligator meat.

_____

5. Polar bears are able to swim _____.

_____

6. Heavy winds blowing _____ caused the waves to hit the house.

_____

7. One student completed her exam _____.

_____

8. A frog jumped _____.

_____

9. The bus was parked _____.

_____

10. Stacks of books were piled _____.

_____

# A.8 Interjections

**Interjections** are words that express emotion or surprise. They are followed by an exclamation point, comma, or period, depending on whether they stand alone or serve as part or all of a sentence. Interjections are used in speech more than in writing.

> <u>Wow</u>! What an announcement!
>
> <u>So</u>, was that lost letter ever found?
>
> <u>Well</u>, I'd better be going.

# B Understanding the Parts of Sentences

A **sentence** is a group of words that must expresses a complete thought about something or someone. A sentence contain a **subject** and a **predicate**.

| Subject | Predicate |
|---|---|
| Telephones | ring. |
| Cecilia | laughed. |
| Time | will tell. |

Depending on their purpose and punctuation, sentences are **declarative**, **interrogative**, **exclamatory**, or **imperative**.

1. **A declarative sentence** makes a statement. It ends with a period.

   Subject  Predicate
   The snow fell steadily.

2. An **interrogative sentence** asks a question. It ends with a question mark (?).

   Subject  Predicate
   Who called?

3. An **exclamatory sentence** conveys strong emotion. It ends with an exclamation point (!).

   Subject  Predicate
   Your photograph is in the company newsletter!

4. An **imperative sentence** gives an order or makes a request. It ends with either a period or an exclamation point, depending on how mild or strong the command or request is. In an imperative sentence, the subject is *you*, but this often is not included.

   Predicate
   Get me a fire extinguisher now! [The subject *you* is understood: (*You*) get me a fire extinguisher now!]

# B.1 Subjects

The **subject** of a sentence is whom or what the sentence is about. It is who or what performs or receives the action expressed in the predicate.

1.  The subject is often a **noun**, a word that names a person, place, thing, or idea.

    > Adriana worked on her math homework.
    >
    > The rose bushes must be watered.
    >
    > Honesty is the best policy.

2.  The subject of a sentence can also be a **pronoun**, a word that refers to or substitutes for a noun.

    > She revised the memo three times.
    >
    > I will attend the sales meeting.
    >
    > Although the ink spilled, it did not go on my shirt.

3.  The subject of a sentence can also be a group of words used as a noun.

    > Reading e-mail from friends is my idea of a good time.

## Simple Versus Complete Subjects

1.  The simple subject is the noun or pronoun that names what the sentence is about. It does not include any **modifiers**—that is, words that describe, identify, qualify, or limit the meaning of the noun or pronoun.

    > Simple subject
    > The bright red concert poster caught everyone's eye.

    > Simple subject
    > High-speed computers have revolutionized the banking industry.

    When the subject of a sentence is a proper noun (the name of a particular person, place, or thing), the entire name is considered the simple subject.

    > Simple subject
    > Martin Luther King Jr. was a famous leader.

    The simple subject of an imperative sentence is *you*.

    > Simple subject
    > [You] Remember to bring the sales brochures.

2.  The **complete subject** is the simple subject plus its modifiers.

    > Complete subject
    > Simple subject
    > The sleek, black limousine waited outside the church.

    > Complete subject
    > Fondly remembered as a gifted songwriter, fiddle player, and storyteller, Quintin Lotus Dickey lived in a cabin in Paoli, Indiana.
    > Simple subject

## Tip for Writers

The simple subject is *reading*, a gerund, a noun made from a verb. It takes a singular verb, in this case, *is*.

## Compound Subjects

Some sentences contain two or more subjects joined with a coordinating conjunction (*and, but, nor, or, for, so, yet*). Those subjects together form a **compound subject**.

Compound subject

Maria and I completed the marathon.

Compound subject

The computer, the printer, and the DVD player were not usable during the blackout.

# B.2 Predicates

The **predicate** indicates what the subject does, what happened to the subject, or what is being said about the subject. The predicate must include a **verb**, a word or group of words that expresses an action or a state of being (for example, *run, invent, build, know, will decide, become*).

Joy swam 60 laps.

The thunderstorm replenished the reservoir.

Sometimes the verb consists of only one word, as in the previous examples. Often, however, the main verb is accompanied by a **helping verb** (see p. 516).

Helping    Main
verb       verb

By the end of the week, I will have worked twenty-five hours.

Helping Main
verb    verb

The training session had begun.

Helping Main
verb    verb

The professor did return the journal assignments.

Tip for Writers

### Tip for Writers

*Did return* is an emphatic past form. This form is often used (instead of the usual past, *returned*) when someone has made a mistake:

Alex said, "The professor didn't return our last essays."

Vera replied, "He did return them. He handed them back the day you were absent."

## Simple Versus Complete Predicates

The **simple predicate** is the main verb plus its helping verbs (together known as the **verb phrase**). The simple predicate does not include any modifiers.

Simple predicate

The proctor hastily collected the blue books.

Simple predicate

The moderator had introduced the next speaker.

The **complete predicate** consists of the simple predicate, its modifiers, and any complements (words that complete the meaning of the verb; see p. 534). In general, the complete predicate includes everything in the sentence except the complete subject.

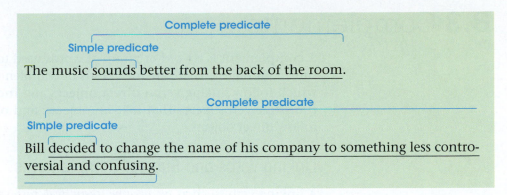

Complete predicate

Simple predicate

The music sounds better from the back of the room.

Complete predicate

Simple predicate

Bill decided to change the name of his company to something less controversial and confusing.

## Compound Predicates

Some sentences have two or more predicates joined by a coordinating conjunction (*and, but, or,* or *nor*). These predicates together form a **compound predicate**.

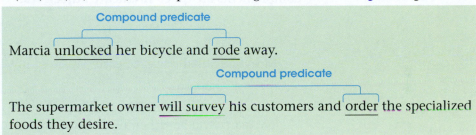

Compound predicate

Marcia unlocked her bicycle and rode away.

Compound predicate

The supermarket owner will survey his customers and order the specialized foods they desire.

**EXERCISE 6**

# Identifying Simple Subjects and Simple and Compound Predicates

**Directions:** Underline the simple subject(s) and circle the simple or compound predicate(s) in each of the following sentences.

 EXAMPLE   Pamela Wong photographed a hummingbird.

1. A group of nurses walked across the lobby on their way to a staff meeting.

2. The campground for physically challenged children is funded and supported by the Rotary Club.

3. Forty doctors and lawyers had attended the seminar on malpractice insurance.

4. Sullivan Beach will not reopen because of pollution.

5. The police cadets attended classes all day and studied late into each evening.

6. Greenpeace is an environmentalist organization.

7. Talented dancers and experienced musicians performed and received much applause at the open-air show.

8. Some undergraduate students have been using empty classrooms for group study.

9. A police officer, with the shoplifter in handcuffs, entered the police station.

10. The newly elected senator walked up to the podium and began her first speech to her constituents.

# B.3 Complements

A **complement** is a word or group of words used to complete the meaning of a subject or object. There are four kinds of complements: **subject complements**, which follow linking verbs; **direct objects** and **indirect objects**, which follow transitive verbs (verbs that take an object); and **object complements**, which follow direct objects.

## Linking Verbs and Subject Complements

A linking verb (such as *be, become, seem, feel, taste*) links the subject to a **subject complement**, a noun or adjective that renames or describes the subject. (See p. 516 for more about linking verbs.) Nouns that function as complements are called **predicate nominatives** or **predicate nouns**. Adjectives that function as complements are called **predicate adjectives**.

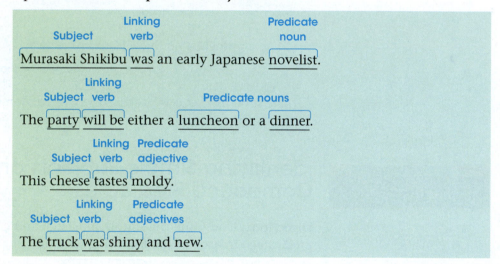

|  | Linking |  | Predicate |
| Subject | verb |  | noun |

Murasaki Shikibu was an early Japanese novelist.

|  | Linking |  | Predicate nouns |
| Subject | verb |  |

The party will be either a luncheon or a dinner.

|  | Linking | Predicate |
| Subject | verb | adjective |

This cheese tastes moldy.

|  | Linking | Predicate |
| Subject | verb | adjectives |

The truck was shiny and new.

## Direct Objects

A **direct object** is a noun or pronoun that receives the action of a transitive verb (see p. 516). A direct object answers the question *What?* or *Whom?*

| Transitive verb | Direct object |

The pharmacist helped us. [The pharmacist helped *whom?*]

| Transitive verb | Direct objects |

Jillian borrowed a bicycle and a visor. [Jillian borrowed *what?*]

## Indirect Objects

An **indirect object** is a noun or pronoun that receives the action of the verb indirectly. Indirect objects name the person or thing *to whom* or *for whom* something is done.

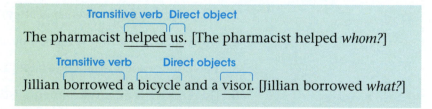

| Transitive | Indirect | Direct |
| verb | object | object |

The computer technician gave me the bill. [He gave the bill *to whom?*]

---

### Tip for Writers

In sentences that tell both *who* and *what* after the verb, follow the word order shown here:

Amir gave his sister a gift. (Do not use *to*.)

Amir gave a gift to his sister. (Use *to*.)

If you mention the person before the thing, don't use *to*.

| Transitive verb | Indirect objects | | Direct objects | |
|---|---|---|---|---|

Eric bought his wife and son some sandwiches and milk. [He bought food *for whom?*]

## Object Complements

An **object complement** is a noun or adjective that modifies (describes) or renames the direct object. Object complements appear with verbs like *name, find, think, elect, appoint, choose,* and *consider.*

| | Direct object | Noun as object complement |
|---|---|---|

We appointed Dean our representative. [*Representative* renames the direct object, *Dean.*]

| | Direct object | Adjective as object complement |
|---|---|---|

The judge found the defendant innocent of the charges. [*Innocent* modifies the direct object, *defendant.*]

# B.4 Basic Sentence Patterns

There are five basic sentence patterns in English. They are built with combinations of subjects, predicates, and complements. The order of these elements within a sentence may change, or a sentence may become long and complicated when modifiers, phrases, or clauses are added. Nonetheless, one of five basic patterns stands at the heart of every sentence.

**PATTERN 1**

| *Subject* | + | *Predicate* |
|---|---|---|
| I | | shivered. |
| Cynthia | | swam. |

**PATTERN 2**

| *Subject* | + | *Predicate* | + | *Direct Object* |
|---|---|---|---|---|
| Anthony | | ordered | | a new desk. |
| We | | wanted | | freedom. |

**PATTERN 3**

| *Subject* | + | *Predicate* | + | *Subject Complement* |
|---|---|---|---|---|
| The woman | | was | | a welder. |
| Our course | | is | | interesting. |

**PATTERN 4**

| *Subject* | + | *Predicate* | + | *Indirect Object* | + | *Direct Object* |
|---|---|---|---|---|---|---|
| My friend | | loaned | | me | | a laptop. |
| The company | | sent | | employees | | a questionnaire. |

**PATTERN 5**

| *Subject* | + | *Predicate* | + | *Direct Object* | + | *Object Complement* |
|---|---|---|---|---|---|---|
| I | | consider | | her singing | | exceptional. |
| Lampwick | | called | | Jiminy Cricket | | a beetle. |

**B. Parts of Sentences**

| EXERCISE 7 | Adding Complements |

**Directions:** Complete each sentence with a word or words that will function as the type of complement indicated.

EXAMPLE   The scientist acted _____*proud*_____ as he announced his latest invention.   predicate adjective

1. The delivery person handed _____ the large brown package.   indirect object

2. Ronald Reagan was an American _____.   predicate noun

3. The chairperson appointed Yesenia our _____.   object complement

4. Protesters stood on the corner and handed out _____.   direct object

5. The secretary gave _____ the messages.   indirect object

6. Before the storm, many clouds were _____.   predicate adjective

7. The beer advertisement targeted _____.   direct object

8. The Super Bowl players were _____.   predicate noun

9. The diplomat declared the Olympics _____.   object complement

10. Shopping malls are _____ before Christmas.   predicate adjective

# B.5 Expanding the Sentence with Adjectives and Adverbs

A sentence may consist of just a subject and a verb.

> Linda studied.
>
> Rumors circulated.

Most sentences, however, contain additional information about the subject and the verb. Information is commonly added in three ways:

■ by using adjectives and adverbs;

■ by using phrases (groups of words that lack either a subject or a predicate or both);

■ by using clauses (groups of words that contain both a subject and a predicate).

### Using Adjectives and Adverbs to Expand Your Sentences

**Adjectives** are words used to modify or describe nouns and pronouns (see p. 521). Adjectives answer questions about nouns and pronouns such as *Which one? What kind? How many?* Using adjectives is one way to add detail and information to sentences.

| | |
|---|---|
| WITHOUT ADJECTIVES | Dogs barked at cats. |
| WITH ADJECTIVES | Our three large, brown dogs barked at the two terrified, spotted cats. |

*Note:* Sometimes nouns and participles are used as adjectives (see p. 517 on participles).

Noun used as adjective

People are rediscovering the milk bottle.

Present participle used as adjective    Past participle used as adjective

Mrs. Simon had a swimming pool with a broken drain.

**Adverbs** add information to sentences by modifying or describing verbs, adjectives, or other adverbs (see p. 524). An adverb usually answers the question *How? When? Where? How often?* or *To what extent?*

| | |
|---|---|
| WITHOUT ADVERBS | I will clean. |
| | The audience applauded. |
| WITH ADVERBS | I will clean very thoroughly tomorrow. |
| | The audience applauded loudly and enthusiastically. |

# B.6 Expanding the Sentence with Phrases

A **phrase** is a group of related words that lacks a subject, a predicate, or both. A phrase cannot stand alone as a sentence. Phrases can appear at the beginning, middle, or end of a sentence.

| | |
|---|---|
| WITHOUT PHRASES | I noticed the stain. |
| | Sal researched the topic. |
| | Manuela arose. |
| WITH PHRASES | Upon entering the room, I noticed the stain on the expensive carpet. |
| | At the local aquarium, Sal researched the topic of shark attacks. |

An amateur astronomer, Manuela arose <u>in the middle of the night</u> to observe the lunar eclipse but, <u>after waiting ten minutes in the cold</u>, gave up.

There are eight kinds of phrases: **noun; verb; prepositional; verbal (participial, gerund,** and **infinitive); appositive;** and **absolute.**

## Noun and Verb Phrases

A noun plus its modifiers is a **noun phrase** (*red shoes, the quiet house*). A main verb plus its helping verb is a **verb phrase** (*had been exploring, is sleeping;* see p. 516 on helping verbs.)

## Prepositional Phrases

A **prepositional phrase** consists of a preposition (for example, *in, above, with, at, behind*), an object of the preposition (a noun or pronoun), and any modifiers of the object. (See p. 527 for a list of common prepositions.) A prepositional phrase functions like an adjective (modifying a noun or pronoun) or an adverb (modifying a verb, adjective, or adverb). You can use prepositional phrases to tell more about people, places, objects, or actions. A prepositional phrase usually adds information about time, place, direction, manner, or degree.

### As Adjectives

The woman <u>with the briefcase</u> is giving a presentation <u>on meditation techniques</u>.

Both <u>of the telephones</u> <u>behind the partition</u> were ringing.

### As Adverbs

The fire drill occurred <u>in the morning</u>.

I was curious <u>about the new human resources director</u>.

The conference speaker came <u>from Australia</u>.

<u>With horror</u>, the crowd watched the rhinoceros's tether stretch <u>to the breaking point</u>.

A prepositional phrase can function as part of the complete subject or as part of the complete predicate, but should not be confused with the simple subject or simple predicate.

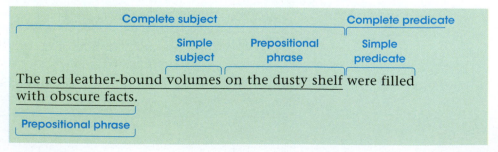

Complete predicate

Simple predicate     Prepositional phrase

Pat ducked quickly behind the potted fern.

## Verbal Phrases

A **verbal** is a verb form that cannot function as the main verb of a sentence. The three kinds of verbals are **participles**, **gerunds**, and **infinitives**. A **verbal phrase** consists of a verbal and its modifiers.

### Participles and Participial Phrases

All verbs have two participles: present and past. The **present participle** is formed by adding *-ing* to the infinitive form (*walking, riding, being*). The **past participle** of regular verbs is formed by adding *-d* or *-ed* to the infinitive form (*walked, baked*). The past participle of irregular verbs has no set pattern (*ridden, been*). (See p. 517 for a list of common irregular verbs and their past participles.) Both the present participle and the past participle can function as adjectives modifying nouns and pronouns.

Past participle               Present participle
as adjective                  as adjective

Irritated, Martha circled the confusing traffic rotary once again.

A **participial phrase** consists of a participle and any of its modifiers.

Participial phrase

participle

We listened for Isabella climbing the rickety stairs.

Participial phrase

Participle

Disillusioned with the whole system, Kay sat down to think.

Participial phrase

Participle

The singer, having caught a bad cold, canceled his performance.

### Gerunds and Gerund Phrases

A **gerund** is the present participle (the *-ing* form) of the verb used as a noun.

Shoveling is good exercise.

Rex enjoyed gardening.

A **gerund phrase** consists of a gerund and its modifiers. A gerund phrase, like a gerund, is used as a noun and can therefore function in a sentence as a subject, a direct or indirect object, an object of a preposition, a subject complement, or an appositive.

Gerund phrase

Photocopying the report took longer than La Tisha anticipated. [Subject]

Gerund phrase

The director considered making another monster movie. [Direct object]

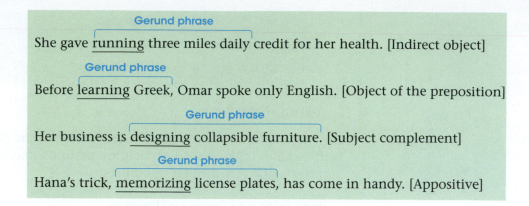

Gerund phrase

She gave running three miles daily credit for her health. [Indirect object]

Gerund phrase

Before learning Greek, Omar spoke only English. [Object of the preposition]

Gerund phrase

Her business is designing collapsible furniture. [Subject complement]

Gerund phrase

Hana's trick, memorizing license plates, has come in handy. [Appositive]

### Infinitives and Infinitive Phrases

The **infinitive** is the base form of the verb as it appears in the dictionary preceded by the word *to*. An **infinitive phrase** consists of the word *to* plus the infinitive and any modifiers. An infinitive phrase can function as a noun, an adjective, or an adverb. When it is used as a noun, an infinitive phrase can be a subject, object, complement, or appositive.

Infinitive phrase

To love one's enemies is a noble goal. [Noun used as subject]

Infinitive phrase

The season to sell bulbs is the fall. [Adjective modifying *season*]

Infinitive phrase

The chess club met to practice for the state championship. [Adverb modifying *met*]

Sometimes the *to* in an infinitive phrase is not written.

Jacob helped us learn the new accounting procedure. [The *to* before *learn* is understood.]

*Note:* Do not confuse infinitive phrases with prepositional phrases beginning with the preposition *to*. In an infinitive phrase, *to* is followed by a verb; in a prepositional phrase, *to* is followed by a noun or pronoun.

## Appositive Phrases

An **appositive** is a noun that explains, restates, or adds new information about another noun. An **appositive phrase** consists of an appositive and its modifiers. (See p. 597 for punctuation of appositive phrases.)

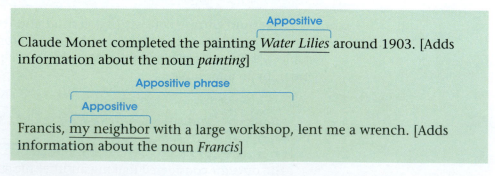

Appositive

Claude Monet completed the painting *Water Lilies* around 1903. [Adds information about the noun *painting*]

Appositive phrase

Appositive

Francis, my neighbor with a large workshop, lent me a wrench. [Adds information about the noun *Francis*]

## Absolute Phrases

An **absolute phrase** consists of a noun or pronoun and any modifiers followed by a participle or a participial phrase (see p. 539). An absolute phrase modifies an entire sentence, not any particular word within the sentence. It can appear anywhere in a sentence and is set off from the rest of the sentence with a comma or commas. There may be more than one absolute phrase in a sentence.

Absolute phrase

The winter being over, the geese returned.

Absolute phrase

Senator Arden began his speech, his voice rising to be heard over the loud applause.

Absolute phrase

A vacancy having occurred, the hotel manager called the first name on the reservations waiting list.

# Expanding Sentences with Adjectives, Adverbs, and Phrases

**Directions:** Expand each of the following sentences by adding adjectives, adverbs, and/or phrases (prepositional, verbal, appositive, or absolute).

EXAMPLE   The professor lectured.

EXPANDED   *Being an expert on animal behavior, the professor lectured about animal-intelligence studies.*

1. Randall will graduate. _____

_____

2. The race began. _____

_____

3. Walmart is remodeling. _____

_____

4. Hillary walked alone. _____

_____

5. Manuel repairs appliances. _____

_____

6. The motorcycle was loud. _____

_____

7. My term paper is due Tuesday. _____

_____

8. I opened my umbrella. _____

_____

**B. Parts of Sentences**

9. Austin built a garage. _____

   _____

10. Lucas climbs mountains. _____

    _____

# B.7 Expanding the Sentence with Clauses

A **clause** is a group of words that contains a subject and a predicate. A clause is either **independent** (also called **main**) or **dependent** (also called **subordinate**).

## Independent Clauses

An **independent clause** can stand alone as a grammatically complete sentence.

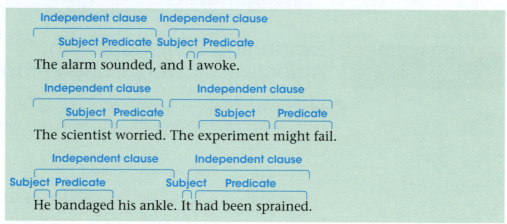

## Dependent Clauses

A **dependent clause** has a subject and a predicate, but it cannot stand alone as a grammatically complete sentence because it does not express a complete thought. Most dependent clauses begin with either a **subordinating conjunction** or a **relative pronoun**. These words connect the dependent clause to an independent clause.

### Tip for Writers

Remember that some of these words have two meanings. For example, *once* can mean "one time" or "after." *While* can mean "at the same time" or "but."

| Common Subordinating Conjunctions | | |
|---|---|---|
| after | in as much as | that |
| although | in case | though |
| as | in order that | unless |
| as far as | in so far as | until |
| as if | in that | when |
| as soon as | now that | whenever |
| as though | once | where |
| because | provided that | wherever |
| before | rather than | whether |

*(continued)*

| Common Subordinating Conjunctions | | |
|---|---|---|
| even if | since | while |
| even though | so that | why |
| how | supposing that | |
| if | than | |

| Relative Pronouns | |
|---|---|
| that | which |
| | who (whose, whom) |
| whatever | whoever (whomever) |

These clauses do not express complete thoughts and therefore cannot stand alone as sentences. When joined to independent clauses, however, dependent clauses function as adjectives, adverbs, and nouns and are known as **adjective** (or **relative**) **clauses**, **adverb clauses**, and **noun clauses**. Noun clauses can function as subjects, objects, or complements.

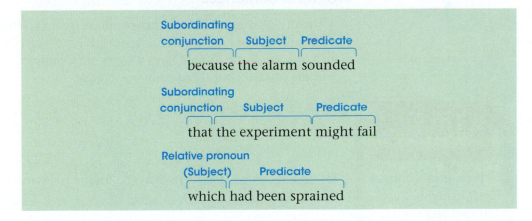

### Adjective Clause

Dependent clause
He bandaged his ankle, <u>which had been sprained</u>. [Modifies *ankle*]

### Adverb Clause

Dependent clause
<u>Because the alarm sounded</u>, I awoke. [Modifies *awoke*]

### Noun Clause

Dependent clause
The scientist worried <u>that the experiment might fail</u>. [Direct object of *worried*]

### Elliptical Clause

Sometimes the relative pronoun or subordinating conjunction is implied or understood rather than stated. Also, a dependent clause may contain an implied predicate. When a dependent clause is missing an element that can clearly be supplied from the context of the sentence, it is called an **elliptical clause**.

**Elliptical clause**

The circus is more entertaining than television [is]. [*Is* is the understood predicate in the elliptical dependent clause.]

**Elliptical clause**

Canadian history is among the subjects [that] the book discusses. [*That* is the understood relative pronoun in the elliptical dependent clause.]

Relative pronouns are generally the subject or object in their clauses. *Who* and *whoever* change to *whom* and *whomever* when they function as objects (see p. 572).

# B.8 Basic Sentence Classifications

Depending on its structure, a sentence can be classified as one of four basic types: **simple**, **compound**, **complex**, or **compound-complex**.

### Simple Sentences

A **simple sentence** has one independent (main) clause and no dependent (subordinate) clauses (see p. 535). A simple sentence contains at least one subject and one predicate. It may have a compound subject, a compound predicate, and various phrases, but it has only one clause.

**Subject  predicate**

Sap rises.

**Subject**        **Compound predicate**

In the spring the sap rises in the maple trees and is boiled to make a thick, delicious syrup.

> **Tip for Writers**
>
> There is no comma before *and* because the subject (*sap*) is not repeated before the second verb (*is boiled*). The phrase after *and* is not a sentence; it is not a complete thought.

### Compound Sentences

A **compound sentence** has at least two independent clauses and no dependent clauses (see p. 535). The two independent clauses are usually joined with a comma and a coordinating conjunction (*and, but, nor, or, for, so,* or *yet*). Sometimes the two clauses are joined with a semicolon and no coordinating conjunction or with a semicolon and a conjunctive adverb like *nonetheless* or *still* followed by a comma. (See p. 525 on conjunctive adverbs and p. 553 on punctuation.)

**Independent clause**

Reading a novel by Henry James is not like reading a thriller, but with patience the rewards are greater.

**Independent clause**

**Independent clause**                              **Independent clause**

I set out to explore the North River near home; I ended up at Charlie's Clam Bar.

## Complex Sentences

A **complex sentence** has one independent clause and one or more dependent clauses (see p. 535). The clauses are joined by subordinating conjunctions or relative pronouns (see p. 542).

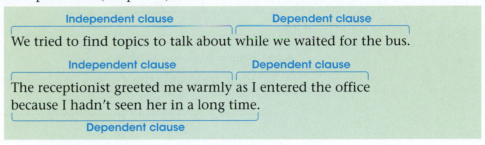

Independent clause | Dependent clause

We tried to find topics to talk about while we waited for the bus.

Independent clause | Dependent clause

The receptionist greeted me warmly as I entered the office because I hadn't seen her in a long time.

Dependent clause

## Compound-Complex Sentences

A **compound-complex sentence** contains two or more independent clauses and one or more dependent clauses (see p. 535).

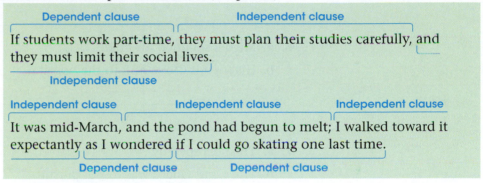

Dependent clause | Independent clause

If students work part-time, they must plan their studies carefully, and they must limit their social lives.

Independent clause

Independent clause | Independent clause | Independent clause

It was mid-March, and the pond had begun to melt; I walked toward it expectantly as I wondered if I could go skating one last time.

Dependent clause | Dependent clause

**EXERCISE 9**

# Combining Sentences

**Directions:** Combine each of the following pairs of sentences into a single sentence by forming independent and/or dependent clauses. You may need to add, change, or delete words.

EXAMPLE      **a.** The levee broke.

                 **b.** The flood waters rose rapidly.

COMBINED    *After the levee broke, the flood waters rose rapidly.*

1. **a.** Margot is a picky eater.

    **b.** Ivan, Margot's cousin, will eat anything.

 _____

 _____

2. **a.** Joe broke his wrist rollerblading.

    **b.** Joe started wearing protective gear.

 _____

 _____

3. **a.** Rick waited in line at the Department of Motor Vehicles.

   **b.** At the same time, Aaliyah waited in line at the bank.

   _____

   _____

   _____

4. **a.** Beer is high in calories.

   **b.** Some beer companies now make low-calorie beer.

   _____

   _____

5. **a.** Keith says he is politically active.

   **b.** Keith is not registered to vote.

   _____

   _____

6. **a.** Miguel sprained his ankle.

   **b.** His friends drove him to the hospital.

   _____

   _____

7. **a.** The boat sped by.

   **b.** The Coast Guard was in hot pursuit.

   _____

   _____

8. **a.** The weather report predicted rain.

   **b.** I brought my umbrella.

   _____

   _____

9. **a.** Graffiti had been spray-painted on the subway wall.

   **b.** Maintenance workers were scrubbing it off.

   _____

   _____

10. **a.** Shoppers were crowding around a display table.

    **b.** Everything on the table was reduced by 50 percent.

    _____

    _____

# Avoiding Sentence Errors

## C.1 Sentence Fragments

A complete sentence contains at least one subject and one verb and expresses a complete thought. It begins with a capital letter and ends with a period, question mark, or exclamation point (see p. 530). A **sentence fragment** is an incomplete sentence because it lacks either a subject, a verb, or both, or it is a dependent (subordinate) clause unattached to a complete sentence. In either case, it does not express a complete thought. Occasionally, a writer may knowingly use a fragment for effect or emphasis. This is known as an **intentional fragment**. However, it is best to avoid fragments in your writing; instead, use complete sentences.

| | |
|---|---|
| FRAGMENT | Walked across campus this afternoon. [This group of words lacks a subject.] |
| COMPLETE SENTENCE | Pete walked across campus this afternoon. |
| FRAGMENT | The car next to the fence. [This group of words lacks a verb.] |
| COMPLETE SENTENCE | The car next to the fence stalled. |
| FRAGMENT | Alert and ready. [This group of words lacks a subject and a verb.] |
| COMPLETE SENTENCE | Juan appeared alert and ready. |
| FRAGMENT | While I was waiting in line. [This group of words is a subordinate clause unattached to a complete sentence.] |
| COMPLETE SENTENCE | While I was waiting in line, I studied the faces of people walking by. |

### How to Spot Fragments

To find sentence fragments in your writing, use the following questions to evaluate each group of words:

1. **Does the group of words have a verb?** Be sure that the verb is a complete sentence verb and not a verbal or part of a verbal phrase (see p. 539).

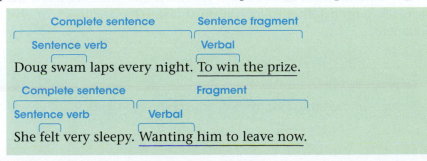

Complete sentence    Fragment

Sentence verb    Verbal

Mateo is excited. Going to the interview tomorrow.

Complete sentence    Fragment

Sentence verb    Verbal

I am starting banjo lessons. Beginning next week.

Each of the underlined phrases needs to be either (1) rewritten as a complete sentence or (2) combined with a complete sentence.

| | |
|---|---|
| REWRITTEN | Doug swam laps every night. He practiced to win the prize. |
| REWRITTEN | She felt very sleepy. She wanted him to leave now. |
| COMBINED | Mateo is excited because he is going to the interview tomorrow. |
| COMBINED | Beginning next week, I am starting banjo lessons. |

To distinguish between a complete sentence verb and a verbal, keep in mind the following rule: a sentence verb can change tense to show differences in time—past, present, and future. A verbal cannot demonstrate these shifts in time. You can change the sentence *I have a lot of homework* to *I had a lot of homework* or *I will have a lot of homework,* but the verbal phrase *riding a horse* cannot be changed to show differences in time.

2. **Does the group of words have a subject?** After you have found the verb, look for the subject. The subject is a noun or pronoun that performs or receives the action of the sentence (see p. 531). To find the subject, ask *who* or *what* performs or receives the action of the verb.

Subject    Verb

The corner bookstore opens at noon. [*What* opens? The bookstore opens.]

Notice, however, what happens when you ask *who* or *what* about the following fragments:

Will study math with a tutor. [*Who* will study? The question cannot be answered; no subject exists.]

And walked away quickly. [*Who* walked away? Again, the question cannot be answered because there is no subject.]

Every sentence must have a subject. Even if one sentence has a clear subject, the sentence that follows it must also have a subject, or else it is a fragment.

Sentence    Fragment

Subject    Verb    Verb

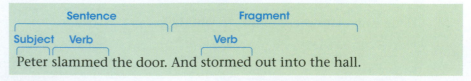

Peter slammed the door. And stormed out into the hall.

You know from the first sentence that it was Peter who stormed out, but the second group of words is nonetheless a fragment because it lacks a subject. Combining it with the first sentence would eliminate the problem.

> COMBINED    Peter slammed the door and stormed out into the hall.

Imperative sentences (sentences that command or suggest) have a subject that is usually not explicitly stated. They are not fragments.

> Follow me. [The subject *you* is understood: (*You*) Follow me.]

3. **Does the group of words begin with a subordinating conjunction (such as *after, although, as, because, however, since,* or *that*)?** A group of words beginning with a subordinating conjunction is a fragment unless that group of words is attached to an independent clause (see p. 524).

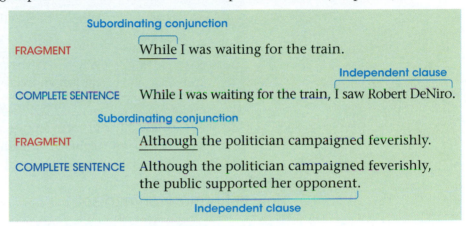

> Subordinating conjunction
>
> FRAGMENT    While I was waiting for the train.
>
> Independent clause
>
> COMPLETE SENTENCE    While I was waiting for the train, I saw Robert DeNiro.
>
> Subordinating conjunction
>
> FRAGMENT    Although the politician campaigned feverishly.
>
> COMPLETE SENTENCE    Although the politician campaigned feverishly, the public supported her opponent.
>
> Independent clause

You can also correct a fragment that is a dependent clause by omitting the subordinating conjunction and making the clause into an independent clause, a complete sentence.

> COMPLETE SENTENCE    I was waiting for the train.
>
> COMPLETE SENTENCE    The politician campaigned feverishly.

4. **Does the group of words begin with a relative pronoun (*that, what, whatever, which, who, whoever, whom, whomever, whose*)?** A group of words beginning with a relative pronoun is a fragment unless it forms a question with a subject and a verb or is attached to an independent clause.

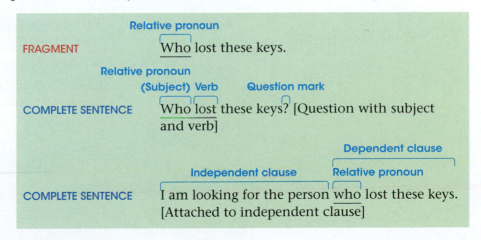

> Relative pronoun
>
> FRAGMENT    Who lost these keys.
>
> Relative pronoun
> (Subject) Verb    Question mark
>
> COMPLETE SENTENCE    Who lost these keys? [Question with subject and verb]
>
> Dependent clause
> Independent clause    Relative pronoun
>
> COMPLETE SENTENCE    I am looking for the person who lost these keys. [Attached to independent clause]

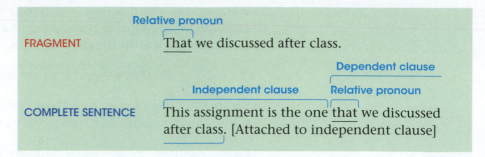

| | Relative pronoun |
|---|---|
| FRAGMENT | That we discussed after class. |

| | Independent clause | Dependent clause / Relative pronoun |
|---|---|---|
| COMPLETE SENTENCE | This assignment is the one that we discussed after class. [Attached to independent clause] | |

Also check groups of words beginning with *how, when, where,* and *why.* If a clause beginning with one of these words neither asks a question nor is attached to an independent clause, then the word group is a fragment.

| | Subordinating word |
|---|---|
| FRAGMENT | Where the meeting will be held. |

| | Verb · Subject · Verb · Question mark |
|---|---|
| COMPLETE SENTENCE | Where will the meeting be held? [Question with subject and verb] |

| | Independent clause · Dependent clause |
|---|---|
| COMPLETE SENTENCE | We peeked into the room where the meeting will be held. [Attached to independent clause] |

## How to Correct Fragments

1. **Attach the fragment to a complete sentence or an independent clause** (see p. 542).

| | Dependent Clause |
|---|---|
| FRAGMENT | While my boss was on the phone. She began to eat lunch. |

| | Dependent clause · Independent clause |
|---|---|
| COMPLETE SENTENCE | While my boss was on the phone, she began to eat lunch. |

| | No sentence verb |
|---|---|
| FRAGMENT | Students who missed five classes. They are ineligible for the final exam. |

| | Subject · Sentence verb |
|---|---|
| COMPLETE SENTENCE | Students who missed five classes are ineligible for the final exam. |

| | No subject |
|---|---|
| FRAGMENT | Sabeen sketched portraits all morning. And read art history all afternoon. |

| | Subject · Compound sentence verb |
|---|---|
| COMPLETE SENTENCE | Sabeen sketched portraits all morning and read art history all afternoon. |

2. Remove the subordinating conjunction or relative pronoun and make sure that the remaining group of words has a subject and a sentence verb—that is, that it can stand alone as a complete sentence.

> FRAGMENT            I did not finish the book. <u>Because its tedious style bored me.</u>
>
> **Independent clause**
>
> **Sentence verb**
>
> COMPLETE SENTENCE   I did not finish the book. Its tedious style bored me.
>
> **Subject**

3. Add the missing subject or verb or both.

> FRAGMENT            The patient refused to pay her bill. <u>And then started complaining loudly.</u>
>
> **Subject added**
>
> COMPLETE SENTENCE   The patient refused to pay her bill. Then she started complaining loudly.
>
> FRAGMENT            The Summer Olympics were held in Beijing. <u>Hot wind blowing every day.</u>
>
> COMPLETE SENTENCE   The Summer Olympics were held in Beijing. A hot wind blew every day.
>
> **Subject added    Sentence verb added**
>
> FRAGMENT            I had to leave the car in the driveway. <u>The snow against the garage door.</u>
>
> COMPLETE SENTENCE   I had to leave the car in the driveway. The snow had drifted against the garage door.
>
> **Sentence verb added**

| EXERCISE 10 | Correcting Fragments |

**Directions:** Make each of the following sentence fragments a complete sentence by combining it with an independent clause, removing the subordinating conjunction or relative pronoun, or adding the missing subject or verb.

> EXAMPLE            Many environmentalists are concerned about the spotted owl. Which is almost extinct.
>
> COMPLETE SENTENCE   Many environmentalists are concerned about the spotted owl, which is almost extinct.

1. Renting a DVD of the movie *Citizen Kane*. _____

_____

2. Spices that had been imported from India. _____

_____

3. The police officer walked to Jerome's van. To give him a ticket.

_____

4. My English professor, with the cup of tea he brought to each class.

_____

5. After the table was refinished. _____

_____

6. Roberto memorized his lines. For the performance tomorrow night.

_____

7. A tricycle with big wheels, painted red. _____

_____

8. On the shelf, an antique crock used for storing lard. _____

_____

9. Because I always wanted to learn to speak Spanish. _____

_____

10. Looking for the lost keys. I was late for class. _____

_____

# C.2 Run-on Sentences and Comma Splices

Independent clauses contain both a subject and a predicate. When two independent clauses are joined in one sentence, they must be separated by a comma and a coordinating conjunction or by a semicolon. Failure to properly separate independent clauses creates the errors known as **run-on sentences** and **comma splices**.

A **run-on sentence** (or **fused sentence**) contains two independent clauses that are not separated by any punctuation or a coordinating conjunction (*and, but, nor, or, for, so, yet*).

A **comma splice** (or comma fault) contains two independent clauses joined only by a comma (the coordinating conjunction is missing). A comma by itself cannot join two independent clauses (see p. 542).

## How to Spot Run-on Sentences and Comma Splices

1. **You can often spot run-on sentences by reading them aloud.** Listen for a pause or a change in your voice. That may signal that you are moving from the first clause to the second. Read the following run-on sentences aloud, and see if you can hear where the two clauses in each should be separated.

| | |
|---|---|
| RUN-ON | We watched the football game then we ordered pizza. |
| CORRECT | We watched the football game, and then we ordered pizza. |

| RUN-ON | My throat feels sore I hope I am not catching a cold. |
|---|---|
| CORRECT | My throat feels sore; I hope I am not catching a cold. |

2. **You can spot a comma splice by looking carefully at your use and placement of commas**. If you see a comma between two independent clauses but no coordinating conjunction after the comma, then you have probably spotted a comma splice.

| COMMA SPLICE | The average person watches 15 hours of television a week, my parents allow my brother only 2 hours a week. |
|---|---|
| CORRECT | The average person watches 15 hours of television a week, |

                        Coordinating conjunction
                        but my parents allow my brother only 2 hours a week.

## How to Correct Run-on Sentences and Comma Splices

There are four ways to correct a run-on sentence or a comma splice. Not every run-on sentence or comma splice can be corrected in the same way. The method you choose will depend on the meaning of the clauses.

1. **Create two separate sentences**. End the first independent clause with a period. Begin the next with a capital letter.

| RUN-ON | We went for a walk in the woods we saw the leaves turning red and orange. |
|---|---|
| CORRECT | We went for a walk in the woods. We saw the leaves turning red and orange. |

2. **Use a semicolon**. Use a semicolon when the thoughts expressed in the independent clauses are closely related and you want to emphasize that relationship. (The word immediately following the semicolon does not begin with a capital letter unless it is a proper noun.)

| RUN-ON | It is unlikely that school taxes will increase this year citizens have expressed their opposition. |
|---|---|
| CORRECT | It is unlikely that school taxes will increase this year; citizens have expressed their opposition. |

*Note:* An independent clause containing a conjunctive adverb (such as *finally, however, meanwhile, otherwise,* or *therefore*) must be separated from another independent clause with a period or a semicolon. (See p. 525 for a list of conjunctive adverbs.) In most cases, the conjunctive adverb itself is set off with a comma or pair of commas.

| COMMA SPLICE | The road crew was repairing potholes, therefore traffic was snarled. |
|---|---|
| CORRECT | The road crew was repairing potholes; therefore, traffic was snarled. |

3. **Insert a comma and a coordinating conjunction (*and, but, for, nor, or, so, yet*).**

| RUN-ON | Americans are changing their eating habits they still eat too much red meat. |
|---|---|

Coordinating conjunction

| CORRECT | Americans are changing their eating habits, but they still eat too much red meat. |
|---|---|

4. **Make one clause subordinate to the other**. This method is especially effective when the idea expressed in one of the clauses is more important than the idea in the other clause. By adding a subordinating conjunction (such as *after, although, because,* or *until*), you can link a dependent clause to an independent clause. (See below for a list of subordinating conjunctions.) Be sure to use a subordinating conjunction that explains the relationship between the dependent clause and the independent clause to which it is joined.

| COMMA SPLICE | I left the store, I shut off all the lights. |
|---|---|

Dependent clause

Subordinating conjunction                Independent clause

| CORRECT | Before I left the store, I shut off all the lights. |
|---|---|

The subordinating conjunction *before* in the above sentence indicates the sequence in which the two actions were performed. In addition to time, subordinating conjunctions can indicate place, cause or effect, condition or circumstance, contrast, or manner.

| MEANING | SUBORDINATING CONJUNCTION | EXAMPLE |
|---|---|---|
| time | after, before, when, until, once, while | After I left work, I went to the mall. |
| place | where, wherever | I will go wherever you go. |
| cause or effect | because, since, so that, that, as | I missed the bus because I overslept. |
| condition or circumstance | if, unless, as long as, in case, whenever, once, provided that | If I get an A on the paper, I'll be happy. |
| contrast | although, even though, even if, whereas, while | Even though I lost my job, I have to make my car payment. |
| manner | as, as if, as though | Ana acted as if she were angry. |

The dependent clause can be placed *before* or *after* the independent clause. If it is placed before the independent clause, put a comma at the end of it. Usually no comma is needed when the independent clause comes first.

| COMMA SPLICE | I studied psychology, I was thinking about some of Freud's findings. |
|---|---|

Dependent clause                Independent clause

| CORRECT | When I studied psychology, I was thinking about some of Freud's findings. |
|---|---|

| | Independent clause | Dependent clause |
|---|---|---|
| CORRECT | I was thinking about some of Freud's findings | when I studied psychology. |

You may add a dependent clause to a sentence that has more than one independent clause (see p. 545).

| | | |
|---|---|---|
| RUN-ON | We toured the hospital we met with its chief administrator she invited us to lunch. | |

| | Dependent clause | Independent clause |
|---|---|---|
| CORRECT | After we toured the hospital, | we met with its chief administrator and she invited us to lunch. |
| | | Independent clause |

**EXERCISE 11**

# Identifying Run-on Sentences and Comma Splices

**Directions:** On the line beside each of the following word groups, identify if it is a run-on sentence (RO), a comma splice (CS), or a correct sentence (C). Revise the word groups that contain errors.

EXAMPLE  ___CS___  The children chased the ball into the street, cars screeched to a halt.

_____  1. Inez packed for the business trip she remembered everything except her business cards.

_____  2. A limousine drove through our neighborhood, everybody wondered who was in it.

_____  3. The defendant pleaded not guilty the judge ordered him to pay the parking ticket.

_____  4. Before a big game, Louis, who is a quarterback, eats a lot of pasta and bread he says it gives him energy.

_____  5. Four of my best friends from high school have decided to go to law school, I have decided to become a paralegal.

_____  6. Felicia did not know what to buy her co-worker for his birthday, so she went to a lot of stores she finally decided to buy him a gift certificate.

_____  7. After living in a dorm room for three years, Jason found an apartment the rent was very high, so he had to get a job to pay for it.

_____  8. The cherry tree had to be cut down, it stood right where the new addition was going to be built.

_____  9. Amanda worked every night for a month on the needlepoint pillow that she was making for her grandmother.

_____  10. Driving around in the dark, we finally realized we were lost, Dwight went into a convenience store to ask for directions.

# C.3 Uses of Verb Tenses

The **tense** of a verb expresses time. It conveys whether an action, process, or occurrence takes place in the present, past, or future. There are 12 tenses in English, and each is used to express a particular time. (See p. 517 for information about how to form each tense.)

The **simple present tense** expresses actions that are occurring at the time of the writing or that occur regularly. The **simple past tense** is used for actions that have already occurred. The **simple future tense** is used for actions that will occur in the future.

| | |
|---|---|
| SIMPLE PRESENT | The chef <u>cooks</u> a huge meal. |
| SIMPLE PAST | The chef <u>cooked</u> a huge meal. |
| SIMPLE FUTURE | The chef <u>will cook</u> a huge meal. |

The **present perfect tense** is used for actions that began in the past and are still occurring in the present or are finished by the time of the writing. The **past perfect tense** expresses actions that were completed before other past actions. The **future perfect tense** is used for actions that will be completed in the future.

| | |
|---|---|
| PRESENT PERFECT | The chef <u>has cooked</u> a huge meal every night this week. |
| PAST PERFECT | The chef <u>had cooked</u> a huge meal before the guests canceled their reservation. |
| FUTURE PERFECT | The chef <u>will have cooked</u> a huge meal by the time we arrive. |

The six progressive tenses are used for continuing actions or actions in progress. The **present progressive tense** is used for actions that are in progress in the present. The **past progressive tense** expresses past continuing actions. The **future progressive tense** is used for continuing actions that will occur in the future. The **present perfect progressive**, **past perfect progressive**, and **future perfect progressive tenses** are used for continuing actions that are, were, or will be completed by a certain time.

| | |
|---|---|
| PRESENT PROGRESSIVE | The chef <u>is cooking</u> a huge meal this evening. |
| PAST PROGRESSIVE | The chef <u>was cooking</u> a huge meal when she ran out of butter. |
| FUTURE PROGRESSIVE | The chef <u>will be cooking</u> a huge meal all day tomorrow. |
| PRESENT PERFECT PROGRESSIVE | The chef <u>has been cooking</u> a huge meal since this morning. |
| PAST PERFECT PROGRESSIVE | The chef <u>had been cooking</u> a huge meal before the electricity went out. |
| FUTURE PERFECT PROGRESSIVE | The chef <u>will have been cooking</u> a huge meal for eight hours when the guests arrive. |

Writing all forms of a verb for all tenses and all persons (first, second, and third, singular and plural) is called **conjugating** the verb. Irregular verbs have an irregularly formed past tense and past participle (used in the past tense and the perfect tenses). (See p. 517 for a list of the forms of common irregular verbs.) Here is the complete conjugation for the regular verb *walk*.

| Conjugation of the Regular Verb *Walk* | | |
| --- | --- | --- |
| | **SINGULAR** | **PLURAL** |
| Simple present tense | I walk<br>you walk<br>he/she/it walks | we walk<br>you walk<br>they walk |
| Simple past tense | I walked<br>you walked<br>he/she/it walked | we walked<br>you walked<br>they walked |
| Simple future tense | I will (shall) walk<br>you will walk<br>he/she/it will walk | we will (shall) walk<br>you will walk<br>they will walk |
| Present perfect tense | I have walked<br>you have walked<br>he/she/it has walked | we have walked<br>you have walked<br>they have walked |
| Past perfect tense | I had walked<br>you had walked<br>he/she/it had walked | we had walked<br>you had walked<br>they had walked |
| Future perfect tense | I will (shall) have walked<br>you will have walked<br>he/she/it will have walked | we will (shall) have walked<br>you will have walked<br>they will have walked |
| Present progressive tense | I am walking<br>you are walking<br>he/she/it is walking | we are walking<br>you are walking<br>they are walking |
| Past progressive tense | I was walking<br>you were walking<br>he/she/it was walking | we were walking<br>you were walking<br>they were walking |
| Future progressive tense | I will be walking<br>you will be walking<br>he/she/it will be walking | we will be walking<br>you will be walking<br>they will be walking |
| Present perfect progressive tense | I have been walking<br>you have been walking<br>he/she/it has been walking | we have been walking<br>you have been walking<br>they have been walking |
| Past perfect progressive tense | I had been walking<br>you had been walking<br>he/she/it had been walking | we had been walking<br>you had been walking<br>they had been walking |
| Future perfect progressive tense | I will have been walking<br>you will have been walking<br>he/she/it will have been walking | we will have been walking<br>you will have been walking<br>they will have been walking |

Following are the simple present and simple past tenses for the irregular verbs *have, be,* and *do,* which are commonly used as helping verbs (see p. 516).

| Irregular Verbs *Have*, *Be*, and *Do* | | | |
| --- | --- | --- | --- |
| | **HAVE** | **BE** | **DO** |
| Simple present tense | I have<br>you have<br>he/she/it has<br>we/you/they have | I am<br>you are<br>he/she/it is<br>we/you/they are | I do<br>you do<br>he/she/it does<br>we/you/they do |
| Simple past tense | I had<br>you had<br>he/she/it had<br>we/you/they had | I was<br>you were<br>he/she/it was<br>we/you/they were | I did<br>you did<br>he/she/it did<br>we/you/they did |

## Special Uses of the Simple Present Tense

Besides expressing actions that are occurring at the time of the writing, the simple present tense has several special uses.

| | |
| --- | --- |
| HABITUAL OR RECURRING ACTION | She works at the store every day. |
| GENERAL TRUTH | The sun rises in the east. |
| DISCUSSION OF LITERATURE | Gatsby stands on the dock and gazes in Daisy's direction. |
| THE FUTURE | He leaves for Rome on the 7:30 plane. |

## Emphasis, Negatives, and Questions

The simple present and the simple past tenses of the verb *do* are used with main verbs to provide emphasis, to form negative constructions with the adverb *not,* and to ask questions.

| | |
| --- | --- |
| SIMPLE PRESENT | Malcolm does want to work on Saturday. |
| SIMPLE PRESENT | He does not want to stay home alone. |
| SIMPLE PRESENT | Do you want to go with him? |
| SIMPLE PAST | Judy did write the proposal herself. |
| SIMPLE PAST | She did not have the money to pay professionals. |
| SIMPLE PAST | Did she do a good job? |

The modal verbs *can, could, may, might, must, shall, should, will,* and *would* are also used to add emphasis and shades of meaning to verbs. Modals are used only as helping verbs, never alone, and do not change form to indicate tense. Added to a main verb, they are used in the following situations, among others:

| | |
| --- | --- |
| CONDITION | We can play tennis if she gets here on time. |
| PERMISSION | You may have only one e-mail address. |
| POSSIBILITY | They might call us from the airport. |
| OBLIGATION | I must visit my mother tomorrow. |

> **Tips for Writers**
>
> The usual simple present tense form is this: Malcolm wants to work on Saturday. The *emphatic form* is sometimes used to correct a mistake:
>
> Ivan says, "Malcolm does not want to work on Saturday."
>
> Maria replies, "He does want to work on Saturday." (or) "Yes, he does."

## Common Mistakes to Avoid with Verb Tense

Check your writing carefully to make sure you have avoided these common mistakes with verb tenses.

1. **Make sure the endings *-d* and *-ed* (for past tenses) and *-s* and *-es* (for third-person singular, simple present tense) are on all verbs that require them.**

   | | |
   |---|---|
   | INCORRECT | I have walk three miles since I left home. |
   | CORRECT | I have walked three miles since I left home. |

2. **Use irregular verbs correctly** (see p. 517).

   | | |
   |---|---|
   | INCORRECT | I will lay down for a nap. |
   | CORRECT | I will lie down for a nap. |

3. **Use helping verbs where they are necessary to express the correct time.**

   | | |
   |---|---|
   | INCORRECT | I go to class tomorrow. |
   | CORRECT | I will go to class tomorrow. |

4. **Avoid colloquial language or dialect in writing.** Colloquial language is casual, everyday language often used in conversation. Dialect is the language pattern of a region or an ethnic group.

   | | |
   |---|---|
   | INCORRECT | I didn't get the point of that poem. |
   | CORRECT | I didn't understand the point of that poem. |
   | INCORRECT | The train be gone. |
   | CORRECT | The train has gone. |

Other common mistakes with verbs are failing to make the verb agree with the subject (see p. 563) and using inconsistent or shifting tenses (see p. 578).

## EXERCISE 12    Correcting Verb Form and Tense Errors

**Directions:** Correct any of the following sentences with an error in verb form or verb tense. If a sentence contains no errors, write "C" for correct beside it.

EXAMPLE    You is *are* next in line.

_____ 1. Mercedes called and ask Jen if she wanted a ride to the basketball game.

_____ 2. Eric went to a party last week and meets a girl he knew in high school.

_____ 3. I cook spaghetti every Wednesday, and my family always enjoys it.

_____ 4. A package come in yesterday's mail for my office mate.

_____ 5. Louisa wears a beautiful red dress to her sister's wedding last week.

_____  6. Marni answered a letter she receive from her former employer.

_____  7. Rob waited until he was introduced, and then he run on stage.

_____  8. The audience laughed loudly at the comedian's jokes and applauds spontaneously at the funniest ones.

_____  9. The group had ordered buffalo-style chicken wings, and it was not disappointed when the meal arrived.

_____  10. Julie spends the afternoon answering correspondence when sales were slow.

# C.4 Active and Passive Voices

When a verb is in the active voice, the subject performs the action of the verb. The direct object receives the action (see p. 534). The active voice expresses action in a lively, vivid, energetic way.

> Subject Active-voice
> (Actor)     Verb        Direct object
> Carlos dropped his calculator.
>
>           Subject    Active-voice
>           (Actor)       Verb        Direct object
> The supermarket gave samples of prepared food.

When a verb is in the passive voice, the subject is the receiver of the action of the verb. The passive voice is formed by using an appropriate form of the verb *be* plus the past participle of the main verb. The actor is often expressed in a prepositional phrase introduced by the preposition *by*. Thus the passive voice tends to be wordier and to express actions in a more indirect way than the active voice.

> Subject     Passive-voice     Object of preposition
> (Receiver)      verb              (Actor)
> The calculator was dropped by Carlos.
>
> Subject                    Passive-voice     Object of preposition
> (Receiver)                     verb              (Actor)
> Samples of prepared food were given by the supermarket.

Sometimes the actor is not expressed in a passive-voice sentence.

> ACTIVE     I did not remove the Halloween decorations until Christmas.
>
> PASSIVE    The Halloween decorations were not removed until Christmas.

As a general rule, you should use the active voice because it is more effective, simpler, and more direct than the passive. In two situations, however, the passive may be preferable: (1) if you do not know who performs the action and (2) if the object of the action is more important than the actor.

PASSIVE     The handle of the dagger <u>had been wiped</u> clean of fingerprints. [It is not known who wiped the dagger.]

PASSIVE     The poem "Richard Corey" by Edwin Arlington Robinson <u>was discussed</u> in class. [The poem is more important than who discussed the poem.]

| EXERCISE 13 | **Changing Verbs from Passive to Active Voice** |

**Directions:** Revise each of the following sentences by changing the verb from passive voice to active voice.

EXAMPLE     The patient was operated on by an experienced surgeon.

REVISED     An experienced surgeon operated on the patient.

1. The coin collection was inherited by Roderick from his grandfather.

_____

_____

2. A large stack of orders was delivered by the staff.

_____

_____

3. The presidential advisers were relied on by the president.

_____

_____

4. Ice cream was served to the children at the birthday party by one of the adults.

_____

_____

5. Tools were packed in a box by Terry.

_____

_____

6. Scuba-diving equipment was handed to the students by the licensed instructor.

_____

_____

7. Alaska was visited by my parents last fall.

_____

_____

8. A large order was placed by Wonderments Gift Shop.

_____

_____

C. Avoiding Sentence Errors

9. The shipment was delivered by United Parcel Service.

_____

_____

10. Trash was collected and disposed of by the picnickers before they left for home.

_____

_____

# C.5 Subjunctive Mood

> **Tip for Writers**
>
> In *subjunctive* (contrary-to-fact) present-tense statements, use a past tense verb in the *if* clause and a modal auxiliary plus an infinitive verb in the main clause:
>
> If I <u>lived</u> in Minnesota, I <u>would need</u> a good pair of winter boots.

The **mood** of a verb conveys the writer's attitude toward the expressed thought. There are three moods in English. The **indicative mood** is used to make ordinary statements of fact and to ask questions. The **imperative mood** is used to give commands or make suggestions. The **subjunctive mood** is used to express wishes, requirements, recommendations, and statements contrary to fact (see p. 519).

| INDICATIVE | Laurel <u>lies</u> in the sun every afternoon. |
| IMPERATIVE | <u>Lie</u> down and rest! |
| SUBJUNCTIVE | It is urgent that she <u>lie</u> down and rest. |

The subjunctive mood requires some special attention because it uses verb tenses in unusual ways. Verbs in the subjunctive mood can be in the present, past, or perfect tense.

| PRESENT | His mother recommended that he <u>apply</u> for the job. <br> If truth <u>be</u> told, Jacob is luckier than he knows. |
| PAST | If she <u>walked</u> faster, she could get there on time. <br> She ran as if she <u>were</u> five years old again. |
| PERFECT | If I <u>had known</u> his name, I would have said hello. |

Here are several rules for using the subjunctive correctly:

1. **For requirements and recommendations, use the present subjunctive (the infinitive) for all verbs, including *be*.**

   Mr. Kenefick requires that his students <u>be</u> drilled in safety procedures.

   The dentist recommended that she <u>brush</u> her teeth three times a day.

2. **For present conditions contrary to fact and for present wishes, use the past subjunctive (the simple past tense) for all verbs; use *were* for the verb *be* for all subjects.**

   I wish that the workday <u>began</u> later.

   If Andrew <u>were</u> not so stubborn, he would admit that Adele is right.

3. **For past conditions contrary to fact and for past wishes, use the perfect subjunctive (*had* plus the past participle) for all verbs, including *be*.**

> **Tip for Writers**
>
> Note that in *contrary-to-fact statements*, the verb in the main clause usually begins with a modal auxiliary or *wish*.

> If Roman <u>had been</u> at home, he would have answered the phone when you called.
>
> When Peter told me what an exciting internship he had abroad last summer, I wished I <u>had gone</u> with him.

# C.6 Subject-Verb Agreement

A subject and its verb must agree (be consistent) in person (first, second, third) and in number (singular, plural). (See p. 512 on the person of pronouns and p. 570 on verb forms in all persons and numbers.) The most common problems with subject-verb agreement occur with third-person present-tense verbs, which are formed for most verbs by adding *-s* or *-es* to the infinitive. (See pp. 517–518 for the present- and past-tense forms for certain irregular verbs.)

## Agreement Rules

1. **Singular subjects.** For a singular subject (one person, place, thing, or idea), use a singular form of the verb: *I dance, he dances, Sally dances, the dog dances; I am, you are, Sally is.*

2. **Plural subjects.** For a plural subject (two or more persons, places, things, or ideas), use the plural form of the verb: *we dance, they dance, the girls dance, the dogs dance; we are, they are, children are.*

## Common Mistakes to Avoid

1. **Third-person singular.** Do not omit the *-s* or *-es* for a present-tense verb used with the pronoun *he, she,* or *it* or any singular noun.

   | INCORRECT | <u>She</u> <u>watch</u> the training video. |
   |---|---|
   | CORRECT | <u>She</u> <u>watches</u> the training video. |

   | INCORRECT | <u>Professor Simmons</u> <u>pace</u> while she lectures. |
   |---|---|
   | CORRECT | <u>Professor Simmons</u> <u>paces</u> while she lectures. |

2. **Compound subjects.** Two or more subjects joined by the coordinating conjunction *and* require a plural verb, even if one or both of the subjects are singular.

   | INCORRECT | <u>Anita</u> and <u>Mark</u> <u>plays</u> cards. |
   |---|---|
   | CORRECT | <u>Anita</u> and <u>Mark</u> <u>play</u> cards. |

   When both of the subjects refer to the same person or thing, however, use a singular verb.

   > The <u>president</u> and <u>chairman of the board</u> <u>is</u> in favor of more aggressive marketing.

   When a compound subject is joined by the conjunction *or* or *nor* or the correlative conjunctions *either/or, neither/nor, both/and, not/but,* or *not only/ but also,* the verb should agree in number with the subject nearer to it.

Neither the books nor the article was helpful to my research.

Sarah or the boys are coming tomorrow.

3. **Verbs before subjects.** When a verb comes before a subject, as in sentences beginning with *here* or *there,* it is easy to make an agreement error. Because *here* and *there* are adverbs, they are never subjects of a sentence and do not determine the correct form of the verb. Look for the subject *after* the verb, and, depending on its number, choose a singular or plural verb.

Singular verb   Singular subject

There is a bone in my soup.

Plural verb   Plural subject

There are two bones in my soup.

4. **Words between subject and verb.** Words, phrases, and clauses coming between the subject and verb do not change the fact that the verb must agree with the subject. To check that the verb is correct, mentally erase everything between the subject and its verb to see if the verb agrees in number with its subject.

Singular subject   Singular verb

The new list of degree requirements comes out in the spring.

Plural subject   Plural verb

Expenses surrounding the sale of the house were unexpectedly low.

Phrases beginning with prepositions such as *along with, as well as,* and *in addition to* are not part of the subject and should not be considered in determining if the verb is singular or plural.

Singular subject

The lamp, together with some plates, glasses, and china teacups, was broken during the move.

Singular verb

5. **Indefinite pronouns as subjects.** Some indefinite pronouns (such as *everyone, neither, anybody, nobody, one, something,* and *each*) take a singular verb (see p. 515).

Everyone appreciates the hospital's volunteers.

Of the two applicants, neither seems well qualified.

The indefinite pronouns *both, many, several,* and *few* always take a plural verb. Some indefinite pronouns, such as *all, any, most, none,* and *some,* may take either a singular or plural verb. Treat the indefinite pronoun as singular if it refers to something that cannot be counted and as plural if it refers to more than one of something that can be counted.

Some of the ice is still on the road.

Some of the ice cubes are still in the tray.

All of the spaghetti tastes overcooked.

All of the spaghetti dishes taste too spicy.

6. **Collective nouns**. A collective noun refers to a group of people or things (*audience, class, flock, jury, team, family*). When the noun refers to the group as one unit, use a singular verb.

> The <u>herd</u> <u>stampedes</u> toward us.

When the noun refers to the group members as separate individuals, use a plural verb.

> The <u>herd</u> <u>scatter</u> in all directions.

7. **Nouns with plural forms but singular meaning**. Some words appear plural (that is, they end in *-s* or *-es*) but have a singular meaning. *Measles, hysterics, news,* and *mathematics* are examples. Use a singular verb with them.

> <u>Mathematics</u> <u>is</u> a required course.

*Note:* Other nouns look plural and have singular meanings, but take a plural verb: *braces, glasses, trousers, slacks, jeans, jodhpurs,* and *pajamas*. Even though they refer to a single thing (to one pair of jeans, for example), these words take a plural verb.

> His <u>pajamas</u> <u>were covered</u> with pictures of tumbling dice.

8. **Relative pronouns in adjective clauses**. The relative pronouns *who, which,* and *that* sometimes function as the subject of an adjective clause. When the relative pronoun refers to a singular noun, use a singular verb. When the pronoun refers to a plural noun, use a plural verb.

> Anita is a person <u>who</u> never <u>forgets</u> faces. [*Who* refers to *person*, which is singular.]

> The <u>students</u> <u>who</u> lost their keys <u>are</u> here. [*Who* refers to *students*, which is plural.]

## EXERCISE 14 | Identifying the Correct Verbs

**Directions:** Circle the verb that correctly completes each sentence.

> EXAMPLE   Everybody (like, (likes)) doughnuts for breakfast.

1. Physics (is, are) a required course for an engineering degree.

2. Most of my courses last semester (was, were) in the morning.

3. The orchestra members who (is, are) carrying their instruments will be able to board the plane first.

4. Suzanne (sing, sings) a touching version of "America the Beautiful."

5. Here (is, are) the performers who juggle plates.

6. Kin Lee and his parents (travel, travels) to Ohio tomorrow.

7. A box of old and valuable stamps (is, are) in the safety deposit box at the bank.

8. The family (sit, sits) on different chairs arranged throughout the attorney's conference room.

9. Elena and Erin (arrive, arrives) at the train station at eleven o'clock.

10. Directions for operating the machine (is, are) posted on the wall.

# C.7 Pronoun-Antecedent Agreement

A pronoun must agree with its **antecedent**, the word it refers to or replaces, in person (first, second, or third), in number (singular or plural), and in gender (masculine, feminine, or neuter).

> Ronald attended the meeting, but I did not have a chance to talk with him. [The third-person, masculine, singular pronoun *him* agrees with its antecedent, *Ronald*.]
>
> We had planned to call our sister, but her line was busy. [*Our* agrees with its antecedent, *We*; *her* agrees with its antecedent, *sister*.]

## Agreement Rules

1.  **Use a singular pronoun to refer to or replace a singular noun.** (A singular noun names one person, place, or thing.)

    > Juanita filed her report promptly.

2.  **Use a plural pronoun to refer to or replace a plural noun.** (A plural noun names two or more persons, places, or things.)

    > The shirts are hung on their hangers.

3.  **Use singular pronouns to refer to indefinite pronouns that are singular in meaning.**

    | | | | | |
    |---|---|---|---|---|
    | another | each | everything | no one | somebody |
    | anybody | either | neither | nothing | someone |
    | anyone | everybody | nobody | one | something |
    | anything | everyone | none | other | |

    **Singular** **Singular**
    **antecedent** **pronoun**

    > Someone left her handbag under this table.

    **Singular antecedent**         **Singular compound pronoun**

    > Everyone in the office must do his or her own photocopying.

    *Note:* To avoid the awkwardness of *his or her,* consider rephrasing your sentence with a plural antecedent and plural pronoun.

    **Plural antecedent**   **Plural pronoun**

    > Office workers must do their own photocopying.

4.  **Use a plural pronoun to refer to indefinite pronouns that are plural in meaning.**

    | | | | |
    |---|---|---|---|
    | both | few | many | several |

    > Both of the journalists said that they could see no violations of the cease-fire.

5.  **The indefinite pronouns *all, any, most, none,* and *some* can be singular or plural, depending on how they are used.** If the indefinite pronoun

refs to something that cannot be counted, use a singular pronoun to refer to it. If the indefinite pronoun refers to something that can be counted, use a plural pronoun to refer to it.

> Most of the voters feel <u>they</u> can make a difference.
>
> Most of the air on airplanes is recycled repeatedly, so <u>it</u> becomes stale.

6. **Use a plural pronoun to refer to a compound antecedent joined by *and*, unless both parts of the compound refer to the same person, place, or thing.**

> Plural antecedent   Plural pronoun
> <u>My girlfriend and I</u> planned <u>our</u> wedding.
>
> Singular antecedent   Singular pronoun
> <u>My neighbor and best friend</u> started <u>her</u> book bindery at the local warehouse.

7. **When antecedents are joined by *or, nor, either/or, neither/nor, both/and, not/but,* or *not only/but also,* the pronoun agrees in number with the nearer antecedent.**

> Neither his brothers nor <u>Sam</u> has made <u>his</u> plane reservations.
>
> Neither Sam nor his <u>brothers</u> have made <u>their</u> plane reservations.

*Note:* Two or more singular antecedents joined by *or* or *nor* require a singular pronoun.

> Neither Larry nor <u>Richard</u> signed <u>his</u> name legibly.
>
> <u>Eva</u> or <u>Anita</u> will bring <u>her</u> saxophone.

8. **Collective nouns refer to a specific group *(army, class, family)*.** When the group acts as a unit, use a singular pronoun to refer to the noun. When each member of the group acts individually, use a plural pronoun to refer to the noun.

> The <u>band</u> marched <u>its</u> most intricate formation.
>
> The <u>band</u> found <u>their</u> seats in the bleachers but could not see the game because the sun was in <u>their</u> eyes.

**EXERCISE 15**

## Correcting Pronoun-Antecedent Agreement Errors

**Directions:** Revise the sentences below that contain agreement errors. If a sentence contains no errors, write "C" for correct beside it.

> EXAMPLE   Somebody dropped ~~their~~ <sup>his or her</sup> ring down the drain.

_____ 1. Many of the residents of the neighborhood have had their homes tested for radon.

_____ 2. Each college instructor establishes their own grading policies.

_____ 3. The apples fell from its tree.

_____ 4. Anyone may submit their painting to the contest.

_____ 5. All the engines manufactured at the plant have their vehicle-identification numbers stamped on.

_____ 6. No one requested that the clerk gift-wrap their package.

_____ 7. Either Professor Judith Marcos or her assistant, Maria, graded the exams, writing their comments in the margins.

_____ 8. James or his parents sails the boat every weekend.

_____ 9. Few classes were canceled because of the snowstorm; it met as regularly scheduled.

_____ 10. Not only Ricky but also the Carters will take his children to Disneyland this summer.

# C.8 Pronoun Reference

A pronoun refers to or replaces a noun or pronoun previously mentioned, called the pronoun's **antecedent**. As you write, you must always make sure that a reader knows to which noun or pronoun a pronoun refers. The antecedent of each pronoun must be clear. Sometimes you may need to reword a sentence to solve a problem of unclear antecedent.

| | |
|---|---|
| INCORRECT | Lois walked with Pam because she did not know the route. [Who did not know the route? The antecedent of _she_ is unclear.] |
| CORRECT | Lois did not know the route, so she walked with Pam. |

## How to Use Pronouns Correctly

1. **A pronoun may refer to two or more nouns in a compound antecedent.**

   Mark and Dennis combined their efforts to fix the leaky faucet.

2. **Avoid using a pronoun that could refer to more than one possible antecedent.**

   | | |
   |---|---|
   | INCORRECT | Rick told Garry that he was right. |
   | CORRECT | Rick told Garry, "You are right." |

3. **Avoid using vague pronouns like _they_ and _it_ that often have no clear antecedent.**

   | | |
   |---|---|
   | INCORRECT | It says in the paper that Kmart is expanding the Williamsville store. |
   | CORRECT | The article in the paper says that Kmart is expanding the Williamsville store. |
   | INCORRECT | They told me that we were required to wear surgeons' masks to view the newborns. |
   | CORRECT | The obstetrics nurses told me that we were required to wear surgeons' masks to view the newborns. |

| INCORRECT | On the bulletin boards, <u>it</u> says that there is a fire drill today. |
|---|---|
| CORRECT | The <u>notice</u> on the bulletin board says that there is a fire drill today. |

4. **Avoid unnecessary or repetitious pronouns.**

| INCORRECT | My sister <u>she</u> said that she lost her diamond ring. |
|---|---|
| CORRECT | My sister said that she lost her diamond ring. |

5. **Be sure to use the relative pronouns *who, whom, which,* and *that* with the appropriate antecedent.** *Who* and *whom* refer to persons or named animals. *That* and *which* refer to unnamed animals and to things.

<u>Mary Anne</u> was the team member <u>who</u> scored the most points this year.

<u>Dublin</u>, <u>who</u> is a golden retriever, barked at everyone.

My sister gave me a ring <u>that</u> has three opals.

Highway 33, <u>which</u> has ten hairpin turns, is difficult to drive.

6. **Use *one* if you are not referring specifically to the reader.** Use the second-person pronoun *you* only to refer to the reader. In academic writing, avoid using *you.*

| INCORRECT | Last year, <u>you</u> had to watch the news every night to keep up with world events. |
|---|---|
| CORRECT | Last year, <u>one</u> had to watch the news every night to keep up with world events. |

7. **Place the pronoun close to its antecedent so that the relationship is clear.**

| INCORRECT | Margaux found a <u>shell</u> on the beach <u>that</u> her sister wanted. |
|---|---|
| CORRECT | On the beach Margaux found a <u>shell</u> <u>that</u> her sister wanted. |

---

**EXERCISE 16**    ## Correcting Pronoun Reference Errors

**Directions:** Revise each of the following sentences to correct problems in pronoun reference. If a sentence contains no errors, write "C" for correct beside it.

EXAMPLE    It said that the grades would be posted on Tuesday.

REVISED     *The professor's note said that the grades would be posted on Tuesday.*

_____ 1. The puppy whom my sister brought home was quite cute.

_____ 2. Laverne and Louise they pooled their money to buy a new stereo system.

_____ 3. They said on the news that the naval base will be shut down.

_____ 4. The street that was recently widened is where I used to work.

_____ 5. Ivan sat on the couch in the living room that he had bought yesterday.

_____ 6. You should highlight in your textbooks for higher comprehension.

_____ 7. Christina handed Maggie the plate she had bought at the flea market.

_____ 8. Bridget found the cake mix in the aisle with the baking supplies that she needed for tonight's dessert.

_____ 9. The answering machine who answered the phone beeped several times.

_____ 10. It said in the letter that my payment was late.

# C.9 Pronoun Case

A pronoun changes **case** depending on its grammatical function in a sentence. Pronouns may be in the **subjective case**, the **objective case**, or the **possessive case**.

| Personal Pronouns | | | |
| --- | --- | --- | --- |
| **SINGULAR** | **SUBJECTIVE** | **OBJECTIVE** | **POSSESSIVE** |
| First person | I | me | my, mine |
| Second person | you | you | your, yours |
| Third person | he, she, it | him, her, it | his, her, hers, its |
| **PLURAL** | **SUBJECTIVE** | **OBJECTIVE** | **POSSESSIVE** |
| First person | we | us | our, ours |
| Second person | you | you | your, yours |
| Third person | they | them | their, theirs |
| **Relative or Interrogative Pronouns** | | | |
| | **SUBJECTIVE** | **OBJECTIVE** | **POSSESSIVE** |
| Singular and plural | who | whom | whose |
| | whoever | whomever | |

## Pronouns in the Subjective Case

Use the **subjective case** (also known as the **nominative case**) when the pronoun functions as the subject of a sentence or clause (see p. 512) or as a subject complement (also known as a predicate nominative; see p. 534). A predicate nominative is a noun or pronoun that follows a linking verb and identifies or renames the subject of the sentence.

**Subject**

She has won recognition as a landscape architect.

**Subject complement**

Cathie volunteers at the local hospital. The most faithful volunteer is she.

The subjective case is also used when a pronoun functions as an appositive to a subject or subject complement (see p. 583).

The only two seniors, she and her best friend, won the top awards.

## Pronouns in the Objective Case

Use the objective case when a pronoun functions as a direct object, indirect object, or object of a preposition (see pp. 534 and 535).

**Direct object**

George helped her with the assignment.

**Indirect object**

George gave her a book.

**Objects of the preposition**

George gave the book to him and her.

The objective case is also used when the pronoun functions as the subject of an infinitive phrase or an appositive to an object.

**Subject of infinitive    Infinitive phrase**

I wanted him to go straight home.

**Direct object        Appositive to object**

The district manager chose two representatives, Marnie and me.

*Note:* When a sentence has a compound subject or compound objects, you may have trouble determining the correct pronoun case. To determine how the pronoun functions, mentally recast the sentence without the noun or other pronoun in the compound construction. Determine how the pronoun functions by itself and then decide which case is correct.

**Subjective case**

They and Teresa brought the beverages. [Think: "*They* brought the beverages."
*They* is the subject of the sentence, so the subjective case is correct.]

**Objective case**

Behind you and me, the drapery rustled. [Think: "Behind *me*." *Me* is the object of the preposition *behind*, so the objective case is correct.]

## Pronouns in the Possessive Case

Possessive pronouns indicate to whom or to what something belongs. The possessive pronouns *mine, yours, his, hers, its, ours,* and *theirs* function just as nouns do.

**Subject**

Hers is the letterhead with the bright blue lettering.

**Direct object**

I liked hers the best.

The possessive pronouns *my, your, his, her, its, our,* and *their* are used as adjectives to modify nouns and gerunds (see p. 522).

Our high-school reunion surprised everyone by its size.

Your attending that reunion will depend on your travel schedule.

### *Who* and *Whom* as Interrogative Pronouns

When *who, whoever, whom,* and *whomever* introduce questions, they are interrogative pronouns. How an interrogative pronoun functions in a clause determines its case. Use *who* or *whoever* (the subjective case) when the interrogative pronoun functions as a subject or subject complement (see p. 534). Use *whom* or *whomever* (the objective case) when the interrogative pronoun functions as a direct object or an object of a preposition.

**Subject**

SUBJECTIVE CASE     Who is there?

**Object of preposition**

OBJECTIVE CASE     To whom did you give the letter?

### *Who* and *Whom* as Relative Pronouns

When *who, whoever, whom,* and *whomever* introduce subordinate clauses, they are relative pronouns. How a relative pronoun functions in a clause determines its case. Use *who* or *whoever* (subjective case) when a relative pronoun functions as the subject of the subordinate clause. Use *whom* or *whomever* (objective case) when a relative pronoun functions as an object in the subordinate clause.

SUBJECTIVE CASE     The lecturer, who is a journalist from New York, speaks with great insight and wit. [*Who* is the subject of the subordinate clause.]

OBJECTIVE CASE     The journalist, whom I know from college days, came to give a lecture. [*Whom* is the direct object of the verb *know* in the subordinate clause.]

# C.10 Correct Adjective and Adverb Use

Adjectives and adverbs modify, describe, explain, qualify, or restrict the words they modify (see pp. 521 and 524). **Adjectives** modify nouns and pronouns. **Adverbs** modify verbs, adjectives, and other adverbs; adverbs can also modify phrases, clauses, or whole sentences.

| ADJECTIVES | <u>red</u> car; the <u>quiet</u> one |
|---|---|
| ADVERBS | <u>quickly</u> finish; <u>only</u> four reasons; <u>very</u> angrily |

## Comparison of Adjectives and Adverbs

**Positive** adjectives and adverbs modify but do not involve any comparison: *green, bright, lively.*

**Comparative** adjectives and adverbs compare two persons, things, actions, or ideas.

| COMPARATIVE ADJECTIVE | Michel is <u>taller</u> than Latoya. |
|---|---|
| COMPARATIVE ADVERB | Antonio reacted <u>more calmly</u> than Robert. |

Here is how to form comparative adjectives and adverbs. (Consult your dictionary if you are unsure of the form of a particular word.)

1. **If the adjective or adverb has one syllable, add *-er.* For certain two-syllable words, also add *-er.***

   cold ⟶ colder      slow ⟶ slower      narrow ⟶ narrower

2. **For most words of two or more syllables, place the word *more* in front of the word.**

   reasonable ⟶ more reasonable      interestingly ⟶ more interestingly

3. **For two-syllable adjectives ending in *-y,* change the *-y* to *-i* and add *-er.***

   drowsy ⟶ drowsier      lazy ⟶ lazier

**Superlative** adjectives and adverbs compare more than two persons, things, actions, or ideas.

| SUPERLATIVE ADJECTIVE | Michael is the <u>tallest</u> member of the team. |
|---|---|
| SUPERLATIVE ADVERB | She studied <u>most diligently</u> for the test. |

Here is how to form superlative adjectives and adverbs:

1. **Add *-est* to one-syllable adjectives and adverbs and to certain two-syllable words.**

   cold ⟶ coldest      fast ⟶ fastest      narrow ⟶ narrowest

2. **For most words of two or more syllables, place the word *most* in front of the word.**

   reasonable ⟶ most reasonable      interestingly ⟶ most interestingly

3. **For two-syllable adjectives ending in *-y,* change the *-y* to *-i* and add *-est.***

   drowsy ⟶ drowsiest      lazy ⟶ laziest

## Irregular Adjectives and Adverbs

Some adjectives and adverbs form their comparative and superlative forms in irregular ways.

---

### Tip for Writers

When writing *superlative statements,* always use *the.* Use *much* only in questions and negatives. In affirmative statements, use *a lot of* or *some.*

Do you have <u>much</u> time for painting now that you're going to school?

Yes, I still have <u>a lot of</u> time for painting. (or) No, I <u>don't have much time.</u>

---

## Tip for Writers

Use *littler* and *littlest* for size; use *less* and *least* for amount (quantity). Use *little/less/least* before noncount nouns; use *few/fewer/fewest* before plural nouns:

The <u>littlest</u> of Lana's eight children is only two years old; Lana has <u>less</u> time to spend with her friends now that she has a big family. She has *fewer* friends now.

| POSITIVE | COMPARATIVE | SUPERLATIVE |
|---|---|---|
| **Adjectives** | | |
| good | better | best |
| bad | worse | worst |
| little | littler, less | littlest, least |
| **Adverbs** | | |
| well | better | best |
| badly | worse | worst |
| **Adjectives and Adverbs** | | |
| many | more | most |
| some | more | most |
| much | more | most |

## Common Mistakes to Avoid

1.  **Do not use adjectives to modify verbs, other adjectives, or adverbs.**

    | | |
    |---|---|
    | INCORRECT | Peter and Mary take each other <u>serious</u>. |
    | CORRECT | Peter and Mary take each other <u>seriously</u>. [Modifies the verb *take*] |

2.  **Do not use the adjectives *good* and *bad* when you should use the adverbs *well* and *badly*.**

    | | |
    |---|---|
    | INCORRECT | Juan did <u>good</u> on the exam. |
    | CORRECT | Juan did <u>well</u> on the exam. [Modifies the verb *did*] |

3.  **Do not use the adjectives *real* and *sure* when you should use the adverbs *really* and *surely*.**

    | | |
    |---|---|
    | INCORRECT | Jan scored <u>real</u> well on the exam. |
    | CORRECT | Jan scored <u>really</u> well on the exam. [Modifies the adverb *well*] |
    | INCORRECT | I <u>sure</u> was surprised to win the lottery. |
    | CORRECT | I <u>surely</u> was surprised to win the lottery. [Modifies the verb *was surprised*] |

4.  **Do not use *more* or *most* with the -*er* or -*est* form of an adjective or adverb.** Use one form or the other, according to the rules above.

    | | |
    |---|---|
    | INCORRECT | That was the <u>most</u> <u>tastiest</u> dinner I've ever eaten. |
    | CORRECT | That was the <u>tastiest</u> dinner I've ever eaten. |

5.  **Avoid double negatives—that is, two negatives in the same clause.**

    | | |
    |---|---|
    | INCORRECT | He did <u>not</u> want <u>nothing</u> in the refrigerator. |
    | CORRECT | He did <u>not</u> want <u>anything</u> in the refrigerator. |

6.  **When using the comparative and superlative forms of adverbs, do not create an incomplete comparison.**

> | INCORRECT | The heater works <u>more efficiently</u>. [More efficiently than what?] |
> |---|---|
> | CORRECT | The heater works <u>more efficiently than it did before we had it repaired.</u> |

7. **Do not use the comparative form for adjectives and adverbs that have no degree.** It is incorrect to write, for example, *more square, most perfect, more equally,* or *most straight.* Do not use a comparative or superlative form for any of the following adjectives and adverbs:

| ADJECTIVES | | | | |
|---|---|---|---|---|
| complete | equal | infinite | pregnant | unique |
| dead | eternal | invisible | square | universal |
| empty | favorite | matchless | supreme | vertical |
| endless | impossible | parallel | unanimous | whole |
| **ADVERBS** | | | | |
| endlessly | infinitely | uniquely | | |
| equally | invisibly | universally | | |
| eternally | perpendicularly | | | |
| impossibly | straight | | | |

## EXERCISE 17    Using Adjectives and Adverbs Correctly

**Directions:** Revise each of the following sentences so that all adjectives and adverbs are used correctly. If the sentence is correct, write "C" for correct beside it.

EXAMPLE    I answered the question polite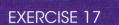.

_____ 1. Michael's apartment was more expensive than Arturio's.

_____ 2. When I heard the man and woman sing the duet, I decided that the woman sang best.

_____ 3. Flowers grow poorly in this soil.

_____ 4. The roller coaster was excitinger than the merry-go-round.

_____ 5. *The Scarlet Letter* is more good than *War and Peace.*

_____ 6. Susan sure gave a rousing speech.

_____ 7. Last week's storm seemed worst than a tornado.

_____ 8. Some women thought that the Equal Rights Amendment would guarantee that women be treated more equally.

_____ 9. Taking the interstate is the most fast route to the outlet mall.

_____ 10. Professor Reed had the better lecture style of all my instructors.

# D Writing Effective Sentences

## D.1 Misplaced and Dangling Modifiers

A **modifier** is a word, phrase, or clause that describes, qualifies, or limits the meaning of another word.

| | |
|---|---|
| WORD | She wore a red dress. [The adjective *red* describes the dress.] |
| PHRASE | I like the taste of vanilla ice cream. [The phrase "of vanilla ice cream" qualifies the word *taste*.] |
| CLAUSE | The boy who fell from the horse was hospitalized. [The clause "who fell from the horse" explains which boy was hospitalized.] |

Modifiers that are not correctly placed can make a sentence confusing.

### Misplaced Modifiers

**Misplaced modifiers** do not describe or explain the words the writer intended them to. A misplaced modifier often appears to modify the wrong word or can leave the reader confused as to which word it does modify.

| | |
|---|---|
| MISPLACED | Max bought a chair at the used-furniture shop that was large and dark. [Was the chair or the furniture shop large and dark?] |
| MISPLACED | The instructor announced that the term paper was due on April 25 at the beginning of class. [Are the papers due at the beginning of class on the 25th, or did the instructor make the announcement at the beginning of class?] |

You can easily avoid misplaced modifiers if you make sure that modifiers immediately precede or follow the words they modify.

| | |
|---|---|
| CORRECT | Max bought a chair that was large and dark at the used-furniture shop. |

| CORRECT | Max bought a <u>large, dark</u> chair at the used-furniture shop. |
|---|---|
| CORRECT | <u>At the beginning of class</u>, the instructor announced that the term paper was due on April 25. |

## Dangling Modifiers

**Dangling modifiers** do not clearly describe or explain any part of the sentence. Dangling modifiers create confusion and sometimes unintentional humor. To avoid dangling modifiers, make sure that each modifier has a clear antecedent.

| DANGLING | <u>Rounding the curve</u>, a fire <u>hydrant</u> was hit by the speeding car. [The modifier suggests that the hydrant rounded the curve.] |
|---|---|
| CORRECT | <u>Rounding the curve</u>, the speeding <u>car</u> hit the fire hydrant. [Modifies *car*] |
| DANGLING | <u>Uncertain of what courses to take next semester</u>, the academic <u>advisor</u> listed five options. [The modifier suggests that the advisor was uncertain of what courses to take.] |
| CORRECT | <u>Uncertain of what courses to take next semester</u>, the <u>student</u> spoke to an academic advisor, who listed five options. |
| DANGLING | Flood <u>damage</u> was visible <u>crossing the river</u>. [The modifier makes it sound as though flood damage was crossing the river.] |
| CORRECT | Flood damage was visible <u>as we crossed the river</u>. |

There are two common ways to revise dangling modifiers:

1. **Add a word or words that the modifier clearly describes.** Place the new material just after the modifier, and rearrange other parts of the sentence as necessary.

| DANGLING | <u>While watching television</u>, the <u>cake</u> burned. |
|---|---|
| CORRECT | <u>While watching television</u>, <u>Sarah</u> burned the cake. |

2. **Change the dangling modifier to a subordinate clause.** You may need to change the verb form in the modifier.

| DANGLING | <u>While watching television</u>, the <u>cake</u> burned. |
|---|---|
| CORRECT | <u>While Sarah was watching television</u>, the cake burned. |

**EXERCISE 18**

## Correcting Misplaced and Dangling Modifiers

**Directions:** Revise each of the following sentences to correct misplaced or dangling modifiers.

| EXAMPLE | Deciding which flavor of ice cream to order, another customer cut in front of Roger. |
|---|---|
| REVISED | <u>While Roger was deciding which flavor of ice cream to order, another customer cut in front of him.</u> |

1. Tricia saw an animal at the zoo that had black fur and long claws.

   _____

2. Before answering the door, the phone rang.

   _____

3. I could see large snowflakes falling from the bedroom window.

   _____

4. Honking, Felicia walked in front of the car.

   _____

5. After leaving the classroom, the door automatically locked.

   _____

6. Applauding and cheering, the band returned for an encore.

   _____

7. The waiter brought a birthday cake to our table that had 24 candles.

   _____

8. Books lined the library shelves about every imaginable subject.

   _____

9. While sobbing, the sad movie ended and the lights came on.

   _____

10. Turning the page, the book's binding cracked.

   _____

# **D.2** Shifts in Person, Number, and Verb Tense

The parts of a sentence should be consistent. Shifts within a sentence in person, number, or verb tense will make the sentence confusing and difficult to read.

## Shifts in Person

**Person** is the grammatical term used to distinguish the speaker or writer (**first person**: *I, we*), the person spoken to (**second person**: *you*), and the person or thing spoken about (**third person**: *he, she, it, they,* and any noun, such as *Joan* or *children*). A sentence or a paragraph should use the same person throughout.

| | |
|---|---|
| SHIFT | If a <u>student</u> studies effectively, <u>you</u> will get good grades. |
| CORRECT | If <u>you</u> study effectively, <u>you</u> will get good grades. |

## Shifts in Number

**Number** distinguishes between singular and plural. A pronoun must agree in number with its antecedent, the word to which it refers (see p. 566). Related nouns within a sentence also must agree in number. (Sometimes you need to change the form of the verb when you correct the inconsistent nouns or pronouns.)

| | |
|---|---|
| SHIFT | When a home owner does not shovel the snow in front of their house, they risk getting fined. |
| CORRECT | When home owners do not shovel the snow in front of their houses, they risk getting fined. |

## Shifts in Verb Tense

The same verb tense should be used throughout a sentence unless meaning requires a shift.

| | |
|---|---|
| REQUIRED SHIFT | *Present* *Future* — After my cousin arrives, we will go to the movies. |
| INCORRECT | *Past* *Present* — After Marguerite bought the health food store, she seems more confident. |
| CORRECT | *Past* *Past* — After Marguerite bought the health food store, she seemed more confident. |
| INCORRECT | *Past* *Present* — Emma heard the clock strike twelve, and then she goes for a midday walk. |
| CORRECT | *Past* *Past* — Emma heard the clock strike twelve, and then she went for a midday walk. |

**EXERCISE 19**

# Correcting Shifts in Person, Number, and Tense

**Directions:** Revise each of the following sentences to correct errors in shift of person, number, or tense. If a sentence contains no errors, write "C" for correct beside it.

EXAMPLE    Boats along the river were tied to their dock. ˢ

_____ 1. When people receive a gift, you should be gracious and polite.

_____ 2. When we arrived at the inn, the lights are on and a fire is burning in the fireplace.

_____ 3. Before Trey drove to the cabin, he packs a picnic lunch.

_____ 4. The artist paints portraits and weaves baskets.

_____ 5. The lobsterman goes out on his boat each day and will check his lobster traps.

_____    6. All the cars Honest Bob sells have new transmissions.

_____    7. Rosa ran the 100-meter race and throws the discus at the track meet.

_____    8. Public schools in Florida have air-conditioning systems.

_____    9. Office workers sat on the benches downtown and are eating their lunches outside.

_____   10. Before a scuba diver goes underwater, you must check and recheck your breathing equipment.

# D.3 Coordination

**Tip for Writers**

Note the inverted (question) word order used with *nor*: She doesn't eat fish, nor does she eat chicken. (This means she doesn't eat either one.) The verb after *nor* is affirmative because *nor* is negative.

**Coordination** is a way to give related ideas equal emphasis within a single sentence. your readers will better understand the flow of your thoughts if you connect coordinate ideas.

## How to Combine Ideas of Equal Importance

There are three ways to combine ideas of equal importance when those ideas are expressed in independent clauses (see p. 542).

1. **Join the two independent clauses with a comma and a coordinating conjunction (*and, but, nor, or, for, so, yet*).**

   Independent clause    Independent clause
   I passed the ball, but Sam failed to catch it.

   You should choose a coordinating conjunction that properly expresses the relationship between the ideas in the two clauses.

**Tip for Writers**

The conjunction *for* is a more formal way to say *because*. Both are followed by a reason. Note the differences in punctuation:

Because I'm tired, I'm going home. (comma)

I'm going home because I'm tired. (no comma)

I'm going home, for I'm tired. (comma)

| COORDINATING CONJUNCTION | MEANING | EXAMPLE |
|---|---|---|
| and | addition; one idea added to another | I went shopping, and I spent too much money. |
| but, yet | contrast | I wanted to grill fish, but Peter was a vegetarian. |
| or | alternatives or choices | Tonight I might go to the movies, or I might work out. |
| nor | not either | Julie was not in class, nor was she in the snack bar. |
| for | cause and effect | We went walking, for it was a beautiful evening. |
| so | result | I was early for the appointment, so I decided to doze for a few minutes. |

D. Writing Effective Sentences

2. **Join the two independent clauses with a semicolon.**

> We decided to see the new Spike Lee film; it was playing at three local theaters.

Use this method when the relationship between the two ideas is clear and requires no explanation. Usually, the two clauses must be very closely related.

*Note:* If you join two independent clauses with only a comma and fail to use a coordinating conjunction or semicolon, you will produce a comma splice. If you join two independent clauses without using a punctuation mark and a coordinating conjunction, or a semicolon, you will produce a run-on sentence (see p. 552).

3. **Join the two independent clauses with a semicolon and a conjunctive adverb followed by a comma.** A conjunctive adverb can also be used at the beginning of a sentence to link the sentence with an earlier one.

| CONJUNCTIVE ADVERB | MEANING | EXAMPLE |
|---|---|---|
| therefore, consequently, thus, hence | cause and effect | I am planning to become a nurse; consequently, I'm taking a lot of science courses. |
| however, nevertheless, nonetheless, conversely | differences or contrast | We had planned to go bowling; however, we went to hear music instead. |
| furthermore, moreover, also | addition; a continuation of the same idea | To save money I am packing my lunch; also, I am walking to work instead of taking the bus. |
| similarly, likewise | similarity | I left class as soon as I finished the exam; likewise, other students also left. |
| then, subsequently, next | sequence in time | I walked home; then I massaged my aching feet. |

**EXERCISE 20**

## Practicing Coordination

**Directions:** Complete each of the following sentences by adding a coordinating conjunction or a conjunctive adverb and the appropriate punctuation.

EXAMPLE    Teresa vacationed in Denver last year; <u>similarly</u>, Jan will go to Denver this year.

1. Our professor did not complete the lecture; _____ he did give an assignment for the next class.

2. A first-aid kit was in her backpack; _____ the hiker was able to treat her cut knee.

3. An opening act began the concert; _____ the headline band took the stage.

4. I always put a light on when I leave the house; _____ I often turn on a radio to deter burglars.

5. Sue politely asked to borrow my car, _____ she thanked me when she returned it.

6. My roommate went to the library; _____ I had the apartment to myself.

7. Steve and Todd will go to a baseball game, _____ they will go to a movie instead.

8. Serena looks like her father, _____ her hair is darker and curlier than his.

9. Maureen took a job at a bookstore; _____ she was offered a job at a museum.

10. Our neighbors bought a barbecue grill; _____ we decided to buy one.

# D.4 Subordination

**Subordination** is a way to show that one idea is not as important as another. When two clauses are related, but one is less important, the less important one can be expressed as a dependent (subordinate) clause (see p. 542). Dependent clauses do contain a subject and a verb, but they do not express a complete thought. They must always be added to a complete sentence or independent clause. If a dependent clause is used alone, it is a fragment and must be corrected (see p. 547).

## How to Combine Ideas of Unequal Importance

1. **Introduce the less important idea with a subordinating conjunction.** Choose a subordinating conjunction that properly shows the relationship of the less important idea to the more important one. Common subordinating conjunctions are *after, although, because, before, unless, when,* and *while.* (See pp. 542–543 for a complete list.)

> Dependent clause
> Subordinating conjunction          Independent clause
> After I finished revising my report, I worked on my oral presentation.

> Dependent clause
> Subordinating conjunction          Independent clause
> Unless I win the lottery, I will not be able to buy a new car.

2. **Introduce the less important idea with a relative pronoun** (such as *who, which, that,* or *what*). A relative pronoun usually introduces a clause that functions as a noun when the clause is attached to an independent clause. (See p. 514 for more on relative pronouns.)

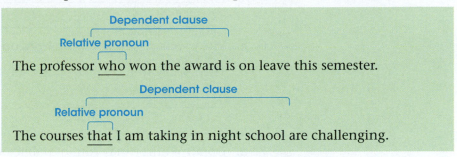

The professor who won the award is on leave this semester.

The courses that I am taking in night school are challenging.

EXERCISE 21

## Combining Sentences Using Coordinating Conjunctions and Relative Pronouns

**Directions:** Combine each of the following pairs of sentences by subordinating one idea to the other with a coordinating conjunction or a relative pronoun.

EXAMPLE  **a.** One kind of opossum can glide like a bird.

**b.** The opossum lives in Australia.

COMBINED  One kind of opossum, which lives in Australia, can glide like a bird.

1. **a.** Trina can get discount movie tickets.

**b.** Trina's husband manages a movie theater.

_____

_____

2. **a.** Rob hit the ground with his tennis racket.

**b.** Rob's tennis racket broke.

_____

_____

3. **a.** The car has satellite radio and a sunroof.

**b.** I bought the car yesterday.

_____

_____

4. **a.** Visitors to the automobile museum can learn a lot about the mechanics of cars.

**b.** Visitors enjoy looking at many old cars.

_____

_____

5. **a.** The sorority will hold its fall picnic next week.

   **b.** The picnic will be held if it does not rain.

   _____

   _____

6. **a.** Vicky went to the library to work on her term paper.

   **b.** Then Vicky went to pick up her son from the day care center.

   _____

   _____

7. **a.** Oprah Winfrey may run for public office someday.

   **b.** Oprah Winfrey is a popular public figure.

   _____

   _____

8. **a.** I will go shopping for a rain slicker tomorrow.

   **b.** I will not go if my roommate has one that I can borrow.

   _____

   _____

9. **a.** Linda and Pablo got divorced.

   **b.** They could not agree on anything.

   _____

   _____

10. **a.** The yacht sailed into the marina.

    **b.** The yacht is owned by the Kennedy family.

    _____

    _____

# D.5 Parallelism

Parallelism is a method of ensuring that words, phrases, and clauses in a series are in the same grammatical form.

## What Should Be Parallel?

1. **Words or phrases in a series.** When two or more nouns, verbs, adjectives, adverbs, or phrases appear together in a sentence connected by a coordinating conjunction (such as *and, or,* or *but*), the words or phrases should be parallel in grammatical form.

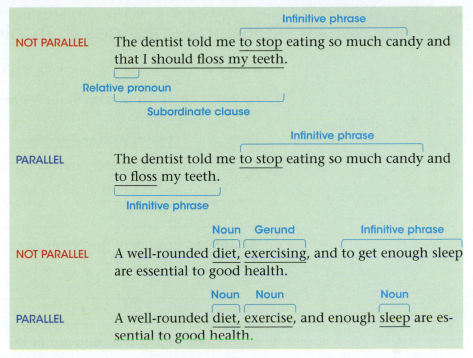

| | Infinitive phrase |
|---|---|
| NOT PARALLEL | The dentist told me to stop eating so much candy and that I should floss my teeth. |

Relative pronoun

Subordinate clause

| | Infinitive phrase |
|---|---|
| PARALLEL | The dentist told me to stop eating so much candy and to floss my teeth. |

Infinitive phrase

| | Noun   Gerund   Infinitive phrase |
|---|---|
| NOT PARALLEL | A well-rounded diet, exercising, and to get enough sleep are essential to good health. |

| | Noun   Noun   Noun |
|---|---|
| PARALLEL | A well-rounded diet, exercise, and enough sleep are essential to good health. |

2. **Independent clauses joined with a coordinating conjunction**. Independent clauses within a sentence should be parallel in tense and in construction.

| | Active voice |
|---|---|
| NOT PARALLEL | The drivers waited patiently as the work crew cleaned up the wreck, but after an hour the horns were honked loudly by all the drivers. |

Passive voice

| | Active voice |
|---|---|
| PARALLEL | The drivers waited patiently as the work crew cleaned up the wreck, but after an hour they honked their horns loudly. |

Active voice

| | Past tense   Present tense |
|---|---|
| NOT PARALLEL | Carlos wanted to go to the concert, but Julia wants to stay home and watch a video. |

| | Past tense   Past tense |
|---|---|
| PARALLEL | Carlos wanted to go to the concert, but Julia wanted to stay home and watch a video. |

3. **Items being compared**. When elements of a sentence are compared or contrasted, use the same grammatical form for each element.

| | Noun   Infinitive phrase |
|---|---|
| INCORRECT | Mark wanted a vacation rather than to save money to buy a house. |

| | Infinitive phrase   Infinitive phrase |
|---|---|
| CORRECT | Mark wanted to take a vacation rather than to save money to buy a house. |

**EXERCISE 22**    # Revising Sentences to Achieve Parallelism

**Directions:** Revise each of the following sentences to achieve parallelism.

> EXAMPLE    Rosa has decided to study nursing instead of going into accounting.
>
> REVISED    *Rosa has decided to study nursing instead of accounting.*

1. The priest baptized the baby and congratulates the new parents.

   _____

   _____

2. We ordered a platter of fried clams, a platter of corn on the cob, and fried shrimp.

   _____

   _____

3. Lucy entered the dance contest, but the dance was watched by June from the side.

   _____

   _____

4. Léon purchased the ratchet set at the garage sale and buying the drill bits there too.

   _____

   _____

5. The exterminator told Brandon the house needed to be fumigated and spraying to eliminate the termites.

   _____

   _____

6. The bus swerved and hit the dump truck, which swerves and hit the station wagon, which swerved and hit the bicycle.

   _____

   _____

7. Channel 2 covered the bank robbery, but a python that had escaped from the zoo was reported by Channel 7.

   _____

   _____

8. Sal was born while Bush was president, and Clinton was president when Rob was born.

   _____

   _____

9. The pediatrician spent the morning with sore throats, answering questions about immunizations, and treating bumps and bruises.

_____

_____

10. Belinda prefers to study in the library, but her brother Marcus studies at home.

_____

_____

# D.6 Sentence Variety

Good writers use a variety of sentence structures to avoid wordiness and monotony and to show relationships among thoughts. To achieve **sentence variety**, do not use all simple sentences or all complex or compound sentences (see pp. 544–545), and do not begin or end all sentences in the same way. Instead, vary the length, the amount of detail, and the structure of your sentences.

1. **Use sentences of varying lengths**.

2. **Avoid stringing simple sentences together with coordinating conjunctions (*and, but, or,* and so on)**. Instead, use some introductory participial phrases (see p. 539).

   | | |
   |---|---|
   | SIMPLE | There was a long line at the deli, so Chris decided to leave. |
   | VARIED | Seeing the long line at the deli, Chris decided to leave. |

3. **Begin some sentences with a prepositional phrase**. A preposition shows relationships between things (*during, over, toward, before, across, within, inside, over, above*). Many prepositions suggest chronology, direction, or location (see p. 527).

   During the concert, the fire alarm rang.

   Inside the theater, the crowd waited expectantly.

4. **Begin some sentences with a present or past participle (*cooking, broken;* see p. 549)**.

   Barking and jumping, the dogs greeted their master.

   Still laughing, two girls left the movie.

   Tired and exhausted, the mountain climbers fell asleep quickly.

5. **Begin some sentences with adverbs (see p. 524)**.

   Angrily, the student left the room.

   Patiently, the math instructor explained the assignment again.

6. **Begin some sentences with infinitive phrases (*to plus the infinitive form: to make, to go;* see p. 540)**.

   To get breakfast ready on time, I set my alarm for 7 A.M.

7. **Begin some sentences with a dependent clause introduced by a subordinating conjunction** (see p. 542).

> <u>Because</u> I ate shellfish, I developed hives.

8. **Begin some sentences with a conjunctive adverb**.

> <u>Consequently</u>, we decided to have steak for dinner.

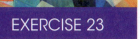

EXERCISE 23

# Practicing Sentence Construction Techniques

**Directions:** Combine each of the following pairs of simple sentences into one sentence, using the technique suggested in brackets.

EXAMPLE    **a.** The dog barked and howled.

**b.** The dog warned a stranger away.
[Use present participle (-*ing* form).]

COMBINED    <u>*Barking and howling, the dog warned a stranger away.*</u>

1.  **a.** Professor Clark has a Civil War battlefield model.

   **b.** He has it in his office.
   [Use prepositional phrase.]

   _____

   _____

2.  **a.** Toby went to Disneyland for the first time.

   **b.** He was very excited.
   [Use past participle (-*ed* form).]

   _____

   _____

3.  **a.** Teresa received a full scholarship.

   **b.** She does not need to worry about paying her tuition.
   [Use subordinating conjunction.]

   _____

   _____

4.  **a.** Lance answered the phone.

   **b.** He spoke with a gruff voice.
   [Use adverb.]

   _____

   _____

5.  **a.** The truck choked and sputtered.

   **b.** The truck pulled into the garage.
   [Use present participle (-*ing* form).]

   _____

   _____

6. **a.** Rich programmed his DVR.

   **b.** He recorded his favorite sitcom.
   [Use infinitive (*to*) phrase.]

   _____

   _____

7. **a.** The postal carrier placed a package outside my door.

   **b.** The package had a foreign stamp on it.
   [Use prepositional phrase.]

   _____

   _____

8. **a.** The instructor asked the students to take their seats.

   **b.** She was annoyed.
   [Use past participle (*-ed* form).]

   _____

   _____

9. **a.** Shyla stood outside the student union.

   **b.** She waited for her boyfriend.
   [Use present participle (*-ing* form).]

   _____

   _____

10. **a.** Bo walked to the bookstore.

    **b.** He was going to buy some new highlighters.
    [Use infinitive (*to*) phrase.]

    _____

    _____

# D.7 Redundancy and Wordiness

Redundancy results when a writer says the same thing twice. Wordiness results when a writer uses more words than necessary to convey a meaning. Both redundancy and wordiness detract from clear, effective sentences by distracting and confusing the reader.

## Eliminating Redundancy

A common mistake is to repeat the same idea in slightly different words.

> The remaining chocolate-chip cookie is the only one left, so I saved it for you. [*Remaining* and *only one left* mean the same thing.]
>
> The vase was oval in shape. [Oval is a shape, so *in shape* is redundant.]

To revise a redundant sentence, eliminate one of the redundant elements.

## Eliminating Wordiness

1. **Eliminate wordiness by cutting out words that do not add to the meaning of your sentence.**

| | |
|---|---|
| WORDY | In the final analysis, choosing the field of biology as my major resulted in my realizing that college is hard work. |
| REVISED | Choosing biology as my major made me realize that college is hard work. |
| WORDY | The type of imitative behavior that I notice among teenagers is a very important, helpful aspect of their learning to function in groups. |
| REVISED | The imitative behavior of teenagers helps them learn to function in groups. |

Watch out in particular for empty words and phrases.

| *Phrase* | *Substitute* |
|---|---|
| until such time as | until |
| due to the fact that | because |
| at this point in time | now |
| in order to | to |

2. **Express your ideas simply and directly, using as few words as possible.** Often by rearranging your wording, you can eliminate two or three words.

the fleas that my dog has ⟶ my dog's fleas

workers with jobs that are low in pay ⟶ workers with low-paying jobs

3. **Use strong, active verbs that convey movement and give additional information.**

| | |
|---|---|
| WORDY | I was in charge of two other employees and needed to watch over their work and performance. |
| REVISED | I supervised two employees, monitored their performance, and checked their work. |

4. **Avoid sentences that begin with "*There is*" and "*There are.*"** These empty phrases add no meaning, energy, or life to sentences.

| | |
|---|---|
| WORDY | There are many children who suffer from malnutrition. |
| REVISED | Many children suffer from malnutrition. |

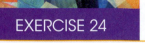

## EXERCISE 24    Eliminating Redundancy and Wordiness

**Directions:** Revise each of the following sentences to eliminate redundancy and wordiness.

EXAMPLE    Janice, who is impatient, usually cannot wait for class to end and packs up all of her books and notebooks in her backpack before the class is over.

REVISED    *Janice is impatient and usually packs everything in her backpack before class ends.*

D. Writing Effective Sentences

1. My co-workers are friendly, nice, and cooperative and always willing to help me.

2. Eva and Joe are returning again to the branch office where they met.

3. Lynn changed from her regular clothes into her shorts and T-shirt in order that she could play basketball.

4. Due to the fact that Professor Reis assigned 100 pages of reading for to-morrow, I will be unable to join the group of my friends at the restaurant tonight.

5. In my mythology class, we discussed and talked about the presence of a Noah's ark–type story in most cultures.

6. Darryl offered many ideas and theories as to the reason why humans exist.

7. There are many children who have not been immunized against dangerous childhood diseases.

8. Scientists have been studying the disease AIDS for many years, but they have been unable to find a cure for the disease.

9. The brown-colored chair was my father's favorite chair.

10. The briefcase that Julio has carried belonged to his brother.

# D.8 Diction

**Diction** is the use and choice of words. Words that you choose should be appropriate for your audience and express your meaning clearly. The following suggestions will help you improve your diction:

1. **Avoid slang expressions.** Slang refers to the informal, special expressions created and used by groups of people who want to give themselves a unique identity. Slang is an appropriate and useful way to communicate in some social situations and in some forms of creative writing. However, it is not appropriate for academic or career writing.

   | | |
   |---|---|
   | SLANG | My sister seems permanently out to lunch. |
   | REVISED | My sister seems out of touch with the world. |
   | SLANG | We pigged out at the ice cream shop. |
   | REVISED | We consumed enormous quantities of ice cream at the ice cream shop. |

2. **Avoid colloquial language.** Colloquial language refers to casual, everyday spoken language. It should be avoided in formal situations. Words that fall into this category are labeled *informal* or *colloquial* in your dictionary.

   | | |
   |---|---|
   | COLLOQUIAL | I almost flunked bio last sem. |
   | REVISED | I almost failed biology last semester. |
   | COLLOQUIAL | What are you all doing later? |
   | REVISED | What are you doing later? |

3. **Avoid nonstandard language.** Nonstandard language consists of words and grammatical forms that are used in conversation but are neither correct nor acceptable standard written English.

| Nonstandard | Standard |
| --- | --- |
| hisself | himself |
| knowed | known, knew |
| hadn't ought to | should not |
| she want | she wants |
| he go | he goes |

4. **Avoid trite expressions.** Trite expressions are old, worn-out words and phrases that have become stale and do not convey meaning as effectively as possible. These expressions are also called *clichés*.

| Trite Expressions | | |
| --- | --- | --- |
| needle in a haystack | sadder but wiser | as old as the hills |
| hard as a rock | white as snow | pretty as a picture |
| face the music | gentle as a lamb | |

**EXERCISE 25**    ## Practicing Correct Diction

**Directions:** Revise each of the following sentences by using correct diction.

EXAMPLE    This here building is Clemens Hall.

REVISED     This building is Clemens Hall.

1. Jean freaked out when I told her she won the lottery.

2. He go to the library.

3. The campus is wider than an occan.

4. Marty sits next to me in chem.

5. Sandy's new stereo is totally cool and has an awesome sound.

6. We went nuts when our team won the game.

7. Them CD players sure are expensive.

8. I think Nathan is as sharp as a tack because he got every question on the exam right.

9. Nino blew class off today to go rock climbing with his pals.

10. Dr. Maring's pager beeped in the middle of the meeting and she had to hightail it to a phone.

# Using Punctuation Correctly

**E** 

## E.1 End Punctuation

### When to Use Periods

Use a period in the following situations:

1. **To end a sentence unless it is a question or an exclamation.**

   > We washed the car even though we knew a thunderstorm was imminent.

   *Note:* Use a period to end a sentence that states an indirect question or indirectly quotes someone's words or thoughts.

   > INCORRECT    Samantha wondered if she would be on time?
   >
   > CORRECT      Samantha wondered if she would be on time.

2. **To punctuate many abbreviations.**

   > M.D.     B.A.     P.M.     B.C.     Mr.     Ms.

   Do not use periods in acronyms, such as *NATO* and *AIDS*, or in abbreviations for most organizations, such as *NBC* and *NAACP*.

   *Note:* If a sentence ends with an abbreviation, the sentence has only one period, not two.

   > The train was due to arrive at 7:00 P.M.

### When to Use Question Marks

Use question marks after direct questions. Place the question mark within the closing quotation marks.

> She asked the grocer, "How old is this cheese?"

*Note:* Use a period, not a question mark, after an indirect question.

> She asked the grocer how old the cheese was.

## Tip for Writers

### Punctuation

Using punctuation incorrectly can sometimes change the meaning of your sentences. Here are two examples:

1. The children who stayed outside got wet. (Only some of the children got wet.) The children, who stayed outside, got wet. (All of the children got wet.)

2. Did she finally marry Roger? Did she finally marry, Roger?

## When to Use Exclamation Points

Use an exclamation point at the end of a sentence that expresses particular emphasis, excitement, or urgency. Use exclamation points sparingly, however, especially in academic writing.

> What a beautiful day it is!                Dial 911 right now!

# E.2 Commas

The comma is used to separate parts of a sentence from one another. If you omit a comma when it is needed, you risk making a clear and direct sentence confusing.

## When to Use Commas

Use a comma in the following situations:

1. **Before a coordinating conjunction that joins two independent clauses** (see p. 580).

   > Terry had planned to leave work early, but he was delayed.

2. **To separate a dependent (subordinate) clause from an independent clause when the dependent clause comes first in the sentence** (see p. 582).

   > After I left the library, I went to the computer lab.

3. **To separate introductory words and phrases from the rest of the sentence**.

   > Unfortunately, I forgot my umbrella.

   > To pass the baton, I will need to locate my teammate.

   > Exuberant over their victory, the football team members carried the quarterback on their shoulders.

4. **To separate a nonrestrictive phrase or clause from the rest of a sentence**. A **nonrestrictive** phrase or clause is added to a sentence but does not change the sentence's basic meaning.

   To determine whether an element is nonrestrictive, read the sentence without the element. If the meaning of the sentence does not essentially change, then the commas are *necessary*.

   > My sister, who is a mail carrier, is afraid of dogs. [The essential meaning of this sentence does not change if we read the sentence without the subordinate clause: *My sister is afraid of dogs.* Therefore, commas are needed.]

   > Mail carriers who have been bitten by dogs are afraid of them. [If we read this sentence without the subordinate clause, its meaning changes considerably: *Mail carriers are afraid of (dogs).* It seems to say that *all* mail carriers are afraid of dogs. In this case, adding commas is not correct.]

5. **To separate three or more items in a series.**

   *Note:* A comma is *not* used *after* the last item in the series.

   > I plan to take math, psychology, and writing next semester.

6. **To separate coordinate adjectives: two or more adjectives that are not joined by a coordinating conjunction and that equally modify the same noun or pronoun.**

   > The thirsty, hungry children returned from a day at the beach.

   To determine whether a comma is needed between two adjectives, use the following test. Insert the word *and* between the two adjectives. Also try reversing the order of the two adjectives. If the phrase makes sense in either case, a comma is needed. If the phrase does not make sense, do not use a comma.

   > The tired, angry child fell asleep. [*The tired and angry child* makes sense; so does *The angry, tired child.* Consequently, the comma is needed.]
   >
   > Sarah is an excellent psychology student. [*Sarah is an excellent and psychology student* does not make sense, nor does *Sarah is a psychology, excellent student.* A comma is therefore not needed.]

7. **To separate parenthetical expressions from the clauses they modify.** Parenthetical expressions are added pieces of information that are not essential to the meaning of the sentence.

   > Most students, I imagine, can get jobs on campus.

8. **To separate a transition from the clause it modifies.**

   > In addition, I will revise the bylaws.

9. **To separate a quotation from the words that introduce or explain it.**

   *Note:* The comma goes *inside* the closed quotation marks.

   > "Shopping," Julia explained, "is a form of relaxation for me."
   >
   > Julia explained, "Shopping is a form of relaxation for me."

10. **To separate dates, place names, and long numbers.**

    > October 10, 1986, is my birthday.
    >
    > Dayton, Ohio, was the first stop on the tour.
    >
    > Participants numbered 1,777,716.

11. **To separate phrases expressing contrast.**

    > Jorge's good nature, not his wealth, explains his popularity.

## EXERCISE 26    Adding Commas

**Directions:** Revise each of the following sentences by adding commas where needed.

   EXAMPLE    Until the judge entered, the courtroom was noisy.

1. "Hello " said the group of friends when Joan entered the room.

2. Robert DeNiro the actor in the film  was very handsome.

3. My parents frequently vacation in Miami  Florida.

4. Drunk drivers  I suppose  may not realize they are not competent to drive.

5. Jeff purchased a television  couch  and dresser for his new apartment.

6. Luckily the windstorm did not do any damage to our town.

7. Frieda has an early class  and she has to go to work afterward.

8. After taking a trip to the Galápagos Islands  Mark Twain wrote about them.

9. The old  dilapidated stadium was opened to the public on September 15  1931.

10. Afterward  we will go out for ice cream.

# E.3 Unnecessary Commas

It is as important to know where *not* to place commas as it is to know where to place them. The following rules explain where it is incorrect to place them:

1. **Do not place a comma between a subject and its verb, between a verb and its complement, or between an adjective and the word it modifies.**

|  | Adjective    Subject |
|---|---|
| INCORRECT | The stunning, imaginative, and intriguing, painting, became the hit of the show. |
|  | Verb |
| CORRECT | The stunning, imaginative, and intriguing  painting  became the hit of the show. |

2. **Do not place a comma between two verbs, subjects, or complements used as compounds.**

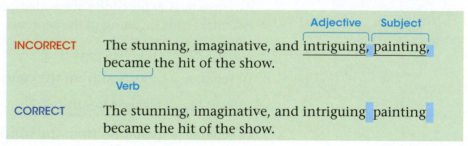

|  | Compound verb |
|---|---|
| INCORRECT | Marisol called, and asked me to come by her office. |
| CORRECT | Marisol called  and asked me to come by her office. |

3. **Do not place a comma before a coordinating conjunction joining two dependent clauses** (see p. 542).

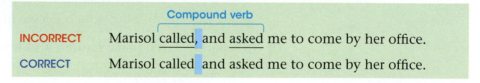

|  | Dependent clause |
|---|---|
| INCORRECT | The city planner examined blueprints that the park designer had submitted, and that the budget officer had approved. |
|  | Dependent clause |
| CORRECT | The city planner examined blueprints that the park designer had submitted  and that the budget officer had approved. |

E. Using Punctuation Correctly

4. **Do not place commas around restrictive clauses, phrases, or appositives.** Restrictive clauses, phrases, and appositives are modifiers that are essential to the meaning of the sentence.

| INCORRECT | The girl, who grew up down the block, became my lifelong friend. |
|---|---|
| CORRECT | The girl who grew up down the block became my lifelong friend. |

5. **Do not place a comma before the word *than* in a comparison or after the words *like* and *such as* in an introduction to a list.**

| INCORRECT | Some snails, such as, the Oahu tree snail, have more colorful shells, than other snails. |
|---|---|
| CORRECT | Some snails, such as the Oahu tree snail, have more colorful shells than other snails. |

6. **Do not place a comma next to a period, a question mark, an exclamation point, a dash, or an opening parenthesis.**

| INCORRECT | "When will you come back?," Dillon's son asked him. |
|---|---|
| CORRECT | "When will you come back?" Dillon's son asked him. |
| INCORRECT | The bachelor button, (also known as the cornflower) grows well in ordinary garden soil. |
| CORRECT | The bachelor button (also known as the cornflower) grows well in ordinary garden soil. |

7. **Do not place a comma between cumulative adjectives.** Cumulative adjectives, unlike coordinate adjectives (see p. 595), cannot be joined by *and* or rearranged.

| INCORRECT | The light, yellow, rose blossom was a pleasant birthday surprise. [*The light and yellow and rose blossom* does not make sense, so the commas are incorrect.] |
|---|---|
| CORRECT | The light yellow rose blossom was a pleasant birthday surprise. |

# E.4 Colons and Semicolons

## When to Use a Colon

A **colon** follows an independent clause and usually signals that the clause is to be explained or elaborated on. Use a colon in the following situations:

1. **To introduce items in a series after an independent clause.** The series can consist of words, phrases, or clauses.

> I am wearing three popular colors: magenta, black, and white.

2. **To signal a list or a statement introduced by an independent clause ending with *the following* or *as follows*.**

The directions are as follows: take Main Street to Oak Avenue and then turn left.

3. **To introduce a quotation that follows an introductory independent clause.**

My brother made his point quite clear: "Never borrow my car without asking me first!"

4. **To introduce an explanation.**

Mathematics is enjoyable: it requires a high degree of accuracy and peak concentration.

5. **To separate titles and subtitles of books.**

*Biology: A Study of Life*

*Note:* A colon must always follow an independent clause. It should not be used in the middle of a clause.

INCORRECT        My favorite colors are: red, pink, and green.

CORRECT          My favorite colors are red, pink, and green.

## When to Use a Semicolon

A **semicolon** separates equal and balanced sentence parts. Use a semicolon in the following situations:

1. **To separate two closely related independent clauses not connected by a coordinating conjunction** (see p. 553).

Sam had a 99 average in math; he earned an A in the course.

2. **To separate two independent clauses joined by a conjunctive adverb** (see p. 524).

Margaret earned an A on her term paper; consequently, she was exempt from the final exam.

3. **To separate independent clauses joined with a coordinating conjunction if the clauses are very long or if they contain numerous commas.**

By late afternoon, having tried on every pair of black checked pants in the mall, Marsha was tired and cranky; but she still had not found what she needed to complete her outfit for the play.

4. **To separate items in a series if the items are lengthy or contain commas.**

The soap opera characters include Marianne Loundsberry, the heroine; Ellen and Sarah, her children; Barry, her ex-husband; and Louise, her best friend.

5. **To correct a comma splice or run-on sentence** (see p. 552).

## EXERCISE 27    Correcting Sentences Using Semicolons

**Directions:** Correct each of the following sentences by placing colons and semicolons where necessary. Delete any incorrect punctuation.

EXAMPLE    Samuel Clemens disliked his name; therefore, he used Mark Twain as his pen name.

1. The large, modern, and airy, gallery houses works of art by important artists, however, it has not yet earned national recognition as an important gallery.

_____

_____

2. Rita suggested several herbs to add to my spaghetti sauce, oregano, basil, and thyme.

_____

_____

3. Vic carefully proofread the paper, it was due the next day.

_____

_____

4. Furniture refinishing is a great hobby, it is satisfying to be able to make a piece of furniture look new again.

_____

_____

5. The bridesmaids in my sister's wedding are as follows, Judy, her best friend Kim, our sister, Franny, our cousin, and Sue, a family friend.

_____

_____

6. Mac got a speeding ticket, he has to go to court next Tuesday.

_____

_____

7. I will go for a swim when the sun comes out, it will not be so chilly then.

_____

_____

8. Carlos was hungry after his hockey game, consequently, he ordered four hamburgers.

_____

_____

9. Sid went to the bookstore to purchase _Physical Anthropology Man and His Makings_, it is required for one of his courses.

_____

_____

10. Here is an old expression, "The way to a man's heart is through his stomach."

_____

_____

# E.5 Dashes, Parentheses, Hyphens, Apostrophes, Quotation Marks

## Dashes (—)

The dash is used to (1) separate nonessential elements from the main part of the sentence, (2) create a stronger separation, or interruption, than commas or parentheses, and (3) emphasize an idea, create a dramatic effect, or indicate a sudden change in thought.

> My sister—the friendliest person I know—will visit me this weekend.
>
> My brother's most striking quality is his ability to make money—or so I thought until I heard of his bankruptcy.

Do not leave spaces between the dash and the words it separates.

## Parentheses ( )

Parentheses are used in pairs to separate extra or nonessential information that often amplifies, clarifies, or acts as an aside to the main point. Unlike dashes, parentheses de-emphasize information.

> Some large breeds of dogs (golden retrievers and Newfoundlands) are susceptible to hip deformities.
>
> The prize was dinner for two (maximum value, $50) at a restaurant of one's choice.

## Hyphens (-)

Hyphens have the following primary uses:

1. **To split a word when dividing it between two lines of writing or typing** (see p. 607).

2. **To join two or more words that function as a unit, either as a noun or as a noun modifier.**

> mother-in-law                    single-parent families
>
> 20-year-old                       school-age children
>
> state-of-the-art sound system

## Apostrophes (')

Use apostrophes in the following situations:

1. **To show ownership or possession.** When the person, place, or thing doing the possessing is a singular noun, add -'s to the end of it, regardless of what its final letter is.

> The man's DVD player                    John Keats's poetry
>
> Aretha's best friend

---

**Tip for Writers**

*Its, your, his,* and *their* are *possessive* forms that go before nouns. Their meanings are possessive, so don't use an apostrophe in these words. On the other hand, *it's, you're, he's,* and *they're* are all contractions of pronouns with *is* or *are,* so an apostrophe is needed in each of these words.

With plural nouns that end in -*s*, add only an apostrophe to the end of the word.

| | |
|---|---|
| the twins' bedroom | postal workers' hours |
| teachers' salaries | |

With plural nouns that do not end in -*s*, add -'*s*.

| | |
|---|---|
| children's books | men's slacks |

Do not use an apostrophe with the possessive adjective *its*.

| INCORRECT | It's frame is damaged. |
|---|---|
| CORRECT | Its frame is damaged. |

2. **To indicate omission of one or more letters in a word or number.** Contractions are used in informal writing, but usually not in formal academic writing.

| | |
|---|---|
| it's [it is] | hasn't [has not] |
| doesn't [does not] | '57 Ford [1957 Ford] |
| you're [you are] | class of '99 [class of 1999] |

## Quotation Marks (" ")

Quotation marks separate a direct quotation from the sentence that contains it. Here are some rules to follow in using quotation marks.

1. **Quotation marks are always used in pairs**.

   *Note:* A comma or period goes at the end of the quotation, inside the quotation marks.

   | |
   |---|
   | Marge declared, "I never expected Peter to give me a watch for Christmas." |
   | "I never expected Peter to give me a watch for Christmas," Marge declared. |

2. **Use single quotation marks for a quotation within a quotation.**

   | |
   |---|
   | My literature professor said, "Byron's line 'She walks in beauty like the night' is one of his most sensual." |

   *Note:* When quoting long prose passages of more than four typed lines, do not use quotation marks. Instead, set off the quotation from the rest of the text by indenting each line one inch from the left margin. This format is called a **block quotation**.

   > The opening lines of the Declaration of Independence establish the purpose of the document:
   >
   > When in the Course of human events it becomes necessary for one people to dissolve the political bonds which have connected them with another, and to assume among the powers of the earth, the separate and equal station to which the Laws of Nature and of Nature's God entitle them, a decent respect to the opinions of mankind requires that they should declare the causes which impel them to the separation.

3. **Use quotation marks to indicate titles of songs, short stories, poems, reports, articles, and essays.** Books, movies, plays, operas, paintings, statues, and the names of television series are italicized (or underlined to indicate italics).

> "Rappaccini's Daughter" (short story)
>
> *60 Minutes* [or <u>60 Minutes</u>] (television series)
>
> "The Road Not Taken" (poem)

4. **Colons, semicolons, exclamation points, and question marks, when not part of the quoted material, go outside of the quotation marks.**

> What did George mean when he said, "People in glass houses shouldn't throw stones"?

---

**EXERCISE 28**    # Adding Appropriate Punctuation Marks

**Directions:** To the following sentences, add dashes, apostrophes, parentheses, hyphens, and quotation marks where necessary.

EXAMPLE    "You are not going out dressed that way!" said Frank's roommate.

1. My daughter in law recently entered medical school.

   _____

   _____

2. At the bar I worked at last summer, the waitresses tips were always pooled and equally divided.

   _____

   _____

3. Youre going to Paris next summer, aren't you?

   _____

   _____

4. The career counselor said, The computer field is not as open as it used to be.

   _____

   _____

5. My English professor read aloud Frost's poem Two Look at Two.

   _____

   _____

6. Frank asked me if I planned to buy a big screen television for our Super Bowl party.

   _____

   _____

7. Rachel the teaching assistant for my linguistics class spent last year in China.

   _____

   _____

8. Macy's is having a sale on womens boots next week.

_____

_____

9. Trina said, My one year old's newest word is bzz, which she says whenever she sees a fly.

_____

_____

10. Some animals horses and donkeys can interbreed, but they produce infertile offspring.

_____

_____

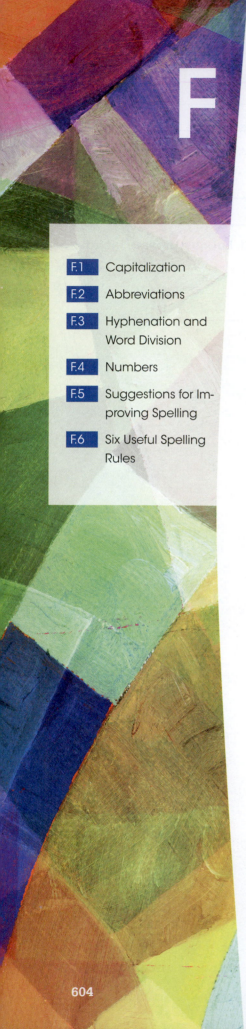

# F Managing Mechanics and Spelling

## F.1 Capitalization

In general, **capital letters** are used to mark the beginning of a sentence, to mark the beginning of a quotation, and to identify proper nouns. Here are some guidelines on capitalization:

| What to Capitalize | Example |
|---|---|
| 1. First word in every sentence | Prewriting is useful. |
| 2. First word in a direct quotation | Sarah commented, "That exam was difficult!" |
| 3. Names of people and animals, including the pronoun *I* | Aladdin<br>Maya Angelou<br>Spot |
| 4. Names of specific places, cities, states, nations, geographic areas, or regions | New Orleans<br>the Southwest<br>Lake Erie |
| 5. Government and public offices, departments, buildings | Williamsville Library<br>House of Representatives |
| 6. Names of social, political, business, sporting, cultural organizations | Boy Scouts<br>Buffalo Bills |
| 7. Names of months, days of the week, holidays | August Tuesday<br>Halloween |
| 8. In titles of works: the first word following a colon, the first and last words, and all other words except articles, prepositions, and conjunctions | *Biology: A Study of Life*<br>"Once More to the Lake" |
| 9. Races, nationalities, languages | African American, Italian, English |
| 10. Religions, religious figures, sacred books | Hindu, Hinduism, God, Allah, the Bible |
| 11. Names of products | Tide, Buick |
| 12. Personal titles when they come right before a name | Professor Rodriguez<br>Senator Hatch |
| 13. Major historic events | World War I |
| 14. Specific course titles | History 201<br>Introduction to Psychology |

## EXERCISE 29   Practicing Capitalization

**Directions:** Capitalize words as necessary in the following sentences.

EXAMPLE   Farmers in the ~~m~~idwest were devastated by floods last summer. *(M above midwest)*

1. My mother is preparing some special foods for our hanukkah meal; rabbi epstein will join us.

2. My american politics professor used to be a judge in the town of evans.

3. A restaurant in the galleria mall serves korean food.

4. A graduate student I know is writing a book about buddha titled *the great one: ways to en*lightenment.

5. at the concert last night, cher changed into many different outfits.

6. An employee announced over the loudspeaker, "attention, customers! we have pepsi on sale in aisle ten for a very low price!"

7. Karen's father was stationed at fort bradley during the vietnam war.

8. Last tuesday the state assembly passed governor allen's budget.

9. Boston is an exciting city; be sure to visit the museum of fine arts.

10. Marcos asked if i wanted to go see the bolshoi ballet at shea's theatre in november.

# **F.2** Abbreviations

An **abbreviation** is a shortened form of a word or phrase that is used to represent the whole word or phrase. The following is a list of common acceptable abbreviations:

| *What to Abbreviate* | *Example* |
| --- | --- |
| 1. Some titles before or after people's names | Mr. Ling <br> Samuel Rosen, M.D. <br> *but* Professor Ashe |
| 2. Names of familiar organizations, corporations, countries | CIA, IBM, VISTA, USA |
| 3. Time references preceded or followed by a number | 7:00 A.M. <br> 3:00 P.M. <br> A.D. 1973 |
| 4. Latin terms when used in footnotes, references, or parentheses | i.e. [*id est*, "that is"] <br> et al. [*et alii*, "and others"] |

Here is a list of things that are usually *not* abbreviated:

| *What Not to Abbreviate* | Example | |
|---|---|---|
| | *Incorrect* | *Correct* |
| 1. Units of measurement | thirty in. | thirty inches |
| 2. Geographic or other place names when used in sentences | N.Y. | New York |
| | Elm St. | Elm Street |
| 3. Parts of written works when used in sentences | Ch. 3 | Chapter 3 |
| 4. Names of days, months, holidays | Tues. | Tuesday |
| 5. Names of subject areas | psych. | psychology |

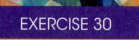

## EXERCISE 30   Correcting Inappropriate Use of Abbreviations

**Directions:** Correct the inappropriate use of abbreviations in the following sentences. If a sentence contains no errors, write "C" for correct beside it.

EXAMPLE   We live 30 ~~mi.~~ outside NYC.

*We live 30 miles outside New York City.*

_____  1.  Frank enjoys going to swim at the YMCA on Oak St.

_____  2.  Prof. Jorge asked the class to turn to pg. 8.

_____  3.  Because he is seven ft. tall, my brother was recruited for the high school b-ball team.

_____  4.  When I asked Ron why he hadn't called me, he said it was Northeast Bell's fault—i.e., his phone hadn't been working.

_____  5.  Tara is flying TWA to KC to visit her parents next Wed.

_____  6.  At 8:00 P.M., we turned on NBC to watch *Dancing with the Stars*.

_____  7.  Last wk. I missed my chem. lab.

_____  8.  The exam wasn't too difficult; only ques. number 15 and ques. no. 31 were extremely difficult.

_____ 9.  Dr. Luc removed the mole from my rt. hand using a laser.

_____

_____10.  Mark drove out to L.A. to audition for a role in MGM's new movie.

_____

# F.3 Hyphenation and Word Division

On occasion you must divide and hyphenate a word on one line and continue it on the next. Here are some guidelines for dividing words.

1. **Divide words only when necessary.** Frequent word divisions make a paper difficult to read.

2. **Divide words between syllables.** Consult a dictionary if you are unsure how to break a word into syllbles.

| di-vi-sion | pro-tect |
|---|---|

3. **Do not divide one-syllable words.**

4. **Do not divide a word so that a single letter is left at the end of a line.**

| INCORRECT | a-typical |
|---|---|
| CORRECT | atyp-ical |

5. **Do not divide a word so that fewer than three letters begin the new line.**

| INCORRECT | **visu-al** |
|---|---|
| CORRECT | **vi-sual** |
| INCORRECT | **caus-al [This word cannot be divided at all.]** |

6. **Divide compound words only between the words.**

| some-thing | any-one |
|---|---|

7. **Divide words that are already hyphenated only at the hyphen.**

| ex-policeman |
|---|

**EXERCISE 31**

## Practicing Division

**Directions:** Insert a diagonal (/) mark where each word should be divided. Mark "N" beside it if the word should not be divided.

EXAMPLE   every/where

_____ 1.  enclose        _____ 6.  disgusted

_____ 2.  house          _____ 7.  chandelier

| | | | |
|---|---|---|---|
| _____ | 3. saxophone | _____ | 8. headphones |
| _____ | 4. hardly | _____ | 9. swings |
| _____ | 5. well-known | _____ | 10. abyss |

# F.4 Numbers

Numbers can be written as numerals (600) or words (six hundred). Here are some guidelines for when to use numerals and when to use words:

| *When to Use Numerals* | *Example* |
|---|---|
| 1. Numbers that are spelled with more than two words | 375 students |
| 2. Days and years | August 10, 2013 |
| 3. Decimals, percentages, fractions | 56.7<br>59 percent<br>1¾ cups |
| 4. Exact times | 9:27 A.M. |
| 5. Pages, chapters, volumes; acts and lines from plays | Chapter 12<br>volume 4 |
| 6. Addresses | 122 Peach Street |
| 7. Exact amounts of money | $5.60 |
| 8. Scores and statistics | 23–6<br>5 of every 12 |

| *When to Use Words* | *Example* |
|---|---|
| 1. Numbers that begin sentences | Two hundred ten students attended the lecture. |
| 2. Numbers of one or two words | sixty students,<br>two hundred women |

## EXERCISE 32 · Practicing Correct Number Usage

**Directions:** Correct the misuse of numbers in the following sentences. If a sentence contains no errors, write "C" for correct beside it.

EXAMPLE    The reception hall was filled with ~~500~~ guests.

   *The reception hall was filled with five hundred guests.*

_____ 1. At 6:52 A.M. my roommate's alarm clock went off.

_____ 2. I purchased 9 turtlenecks for five dollars and fifty-five cents each.

_____ 3. 35 floats were entered in the parade, but only 4 received prizes.

_____ **4.** Act three of _Othello_ is very exciting.

_____ **5.** Almost fifty percent of all marriages end in divorce.

_____ **6.** The Broncos won the game 21–7.

_____ **7.** We were assigned volume two of _Don Quixote,_ beginning on page 351.

_____ **8.** The hardware store is located at three forty-four Elm Street, 2 doors down from my grandmother's house.

_____ **9.** Maryanne's new car is a 2-door V-8.

_____ **10.** Our anniversary is June ninth, nineteen eighty-nine.

# **F.5** Suggestions for Improving Spelling

Correct spelling is important to a well-written paragraph or essay. The following suggestions will help you submit papers without misspellings:

1. **Do not worry about spelling as you write your first draft.** Checking a word in a dictionary at this point will interrupt your flow of ideas. If you do not know how a word is spelled, spell it the way it sounds. Circle or underline the word so you remember to check it later.

2. **Keep a list of words you commonly misspell.** This list can be part of your error log.

3. **Every time you catch an error or find a misspelled word on a paper returned by your instructor, add it to your list.**

4. **Study your list.** Ask a friend to quiz you on the words. Eliminate words from the list after you have passed several quizzes on them.

5. **Develop a spelling awareness.** You'll find that your spelling will improve just by your being aware that spelling is important. When you encounter a new word, notice how it is spelled and practice writing it.

6. **Pronounce words you are having difficulty spelling.** Pronounce each syllable distinctly.

7. **Review basic spelling rules.** Your college library or learning lab may have manuals, workbooks, or computer programs that cover basic rules and provide guided practice.

8. **Be sure to have a dictionary readily available when you write.**

9. **Read your final draft through once, checking only for spelling errors.** Look at each word carefully, and check the spelling of those words of which you are uncertain.

# **F.6** Six Useful Spelling Rules

The following six rules focus on common spelling trouble spots:

1. **Is it *ei* or *ie*?**

   *Rule:* Use *i* before *e*, except after *c* or when the syllable is pronounced *ay* as in the word *weigh*.

   > *i* before *e*: believe, niece
   >
   > except after *c*: receive, conceive
   >
   > or when pronounced *ay*: neighbor, sleigh

   | *Exceptions:* | either | neither | foreign | forfeit |
   |---|---|---|---|---|
   | | height | leisure | weird | seize |

2. **When adding an ending, do you keep or drop the final *e*?**

   *Rules:* a. Keep the final *e* when adding an ending that begins with a consonant. (Vowels are *a, e, i, o, u,* and sometimes *y*; all other letters are consonants.)

   | hope → hopeful | aware → awareness |
   |---|---|
   | live → lively | force → forceful |

   b. Drop the final *e* when adding an ending that begins with a vowel.

   | hope → hoping | file → filing |
   |---|---|
   | note → notable | write → writing |

   | *Exceptions:* | argument | truly | changeable |
   |---|---|---|---|
   | | awful | manageable | courageous |
   | | judgment | noticeable | outrageous |
   | | acknowledgment | | |

3. **When adding an ending, do you keep the final *y*, change it to *i*, or drop it?**

   *Rules:* a. Keep the *y* if the letter before the *y* is a vowel.

   | delay → delaying | buy → buying | prey → preyed |
   |---|---|---|

**Tip for Writers**

The final *e* must remain on a word (before adding an ending) if the *e* is needed to keep a "soft" *c* sound (like *s*) or a "soft" *g* sound (like *j*) on the preceding letter. Two examples are *noticeable* and *manageable*.

**b.** Change the *y* to *i* if the letter before the *y* is a consonant, but keep the *y* for the *-ing* ending.

> defy → defiance          marry → married
>
>     → defying               → marrying

4. **When adding an ending to a one-syllable word, when do you double the final letter if it is a consonant?**

   *Rules:* **a.** In one-syllable words, double the final consonant when a single vowel comes before it.

   > drop → dropped          shop → shopped          pit → pitted

   **b.** In one-syllable words, *don't* double the final consonant when two vowels or a consonant comes before it.

   > repair → repairable          sound → sounded
   >
   > real → realize

5. **When adding an ending to a word with more than one syllable, when do you double the final letter if it is a consonant?**

   *Rules:* **a.** In multisyllable words, double the final consonant when a single vowel comes before it *and* the stress falls on the last syllable. (Vowels are *a, e, i, o, u,* and sometimes *y.* All other letters are consonants.)

   > begin' → beginning          transmit' → transmitted
   >
   > repel' → repelling

   **b.** In multisyllable words, do *not* double the final consonant (a) when two vowels or a vowel and another consonant come before it *or* (b) when the stress is not on the last syllable.

   > despair → despairing          ben'efit → benefited
   >
   > conceal → concealing

6. **To form a plural, do you add *-s* or *-es*?**

   *Rules:* **a.** For most nouns, add *-s.*

   > cat → cats          house → houses

   **b.** Add *-es* to words that end in *-o* if the *-o* is preceded by a consonant.

   > hero → heroes          potato → potatoes

   *Note: Zoos, radios, ratios,* and other words ending with two vowels are made plural by adding *-s.*

   **c.** Add *-es* to words ending in *-ch, -sh, -ss, -x,* or *-z.*

   > church → churches          fox → foxes          dish → dishes

# Credits

## Photo Credits

**Abstract painting graphic, used throughout:** iStock-photo; **Connections Box Icons (top):** © Exactostock/Superstock; **(middle):** © Digital Vision/Photolibrary; **(bottom):** © Radius/Superstock; **Need to Know icon:** Roman Sotola/Shutterstock; **Visualize It icon:** iStockphoto, Shutterstock; **Thinking Visually icon:** Kak2s/Shutterstock.com; **p. 1 (top left):** © Mike Hill/Alamy; **(top middle):** © Diego Cervo/Shutterstock; **(top right):** © GoGo Images Corporation/Alamy; **(bottom):** © Photo and Co/Getty Images; **p. 3:** Courtesy Kate Atkinson; **p. 5 (top):** age fotostock/SuperStock; **(bottom):** Courtesy Nora Edge; **p. 6:** Courtesy Nina Paus-Weiler; **p. 7:** © Otna Ydur/Shutterstock; **p. 8 (top):** Courtesy Ben Howard; **(bottom):** © Arcady31/Dreamstime.com; **p. 9 (top):** Courtesy Jordan Bobbitt; **(bottom):** © Strauski/Dreamstime.com; **p. 11 (top):** Courtesy Sharlinda Thompson; **(bottom):** Opla/iStockphoto; **p. 12:** Courtesy Santiago Quintana; **p. 13:** Opla/iStockphoto; **p. 28:** Dante Terzigni; **p. 34:** Tom Wang/Shutterstock; **p. 35:** Phil Date/Shutterstock; **p. 36:** Bragin Alexey/Shutterstock; **p. 37:** Jirsak/Shutterstock; **p. 38:** Ene/Shutterstock; **p. 39:** Alfonso de Tomas/Shutterstock; **p. 40:** Rido/Shutterstock; **p. 41 (top):** Moises Fernandez Acosta/Shutterstock; **(bottom):** Eky Studio/Shutterstock; **p. 42:** PozitivStudija/Shutterstock; **p. 44:** Steven Frame/Shutterstock; **p. 45:** Steven Frame/Shutterstock; **p. 46:** Lori Carpenter/Shutterstock; **p. 47:** Andresr/Shutterstock; **p. 48:** Karuka/Shutterstock; **p. 49:** Dja65/Shutterstock; **p. 50:** Henrik Lehnerer/Shutterstock; **p. 51:** Ingrid Prats/Shutterstock; **p. 52:** AVAVA/Shutterstock; **p. 53:** CREATISTA/Shutterstock; **p. 54:** Monkey Business Images/Shutterstock; **p. 55:** © Kemalbas/iStockphoto.com; **p. 75:** Courtesy Doug Mello; **p. 78:** © Michael Willis/Alamy; **p. 83:** © Asia Images/Getty Images; **p. 93:** © Stephen Coburn/Shutterstock.com; **p. 120 (top):** © Ethel Wolvovitz/The Image Works; **(bottom):** © Jim Bryant/epa/Corbis; **p. 126:** Mandy Godbehear/Shutterstock; **p. 132:** TPH/allOver Photography/Alamy Images; **p. 134:** Peter Steiner / The New Yorker Collection / www.cartoonbank.com; **p. 136:** Los Angeles Times photo by Mark Boster; **p. 138:** © Niels Poulsen std / Alamy; **p. 143:** Richard Cartwriting/CBS/Everett Collection; **p. 162:** Courtesy Kate Atkinson; **p. 166:** Paula Burch-Celentano/Tulane University; **p. 171:** PictureNet/Corbis; **p. 200:** Courtesy James Sturm; **p. 202:** Suzie Maeder/Lebrecht Music and Arts Photo Library; **p. 207:** Sharrocks/Dreamstime; **p. 209:** Dave King/DK Images; **p. 222:** Vismax/Dreamstime; **p. 231:** Courtesy Yesenia De Jesus; **p. 235:** age fotostock/SuperStock; **p. 241:** Broker/Dreamstime.com; **p. 274:** Courtesy Jessica Nantka; **p. 277:** Chris Jordan; **p. 282 (top and bottom):** Richard Hutchings/Corbis; **p. 299:** AP Images/Dale Sparks; **p. 304:** Tony Law/Redux Pictures; **p. 309:** Richard Borge/www.richardborge.com; **p. 327:** Courtesy Ted Sawchuck; **p. 329 (laptop):** Shortkut/Shutterstock; **(faucet):** Jozsef Szasz-Fabian/Shutterstock; **p. 335:** Nobor/Shutterstock; **p. 356:** Courtesy Ted Sawchuck; **p. 360:** ilker canikligil/Shutterstock; **p. 365:** © Exotica.im 8/Alamy; **p. 367:** Ronen/Shutterstock; **p. 390:** Rawdon Wyatt/Alamy; **p. 395:** Gino Domenico/Bloomberg via Getty Images; **p. 416:** Courtesy Santiago Quintana Garcia; **p. 419:** Blend Images/Alamy; **p. 424:** Julio Donosco/Corbis; **p. 441:** Courtesy Aurora Gilbert; **p. 444:** WaterFrame/Alamy; **p. 449:** LHB Photo/Alamy; **p. 473:** Courtesy Quinne Sember; **p. 484:** Greg Epperson/Shutterstock.

## Text Credits

### Chapter 1

**p. 16:** Michael R. Solomon, Mary Anne Poatsy, and Kendall Martin, *Better Business*, 2nd ed., pp. 279–280, © 2012. Reprinted and electronically reproduced by permission of Pearson Education, Inc. Upper Saddle River, New Jersey.

**p. 26:** Rebecca J. Donatelle, *Health: The Basics*, Green Edition, 9th ed., p. 255, © 2011. Reprinted and electronically reproduced by permission of Pearson Education, Inc., Upper Saddle River, New Jersey.

**p. 28:** Ashley Womble, "A Brother Lost," as it appears in *Utne Reader*, excerpted from the original article "The Homeless Brother I Cannot Save," Salon.com, July 27, 2010. This article first appeared in Salon.com, at http://www.Salon.com. An online version remains in the Salon archives. Reprinted by permission.

### Vocabulary Workshops

**p. 42:** H. L. Capron, *Computers: Tools for an Information Age*, 5th ed. Reading, MA: Addison-Wesley, 1998.

**p. 43:** William J. Germann and Cindy L. Stanfield, *Principles of Human Physiology*. San Francisco: Benjamin Cummings, 2002, p. 9.

**p. 43:** Alex Thio, *Sociology*, 5th ed. New York: Longman, 1998, p. 235.

**p. 44:** James M. Henslin, *Sociology: A Down-to-Earth Approach*, 10th ed., p. 386, © 2010. Reprinted and electronically reproduced by permission of Pearson Education, Inc., Upper Saddle River, New Jersey.

**p. 44:** Michael R. Solomon, *Consumer Behavior: Buying, Having, and Being*, 8th ed. Upper Saddle River, NJ: Pearson Prentice Hall, 2009, p. 19.

**p. 45:** Rebecca J. Donatelle, *Health: The Basics*, Green Edition, 9th ed., p. 57, © 2011. Reprinted and electronically reproduced by permission of Pearson Education, Inc., Upper Saddle River, New Jersey.

**p. 53:** James M. Henslin, *Sociology: A Down-to-Earth Approach*, 10th ed., p. 52, © 2010. Reprinted and electronically reproduced by permission of Pearson Education, Inc., Upper Saddle River, New Jersey.

**p. 54:** Michael R. Solomon, *Consumer Behavior: Buying, Having, and Being*, 8th ed. Upper Saddle River, NJ: Pearson Prentice Hall, 2009, pp. 62–63.

**p. 54:** Rebecca J. Donatelle, *Health: The Basics*, Green Edition, 9th ed., p. 34, © 2011. Reprinted and electronically reproduced by permission of Pearson Education, Inc., Upper Saddle River, New Jersey.

**p. 54:** Jenifer Kunz, *Think Marriages & Families*, 1st ed., pp. 278–279, © 2011. Reprinted and electronically reproduced by permission of Pearson Education, Inc., Upper Saddle River, New Jersey.

## Chapter 2

**p. 68:** Doug Mello, First Draft. Reprinted by permission of the author.

**p. 75:** Doug Mello, "Education: The Open Road." Reprinted by permission of the author.

**p. 77:** "Credit Card Smarts: Take Charge of Your Cards," www.collegeboard.org. Copyright © 2012. The College Board. Reproduced with permission.

## Chapter 3

**p. 91:** Rebecca J. Donatelle, *Health: The Basics*, 5th ed., p. 286, © 2003. Reprinted and electronically reproduced by permission of Pearson Education, Inc., Upper Saddle River, New Jersey.

**p. 92:** Steve Russo and Mike Silver, *Introductory Chemistry: Essentials*, 2nd ed. San Francisco: Benjamin Cummings, 2001, pp. 3–4.

**p. 93:** Sharon S. Brehm, Saul Kassin, and Steven Fein, *Social Psychology*, 6th ed. Boston: Houghton Mifflin, 2005.

**p. 94:** Jenifer Kunz, *Think Marriages & Families*, 1st ed., p. 207, © 2011. Reprinted and electronically reproduced by permission of Pearson Education, Inc., Upper Saddle River, New Jersey.

**p. 97:** Joseph A. DeVito, *Messages: Building Interpersonal Communication Skills*, 5th ed. Boston: Allyn and Bacon, 2002, p. 317.

**p. 98:** Teresa Audesirk, Gerald Audesirk, and Bruce E. Byers, *Life on Earth*, 5th ed. San Francisco: Pearson Benjamin Cummings, 2009, pp. 584–585.

**p. 100:** James N. Gilbert, *Criminal Investigation*, 8th ed., pp. 64–65, © 2010. Reprinted and electronically reproduced by permission of Pearson Education, Inc., Upper Saddle River, New Jersey.

**p. 104:** Saul Kassin, *Psychology*, 4th ed. Upper Saddle River, NJ: Pearson Prentice Hall, 2004, p. 252.

**p. 106:** Edward F. Bergman and William H. Renwick, *Introduction to Geography: People, Places, and Environment*, updated 2nd ed. Upper Saddle River, NJ: Prentice Hall, 2003, pp. 495–496.

**p. 106:** Rebecca J. Donatelle, *Health: The Basics*, 5th ed., p. 350, © 2003. Reprinted and electronically reproduced by permission of Pearson Education, Inc., Upper Saddle River, New Jersey.

**p. 107:** Deborah Tannen, *You Just Don't Understand: Women and Men in Conversation*. New York: Morrow, 1990, p. 246.

**p. 110:** Carole Wade and Carol Tavris, *Invitation to Psychology*, 5th ed., pp. 292–293, © 2012. Reprinted and electronically reproduced by permission of Pearson Education, Inc., Upper Saddle River, New Jersey.

**p. 110:** Pennies figure. Reprinted from *Cognitive Psychology*, vol. 11, Nickerson, R. S., & Adams, M. J., "Long-term memory for a common object," pp. 287–307, Copyright 1979, with permission from Elsevier. http://www.science-direct.com/science/journal/00100285

## Chapter 4

**p. 117:** James M. Henslin, *Sociology: A Down-to-Earth Approach, Core Concepts*, 3rd ed., Figure 7.7, p. 222, © 2009. Reprinted and electronically reproduced by permission of Pearson Education, Inc., Upper Saddle River, New Jersey. Figure by Henslin based on *Statistical Abstract of the United States 2007*: Table 694.

**p. 121:** Jeffrey O. Bennett, William L. Briggs, and Mario F. Triola, *Statistical Reasoning for Everyday Life*, 3rd ed., Figure 3.23, p. 116, © 2009. Reprinted and electronically reproduced by permission of Pearson Education, Inc., Upper Saddle River, New Jersey.

**p. 122:** William E. Thompson and Joseph V. Hickey, *Society in Focus: 2010 Census Update*, 7th ed. Boston: Allyn & Bacon, 2011, p. 9. Data source: U.S. Census Bureau, *Statistical Abstract of the United States 2011*.

**p. 124:** Jenifer Kunz, *Think Marriages & Families*, 1st ed., p. 173, © 2011. Reprinted and electronically reproduced by permission of Pearson Education, Inc., Upper Saddle River, New Jersey. Data source: U.S. Census Bureau.

**p. 125:** William E. Thompson and Joseph V. Hickey, *Society in Focus: An Introduction to Sociology*, 7th ed., Figure 10.5, p. 282, © 2011. Reprinted and electronically reproduced by permission of Pearson Education, Inc., Upper Saddle River, New Jersey. Data source: Office of Immigration Statistics, U.S. Department of Homeland Security, *2008 Yearbook of Immigration Statistics*.

**p. 126:** Abigail A. Baird, *Think Psychology*, 2nd ed., p. 186, © 2011. Reprinted and electronically reproduced by permission of Pearson Education, Inc., Upper Saddle River, New Jersey. Derived from information in Rollins & Feldman, 1970.

**p. 127:** Adapted from William E. Thompson and Joseph V. Hickey, *Society in Focus: An Introduction to Sociology*,

7th ed., Figure 1.1, p. 10, © 2011. Reprinted and electronically reproduced by permission of Pearson Education, Inc., Upper Saddle River, New Jersey. Data source: Adapted from Table 1089, U.S. Bureau of Census, *Statistical Abstract of the United States 2009* (128th ed.). Washington, DC, 2008.

**p. 129:** Michael C. Mix, Paul Farber, and Keith I. King, *Biology: The Network of Life*, 1st ed., Figure 39.5, p. 752, © 1992. Reprinted and electronically reproduced by permission of Pearson Education, Inc., Upper Saddle River, New Jersey.

**p. 130:** Courtland L. Bovée and John V. Thill, *Business Communication Today*, 9th ed., Figure 12.13, p. 379, © 2008. Reprinted and electronically reproduced by permission of Pearson Education, Inc., Upper Saddle River, New Jersey.

**p. 131:** Courtland L. Bovée and John V. Thill, *Business Communication Today*, 9th ed., Figure 12.12, p. 379, © 2008. Reprinted and electronically reproduced by permission of Pearson Education, Inc., Upper Saddle River, New Jersey.

**p. 132:** Rebecca J. Donatelle, *Health: The Basics*, Green Edition, 9th ed., p. 241, © 2011. Reprinted and electronically reproduced by permission of Pearson Education, Inc., Upper Saddle River, New Jersey.

**p. 136:** James M. Henslin, *Sociology: A Down-to-Earth Approach*, 10th ed., pp. 580–581, © 2010. Reprinted and electronically reproduced by permission of Pearson Education, Inc., Upper Saddle River, New Jersey.

**p. 137:** Leah McLaughlin, "Soft Addictions: Are You Hooked?" From *Working Mother*, April 2010. © 2010 Working Mother. All rights reserved. Used by permission and protected by the Copyright Laws of the United States. The printing, copying, redistribution, or retransmission of this Content without express written permission is prohibited. www.workingmother.com

## Chapter 5

**p. 145:** Joseph A. DeVito, *Human Communication: The Basic Course*, 9th ed. Boston: Allyn and Bacon, 2003, p. 182.

**p. 148:** Joseph A. DeVito, *Human Communication: The Basic Course*, 9th ed. Boston: Allyn and Bacon, 2003, p. 178.

**p. 148:** John D. Carl, *Think Sociology*. Upper Saddle River, NJ: Pearson Prentice Hall, 2010, p. 211.

**p. 148:** Jenifer Kunz, *Think Marriages & Families*, 1st ed., p. 8, © 2011. Reprinted and electronically reproduced by permission of Pearson Education, Inc., Upper Saddle River, New Jersey.

**p. 149:** Jenifer Kunz, *Think Marriages & Families*, 1st ed., p. 82, © 2011. Reprinted and electronically reproduced by permission of Pearson Education, Inc., Upper Saddle River, New Jersey.

**p. 149:** George C. Edwards III, Martin P. Wattenberg, and Robert L. Lineberry, *Government in America: People, Politics, and Policy*, 14th ed. New York: Pearson Longman, 2009, p. 313.

**p. 150:** X. J. Kennedy and Dana Gioia, *Literature: An Introduction to Fiction, Poetry, Drama, and Writing*, 11th ed. New York: Pearson Longman, 2010, p. 1243.

**p. 151:** Jenifer Kunz, *Think Marriages & Families*, 1st ed., p. 36, © 2011. Reprinted and electronically reproduced by permission of Pearson Education, Inc., Upper Saddle River, New Jersey.

**p. 151:** Richard T. Wright and Dorothy Boorse, *Environmental Science: Toward a Sustainable Future*, 11th ed., p. 247, © 2011. Reprinted and electronically reproduced by permission of Pearson Education, Inc., Upper Saddle River, New Jersey.

**p. 152:** Richard T. Wright and Dorothy Boorse, *Environmental Science: Toward a Sustainable Future*, 11th ed., p. 150, © 2011. Reprinted and electronically reproduced by permission of Pearson Education, Inc., Upper Saddle River, New Jersey.

**p. 152:** Colleen Belk and Virginia Borden Maier, *Biology: Science for Life*, 3rd ed. San Francisco: Benjamin Cummings, 2010, p. 334.

**p. 153:** James N. Gilbert, *Criminal Investigation*, 8th ed., p. 33, © 2010. Reprinted and electronically reproduced by permission of Pearson Education, Inc., Upper Saddle River, New Jersey.

**p. 153:** Shirley Badasch and Doreen Cheesebro, *Health Science Fundamentals: Exploring Career Pathways*. Upper Saddle River, NJ: Pearson, 2009, p. 88.

**p. 153:** Jason B. Loyd and James D. Richardson, *Fundamentals of Fire and Emergency Services*. Upper Saddle River, NJ: Pearson, 2010, p. 12.

**p. 153:** Mike Johnson, et al., *The Pharmacy Technician: Foundations and Practices*. Upper Saddle River, NJ: Pearson Prentice Hall, 2009, p. 455.

**p. 154:** Louis D. Giannetti, *Understanding Movies*, 12th ed. Boston: Pearson Allyn & Bacon, 2011, p. 251.

**p. 154:** Rebecca J. Donatelle, *Health: The Basics*, Green Edition, 9th ed., p. 6, © 2011. Reprinted and electronically reproduced by permission of Pearson Education, Inc., Upper Saddle River, New Jersey.

**p. 154:** Robert C. Nickerson, *Business and Information Systems*. Reading, MA: Addison-Wesley, 1998, p. 249.

**p. 154:** Rebecca J. Donatelle, *Health: The Basics*, Green Edition, 9th ed., p. 66, © 2011. Reprinted and electronically reproduced by permission of Pearson Education, Inc., Upper Saddle River, New Jersey.

**p. 155:** Thomas F. Goldman and Henry R. Cheeseman, *The Paralegal Professional*, 3rd ed., p. 459, © 2011. Reprinted and electronically reproduced by permission of Pearson Education, Inc., Upper Saddle River, New Jersey.

**p. 155:** Steven A. Beebe, Susan J. Beebe, and Mark V. Redmond, *Interpersonal Communication: Relating to Others*, 3rd ed. Boston: Allyn and Bacon, 2002, pp. 243, 248.

**p. 155:** John Vivian, *The Media of Mass Communication*, 10th ed. Boston: Pearson Allyn & Bacon, 2011, pp. 278–279.

**p. 162:** Kate Atkinson, "The Russian and U.S. School Systems." Reprinted by permission of the author.

**p. 165:** John Robbins, "Greed, Cancer, and Pink KFC Buckets," *The Huffington Post*, May 17, 2010. Reprinted by permission of the author. John Robbins is the author of *No Happy Cows*, see www.johnrobbins.info

**Chapter 6**

**p. 174:** Joseph A. DeVito, *Messages: Building Interpersonal Communication Skills*, 4th ed. New York: Longman, 1999, p. 159.

**p. 174:** Joseph A. DeVito, *Messages: Building Interpersonal Communication Skills*, 4th ed. New York: Longman, 1999, p. 130.

**p. 175:** B. E. Pruitt and Jane J. Stein, *Health Styles: Decisions for Living Well*, 2nd ed. Boston: Allyn & Bacon, 1999, pp. 108, 110.

**p. 176:** Hugh D. Barlow, *Criminal Justice in America*. Upper Saddle River, NJ: Prentice Hall, 2000, p. 238.

**p. 177:** John R. Walker and Josielyn T. Walker, *Tourism: Concepts and Practices*. Upper Saddle River, NJ: Pearson, 2011, p. 11.

**p. 178:** George C. Edwards III, Martin P. Wattenberg, and Robert L. Lineberry, *Government in America: People, Politics, and Policy*, 14th ed. New York: Pearson Longman, 2009, p. 239.

**p. 178:** Thomas F. Goldman and Henry R. Cheeseman, *The Paralegal Professional*, 3rd ed., pp. 736–737, © 2011. Reprinted and electronically reproduced by permission of Pearson Education, Inc., Upper Saddle River, New Jersey.

**p. 178:** Saundra K. Ciccarelli and J. Noland White, *Psychology: An Exploration*, 1st ed. Upper Saddle River, NJ: Pearson Prentice Hall, 2010, p. 249.

**p. 179:** Thomas F. Goldman and Henry R. Cheeseman, *The Paralegal Professional*, 3rd ed., p. 81, © 2011. Reprinted and electronically reproduced by permission of Pearson Education, Inc., Upper Saddle River, New Jersey.

**p. 179:** Paul G. Hewitt, *Conceptual Physics*, 5th ed. Boston: Little, Brown, 1985, p. 15.

**p. 180:** James M. Henslin, *Sociology: A Down-to-Earth Approach*, 6th ed. Boston: Allyn & Bacon, 2003, p. 383.

**p. 180:** Paul G. Hewitt, *Conceptual Physics*, 5th ed. Boston: Little, Brown, 1985, pp. 234–235.

**p. 181:** Paul G. Hewitt, *Conceptual Physics*, 5th ed. Boston: Little, Brown, 1985, p. 259.

**p. 181:** George C. Edwards III, Martin P. Wattenberg, and Robert L. Lineberry, *Government in America: People, Politics, and Policy*, 9th ed. New York: Longman, 2000, pp. 458–459.

**p. 181:** Roy A. Cook, Laura J. Yale, and Joseph J. Marqua, *Tourism: The Business of Travel*, 4th ed. Upper Saddle River, NJ: Pearson Prentice Hall, 2010, p. 209.

**p. 181:** Rebecca J. Donatelle and Lorraine G. Davis, *Access to Health*, 6th ed. Boston: Allyn and Bacon, 2000, pp. 358, 371.

**p. 182:** John A. Garraty and Mark C. Carnes, *The American Nation: A History of the United States*, 10th ed. New York: Longman, 2000, p. 706.

**p. 182:** Palmira Brummett, et al., *Civilization: Past & Present*, 9th ed. New York: Longman, 2000, p. 348.

**p. 183:** Jenifer Kunz, *Think Marriages & Families*, 1st ed., p. 83, © 2011. Reprinted and electronically reproduced by

permission of Pearson Education, Inc., Upper Saddle River, New Jersey.

**p. 183:** Janice Thompson and Melinda Manore, *Nutrition for Life*, 2nd ed. San Francisco: Pearson Benjamin Cummings, 2010, p. 302.

**p. 184:** Richard T. Wright and Dorothy Boorse, *Environmental Science: Toward a Sustainable Future*, 11th ed., p. 604, © 2011. Reprinted and electronically reproduced by permission of Pearson Education, Inc., Upper Saddle River, New Jersey.

**p. 185:** H. Edward Reiley and Carroll L. Shry, Jr., *Introductory Horticulture*. Albany, NY: Delmar Publishers, 1979, p. 114.

**p. 188:** Joseph A. DeVito, *Messages: Building Interpersonal Communication Skills*, 5th ed. Boston: Allyn and Bacon, 2002, p. 290.

**p. 189:** Josh Gerow, *Psychology: An Introduction*, 3rd ed. New York: HarperCollins College Publishers, 1996, p. 319.

**p. 189:** Nora Newcombe, *Child Development: Change Over Time*, 8th ed. New York: HarperCollins College Publishers, 1996, p. 354.

**p. 189:** Michael R. Solomon, *Consumer Behavior: Buying, Having, and Being*, 8th ed. Upper Saddle River, NJ: Pearson Prentice Hall, 2009, p. 189.

**p. 190:** Michael R. Solomon and Elnora W. Stuart, *The Brave New World of E-Commerce* (Supplement to *Marketing: Real People, Real Choices*). Upper Saddle River, NJ: Prentice Hall, 2001, p. 13.

**p. 190:** Stephen A. Beebe and John T. Masterson, *Communicating in Small Groups: Principles and Practices*, 6th ed. New York: Longman, 2000, p. 150.

**p. 190:** Colleen Belk and Virginia Borden Maier, *Biology: Science for Life with Physiology*, 3rd ed. San Francisco: Pearson Benjamin Cummings, 2010, p. 236.

**p. 191:** Robert A. Divine, et al., *America Past and Present*, Combined Volume, 9th ed. New York: Pearson Longman, 2011, p. 449.

**p. 191:** Rebecca J. Donatelle and Lorraine G. Davis, *Access to Health*, 6th ed. Boston: Allyn and Bacon, 2000, p. 42.

**p. 200:** James Sturm, "The China Bug." Reprinted by permission of the author.

**p. 202:** Amy Tan, "The Most Hateful Words." Copyright © 2003 by Amy Tan. First appeared in *The New Yorker*. Reprinted by permission of the author and the Sandra Dijkstra Literary Agency.

**Chapter 7**

**p. 210:** Mark C. Carnes and James A. Garraty, *The American Nation: A History of the United States*, 11th ed. New York: Pearson Longman, 2003, p. 518.

**p. 211:** Roy A. Cook, Laura J. Yale, and Joseph J. Marqua, *Tourism: The Business of Travel*, 2nd ed. Upper Saddle River, NJ: Prentice Hall, 2002, p. 102.

**p. 212:** Elaine N. Marieb, *Human Anatomy & Physiology*, 5th ed. San Francisco: Benjamin Cummings, 2001, p. 13.

**p. 212:** Mark C. Carnes and James A. Garraty, *The American Nation: A History of the United States*, 11th ed. New York: Pearson Longman, 2003, p. 455.

**p. 212:** Rebecca J. Donatelle, *Access to Health*, 7th ed. San Francisco: Benjamin Cummings, 2002, p. 533.

**p. 215:** Roger LeRoy Miller, Daniel K. Benjamin, and Douglass C. North, *The Economics of Public Issues*, 16th ed. Upper Saddle River, NJ: Pearson Prentice Hall, 2010, pp. 163–164.

**p. 215:** James M. Henslin, *Essentials of Sociology: A Down-to-Earth Approach*, 8th ed. Boston: Pearson Allyn and Bacon, 2009, p. 337.

**p. 215:** Janetta Rebold Benton and Robert DiYanni, *Arts and Culture: An Introduction to the Humanities*, 4th ed. Upper Saddle River, NJ: Pearson Prentice Hall, 2012, p. 576.

**p. 220:** Richard Paul Janaro and Thelma C. Altshuler, *The Art of Being Human*, 9th ed. New York: Pearson Longman, 2009, p. 136.

**p. 220:** Frederick K. Lutgens, Edward J. Tarbuck, and Dennis Tasa, *Essentials of Geology*, 10th ed. Upper Saddle River, NJ: Pearson Prentice Hall, 2009, p. 272.

**p. 220:** Margaret McWilliams, *Food Around the World: A Cultural Perspective*, 3rd ed. Upper Saddle River, NJ: Pearson Prentice Hall, 2011, p. 149.

**p. 226:** Edward F. Bergman and William H. Renwick, *Introduction to Geography*, 2nd ed. Upper Saddle River, NJ: Pearson Prentice Hall, 2002, p. 356; and Mark C. Carnes and John A. Garraty, *The American Nation: A History of the United States*, 10th ed. New York: Longman, 2000, p. 916.

**p. 227:** Richard T. Wright and Dorothy Boorse, *Environmental Science: Toward a Sustainable Future*, 11th ed., pp. 56–57, © 2011. Reprinted and electronically reproduced by permission of Pearson Education, Inc., Upper Saddle River, New Jersey.

**p. 228:** Richard T. Wright and Dorothy Boorse, *Environmental Science: Toward a Sustainable Future*, 11th ed., p. 57, © 2011. Reprinted and electronically reproduced by permission of Pearson Education, Inc., Upper Saddle River, New Jersey.

**p. 231:** Yesenia De Jesus, "From Bullet to Blue Sky." Pearson Writing Rewards Student Essay Contest. Copyright © Pearson Education, Inc.

**p. 235:** Amanda Fields, "Cairo Tunnel," *Brevity* 30, May 2009. Reprinted by permission of the author.

**Chapter 8**

**p. 240:** Gerald Audesirk, Teresa Audesirk, and Bruce E. Byers, *Biology: Life on Earth with Physiology*, 8th ed., Figure 28-11, p. 570, © 2008. Reprinted and electronically reproduced by permission of Pearson Education, Inc., Upper Saddle River, New Jersey.

**p. 244:** Edward F. Bergman and William H. Renwick, *Introduction to Geography: People, Places, and Environment*, updated 2nd ed. Upper Saddle River, NJ: Pearson Prentice Hall, 2003, p. 280.

**p. 245:** Rebecca J. Donatelle, *Access to Health*, 7th ed. San Francisco: Benjamin Cummings, 2002, p. 65.

**p. 245:** Jenifer Kunz, *Think Marriages & Families*, 1st ed., p. 119, © 2011. Reprinted and electronically reproduced by permission of Pearson Education, Inc., Upper Saddle River, New Jersey.

**p. 246:** Jeffrey Bennett, et al., *The Cosmic Perspective*, Brief Edition. San Francisco: Addison Wesley Longman, 2000, p. 28.

**p. 246:** X. J. Kennedy and Dana Gioia, *Literature: An Introduction to Fiction, Poetry, and Drama*, 3rd Compact Edition. New York: Pearson Longman, 2003, p. 7.

**p. 246:** Elaine N. Marieb, *Human Anatomy & Physiology*, 5th ed. San Francisco: Benjamin Cummings, 2001, p. 387.

**p. 251:** David Krogh, *Biology: A Guide to the Natural World*, 4th ed. San Francisco: Pearson Benjamin Cummings, 2009, p. 429.

**p. 251:** Gerard J. Tortora, *Introduction to the Human Body: The Essentials of Anatomy and Physiology*, 2nd ed. New York: HarperCollins College Publishers, 1991, p. 56.

**p. 251:** James M. Henslin, *Sociology: A Down-to-Earth Approach*, 10th ed., pp. 109, 111, © 2010. Reprinted and electronically reproduced by permission of Pearson Education, Inc., Upper Saddle River, New Jersey.

**p. 256:** Jeffrey Bennett, *The Cosmic Perspective*, 2nd ed. San Francisco: Addison-Wesley, 2002, p. 249.

**p. 258:** Rebecca J. Donatelle, *Health: The Basics*, 5th ed., p. 324, © 2003. Reprinted and electronically reproduced by permission of Pearson Education, Inc., Upper Saddle River, New Jersey.

**p. 263:** William J. Germann and Cindy L. Stanfield, *Principles of Human Physiology*. San Francisco: Benjamin Cummings, 2002, p. 622.

**p. 270:** Thomas F. Goldman and Henry R. Cheeseman, *The Paralegal Professional*, 3rd ed., p. 183, © 2011. Reprinted and electronically reproduced by permission of Pearson Education, Inc., Upper Saddle River, New Jersey.

**p. 270:** James M. Henslin, *Sociology: A Down-to-Earth Approach*, 6th ed. Boston: Allyn & Bacon, 2003, p. 637.

**p. 270:** Edward F. Bergman and William H. Renwick, *Introduction to Geography: People, Places, and Environment*, 3rd ed. Upper Saddle River, NJ: Pearson Prentice Hall, 2005, p. 430.

**p. 271:** William J. Germann and Cindy L. Stanfield, *Principles of Human Physiology*. San Francisco: Benjamin Cummings, 2002, pp. 303–304.

**p. 274:** Jessica Nantka, "Benefits of Joining the Military." Reprinted by permission of the author.

**p. 277:** Jay H. Withgott and Scott R. Brennan, *Environment: The Science Behind the Stories*, 4th ed., pp. 633, 635, © 2011. Reprinted and electronically reproduced by permission of Pearson Education, Inc., Upper Saddle River, New Jersey.

**p. 439:** Christine Haugen, "Logging Illogic," *World Watch*, September/October 2002.

**p. 441:** Aurora Gilbert, "From Ignorant Bliss to Painful Awareness." Reprinted by permission of the author.

**p. 443:** Virginia Sole-Smith, "Sweatshops at Sea" in *Utne Reader*, September-October 2010. Research support for this article provided by The Nation Institute's Investigative Fund. Reprinted by permission of the author.

## Chapter 15

**p. 464:** Timothy Denesha, "From a Vegetarian: Looking at Hunting from Both Sides Now," *Buffalo News*, November 24, 1996. Reprinted by permission of the author.

**p. 469:** William E. Thompson and Joseph V. Hickey, *Society in Focus: An Introduction to Sociology*, 7th ed., Boston: Pearson Allyn & Bacon, 2011, pp. 328–329.

**p. 473:** Quinne Sember, "Marijuana: An Argument for Legalization." Reprinted by permission of the author.

**p. 478:** Sen. Joseph I. Lieberman, "Should Online Sites Ban Postings by Groups the Government Identifies as Terrorists?" *CQ Researcher*, vol. 18, no. 27 (August 1, 2008), p. 641. From http://hsgac.senate.gov

**p. 480:** Leslie Harris and John Morris, "Should Online Sites Ban Postings by Groups the Government Identifies as Terrorists?" as appeared in *CQ Researcher*, vol. 18, no. 27 (August 1, 2008), p. 641. The entire article appeared at HuffingtonPost.com (May 28, 2008). Reprinted by permission of Center for Democracy & Technology.

## Chapter 16

**p. 491:** Sharon S. Brehm, Saul Kassin, and Steven Fein, *Social Psychology*, 6th ed. Boston: Houghton Mifflin, 2005.

**p. 491:** Richard L. Weaver II, *Understanding Interpersonal Communication*, 7th ed. New York: HarperCollins College Publishers, 1996.

**p. 492:** Teresa Audesirk, Gerald Audesirk, and Bruce E. Byers, *Life on Earth*, 5th ed. San Francisco: Pearson Benjamin Cummings, 2009, pp. 249–251.

**p. 493:** Sierra Club, excerpt from Sierra Club, http://www.sierraclub.org/habitat/habitatloss.asp, August 16, 1999.

**p. 503:** Adam Simmons, "Weighing the Consequences of Censorship in Media." Reprinted by permission of the author.

# Index